Y0-BXI-709

The Birth of Orientalism

ENCOUNTERS WITH ASIA

Victor H. Mair, Series Editor

Encounters with Asia is an interdisciplinary series dedicated to the exploration of all the major regions and cultures of this vast continent. Its timeframe extends from the prehistoric to the contemporary; its geographic scope ranges from the Urals and the Caucasus to the Pacific. A particular focus of the series is the Silk Road in all its ramifications: religion, art, music, medicine, science, trade, and so forth. Among the disciplines represented in this series are history, archeology, anthropology, ethnography, and linguistics. The series aims particularly to clarify the complex interrelationships among various peoples within Asia, and also with societies beyond Asia.

A complete list of books in the series is available from the publisher.

The Birth of Orientalism

Urs App

PENN

UNIVERSITY OF PENNSYLVANIA PRESS

PHILADELPHIA · OXFORD

Published by
University of Pennsylvania Press
Philadelphia, Pennsylvania 19104-4112

Printed in the United States of America on acid-free paper
10 9 8 7 6 5 4 3 2 1

Library of Congress Cataloging-in-Publication Data
App, Urs, 1949–
   The birth of orientalism / Urs App.
      p.   cm. — (Encounters with Asia)
   Includes bibliographical references and index.
   ISBN 978-0-8122-4261-4 (acid-free paper)
   1. Asia—Religion—Study and teaching—History—18th
century.   2. Orientalism—Europe—History—18th century.
3. Europe—Intellectual life—18th century.   4. Religions—
Study and teaching—History—18th century.   I. Title.
BL1033.A66   2010
294—dc22   2010004556

To my sensei
YANAGIDA Seizan
(1922–2005)

Fact Is Fiction—And Fiction Is Fact

Contents

Figures and Tables

Figures

Tables

Preface

"Orientalism" has been a buzzword since Edward Said's eponymous book of 1978. Critics have pointed out that Said's "Orient" is focused on the Arab world and excludes most of what Westerners mean by the word. A more recent history of Orientalism, Robert Irwin's *For Lust of Knowing*, criticizes Said's narrow view of orientalists as "those who travelled, studied or wrote about the Arab world" (2006:294) but goes on to use the same "somewhat arbitrary delimitation of the subject matter" (p. 6), which leaves out India, China, Japan, Tibet, Central Asia, North Asia, and Southeast Asia—in other words, most of what we mean by Asia and more than half of humankind.

The term "Orientalism" also has many other connotations, for example, in the context of "oriental" fashions of the seventeenth and eighteenth centuries or the imitation of oriental styles in garden architecture and painting. The Orientalism whose birth process is examined in this book is modern Orientalism, that is, the secular, institutionalized study of the Orient by specialists capable of understanding oriental languages and handling primary-source material. Its genesis—and, more generally, the history of premodern Europe's encounter with Asia—is still barely known. The present book does not claim to furnish a history of Orientalism as a whole. Its much more modest aim is to elucidate through relatively extensive case studies a crucial phase of the European encounter with Asia: the century of Enlightenment. The focus is on the European discovery of the regions east of Said's and Irwin's "Orient," in particular on Europe's discovery of non-Islamic Asian religions. The facets of Asian religions treated are, needless to say, determined by the interests of the protagonists of the included case studies. Unlike Immanuel Kant (App 2008a), they showed little interest in Tibetan religion; hence there is little discussion of it in this book.

Why the focus on religion? Because the role of colonialism (and generally of economic and political interests) in the birth of Orientalism dwindles to insignificance compared to the role of religion. Modern Orientalism is the successor of earlier forms of Orientalism involving the study of Asian languages and texts. Christian Europe had been wrestling with Islam for many centuries; from the sixteenth century many of its universities prided themselves on having an "orientalist" professor who specialized in Hebrew and other Bible-related languages such as Aramaic, Syriac, and sometimes even Arabic or Persian. Such premodern academic Orientalism was generally a handmaiden of Bible studies and theology—which explains its almost exclusive focus on regions, languages, and religions that play a role in the Old and New Testaments. Studies of Oriental texts and languages beyond the "biblical" region usually—though not exclusively—occurred in the context of Christian missions.

The eighteenth century brought a momentous change that opened the door to a new kind of Orientalism, less shackled by theology, Bible studies, the frontiers of the Middle East, and Europe's time-honored Judeo-Christian worldview. This new or "modern" Orientalism was prepared by a growing interest in India as the cradle of civilization, an interest that was promoted by Voltaire (1694–1778) in his quest to denigrate the Bible and destabilize Christianity (see Chapter 1). After the appearance of a number of purportedly very ancient texts of Indian origin in the 1760s and 1770s (Chapters 6 and 7), the idea of Indian origins of civilization gained ground. The research by early British Sanskritists in Calcutta and their articles in the *Asiatick Researches* added oil to the fire, and in 1795 Europe's first secular institution for the study of Oriental languages was established: the École Spéciale des Langues Orientales Vivantes in Paris. Its first director, Louis-Mathieu Langlès (1763–1824), was inspired both by Voltaire's idea of Indian origins and the new approach of the British gentlemen scholars, and he regarded the Bible as an imitation of the far older Veda (see Chapter 8). With the support of Constantin-François Volney (1757–1820), the noted Orientalist and author of the law expropriating the French Catholic Church, the École Spéciale officially sought to divorce the study of Asia, its languages, and its textual heritage from the realm of theology and biblical studies. At the beginning of the nineteenth century, this school quickly became the Mecca of secular Orientalist philology, and further progress was made with such developments as the creation of the first European university chairs in Indology and Sinology (Paris, 1814). However, as the recent studies of Mangold (2004), Polaschegg (2005), and Rabault-Feuerhahn (2008) show for the case of Germany, the emancipation of Orientalism from theology and its establishment as a discipline in its own right required many decades. Indeed, the complicated relationship between "theology," "religious studies," and "Asian studies" in today's academic environment would indicate that this emancipation process is far from finished.

It is easily forgotten that even in the 1820s Europeans believed with few exceptions that the world is only a few thousand years old, that all the world's peoples can be traced back to Noah's Ark, and that Christianity is the fulfillment and goal of all religion. Even well-informed people like the philosopher Georg Wilhelm Friedrich Hegel (1770–1831) had no doubt about this, as his lectures on the philosophy of history and on oriental religions show (App 2008a). Fundamental views about where we come from, where we stand, and where we are headed played an extraordinary role in the discovery of other cultures and religions. The notion of a soul that, once created, goes on living forever, or of a future state in which acts committed during life will be rewarded or punished, were incomparably more important in the European discovery of Asian religions than were commercial greed and imperialist ambitions. The same is true for the conviction that there is a God who created the universe out of nothing, manages its smooth functioning, foresees everything, punishes man's evil deeds by natural disasters such as floods, and sent his son to atone for man's sins. Such notions form the ideological background of the European discovery of Asian religions, and the history of Orientalism is to a substantial degree also a history of the West's gradual detachment from this traditional ideology.

It is a central thesis of this book that Europe's discovery of Asian religions was deeply linked to the development of Orientalism and its gradual emancipation from biblical studies. The birth of modern Orientalism was not a Caesarean section performed by colonialist doctors at the beginning of the nineteenth century when Europe's imperialist powers began to dominate large swaths of Asia. Rather, it was the result of a long process that around the turn of the eighteenth century produced a paradigm change. Our case studies show a centuries-long, gradual broadening of perspectives beyond the sphere circumscribed by Abrahamic religions and the Bible. As in all discoveries, the familiar determined to a large extent the appearance of the new. But Europe's Bible-based worldview with its creation, paradise, fall, deluge, monotheist orthodoxy, and satanic idolatry—the mirror in which Asian religions appeared—was also gradually changing. Hence, our case studies reflect not only evolving images of Asia's religious landscape but also a transformation of the worldview of the perceivers. In the course of the eighteenth century, Europe's dominant ideological matrix experienced a deepening crisis, and its hitherto unassailable biblical foundations showed ever more threatening fissures. The loss of biblical authority, which was due to many factors, occurred at a time when Judaism and Christianity themselves began to be increasingly viewed as local phenomena on a dramatically expanded, worldwide canvas of religions and mythologies. At the end of the eighteenth century, Volney—the subject of our last case study—portrayed Christianity as a relatively insignificant and young local religion based on local varieties of solar myth, and Langlès officially promoted a new Orientalism liberated from the shackles of theology and biblical studies.

The study of the European discovery of Asia's non-Abrahamic religions—especially religions with sacred scriptures that were possibly older than the Old Testament—thus not only is crucial for understanding the genesis of modern Orientalism but also opens a hitherto neglected perspective on the profound changes characterizing Europe's age of Enlightenment and path to modernity. Though some of this book's protagonists may on the surface appear to be little concerned with religion, a closer look soon reveals the religious coloring of their convictions and motivations. Each case study aims not only at elucidating the protagonist's sources for and understanding of Asian religions but also the underlying motivations and approaches (such as, in the case of Voltaire and John Zephaniah Holwell, the promotion of deism and reform of Christianity).

The choice of protagonists crystallized over a dozen years of very enjoyable research. Though some of them are hardly household names, they all played significant roles in the genesis of modern Orientalism and deserve to be better known. The case studies do not follow a chronological sequence, but the synoptic list of major figures just before the notes ought to facilitate orientation. Each case study throws light on some facets of premodern views of Asian religions and thus forms a piece of a mosaic contributing to an overall picture unlike any the reader will hitherto have encountered. Other figures might have added detail and color, for example, Nicolas Fréret, Nathaniel Brassey Halhed, Johann Gottfried Herder, or Thomas Maurice, but a few have already been studied in detail (Rosane Rocher's studies of Hamilton and Halhed). A chapter on William Jones is published elsewhere[1] because of space limitations, and other figures (such as Paulinus a Sancto Bartholomaeo) await further research by indologists. Little effort was expended on disputing or discussing mistaken ideas, for example, the notion of the Egyptian origin of metempsychosis, the view that Buddhist sutras reproduce the words of the historical Buddha, or the legends that Vyasa wrote the Vedas and Moses the Pentateuch. I cheerfully and gratefully delegate this task to authors of textbooks and encyclopedias, while I enjoy tracing the adventures of wayward ideas, traditions made of whole cloth, apocryphal texts, invented saints, and other miracles of imagination.

Almost all the figures studied in this book were very much interested in origins; this question was a central one for the eighteenth century and beyond, and it often arose when the traditional Bible-based answers were questioned and became suspect. Where do European languages and our alphabet come from? Was there ever a descendant of Noah called Tuisco who was the forefather of all Germans? Why do the German and Persian languages seem related? How did marine fossils and sharks' teeth turn up on the peaks of the Alps? How did mountains form, and how long did this take? Why did giant "elephants" and tropical fauna end up frozen in Siberian ice? How much could the creation story of the Old Testament be trusted? Were Christianity and Judaism influenced by far older Egyptian, Persian, or Indian religions? If not the Bible, what are the world's oldest books, and what do they contain? Are there alternative sources for the understanding of ultimate origins?

Since candidates in the competition for the world's oldest book inevitably include religious scriptures, such texts form a second set of protagonists whose fate is traced in the chapters of this book. Most fundamental is, of course, the Bible, particularly its "books of Moses" (the Pentateuch), whose authority as well as its gradual loss determined so much of the outlook of Europeans on Asian religions. But hot candidates in the race for the world's oldest book also come from the antediluvian world and possibly even Paradise (the book of Enoch), from China (the *Yijing* or Book of Changes), and from mother India (the Vedas, Voltaire's *Ezour-vedam*, Holwell's *Shastah*, and Abraham Hyacinthe Anquetil-Duperron's *Oupnek'hat*). Buddhism also had a book in the race, even though it was only thought to be the oldest Buddhist text: the *Forty-Two Sections Sutra*. These competitors all play central roles in some of this book's chapters as they were revealed, invented, discovered, studied, unmasked, admired, or despised. Modern Orientalism owes them a great debt that was hitherto rarely explored due to excessive valuation of genuineness, positivism, divine inspiration, and so forth. Yet their biographies can be as touching, funny, wonderful, and interesting as any saint's, and I hope the joy of discovery infects some of my readers as they follow the intertwined fates of men, books, and ideas. The history of religions demonstrates with sufficient clarity that invented facts, dubious claims, and mistaken assumptions can occasionally work wonders. This book shows how much modern Orientalism, too, is indebted to them. More generally, they appear to be central factors in the history of humanity. Indeed, where would we be without them?

Readers used to the Eurocentric horizon of discussion as well as Orientalists will find that this book contains a substantial number of unknown or little known names and texts. It is the fate of pioneering studies to burden the reader with such "unknowns" and much detail that may at first sight seem peripheral and inconsequential. This was also the case, for example, with studies on the role of clandestine literature in the formation of the age of Enlightenment. However, such studies not only put the spotlight on many seminal texts and personages but demonstrated that they formed the pillars on which the Enlightenment was erected. Europe's encounter with non-Abrahamic Asian religions is a far more complex affair whose roots reach back to antiquity; and if the huge crowds flocking to talks by the Dalai Lama in Western stadiums are a valid indicator, it is not only still alive but still young. Though it can without exaggeration be called the largest-scale religio-cultural encounter in human history, it has so far received surprisingly little attention—which is why some of its major features are here described for the first time. That serious scientific study of this encounter has barely begun may be connected with this encounter's intimidating cultural, religious, historical, and linguistic bandwidth. For example, one of the most influential texts both in East Asian Buddhism and in the religion's Western reception was the *Forty-Two Sections Sutra*, a Chinese text whose history in the East and West is for the first time traced in this book.

Not just books but also ideas have fates that sometimes deserve to be traced. One of the dominant ideas of eighteenth-century views of Asian religions—the idea that Brahmanism and Buddhism are two sects of one religion—was to a substantial extent based on notes from a casual conversation with a Jesuit in China. These notes were used, heavily edited and without attribution, in Charles Le Gobien's book about the Chinese emperor's tolerance edict. Religious tolerance happened to be a theme of extreme interest to Pierre Bayle whose Protestant father had died in a French prison after the revocation of the Edict of Nantes. Thus, an idea uttered by an obscure missionary in the Chinese boondocks found its way into Bayle's dictionary and reached an enormous public all over Europe. Not only that, it appeared to confirm the opinion of Athanasius Kircher; Johann Jacob Brucker used it in his pioneering history of philosophy; Denis Diderot put it into the limelight in a seminal article of the *Encyclopédie*; Anquetil-Duperron wanted to go to

China because of it; Joseph de Guignes was led astray by it; and Herder built his view of Asian religions on it. Some of the ideas and sources whose roots are for the first time probed in this book were thus very influential despite their humble origins as unpublished notes. That such manuscripts could, under the right circumstances, be powerful forces even before publication is also shown by Voltaire's *Ezour-vedam* (see Chapters 1 and 7), which was best known and most influential before its 1778 appearance in print. Holwell's *Shastah* of 1767, too, attracted attention as a partial translation of a supposedly extremely ancient but lost manuscript (see Chapter 6).

There is much material in this book that was translated from a variety of languages into English for the first time.[2] Unless another translator is indicated, all quotations from sources with non-English titles were translated into English by me. The inclusion of texts in original languages would have added too much bulk, which is why only a few crucial passages or terms (usually in square brackets) are provided. I trust that Google Books (books.google.com), archive.org, and similar initiatives, which have made a brilliant start particularly with old books, already (or will in the near future) allow access to many primary sources that I was still obliged laboriously to locate, photograph, and even type out at numerous libraries and archives in Asia, Europe, and the United States, whose personnel I wish to thank on this occasion for their kind help. Equal thanks go to the many people involved in the scanning and free Internet publishing of old books.

The spelling of historical texts is often different from that in their modern cousins. A modern reader might be shocked to see words like "le Cahos ou le Vuide" instead of "le chaos ou le vide," as well as "wrong" or missing accents ("matiere," "premiére," etc.) or "superfluous" letters ("bee" instead of "be"). The reader can rest assured that every effort was made to reproduce original spellings accurately and that a sea of *sics* is therefore unnecessary. Those who suspect insufficient knowledge on my part of spellings, modern and historical, of various languages are welcome to check them against the originals. Inline references consisting only of page numbers always refer to the last given full reference. Unless otherwise noted all illustrations are by the author or reproduce materials from his private library.

Many institutions, colleagues, and friends were of direct and indirect help in the genesis of this book. In its initial stages, I was working at Hanazono University in Kyoto under Prof. Seizan Yanagida, to whom this book is dedicated, and toward the end, I received the financial support of the Swiss National Research Fund (grant No. 101511-116443). Through the years, I ben-

efited from the aid of my parents, my ever generous brother Pius, Akifumi
Takagi, the family of Dr. Kazuko Arai in Tokyo, Haruko Torii, and Rev.
Taizan Egami in Kyoto. I also wish to thank my son Alexander Huwyler and
many friends, including Prof. Steven Antinoff, Prof. Antonino Forte, Prof.
Hubert Durt, Prof. Silvio Vita, Naomi Maeda, Prof. Lee Roser, Mark
Thomas, John Gorman, Patricia Lutkins, Dr. Joseph Osterwalder, André
Wicky, Satoshi Sakai, Yves Ramseier, Dr. René Bischofberger, Drs. Valerio
and Adriana Pozza, Ursula Ilg, Kunio and Yoko Murakoshi, Stefanie Osterwalder, Dr. Pius Bischof, James V. Stokes, Dr. Christine Mollier, Dr. Nathalie Monnet, and Dr. Hubert Delahaye. I am also obliged to the editor of the
series, Prof. Victor Mair, and the readers of the University of Pennsylvania
Press as well as to Prof. Jonathan Silk for their suggestions and corrections.
My deepest gratitude is due to my wife, Dr. Monica Esposito, who continu-
ously encouraged and stimulated my research and helped to improve this
book through countless suggestions and discussions.

Introduction

When a dozen years ago I began to study oriental influences on Richard Wagner's operas in the mid-nineteenth century, I had no idea where my investigations would lead. Having done some research on the Western discovery of Japanese religions in the sixteenth century, it did not take me long to find traces of this discovery in the nineteenth century. But Raymond Schwab's *La renaissance orientale* and studies on the history of the Western encounter with Asian religions such as Henri de Lubac's *La rencontre du bouddhisme et de l'Occident* presented an utterly confusing mass of data arranged according to modern notions such as "Buddhism" or "Hinduism" and to modern geographical units such as "India" or "China."

A major reason for this confusion was the fact that the primary sources seem to come from a different world where such neat delimitations do not exist. They tend, for example, to distinguish between esoteric and exoteric "branches" of a pan-Asian religion or to connect the creeds of various countries of "the Indies" to some descendant of Noah. Another factor that complicated matters was the sheer mass of data in many European languages that used different local pronunciations and transcriptions for the same person or thing. Thus, the Portuguese missionaries in Japan often called the Buddha "Xaca," the French missionaries in China "Xekia" or "Foe," the Italians in Vietnam "Thicca," and so on. Some were aware of their identity, others not; and again, others claimed that the Indian god Vishnu, the Persian prophet Zoroaster, or the Egyptian Hermes Trismegistos were alternative names of Buddha. An additional complicating factor was the maze of authors and texts. Trying to distinguish the trailblazers from imitators, embellishers, copyists, and plagiarists turned into a laborious enterprise that involved burrowing through heaps of multilingual literature in libraries on several continents in order to find out where specific items of information came from. This often was difficult. However, patient investigative work over a decade clarified matters to a certain extent and allowed me to isolate a number of ideas, figures, and texts that played key roles in the drawn-out and complex process of the premodern European discovery of Asian religions. These I will present in this introduction.

Key Ideas

1. Esoteric and Exoteric Forms of Religion

One of the ideas repeated in countless European sources about Asian religions is the distinction between "outer" or "exoteric" and "inner" or "esoteric" forms. It was already used in early Christian literature, for example, by Eusebius of Caesarea and Lactantius, to characterize heathen creeds around the Mediterranean. But its roots lie in ancient Greek views of Egyptian religion where Egyptian priests are said to have encoded secret esoteric teachings in hieroglyphs while feeding the outer, exoteric bark of religion to the people. This idea gained renewed popularity in the Renaissance when texts attributed to Hermes Trismegistos ("hermetic texts") were translated into Latin and portrayed as vestiges of ancient Egyptian "esoteric" monotheism. In Europe, this inspired proponents of ancient theology (*prisca theologia*) like the seventeenth-century Jesuit Athanasius Kircher as well as many missionaries.

Several case studies in this book will show how this notion of esoteric and exoteric teachings allied itself with sixteenth-century reports about Japanese Buddhism and became one of the dominant ideas about Asian religions. The Japanese views, in turn, have roots in Chinese and Indian Buddhism and are thus about as old as their European counterparts. Having heard of this Buddhist distinction in the second half of the sixteenth century, the missionaries to Japan used it to classify the Buddhist sects of that country. At the beginning of the seventeenth century, a long-time resident of Japan, João Rodrigues, first applied it to all three major religions of China (which today are called Confucianism, Daoism, and Buddhism). In the 1620s, the Italian Jesuit Cristoforo Borri in Vietnam used the esoteric/exoteric distinction to characterize two phases of the Buddha's life and to classify religious movements in India, Vietnam, China, and Japan. In the course of the seventeenth and eighteenth centuries, this distinction became not only the most conspicuous feature of the Buddha's biography (the story of his deathbed confession) but also the dominant way of explaining the connection between various religions of Asia in terms of esoteric and exoteric branches of a huge pan-Asian religion. The importance of this distinction (as well as of other key ideas mentioned below) for the European discovery of Asian religions cannot be overestimated. It had a far deeper influence than the politico-economic motives that tend to stand in the limelight of current "Orientalism" literature.

2. The Bible-Based Perspective

A fundamental factor in the premodern European discovery of Asian religions is easily overlooked just because it is so pervasive and determines the outlook of most discoverers: the biblical frame of reference. All religions of the world had to originate with a survivor of the great deluge (usually set circa 2500 B.C.E.) because nobody outside Noah's ark survived. In Roman times, young Christianity was portrayed as the successor of Adam's original pure monotheism, thus stretching its roots into antediluvian times. In the Renaissance and its aftermath, Egyptian religion, hermetic texts, and other "ancient" writings such as the Chaldaic oracles were seen as a confirmation of, or a threat to, such claims.

After the discovery of America and the opening of the sea route to India at the end of the fifteenth century, new challenges to biblical authority arose. It was difficult to establish a connection between hitherto unknown people and animals and Noah's ark. But an equally tough nut to crack were the Chinese annals which in the seventeenth century caused much consternation as claims were published that they might be as old as, or even older than, Noah's flood. Our case studies show different ways in which Europeans tried to rise to such challenges: missionaries who attempted to incorporate ancient Asian cultures and religions into Bible-based scenarios; others who tried to move the starting shot of biblical history backward to beat the Chinese annals; people like Isaac La Peyrère and Baruch de Spinoza who concentrated on cracks in the biblical edifice; deists and reformers like Voltaire and John Zephaniah Holwell who attempted to use Asian texts as older and better Old Testaments; and skeptics like Constantin-François Volney who came to see the Old Testament as just another outgrowth of the Oriental imagination.

Asian phenomena and texts, invented or not, were operative not only in the European discovery of Asian religions but also in that of Europe's own religions, languages, and cultures. Just as a people on an isolated island tends to question its own origin and customs only after contact with aliens, Europe's changing worldview and obsession with origins were intimately linked to its confrontation with other cultures and religions—particularly with non-Abrahamic religions far older than Islam and possibly even than the religion of Abraham. In the course of this confrontation and the crumbling of previous certainties (for example, that Hebrew is the mother of all languages and the Bible the world's most ancient book), even the traditional sequence from initial paradisiacal perfection to the Fall and eventual regeneration came increasingly under attack. The traditional European worldview and even Christianity itself were in danger of being relativized, destabilized, and marginalized.

Of course, the discovery of Asian religions was far from the only factor in this process of erosion. But the influence of this discovery on the view of eighteenth-century opinion leaders and innovators such as Pierre Bayle, Giambattista Vico, David Hume, Voltaire, Denis Diderot, Immanuel Kant, and Johann Gottfried Herder is well documented. Nevertheless, it remains little studied. The same can be said of the role of the discovery of Asian religions in the birth of Europe's modern Orientalism. This discovery may appear to be an exotic topic, but in its time it broadened perspectives far more than the Hubble space telescope is expanding ours. It contributed to a change in the very lens apparatus through which the Orient, Europe, the origin of peoples and their cultures, and the world as a whole were seen. Not just traditional religious convictions and ideas about other religions were at stake but the very identity of the Europeans.

3. The Oriental System

Boosted by seventeenth-century Jesuits like Rodrigues, Kircher, and Charles Le Gobien, the notion of a pan-Asian "oriental system" or *doctrina orientalis* with possible Mesopotamian or Egyptian roots became a major factor in eighteenth-century views of Asian religions. Facets of this complex of ideas include theories of an Egyptian origin of Buddhism (Kircher, Mathurin Veyssière de La Croze, Engelbert Kaempfer, Johann Jacob Brucker, Diderot), the view that Brahmanism is a form of exoteric Buddhism (Diderot, Herder, etc.), the notion that some Buddhist texts of China are translations from the Veda (Joseph de Guignes), and the suspicion that Greek philosophy and particularly Plato were inspired by oriental ideas (A. M. Ramsay) or even by Buddhism (la Créquinière). The "inner" teachings of this *doctrina orientalis* were first modeled on the purported monism, emanatism, and "quietism" of Japanese Zen Buddhism and later also of Vedanta and Sufism. In 1688 François Bernier linked such oriental quietism to the teachings of Miguel de Molinos, François Fénelon, and Madame Guyon as well as the philosophy of Spinoza.

The "Spinoza" article in Bayle's dictionary of 1702—one of the most famous and controversial articles in one of the most noted works of eighteenth-century Europe—is a good example for both the broad use of missionary and secular sources about Asia and the deep influence of the linkage between features of Asian religions and raging theologico-philosophical controversies of Christian Europe. Bayle's influence is palpable not only in Brucker's influential histories of philosophy of the 1730s and 1740s and in Diderot's articles for the *Encyclopédie* of the 1750s, but also in Johann Lorenz Mosheim's *Ecclesiastical History* of 1755, François Pluquet's *Examen du fatalisme* of 1757, and many later European works including Herder's philosophy of history (1784–91) and Friedrich Schlegel's pioneering work on the language and wisdom of the Indians (1808). Schlegel, with Volney one of continental Europe's first students of Sanskrit, saw this *doctrina orientalis* as the ultimate source not only of Oriental philosophy and religion but also of their ancient Greek counterparts (Schlegel 1808:114–23).

At the beginning of the nineteenth century, India had thus for some become not only the cradle of human civilization, as Voltaire had so insistently argued, but of all ancient religion and philosophy—a notion that inspired Europe's romantic indomania. The birth of modern Orientalism is intimately linked to this idea of Indian origins as an alternative to the biblical narrative. It is not by chance that one of the most ardent propagators after Voltaire of Indian origins was Louis Langlès, director of Bible-independent Orientalism's first institution on European soil, the École Spéciale des Langues Orientales Vivantes, founded in 1795.

4. *Emanation and Transmigration*

Bayle (1702), Brucker (1744), Pluquet (1757), F. Schlegel (1808), and many others identified two of the core features of the "oriental doctrine" as emanation and metempsychosis or transmigration of souls. Both were linked to Platonism, pantheism, and Spinozism; thus, they aroused much discussion when all these came under increasing attack. Bayle's 1702 article on Spinoza explicitly established this link in combining information about Greek philosophers and Christian heretics with extensive data from the Orient (François Bernier, Philippe Couplet, Simon de La Loubère, Louis Daniel Le Comte, Le Gobien, Antonio Possevino, Guy Tachard) and became a central source not only for Brucker's and Mosheim's discussion of "oriental doctrine" but also for Diderot's article on "philosophie asiatique" (1751) that is discussed in Chapter 3.

In the course of the eighteenth century, the old idea that emanation and transmigration had been brought by Pythagoras via Egypt to India got reversed, and India became the ultimate point of origin. Emanation and the thought of a first principle adopting myriad forms had long been linked to the teaching of Buddha, as was the doctrine of transmigration. The idea of the Egyptian origin of such teachings (and by consequence also of Buddhism)—which had prominent supporters like Kircher (1667), La Croze (1724), Kaempfer (1729), and Brucker (1744)—lingered on, but in the second half of the eighteenth century, the notion of an Indian cradle carried the day.

Regardless of such controversies about origins, it can be said that, from the sixteenth to the nineteenth centuries, the doctrines of emanation and transmigration constituted a crucial link between East and West extending from Japan in the Far East (where these two ideas had since the sixteenth century been associated by missionaries with the esoteric and exoteric teachings of Xaca or Buddha) via China, Vietnam, Siam, India, and Persia to Egypt and Greece. In the thought of Ramsay (Chapter 5) and Holwell (Chapter 6), this link took on a particularly poignant form since these authors identified transmigration as a most ancient and universal pre-Mosaic teaching concerning the fall of angels before the creation of the earth—a teaching that in their view forms the initial part of the biblical creation story that Moses omitted. They regarded human souls as the souls of fallen angels imprisoned in human bodies who have to migrate from one body to the next until they achieve redemption and can return to their heavenly home.

5. Origins and Lines of Transmission

Almost all European writers about Asian religions addressed questions of origin and transmission. They were concerned, among other things, with the connection between secular and sacred history and the problem of national and religious identity. In 1498, just after the discovery of America, Annius of Viterbo produced a number of forged texts that linked the national histories of Spain, Italy, France, and Germany to Noah. While European kings and nations were beneficiaries of the "good" transmission line originating with Adam, his good son Seth, and Noah (who according to Annius had traveled to blessed Italy to transmit antediluvian wisdom), other nations were not so lucky since they received their religion from Noah's son Ham, the pivotal member of the "evil" transmission line originating with Cain. Though Annius did not invent the idea that Noah's son Ham is identical with Zoroaster, as Schmidt-Biggemann claims (2006:93), he certainly gave new life to an idea already popular with Clement of Alexandria and other early Christian writers (Rodrigues 2001:356).

Annius published his concoctions just when Vasco da Gama was sailing around Africa to India. Though he knew little about Oriental religion, Annius must have sensed its subversive potential and cleared a path to its understanding that was adopted by many. Among them was João Rodrigues, who in the early seventeenth century also identified Zoroaster with Ham and regarded the Chinese as his descendants (p. 356). This meant that the religions of India, China, and Japan were seen as part of a kind of "axis of evil." In this respect, Rodrigues was opposed to Matteo Ricci and the "accommodationist" Jesuit missionaries who, like their extremist figurist successors, put China in the "good" transmission line of original monotheism and Adamic wisdom. These two opposing views form the heart not only of the famous Chinese Rites controversy around the beginning of the eighteenth century but also of the black-and-white pattern underlying the vast majority of European views of Asian religions.

The question of transmission was often linked to ancient texts. The oldest ones were said to have been carved on two pillars even before the deluge, and Rodrigues was not the only European to think that the ancient Chinese had inherited their mysterious writing system and astronomical knowledge from antediluvian times. As the age of Moses and the Old Testament dwindled in the face of Asian claims of antiquity, the search for older texts and records of divine revelation became ever more urgent. The focus of this search moved from Egyptian hermetic texts, Chaldaic oracles, and so on toward the Chinese *Yijing* and eventually to the Indian Vedas.

This overall movement reflects major stages in the evolution of European interest in Asian religions and its oldest texts, and I argue in this book that this interest formed a decisive factor in the genesis of modern Orientalism. One of its many effects was that it furnished the motivation for Abraham Hyacinthe Anquetil-Duperron's 1754 trip to India, the first journey of a European beyond the Middle East with the sole objective of finding and translating ancient sacred texts. But even European opinion leaders like Bayle and Voltaire, who only traveled within Europe, tended to be profoundly affected by the discovery of Asian religions and ancient sacred texts. The impact of this discovery in such domains as the genesis of European atheism, the formation of the modern conception of religion, and the quest for a modern, less Bible-dependent European identity cannot be grasped on the basis of a few case studies. However, my studies indicate that this hitherto neglected perspective has a considerable potential to enhance our understanding of such developments.

6. Ur-Traditions

An increasing number of studies focus on the role of "ancient theology" (often called *prisca theologia* or *prisca sapientia* and linked to the *philosophia perennis*) in Europe's history of ideas. Since D. P. Walker's *The Ancient Theology*, which focused on Christian Platonism from the fifteenth to the eighteenth century and devoted a chapter each to the Jesuit figurists and to Chevalier Ramsay, this movement was usually associated with "a certain tradition of Christian apologetic theology that rests on misdated texts" (Walker 1972:1) and that flourished from the early Church fathers to the early eighteenth century. This grounding in Christian theology and Neoplatonism is also apparent in the case studies ranging from Proklos in the fourth century to Friedrich Schelling in the nineteenth featured in Schmidt-Biggemann's *Philosophia perennis* (1998). Though Schmidt-Biggemann draws the circle somewhat wider and also mentions Judaism and Islam, the overall scope remains thoroughly theological and Christian.

In the course of my studies on this subject, I noticed that Church fathers like Eusebius and Lactantius, Renaissance admirers of hermetic literature like Marsilio Ficino, Jesuits like Athanasius Kircher and the figurist Joachim Bouvet, and numerous other "ancient theologians" including Chevalier Ramsay (Chapter 5) were all confronting other religions and tried to link their own religion to an "ancient" (*priscus*), "original," and "pure" teaching of divine origin. Reputedly extremely ancient texts such as hermetic literature, Chaldaic oracles, and the Chinese *Yijing* (*Book of Changes*) played a crucial role in establishing this link to primordial wisdom. However, I found the same endeavor also in non-Abrahamic religions such as Buddhism where neither the creator God nor Adam, Noah, or the Bible plays a role.

A good example is the *Forty-Two Sections Sutra*, one of the most important texts in East Asian Buddhism, which also happens to be the first Buddhist sutra translated into a European language. Though the text originated roughly 1,000 years after the birth of Buddhism and in China, it came to be presented as the original teaching of the Buddha (his first sermon after enlightenment) and thus also formed a link to an "original teaching." The case studies of this book show that such misdated texts—and the urge to establish a link between one's own creed and a most ancient teaching— played an extraordinary role in the Western discovery of Asian religions.

Many texts mentioned in our pages are concerned with some "Ur-tradition"—God's instructions to Adam, Buddha's instructions to his closest disciples, the "original" doctrine of the Vedas revealed by Brahma, and so on. These texts are covered with the fingerprints of various reformers and missionaries. On the *Forty-Two Sections Sutra* I found fingerprints of an eighth-century reformist Zen master; on the *Yijing* those of Jesuit figurists; on the Upanishads those of Shankara and the Sufi Prince Dārā; on the *Ezour-vedam* those of Jean Calmette and Voltaire; and on the *Shastah of Bramah* those of Holwell. As much as their respective agendas differ, they possess a common denominator in the obsession with vestiges of an ancient true religion that happens to support their mission. As discussed in Chapter 5, "ancient theology" thus reveals itself not as a unique European phenomenon but rather as a local form of a universal mechanism operative in the birth of religious or quasi-religious movements. This mechanism is characterized by the use of supposedly very ancient texts and unique transmission lines designed to legitimize new or reformist views by linking such views to a founder figure's old, "original" teaching.

Key Figures and Texts

1. The Japanese Impetus (Sixteenth Century)

Numerous recent publications stress the role of the nineteenth century when religions such as Buddhism and Hinduism became known under their modern names to a broader public. But the case studies of this book show that such identities were not suddenly discovered (or even "invented") by Europeans in the first decades of the nineteenth century. They developed over centuries, and even searching for roots as far back as the thirteenth century and the writings of people like William Rubruck and Marco Polo would be appropriate. This book argues that the systematic study of non-Abrahamic oriental religions and languages by Europeans began in sixteenth-century Japan, and that several key ideas shaping the European discovery of Asian religions in the subsequent centuries have their roots there. Helped by learned native informers familiar with Buddhist literature, the Jesuits wrote reports and letters about Japanese sects that were published in various languages and compendia across Europe. Unlike sixteenth-century reports from Africa, India, and America, they described a religious culture that was surprisingly similar to Europe's. It featured monks and nuns, monasteries and bells, rosaries and sermons, sects and sacred texts, baptisms and funerals, processions and temple services, and even heaven and hell. The dominant Buddhist denomination among Japan's ruling class was Zen. Its cartooned teachings became Europe's model for the "esoteric" doctrine of the Orient: quiet meditation, passivity, nothingness, all-oneness, no meritorious acts, no yonder. Such were, according to mid-sixteenth-century reports, the "real" teachings of Buddhism's founder Xaca, whose creed had come from India via China to Japan. But other sects of the same religion stressed worship, merit, retribution in a future state, and transmigration, and they even mentioned heaven and hell. These were said to be "outer" or "provisional" teachings of the founder. In Alessandro Valignano's catechism of 1586, this distinction between real/esoteric and provisional/exoteric teachings was touted as the master key to understanding Japanese religions. This catechism was reprinted in Possevino's *Bibliotheca selecta* of 1593, a textbook used by every aspiring Asia missionary and every student in Jesuit schools. It is one of the hitherto overlooked key texts of the European discovery of Asian religions. Early European perceptions of Japanese religion were extremely influential and also shaped the perception of Chinese religions (from the 1590s) and Indian religions (particularly by Roberto de Nobili in the first decades of the seventeenth century). They created patterns of understanding whose effects are shown to be pervasive in the seventeenth and eighteenth centuries and did not abate in the nineteenth century.

2. The Chinese Model (Seventeenth Century)

The man who most systematically applied Japanese insights to Chinese religions, João Rodrigues, did extensive research on Japanese and Chinese religions and was an exceptional linguist capable of handling primary sources in both languages. He is a hitherto mostly ignored key figure whose views exerted a profound and lasting influence on European perceptions of Asian religions. Unlike Matteo Ricci, whose 1615 report about China and its religions had gained a broad readership in Europe and opened many a European's eye, Rodrigues remained in the background. His groundbreaking research on the history of Chinese religions, chronology, and geography was used by others but rarely credited to him. However, in the form of Martino Martini's publications and of documents that proved decisive in the Chinese Rites controversy, Rodrigues's ideas reached a relatively broad readership. His reports were intensively studied in missionary circles, and his distinction between esoteric and exoteric forms of Chinese and Japanese religions became widely adopted.

The two major divergent views of the China and India missions—Ricci's and de Nobili's "good" monotheist transmission model versus Rodrigues's "evil" idolatry model—spilled over into other realms and also had important repercussions in Rome, where Athanasius Kircher in 1667 published under the title of *China Illustrata* a synthesis of an enormous amount of data from the Jesuit archives and personal communication with travelers and missionaries. He thought, like Rodrigues, that the Brahmans of India were representatives of Xaca's religion who had infected the entire East with their creed. A Chinese Buddhist text helped in fostering this mistaken view: the *Forty-Two Sections Sutra*. Its preface explained that Buddhism was introduced to China from India in the year 65 C.E. This text played an extraordinary role not only in the European discovery of Buddhism but also in that of China, Japan, and even America (see Chapter 4).

Of course, books attributed to Confucius also elicited major interest in Europe when they appeared in Latin translation, but even more influential was the portrait of Chinese religions in the preface to Couplet's *Confucius Sinarum philosophus* of 1687 (see Chapters 2 and 3). This book appeared at a time when scholarly journals such as the *Acta eruditorum* and the *Journal des sçavans* published extensive reviews of books on Asia and disseminated such information in the pan-European "republic of letters." The entries on "Spinoza," "Brachmanes," and "Japan" in Bayle's dictionary (1702 edition) quoted such reviews at length and drew a compelling picture of Asian religions while linking them to some of the hottest topics of European philosophical controversy. Bayle used reports from sixteenth-century Japan and seventeenth-century China along with information from Vietnam, Siam, Tibet, and India; among his sources was also Le Gobien's 1698 report about the religious tolerance edict of the Chinese emperor. Rodrigues had in his *Historia da Igreja do Japão* of 1620–21 already called the Brahmans "disciples of Shaka's doctrine" (Rodrigues 2001:360), but it was Le Gobien's preface to the book on China's imperial tolerance edict that became the main European conduit for the idea that Brahmans were Buddhist missionaries. This identification became one of the key ideas of the eighteenth-century pan-European reception of Asian religions, and it is a major reason why studies about "British," "French," or "German" discoveries of "Hinduism" or "Buddhism" in "India" or "China" are largely modern fictions.

3. The Indian Connection (Eighteenth Century)

The need to understand Japanese religions in order to criticize them had promoted the study of Japanese and classical Chinese among missionaries to Japan in the sixteenth century and led to the production of grammars and dictionaries. In the seventeenth century, the European spotlight had turned to China. The controversy about ancient Chinese religion had elicited acute interest in Chinese historical annals, in ancient texts such as the *Yijing*, and in philological methods to deal with such ancient sources. Claude de Visdelou and other talented French Jesuits were obliged to become competent Sinologists in order to translate and analyze such texts in a reliable fashion, and two of them (Jean-François Foucquet and Joseph-Henri Prémare) became informants of Voltaire (Chapter 1) and Ramsay (Chapter 5). But their know-how, books, and manuscripts were also used—though mostly without explicit acknowledgment—by Paris-based Sinologists such as Étienne Fourmont, Joseph de Guignes, and Michel-Ange-André Deshauterayes (see Chapter 4).

In the course of the eighteenth century, the spotlight turned to India. Early in the century, the German Protestant missionary Bartholomäus Ziegenbalg engaged in the study of South Indian religion, and his reports about India's monotheism caused a sensation. Ziegenbalg was standing on the shoulders of seventeenth-century Catholic as well as Protestant missionaries,[1] but he made extensive use of native informers and teachers and became able to study Indian texts independently. Many results of Ziegenbalg's specialized research were published later; but his manuscripts were made available to the royal librarian of Prussia, the noted linguist Mathurin Veyssière de La Croze, who recognized the novelty and extraordinary value of Ziegenbalg's work and intensively used his manuscripts for a groundbreaking treatise about Indian religions (La Croze 1724). Ziegenbalg and La Croze played important roles in the delimitation of the traditions that are now called "Hinduism" and "Buddhism" (see Chapter 2).

If the seventeenth century had its "good" and "bad" transmission factions, the eighteenth tended to pitch proponents of a single pan-Asian religion with different branches against people who, in the wake of Ziegenbalg and La Croze, distinguished the followers of Buddha in various regions of Asia outside India from the religions of India proper. An influential member of the "pan-Asian" faction was the German medical doctor Engelbert Kaempfer, who saw an "Oriental paganism" extending from Egypt via India and Siam to China and Japan (see Chapter 3). The English translation of Kaempfer's manuscript was published in 1727. Soon afterward, in the 1730s, the French missionaries and early students of Sanskrit Jean François Pons and Jean Calmette got hold of a copy of the hitherto elusive Vedas and researched India's oldest religious literature. A testament of their study is catechetic material such as the *Ezour-vedam*, whose main publicist was Voltaire. Voltaire used this text for his campaign to marginalize Judeo-Christianity by claiming Indian origins (see Chapter 1).

Just around that time, the British exploited the 1756 Black Hole of Calcutta incident as a starting shot for their empire. The writer of that report, John Zephaniah Holwell, also made a name for himself as publisher of a mysterious text: the *Shastah of Bramah*. The published fragments were introduced by the stunning claim that this text was far older than the Veda. Though the *Ezour-vedam* (published by Guillaume Sainte-Croix in 1778) and Holwell's *Shastah* (published in 1767) are not exactly divine revelations (see Chapters 6 and 7), they played an extraordinary role in focusing attention on India and its ancient religious literature. The study of Sanskrit texts by the English, which began in the 1780s and astonished Europe by such gems as Charles Wilkins's *Bhagavad gita* (1785) and William Jones's *Institutes of Hindu Law* (1796), opened the era of modern Indology.

Just before the first Europeans began receiving Sanskrit lessons from Alexander Hamilton in Paris, the last major translation of a Persian version of an Indian text was published: Anquetil-Duperron's pioneering Latin translation of the Upanishads (1801–2; see Chapter 7). It marked the end of an era, not only because ancient India, thanks to the study of Sanskrit, finally began to reveal its secrets but also because Anquetil-Duperron once more sought to prove the existence of an ancient pan-Asian monotheistic religion. By that time, the first secular institutions offering systematic instruction in oriental languages already existed: the Benaras Hindu College (1791; J. Duncan), the École Spéciale des Langues Orientales Vivantes in Paris (1795; Louis-Mathieu Langlès), and Fort William College (1800–1801; H. T. Colebrooke). They were soon followed by the East India College of London (1805–6; Hamilton) and, finally, in 1814 by the creation of Europe's first university chairs in Sanskrit (Antoine Leonard de Chézy) and Chinese (Jean-Pierre Abel-Rémusat) in Paris.

The Case Studies

The first of the included case studies explores Voltaire's role in the promotion of India as the perceived cradle of human culture. This idea played a major role in the second half of the eighteenth century and in the genesis of modern Orientalism. This chapter introduces some of the key ideas, figures, and texts and points to the importance of the contribution by missionaries. The second chapter focuses on the role of an early Protestant Indologist, Bartholomäus Ziegenbalg, whose ideas and writings were falsely thought to have had little impact. They were used, partly in manuscript form, by the linguist La Croze. These two men played pioneering roles in the delineation of Hinduism and Buddhism. The third case study presents Denis Diderot's view of Asian philosophy as presented in the French *Encyclopédie*. While tracing some of its sources back in time, it shows how the idea of a pan-Asian religion gained traction. The fourth chapter looks at a man who usually goes unmentioned in histories of Orientalism: Chevalier Andrew Ramsay, a pioneering freemason and secretary of two famous "quietists." It throws light on the European search for humanity's oldest religion and the role of Chinese and other ancient Asian sources in this quest. Chapter five shows how Joseph de Guignes, a pioneering Paris-based Sinologist, produced the first European translation of a Buddhist sutra (the *Forty-Two Sections Sutra*) and attempted to elucidate Asia's ancient religious landscape (and to confirm biblical authority) with the help of Chinese Buddhist sources. The sixth case study focuses on an early member of the British colonial enterprise, John Zephaniah Holwell, and his connection to a text that he hailed as the world's oldest sacred scripture, the *Shastah of Bramah*. The seventh case study looks at the motivations and aims of the first European who traveled to India in search of ancient sacred scriptures, Abraham Hyacinthe Anquetil-Duperron, and discusses what he found (as well as what he thought he found). The eighth and last case study examines the evolution of views about Asian religions in the work of Constantin-François Volney, who was not only a prime mover of the French Revolution, bestselling author, and friend of Benjamin Franklin and Thomas Jefferson but also a well-known Orientalist and promoter of the institutionalization of modern, Bible-independent Orientalism.

Chapter 1

Voltaire's Veda

François Marie Arouet—better known as VOLTAIRE (1694–1778)—was a superstar in eighteenth-century Europe and for a time one of its most read and translated authors. His plays were performed across the continent, and his view of world history was so influential that the Russian Czar, upon reading Voltaire's *Essai sur les moeurs*, sent an embassy to China to verify some of its claims. This chapter will highlight a little known side of this multifaceted man. Though current histories of Orientalism barely mention him,[1] Voltaire played an important role in the genesis of modern Orientalism. Since some of Voltaire's sources and his particular approach are deeply connected with the missionary discovery of Asian religions and mission literature, relevant facets of this missionary basis will first have to be examined in some detail. In Voltaire's time, much of Asia was still called "the East Indies," and the focus of previous scholarly discussion on India proper and on religions that are today associated with the Indian subcontinent must be widened in order to understand eighteenth-century views and images. The influence and staying power of old ideas have hitherto been underestimated. Not just the study of the Orient in Voltaire's time but even modern Orientalism is shaped by earlier impressions and approaches in profound and sometimes pernicious ways. It is a mistake to regard—in the manner of Schwab (1950), de Jong (1987), and many others—the onset of modern Orientalism as a clean break from a "nonscientific" past. As the examples of William Jones (App 2009) and Anquetil-Duperron (see Chapter 7) show, the pioneers of modern Orientalism raised the curtains and set a new stage; but much of the stage set seems recycled from earlier productions, and many actors in this play wear costumes of the sixteenth, seventeenth, and eighteenth centuries while expressing ideas that fit those times. The lack of appreciation regarding some of the crucial underpinnings of Voltaire's venture—particularly of missionary approaches and sources—gave rise to misunderstandings not only concerning his use of India-related sources but also the role he played in the genesis of modern Orientalism. Hence, the first task will be to discuss in some detail a number of facets of the missionary discovery of Asian religions that came to influence Voltaire's views and sources.

Valignano's Catechism

Partly due to the summary dismissal of missionary portrayals of Asian religions as biased, some of the basic events of the missionary discovery of these religions are still ignored even by today's Orientalists. It is, for example, a fact that the first systematic exploration of non-Islamic Asian religions happened not in India or some other land at a manageable distance from continental Europe but at the very end of the world as it was known at the time, namely, in sixteenth-century Japan. From the beginning of the sixteenth century, Catholic missionaries had settled in India and subsequently in various parts of Southeast Asia; but these were regions where even knowledge of the local vernacular did not yet entail access to sacred literature. Besides, the heathen cults were regarded as works of the devil to be exterminated rather than studied. In Japan, by contrast, the need for study arose from the fiasco of St. Francis Xavier's Jesuit mission.[2] FRANCIS XAVIER (1506–1552) and his Jesuit companions had arrived in the summer of 1549 in Japan with high hopes and accompanied by Anjirō, a Japanese man of modest education who served as their interpreter. He had translated "God" as "Dainichi" (the Sun-Buddha, the principal Buddha venerated by the Shingon sect of Buddhism), "heaven" and "paradise" as *jōdo* (the Pure Land of Buddhism), and "Christianity" as *buppō* (the Buddha dharma or Buddhist law); consequently, the Japanese were convinced that the Jesuits were Buddhist sectarian reformers from India. They had indeed come to Japan from Goa in India, and the Japanese (whose world at the time ended in India alias "Tenjiku") consistently called Xavier and his companions "Indians" ("Tenjiku's" or "Tenjikujin") (App 1997a:55–58). The Japanese Shingon priests were so delighted with their new cousins from India that the Jesuits became suspicious; but even after Francis Xavier's departure toward the end of 1551, the missionaries were still viewed as a bunch of zealous Buddhist sectarians. The document that supposedly proves their most notable success, the donation of a "church"

TABLE 1. EDICT OF THE DUKE OF YAMAGUCHI TRANSLATED FROM JAPANESE AND
PORTUGUESE

English translation of Japanese text (actual content of edict)	Translation of published Portuguese text (how missionaries translated edict)
The bonzes[a] who have come here from the Western regions may, for the purpose of promulgating the Buddhist law, establish their monastic community [at the Buddhist monastery of the Great Way].	[The Duke] accords the great Dai, Way of Heaven, to the fathers of the occident who have come to preach the law that produces Saints in conformity with their wish until the end of the world.

[a] The term "bonze" (from Jap. *bōzu*) has been in use since the sixteenth century for Buddhist priests or monks (originally of Japan or China, but later increasingly as a generic term). In this book we will also encounter such equivalents as "heshang" for China, "lama" for Tibet, and "talapoin" for Southeast Asia.

(in reality, a Buddhist monastery) by the regent of Yamaguchi, became an object of widespread interest in Europe as it was printed in various letter collections all over the continent and became the first document in Chinese characters to be printed in Europe (Schurhammer 1928:26–27; App 1997b:236). The confrontation of the crucial portion of the published Portuguese rendering with my translation of the original Japanese text in Table 1 illustrates the heart of the problem: the Japanese regarded the missionaries as Buddhist bonzes intent on promulgating the Buddha dharma, whereas the Jesuit missionaries believed that the donation of a Buddhist temple signaled acceptance of their stated aim of producing Christian saints.[3]

Only in 1551, when Francis Xavier was getting ready to leave Japan in order to convert the Chinese, did the missionaries begin to use the word "Deus" instead of "Dainichi" (App 1997b:241–42). Their fiasco triggered a "language reform" that consisted in figuring out which terms were Buddhist, what they signified, and which were safe for use in a Christian context. This could only be achieved by some degree of systematic study and with the help of native informers familiar with Buddhist doctrine and texts. By 1556, eight years after the beginning of the Japan mission, the first report about the country's religions was sent via Goa to Europe, where it arrived in 1558 (Bourdon 1993:261).[4] This *Sumario de los errores* (Summary of Errors) contained a first survey of Japanese religions including Shinto and listed eight sects of Japanese Buddhism. They were all identified as belonging to "bupō" (Buddha dharma) and associated with a founder called Shaka (Shakyamuni Buddha) (Ruiz-de-Medina 1990:655–67). The *Sumario* also furnished information about the clergies of these sects, the texts they used, and some of their doctrines including a topic that was to have extraordinary repercussions well into Voltaire's time: the distinction between two significations of Buddhist doctrines, an exoteric or outer one for the simple-minded people and an esoteric or inner one for the philosophers and literati (pp. 666–67). The esoteric teaching, which was associated with Zen Buddhism and its use of meditation and *kōans*, was said to lead to the realization that there is nothing beyond life and death and that "all is nothing" (p. 666). This is an early seed of the European misconception of an esoteric "cult of nothingness"[5] with a secret teaching that later turned into the legend about the Buddha's deathbed confession (see Chapter 3).

When the Jesuit Alessandro VALIGNANO (1539–1606) visited Japan for the first time between 1579 and 1582, he quickly realized that the study of the native language and religions was of paramount importance. He reported, "The first thing that I addressed and ordered after arriving in Japan . . . was that the European brothers study [the language] with great care and that a grammar and vocabulary of Japanese be produced" (Schütte 1951:321). Valignano promoted the admission of Japanese novices and, helped by P. Luis Frois who translated his words into Japanese, in 1580–81 held a course of intensive instruction for both European and Japanese novices (Schütte 1958:84–85). One of Valignano's eight new novices, the middle-aged Japanese doctor Paulo Yōhō, was knowledgeable about Japanese religions and provided information about Buddhism to both Valignano and the novices. Together with his son Vicente Tōin, Paulo helped Valignano craft a catechism whose overall structure interests us here. Since Valignano had studied Francis Xavier's fiasco and realized the importance of clearly separating truth from error, he decided to write a catechism and devote the first of its two books to the sects and religions of the Japanese in order to build a firm basis for their refutation through rational argumentation (Valignano 1586:3–76). It is a detailed presentation and critique of (mostly Buddhist) Japanese religious doctrine and shows how much knowledge the Jesuits had accumulated since the days of Francis Xavier. The catechism's second book then treats of Christian life and its basis in the Ten Commandments and other doctrines.

An interesting and influential observation that Valignano made at the beginning of the first part was that, in spite of the multitude of sects in Japan and the confusing doctrines of Buddhism, there was a key that facilitated understanding all of them. This key was the distinction between an "outer" or provisional teaching for the common people (Jap. *gonkyō*) and the "inner" or true teaching for the clergy (Jap. *jikkyō*) (p. 4v).[6] Valignano's entire presentation of doctrines and sects is based on this "gon-jitsu" distinction, which he, of course, decries as "fallacious, mendacious, and deceptive" (*fallax, mendax, hominum deceptrix*) (p. 34v).

Without going into more detail, we note that this catechism is proof that Buddhism was already quite intensively studied by Westerners in the sixteenth century with the help of native experts. For his reform of the Jesuit Japan mission, Valignano even researched and copied some features of the organizational structure of Zen monasteries. Such study continued in the following decades until the expulsion of all missionaries from Japan in the early seventeenth century, and among its major fruits was a Japanese-Portuguese dictionary with about 32,000 entries (*Vocabulario da Lingoa de Iapam*, 1603; Jap. *Nippo jisho*). In this dictionary, all Buddhist terms are identified by the marker "*Bup*," for *buppō* (Buddhism)—which proves how aware the missionaries were of Buddhism's identity as a religion. This dictionary alone should lay forever to rest all claims that Buddhism was not perceived as a religion by Westerners before the nineteenth century. It is easy, however, to overestimate the influence of such mission documents since many of them soon ended up in dusty mission archives. While reports such as the *Sumario de los errores* got relatively little public exposure, Valignano's catechism enjoyed the opposite fate. Its first edition, printed in Lisbon in 1586, is exceedingly rare, but the work was included almost unchanged in Antonio Possevino's *Bibliotheca selecta* of 1593, a major textbook for generations of Jesuits and for Europe's educated class (Possevino 1593:459–529; Mühlberger 2001:137–38). At the time, this was just about the most powerful megaphone anyone could wish for, and all the Jesuit protagonists in this chapter heard the message.

Ricci's Rebranding

When Matteo RICCI (1552–1610) arrived in China in the summer of 1582 and began to learn Chinese, he benefited from a special introduction to Asian religions since Valignano, who was also in Macao at the time, made him copy the conclusions ("Risolutioni") that he had drawn from his three-year stay in Japan (Schütte 1958:63). But when Ricci in the same year moved with another Italian missionary, Michele Ruggieri,[7] to Canton and then to Zhaoqing in South China, history seemed to repeat itself with a vengeance: the two

Jesuits adopted the title and vestments of the Chinese *seng*—that is, they identified themselves and dressed as ordained Buddhist bonzes. Even their Ten Commandments in Chinese contained Buddhist terms; for example, the third commandment read that on holidays it was forbidden to work and one had to go to the Buddhist temple (*si*) in order to recite the sutras (*jing*) and worship the Master of Heaven (*tianzhu*, the Lord of devas).[8] Ruggieri's and Ricci's first Chinese catechism, the *Tianzhu shilu* of 1584—the first book printed by Europeans in China—also brimmed with Buddhist terms and was signed by "the bonzes from India" (*tianzhuguo seng*) (Ricci 1942:198). The doorplate of the Jesuit's residence and church read "Hermit-flower [Buddhist] temple" (*xianhuasi*), while the plate displayed prominently inside the church read "Pure Land of the West" (*xilai jingdu*).[9] As can be seen in the report about the inscriptions on the Jesuit residence and church of Zhaoqing (Figure 1),[10] Ruggieri translated "hermit" (*xian*), a term with Daoist connotations, by the Italian "santi" (saints), and the Buddhist temple (*si*) became an "ecclesia" (church). Even more interesting is his transformation of the Buddhist paradise or "Pure Land of the West" into "from the West came the purest fathers."[11] This presumably referred to the biblical patriarchs, but it is not excluded that a double-entrendre (Jesuit fathers from the West) was intended.

Nine years later, in 1592, when Ricci was translating the four Confucian classics, he decided to abandon his identity as a Buddhist bonze (*seng*); and during a visit in Macao, he asked his superior Valignano for permission also to shed his bonze's robe, begging bowl, and sutra recitation implements. The Christian churches were renamed from *si* to *tang* (a more neutral word meaning "hall"), and in 1594 the final step in this rebranding process was taken when Ricci received Valignano's permission to present himself and dress up as a Chinese literatus (Duteil 1994:85–86). It was the year when Ricci finished his translation of the four Confucian classics, the books that any Chinese wishing to reach the higher ranks of society had to study. In Ricci's view, these books contained unmistakable vestiges of ancient monotheism. In his journals he wrote,

> Of all the pagan sects known to Europe, I know of no people who fell into fewer errors in the early stages of their antiquity than did the Chinese. From the very beginning of their history it is recorded in their writings that they recognized and worshiped one supreme being whom they called the King of Heaven, or designated by some other name indicating his rule over heaven and earth. . . . They also taught that the light

Avanti la porta della casa nostra

Ecclesia e fior novello degli Santi

Figure 1. Inscriptions for the Jesuit residence and church in Zhaoqing, 1584.

of reason came from heaven and that the dictates of reason should be hearkened to in every human action. (Gallagher 1953:93)

The Jesuit language reform in China took a different direction from the earlier one in Japan; instead of intensively studying the Buddhist and Daoist competition in order to defeat it, Ricci and his companions focused on cozying up to the Confucians. On November 4, 1595, Ricci wrote to the Jesuit Father General Acquaviva: "I have noted down many terms and phrases [of the Chinese classics] in harmony with our faith, for instance, 'the unity of God,' 'the immortality of the soul,' the glory of the blessed,' and the like" (Ricci 1985:14). Ricci intended to identify appropriate terms in the Confucian classics to give the Christian dogma a Mandarin dress and to illustrate his view that the Chinese had successfully safeguarded an extremely ancient knowledge of God. The portions of Ruggieri and Ricci's old "Buddhist" catechism dealing with God's revelation and requiring faith rather than reason were removed, while topics such as the "goodness of human nature" that appealed to Confucians were added (p. 15). Ricci systematically substituted Buddhist terminology with phrases from the Chinese classics. But rather than as a revision of his earlier "Buddhist" catechism, Ricci's *True Meaning of the Lord of Heaven* should be regarded as a new work reflecting his view of China's ancient theology. It was crafted in the mold of the first part of Valignano's catechism of 1586, and exactly ten years after the publication of that work, Ricci's supervisor Valignano examined and approved Ricci's new text for use in China. It was not a catechism in the traditional sense but a *praeparatio evangelica*: a way to entice the rationalist upper crust of Chinese society and to refute the "superstitious" and "foreign" forms of Chinese religion (such as Daoism and Buddhism) by logical argument while interpreting "original" Confucianism as a kind of Old Testament to Christianity. Ricci's "catechism" was thus not yet the Good News itself but a first step toward it. It argued that Chinese religion had once been thoroughly monotheistic and that this primeval monotheism had later degenerated through the influence of Daoism and Buddhism. In Ricci's view Christianity was nothing other than the fulfillment of China's Ur-monotheism.

Ricci decided to cast this preparatory treatise in Renaissance fashion as a dialogue between a Western and a Chinese scholar who discuss various aspects of Chinese religion. Ricci's Western scholar analyzes Daoist, Buddhist, and Neoconfucianist beliefs and practices and proceeds to demolish them by rational argument, thus exposing their inconsistency and irrationality. When Ricci's work was completed and his new manuscript began to circulate in preparation for the printing, the old "Buddhist" catechism was no longer used.

Rodrigues's Two Transmissions

When the first copies of Ricci's *True Meaning of the Lord of Heaven* arrived in Japan, one of Valignano's erstwhile novices, João RODRIGUES (1561–1633), studied it with much interest. Having arrived in Japan in 1577 at the young age of 16, he had at the turn of the seventeenth century already spent a quarter-century in the Far East and had become the best foreign speaker, reader, and writer of Japanese in the Jesuit mission. He had become not only procurator of the Japan mission but also court interpreter for Japan's auto-cratic ruler Tokugawa Ieyasu. When Valignano left Japan for the last time in 1603, Rodrigues was just putting the finishing touches on his remarkable Japanese grammar *Arte da Lingoa de Iapam*, which was first printed in 1604 (Cooper 1994:228). Like any educated Japanese of the time, Rodrigues had also studied classical Chinese and sprinkled his grammar with examples from Confucius's *Analects*. The depth of his knowledge of Japanese language and religion is apparent in his advice on letter writing style, which includes an introduction to the various kinds and degrees of Buddhist clergy and the correct ways of addressing them (Rodrigues 1604:199r–201r). His grammar also features a masterly treatise on Japanese poetry that is "the first compre-hensive description of Far Eastern literature by any European" and includes a section on the translation of Chinese poetry into Japanese (Cooper 1994:229–30). Rodrigues was very much interested in the origins of Asian religions and peoples, and for this a firm grasp of chronology was needed. The third part of his grammar (Rodrigues 1604:232v–239r) contains Ro-drigues's chronological tables based on both Western and Far-Eastern sources.[12] In the section on Chinese chronology, Rodrigues made the first known attempt to relate Japanese, Chinese, and Western chronologies. His aim was to position the founders of China's three major religions (Confucian-ism, Daoism, and Buddhism) in the framework of biblical history and its accepted chronological sequence (pp. 235r–236r).

After being forced out of Japan in 1610, he spent the rest of his life in China. He thus lived a total of thirty-three years in Japan and twenty-three in China. Even though his name is seldom if ever mentioned in books about the discovery of Oriental religions, it is clear that, during his fifty-six years in Asia, he became by far the most knowledgeable Westerner of his time about the religions of Japan and China. Even in his late teens, he had the chance of participating in Valignano's lecture series leading to the 1586 catechism and was instructed by Japanese experts on Buddhism.[13] When Ricci's Chinese books made their way to Japan, Rodrigues thus was one of the few people capable of studying and criticizing them.[14] He noticed a number of "grave things":

These things arose on account of the lack of knowledge at that time and the Fathers' ways of speaking and the conformity (as in their ignorance they saw it) of our holy religion with the literati sect, which is diabolical and intrinsically atheistic, and also contains fundamental and essential errors against the faith. (Cooper 1981:277)

Rodrigues's early doubts about Ricci's view of Confucianism as a vestige of primeval monotheism were reinforced when he spent two entire years ·(June 1613–June 1615) traveling in China "deeply investigating all these sects, which I had already diligently studied in Japan" (p. 314). His "three sects of philosophers" are Confucianism, Daoism, and Buddhism, which Rodrigues not only studied in books but also through extensive field research: "To this end I passed through most of China and visited all our houses and residences, as well as many other places where our men had never been so far" (p. 314). The catechism that Rodrigues compiled (pp. 306, 315), a detailed atlas of Asia with tables of longitudes and distances (pp. 302–3), and a small report (p. 321) as well as a voluminous treatise (pp. 310, 277) about Far Eastern religions seem to be lost. However, some of their content survived. Maps and other geographical materials by Rodrigues were used without attribution by his ambitious fellow Jesuit Martino Martini,[15] and his reports about Asia's religions formed a principal source of Niccolò Longobardi's famous essay that was written in the early 1620s but published in 1701 at the height of the "Chinese Rites" controversy raging in Voltaire's youth.[16] A number of Rodrigues's letters from China survived and are of considerable help in our reconstruction of the basic direction of his argument.

Contradicting Ricci, Rodrigues maintained that all reigning religions of China, including Confucianism, were fundamentally atheist and thus incompatible with Christianity. Influenced by what he had learned about the provisional (outer) and true (inner) teachings of Buddhism in Japan (the *gonjitsu* dichotomy underlying the first part of Valignano's catechism), Rodrigues detected the same two types of doctrines in all China's religions (pp. 311–12). According to Rodrigues, Ricci's problems were a result of his failure to understand this fundamental distinction and of his ignorance about the inner teachings:

Until I entered China, our Fathers of China knew practically nothing about this [distinction between exoteric and esoteric teachings] and about the speculative doctrine. They knew only about the civil and popular doctrine, for there was nobody to explain it to them and enlighten them. The above-mentioned Fr. Matteo Ricci worked a great deal in this field and did what he could, but, for reasons only known to Our Lord, he was misled in this matter. All these three sects of China are totally atheistic in their speculative teaching, denying the providence of the world. They teach everlasting matter, or chaos, and like the doctrine of Melissus, they believe the universe to contain nothing but one substance. (pp. 311–12)

The disappearance of Rodrigues's religion report is very likely due to his fierce opposition to a Ricci-style accommodation with Confucianism that was the central bone of contention in the controversy about Chinese Rites that filled so many book shelves from the mid-seventeenth century onward. The whole question of the acceptability of Confucian rites depended on Confucianism's pedigree. If it could be traced to monotheism, as Ricci thought it could, then its ancient rites posed hardly a problem. But if Rodrigues was right and Confucianism's inner doctrine was pure atheism (complete with eternity of matter, lack of a creator God, and absence of providence), then any rite connected to such a religion was to be condemned.

In his letters from China and some of his printed works, Rodrigues identified all three major religions of China as descendants of ancient heathen cults of the Middle East. While Ricci viewed Confucianism as a child of original monotheism and the Chinese literati as relatively free from heathen superstition prior to the influence of Daoism and Buddhism, Rodrigues envisioned a very different pedigree reaching back to Chaldean diviners:

There does not seem to be any other kingdom in the whole world that has so many [superstitions] as this kingdom [of China], for it appears that all the ancient superstitions that ever existed have gathered here, and even modern superstitions as well. The sect of Chaldean diviners flourishes here. The Jesuits call it here the Literati Sect of China. Like them it philosophizes with odd and even numbers up to ten and with hieroglyphic symbols and various mathematical figures, and with the principal Chaldean deities, Light and Darkness, and these two deities are called the Virtue of Heaven and the Evil of Earth. This sect has thrived in China for nearly four thousand years, and it seems to have originated from Babylon when those people came to populate this kingdom. (p. 239)[17]

Daoism, by contrast, was identified as "the sect of the Magicians and Persian evil wizards" that "seems to be a branch of the ancient Zoroaster" and Buddhism as "the sect of the ancient Indian gymnosophists" that spread all over Asia but had Egyptian roots since it professes "a part of the doctrine of the Egyptians" (p. 238). This may well be the earliest example of an Egyptian genealogy for Buddhism—an idea that had a great career in the seventeenth and eighteenth centuries (see Chapters 2, 3, and 4). For Rodrigues, all three Chinese religions thus had their roots in the Middle East: Confucianism in Mesopotamia, Daoism in Persia, and Buddhism in Egypt.

Since no one except Noah and his family had survived the great deluge, all three religions could not but have their ultimate origin with someone on the ark. The usual suspect was Ham, the son of Noah who had seen his father naked while drunk and whose son Canaan had been cursed by Noah (Genesis 9:25). According to Rodrigues, the Chinese people were descendants of Belus who "is the same as Nimrod, the grandson of Ham" who began to reign just after the confusion of tongues in Babel. The Chinese settled in their land after traveling "from the Tower of Babel straight after the Confusion of Tongues" and were "the first to develop . . . astrology and other mathematical arts and other liberal and mechanical arts" (Rodrigues 2001:355). Especially the "science of judicial astrology" that Chinese Confucians still practice "after the fashion of the Chaldeans with figures of odd and even numbers" was "spread throughout the world by Ham, son of Noah" (p. 356). All this led Rodrigues to the expected conclusion:

> According to this and the other errors that they [the Chinese] have held since then concerning God, the creation of the universe, spiritual substances, and the soul of man, as well as inevitable fate, the Chinese seem to be descendants of Ham, because he held similar errors and taught them to his descendants, who then took them with them when they set off to populate the world. (p. 356)

But how did such knowledge reach China? As Noah's descendants dispersed to populate the world after the Confusion of Tongues in Babylon, "the wiser families" according to Rodrigues took along such knowledge (and possibly also books) and proceeded to spread them throughout the world. In some places this knowledge was lost, but in others (like China) it was preserved (p. 378). If the transmission of genuine religion extended from God via

Adam, Seth, and Enoch to Noah, how about the antediluvian transmission of false religion?

> In addition to this astrological truth acquired through experience by the good sons of Seth, the wicked sons of Cain invented many conceits, innumerable superstitions, and errors. . . . they would commit many evil deeds and offences against God with the encouragement of the devil, to whom they had given themselves. For as it is written about him [Ham] and Cain, they were the first idolaters in the world and inventors of the magical arts. As he was evilly inclined, Ham, the son of Noah, was much given to this magical and judicial art, which he learnt from Cain's descendants before the Flood. (p. 378)

While the Chinese had safeguarded some useful scientific knowledge and the use of writing (p. 331) from the good transmission and thus had possibly managed to develop the world's earliest true writing system (p. 350), their religions, including Confucianism, unfortunately carried the strong imprint of Ham and the evil transmission. Rodrigues knew little about India, which he had only briefly visited on the way to Japan as a teenager. For him India's naked philosophers or gymnosophists and the Brahmans were all "disciples of Shaka's doctrine" (p. 360), and since Shaka (Shakyamuni Buddha) had "lived long before them," it was from him that they had learned such mistaken doctrines as that of a multitude of worlds (p. 360)—one of the views, *nota bene*, that around this time (1600) landed Giordano Bruno on the stake. Rodrigues thus regarded all three religions of China as descendants of the Hamite line that ultimately goes back to Cain, the slayer of his brother Abel. Though Buddhism was transmitted via India and reached China later than Confucianism and Daoism, it had the same ultimate root and atheist core. As we will see in Chapter 3, Rodrigues's vision of an underlying unity of Asian religions had a great future in the eighteenth century.

While Rodrigues fought against the ancient theology of Ricci and other Jesuits in China, a similar battle unfolded on the Indian subcontinent. In India, too, missionaries who were convinced that India's ancient religion belonged to the evil transmission fought against colleagues who believed that India had once been strictly monotheistic. The latter saw it as a land of pure primeval monotheism that, alas, had in time become clouded by the fumes of Brahmanic superstition.[18] The most famous Jesuit in India to hold the latter view was Roberto DE NOBILI (1577–1656), who was later falsely accused of having authored Voltaire's *Ezour-vedam*. The real authors of the *Ezour-vedam*, French Jesuit missionaries in India,[19] were also partisans of Indian Ur-monotheism—and so was their contemporary and critic in France, Voltaire.

Abrahamic Brahmans

One of Voltaire's favorite teachers at the Jesuit college Louis-le-Grand in Paris was Father René Joseph DE TOURNEMINE (1661–1739), the chief editor of the journal *Mémoires de Trévoux*. Father Tournemine had been involved in the controversy about the Chinese Rites that culminated in 1700 with the banning of several books on China at the Sorbonne. This so-called Querelle des rites had been accompanied by the publication of reams of pamphlets and books and is a striking example of public attention to oriental issues in Voltaire's youth and of their impact on the established religion in Europe (Étiemble 1966; Pinot 1971; Cummins 1993).

On the losing side of the rites controversy, which came to a peak one century after Ricci in Voltaire's school years, were those who agreed with his idea that the ancient Chinese had from remote antiquity venerated God and abandoned pure monotheism only much later under the influence of Persian magic (Daoism) and Indian idolatry (Buddhism). They liked to evoke Ricci's statement about having read with his own eyes in Chinese books that the ancient Chinese had worshipped a single supreme God. In order to explain how this pure ancient religion had degenerated into idolatry, they cited Ricci's story about the dispatch in the year 65 C.E. of a Chinese embassy to the West in search of the true faith (Trigault 1617:120–21). Instead of bringing back the good news of Jesus, the story went, the Chinese ambassadors had stopped short on the way and returned infected with the idolatrous teachings of an Indian impostor called Fo (Buddha). In the following centuries, this doctrine had reportedly contaminated the whole of East Asia and turned people away from original monotheism. Since Ricci's story[20] was told in one of the seventeenth century's most widely translated and read books about Asia, Nicolas Trigault's edition of Ricci's *History of the Christian Expedition to the Kingdom of China* (first published in Latin in 1615), it had an enormous influence on the European perception of Asia's religious history.

Ricci's extremist successors, the so-called Jesuit figurists (see Chapter 5), sought to locate the ancient monotheistic creed of the Chinese not just in Confucian texts but also in the Daoist *Daodejing* (Book of the Way and Its

Power) and of course in the book that some believed to be the oldest extant book of the world, the *Yijing* (or *I-ching*; Book of Changes). These figurists included the French China missionaries Joachim Bouvet (1656–1730), the correspondent of Leibniz, and younger Jesuit colleagues like Joseph-Henri Prémare (1666–1736) and Jean-Francois Foucquet (1665–1741), the man to whom Voltaire later falsely attributed the translation of his own "Chinese catechism."[21] The Jesuits of the Ricci camp thought that since genuine monotheism had existed in a relatively pure state at least until the time of Confucius, their role as missionaries essentially consisted in reawakening the old faith, documenting its "prophecies" regarding Christ, identifying its goal and fulfillment as Christianity, and eradicating the causes of religious degeneration such as idolatry, magic, and superstition. Ritual vestiges of ancient monotheism were naturally exempted from the purge and subject to "accommodation."

By contrast, the extremists in the victorious opposite camp of the Chinese Rites controversy held that—regardless of possible vestiges of monotheism and prediluvian science—divine revelation came exclusively through the channels of Abraham and Moses, that is, the Hebrew tradition, and was fulfilled in Christianity. This meant that the Old and New Testaments were the sole genuine records of divine revelation and that all unconnected rites and practices were to be condemned. From this exclusivist perspective, the sacred scriptures of other nations could only contain fragments of divine wisdom if they had either plagiarized Judeo-Christian texts or aped their teachers and doctrines.

But China was not the only country whose religious pedigree was questioned. As early as the Renaissance, Marsilio Ficino (1433–99) had pored over the texts attributed to Hermes Trismegistos and oracular texts reputed to contain vestiges of pre-Judaic monotheism. In those days the focus of interest was mostly on Egypt, which (at least in heathen circles) had long been regarded as the cradle of humankind. After the discovery of the Americas ("West Indies") (1492) and the exploration of the "East Indies" following Vasco da Gama's circumnavigation of Africa and arrival in India (1498), the possibility of finding pre-Mosaic texts containing vestiges of God's revelation in other civilized regions had to be considered seriously. Following the lead of Epiphanius, who had first identified the Brahmans as descendants of Abraham and Keturah (Paulinus a Sancto Bartholomaeo 1797:63), Guillaume Postel (1510–81) speculated in his interesting book *De originibus* (On the Origins) that the Indian Brahmans ("Abrahmanes") are direct descendants of Abraham (Postel 1553b:68–69). Postel was the first to suggest that India might harbor extremely ancient scriptures that could finally bring "absolute clarity" to the Mosaic narrative (p. 72). He thought that India was a land in which "infinite treasures of history and antediluvian books are hidden" and surmised that Enoch's books could be found there (p. 72). Though his idea was not exactly orthodox, Postel clearly stayed within the biblical framework since Enoch is one of the antediluvian heroes praised in the Bible and revered in Christianity as a pre-Judaic "pagan saint."[22] However, the emphasis on antediluvian texts by Enoch and possibly even older figures such as Seth, the good son of Adam, could also be interpreted as an attack on Mosaic authority and the Old Testament. At any rate, Postel postulated two Abrahamic transmissions: a familiar one in the Middle East and an alternative one to the "sons of the Orient" (p. 64) who were none other than the Indian Brahmans. Though it remained unclear what texts and doctrines this oriental lineage of Abraham had actually transmitted or produced, the tantalizing possibility remained in the air that a kind of alternative (and possibly more ancient) Old Testament could exist in India.

Postel's Abrahamic Brahmans soon became the object of criticism, for example, in Henry Lord's *A Discoverie of the Sect of the Banians*, which asserted that the Indians had never heard of Abraham (Lord 1630:71–72). Despite the criticism, in Voltaire's time there were still supporters of this rather effective way of incorporating the Indians (and other Asians linked to them) into the biblical lineage. One of them was Isaac Newton,[23] who wrote in his famous *Chronology* that was studied by Voltaire,

> This religion of the Persian empire was composed partly of the institutions of the Chaldaeans, in which Zoroastres was well skilled, and partly of the institutions of the ancient Brachmans; who are supposed to derive even their name from the Abrahamans, or sons of Abraham, born of his second wife Keturah, instructed by their father in the worship of ONE GOD without images, and sent into the east, where Hystaspes was instructed by their successors. (Newton 1964:5.247)

Another supporter of Postel's hypothesis was the Jesuit Jean Venant Bouchet (1655–1732), one of the major contributors to the large collection of Jesuit mission letters entitled *Lettres édifiantes et curieuses*, which was required reading for men like Voltaire, Abraham Hyacinthe Anquetil-Duperron, Constantin-François Volney, William Jones, and anyone interested in Asia and its religions. The India part of this collection contains a total of nine letters by Bouchet. By far the most famous and influential ones are those to the bishop of Avranches, Pierre-Daniel Huët (1630–1721). Huët's *Demonstratio evangelica* of 1678 attempted to prove the unbeatable antiquity of the Old Testament by asserting that all pagan gods derive from Moses (and occasionally other Hebrew patriarchs) or from Moses's wife or sister. D. P. Walker (1972:216) wrote of being "lulled into a coma by the monotony of 'Vulcanus idem ac Moses. Typhon idem ac Moses . . . Zoroastres idem ac Moses . . . Apollo idem ac Moses. Pan idem ac Moses . . .'."[24] Huët's purpose was not the coma of his readers but the fortification of his (and some readers') wobbling faith in the trustworthiness of Moses. The onslaught could not be ignored: there were, of course, Isaac La Peyrère (1596–1676) with his theory of pre-Adamites (1655) and Baruch de Spinoza (1632–77) with his *Tractatus theologico-politicus* (1670), who both attacked the Old Testament's value as a textual source. But hardly less dangerous were assertions by the likes of Martino MARTINI (1614–1661), the Jesuit missionary who shocked Europe by his report that Chinese historical records reached back to antediluvian times (Martini 1658; Collani 2000). Huët's herculean effort had filled his house with so many books that it ended up collapsing, and Bouchet's letters from India may have been designed to prevent Huët's precarious faith (Walker 1972:219) from suffering the same fate. Additionally, these letters mark the onset of a gradual shift from interest in China—which had dominated the second half of the seventeenth century and the first decades of the eighteenth century—to the focus on India promoted by Voltaire that fed the orientalist revolution described in this book.

Deist Mission and Universal History

Voltaire's *Sermon des cinquante*, the earliest print of which has been backdated to 1749,[25] is something like a prayer book of a society of fifty "pious and reasonable learned people" who meet every Sunday, pray together, and then listen to a sermon before dining and collecting money for the poor. If one replaces "dining" by "breaking bread," one immediately gets Voltaire's point: this is the Sunday service of his religion for "reasonable learned people." After the initial prayer to the one unborn and undying God who rewards good and punishes evil, the president of the society begins his sermon as follows:

My brothers, religion is the secret voice of God who speaks to all human beings; it must unite them all, not divide them. Thus any religion that belongs only to a single people is false. Ours is in principle the religion of the entire universe; because we venerate a Supreme Being, like all nations do; we practice the justice which all nations teach, and we reject all the lies that the peoples accuse each other of. In agreement with them about the principle that unites them, we differ from them with regard to everything that makes them fight. The point that unites all people of all times must necessarily be the unique core of truth, and the points in which they differ, the standards of lie: religion must be in accordance with morality, and it must be universal like morality. Thus any religion that offends morality is necessarily false. It is under this double perspective of perversity and falsity that in this discourse we will examine the books of the Hebrews and those who have succeeded to them. (Voltaire 1749:4–5)

This pamphlet is Voltaire's deist manifesto, whose beginning already indicates that it entails a harsh indictment against Jewish and Christian exclusivism. It is an impassioned plea against the sects of Moses and Jesus and all their superstitions, divisions, hatred, persecutions, and brutality, and ends with a call to return to a pure, united religion:

Oh my brothers! can one commit such outrages against mankind? Have not our fathers already relieved the people from transsubstantiation, the veneration of creatures and bones of the dead, and from oral confession, indulgences, exorcisms, false miracles, and ridiculous images? Have not the people become accustomed to be deprived of such superstition? One must have the courage to take some further steps. The people are not as idiotic as one might think. They will easily accept a wise and simple cult of a unique God that, we are told, the sons of Noah professed and all the sages of antiquity practiced, as all scholars in China accept. (p. 26)

Voltaire was a convinced deist, and the deists' creed was thoroughly inclusive: not just those born into a certain region or era or religion had received God's revelation but all humankind. True religion thus had to be natural religion, that is, the religion that God had poured into the heart of every human being. For this religion, the concept of universal consent was crucial, as the beginning of Voltaire's sermon shows: all nations and men belong to God's axis of good. Voltaire was not only in search of a universal history but also of a universal religion; and as soon as he embarked on his quest for a universal history during the 1740s, he also began to examine the religions of the world, particularly those of ancient Asia. Thanks to the writings of Ricci and his successors, he found that in China a pure veneration of God without any superstition and accompanied by excellent morality had once existed. However, as in other countries, this initial purity had become adversely affected through priestcraft and "the superstition of the bonzes" (Pomeau 1995:158). Voltaire was not interested in a simple extension of the biblical narrative to other countries, as was the case with the figurists in China or Father Bouchet in India who sought a link to a "good" son of Noah. That would have been tantamount to letting the Jews and their exclusivist divinity continue monopolizing human origins. For him it was not a question of the transmission of exclusively revealed truths or of the plagiarism of sacred scriptures in the sole possession of one people. Voltaire's eye was set on a true universal religion, a pure theism forming the root of all creeds. Already in a pamphlet of 1742 he had written,

> Deism is a religion that is present in all religions; it is a metal that alloys with all others and whose veins run underground to the four corners of the world. This mine is more exposed, more dug in China; everywhere else it is hidden and the secret is only in the hands of the adepts. There is no land with more adepts than England. (p. 159)

One of these "adepts" was Edward HERBERT, Baron of Cherbury (c. 1600–1655), who had built his central argument on "universal consent," that is, a common (monotheist) denominator to all religions of past and present. Voltaire thought that a pure, uncluttered monotheism suited to the taste of modern deists had existed in the remote past and that traces of it could be found in the most ancient cultures. Like his teacher Tournemine, Voltaire had with much interest studied the observations of Thomas HYDE (1636–1703) on the religion of Persia (1700) and found himself in agreement with the English scholar's argument that monotheism had anciently existed everywhere and left vestiges in the form of texts, myths, and rituals far older than those of Judaism. Of course he was also interested in such vestiges because they offered a chance to undermine biblical authority and its monopoly on ancient history. Was God less intolerant, cruel, and vindictive in texts other than the Old Testament—texts that were potentially much older than the scribblings of Moses and far less offensive to a modern deist who believed in God's universal revelation in the form of natural law for all rather than a secret communication to an individual or tribe?

Voltaire's search for vestiges of ancient monotheism thus formed part and parcel of his quest for a universal history that began in earnest in the 1740s. "Universal histories" such as the pioneering work by Jacques-Bénigne BOSSUET (1627–1704) tended to begin with the creation of the world in 4004 B.C.E. (Bossuet 1681:7) and to feature events such as Enoch's miraculous ascension in 3017 B.C.E. (pp. 8–9) and the universal deluge of 2348 B.C.E. For Bossuet, the time up to 1491 B.C.E., when Moses wrote down God's law, was "the period of natural law [Loy de Nature] when people had only natural reason [la raison naturelle] and the traditions of their ancestors to govern themselves" (pp. 17–18). From Bossuet's perspective, the histories and religions of all people were rooted in the events described in the Old Testament. Bossuet was well informed about the Chinese and had a hand in the campaign to condemn the Chinese Rites as idolatrous; indeed, it was through his offices that a "Letter to the Pope about the Chinese idolatries and superstitions" was printed (Hazard 1961:197). He was incensed that the Jesuits had dared to write of a "Chinese church" and thundered, "Strange kind of church without faith, without promise, without covenant, without sacraments, without the slightest sign of divine testimony. . . . After all, this is nothing but a confused pile of atheism, politics, irreligion, idolatry, magic, divination, and spells!" (p. 197). In the first edition of his universal history, Bossuet simply ignored this pile of refuse. But when he published the third edition of his history in 1700, at the height of the Chinese Rites controversy, he was forced to add alternative year numbers from the Septuagint version of the Old Testament. The Jesuit China missionaries had long made use of Septuagint chronology because it added 959 years to the world's age and thus guaranteed that the starting shot of biblical history rang before that of the Chinese annals. Thus Bossuet's pupil, the French royal heir apparent, and his numerous other readers needed to be informed that there was a second biblically supported date for the world's creation, namely, 4963 B.C.E. Bossuet's twelve epochs of world history, which so beautifully show his biblical and Mediterranean bias (1. creation; 2. deluge; 3. Abraham; 4. Moses; 5. Troy; 6. Salomo; 7. Romulus and Rome; 8. Cyrus; 9. Scipio and Carthago; 10. Jesus; 11. Constantine; 12. Charlemagne), thus all received a second, alternative date. As Kaegi (1938:82) aptly put it, these double numbers exposed "a small crack in the royal edifice that within a few decades deepened and eventually led to its collapse." But Bossuet's universal history was not the only one that featured a staunchly biblical narrative of origins. Even some more recent works such as the gigantic English *An Universal History from the Earliest Accounts to the Present* whose publication began in 1730 featured chapters titled "From the Creation to the Flood" and "From the Deluge to the Birth of Abraham" (Sale et al. 1747:1.1–153).

When Voltaire in the early 1740s set out to write his *Essai sur les moeurs et l'esprit des nations et sur les principaux faits de l'histoire depuis Charlemagne jusqu'à Louis XIII* (which in the following will simply be called *Essai*), he intended not to supplant Bossuet's history but rather to supplement it; but it irked him no end that a few rather insignificant nations around the Mediterranean Sea had hijacked the early history of humankind. In the introduction to the first fragments for his new beginning of universal history, Voltaire wrote,

> Until now, the majority of Universal Histories treated other peoples as if they did not exist at all. Greece and the Romans have seized all of our attention, and when the famous Bossuet says a word about the Mohammedans, he speaks of them only as an inundation of barbarians, even though many of these nations possessed useful arts that we inherited from them. . . . We are neither just nor wise to ignore them. (Voltaire 1745:8)

While getting ready to remedy this state of affairs, Voltaire wanted to collect what his predecessors had neglected (p. 5) in order to furnish a truly universal history of "the customs of man and the revolutions of the human spirit" (p. 5). The first draft chapters of this new history dealt not with Adam and creation but with China and India, which pointed to a looming revolution in Europe's perception of origins. Voltaire's central and most influential work is without any doubt the *Essai*. With regard to his view of Asian religions and to the development of his vision of India and its religions, the *Essai* is most interesting because its different editions reflect different stages of Voltaire's outlook. We will thus focus on this central text of Voltaire and adduce other works as needed. Table 2 lists the stages of the *Essai*'s genesis with brief remarks about the relevance for our inquiry.

TABLE 2. VOLTAIRE'S *ESSAI SUR LES MOEURS* AND ASIAN RELIGIONS

1745	The *1745 fragments* (later used in the *Essai*) published in the *Mercure de France* contain an introduction and the first two chapters on China and India which reflect Voltaire's early view of Asian religions and literature.
1756	The *first edition* of the *Essai sur les moeurs* contains many changes and additions to the 1745 texts on China and India reflecting Voltaire's intensive study of missionary and travel literature before his encounter with the *Ezour-vedam*. Apart from the China and India chapters, ch. 120 on Japan contains information about Voltaire's view of India and its sacred literature.
1761	The *second edition* of the *Essai sur les moeurs* reflects Voltaire's study of the *Ezour-vedam* and contains—apart from a new chapter on the Brahmans, the Veda, and the *Ezour-vedam*—also many interesting revisions and additions. The Indies part of the Japan chapter now forms a separate chapter (ch. 139) and contains some revisions and additions.
1765	Voltaire's *La philosophie de l'histoire* (published separately under the pseudonym of Abbé Bazin but in 1769 incorporated into the *Essai sur les moeurs*) contains Voltaire's views on the early history of religion and contains a chapter on "Bram, Abram, Abraham" and one each on India and China. (Voltaire's 1767 *La défense de mon oncle* is a defense against a critic of the *La philosophie de l'histoire* and, besides adding some relevant information, represents the apex of *Ezour-vedam* influence)
1769	The *third edition* of the *Essai sur les moeurs* newly features the 1765 *La philosophie de l'histoire* as Introduction to the *Essai*. The *Essai* itself also contains numerous passages reflecting Voltaire's study of Holwell's *Interesting historical events* and its fragments of the *Chartah Bhade*.
1775	For collective editions of his works, Voltaire revised his *Essai* text three more times and added some polemics (Pomeau 1963:xviii); these revisions are of little importance to our inquiry.

China and India in 1745

Voltaire's admiration of India is often described in the context of his purported shift from a similar but earlier admiration of China. In the eyes of Wilhelm Halbfass, this transition from infatuation with China to indomania happened in 1760 on contact with the *Ezour-vedam*:

> China at first appeared much more attractive and important than India in Voltaire's eyes, and he played an active role in helping to idealize the

"practical philosophy" and civic institutions of the Chinese. However, after studying the manuscript of the *Ezourvedam* which the Chevalier de Maudave had given him in 1760, he became convinced that the world's oldest culture and most pristine religious thought was to be found in India and not in China. (Halbfass 1990:57)

However, Daniel Hawley detected some admiration for India already in the 1756 version of Voltaire's *Essai*. But in support of his thesis that until the encounter with the *Ezour-vedam* Voltaire's India was the "exotic India" of *Bababec and the Fakirs* (1750), Hawley states that "before 1756 the majority of references to India in the *Essai* were no more than exotic details" (1974:166). A closer look at Voltaire's 1745 *Essai* chapters on China and India, however, results in a completely different picture.

Since Voltaire took the revolutionary step of beginning his universal history not with the creation story and Adam but rather with a chapter on China, questions of chronology were of great importance. Voltaire used information furnished by the learned Father Antoine Gaubil of the Jesuit China mission to characterize the accuracy of Chinese historiography as "indisputable" because it is "the only one based on astronomical observations" (Voltaire 1745:9). As we have seen, Bossuet (1681:17–18) had Moses write down God's law in 1491 B.C.E. or, if one used the Septuagint-based calculation, in 2450 B.C.E. At the beginning of Voltaire's China chapter of 1745, Gaubil's information is used to show that China's first king reigned twenty-five centuries before Christ. The fact that he already united fifteen kingdoms, Voltaire wrote, "proves that several centuries earlier this region was very populated, governed, and partitioned in numerous sovereign countries" (p. 11). Voltaire adduced China's gigantic population and towns, the Great Wall, its ancient use of paper and printing, and many other facts to convince his readers of both the antiquity and excellence of Chinese civilization (pp. 11–18). But near the end of his litany comes the surprising statement that there is one thing that might merit more attention than all China's mentioned achievements: "that from time immemorial they partition the month in weeks of seven days" (p. 18). This statement persisted unrevised through all subsequent editions of the *Essai*, but an explanation added in the 1769 version clarifies its significance: "The Indians used this; Chaldea modeled its method on it and passed it on to the small country of Judea; but it was not adopted in Greece" (Voltaire 1829:15.268).[26] The fact that Voltaire paid so much attention to this and mentioned it once more in his India chapter of 1745 ("their weeks always had seven days," Voltaire 1745:29) indicates that already in 1745 Voltaire was determined to use ancient India and China to destabilize biblical authority. The idea that the basic scheme of the Old Testament's creation story, the tale of seven days, was derived from far older peoples further east was a direct attack on Judeo-Christianity.

While Judea clearly was no more in competition for the oldest human culture, Voltaire was at this point still vacillating between India and China. Yet there were already signs that India was about to gain the upper hand. Voltaire mentioned that the ancient Greeks had traveled to India for instruction in the sciences and that the Arabs had adopted Indian numbers; but what most attracted his interest was the report that the Chinese emperor treasured Indian antiquities: "Perhaps the ancient Indian medals, which the Chinese make such a fuss about, are proof that the arts were cultivated in India before they became known to the Chinese" (p. 8). Regarding the other competitor, Egypt, Voltaire argued,

> If one had to decide between the Indies and Egypt, I would think that the sciences are much older in the Indies; my conjecture is based on the fact that the land of the Indies is much easier to inhabit than that in the vicinity of the Nile River whose inundations doubtlessly deterred the first colonizers until they tamed this river by digging canals; besides, the soil of the Indies shows a much more varied fertility and must have stimulated human curiosity and industry to a greater degree. (p. 29)

Even though Voltaire as early as 1745 suspected that the earliest human civilization was in India, his idealization of China held up as he added to the above quotation that in India "the science of government and of morals does not seem to have been as sophisticated as with the Chinese" (p. 29). But the question of origins was far from solved in Voltaire's mind. Eleven years later, in the 1756 version, he was to replace this last sentence about Chinese sophistication with the following:

> Some have believed that the human race originated from Hindustan, arguing that the weakest animal had to be born in the mildest climate; but all origin is veiled for us. Who is able to say that there were no insects, no grass, no trees in our climates when they were present in the orient? (p. 30)

This argument about insects points to Voltaire's belief that human beings of different races could, just like insects, have originated anywhere on the globe. In the 1761 version, he added a long paragraph in which he mocked Bible-inspired monogenetic ideas, including that of the *Ezour-vedam*. Voltaire's dismissive attitude toward the *Ezour-vedam* is at odds with the kind of admiration and complete trust that Halbfass's and Hawley's narratives make readers expect. Voltaire's trenchant critique of the *Ezour-vedam* tale of Adimo (here misprinted Damo but later corrected) clearly shows his unwillingness to replace biblical monogenesis with an Indian equivalent:

> All these considerations [about the fertility and easy life in India] seem to strengthen the old idea that mankind was born in a land where nature did everything for men and left them with almost nothing to do; but this only proves that the Indians are indigenous, and it does not prove at all that other kinds of people came from these regions. The whites, negroes, reds, Laplanders, Samoyedes, and Albinos certainly do not stem from the same land. The difference between all these species is as marked as that between a greyhound and a mullet; thus, only a badly instructed and pigheaded Brahman would pretend that all humans descend from the Indian Damo and his wife. (Voltaire 1761:1.44)

Returning to the 1745 India chapter after this foretaste of Voltaire's critical attitude toward the *Ezour-vedam* and his rejection of any monogenetic conception of origin, we note that in 1745, too, Indian religion was harshly criticized. From 1745 to the end of his life, Voltaire used the term "Bracmanes" or "Brachmanes" for the ancient clergy of India and "Bramins" for their modern successors. In 1745, he accused both the "Bonzes" (Buddhist clergy) and Brachmanes of fostering superstition, believing in metempsychosis or transmigration of souls and thus "spreading mindless stupidity [abrutissement] together with error" (Voltaire 1745:30): "Some of them are deceitful, others fanatic, and several of them are both;" and all "still prod, whenever they can, widows to immolate themselves on the body of their husbands" (p. 30).

We have already encountered several avatars of the idea that priests believe in a secret "inner" doctrine while misleading the people with "outer" lies and superstitious practices. This idea did not originate in the missions but already forms the basis of Plutarch's portrayal of Egyptian priests in his *Isis and Osiris* and runs like a thread via Lactantius, Augustine's *City of God*, and many other texts to the eighteenth century with its Jesuit figurists, John Toland's *Letters to Serena* (1704), and Ramsay's *Voyages de Cyrus* (1728) to Voltaire's *Essai*. We will see in Chapters 2, 3, and 5 that one of these avatars, the Buddha's deathbed confession story, played an important role throughout the eighteenth century. Of course, the conception of an "inner" doctrine appreciated by the elite and an "outer" one for the ignorant masses was also fundamental for Ricci and other missionaries who portrayed Chinese or Indian religions in this manner and produced the reading material that inspired Voltaire. Thus, it is by no means surprising that he adopted this very scheme in his 1745 portrait of Indian and Chinese religions. With regard to the Indians, Voltaire wrote,

> These Brahmins, who maintain the populace in the most stupid idolatry nevertheless have in their hands one of the most ancient books of the world, written by one of their earliest sages, in which only one Supreme Being is recognized. They preserve with great care this testimony that condemns them. (Voltaire 1745:30)

As Pomeau (1995:161) pointed out, Voltaire here probably amalgamated information about two Indian books from a letter of January 30, 1709, by Father Lalane included in the *Lettres édifiantes et curieuses* collection. The first concerns a book called *Panjangan* that proves the Indian recognition of one supreme being. Very much in the tracks of his Jesuit colleagues in China, Father Lalane wrote,

> Based on the evidence from several of their books, it seems evident to me that they [the Indians] formerly had quite distinct knowledge of the true God. This is easy to see from the beginning of a book called *Panjangan* whose text I have translated word for word: "I venerate this Being that is subject neither to change nor anxiety [inquiétude]; this Being whose nature is indivisible; this Being whose simplicity does not admit of any composition of qualities; this Being who is the origin and the cause of all beings and who surpasses all in excellence; this Being who is the support of the universe and the source of the three-fold power." (Le Gobien 1781–83:11.219)[27]

The second refers to the Veda, which Father Lalane described as follows:

> The most ancient books, which contained a purer doctrine and were written in a very ancient language, were gradually neglected, and the use

of this language has entirely disappeared. This is certain with regard to the book of religion called *Vedam*, which the scholars of the land understand no more; they limit themselves to reading it and to learning certain passages by heart, which they then pronounce in a mysterious manner to dupe the people more easily. (p. 220)

For Voltaire's China the same distinction applied. On one hand, he was enchanted with China's "morality, this obedience to the laws joined to the veneration of a supreme Being" that "form the religion of China, of its emperors and scholars [lettrés]" (Voltaire 1745:22). In the 1745 *Essai* fragments, Confucius is said to have "established" this religion "which consists in being just and benevolent [bienfaisant]" (p. 22) and conveyed "the sanest ideas about the Divinity that the human spirit can form without revelation" (p. 23). As Voltaire did not believe in any divine revelation other than the laws of nature, reason, and the moral principles in everyone's heart, it is clear that in 1745 he regarded this idealized Confucianism as the model of a religion. On the other hand, China also had its superstitions for the masses. Sects like the cult of "Laokium" (Laozi; Daoism) that "believe in evil spirits and magic spells [enchantements]" and "the superstition of the Bonzes" who "offer the most ridiculous cult" to the Idol Fo (Buddha) (p. 23) are certainly not to the liking of the "magistrates and scholars who are altogether separate from the people." But these members of the elite who "nourish themselves with a purer substance" nevertheless insist that superstitious sects "be tolerated in China for use of the vulgar people, like coarse food apt to feed them" (p. 25). In Voltaire's religion there was no tolerance for intolerance.

The 1756 *Essai* and Dreams of the Veda

Unlike the scattered chapters published in 1745, the 1756 *Essai* was the first complete version that Voltaire submitted to the public. It resounded, as we will see in Chapter 7, not only throughout Europe but even elicited an interesting echo in far-away India.

The most striking change in the *Essai*'s India chapter is found at its end where Voltaire eliminated two passages that were cited above. The first is about the bonzes and brachmanes who spread mindless stupidity and are deceitful, fanatic, or both; and the second is about the brahmins who maintain the populace in the most stupid idolatry even though they safeguard a book that recognizes a supreme being. In place of such critique, Voltaire in 1756 almost justifies the Brahmins:

> It would still be difficult to reconcile the sublime ideas which the brah-
> mins preserve about the supreme being with their garrulous mythology
> [mythologie fabuleuse] if history would not show us similar contradic-
> tions with the Greeks and Romans. (Voltaire 1756:1.32)

What had happened in the eleven years between 1745 and 1756? How did the Brahmins get rid of their superstitions, fanaticism, and evil instigation of the ritual suicide of widows (*sati*)? And how did the "most stupid idolatry" get transformed into a "garrulous" or "fabulous" mythology whose contra-dictions are not worse than those of the Greeks and Romans? A partial answer is not found in the India and China chapters at the beginning of the 1756 *Essai* but rather way back in chapter 120, "On Japan." For some reason, in this unlikely place Voltaire included new information on India, and here he also mentions a lesson learned through experience:

> It is true that one must read almost all reports that arrive from faraway
> lands with a spirit of doubt. People are busier sending us goods from the
> coasts of Malabar than truths. A particular case is often portrayed as a
> general custom. (Voltaire 1756:3.203)

Voltaire was now informed about some of the most striking features of Asian religions. He saw "almost all peoples steeped in the opinion that their gods have frequently joined us on earth": Vishnu had gone through nine incarnations, and the god of the Siamese, Sammonocodom (Buddha), report-edly took human form no less than 150 times (p. 204). Voltaire noted that the ancient Egyptians, Greeks, and Romans had very similar ideas, and he sought to interpret this "error" amiably and monotheistically:

> Such a rash, ridiculous, and universal error nevertheless comes from a
> reasonable feeling that is at the bottom of all hearts. One feels naturally
> one's dependence on a supreme being; and the error which always joins
> truth has almost everywhere caused people to regard the gods as lords
> who came at times to visit and reform their domains. (p. 205)

Another characteristic common to many religions is identified as atone-ment: "Man has always felt the need for clemency. This is the origin of the frightening penances to which the bonzes, brahmins, and fakirs subject themselves" (p. 205). For the Indian cult of the *lingam*, he also found Mediterranean counterparts in "the procession of the *phallum* of the Egyptians and the *priapus* of the Romans" (p. 205). Voltaire thought it "probable that this custom was introduced in times of simplicity and that at first people only thought of honoring the divinity through the symbol of the life it gave to us" (p. 205). These interpretations show how eager Voltaire was to find vestiges of monotheism even in ideas and cults that not so long ago would have elicited harsh words of condemnation or ridicule. Now he not only tried to interpret them as signs of ancient monotheism but also pointed to an ancient source:

> Would you believe that among so many extravagant opinions and bizarre superstitions these Indian heathens all recognize, as we do, an infinitely perfect being? Whom they call *the being of beings, the sovereign being, invisible, incomprehensible, formless, creator, and preserver, just and merciful, who deigns to impart himself to the people to guide them to eternal happiness*? These ideas are contained in the Vedam, which is the book of the ancient brachmanes. They are spread in modern books of the brahmins. (p. 206)

Voltaire then hints at the source of this information: "A learned Danish missionary on the coast of Tranquebar" who "cites several passages and several prayer formulae that seem to come from straightest reason and purest holiness." Had he finally found an alternative to the Jewish Old Testament? While in 1756 he had quoted only the first five words of a single prayer from a book called *Varabadu*—"O sovereign of all beings, etc." (p. 206)—the 1761 *Essai* features the whole prayer; and though the source is not further identified, it appears that Voltaire got all this information from the book published in 1724 by Mathurin Veyssière de LA CROZE (1661–1739) that will be analyzed in the next chapter.

Voltaire already appears to have used La Croze's book when writing his brief 1745 portrayal of the cult of Fo or Foe (Ch. Buddha) that described its Indian origin around 1000 B.C.E. and its popularity in most of Asia (Voltaire mentions Japan, China, Tartary, Siam, and Tibet; 1745:23–25). Such information was found in La Croze's survey of "Indian idolatry" (1724:424–519) that contained an early synthesis of ancient and contemporary information about phenomena that we today associate with Buddhism. But it also featured much information on Indian religion that Voltaire used for the 1756 version of his *Essai*. La Croze, a former Benedictine monk who had converted to Protestantism, had read early accounts of the sacred scriptures of India, the Vedas, and his status as Prussia's royal librarian helped him get access to a treasure trove of recent information on India's religions. These were the unpublished manuscripts of the German Lutheran missionary Bartholomäus ZIEGENBALG (1682–1719), who in 1706 had arrived in South India as India's first Protestant missionary and spent thirteen years in the Danish enclave of Tranquebar on India's southeastern coast (Tamil Nadu). Just two months after his arrival, Ziegenbalg proclaimed in a letter what was to become the tenor of his extensive studies of Hinduism: "They have many hundreds of gods yet recognize only a single divine Being as the origin of all gods and all other things" (Bergen 1708:19).[28] This assertion of ancient Indian monotheism was not only repeated and documented in Ziegenbalg's manuscripts but also found its way into two of Voltaire's major sources, namely, La Croze (1724) and Niecamp (1745).

Near the beginning of La Croze's investigation about the "idolatry of the Indies," Voltaire read that "in spite of the grossest idolatry, the existence of the infinitely perfect Being is so well established with them [the Indians] that there is no room for doubt that they have preserved this knowledge since their first establishment in the Indies" (La Croze 1724:425). Calling the Indians "one of the oldest people on earth," La Croze thought it "a very probable fact that in ancient times they had a quite distinct knowledge of the true God and that they offered an inner cult [culte interieur] to him which was not mixed with any profanation" (p. 426). To find out more about this, La Croze suggested, one would have to get access to the *Vedam*, "which is the collection of the ancient sacred scriptures of the Brachmanes" (p. 427). In the *Vedam* "in all likelihood one would find the antiquities [Antiquitez] which the superstitiously proud Brahmins conceal from the people of India whom they regard as profane" (p. 427). Consequently, the Brahmins (the modern successors of the ancient Brachmanes) introduce ordinary people only to "the exterior of religion enveloped in legends [fables] that are at least as extravagant as those of Greek paganism" (p. 428). According to La Croze, the *Vedam*, which can be read only by Brahmins who are its guardians, "enjoys the same authority with these idolaters as the Sacred Writ does with us" (p. 447). Always following Ziegenbalg's and his fellow missionaries' manuscripts, La Croze quoted a passage "from one of the [Indian] books" about God whom the Indians call "Barabara Vástou, that is, the Being of Beings" (p. 452).[29] La

Croze did not identify this book, but Voltaire must have been so impressed by the information about the monotheistic Vedas that, in the 1756 *Essai*, he jumped to the conclusion (Voltaire 1756:3.206): "These ideas are contained in the *Vedam*, which is the book of the ancient brachmanes."[30] In fact, the ideas mentioned by Voltaire—"*the being of beings, the sovereign being, invisible, incomprehensible, formless, creator, and preserver, just and merciful, who deigns to impart himself to the people to guide them to eternal happiness*"—were culled in almost identical sequence from a longer passage in La Croze, which reads as follows (words taken over by Voltaire are italicized):

> The infinitely perfect Being is known to all these gentile pagans. They call it in their language Barabara Vástou, that is, the *Being of Beings*. Here is how they describe it in one of their books. "*The Sovereign Being* is *invisible* and *incomprehensible*, immobile and *without* shape or exterior *form*. Nobody has ever seen it; time has not included it: his essence fills all things, and all things have their origin from him. All power, all wisdom, all knowledge [science], all sanctity, and all truth are in him. He is infinitely good, *just*, and *merciful*. It is he who has *created* all, *preserves* all, and who enjoys to *be among men* in order to *guide them to eternal happiness*, the happiness that consists in loving and serving him." (La Croze 1724:452)

With regard to the *lingam* cult Voltaire also followed La Croze and indirectly Ziegenbalg. La Croze had explained that "the *lingum* . . . is a symbolic representation of God . . . but only represents God as he materializes himself in creation," (p. 455) while Voltaire speculated that this cult "was introduced in times of simplicity and that at first people only thought of honoring the divinity through the symbol of the life it gave to us" (Voltaire 1756:3.205).

At this point, Voltaire leaned toward India as the earliest human civilization (1756:1.30) and believed that the most ancient text of this civilization was called *Vedam* and contained a simple and pure monotheism. So he must have been elated when a reader of his 1756 *Essai*, Louis-Laurent de Féderbe, Chevalier (later Comte) DE MAUDAVE (1725–77), wrote to him from India two or three years after publication of the *Essai*. Maudave had left in May 1757 for India and in 1758 participated in the capture of Fort St. David and the siege of Madras (Rocher 1984:77). While stationed in South India, Maudave had gotten hold of French translations from the Veda[31] and decided to write a letter to Voltaire. Having read the Japan chapter of the 1756 *Essai*, he knew how interested Voltaire was in finding documentation for ancient Indian monotheism through the *Vedam*. In the margin of a page of his *Ezour-vedam* manuscript (which he later passed on to Voltaire), Maudave scribbled next to two prayers to God: "Copy these prayers in the letter to M. de Voltaire" (p. 80).[32] Though these prayers are not found in the extant fragment of Maudave's letter, it is likely that Maudave included them in order to document the existence of pure monotheism in the *Vedam*. The second major point of Voltaire's 1756 *Essai* that Maudave addressed in his letter was the cult of the lingam.[33] In his discussion, Maudave quoted the *Ezour-vedam* as textual witness and offered to send Voltaire a replica of a *linga* and a copy of the *Ezour-vedam* (Rocher 1984:48).

Discoveries of the *Ezour-vedam*

Maudave's letter to Voltaire described the *Ezour-vedam* as a dialogue written by the author of the Vedas: "This Dialogue presupposes that Chumontou is the author of the Vedams, that he wrote them to countervail the empty superstitions that spread among men and, above all, to halt the unfortunate progress of idolatry" (p. 49). Maudave also specifically mentioned the author of the text's French translation: "Its author is Father Martin, the former Jesuit missionary at Pondichéry" (p. 49). Since this missionary had died in Rome in 1716, Maudave must have thought that the translation from the Sanskrit original was about fifty years old. This missionary connection clearly disturbed Maudave. First of all, a strange agreement with Christian doctrine made Maudave suspicious about the quality of the translation. More than that, he let Voltaire know that his doubts were specifically connected with the tendency of the translator's Jesuit order to find traces of their own faith in just about every part of the world—in Chinese books, in Mexico, and even among the savages of South America (p. 80)! Maudave had carefully studied the Jesuit letters including those of Calmette that announced the dispatch of the four Vedas to Paris and wrote the following about their content to Voltaire:

> This body of the religion and regulations of the country is divided in four books. There is one at the Royal Library. The first contains the history of the gods. The second the dogmas. The third the morals. The fourth the civil and religious rites. They are written in this mysterious

language which is here discussed and which is called the *Samscrout*. (Ms 1765, Musée d'Histoire Naturelle, Paris, 118v)

hat puzzled Maudave above all was that this information about the content of the Vedas was in total contradiction with what he saw in the *Ezour-vedam*. He wrote to Voltaire that the *Ezour-vedam* was a dialogue between two Brahmes, one of whom "believes in the religion of the Indies" while the other "defends the unity of God" (p. 122r). Maudave thought "this dialogue assumes that Chumontou is the author of the Vedams and that he wrote them to remedy the vain superstitions that spread among men and above all to stop the unfortunate progress of idolatry" (p. 122r). The Chumontou of the *Ezour-vedam* was both a fierce critic of rites and seemed to be the author of the Vedams. Maudave observed, "Here there is a very manifest contradiction since one book of the Vedams contains all the religious rites of which the cult of God forms a part" (p. 122v).

Maudave felt a problem that bothered many who read the *Ezour-vedam* and that will be explained in Chapter 7: somehow Chumontou seemed to be both the author of the Veda and its critic. At any rate, what Maudave knew about the content of the Veda must have made him think that the *Ezour-vedam* was not the real Veda. He was suspicious of some kind of foul play and continued:

> In spite of this [contradiction], I admit that the manuscript is quite singular. But I find in it propositions about the unity of God and the creation of the universe that are too direct and too conforming to our sacred scriptures to have complete trust in the fidelity of the translation. If you have some interest in seeing this manuscript, I will have it copied and will send it to you. (p. 122v)

Maudave thus expressed his doubts about the authenticity of the *Ezour-vedam*, the quality of Father Martin's translation, and the general tendency of Jesuits to find in texts exactly what they needed to find. Though by his own admission Maudave lacked the knowledge necessary to explain "the foundations of Indian religion" and wrote to Voltaire that the subject "had roused my curiosity only intermittently," he expressed his disapproval of Jesuit accommodation strategy and let the patriarch of Ferney know that "the abominable superstitions of these peoples arouse my indignation" (Rocher

1984:79). Maudave knew of Voltaire's strong interest in the Veda, and in this letter he both maintained that it must have been translated from Sanskrit and found that this text did not at all match his idea of the four Vedas. The depth of Maudave's doubts about the *Ezour-vedam*'s quality of translation and possibly its authenticity was such that he offered to have a copy made for Voltaire only if he was at all interested in the manuscript (p. 48).

On the occasion of Maudave's visit to Voltaire in late September or early October 1760, Voltaire received the *Ezour-vedam* along with an additional text called *Cormo-Vedam*.[34] During the winter he studied the manuscript, and in the following spring, he reported that he had found a way to "make good use of it" (Voltaire 1980:6.287). He had decided to include a new chapter about "the Brachmanes, the Vedam, and the Ezourvedam" in the *Essai*'s 1761 edition and wrote this chapter during the summer of 1761. He then had a copy of Maudave's texts made and on August 14 sent the original Maudave manuscripts to the Royal Library in Paris (Sinner 1771:128–29).

In 1762 Voltaire's nephew, Abbé Vincent Mignot, mentioned the *Ezour-vedam* in two of his five papers read at the Royal Academy of Inscriptions about the ancient philosophers of India. He thought that India had been inhabited earlier than Egypt but traced both the Indian and Egyptian religions back to the plain of Shinar (Sennaar) near the landing spot of Noah's ark (Mignot 1768:122, 144). For Mignot the *Ezour-vedam* proved the early presence of monotheism in ancient India; in support of this view, he quoted one of its prayers: "You are the savior, the father, and the lord of the world; you see everything, you know everything, you rule over everything" (p. 263; transl. Rocher 1984:7). But some readers of the *Ezour-vedam* manuscript also noted a number of strange passages that betrayed a Western author. For example, Anquetil-Duperron[35] remarked that Chumontou "does no more than to confront them [Indian legends] with the doubts of a philosopher who cannot be held to represent the religion of India" (Rocher 1984:8–9) and detected some passages that clearly stemmed from a European.[36] But as early as 1762, Abbé Mignot made the connection betweeen the *Ezour-vedam* and the monotheistic "gnanigöl."[37] In one of his papers on the ancient philosophers of India, he described these Indians as modern successors of the ancient Brachmans. They are "intimately convinced of God's oneness" and are regarded as "the sages and saints of India" who "openly reject the cult of idols and all superstitious practices of the nation in order to worship only God whom they call 'Being of beings' [l'être des êtres]" (Mignot 1768:218–19). In 1771 Anquetil-Duperron published his opinion that the text's author was one of these "Ganigueuls" or "gnanigöl" described by Ziegenbalg and La Croze (Anquetil-Duperron 1771:1.lxxxv), and this opinion was later supported in the preface to the *Ezour-vedam*'s first printed edition of 1778 where Sainte-Croix informed the readers:

> Everywhere in the *Ezour-Védam* we find the principal articles of the doctrine of the Ganigueuls . . . and therefore one cannot doubt that it was a philosopher of this sect who composed this work. A man immersed in the darkness of idolatry reports, under the name of *Biache*, the most accepted fables of India and exposes the entire system of popular theology of this country. The philosopher Chumontou rejects this mythology as contrary to good sense, or because he has not read of it in the ancient books, and expounds the fabulous accounts in a moral sense. . . . Responding to the questions of Biache, the Ganigueul philosopher explains the doctrine of the unity of God, creation, the nature of the soul, the dogma of punishment and reward in a future state, the cult appropriate for the supreme being, the duties of all states, etc. (Sainte-Croix 1778:1.146–47)

The association of these Gnanigöl with the *Ezour-vedam* will be discussed in Chapters 2 and 7; here I just note that anybody familiar with the arguments of deists and their opponents will immediately recognize the themes mentioned in this last phrase as central to the debate about Christianity. Though Sainte-Croix did not ascribe the text to a missionary, he regarded this teaching as quite different from that of the *Vedam* and explained that "Chumontou pretends to teach the *Vedam* by establishing his own system, and he does not bother to prove if it is really conform to the doctrine of that sacred book" (1.149). Such doubts led to the following conclusion about the text's authorship and age: "This work which contains the exposition of the principles of the philosophy of the Ganigueuls, as opposed to the actual beliefs of Indian people, can certainly not be very old" (1.150). In his footnotes to the text of the *Ezour-vedam*, Sainte-Croix also added various critical remarks; for example, an argument of Chumontou is dismissed in the editor's note by "Nothing more arbitrary and worse reasoned than this" (1.211), and exclamations such as "bad reasoning" (1.284) or "funny cosmography!" (1.254) pepper the notes. Furthermore, Sainte-Croix omitted some passages from the *Ezour-vedam* text because of his conviction that they were interpolations written by a European (1.267; 2.163).

Four years after the *Ezour-vedam*'s 1778 publication, Sonnerat (1782:1.215) described it as "definitely not one of the four Vedams" and as "a book of controversy, written by a missionary of *Masulipatam*" who "tried to reduce everything to the Christian religion" (Rocher 1984:13). In 1784, Gottfried Less wrote that the text reminds us of the Bible, must be based on that source, and is distinctly European and specifically French both in content and expression (pp. 15–16). Barely eight years after the *Ezour-vedam*'s publication and Voltaire's death, August Hennings claimed that "today no one believes any longer in the authenticity of the Ezurvedam" (p. 16). Although this statement is exaggerated,[38] it shows that harboring doubts about the text was normal among men who were far less skeptical and discerning about historical sources than Voltaire and had no inkling of Maudave's reservations before he brought this manuscript to Europe. Like Maudave in the late 1750s, these readers tended to become suspicious as soon as they studied the text with some attention.

The *Ezour-vedam* is set up as a conversation between Chumontou (Sumantu) and Biache (Vyāsa). Like Ricci's Western scholar, Chumontou presents himself as a reformer who wants to restore primeval monotheism to its pristine purity. The interlocutor Biache represents the degeneration of primeval purity into idolatry, polytheism, and priestcraft. Many of the themes discussed in the *Ezour-vedam* show such a strong Christian slant that one readily understands why Maudave wrote to Voltaire from India that he found the manuscript strange because it reminded him so much of the Bible and conformed so suspiciously to Jesuit mission strategy. A good example is the following explanation by Chumontou about the difference between man and animal that could hardly be more un-Indian:

> In creating man, God has created everything for his use. The animals have been created to serve him. Trees, plants, fruit, the different foodstuffs and in the end everything on earth has been made to cater to his needs. The distress and pain that animals feel is inseparable from their state since they are made to serve man; but they are not a [karmic] effect or consequence of sin. Here is why: the punishment of sin is eternal in its nature but the distress that animals feel is only temporary. Trees, etc., do not have a soul and are thus incapable of committing sins. However vile and despicable man may be, he has a soul and is always endowed with reason. He has a propensity for sin, commits it, and after death he reaps eternal punishment. Likewise with virtue: a good man practices it

during his life; and the moment of death is the happy instant when he begins to taste the fruit [of virtue] and to enjoy it in all eternity. (Sainte-Croix 1778:2.9–11)

Even a person like Maudave—who admitted at the end of his letter to Voltaire that he was more interested in the political situation of the country and in commerce (Rocher 1984:79)—must have felt skeptical when reading such an obviously Christian view of man's relation to animals and of soul, hell, and paradise along with such an unequivocal refutation of rebirth and karma. But what would a man like Voltaire, the famous critic of the Jesuits and one of the most discerning and mischievous readers of religious texts of his time, see in this text?

Voltaire's Indian Gospel

If Maudave "was puzzled by the French *Ezour-vedam* to the point of doubting its authenticity" (Rocher 1984:80), Voltaire's reaction on receiving the text from Maudave in the fall of 1760 is even more puzzling. We do not know what Maudave told him during his visit, but there is no doubt that he had informed Voltaire in writing (1) that the translator of the text was the Jesuit Pierre Martin (who had died in 1716) and (2) that he had doubts about the accuracy of the translation because of Jesuit involvement. However, shortly after Maudave's visit, Voltaire wrote in a letter that he was going to establish contact with the Indian translator ("my brahmin") and joked that he hoped that this Brahmin would be more reasonable than the professors at the Sorbonne (Voltaire 1980:6.20; October 10, 1760). Four months later, when he had thoroughly studied the text and expressed his confidence that he could "make good use of it," he described the translator as a "Brahmin of great esprit" who knows French very well (6.287; February 22, 1761) and who produced "a faithful translation" (6.298; March 3, 1761). In July 1761, at the time when he had decided to add a new chapter to the *Essai* about the *Ezour-vedam* and then to present his copy of the manuscript to the Royal Library in Paris, he claimed that Maudave had received the *Ezour-vedam* from a Brahmin who was a correspondent of the French Compagnie des Indes and had translated it (6.470; July 1761). After sending the manuscript to the Royal Library, Voltaire for the first time located this Brahmin translator in Benares, the center of Brahman orthodoxy (6.602; October 1, 1761). He repeated this last version until he encountered Holwell's work and learned that the *Shastah* was far older than the *Vedam* and its commentary, the *Ezour-vedam*. As we will see in Chapter 6, Holwell claimed that the *Vedam* contained the relatively corrupt teaching of South India, whereas his *Shastah* was expounded by the orthodox Brahmins of Benares in the north. In 1769, after having read this, Voltaire once more changed his translator story. Since (according to Holwell) Benares and Northern India are the home of the ancient *Shastah* and Southern India that of the far younger *Vedam*, Voltaire came up with a new narrative: the man who had translated the *Ezour-vedam* from the sacred Sanskrit language into French was now suddenly no more an orthodox successor to the oldest Brachman tradition from Benares but rather a mysterious "old man, 100 years of age" who was "arch-priest [grand prêtre] on the island of Seringham [Chérignan] of Arcate province" in South India—a man "respected for his incorruptible virtue" who "knew French and rendered great services to the Compagnie des Indes" (Voltaire 1769:2.68).[39] One would expect such a rare creature—an eminent old Brahmin heading a huge clergy who wrote perfect French and rendered great services to the colonial administration—to turn up somewhere in the French colonial records; but Rocher (1984:28) failed to find any trace of this man, even though, according to Voltaire, he had been a witness for the chevalier Jacques François Law in his conflict with Joseph François Dupleix.

What are we to make of this? Today we know, thanks to the efforts of many scholars, that Voltaire's *Ezour-vedam* was definitely authored by one or several French Jesuits in India, and Ludo Rocher has convincingly argued that the text was never translated from Sanskrit but written in French and then partially translated into Sanskrit (Rocher 1984: 57–60). Consequently, there *never was a translator* from Sanskrit to French—which also makes it extremely unlikely that any Brahmin, whether from Benares in the north or Chérignan (Seringham) in the south, ever gave this French manuscript to Maudave. Whether Maudave was "a close friend of one of the principal brahmins" and how old and wise that man was appear equally irrelevant. Voltaire's story of the Brahmin translator appears to be entirely fictional and also squarely contradicts the only relevant independent evidence, Maudave's letter to Voltaire, which (rightly or wrongly; see Chapter 7) named a long-dead French Jesuit as translator and imputed Jesuit tampering with the text. Since it is unlikely that Maudave would arbitrarily change such central elements of his story when he met Voltaire, the inevitable conclusion is that

Voltaire created a narrative to serve a particular agenda and changed that story when the need arose.

In this light it is doubly surprising that Voltaire has hitherto almost unanimously been accused of uncritical trust in tainted sources. Raymond Schwab, who rightly credited Voltaire with the "launch of India," took him severely to task: "Voltaire, as usual, was simplifying and . . . poses no questions of authenticity; never has a mind been less bothered by critique, never has critique been more hasty: as long as a text was not of semitic origin, he saw no reason to discuss its value" (Schwab 1950:146).

Schwab, an ardent Christian himself, reveled in the irony that "the main weapon of his [Voltaire's] arsenal," the supposedly very ancient *Ezour-vedam*, was unmasked by Ellis (1822) as a modern Jesuit creation (Schwab 1950:168). Leslie Willson's book about the creation of an idealized image of India in romantic Germany also hails Voltaire as a pioneer who affirmed the probability that "the Persians, the Egyptians, the Greeks themselves, and perhaps the Chinese originally received their wisdom from Hindustan" and derides him for his trust in fake texts (1964:25). Likewise, Alex Aronson's *Europe Looks at India* lauds him for his pioneering role in claiming "that India was once the cradle of civilization" (1946:20) but scolds him as superficial and ignorant: "Voltaire was not what we could call today a profound writer. He could hide, with a cleverness which seems to us incredible today, his own ignorance as well as the utter stupidity of the sources from which he gathered his information about India" (p. 16). More recent publications tend to rely on Daniel S. Hawley's groundbreaking study "L'Inde de Voltaire" of 1974, which states that it was Voltaire "who launched the India craze [la mode de l'Inde] in France" (1974:173) and describes his involvement with India in four phases (p. 140): an initial phase of exoticism (before 1760); a second phase under the spell of the *Ezour-vedam* (1761–66); a third phase influenced by Holwell (1767–69); and a final blossoming of Voltaire's India (1770–78). Like virtually all recent authors, Hawley takes it as a fact that Voltaire was blindly trusting spurious sources,[40] especially the *Ezour-vedam*—"unfortunately . . . only a literary hoax" (p. 144)—and Holwell, whose work is described as a "twaddle [galimatias] of puranic, vedic, and even Persian traditions without resemblance to any Indian cosmogony" (p. 146). Though Hawley took some note of Voltaire's manipulation of such sources, he was utterly convinced that "Voltaire trusted his *Ezour-Vedam*" and other supposedly ancient texts (p. 153).

While such criticisms certainly have some justification, we must ask what exactly Voltaire meant by "making good use" of the *Ezour-vedam* and how he portrayed the text over time. Immediately after Maudave's visit, Voltaire was already fully aware that the two texts that he had received were not the Veda itself but rather commentaries. In his letter to Jean le Rond d'Alembert (who had introduced Maudave to him), Voltaire remarked with his customary dose of sarcasm that Maudave gave him "commentaries of the Vedam which are every bit as good as others, and a god that is every bit as good as another one. It is the phallum" (Voltaire 1980:6.14; October 8, 1760). A few months later, when Voltaire knew what use he was going to make of the manuscript, he portrayed the *Ezour-vedam* not as a simple commentary but as "the Gospel of the ancient brachmanes" and "the most curious and most ancient book that we possess, except for the Old Testament whose sanctity, truth, and antiquity you know" (6.289; February 24, 1761). Since his addressee was, of course, familiar with Voltaire's scathing critique of the sanctity, truth, and antiquity of the Old Testament, we can imagine what his friend thought about this Indian gospel. In July of the same year, Voltaire promised to donate the *Ezour-vedam* manuscript to the Royal Library and informed librarian Jean-Augustin Capperonnier that this "commentary of the Vedam is for the Indians what the Sader is for the Guèbres"—that is, an important foundational religious text—and that it was "in all likelihood older than the expedition of Alexander" (6.470; July 13, 1761). But inflation soon struck also in this respect: in mid-September, when he sent his new *Essai* chapter to the Marquise Deffand, he called the *Ezour-vedam* "possibly the oldest book in the world" (6.579; September 16, 1761), and two weeks later he dated it to "several centuries before Pythagoras." Boasting that "it will be the only treasure that will survive of our Compagnie des Indes," he even claimed that the Royal Library regarded his "very authentic" *Ezour-vedam* manuscript as "the most precious monument it possesses" (6.602–3; October 1, 1761)!

The World's Oldest Monotheism

The new fourth chapter of the 1761 *Essai*, "On the Brachmanes; of the Vedam; and the Ezourvedam," begins with Voltaire's influential assertion about the antiquity of Indian culture and religion:

> If India, of which the entire earth is dependent and which alone is not in need of anybody, must, on account of this very fact, be the most

anciently civilized region, then it must also have had the most ancient form of religion. It is very likely that for a long time this religion was the same as that of the Chinese government and consisted only in a pure cult of a supreme Being, free of any superstition and fanaticism. (Voltaire 1761:49)

This oldest religion of the world was "founded by the Bracmanes" and subsequently "established in China by its first kings" (p. 49). Voltaire portrayed this religion as if it were his own: since it was built on "universal reason" (p. 50), it "had to be simple and reasonable," which was easy enough since "it is so natural to believe in a unitary God, to venerate him, and to feel at the bottom of one's heart that one must be just" (p. 49). Long before Alexander's India adventure, this pure, original monotheism began to degenerate when the cult of God "became a job" and the divinities multiplied; but even under the reign of polytheism and popular superstition, a "supreme God was always acknowledged" (p. 50) and is still venerated today (p. 51).

Luckily, an authentic record of India's ancient pure monotheism had fallen precisely into the hands of the person whose religion resembled it most:

I have in my hands the translation of one of the most ancient manuscripts in the world; it is not the *Vedam* which in India is so much talked about and which has not yet been communicated to any scholar of Europe, but rather the *Ezourvedam*, the ancient commentary by Chumontou on the *vedam*, the sacred book which was given by God to humans, as the Brahmins pretend. This commentary has been redacted by a very erudite Brahmin who has rendered many services to our Compagnie des Indes; he has translated it himself from the sacred language into French. (pp. 52–53)

To prove his point, Voltaire in the 1761 *Essai* for the first time published eight "quotations" from the *Ezour-vedam*.[41] In view of his privileged access to the text and his assurances about the authenticity and age of the *Ezour-vedam*, one would expect faithful quotations from the sacred scripture. But already Voltaire's first two "quotations" (which he used again in several other works) prove such expectations wrong. The first ends with "etc."; though it might seem otherwise because of the table-form arrangement shown, Voltaire presents both passages as continuous quotations from the *Ezour-vedam* that supposedly furnish "the very words of the *Veidam*" rather those of two interlocutors. In the juxtaposition in Table 3, text omitted by Voltaire is shown on gray, and added or changed text is underlined.

Some of Voltaire's numerous omissions are clearly related to his presentation of this creation account as continuous quotations from the *Vedam*. In the *Ezour-vedam* text, however, Chumontou does not quote anything but simply responds to Biache's questions. To maintain his fiction, Voltaire had to omit not only the questions but also phrases (for example, those before the "four different ages") that clearly show this text to be part of a conversation. The *Ezour-vedam* "quotation" beginning with "At the time when God alone existed" shows that he systematically misled his readers: the text that Voltaire presents as a continuous quotation from the *Ezour-vedam* actually shrinks eight pages of the Sainte-Croix edition (1778:1.189–96) to a fraction of their original volume. Some of Voltaire's additional changes are stylistic; but the majority is clearly related to content that Voltaire chose to omit or add for a variety of reasons. For example, he cut the *Ezour-vedam*'s explanation that after the creation of time, water, and earth, "the earth was completely submerged" and omitted God's order "that the water retract on one side and that the earth become stable and solid" (1.189–90). This passage did not please Voltaire who opposed theories of universal flood and models of earth formation that involved total submersion in water.[42] Likewise, Voltaire did not like the idea that God created three worlds, which is why he eliminated the information about the superior, inferior, and central world. The idea of monogenesis and primitive man's god-given wisdom also bothered him (Voltaire 1969:59.121); thus, he omitted the *Ezour-vedam*'s "In creating him he endowed him with extraordinary knowledge and put him on earth in order to be the principle and origin of all other men." The presentation of Adimo as father of Brahma, Shiva, and Vishnu and of their birth from his navel and flanks certainly fit the agenda of the *Ezour-vedam*'s Jesuit author(s) who wanted to highlight the absurdity of Indian mythology; but this was very much contrary to Voltaire's intention of presenting the wisdom of the *Vedam* as somewhat conforming to a deist's ideal of rationality. Therefore, he drastically demoted Adimo from father of India's three supreme gods to father of "Brama who was the legislator of nations and the father of the brahmins."

This pattern of Voltaire's editorial policy is repeated in much of the rest of his "quotations" from the *Ezour-vedam*. A passage that explains the origin of the four Indian castes is falsely portrayed by Voltaire not as Chumontou's commentary but as "one of the most singular pieces from the Vedam" (Voltaire 1761:54)—but, singular or not, Voltaire decided to omit about half of the

TABLE 3. VOLTAIRE'S EDITION OF THE *EZOUR-VEDAM*'S CREATION ACCOUNT

Voltaire (*Essai* 1761:53)	*Ezour-Vedam* (1.188–196)
In this Ézour-Veidam, in this commentary, Chumontou fights against idolatry quoting the very words of the Veidam.	
"It is the Supreme Being that has created everything, the perceptible and the imperceptible;	*Chumontou.* It is God, it is the Supreme Being that has created everything, the perceptible and the imperceptible things. In a word, all that exists owes him its being and life. It's beyond me to give you the exact details, but I will nevertheless give you a short summary. So give up all other affairs and lend all your attention to what the Vedam taught us about it.
there were four different ages; everything perishes at the end of each age, everything is submerged, and the deluge is a passage from one age to the other, <u>etc.</u>"	One must first of all distinguish four different ages. At the end of each age everything perishes, everything is submerged; this is why the passage from one age to the other is called deluge. Time is also regarded as a kind of sleep of the Supreme Being because he is the only one that exists, and nothing exists beside him.
"At the time when God alone existed and no other being existed beside him, he formed the plan to create the world: he first created time, then water and the earth;	Thus, at the time when God alone existed and no other being existed beside him, having formed the plan to create the world, he first created time and nothing else; then he created water and the earth.
	When he examined his work he saw that the earth was completely submerged and that it was not yet inhabited by any living being. He thus ordered that the water retract on one side and that the earth become stable and solid.
and from the mixture of the five elements, i.e., earth, water, fire, air, and light he formed different bodies and gave them the earth as their base.	From the mixture of the five elements, i.e., earth, water, fire, air, and light he formed different bodies and gave them the earth as their base.
	It is also on this earth that the Master of the universe has created the three worlds, i.e., the Chvarguam or superior world, the Patalan or inferior world, and the Mortion or central world which is the one that we inhabit.

TABLE 3. (CONTINUED)

He made the earth which we inhabit in an oval form like an egg. At the center of the earth is the highest of all mountains, called Mérou (that is Immaüs).	The earth is of round shape, but a bit oblong; which is why the scholars have compared it to an egg. At the center of the earth is the highest of all mountains, called Merou; that is where the country named Zomboudipo is situated, India. (here follow more than four pages of geographical explanations) Biache. Nothing escapes your knowledge and you weigh everything on the scale of reason. Now tell me, who is the first human whom God created? What are the orders he gave to him? Who was his wife, and what is her name?
Adimo is the name of the first human issued from the hands of God: Procriti is the name of his wife.	Chumontou. Adimo is the name of the first human issued from the hands of God. In creating him he endowed him with extraordinary knowledge and put him on earth in order to be the principle and origin of all other men. Prokriti is the name of his wife. That's what the Védam teaches us. You have hitherto cheated the world by teaching that Rada, Dourga, Chororboti, etc. were this Prokriti. But I've agreed to drop the curtain on all this. But from now on you must disabuse men of the errors you have plunged them into, or at least you must be wise enough to keep them hidden and not talk of them anymore.
From Adimo was born Brama, the legislator of nations and father of the brahmans [brames]."	From Adimo first Dokio-Bramma was born. He was the father of several children and was born of his [Adimo's] belly button. From the right flank of the same Adimo Vichnou was born, and from his right flank Chib. One gave them the names of creator, preserver, and destroyer. I will prove to you later that they are nothing of all this. That's all regarding the first creation.

Ezour-vedam's text (which, of course, was no Vedic quotation at all). Another flagrant example is Voltaire's fifth excerpt (p. 55), which is a hodgepodge from the *Ezour-vedam*'s sixth and seventh chapters (Sainte-Croix 1778:I.222–26) presented as a continuous citation from the Vedam. Voltaire introduces this as follows:

> The Vedam continues and says: "The supreme Being has neither body nor form," and the *Ezourvedam* adds: "All those who ascribe him feet

and hands are insane." Chumontou then cites the following words of
the Vedam: . . . (p. 55)

However, in the text of the *Ezour-vedam* all this forms part of Chumontou's conversation. Once again, Voltaire's transmutation forced him to elimi-
nate all phrases proving that Chumontou was not citing the Veda but simply
talking to Biache. Thus, he had to delete statements like "That's what the
Vedam teaches. The sun which you have divinized is no more than a body"
(Sainte-Croix 1778:1.226). More than half of the *Ezour-vedam*'s text (pp. 222–
27) in this supposedly continuous quotation suffered the same fate. Instead of
a faithful presentation of "Vedic" text, Voltaire's readers thus got a blatantly
tendentious pastiche of conversation fragments taken from two different
chapters of a "commentary" containing not a single genuine quotation from
the Veda.

In contrast to the *Ezour-vedam*, which in Voltaire's 1761 *Essai* was massaged until it fit Voltaire's idea of ancient monotheism and could please a
deist, the "Cormorédam" (which is a misprint for Cormovédam) is severely
criticized as a product of degeneration. This second text that Voltaire received
from Maudave was presumably also donated to the French national library.
In his 1761 *Essai*, Voltaire describes it as follows:

> The Brahmins degenerated more and more. Their *Cormorédam*, which
> is their ritual, is a bunch of superstitious ceremonies that make anybody
> who is not born on the banks of the Ganges or Indus laugh—or rather,
> anyone who, not being a *philosophe*, is surprised about the stupidities
> of other peoples and not amazed at those of his own country. As soon as
> an infant is born, one must recite the word *Oum* over him to prevent his
> being unhappy forever; one must rub his tongue with consecrated flour,
> say prayers over him, and pronounce at each prayer the name of a divin-
> ity. Subsequently one must put the infant outside on the third day of
> the moon and turn his head toward the north. The minute detail is
> immense. It is a hodgepodge of all the lunacies with which the senseless
> study of judicial astronomy could inspire ingenious but extravagant and
> deceitful scholars. The entire life of a Brahmin is devoted to such super-
> stitious ceremonies. There is one for each day of the year. (Voltaire
> 1761:57)[43]

It is possible that Maudave gave Voltaire a copy of the manuscript described
by Ellis (1822:19) as follows: "This manuscript [No. 2] is a quarto volume

bound in black leather. It contains that part of the *"Zozochi Kormo Bédo,"* which treats on the *Sandhya,* &c. the whole of the *Ezour Védam* . . . and the supplement of the *Ezour Védam.* All in *French* only without the *Sanscrit."* However, Voltaire's description of the *Cormo Veidam* has a perfect match in another Pondicherry text, the *"Zozochi Kormo Bédo,"* whose first part is entitled "Rite of the Ezour Vedam" (Castets 1935:26–27). According to the Jesuit Jean Castets, this part features detailed descriptions of rites (including those required at the birth of a male child) as well as long lists of prescribed/auspicious or prohibited/inauspicious activities on particular days of the year (pp. 28–32).

Bowing to Voltaire's will, the *Ezour-vedam* thus became a monument of a protodeist's monotheistic Ur-religion (primeval religion), while the *Cormo-Vedam* had the role of representing what India's deceitful clergy is catering to the superstitious masses. Voltaire's commentary shows to what degree he identified with the reformer Chumontou:

The ancient purity of the religion of the first Bracmanes survived only with some of their philosophers; and they do not make the effort to instruct a people that does not want to be taught and does not merit it either. Disabusing it would even carry a risk; the ignorant Brahmins would rise up, and the women attached to their temples and their little superstitious practices would cry heresy. Whoever wants to teach reason to his fellow citizens is persecuted unless he is the strongest; and it almost invariably happens that the strongest redoubles the chains of ignorance instead of breaking them. (Voltaire 1761:59)

In the years between the publication of the 1761 *Essai* and the *Homélies* of 1767, Voltaire continued to exploit the *Ezour-vedam* for his purposes. Chapter 13 of the *Défense de mon oncle* (1767) is the last statement of his views before the effect of Holwell set in. Here the *Ezour-vedam* is called "the most precious manuscript of the Orient" that "indisputably is from the time when the ancient religion of the gymnosophists began to be corrupted" and represents "apart from our sacred scriptures the most respectable monument of faith in the unity of God" (Voltaire 1894:27.164). Voltaire once more presented the first two of his sanitized quotations from the *Ezour-vedam* and defended his absurd argument from the *Philosophie de l'histoire* (1765) that the *Ezour-vedam* had to stem from the period before Alexander because its place names are not Greek-influenced.

Transformations

Discussions of Voltaire's view of the *Ezour-vedam* have hitherto been marred
by the assumption that Voltaire's propaganda campaign for the *Ezour-vedam*
implied his unquestioning trust in the text's authenticity. Paulinus a Sancto
Bartholomaeo was already of this opinion when he wrote in 1791: "Does he
[Voltaire] know what is in the book? Does he know its author? Has he read
the book? Did he make sure that it is an authentic book?" (Rocher 1984:16).
If Voltaire made such a fuss about this text and regarded it as such a powerful
weapon against biblical authority, so the argument went, he must have believed it genuine. But Voltaire was certainly a much more discerning reader
of religious texts than young Maudave and a better informed critic of the
Jesuits to boot. His selection of a few fragments of the *Ezour-vedam* and his
very invasive editing of them lead one almost to suspect that he sensed Jesuit
involvement and perhaps even relished the thought of surreptitiously perverting their fundamental intention. The student and enemy of the Jesuits, it
turns out, had a missionary agenda of his own. He, too, was eager to advocate
ancient monotheism and to denounce its later degeneration. But for him
such degeneration included not just the theology of the "stupid Brahmins"
but rather the *infâme* itself: Judeo-Christianity, complete with its cruel God,
deluded prophets, plagiarized texts, degenerate clergy, intolerant worldview,
and parochial conception of history.

Voltaire's "transformations" as well as his remarks about the *Ezour-
vedam* indicate a cynical rather than a credulous stance and may reflect Father
Bouchet's view that "even lies serve us to make truth known" (Le Gobien
1781–83:12.238). As mentioned above, Voltaire mocked the text's story about
the first man Adimo already in 1761 by calling it the tale of a "badly instructed
and pigheaded Brahmin" (Voltaire 1761:44). In the *Ezour-vedam* chapter of
his 1761 *Essai*, Voltaire showed his hand when writing of St. Ambrose's
method:

> Perhaps it is one of these exaggerations that one indulges in sometimes
> to make one's fellow citizens ashamed of their mess; one praises the
> bracmanes in order to correct the [Christian] monks: and if Saint Am-
> brose had lived in India, he probably would have praised the monks to
> put shame on the bracmanes. (p. 51)[44]

Voltaire's use of short and heavily edited excerpts of the *Ezour-vedam*
certainly seems designed to employ Chumontou's religion as a whip to chas-

tise Europe's conventional Christians. The *Ezour-vedam* was far from an ideal candidate as an Old Testament for Voltaire's religion; judging from the very few (and heavily edited) excerpts that he presented of this supposedly extremely important and unique source, it would seem that, for Voltaire's taste, it simply contained too much rubbish. He wrote that in spite of their sublime morality, "the ancient brahmins were without any doubt just as terrible metaphysicians and ridiculous theologians as the Chaldeans and Persians and all the nations west of China" (Voltaire 1767:318). In his view, the Chinese should have done a bit better; but Confucius was too prosaic, the Chinese emperor's "Adore God and be just" (p. 319) admirable but no substitute for a gospel, and the *Yijing* ancient but full of superstition. But it so happened that the *Ezour-vedam*—which, as already Maudave had noted, reflected the Jesuit agenda of emphasizing primeval monotheism and its subsequent degeneration—fell into Voltaire's hands just when he needed it most, that is, when the battle against "l'infâme" heated up and he was eager to get whatever ammunition against biblical authority that he could lay his hands on. Since the *Ezour-vedam* was still unpublished,[45] he could cherry-pick and massage the text at will to suit his purpose. When even his short, edited extracts proved unsatisfactory, Voltaire did not shy away from cruder methods in pursuit of his goals. For example, in the "Defense of my uncle" of 1767,[46] he quoted the *Ezour-vedam* to the effect that each world age ends in a deluge in which everything is submerged (Voltaire 1894:27.165). But a few pages later, he brazenly stated:

> There are even those who pretend that the Indians mentioned a universal deluge before that of Deucalion. It is said that several brachmanes believed that the earth had experienced three deluges. Nothing of that is said in the *Ezour-Veidam* nor in the *Cormo-Veidam* which I have read with great attention; but several missionaries who were sent to India agree that the brahmins recognize several deluges. (27.183)

It had certainly not escaped Voltaire's "great attention" that the *Ezour-vedam* contains no less than four passages[47] that unequivocally speak of universal deluges and that he had quoted one of them repeatedly since the 1761 *Essai*—even in the very book containing this denial! Sainte-Croix was so incensed about this blatant contradiction and Voltaire's custom of "suppressing some details that in his eyes did not do enough honor to the Indian work" that he denounced this whopper in a detailed "clarification" (Sainte-

Croix 1778:2.203–6). Since Voltaire had sanitized the deluge quotation so carefully and used it several times, it certainly was not a "copyist's mistake" (as Sainte-Croix politely suggested). Rather, it is an example of Voltaire's "making good use" of the text on St. Ambrose's line. Had he been such an ardent believer in the *Ezour-vedam*'s authenticity, he would without any doubt have been eager to supply the curious public with more (and more accurate) quotations from this most valuable text of antiquity.

Exactly in the year when Voltaire received his *Ezour-vedam* manuscript, James Macpherson's famous forgery of the poems of Ossian (1760) made its appearance. Though these two texts had a similar fate and share some characteristics, the *Ezour-vedam* does not belong in the category of literary hoaxes. In fact, it exhibits many characteristics of a genre of missionary literature cultivated by the Jesuits in Asia. Exactly like the Western scholar in Ricci's catechism, Chumontou in the *Ezour-vedam* explains that pure monotheism once reigned in the land and needs to be restored now. The first step toward such a restoration consists in the careful examination of the teachings that had clouded and perverted the original creed and in their refutation on rational grounds—exactly what the *Ezour-vedam* tries to do. The Evora fragments of Japan mentioned above[48] show that detailed presentations of native religions and their dogmas, rites, myths, and terminology were employed in the education of missionaries and catechists. They presented the best strategies to demolish them rationally in order to prepare the ground for the presentation of genuine (that is, Christian) truth. Since the early days of the Japan mission, explanations about the reasons for various natural phenomena and news about geography and history were used as effective means to prove the superiority of the missionaries' knowledge of the here-and-now (and by implication, their knowledge of the remote past and future as well as heaven and hell). The *Ezour-vedam* also appears to use fictional dialogues about local religions and the world at large for the education of native catechists and missionaries (see Chapter 7).

Sonnerat showed an intuition of this when he characterized the *Ezour-vedam* in 1782 as "a book of controversy written . . . by a missionary" (Sonnerat 1782:1.360), and in 1791 Paulinus a Sancto Bartholomaeo stated that "the book in question is more likely a Christian catechism than a Brahmanic book" (1791:316). Paulinus's opinion was based on his experience as a missionary and especially his perusal of the Pondicherry manuscripts and was far more informed than that of his critics.[49] Since questions related to the genesis and authorship of the *Ezour-vedam* will be discussed in Chapter 7, the focus is here on Voltaire's role in its rise to fame. Whatever the intentions of its authors were, it was Voltaire who almost single-handedly transformed some missionary jottings from the South Indian boondocks into the "world's oldest text," the Royal Library's "most precious document," and (as a well-earned bonus for the promoter) into the Old Testament of his deism! So far, there is no evidence of any influence of this text before Maudave and Voltaire. But soon after Maudave's manuscript got into Voltaire's hands, the *Ezour-vedam*'s brilliant career began. For Voltaire it was, for a few years, a potent weapon to undermine biblical authority and to attack divine partiality for Judeo-Christianity. It was no Jesuit missionary but rather Voltaire, the missionary of deism, who trumpeted extraordinary claims into the world about the *Ezour-vedam*'s authenticity, antiquity, and supreme value. Paulinus a Sancto Bartholomaeo saw this quite clearly when in 1791 he called the *Ezour-vedam* "the notorious gift from the most learned prince of philosophers, Voltaire"—a poisoned gift "that found its way into the Royal library in Paris, or rather which he pressed upon them to use it as the foundation for his own philosophical superstructure" (Rocher 1984:16). It was a calculated move on the Indian flank of Voltaire's war against "l'infâme," and as we will see in the remainder of this book, it was rather successful in inciting European enthusiasm for India as the cradle of civilization and preparing the ground for "indomania."[50] Further boosted by virulent orthodox reactions near the end of the eighteenth century, Voltaire's "Indian" campaign ended up playing a crucial role in raising the kind of questions about origins and ancient religions that played at least as important a role in the establishment of state-supported, university-based Orientalism as did the much-touted colonialism and imperialism. Rather than thirst for political and economic power, what was primarily at work here was ideological power: the power of Europe's long-established worldview and religious ideology that Voltaire provocatively labeled "l'infâme" and that he tried to destabilize through an avalanche of articles, pamphlets, and books.

History Versus Propaganda

For Europeans, the first chapters of the Old Testament had for many centuries conclusively explained the origin of the world and of humankind, including its achievements such as language, religion, and civilization. Such certainties gradually came to be undermined not only through critique of the

Bible by the likes of Baruch de Spinoza, Richard Simon, and Pierre Bayle but also through discoveries about our earth and its inhabitants. By the middle of the eighteenth century, the time was ripe for an overall reassessment, which is what Voltaire undertook in *La philosophie de l'histoire* of 1765.[51] The work begins with an examination of the geological history of the earth that includes Voltaire's theory of fossils, his rejection of the idea that the whole earth was once covered by water, and his critique of the theory by Buffon and others that the earth had anciently been hot and luminous (Voltaire 1969:59.39).[52] Voltaire drew an overall picture that was diametrically opposed to the biblical scenario. His chapter on "The Savages" provides a glimpse of a chronology that pulverizes all biblical limits. Voltaire regarded the human race as immeasurably old, thought it "very likely that man has been rustic for thousands of centuries," and was convinced that that all nations were once savages roaming the forests (p. 112). "Without any doubt," he stated, early man spoke "for a very long time no language" and communicated only by "shouts and gestures" (p. 113).

Religion, too, began only "after a great many centuries" when "some societies had been established" and "some kind of religion, a sort of gross cult" formed (p. 99). "All peoples were thus what the inhabitants of several southern coasts of Africa, some islanders, and half of the Americans are today. These people have not the slightest idea of any unitary God" (p. 100). Ignorant of the reasons for good and bad events, people began to appease unknown powers and venerate all kinds of beings until they came up with the idea of a single Master or Lord (pp. 100–101). According to Voltaire, the recognition of a punishing and rewarding creator God was thus a very late development in human history (p. 100). It first arose in temperate regions like India, China, and Mesopotamia that had long been densely populated while the rest of the globe still was almost deserted (p. 97). In Voltaire's view, "the Indians around the Ganges River were possibly the earliest humans forming a people" (p. 145), and he regarded Indian civilization as substantially older than its Egyptian (p. 159), Greek (p. 146), and probably even Chinese (p. 146) counterparts. The three regions with the earliest mass population also produced the oldest writing systems and sacred texts. According to Voltaire, who praised the Chinese religion as "simple, wise, august, free from all superstition and barbarism" (p. 155), the Indian religion was still the least known:

> We know almost nothing of the ancient brahmanic rites that are preserved today. [The brahmins] communicate little about the Sanskrit

books that they still possess in this ancient sacred language; for a long time, their *Veidams* remained as unknown as the *Zend* of the Persians and the five *Kings* of China. (p. 149)

Voltaire's portrayal of the history of religion in 1765 was deeply influenced by David Hume's *Natural History of Religion* (1757) and stands in marked contrast to his "propaganda mode" output. Propaganda is, of course, not absent in the *Philosophy of History*, but the tone is rather sober:

A stroke of luck has brought an ancient book of the brahmans to the library in Paris: the *Ezour-Veidam* that was written before the expedition of Alexander to India, with a ritual of all ancient rites of the brachmanes with the title *Cormo-Veidam*. This manuscript, translated by a brahman, is not really the *Veidam* itself, but a summary of the opinions and the rites contained in this law. . . . [The author] certainly does not flatter his sect; he does not attempt to disguise his superstitions, to give them some plausibility through forced explanations, or to excuse them via allegories. He describes the most extravagant laws with the simplicity of candor. Here the human spirit appears in all its misery. (pp. 149–50)

In Voltaire's "historical mode," the world's "oldest religion" was not pure monotheism but rather a primitive cult by people wholly ignorant of a unitary God—a cult designed to appease unknown powers. Monotheism was a comparatively late phenomenon that possibly first arose in India and was possibly documented in the still unknown *Veidam*. In Ambrosian "propaganda mode," by contrast, this late development in India acquired disproportionate importance since, appropriately massaged and edited, even a flawed and relatively recent text like the *Ezour-vedam* could serve to show that far younger religions such as Judaism and Christianity had borrowed central doctrines and rites from India and to portray the Bible as a late and derivative product. This view undermined claims of a Hebrew "chosen people" and contradicted the vision of a God partial to a single people—a God who continually interferes in history by teaching, guiding, and indulging a group of uncivilized, stubborn peasants and nomads around the eastern Mediterranean.

However, by 1765 Voltaire's propaganda campaign began to show signs of stress, as he had to struggle on two fronts. On one hand, he was fighting against biblical authority and was in need of monotheistic religions, rites, and especially sacred scriptures that were old and flexible enough to serve as Ambrosian whips for Judaism and Christianity. The second front had opened among Voltaire's erstwhile sympathizers and friends in Paris who were resolutely materialist and atheist (see Chapter 8). Their view of the history of humankind and of primitive religion was rather similar to the first chapters of Voltaire's *Philosophy of History*, but they regarded Voltaire's insistence on a punishing and rewarding creator God and on inspired scriptures, whether from Israel or India, as a ridiculous and an old-fashioned obsession. On both fronts Voltaire felt the need for historical evidence in the form of ancient texts proving the widespread presence of pure monotheism and excellent morality. If a good creator God had, like a supreme mechanic, fashioned a world as he intended it to remain, that is, a world without any need for further intervention and maintenance, then the religion and morality he had endowed humanity with needed somehow to show up in history. Like his fellow English deists, Voltaire was thus keen to find signs of "universal consent" in different civilizations, particularly ancient and important ones. Had not all of them come to believe in monotheism? Did they not all follow identical, universal rules of morality and justice? And were they not all devoted to the reign of universal reason and the ideal of tolerance? Or, in starker terms, could history not be forced to cough up a decent proof (or at least support) of Voltaire's own religion? Voltaire's vision of humanity's very slow progress from total primitivity to a semblance of civilization squarely contradicted his championship of a purely monotheistic Ur-religion, but this does not seem to have overly bothered him; the "Ambrosian" use of India and the *Ezour-vedam* in his propaganda war against the "infâme" apparently did not affect this level-headed acceptance of humanity's slow progress from primitivity to some kind of rationality and eventually to the watchmaker argument or some other "proof" of the existence of a creator God. Faced with French Catholics who supported and justified the execution of innocent men like Jean Calas, Voltaire was not too picky about countermeasures. His unrelenting effort to promote India as the cradle of civilization formed part of this battle, and—as in most wars—the ends tended to justify the means.

Veidam Versus Shastah

The editors of the *Annual Register* of 1766 published part of Voltaire's *Philosophy of History* in English translation, and in that very issue Voltaire discovered lengthy excerpts from a text that soon was to replace the *Ezour-vedam* in his propaganda war: the so-called *Shastah of Bramah* contained in John Zephaniah Holwell's *Interesting historical events* (see Chapter 6). The review of Holwell's book mentioned that he had spent thirty years in Bengal and procured "many curious manuscripts relating to the philosophical and religious principles of the Gentoos, particularly two correct copies of their Bible, called the Shasta" (Burke 1767:306–7). Having lost both the originals and his translation at the capture of Calcutta in 1756, Holwell "recovered some MSS. by accident" during his last eight months in Bengal. This enabled him to repair his loss "in some degree" and to present the hitherto best account "of the religion of the Gentoos, both in its original simplicity, and its present corruption" (p. 307). After an outline of the content of the *Shastah*'s creation story and Holwell's genealogy of Indian sacred literature (pp. 317–19), the *Annual Register*'s anonymous reviewer (Edmund Burke) included the entirety of Holwell's translation from the *Shastah* (pp. 310–16) along with his lengthy report of the burning of a widow (pp. 317–19).

Daniel Hawley argued that Voltaire had "blind faith in what Holwell asserted" (Hawley 1974:161) and that his "enthusiasm for Holwell became more and more marked each time he cited him" (p. 161). In the terminal phase of Voltaire's infatuation with India, according to Hawley, Voltaire's trust in Holwell's and Alexander Dow's translations from Indian texts was so complete that he compared doubts about them to the skepticism and stupid disbelief that greeted Newton's experiments in Paris: "That Voltaire would put Newton's experiments and the books of Dow and Holwell on the same level cannot but astonish us and must convince us of the great importance that Voltaire attached to the veracity of his sources" (p. 162).

Even Voltaire's decision to overlook Dow's devastating critique of Holwell and to pass silently over the grave differences between Dow's and Holwell's portrayals of Indian religion were interpreted by Hawley as proofs of Voltaire's complete trust in his sources:

> Leaving aside the contradictions between the two Englishmen, Voltaire's attitude toward the work by Dow is exactly identical to his judgment about the work by Holwell: blind faith and frank admiration. After having quoted some passages from Dow's *Bedang shaster*, Voltaire notes, "Such is this catechism, the most beautiful monument of all antiquity!" (p. 162)

The question of Voltaire's attitude toward his sources is, of course, also crucial for any judgment about his particular use of them. Hawley noted that Voltaire's three major sources (the *Ezour-vedam*, Holwell's *Shastah*, and Dow's *Bedang shasta*) "gave so very different accounts of the first creation" (p. 164) that Voltaire's indiscriminate praise poses a problem. How could a man as critical as Voltaire proclaim complete trust in sources that so blatantly contradicted each other? If Voltaire simply "made use of India rather than studying it" (p. 139), what were his motives? Hawley identified four major goals of Voltaire:

> The attack of Voltaire focuses on four problems: the chronology of the sacred scriptures; the election of the Jews by Jehovah according to which they alone know the divine revelation; the true origin of our religious traditions; and the genesis and diffusion of our mythology which involves the problematization of the historical importance of the Jews. (Hawley 1974:140–41)

This portrayal again relies on the question of Voltaire's evaluation of his sources since, for Hawley, Voltaire's admiration of "the sublime character of Indian philosophy and morality" forms the basis for the "justification and verification of his new interpretation of the historical value of the Judeo-Christian tradition which, according to him, is but an insipid imitation of Indian wisdom" (p. 140).

But if Voltaire's use of the *Ezour-vedam* has made us suspicious, we might as well ask to what degree he trusted Holwell's revelations. Voltaire first mentioned this new source in the *Homily on Atheism* (Voltaire 1768:293–316), which is an early effort on his second front. After stating flatly that "we must begin with the existence of a God" and that this "subject has been treated by all nations" (p. 293), Voltaire lectures his atheist readership that "this supreme artisan who has created the world and us" is "our master" and "our benefactor" because "our life is a benefit, since we all love our life, however miserable it might get" (p. 298). Thus, "one must recognize a God who remunerates and avenges, or no God at all." For Voltaire there was no middle ground: "either there is no God, or God is just" (p. 303). To support his radical theism, Voltaire always used the argument of universal consent: "all civilized people [peuples policés], Indians, Chinese, Egyptians, Persians, Chaldeans, Phoenicians: all recognized a supreme God" (p. 311). And it is exactly here that the sacred literature of such people as Holwell's ancient Indians came in handy. Voltaire wrote,

> The Indians who boast of being the oldest society of the universe still have their ancient books that according to their claim were written 4,866 years ago. According to them, the angel Brama or Abrama, the envoy of God and minister of the supreme Being, dictated this book in the Sanskrit language. This sacred book is called Chatabad, and it is much more ancient than even the Vedam that since such a long time is the sacred book on the banks of the Ganges. These two volumes [the Chatabad and the Vedam], which are the law of all sects of the brahmans, [and] the Ezour-Vedam which is the commentary of the Vedam, never mention anything other than a unique God. (p. 310).

As an illustration of universal consent on monotheism, Voltaire presented the first section of his newly found "oldest" text, Holwell's *Chartah Bhade Shastah*, which "was written one thousand years before the Vedam" and "treats of God and his attributes" (pp. 310–11). But, as seen in Table 4, already Voltaire's first quotation from this oldest testament shows that he had not abandoned his efforts to improve on supposedly genuine ancient texts.

As with the *Ezour-vedam*, Voltaire molded the text to suit his views; but since Holwell's text had already appeared in print, the changes needed to be a bit more subtle. Voltaire did not like that the God of Holwell's *Shastah* rules the world by providence and replaced "providence" by "general wisdom." As he was intent on proving *the existence* of God to atheists, he transformed the *Shastah*'s prohibition to inquire into "the essence and nature of the *existence* of the Eternal One" into one that concerned only "his essence and his nature." As a Newtonian, he was—unlike Holwell—in favor of exploring the laws of nature; thus, the prohibition to inquire "by what laws he governs" was not acceptable to him and had to be eliminated. Since Voltaire missed God's goodness in Holwell's *Shastah* text and firmly believed in divine punishment and reward, he replaced Holwell's "mercy" by "goodness." Finally, Voltaire's religion focused not on base self-benefit but rather on devoted worship of God and excellent morality—which may be why Holwell's "benefit thereby" was supplanted by "Be happy in worshipping him."

In 1774 Voltaire published another translation of this text (see the right column of Table 4). It was destined for a different public, and Voltaire had heard that a French translation of Holwell's *Shastah* had in the meantime

TABLE 4. FIRST SECTION OF HOLWELL'S *SHASTAH* WITH TWO DIFFERING TRANSLATIONS BY VOLTAIRE IN HIS FIRST *HOMÉLIE* (1768) AND THE *FRAGMENS SUR L'INDE* (1774)

Holwell, vol. 2, p. 31	Voltaire 1768:6.311	Voltaire 1774:143[a]
"God is ONE.—Creator of all that *is*.—[b]	God is one; he has formed all that is.	God is *the one who always was*; he created all that is.
God is like a perfect sphere, without beginning or end.—	He resembles a perfect sphere without beginning or end.	A perfect sphere, without beginning or end, is his feeble image.
God rules and governs all creation by a general providence resulting from first determined and fixed principles.—	He governs everything by a general *wisdom*.	God animates and governs all creation by the general providence of his unchanging and eternal principles.
Thou shalt not make inquiry into the essence and nature of the existence of the ETERNAL ONE, nor by what laws he governs.—	You shall not seek his essence and his nature,	Do not probe the nature of the existence of him who always was:
An inquiry into either is vain, and criminal.—	this enterprise would be vain and criminal.	such inquiry is vain and criminal.
It is enough, that day by day, and night by night, thou seest in his works, his *wisdom, power,* and his *mercy*.—	It is enough for you to admire day and night his works, his wisdom, his power, *his goodness*.	It is enough that day by day and night by night his works announce to you his wisdom, his power, and his mercy.
Benefit thereby."	Be happy in worshipping him.	Benefit thereby.

[a] For this translation in the 1774 *Fragmens sur l'Inde*, Voltaire used the text of the 1766 *Annual Register* (p. 310) whose first paragraph differs from Holwell's 1767 edition. It reads: "God is the one that ever was, creator of all that *is*.—" (see Chapter 6). In his *Lettres chinoises* of 1776 he once more sang the praises of "the *Shasta-bad*, the most ancient book of Hindustan and of the entire world" and included another translation modeled on that of 1768; he also eliminated the prohibition to inquire about the existence of God (Voltaire 1895:30.149–50).
[b] Voltaire's translation shows that for this translation of the *Homélies* he used the 1767 edition of Holwell's book and not, as Hawley argued (1974:154), the text in the *Annual Register*.

appeared in Amsterdam (Holwell 1768).[53] Voltaire's new translation proves that the changes in his first translations were not due to the level of his knowledge of English. Rather, as is also evident from many letters containing very different portrayals of particular events depending on the addressee, Voltaire was extremely adept at tailoring information to fit specific needs (Stackelberg 2006:21–32). As if to prove this last point, Voltaire published one more translation in 1776 that again edits out the *Shastah*'s prohibition to inquire about God's existence.

After his discovery of Holwell's *Shastah*, Voltaire's interest in the *Ezour-vedam* abruptly ceased. It had done its duty and was rather unceremoniously dismissed before it was even published. The article on the *Ezour-vedam* in Voltaire's *Questions sur l'encyclopédie* of 1771 is exceedingly short (Voltaire 1775:4.255–56); in fact, almost the only information it offers is a joke about Adimo and his wife. Voltaire, whose critique of such monogenetic tales invented by pigheaded Brahmins has already been mentioned, asked the reader whether the Jews had copied their Adam and Eve story from the Indians or the Indians their Adimo story from the Jews—only to add sarcastically a third possibility: "Or can one say that both have originally invented it and that the beautiful minds have met?" (pp. 256). While the *Ezour-vedam* passed into oblivion because the Veda is only "a recent law given to the brachmanes 1,500 years after the first law called *shasta* or *shasta-bad*" (Voltaire 1775:1.52), Voltaire turned into an ardent champion of Holwell's *Shastah* whenever the argument required it. In his letter to Bailly of December 15, 1775, he calls the fragments of the *Shastah* that were "written about 5,000 years ago" nothing less than "the only monument of some antiquity that is extant on earth" (Bailly 1777:3).

In his campaign for Indian origins, Voltaire in the 1770s kept evoking the perfect accord of two excellent Englishmen who both had studied Sanskrit, spent decades in India, and supposedly translated the same extremely ancient Indian text called *Shastah* or *Shastah-bad*. However, the two gentlemen in question, John Zephaniah HOLWELL (1711–98) and Alexander DOW (1735/6–76), never claimed that they knew Sanskrit; in fact, Dow unequivocally states at the beginning of his "Dissertation concerning the customs, manners, language, and religion of the Hindoos" of 1768 that he originally intended to acquire "some knowledge in the Shanscrita language" but soon found that his time in India "would be too short to acquire the Shanscrita," which is why he decided to inform himself "through the medium of the Persian language, and through the vulgar tongue of the Hindoos" about the mythology and philosophy of the Brahmins (Dow 1770:xxi). Dow even explained his procedure: he "procured some of the principal Shasters, and his pundit explained to him, as many passages of those curious books, as served to give him a general idea of the doctrine which they contain" (p. xxii). Dow's "most beautiful monument of antiquity" (Voltaire 1774:172) was thus by no means a "translation" from the "sacred Sanskrit language," as Voltaire claimed.

In fact, the two English gentlemen whose "translations" replaced the *Ezour-vedam* as the world's oldest book were so much at odds about Indian religion that Dow felt "obliged to differ almost in every particular concerning the religion of the Hindoos, from that gentleman [Holwell]" (Dow 1770:xxx). These differences, consistently papered over by Voltaire, also extend to the crucial "oldest text of the world" (see chapter 6). Holwell usually called it *Shastah* or *Shasta-bad* and portrayed it as a single text, far older and more authentic than the Vedas, of which he supposedly had salvaged and translated some fragments. Dow, by contrast, stressed that there are many *Shasters* since that word simply "signifies Knowledge":

> There are many Shasters among the Hindoos, so that those writers who affirmed, that there was but one Shaster in India, which, like the Bible of the Christians, or Koran of the followers of Mahommed, contained the first principles of the Brahmin faith, have deceived themselves and the public. (p. xl)

This critique is without any doubt directed at Holwell; but Dow does not help his case when later in his dissertation he explains that "the most orthodox, as well as the most ancient" of the "two great religious sects" of the Hindoos are "the followers of the doctrine of the Bedang" (p. xl) and then presents "extracts literally translated from the original *Shaster*, which goes by the name of Bedang" (p. xli). If the reader is not confused by now, he or she should be. Not so, apparently at least, Voltaire who—in spite of Dow's wholesale critique of Holwell and their totally different creation accounts—happily continued to assert that both Englishmen had translated the same text. He even turned Dow's dire view of Holwell on its head, claiming without any foundation that Dow had "recognized the faithfulness of [Holwell's] translation" and noting that Dow's "avowal carries even more weight since the two differ with regard to some other articles" (Voltaire 1774:143). These "other articles," he explains in a passage that proves how closely he had read both texts, include the dispute "about the way of pronouncing shasta-bad or shastra-beda, and if *beda* signifies science or book" (p. 172).

The Indian Cradle

Toward the end of his life, in the *Lettres chinoises, indiennes et tartares* of 1776, Voltaire recapitulated his view of Indian sacred literature. The oldest source, "written in the sacred language during the present world-age [iogue] by a king on the banks of the Ganges named Brama," is the holy *Shasta-bad* translated by Holwell and Dow; it is 5,000 years old. As much as 1,500 years later "another brachmane who, however, was not king" proclaimed the "new law of the *Veidam*" (Voltaire 1895:40.154). What Voltaire had long regarded as the world's most valuable and ancient sacred text, the Veda, was now presented as a much later product, a "new law" that Voltaire butchered as follows:

> This *Veidam* is the most boring hodgepodge [fatras] that I have ever read. Imagine the *Golden Legend*, the *Conformities of St. Francis of Assisi*,[54] the *Spiritual Exercises* by St. Ignace, and the *Sermons* of Menot [1506] all put together, and you will still only have a faint idea of the impertinence of the *Veidam*. (p. 154)[55]

The *Ezour-vedam*, which Voltaire had long showered with praise as a commentary of the Veda that supposedly contained genuine Vedic quotations, was now elegantly moved to the realm of enlightened philosophy:

> The *Ezour-Veidam* is a completely different thing. It is the work of a true sage who powerfully rises up against the stupidities of the brachmanes of his time. This *Ezour-Veidam* was written some time before Alexander's invasion. It is a dispute of philosophy against Indian theology; but I bet that the *Ezour-Veidam* receives no credit at all in its country and that the *Veidam* is regarded as a heavenly book. (p. 154)

But neither India's philosophy nor its ancient theology managed to live up to Voltaire's idea without considerable help. Although Voltaire praised Dow's text as the "catechism" of India and "the most beautiful monument of all antiquity" (p. 172), he sanitized it in his usual manner (pp. 168–71) and concluded: "You can traverse all nations of the universe, and there will not be a single one whose history does not begin with fables worthy of the four sons of Aymon and Robert-the-devil" (p. 191). Holwell's *Shasta-bad*, the *Ezour-vedam*'s successor as "India's and the whole world's oldest book" (Voltaire 1895:30.149), also received its share of criticism.

Already in 1771, while Voltaire continued to trumpet the wonders of the *Shasta-bad*, he slipped an insidious couple of questions into his discussion of Indian sacred doctrine (Voltaire 2006:352): "How could God provide a second law in his Veidam? Was his first one [in the *Shasta-bad*] therefore no good?" A year later he targeted Holwell's *Shasta-bad* when he joked about "novels [romans] about the origin of evil" whose "extreme merit" is that "there never was a commandment that one must believe them" (Voltaire 1894:29.203). Thus, even Holwell—the man who according to Voltaire "had not only learned the language of the modern brahmins but also that of the ancient bracmanes, who has since written such precious treatises about India and who translated sublime pieces from the oldest books in the sacred language, books older than those of Sanchuniathon of Phoenicia, Mercury of Egypt, and the first legislators of China"—even the heroic Holwell "cannot be trusted blindly" (Voltaire 1774:72). And in an aside that reveals for a moment his true opinion about Holwell's *Shasta-bad*, Voltaire mischievously added, "But at any rate he has demonstrated to us that 5,000 years ago the people living on the Ganges [Gangarides] wrote a mythology, whether good or bad" (p. 72).[56]

However Voltaire evaluated such "oldest texts of the world," his conviction that India is the world's oldest civilization did not budge even when Jean Sylvain Bailly challenged it in a series of letters. They were published in 1777, one year before Voltaire's death, in Bailly's *Letters on the origin of the sciences and of the peoples of Asia*. Insisting that Holwell is "truth and simplicity in person" (Bailly 1777:4) Voltaire used Holwell's *Shastah* to support his rejection of Bailly's argument for the Siberian origins of humankind. Whatever arguments Bailly pressed upon him, Voltaire politely but firmly clung to his idea and declined to change his view of India as the cradle of civilization (pp. 9–14). It was this opinion of his that, hammered into public consciousness through a ream of books and pamphlets, played a seminal role in turning the European public's gaze toward India and its religious literature. Voltaire's influence is conspicuous in several figures studied in this book. Joseph de Guignes, Anquetil-Duperron, Gaston Laurent Coeurdoux, Volney, Louis-Mathieu Langlès, and William Jones were all readers of Voltaire and reacted to his views in one way or another. Countless quotations from his books and numerous reactions to his views show that his propaganda campaign was, for his time and purpose, a smashing success. Even in the nineteenth century, long after the *Ezour-vedam*'s publication by Sainte-Croix, there are instances where Voltaire's doctored "quotations" from the *Ezour-vedam* rather than the correct text were used (Fortia d'Urban 1807:289–89). His propaganda, as well as the reaction it created among Christians (including, for example, Johann Gottfried Herder, Thomas Maurice, and Joseph Priestley), was instrumental in promoting interest in India and its ancient texts. Whether these texts, in retrospect, are regarded as genuine or not, this interest fertilized the soil for the phenomenon that Thomas Trautmann aptly labeled "indomania" and for the "new Orientalism" it helped foster. Discoveries of Asian sources promising Bible-independent insight into the history of humanity (and generally into questions of origin) were intimately linked to a crisis of biblical authority and an upheaval of Europe's long-dominant worldview. While the Bible's explanatory power was still intact, many of these questions neither arose nor required a new answer. But as a string of nonbiblical texts were touted as "the world's oldest"—the Chinese *Yijing* in the late seventeenth century and the eighteenth century's *Ezour-vedam* of Voltaire, *Shasta-bad* of Holwell, *Desatir* of William Jones,[57] and *Zend Avesta* as well as *Oupnek'hat* of Anquetil-Duperron—the solid study of Asian languages and literatures became ever more pressing. Voltaire's Indian campaign was an important force in the momentous shift of focus away from the biblical area toward India that prepared the ground for the modern, Bible-independent Orientalism envisaged by an outspoken admirer of Voltaire's view, Louis-Mathieu Langlès, the founding director of modern Orientalism's first institution, the École Spéciale des Langues Orientales Vivantes in Paris.[58]

Chapter 2

Ziegenbalg's and La Croze's Discoveries

Studies about the European discovery of Buddhism tend to belong to one of two categories. The first depicts a gradual unveiling of what we today know about Buddhism (its founder, history, geographical reach, texts, rituals, art, and so forth) in form of a three-act play. Act 1 deals with antiquity and the Middle Ages, act 2 with the missionary discovery until about 1800, and act 3 with the "scientific" discovery of Buddhism of the nineteenth and twentieth centuries. Such a three-stage scenario characterizes, for example, the studies of de Lubac (2000) and Batchelor (1994). Lately this kind of scenario came to be replaced by one that begins in the early nineteenth century and features a single act with an inconsequential prelude. Such one-act scenarios claim that the "phenomenon" of Buddhism only became a reality for Europeans around 1820 when the term "Buddhism" (and its equivalents in other languages) came into common use in Europe. They underlie, for example, the studies of Almond (1988) and Droit (1997 and 2003). The first decades of the nineteenth century represent a crucial turning point in both scenarios since they mark the beginning of modern "scientific" study of Buddhism. Welbon's *The Buddhist Nirvāṇa and Its Western Interpreters* devotes fewer than five pages to the eighteenth century and squarely focuses on the "beginnings of a scientific study" in the nineteenth century, which it portrays as a clean break from a worthless prelude of "fabulous reports, desultory descriptions, and unfounded conjectures" (Welbon 1968:23).

> The ideas and discussions of pre-nineteenth-century "commentators" on Buddhism—whatever their interest may be for antiquarians of our own time—patently had not been widely circulated, nor had they aroused sustained interest on the part of scholars and laymen. Only the most

ingenious enthusiast would attempt to make a case for the ordered development of a body of knowledge concerning Buddhism before the end of
the eighteenth century. (p. 23)

A similar "sudden" scenario has come to dominate portrayals of
the discovery (or, to underline the break with the past, the "creation") of
Hinduism by Europeans. Interestingly, this discovery is usually regarded as a
separate play on a different stage and with a different set of actors. Since
Buddhism was supposedly discovered later than Hinduism, publications
about the discovery of Hinduism usually make no mention at all of Buddhism. Numerous recent publications place the "discovery" or "creation" of
Hinduism some decades earlier than that of Buddhism. According to Will
Sweetman, "the concept of a unified pan-Indian religion is firmly established
by the 1770s, when 'Holwell's Gentooism' appeared," and the first use of
the word "Hindooism" occurred in 1787 (2003:163). In this view the identification of "Hinduism" as India's "national religion" ran parallel to the establishment of "India" as a meaningful geographical entity: "The concept of
'Hinduism' and the concept of 'India' in its modern sense, are coeval" (p.
163). This roughly coincides with the period when, according to Thomas
Trautmann, a "new Orientalism" raised its head. It is characterized by a
double shift: a shift of interest from "European fascination with China that
was so marked in the seventeenth and early eighteenth centuries" to "a fascination with India" and, second, "a titanic shift of authority" (Trautmann
1997:30) involving the knowledge of indigenous languages and texts. This
"new claim of authority" focused first on Persian and then on Indian texts;
and the pioneers of this "new Orientalism" were, according to Trautmann, a
Frenchman and three Englishmen:

> The first works of the new Orientalism, prior to the formation of the
> Asiatic Society at Calcutta, were mostly translations from Persian: Abra-
> ham Hyacinthe Anquetil-Duperron's translation of the *Zend-Avesta*
> (1771) with the help of Parsi scholars in India; John Zephaniah Holwell's
> *Interesting historical events, relative to the provinces of Bengal, and the em-
> pire of Indostan* (1765–71), which relies on Persian sources in part, al-
> though it also contains what purport to be translations from a mysterious
> ancient Hindu text, *Chartah Bhade Shastah* (Sanskrit, *Catur Veda Śāstra*),
> a work not heard of since; Alexander Dow's translation of Firishtah's
> Persian *History of Hindostan* (1768); and the *Code of Gentoo laws* (1776),

translated by Nathaniel Brassey Halhed from a Persian translation of a Sanskrit digest of Hindu law compiled by pandits on commission from the East India Company. (Trautmann 1997:30)

Since it was "based on direct interchange with the pandits in India" who taught the pioneers the necessary languages, this new Orientalism "in its own propaganda . . . drew its authority from its knowledge of the languages of India and opposed it to that of the travelers and missionaries" (p. 32).

However, studies such as those by Rubiés (2000) and Sweetman (2003) amply document that this "discovery" play of the latter half of the eighteenth century had significant earlier acts. For example, Sweetman shows that Jesuit letters of the early eighteenth century already exhibit an understanding of Hinduism *avant la lettre* and states that the speculations of Father Jean Ven- ant Bouchet around 1702 (see Chapter 1) "strongly suggest a unified concep- tion of 'the system of religion recognized among the Indians'" (Sweetman 2003:140). But what about the "titanic shift of authority" that, according to Trautmann (1997:30), took place in the second half of the eighteenth century? Were Holwell's publications of 1765–71 really "one of the first statements of this new authority claim" (p. 33)? And was Anquetil-Duperron's translation of the *Zend-Avesta* of 1771 indeed "the first approach to an Asian text that was totally independent both of the biblical and the classical tradition," as Raymond Schwab claimed in his groundbreaking study *La Renaissance orien- tale* (1950:25)?

Many questions about the development of Western conceptions of "Buddhism" and "Hinduism" during the eighteenth century have either not yet been posed or remain unanswered. The retroprojection of a strict separa- tion of "Hinduism" and "Buddhism" may form a major stumbling block. Other (seemingly solid) boundaries such as those between nations and lan- guages are also frequently brought into play and led to book titles such as *The British Discovery of Buddhism* (Almond 1988), *The British Discovery of Hinduism in the Eighteenth Century* (Marshall 1970), or *Nirwana in Deutsch- land* (Lütkehaus 2004). Regardless of their value as collections of sources, such endeavors convey the wrong impression that such discoveries had much to do with national boundaries and particular languages. The two protago- nists of this chapter, Bartholomäus Ziegenbalg and Mathurin Veyssière de La Croze, show how effortlessly such boundaries were crossed. Ziegenbalg was a German working for a Protestant Danish mission in India whose correspon- dence was first published in German but found a broad pan-European reader-

ship through English, French, and Latin translations. La Croze was a
multilingual Frenchman living in Berlin who wrote in French and Latin, was
read by many intellectuals throughout Europe, and deeply influenced the
Western perception of Asian religions from the 1720s well into the nineteenth
century.

While Bartholomäus ZIEGENBALG (1682–1719) received some attention
from Indologists and researchers of Hinduism (for example, Dharampal-
Frick 1994, Jeyaraj 2003, and Sweetman 2003), the influence of his work on
the discovery of Buddhism remains unexplored. Mathurin Veyssière de LA
CROZE (1661–1739) usually plays no role at all in the fashionable "discovery
of Buddhism" and "discovery of Hinduism" tales. He died in 1739, half a
century before the first use of the word "Hindooism," and his *Histoire du
Christianisme aux Indes* (whose sixth chapter we will mainly examine) was
published in 1724, that is, a full century before—according to Roger-Pol
Droit—the "word Buddhism" and the "phenomenon itself" were "simultaneously" born in the "scholarly gaze" of Europe (1997:36). What did Ziegenbalg and La Croze discover? Can one speak at all of a discovery of Hinduism
and of Buddhism in the first decades of the eighteenth century? And if one
can, how did such discoveries take place? Did they happen decades apart on
separate stages and with different scripts, stage sets, and actors?

Indian Monotheism

Chapter 6 of La Croze's *History of Christianity of the Indies* has the title "Of
the idolatry of the Indies," and it is worth noting that "idolatry" is in the
singular and "Indies" in the plural. These are symptoms of La Croze's view
of a pan-Asian phenomenon whose history, character, and dimensions will
be explored in this chapter. He felt that this "idolatry of the Indies" merited
at least as much attention by Europeans as its Greco-Roman counterpart,
since "one finds in it vestiges of antiquity that lead to solid research about
ancient history and the origin of errors in the field of religion" (La Croze
1724:425). The question of origins concerned not only idolatry but also
monotheism. Like Voltaire three decades later, La Croze was convinced that
vestiges of early monotheism could be found in the Indies and that they
would throw light on the earliest phase of human history:

> Nothing . . . should evoke more interest for them [the Indians] than to
> see that, in spite of the grossest idolatry, the existence of the infinitely

perfect Being is so well established with them that there can be no doubt that they have preserved such knowledge since their first establishment in the Indies. (p. 425)

Whereas with the Greeks and Romans "the existence of the true God" was "known only to a small number of philosophers and played no role at all in the religion of the people," evidence from India indicated to La Croze that the Indians not only had pure monotheism in the remote past but preserved it ever since. Their antiquity far surpassed that of the Greeks:

One sees them form a large crowd [multitude nombreuse] from the centuries when Greek history begins to emerge from the darkness of ancient mythology, and this—in combination with other reflections—gives one the right to regard them as one of the most ancient peoples of the world. (p. 426)

While La Croze did not want to discuss the exact origin of this monotheism and found that it would be "badly managed erudition" to pinpoint exactly which son of Noah had transmitted his religion to the Indies (p. 426), it is clear that the ark of Noah and the biblical creation story loomed in the back of his mind. All signs indicated that Noah's pure religion had made its way to the Indies soon after the deluge and was preserved there:

One can even suppose, as a very probable fact, that in ancient times they had a quite distinct knowledge of the true God and that they worshipped him in an inner cult [culte intérieur] that at the time was mixed with no profanation at all. Some of their sages who until today preserve this doctrine . . . make this conjecture so probable that there seems to be no possible counterargument. (p. 426)

The other momentous transmission from the shores of the Mediterranean to larger Asia was that of idolatry. La Croze's view of it resembles that of Athanasius Kircher (1667) and of François Catrou (1708:54) and needs to be discussed briefly before we return to pure original monotheism and its vestiges in the Indies. La Croze was convinced "that the ancient Indians had been colonies of Egypt" and that "the origin of the superstitions of the Indies must be attributed to those of the Egyptians with which they maintain to this day a surprising conformity" (La Croze 1724:427). Among the superstitions mentioned by La Croze, we find not only "Egyptian-style" metempsychosis or transmigration of souls[1] but also the mortifications that fascinated and repelled so many Europeans:

> Furthermore, the Egyptians professed marvelous abstinence and treated their body as enemy. This is what we will later see practiced by the Indians, not only in antiquity but until the present times. No slackening whatsoever has since taken place in the observation of these mortifications that are so contrary to sane reason and to the affection that should make every human interested in self-preservation. (pp. 428–89)

La Croze also saw an Egyptian origin of Indian phallic worship, animal worship, the distinction of castes, vegetarianism, and monasticism complete with tonsure and celibacy (pp. 430–37). All this convinced La Croze—who as a Protestant of course also remarked on the Egyptian origins of Catholic monasticism and rites—that Egypt is "the mother and the origin of ancient superstitions and of all sorts of errors and idolatries" (p. 436). If this was the source of a misguided cult that "the Bramines entertain for their own particular interests" (p. 462), they were also the guardians of an ancient monotheistic teaching that the priests kept hidden from the common people (pp. 454–59). This theme of an exoteric and an esoteric teaching (the latter of which is hidden and encoded by priests) was already present in Plutarch's book on Isis and Osiris and was widely regarded as a characteristic feature of Egyptian religion. In Kircher's misguided efforts to translate Egyptian hieroglyphs—for example, in his *Obeliscus Pamphilius* of 1650—it played a central role, since his whole method rested on the dichotomy of exoteric and esoteric teachings and the idea that the latter represented primeval monotheism encoded in sacred symbols. Kircher detected few signs of humankind's original monotheism in Asia and saw the continent as a vast repository of Egyptian superstition; but believers in a God with a less discriminatory revelation policy emphasized, in the footsteps of Matteo Ricci and Roberto de Nobili, the ancient monotheistic heritage of China and India.

Already in Ricci's and de Nobili's time, around the beginning of the seventeenth century, the claim surfaced that the Vedas of India were the repository of ancient Indian monotheism. Of course, the approach of Nobili and his successors in the Jesuit Madurai mission was anchored in the idea that India had once been a land reigned by pure monotheism; but the *locus classicus* for the monotheism of the Vedas is the description in Diogo do

Couto's *Decada Quinta da Asia* of 1612 (124v ff.). Schurhammer (1977:614–18) has shown that Couto plagiarized the report by the Augustinian missionary Agostinho de Azevedo, but it was through Couto that this view of the Vedas as a monotheistic scripture, hidden by the Brahmans from the people to whom they preached polytheism, became popular. Since Couto's description was a central source for Holwell, I will discuss it in more detail in Chapters 5 and 6; here its summary by Philip Baldaeus will suffice:

> The first of these Books treated of God and of the Origin and Beginning of the Universe. The second, of those who have the Government and Management thereof. The third, of Morality and true Virtue. The fourth of the Ceremonials in their Temples, and Sacrifices. These four Books of the *Vedam* are by them call'd *Roggo Vedam*, *Jadura Vedam*, *Sama Vedam*, and *Tarawana Vedam*; and by the Malabars *Icca*, *Icciyxa*, *Saman*, and *Adaravan*. The loss of this first Part is highly lamented by the Brahmans. (Baldaeus 1703:891)

Though various descriptions based on Azevedo and Giacomo Fenicio made the rounds, no European had yet managed to get access to more than fragments of these prized Vedas. Some hoped that eventually an apostate Brahman would communicate them in toto, and La Croze was certain that this would bring about a revolution in knowledge not only about India but also antiquity in general:

> There is hardly any doubt that in this respect one could go much further if the *Vedam*, which is the collection of the ancient sacred books of the Brachmans, was translated into Latin or one of Europe's [living] languages. It is likely that one would find in it antiquities [Antiquitez] that the superstitiously proud Brahmins withhold from the people of the Indies whom they regard as profane and to whom nothing but the exterior [exterieur] of religion is conveyed, buried in fables that are at least as extravagant as those of Greek paganism. (La Croze 1724:427–28)

For La Croze, the Vedas represented the monotheistic core of Indian religion that the Brahmans jealously guarded as a secret while feeding the exoteric surface to the crowds. But since this "interior" doctrine of the Vedas was still unknown, information from other sources was all the more important. As royal librarian of Prussia, La Croze could make use of a very broad range of

The Idol of Vishnum.

Figure 2. Vishnu recuperates the Veda from the sea (Baldaeus 1703:844).

publications, but as a linguist and philologist, he was partial to authors who could read local languages. Abraham ROGER (d. 1649), though "having given a kind of system" of the religion of the Brahmans in a "work that was composed with care" and "translated into several languages," is criticized because "he did not himself read the religious books of the Indians and admits having relied on what he learned from the mouth of a Brahmin called Padmanaba"

(p. 444). Philip BALDAEUS (1632–72), the Dutch missionary and author of a description of South India and Ceylon (1672), is reprimanded for having "based his dissertations [Mémoires] about the island of Ceylon on the manuscripts of Portuguese missionaries who disfigured the Indian pronunciation to accommodate their way of writing and in various respects were not exactly well enough informed about the facts" (pp. 444–45). Vincenzo MARIA (d. 1680), the Carmelite author of *Il viaggio all'Indie orientali* (1678) "also described at length the religion of the Indians in Malabar and even gave some extracts from some of their books"; but he "ignored the language of the land and frankly admitted to have done no more than copy the Portuguese dissertations communicated to him by Don Francis Garzia, the Jesuit archbishop of Cranganor" (p. 445).

Ziegenbalg's Evidence

While using all these major authors, La Croze prized the information furnished by Bartholomäus ZIEGENBALG most highly: "He is preferable due to his accuracy and the care he took to report only what he had himself observed and what he read in the books written in a language that had become as natural to him as the one he sucked with his mother's milk" (p. 445). This is exactly the kind of new authority claim that, according to Trautmann, characterized the rise of a "new Orientalism" in the second half of the eighteenth century (1997:32–34). But fifty years before the publication of Holwell's dubious work, La Croze had already corresponded with Ziegenbalg, who recommended the perusal of the manuscript of his *Bibliotheca Malabarica* (letter of February 1716; Jeyaraj 2003:317). This was an annotated list of 119 Indian texts in the Tamil language collected by Ziegenbalg in the two-year span between his arrival in India (1706) and 1708.[2] A modern expert on Tamil literature, Kamil Veith Zvelebil, described this as "a relatively complete account of Tamil literature" (Zvelebil 1973:2), and we can imagine how impressed an early eighteenth-century linguist such as La Croze must have been. While the larger European public got news about the Danish Malabar mission mainly via the *Malabar Correspondence* and related materials that were first published in German and then partly translated into English (Philipps 1717; Ziegenbalg and Gründler 1719) and French (Niecamp 1745), La Croze enjoyed full access to all the major manuscripts that Ziegenbalg had sent to Europe: his travel account, the *Bibliotheca Malabarica*, the translations from

Tamil morality books, the *Malabar Correspondence*, the manuscript of the *Malabar Heathendom*, and of course also the manuscript of the second main work of Ziegenbalg, the *Genealogy of Malabar Divinities* (Jeyaraj 2003:318).

Ziegenbalg had studied Baldaeus (1672) before arriving in India as a young man of twenty-four years, and in his first letter (September 2, 1706); he described "the content of the four books of law [Vedas] according to his opinion" (Ziegenbalg 1926:14). But he soon realized that Baldaeus "got most [of his information] from the Portuguese fathers who were forced to leave it when they were chased out of Ceylon by the Dutch" and that the rest stemmed "from his dealings with Brahmans who oftentimes know very little of their dogmas" (pp. 14–15). His own work, so the young man decided, would not be such a pastiche (Schmierewerck) cobbled together from other authors but had to be based on reliable sources: "Everything that I have written I have either transcribed word for word from their own books and translated from the Malabar language into German, or I have heard it during frequent discussions from the very mouth of the heathen and had it told to me by people of understanding" (p. 15). That Ziegenbalg knew very little about the Vedas is evident from his manuscript on Malabar heathendom (1711) where he described them as "four small books of law" called "1. *Urukkuwedum*. 2. *Iderwedum*. 3. *Samawedum*. 4. *Adirwannawedum*" (p. 34).[3] But while "the four law books and the six *Sastirangöl* [*cāstiraṅkaḷ*] get into the hands of few persons and are only found with some priests who show such books to nobody," he wrote, "the eighteen *Paranen* [*purāṇas*] and other history books are ubiquitous, and parts of them can also be found with the common people" (p. 36).

It was thus not in Vedic literature that Ziegenbalg found support for his idea of Indian monotheism but rather in certain Tamil texts (see below) and in assertions of his Indian informants. Via the *Malabar Correspondence* in the *Hallesche Berichte*, its translations and summaries, and through passages of Ziegenbalg's works quoted in La Croze, such information from southern India eventually reached the desks of men like Voltaire, Joseph de Guignes, Anquetil-Duperron, Immanuel Kant, Johann Gottfried Herder, William Jones, and Constantin-François Volney.[4]

While partly modeling his *Genealogy of Malabar Divinities* of 1713 on the lists of gods in the "*Diwagaram* [*Tivākaram*]" (p. 286), Ziegenbalg omitted the "symbol of Tamil religiosity," Murukan̲, from his list (p. 299). Instead he began his *Genealogy* in the manner of a Christian theology book, with a chapter on "Barábarawástu" who in Ziegenbalg's view is "the supreme divine being and origin of all divinities" [das höchste göttliche Wesen und der Ursprung aller Götter] (p. 37), even though it is not listed in the *Tivākaram*. As natural monotheists, so Ziegenbalg thought, the Indians must since antiquity have worshiped a supreme divine being who was not just one god among others but rather the very origin of all gods and the world.

> These heathen know by the light of nature that there is one God. This truth has not only been communicated to them by Christians but is so firmly implanted in their mind [Gemüthe] by the evidence of their conscience that they would regard it as the greatest impiety [Gottlosigkeit] if they would learn that there are people in this world who do not posit a divine being who is the origin of everything, preserves everything, and reigns over everything—the kind of *atheism* [Atheistreÿ] that has found entry even among Christians and particularly among learned people here and there. (Ziegenbalg 2003:37).

Ziegenbalg compared such European atheists of the early eighteenth century with "heathen" Indians who are not only naturally monotheist but even profess faith in the very same God that the German pastors evoked in their sermons: "a God who created everything, reigns over everything, punishes evil, rewards good deeds, and who must be feared, loved, worshipped, and prayed to" (p. 37). The faith in this God had not only led the Indians to "establish a law and write many books of religion" but also to "introduce all kinds of sacrifices, build pagodas, and establish everywhere in their lands a *formal* service that in their opinion serves God" (p. 37). Because they relied exclusively on reason that "since the Fall is entirely misguided and spoiled," they eventually "let themselves be seduced by Satan in various ways." Nevertheless, from time immemorial, they fundamentally accept and worship an invisible divine being and have texts to prove this:

> Such truth gained from the light of nature is not a recent thing with them but a very ancient one; they have books that are said to be more than 2000 years old. These form the basis of their opinions in these matters, and they hold that their religion is the oldest of all; it may have originated not long after the deluge. They not only believe in one God but have by the light of nature come so far as to accept no more than one single divine being as the origin of all things. Even though they worship many gods, they hold that all such gods have sprung from a

single divine being and will return therein; so that in all gods only that single divine being is worshipped. Those among them who are a bit learned will defend this very obstinately even though they cannot deliver any proof of it. (pp. 37–38)

The best among the Indians regard "this *Barábarawástu*, which means Highest Being [*Ens Supremum*] or Being of beings [*Ens Entium*]" as an immaterial being [unmaterialisches Wesen] without any shape. They have hundreds of names for it, for example "*Savuvésuren*, the Lord over everything; *Niddia Anánder*, the eternally supreme one; or *Adināiagen*, the first lord of all who is supreme" (pp. 38–39).[5] Asked what this supreme God or Being of all Beings [Wesen aller Wesen] is, an Indian informer wrote in a letter to Ziegenbalg:

The supreme God, or the Being of all Beings, has a form yet is without form. He cannot be compared to anything. One cannot describe him nor say that he is this or that. He is neither male nor female, neither heaven nor earth, neither man nor any other creature. This God is not subject to destruction or death. He does not need to rest or sleep. He is omnipotent and omnipresent. He is without beginning and remains unchanged in eternity. His form can neither be seen nor described nor pronounced, etc. (pp. 39–40)

Together with excerpts from Indian scriptures, such letters by Indian "heathen" to Ziegenbalg constituted evidence that deeply impressed European readers including Voltaire. The *Malabar Correspondence* contained numerous Indian descriptions of God and prayers that for the first time gave voice to the Indians themselves. Bothered by resistance both of Danish administrators in Tranquebar on India's southeastern coast and of Pietist Europeans who questioned the value of the mission, Ziegenbalg and his companion Johann Ernst Gründler had decided to drum up support by having Indians answer written questions and ended up sending translations of no fewer than 104 such letters by Indians to Europe. Ninety-nine of them were published in two installments (1714 and 1717). Some of them appeared also in English and French, and central passages (such as the one just cited) were quoted in Ziegenbalg's manuscripts and in La Croze's book. Given the deist leanings of many European intellectuals, including Voltaire, such documentation of natural monotheism in one of the world's oldest nations did not go unnoticed and substantially contributed to eighteenth-century Europe's gradual shift of interest from China to India. It probably also formed a reason for August Hermann FRANCKE (1663–1727) to decide against the immediate publication of Ziegenbalg's manuscripts. Ziegenbalg may have been unaware of this problem, and his introduction to *Malabar Heathendom* shows him more concerned about atheists than deists:

> The fourth reason [for transmitting such information] is that teachers and preachers of atheism, which is fashionable among many in Europe, can be refuted through the principles of these heathen. Even though they are heathen, one will see consistently in these books that they believe in a divine Being who created all, reigns over everything, and eventually will reward virtue and punish evil; and that bliss awaits the faithful and damnation the evil. All of this, as a matter of fact, is denied by many Christians who rely on chance [fortuitum] and live much worse than the heathen. (Ziegenbalg 1926:13)

This sounds a bit like Voltaire's "Ambrosian" method of praising the heathen Indians in order to chastise degenerate European Christians. We have seen in Chapter 1 that, in order to support his claims of ancient Indian monotheism, Voltaire first used Indian prayers and quotations from Indian texts that he found in La Croze; subsequently, it was the *Ezour-vedam* that provided additional evidence; and finally, Voltaire lionized the pure monotheism of the "Indian" texts by Holwell and Dow. Though Ziegenbalg's admiration for monotheism in India resembles that of Voltaire, the German clergyman's mission was more straightforward. But he also had a little problem with his sources.

Ziegenbalg's Founts of Wisdom

Since La Croze's idea of the religion of the Indies was so much based on Ziegenbalg's published and unpublished writings and on letters written by Indians, some basic questions about them need to be posed. Who were these "numerous Indians" who in a short timespan wrote so many letters to Ziegenbalg and insisted so stridently on the monotheism of Indian religion that god-fearing Europeans including Voltaire were astonished? And who were these Gnanigöl, the authors of the Indian texts whose translations so much inspired Ziegenbalg, La Croze, and their readers?

When Ziegenbalg arrived in the small Danish colony of Tranquebar on the coast south of Madras (Chennai) in 1706, he first had to learn some Portuguese; but before long he decided that only a thorough knowledge of the local Tamil language would let him communicate freely with the natives. His first teacher of Tamil did not understand Portuguese, and progress was very slow because of the lack of a dictionary and grammar. But he soon met an eminent native who seemed to be the answer to his prayers:

> We got to know a Malabar who used to be the head [of the Tamil community] here [in Tranquebar] but had been evicted from the town and county [by Danish authorities] because of a certain reason. Since he spoke good Portuguese, Danish, Dutch, and German, we employed him as *translator* and managed to get permission for him and his family to return to town. (Letter of Sept. 22, 1707; Jeyaraj 2003:281)

It was this gifted man, Alakappan or Aleppa, who introduced Ziegenbalg to the intricacies of the Tamil language and to the vocabulary needed for his mission. Three months after his arrival Ziegenbalg wrote,

> My old schoolmaster often discusses with me all day long, and this has already allowed me to become relatively familiar with their forms of religious worship [Götterdienste]. I intend to make a Christian of him, and he has the hope to eventually turn me into a Malabar. Therefore he seeks to demonstrate everything so distinctly that I could not wish for anything better. (Lehmann 1956:40)

Daniel Jeyaraj thinks that, on the basis of the man's name, Aleppa was a Shaivite and argues that this could explain why Ziegenbalg dealt more with this branch devoted to the worship of the god Shiva than with rival forms of Hinduism (Jeyaraj 2003:282). The importance of Aleppa exceeds that of the Japanese Anjirō to Francis Xavier (who, as explained in Chapter 1, caused such a fiasco in the early Japan mission). Aleppa was born around 1660 into a family (probably of higher Tamil Shudra caste) that had long worked for Europeans. Around 1700 he was "Ober-Tolk" (head translator) of the Danish trading company and the top representative of the Tamil inhabitants of the city (Gründler and Ziegenbalg 1998:18). It is not clear for what grave reasons this influential man was banished from Tranquebar; but his value to the mission is reflected both in the decision to let him return to the city and in his extraordinarily high yearly salary of 100 thalers, which surpassed even that of European employees (p. 20). After two years of work with the missionaries, Aleppa was again expelled in 1709. However, the missionaries managed to keep him on their payroll as collaborator from afar. And collaborate he did: in 1710–11 he was even imprisoned by the king of neighboring Tañcāvūr for having "revealed all the secrets of their law and worship [Gesetzes und Gottesdienstes]" to the missionaries (p. 21).

Aleppa clearly played a central role in Ziegenbalg's introduction to the Malabar language and religion, but his influence did not end there. When Ziegenbalg and his associate Gründler needed more European support and were preparing for Ziegenbalg's journey to Germany, Denmark, and England, they paid Aleppa to write letters from exile in answer to the missionaries' questions. These answers were almost immediately translated or edited, annotated, and sent to Europe where they were published; but since Aleppa was in exile and could for various reasons not be named as a source, the missionaries decided to omit all names of correspondents. They tried to create the impression that these letters came from many different informants, and their habit of sometimes splitting a single letter into several pieces (p. 27) that supposedly came from different correspondents enhanced the readers' impression that a substantial number of Indians were involved. The first batch of fifty-five letters was printed in 1714 with a preface emphasizing that "all of these letters without exception are from heathens of the most understanding kind" who write so excellently about God that "one could hardly find better ones with the ancient Greeks and Romans, and many so-called Christians will rightly feel ashamed" (pp. 42–43). Though the Indian heathens had no way of knowing Christ "through the light of nature" and had to be saved "from their misery and blindness," the "Christian readers could not but be pleased, and the atheists ashamed, that even these heathens recognize a single supreme being and are convinced that all men can know with absolute certainty that there is a lord who created this world and everything in it" (p. 44).

Here the letter collection's preface refers to letter number 6, which is "written by someone who read and copied many books of the Christian religion in his language" (p. 115). Though unnamed, this man was, of course, Aleppa; and as in many other letters, he wonders why the missionaries, whom he had orally informed in such detail, wanted him to write about things that they already perfectly knew. The missionaries had obviously asked him to send, against payment of course, a whole series of letters with answers to their questions. The task set for this particular letter was to explain the difference between Christianity and his own religion (p. 116). Aleppa began his explanation as follows:

> You know me very well and are already well aware of the limits of my knowledge and my utter incapacity of demonstrating such a difference of religion [Gesetz]—all the more since I was about 15 years old when I entered your [colonial] services and could not yet read nor write well, not to speak of knowing something about the doctrines of our religious texts [Gesetzbücher]. . . . Since I know many things of your religion [Gesetz] and was educated in my best years not so much according to our but rather according to your ways, it is very difficult and even impossible for me to write about a true difference between these religions [Gesetze] based on your and our religious texts [Gesetzbücher]. But to show you my good will, I will briefly write down my opinion. . . . All men can know with the utmost certainty that there is a lord who created the world and everything in it. (pp. 116–17)

Time and again, Aleppa wrote to the missionaries that they already knew what they wanted him to explain, and I think that this was not just a polite formula: "You know everything much better than what I can write" (p. 49); "I also know that you already know more about our doctrines [Lehrsätze] than I can write" (p. 89); "You are those who know everything and understand what can be learned by men. . . . Concerning theology, wisdom, and virtue, I know nothing that you do not already know and understand; you have read and understood much more about this, and I do not presume to instruct people such as you" (p. 114).

Of course, Aleppa was well informed about the missionaries' knowledge; after all, he had been instrumental in teaching them his language and religion, and as their highest-paid, best connected, and most knowledgeable employee, he was also deeply involved in their effort to collect and study the Tamil texts listed in the *Bibliotheca Malabarica* of 1708. Ignorant about the planned use of his letters for raising mission funds in Europe, he could not figure out why the missionaries wanted letters about things he had so much discussed with them over the years. He expressed his puzzlement once more at the beginning of the twelfth letter:

In the year Nándanawáruschúm [1712], October 15. I, N., inform the two reverends in Tranquebar that thanks to your prayers I am to date well and without the slightest ill. You desire to know something from me, namely, if we Malabars worship one God or many gods. But can it be that you are in this matter ignorant, you who have for such a long time heard all our doctrines and read in our books and have also preached against [our doctrines] to us? But since you so desire, I will write what I know about it and what everybody knows. (p. 141)

After this interesting introduction, Aleppa repeats what he apparently learned so well since his youth and discussed so many times with the missionaries:

The fact that God is a unique God [einiger Gott] is known and professed by all. . . . We also say that among all [gods] there is only one who is the highest being, called at times *Bárabarawástu* [Skt. *parāparavastu*, divine substance] and at times *Tschiwén* [Shiva], *Tschatátschiwum* [Skt. *sadā-śiva*, eternally graceful one], or *Barabirúma* [Skt. *para-brahmā*, supreme Brahman]. This God has created all others, given each of them his duties and tasks, and ordered that they must be worshipped and prayed to. All of this is written in our law [Gesetz] and is commanded in old history books. Therefore it is among us everywhere customary to pray to the said persons. At the same time it is written in our books of law that God promised various modes of recompensation to those who worship such persons and accept them in faith and love. (p. 142)

The ordinary people of South India were thus depicted as fundamentally monotheistic, even though they had a tendency to worship the true God under different names and forms. But Aleppa also mentioned radical mono-theists:

Other than that, there are also people among us who worship God the supreme being alone and always honor only this lord while they re-nounce everything in the world in order to keep contemplating God in their heart at all times. It is said of these [*Gnanigöl*] that God unites with them and transforms them into himself [in sich verwandele], and also that they become invisible in the world. (p. 142)

The first fifty-five Malabar letters were published in 1714 (reprints in 1718 and 1735) and the remaining forty-four in 1717 (reprints in 1718 and 1735). A number of them soon were excerpted in English translation (Philipps 1717; Ziegenbalg and Gründler 1719), and in 1724, La Croze quoted numerous passages from Ziegenbalg's correspondence and manuscripts.[6] Only in 1729, five years after the publication of La Croze's book, did readers of the Halle mission reports first learn that these letters "were mostly written by the translator of the erstwhile missionaries, Arhagappen [Aleppa], who remains a heathen, when he lived nearby and earned his living from this [letter writing] while in exile" (Gründler and Ziegenbalg 1998:17). Though some scholars still believe that many different letter authors were involved, the tone and content of the vast majority of the letters point to a single author who on occasion interviewed knowledgeable persons in his vicinity. The sequence of the first fifty-five letters supports this; the first is from October 2, 1712, and the fifty-fifth from December 10 of the same year. This comes to a bit less than one letter a day, and I may not be too wrong in hypothesizing that Aleppa was contracted to write about one letter per day. In October 1712, twenty-three letters were written, and a letter-free day is often followed by a day with two letters. Though Aleppa certainly integrated information gained from others and sometimes apologizes for drawing only on his own knowledge, these letters for the most part reflect Aleppa's views, which were, of course, developed during his long acquaintance with Europeans, his Western-style education, his years as an official interpreter, and especially his prolonged daily contact with the missionaries in his function as teacher, informant, and translator. He clearly tried to present his own religion in the best light and had adopted the Europeans' fundamental conviction that monotheism was good, while polytheism and idol-worship were evil and the devil's work. In this way European readers, including La Croze, thus read, in a manner of saying, Aleppa's correspondence course on Tamil religion that reflects his earlier lessons to the German missionaries and their discussions. The European readership learned about Indian monotheism from the very man who had introduced Ziegenbalg to Indian religions and had helped him find texts that supported this idea of Indian monotheism.

Ignorance and Wisdom

Ziegenbalg's Tamil treatises are a sort of correspondence course in the opposite direction. To explain how heathendom arose, for example, the missionary informed his Tamil readers that *Añānam* (Skt. *ajñāna*, ignorance) came into this world through the cunning of Picācu (Skt. *piśāca*, ghost, goblin) and man's offense. Ziegenbalg pointed out that *ajñāna* (which for him signified idolatrous heathendom) is present when, instead of the true God, only his creatures are worshipped. Only the *manuṣa-avatāram* (Skt. *manuṣāvatāra*, human manifestation) of Christ could bring true *mōṭcam* (Skt. *mokṣa*, liberation) and conclusively exterminate *ajñāna* (Jieyaraj 2003:311–12).

Aleppa was not the only source of this kind of terminology. Though Ziegenbalg had expected to be sent to Africa and came to India quite unprepared for his task, he was a fast learner—and a lucky one to boot. During a phase of persecution in a neighboring region, a Jesuit missionary's library was stored in Tranquebar, and Ziegenbalg found himself suddenly in possession of much interesting materials that included a Tamil translation of the New Testament. This stroke of luck made him an heir to Jesuit research on terminology that had flourished since the days of Roberto de Nobili. In the *Bibliotheca Malabarica* of 1708, Ziegenbalg already listed sixteen Roman Catholic works and wrote that he had corrected five of them to such an extent that they could be used by his Protestant flock "without any problem" (p. 291–92). At this early stage he thus began to employ de Nobili's loaded terminology; for example, he often used the word Caruvēcuraṉ (Skt. *sarveśvara*, lord of all) for God. According to Jeyaraj (2003:292), the twenty-six Tamil sermons of de Nobili contain many words picked up by Ziegenbalg—for example, the Tamil words for God, angels, devil, world, man, soul, death, salvation, remission, and eternal life. Ziegenbalg's Tamil community was likely to learn, just like de Nobili's flock a century earlier, how important it is for *manuṣaṉ* (Skt *manuṣa*, man) to avoid *pāvam* (Skt. *pāpa*, evil), to embrace *puṇṇiyam* (Skt. *puṇya*, virtue), and to worship Caruvēcuraṉ (Skt. *sarveśvara*, lord of all) in the form of Barábarawástu (Skt. *parāparavastu*, divine substance) because there is no other path to the other shore (*karai-ērutal*) of *mōṭcam* (Skt. *mokṣa*, liberation) (p. 292).

Apart from terms for God such as Caruvēcuraṉ and Barábarawástu, the juxtaposition of *jñāna* (knowledge, wisdom) and *ajñāna* (ignorance) was particularly important for Ziegenbalg's view of Indian religions and his mission enterprise. The title of the first pamphlet from the brand-new Tamil mission press in Tranquebar reads: "The *Vēta-pramāṇām* (Skt. *vedapramāṇa*, Vedic norm) demonstrating that *akkiyāṉam* [*ajñāna*] must be detested and how those in *akkiyāṉam* can be saved" (pp. 309–10). In the very first sentence Ziegenbalg comes straight to the point: "We have come to you in order to save you from *akkiyāṉam*" (Grafe 2004:83–84). Grafe summarizes the pamphlet's contents as follows:

> (1) What is *a-jnana*?—It is idol worship and moral perversion according to Rom. 1:21–32. (2) How *a-jnana* spread in this world.—It did so because of the devil's deceit and men's guilt and not because of God. (3) There is much *a-jnana* in the whole of Tamilnadu. (4) How detestable *a-jnana* is.—Because by *a-jnana* soul and body will be perverted and punished. (5) How God is helping those in *a-jnana* to be saved.—Jesus Christ took upon himself the burden of *a-jnana* and delivers from *a-jnana* saving soul and body. (6) What the things are which those who wish to be saved from *a-jnana* have to do. . . . (7) The trials and tribulations which those who give up *a-jnana* and enter the Church experience in the world for the sake of righteousness. (8) The benefits promised to those who give up *a-jnana*, accept true religion and stand in the Christian faith unshaken. (p. 84)

It is clear that Ziegenbalg used the word *ajñāna* (ignorance) for sin, heathendom, and idolatry. On the other hand, *jñāna* (knowledge or wisdom) stood for monotheism and the acceptance of Jesus as savior. For Ziegenbalg, *ajñāna* involves the veneration of false devas and the worship of *vikrakams* (Skt. *vigraha*, forms or shapes) made of earth, wood, stone, and metal. By contrast, *jñāna* signifies the exclusive worship of Barábarawástu (Skt. *parāparavastu*, divine substance). The point Aleppa kept making in his apologetic letters was exactly that his native religion was fundamentally a monotheistic *jñāna*, rather than a heathen *ajñāna*, and it seems that he was highly motivated to help the missionaries find Tamil texts that proved exactly this point. The text that Ziegenbalg most often quotes to illustrate Indian monotheism was already used by de Nobili for the very same purpose: the *Civavākkiyam*, a fourteenth-century collection of poems by Civavākkiyar who belongs to the Tamil Siddha tradition.

Although the Tamil tradition speaks of eighteen Siddhas and posits a line of wandering saints and *sannyāsis* from Tirumular (sixth century) to Tayumanavar (1706–44), most of the noted Siddhas flourished between the fourteenth and eighteenth centuries (Kailasapathy 1987:387). From the beginning, the antibrahmanical and antihierarchical tendency of Siddha writings was prominent, as in Tirumular's oft-quoted lines, "Caste is one and God is one" (p. 386). But the God referred to here is not exactly the one whom de

Nobili and Ziegenbalg worshipped, and this saying does not signify "mankind is one and God is one." Rather, as Kailasapathy explains, Tirumular meant that "insofar as religious worship was concerned, all castes are equal and the only god is Shiva" (p. 386). Yet this movement fought against "the extreme antagonism between the Vedic religions (Shaivism, Vaishnavism) and the non-Vedic or heterodox religions (Buddhism, Jainism and the Ajivika faith)" and tried to overcome virulent sectarianism of various sorts. Its poetry, written in colloquial style, was attractive and quite popular. For example, verse 1533 of Tirumular reads:

> Those who follow the six religions know him not
> Nor is he confined to those six faiths.
> Seek and having sought cogitate in your mind
> And then without doubt you will gain salvation. (p. 387)

Of the more than fifty names associated with the way of the Siddhas (Siddha *mārga*), that of the author of the *Civavākkiyam* (Aphorisms on Shiva) is best known. The author of these aphorisms, Civavākkiyar or Sivavakkiyar, is "without doubt the most powerful poetic voice in the entire galaxy of the Siddhas" and is best known for his skill in criticizing and ridiculing Hindu orthodoxy (p. 387–89). Though not forming a well-defined school of thought, the Siddhas "challenged the very foundations of medieval Hinduism: the authority of the Shastras, the validity of rituals and the basis of the caste system" (p. 389). According to Zvelebil, "almost all of them manifest a protest, often in very strong terms, agains the formalities of life and religion; denial of religious practices and beliefs of the ruling classes" (1973:8). Tamil Siddhas were basically "all theists and believed in a transcendental God and his grace towards man," but they were not "idol-worshippers or believers in a supreme Person"; rather, they "believed in a supreme Abstraction" that they referred to as *civam* (Kailasapathy 1987:393).

> The recurrent use by the Siddhas of the word *civam* (an abstract noun meaning "goodness," "auspiciousness" and the highest state of God, in which he exists as pure intelligence) in preference to the common term *civan* (meaning Shiva) makes this point very clear. In other words, they believed in an abstract idea of Godhead rather than a personal God. (p. 393)

Among the three Hindu religious paths to salvation (*jñāna*, the way of knowledge; *karma*, the way of work; and *bhakti*, the way of devotion), the Siddhas emphasized the path of knowledge (p. 393). In the light of such explanations, it is easy to see why de Nobili and Ziegenbalg felt attracted to such poetry and in particular to Civavākkiyar who dared to refute deeply entrenched dogmas such as transmigration:

> Milk does not return to the udder,
> Likewise butter can never become butter-milk;
> The sound of the conch does not exist once it is broken;
> The blown flower, the fallen fruit do not go back to the tree;
> The dead are never born again, never! (p. 401)

Siddha Civavākkiyar's work promotes *civam* mysticism and is critical not only of the worship of images and brahmans but also of the Vedas and Vedic practices. Zvelebil translates a typical verse as follows:

> In the Four Eternal Vedas,
> In the study and reading of scripts,
> In sacred ashes and in Holy Writs
> And muttering of prayers
> You will not find the Lord!
> Melt with the Heart Inside
> and proclaim the Truth.
> Then you will join the Light—
> Life without servitude. (Zvelebil 1973:83)

Such Tamil Siddhas belonged to the class of men that Ziegenbalg referred to as "*Gnanigöl* or the Wise" (Ziegenbalg 2003:40). "Gnanigöl" is Ziegenbalg's transcription of the Tamil *ñāṇikaḷ*, which is the plural of *ñāṇi* (Skt. *jñānin*, a wise or knowing one). They are saints in the fourth path (*pāda*) of Shaivite Siddhānta *āgama*. Ziegenbalg called these four paths "Tscharigei" (*caryā*, proper conduct), "Kirigei" (*kriyā*, rites), "Jógum" (*yoga*, discipline), and "Gnánum" (*jñāna*, knowledge). The Gnanigöl are most frequently mentioned by Ziegenbalg, and quotations from their texts make up the bulk of his evidence for Indian monotheism. In the first chapter of his *Genealogy*, where he discusses the pure Indian conception of monotheism, Ziegenbalg explains:

One still finds here and there a few who destroy all idolatry [Götzen-Wesen] and venerate this sole divine Being without images. Among them are those called *Gnanigöl* or the Wise who have written only such books that lead exclusively to a virtuous life wherein only the sole God is to be worshipped. The most excellent among such books are: 1) The *Tschiwa-wāikkium* [Civa-vākkiyam], in which polytheism along with many heathen errors is totally rejected in thoughtful verses and the worship of a single God is advocated. 2) The *Diruwalluwer*,[7] which treats of morality. 3) *Nidishárum*[8] which presents some rules of life in in the form of parables. 4) *Gnanawenpa*[9] which contains wisdom teachings and testimonies of the one God. (Ziegenbalg 2003:40)

The book that leads this list, the *Civavākkiyam*, is also the one that Ziegenbalg most frequently adduced in his discussions of Indian monotheism. La Croze's argument for Indian monotheism, too, is almost entirely illustrated by quotations from Ziegenbalg's rendering of verses by Civavākkyar.[10] But there were also many other textual sources consulted by Ziegenbalg since he had become proficient in the Tamil language. In 1708, two years after his arrival in India, he wrote in the preface to his first translation of a Tamil morality text:

> As soon as I became a bit familiar with their language and could converse with these heathen [in Tamil] about various topics, I was gradually freed from this prejudice [that they are a barbaric people] and could thus think better of them. When I finally arrived at the point where I could read their own books I became aware that the same philosophical disciplines as those of the learned in Europe are quite well taught among them and that they have a proper written law from which all theological matters must be derived and demonstrated. I was very much surprised by this and developed an enormous desire to become thoroughly instructed through their own scriptures regarding their heathendom. Acquiring one book after another, I spared neither time nor money; and now I have come to the point that, through diligent reading of their books and constant disputing with their Brahmans or priests, I am able to gain certain knowledge about them and discuss it rationally. (Ziegenbalg 1930:11)

As previously mentioned, having arrived in India in 1706 with a smattering of knowledge about Indian religions gathered mainly from Baldaeus and

Alexander Ross's *Pansebeia* (1701)—both of which also contained information from Abraham Roger (1651)—Ziegenbalg thus soon found himself in a position not only personally to observe rituals and customs in and around Tranquebar but also to question knowledgeable Indians and to study Tamil scriptures intensively. In this way he could form an image of South Indian religion that was better informed than that of all predecessors. He was conscious of this when he asserted in the preface of *Malabar Heathendom* that his work was "not a pastiche cobbled together from other authors" but rather an account based on oral and written information from reliable Tamil sources (Ziegenbalg 1926:15). As he was quite aware that "his work could not be free of mistakes," he reserved the right to correct the given information "if in the future I should observe that I have erred," adding,

> These heathens are very shifting [variabel] in their discourses. One tells me one thing and another something different. This is why I do not put much trust in their tales unless I heard something unanimously from many mouths. What I have read myself in their books is most worthy of trust. Since few heathens are very familiar [versiret] with their books, one must not rashly conclude that information in books is wrong when it is unfamiliar to these heathens. As soon as one discusses these matters with persons who are well read, one will see and hear that they confirm everything that I here allege on the basis of their books. (p. 15)

This kind of attitude motivated modern scholars to call Ziegenbalg's work "close to science" (wissenschaftsnah) and to praise his portrayal of Hindu practices and forms of faith as having been produced "from the inside, and relying on oral informants as well as (partly classical but partly also quite rare) indigenous textual sources" (Dharampal-Frick 2004:131). Such praise is often tempered by the observation that the late publication of Ziegenbalg's *Malabar Heathendom* (1926) and his other books prevented them from having a major influence on eighteenth-century Europe's view of Indian religions. However, Ziegenbalg's views found other channels to seep into the European mindset and ended up having a major impact both in Europe and in India.

Hinduism Avant la Lettre

Today Ziegenbalg's surprisingly modern approach and his innovative portrayal of Indian religion get increasing attention from reseachers studying the

European reception of Indian religion and particularly the Western "discovery" or "creation" of Hinduism. But neither the word "Hinduism" nor any of its cognates ever appear in Ziegenbalg's writings. Is the semantic field of what he calls "Malabar heathendom" more or less congruent with the modern concept of Hinduism? In the preface of *Malabar Heathendom*, Ziegenbalg uses, possibly as the first European author (Sweetman 2003:109), the term "Welt Religionen" (sic; world religions).

> All inhabitants of the whole Earth are classified in four main religions [4 haupt Religionen], which are Jews, Christians, Mahometans, and heathens. The Jews are the least numerous people and are dispersed everywhere in the world. The Christians are a bit more numerous and have not only filled the whole of Europe but are also scattered in the other three parts of the world. The Mahometans are a very large people, have subjugated almost a one-third of the world, and spread everywhere. The heathens form the largest people and reside in the majority of regions on the globe. Among all of these four great world religions, the Devil has shown himself very busy trying to confuse the souls of men and seduce them to eternal damnation. (Ziegenbalg 1926:10)

Ziegenbalg's *Malabar Heathendom* shows him as an heir to earlier classification schemes. His classification of the world's religions is similar in structure to that of Bernhard Varenius (1649); his view of natural religion agrees with Edward Herbert's "five common notions" (1663); his conception of the heathen's symbolic worship and critique of Brahman priestcraft also conforms with Herbert's arguments; and his view of the fundamental theism of heathendom and the positive role of its knowledge in the fight against atheism has its counterpart in Alexander Ross (1653). Furthermore, his portrayal of the devil as the prime culprit in the degeneration process from a fundamentally good and monotheistic heathendom to polytheistic cults with abhorrent practices mirrors a tract by David Nerreter in the enlarged 1701 edition of Ross. But while Ziegenbalg's classification shows little originality in its overall structure and theoretical foundation, it features a very innovative view of Indian religions whose description in Ross was woefully inadequate and included hardly any knowledge gained since the sixteenth century.

Like Brerewood (1614) and many others, Ziegenbalg divided the world's religions in four basic categories (see Figure 3). The first three (Judaism, Christianity, and Islam) are based on divine revelation and rely on the whole

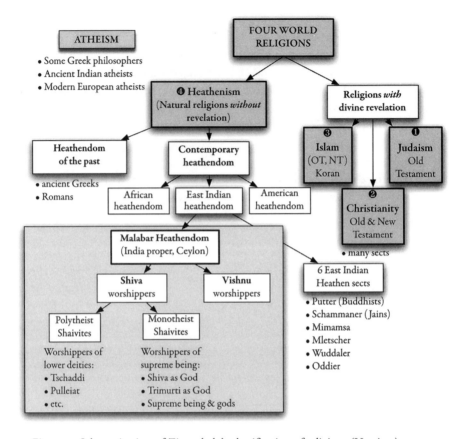

Figure 3. Schematic view of Ziegenbalg's classification of religions (Urs App).

or on parts of the Bible. But in spite of the dispersion of Christianity and the size of Islam, which has "subjugated almost one-third of the world," "heathendom"—the fourth of Ziegenbalg's "great world religions"—is by far the biggest and "occupies the largest part of the world" (Ziegenbalg 1926:9). While the devil played his part also in the Abrahamic religions by fracturing and perverting them and putting particularly the followers of Islam under his domination, the heathens were even more deceived by him (p. 10). Because they were deprived of God's revelation, it was even easier to pervert their natural monotheism and turn their sane reason toward various abominations. Ziegenbalg mentioned some major forms of heathendom (African, American, old European) but did not offer any scenarios of origin other than pointing to the devil. Instead he zoomed in on his area of expertise, the heathendom of the East Indies and the religious complex he called "Malabar heathendom."

This "Malabar heathendom" is distinguished in various ways from other religions. One way is geographical. According to Ziegenbalg, Malabar heathendom is prevalent in an area that more or less corresponds to the Indian subcontinent: "Malabar heathendom is spread far and wide in India so that many kingdoms, islands, peoples, and languages fall into its sphere. This heathendom reaches over the whole Coromandel coast far into Bengal; one reads in their books very many stories that are said to have happened there" (p. 23). But it spread beyond Bengal since "one also reads that many of their saints stayed in the large forests that are said to be beyond Bengal and underwent severe penances there" (p. 23). On the west coast of the Indian subcontinent, Malabar heathendom reigns from Ceylon all the way up north: "Thus all heathens in the Mogul empire are included in this heathendom; even though they otherwise are in many ways different and have separate sects among them, they worship the same gods" (p. 23).

In view of the obviously inconsistent usage of words such as "religion," "law" (Gesetz), and "sect," in the writings of Ziegenbalg, his associates, and Aleppa, it appears wise not to retroproject modern meanings on such terms and to dissect them. Rather, the multiple dimensions of Ziegenbalg's delimitation and characterization of Malabar heathendom deserve attention. So far we have seen that Ziegenbalg defined Malabar heathendom in terms of geography and worshipped divinities. Next he distinguishes two main traditions:

> This whole widespread heathendom is divided into two important main sects. The first sect is called *Tschiwasámeian* [*Civacamayam*; system of Shiva] and the second *Wischtnusameiam* [*Viṣṇucamayam*; system of Vishnu]. All those who belong to the first sect regard Shiva or Ishvara as supreme God and pray to all gods that he befriended or stem from his lineage. In all their sacrifices, prayers, external ceremonies, fasts, and tenets [Lehrsätzen] they follow those books whichare written about Shiva. All who belong to this sect smear ashes from burnt cow-dung on their forehead and on various parts of their body. (p. 23)

The second main sect of Ziegenbalg's Malabar heathendom regards Vishnu as the supreme God and follows the practices and doctrines prescribed in Vishnu-related texts. In general its adherents do not smear the ash of cow-dung on their bodies but rather draw symbols for their God on their forehead and other body parts using a particular kind of clay from the Mogul domain that is specially prepared for use as color. These colored symbols as well as signs burned into the skin characterize the outer appearance of the worshippers of Vishnu (p. 24).

Instead of pursuing Ziegenbalg's intricate descriptions of these two main traditions and their various subsects, doctrines, sanctuaries, secondary divinities, practices, and intersectarian conflicts, we now turn to some elements that link them and define them as parts of a single religious unit called "Malabar heathendom." Though Ziegenbalg wrote that the two main divisions of Malabar heathendom are "again divided into four kinds that are found both among the followers of Shiva (Tschiwapaddikaren) and those of Vishnu (Wischtnupaddikaren)" (p. 26) his explanations show that these "kinds" are not subsects but rather "differens états de la vie" (different stages of life), as La Croze put it (1724:450). As we have seen, these four stages on the religious path are "Tscharigei" (*caryā*, proper conduct), "Kirigei" (*kriyā*, rites), "Jógum" (*yoga*, discipline), and "Gnánum" (*jñāna*, knowledge); and according to Ziegenbalg, these stages are identical for the followers of Shiva and Vishnu. The observances at each stage are different. The first stage is for householders who cannot strictly follow the prescribed observances; the second for those who strictly follow outer observances, for example, clergy like "the Brahmanes, Pantaren, and Antigöl"; the third for those who do not care about the many divinities and ceremonies but rather devote themselves singlemindedly to meditation, remain or become again celibate, and perform manifold austerities; and the fourth for those who have abandoned everything and reached "*Gnánum* or wisdom" (Ziegenbalg 1926:27). This fourth and highest stage is that of the Gnanigöl who have left behind all ignorance (*ajñāna*) and who for Ziegenbalg represent the purest wisdom (*jñāna*) of monotheism:

> Those who have thus become *Gnanigöl* not only consider the ways of the world as foolish but also every other thing in which people seek bliss. They reject the many gods that others revere so much; as one of them writes in a book called *Tschiwawáikkium* [Civavākkyiam]: You are nothing but lies, prayer-formulas are lies, the disciplines of erudition are lies. Bruma and Wischtnum [Brahma and Vishnu] are fabricated lies, and Dewandiren [Devendra] too. Whoever abandons the lusts of the flesh that seem sweet as honey, dies to that which seems beautiful to the eyes,

and hates the habits of man while worshipping only the True supreme being: to him all of these things appear as false and full of lies. (pp. 27–28)

Such saintly Gnanigöl, Ziegenbalg emphasized, are found among both the worshippers of Shiva and those of Vishnu; "they lead a virtuous life after their fashion, worship only the supreme being of all beings, and lead their disciples and pupils toward a worship of God that is completely interior (p. 28). Clearly Ziegenbalg, the German Protestant and Pietist, found himself much attracted by such pure and austere piety, which stood in stark contrast to the somewhat Catholic ceremonies and the seemingly Jesuit haughtiness of the Brahmans.

Interestingly, Ziegenbalg linked these four stages of the religious path to the four Vedas, about whose content he knew practically nothing:

These heathens have among them four small books of law: 1. the *Urukkuwedum* [Ṛg veda]; 2. *Iderwedum* [Yajur veda]. 3. *Samawedum* [Sāma veda]; 4. *Adirwannawedum* [Atharva veda]. From these four books of law originated the four kinds [Sorten] . . . among the worshippers of Shiva and of Vishnu, that is, 1. Tscharigei; 2. Kirigei; 3. Iogum; 4. Gnanum. The first law (Veda), according to some, contains what the Tscharigeikárer or people of worldly professions ought to do in order to reach bliss through their worldly tasks. (p. 35)

The first Veda, according to Ziegenbalg's information, thus contained mainly "*Mandirum* [mantras] or prayer formulas" and the second Veda what was needed for those who wanted to be saved by works [Werckheilige] (p. 34). The third Veda, "according to some," has the instructions for Yogic practices, and "the fourth book of law is said to contain everything which the *Gnanigöl* who have reached wisdom and sainthood ought to perform and do" (p. 35). Though Ziegenbalg repeatedly used formulae indicating that he had not himself seen any Veda and depended on unconfirmed information, the four Vedas were thus seen as the basic sacred scriptures for both main branches of Malabar heathendom. Together with "the six *Sastirum* which are called theological systems" and the "Eighteen *Puranen*" containing "the manifestations and miracles of their gods," they form a body of scriptures "of which they say and write that they stem from the gods inspiring their disciples who wrote them down" (p. 35). While the four Vedas and six Shastras are written in an ancient language (Sanskrit) and are "in very few people's hands" (p. 36), the eighteen Puranas are readily accessible even for the common people. Ziegenbalg writes that the Indians "regard these books as canonical," "revealed by the gods," and written down many hundreds of thousands of years ago in former world ages (p. 35). By contrast, the twenty-four *Ágamangöl* [āgama] and the sixty-four *Kaleikkianum* or Books of Art are only read by scholars and are not regarded as revealed (pp. 35–36). Though Ziegenbalg does not use these terms and though attributions of texts vary, these two different kinds of texts are known as *śruti* (what is heard directly), that is, revealed scriptures, and *smṛti* (memorized tradition), that is, texts by human authors.

In addition to the geographical definition, the fundamental faith in a supreme God, the common divinities, and the shared four stages of the religious career, Ziegenbalg's Malabar heathendom is thus also characterized by a common basis of divinely inspired sacred scriptures called Vedas that prescribe practices valid for all branches. Further characteristics of Malabar heathendom in Ziegenbalg's description are the caste system, the Brahman clergy, and the veneration of cows. Regardless of Ziegenbalg's use of terms like "religion" or "sect"—and regardless of whether one finds the term Hinduism appropriate—I thus conclude that the geographic as well as the semantic field of Ziegenbalg's "Malabar heathendom" matches that of "Hinduism" rather closely. But this is an appraisal that we can make only today on the basis of privileged access to Ziegenbalg's major works. Materials by Ziegenbalg that were published in the eighteenth century could not yet lead to such a conclusion. "Hinduism" was not yet born as a European category. Its creation in the European mind—though not quite ex nihilo—had to await an Irish gentleman by the name of Holwell (see Chapter 6).

La Croze's Scenario

In his readings of Tamil texts, Ziegenbalg also came across some Indian religions that did *not* form part of Malabar heathendom and thus delimited it in one more way:

> Apart from the above-mentioned sects [Shaiva and Vaishnava], there are several others among the East Indian heathens which the Malabarians entirely exclude from their religion, taking them for heathens while re-

garding themselves as a people with an extremely ancient religion and worship [Gottesdienst]. Apart from themselves, they enumerate six other religion-sects [Religions-Secten], several of which are said still to exist in faraway countries, while others among them were completely extinguished and absorbed into their religion. The first sect is called *Putter* [Buddhism] from which they say they have their poetry. The second sect is called *Schammaner* from which they got the art of arithmetic along with other arts and learning. The third sect is called *Minmankuscher* [Mīmāṃsakas], the fourth *Miletscher* [mlecchas] or the sect of barbarians, the fifth *Wuddaler*, and the sixth *Oddier*. (p. 29)

It is interesting that Ziegenbalg's informants labeled religions that differed from their "Malabar heathendom" as *ajñāna* or heathen. This is not just a case of the missionaries' "heathen" chicken coming home to roost but a symptom of boundaries perceived by the Indians themselves. Of particular interest in our context are the first two religions regarded as *ajñāna* by the Indian informants and in texts consulted by Ziegenbalg. The Putter, also called "Buddergöl"[11] by Ziegenbalg, are said to have been expelled from India long ago. In recounting the ten transformations (Verwandlungen) of Vishnu, the missionary says about the sixth avatar: "*Wegudduwa Awatarum*, when he was born as a priest in the world, chased away the religion of *Buddergöl* and *Schammanergöl*, and had his twelve disciples, called *Banirentualwahr*, establish his religion everywhere" (p. 47). Ziegenbalg here uses the singular "religion" for both groups. Did he think they professed the same religion? Today we identify the Buddergöl as Buddhists; but who were these Schammanergöl?[12] In Ziegenbalg's *Malabar Heathendom* there is little information about this "religion of the *Schammaner*" except that it was founded by a "*Kánánder* by the name of *Tschánkuden*" (p. 193), brought some arts to India (p. 193), and was already long dead in Ziegenbalg's time (p. 146). However, in the *Genealogy of Malabar Divinities*, Ziegenbalg goes into greater detail about the sixth transformation of Vishnu and summarizes what he found in a Tamil text:

There once were two nations called *Buddergöl* and *Schammanergöl*. They had a noxious *religion* and created evil *sects*. They blasphemed *Vishnudom* and *Shiva's religion* and forced the rest of the Malabars to take on their *religion*. Those who did not adopt it were much harassed. They neither put on Dirunúru [holy ash] nor *Dirunámum* [the Vaishnavite mark on the forehead]. They did not observe purity of the body. Though they worship images, they seemed to be of no *religion*. They did not differentiate between castes [Geschlechten] but regarded all as equally good. Thus all respect and esteem between high and low and between wise and unwise was effaced. They blasphemed the books of *theology* and wanted all men to like their ways. (Ziegenbalg 2003:97)

It is noteworthy that Ziegenbalg again attributes a single religion to the Buddergöl and Schammanergöl "nations." This religion lacked some of the basic characteristics of Malabar heathendom and was opposed to (1) the worship of Vishnu and Shiva; (2) the display of their outward signs; (3) ritual bathing; (4) the division of castes; (5) the authority of Vedic scriptures; (6) the worship of cows; and (7) the idea that one belongs to the religion of one's fathers. The last point may not seem so obvious, but the attempt to convert people to another religion was also something that distinguished the Buddergöl/Schammanergöl religion from Ziegenbalg's Malabar heathendom; Indians were born into that religion rather than converting to it. According to Ziegenbalg, his Indian texts and informants thus regarded the Buddergöl/Schammanergöl religion not only as different from their Malabar heathendom but as opposed to it:

Their *religion* had no similarity with our Malabar religion nor with the moorish [Islam] and Christian *religion*; rather, it was the ruin [Verderb] of all *religions*. Therefore Vishnu wanted to exterminate it, adopted the shape of a human, joined them as if he were one of their priests, was with them for a long time, and ate and drank with them. Once he had well seen their doctrine and behavior [Wandel], he summoned his twelve disciples, called *Banirentualwahr*, and completely exterminated such *religion*. (p. 97)

Ziegenbalg knew very little about the Buddergöls, and it seems that what he associated directly with them is that they "brought poetry," disappeared from India at some point, and may belong to those Indian religions that "still exist in faraway countries" (Ziegenbalg 1926:29). With respect to the Schammanergöls, he read the tales about their forced conversion, extermination, or expulsion from India. When the missionaries posed the question "what Heathenism is, which nations are to be called heathens, and if the

Malabarians are not also to be known as heathens," the reply included the following statement:

> The Schámmaner [camaṇar] were a nation that had a religion apart from the above-mentioned two main religions [Shaiva and Vaishnava]. One reads very much about them in books. The Malabarians have poetry, the art of arithmetic, and most philosophical *disciplines* stem from these Schammaner. But they were partly extinguished and partly converted to Shiva's religion by a young man called Schammándaperumal [Ñāṉacam-pantar] who had 16,000 disciples. Such a story is described in detail in a book called *Arubaddunálu diruwileiádel* [Aṟupattuṉālu Tiruviḷaiyātar]. (Ziegenbalg 2003:441)

The description of the Schammaner and "the reference to Ñāṉacampatar and the *Aṟupattuṉālu Tiruviḷaiyātar*, a sixteenth-century collection of hymns of Śaiva poet-saints attributed to Parañcōti Muṉivar," show that Ziegenbalg's Schammaner designate Jain renouncers (Sweetman 2003:121). Already in 1708 Ziegenbalg had a copy of this hymn collection and commented, "I have studied it well and copied several thousand words and beautiful phrases from it. The Malabaris consider it a very precious book and wonder how I could get hold of it" (p. 121). The twenty-second chapter of this book describes the destruction of Buddhism and Jainism, and the sixty-second and sixty-third chapters tell the story (which Ziegenbalg partly translated) of the defeat of the Jains by Ñāṉacampantar (p. 121). In these chapters the missionary found the passage about the "six religion-sects" (Religions-Secten) where the Putter or Buddhists are clearly distinguished from the Schammaner or Jains (Ziegen-balg 1926:29).

But apart from such tales in Shaivite sources, Ziegenbalg could not learn much about the religion and history of the Schammaner. He did not know that the Sanskrit word *śramaṇa* ("one who strives") denotes a wandering monk or ascetic in the religious traditions of ancient India and that Mahāvīra (599–527 B.C.E.), the founder of Jainism, and also Gautama Buddha had been leaders of *śramaṇa* movements. Some such movements shared several of the characteristics mentioned by Ziegenbalg: they denied a creator God and some traditional divinities, rejected the Vedas as revealed texts, were by vary-ing degrees critical of the caste system, and opposed some traditional beliefs, sacrifices, rituals, and customs as well as Brahmanic authority. Today we also know that, in the context of Jainism and Buddhism, the word *śramaṇa* had come to signify "Jaina ascetic" or "Buddhist monk."

Among the burning questions of La Croze, the avid reader of Ziegenbalg, was the age and origin of "Malabar heathendom." We recall his statement near the beginning of the sixth chapter of his *History of the Christianity of the Indies* in which he stated he did not want to discuss which son of Noah had brought pure antediluvial monotheism to India. Still, he insisted that one must regard the Indians as "one of the most ancient peoples of the world" (La Croze 1724:426). Calling it a "very probable fact" that the ancient Indians had "a quite distinct knowledge of the true God and offered him an inner cult [culte interieur] which at the time was not mixed with any profanation," La Croze added that "some of their sages who until today preserve this doctrine make this conjecture so probable that no counterargument seems possible" (p. 426).

In his discussion of these sages, several pages of translations from Tamil Siddha (Gnanigöl) texts are adduced as proof that ancient India was indeed a repository of the world's original monotheism. La Croze had read in Ziegenbalg's *Genealogy of Malabar Divinities* that Indian monotheism was likely to be "a very ancient affair" since the Indians have books "that are said to be more than 2,000 years old" and regard their religion as "the oldest of them all" (Ziegenbalg 2003:37–38). Ziegenbalg also regarded Indian monotheism as old enough to have begun "not very long after the deluge" (p. 38), and it is no surprise that the Gnanigöl described by Ziegenbalg appeared to La Croze as heirs of the world's oldest religion, the religion of Adam and Noah, who had safeguarded its pure "inner cult."

But if the religion of the Gnanigöl is the heir of the oldest religion of India, what is its relation to the Brahmans and the other Indian religions mentioned by Ziegenbalg? Given that the Gnanigöl attacked central facets of Ziegenbalg's Malabar heathendom and fiercely criticized Vedic authority, the caste system, the Brahmans, etc., it was puzzling that they represent the fourth and highest stage of Malabar heathendom, are entrusted with the fourth Veda, and are revered by both of its great branches as saints. Such questions must have bugged La Croze as he read Ziegenbalg's manuscripts; but the missionary did not offer much help to the historian. While he delivered a trustworthy and detailed picture of the living religion in South India and made educated conjectures about the north on the basis of Indian texts and informants, Ziegenbalg had almost nothing to say about the relationship of his Malabar heathendom with the religions of greater Asia whose descriptions by missionaries and travelers La Croze had studied. Having his hands full with mission work and the intensive study of Indian texts, Ziegenbalg had neither the time nor the interest and access to materials to engage in such research. The opposite was true for La Croze. He made full use of his connections as royal librarian in Berlin, his proverbially stunning powers of memory, and a voracious appetite for information. If the title of his sixth chapter, "About the idolatry of the Indies," already points to the larger scope of his inquiry, his introductory paragraphs leave no doubt that he intended to put Ziegenbalg's findings into a broader geographical, historical, and religious context. His remarks about the Egyptian origin of many facets of Indian religion (see the beginning of this chapter) already demonstrated his keen interest in the origins of specific phenomena.

Although La Croze was one of the foremost linguists of his century, he indulged in surprisingly few etymological fantasies except for trying to link Shiva/Ishvara to Osiris of Egypt (p. 430) and Vishnu to Vihishtoush of Persia (p. 439). He also hypothesized on the basis of the Indian writing system that "the Indians received their sciences, their religion, and their literature from the Egyptians" (p. 442) but shied away from the kind of historical speculation that marred the work of Kircher (1667) and Kaempfer (1729).

Another question in La Croze's mind concerned the sequence of events. Piecing information together mainly from Ziegenbalg's manuscripts and letters, he came up with a comprehensive scenario that attempted to integrate all data and place Ziegenbalg's Malabar heathendom in a pan-Asian context. This much is already made clear in La Croze's definition of Malabar heathendom, which went far beyond the boundaries set by Ziegenbalg:

> The Malabar Heathendom [Paganisme du Malabar] has a great extension in the Indies. It is the ancient religion of the entire subcontinent West of the Ganges and of almost the entire Mogul empire or Indostan, where it certainly originated; of the kingdom of Bengala; of the island of Ceylon and several other places; to which one can add a part of Asian Tartary, the kingdoms of Aracan, Siam, Pegu, Laos, Cambodia, Tonkin, Cochin China, and even China and Japan. The religion of these last-mentioned places differs in various things from that of Malabar which is purer and, if I dare using that term, more orthodox. However, it has its origin in the same [Indian] locations. (La Croze 1724:445–46)

This passage should explain why La Croze used the singular for "idolatry" and the plural for "Indies" in his chapter title "Of the Idolatry of the

Indies." His description of Malabar heathendom portrays it as the religion of very large parts of Asia that include India and Ceylon in South Asia; Burma, Siam, Laos, Cambodia, and Vietnam in Southeast Asia; parts of Central and North Asia; and China and Japan in East Asia. This religion is characterized as an "idolatry" that centers on "the recognition and worship of three false gods under an infinity of different names" and is split into two main branches of which one worships Shiva and the other Vishnu (p. 446):

> These two sects agree on honoring the Brahmans and accepting the dogmas contained in the Vedam, which among these idolaters has the same authority as the Sacred Writ has with us; though the Brahmans, who are its guardians [depositaires], reserve [the right of] reading [the Vedam] for themselves alone. (pp. 446–47)

La Croze goes on to describe this pan-Asian idolatry of Indian origin based on Ziegenbalg's information about Malabar heathendom and devotes no less than ten pages (pp. 451–61) to the "Gnanigueuls [Gnanigöl], i.e. the sages and saints . . . who reject with scorn the cult of idols and all the other superstitious practices of their nation" (p. 451). La Croze uses numerous passages from Ziegenbalg's renderings of the *Civavākkiyam* and other Tamil Siddha texts to impress as strongly as possible on his readers that some pagans of the Indies not only had "much more sublime and correct ideas about the Divinity than most of the ancient Greeks and Romans" (p. 461) but even perfectly knew "the greatness and majesty of God" (p. 460) and possessed "the Vedam, which is the ancient Book of their Law" containing "these sublime ideas of God" (p. 454).

Why, then, one might ask, does La Croze call the Malabar heathendom an "idolatry" with "false gods" and a "cult of idols"? Because he saw it as a degenerated form of religion, a form that at some point had replaced the ancient monotheism that probably came straight from Noah's ark to India. The vestiges of this ancient monotheism were found, according to La Croze, in the Vedam and the books of the Gnanigöl. But how did this degeneration take place—and why were the Gnanigöl so critical of the Brahmans, the very guardians of the Veda? We have seen that Ziegenbalg, who also believed in an original monotheism and a subsequent degeneration, put the blame on the devil and the Brahmans. But La Croze, more ingenious and more interested in history, cooked up an elaborate scheme to explain it all. His scenario begins, like Ziegenbalg's, with an age of pure monotheism whose heirs are the Gnanigöl. Instead of the devil, La Croze saw the reason for the decline of this pure original religion in two migrations that invaded India. The first was by the "Nation of Sammanéens" and the second by "the Brahmans who recognize that their cult in Malabar followed that of a certain people that they regard as heathen and that they call the Nation of the Sammanéens" (491).

> It seems from the Malabar books that the Sammanéens were skilled because they [the Malabaris] acknowledge that all their sciences and arts came from that [Sammanéen] people. The migration of the Brachmanes must thus be posterior to that of the Sammanéens; or they [the Brachmanes] felt the need of a reformation because the first principles of their religion had been corrupted by them [the Sammanéens] and the people had fallen into ignorance of the Sovereign God. This latter feeling seems most probable provided that what the Malabaris say is true, namely, that they regard their religion as infinitely more ancient than that of the Sammanéens whom they call in their language *Schammanes*. (p. 493)

This statement is a bit difficult to decode. La Croze's two alternative scenarios both see a pure monotheism that is corrupted by immigrant Sammanéens who brought culture to India. The two possibilities mentioned by La Croze concern only the Brahmans. In the first scenario these Brahmans migrated to India after the Sammanéens and were thus not yet present in India when the Sammanéens first flourished. In the second scenario the Brahmans had migrated to India before the arrival of the Sammanéens. Witnessing the degradation of the original religion through Sammanéen influence, they then pushed for a reform and eventually managed to expel the Sammanéens. Since the Malabaris claim that their religion, that is, Malabar heathendom, is much more ancient than that of the Sammanéens, La Croze regards the second scenario with the Brahmans being the earlier immigrants as more likely. But he is not quite sure because this would mean that the Brahmans were quite uncultured when they migrated to India.

Both of La Croze's scenarios offered a historical explanation in the golden age/degeneration/regeneration mould that was very popular in Europe since the Middle Ages and will be further discussed below. This mould also shaped the vision of many missionaries, for example, de Nobili and the Madurai Jesuits, Athanasius Kircher, and the Jesuit figurists in China. They saw themselves as restorers of a pure "golden-age" monotheism that had degenerated through the influence of Brahmans or an impostor such as Shaka (Buddha). In this respect they resemble Chumontou of the *Ezour-vedam* and Voltaire (see chapter 1) as well as Isaac Newton (see Chapter 5), who all were critical of established religion and dreamed of restoring pure original monotheism. But the explanation of the relationship between the Gnanigöl and the Brahmans as well as the label of "idolatry" on the end result also called for another time-honored explanatory scheme: the distinction between exoteric and esoteric doctrines and practices. La Croze made copious use of all these elements to forge his scenario designed not only to explain the origin and history of the reigning religion of India but also the "idolatry" that had infected much of the Asian continent.

Egyptian Repercussions

We have seen that La Croze, like Kircher, saw Egypt as the ultimate source of many central elements of Malabar heathendom and that he also suggested Persian influence. Though La Croze does not discuss this, a "migration" of Brachmanes to India, regardless of its chronology, would thus probably have originated in Egypt and reached India via Persia. Their restoration project in India was, as one would expect in view of their Egyptian background, a duplicitous one. Though convinced of the "unity of God" and in possession of the Vedas containing this teaching, they treated it as an esoteric secret, safeguarded and used for their own advantage. Instead of teaching the original monotheist creed to the people, the Brahmans claimed, exactly like the Egyptian priests of Plutarch, that common people were incapable of grasping the truth and were in need of a "fabulous idolatry" (p. 460). Accordingly, they created for the people a cult of idols as grotesque as any that the world had ever seen.

> It is also because of this pretended incapacity [of the common people] that the exterior cult was formed which the Brahmins entertain for their particular interests. The immateriality of God and materiality of the world, of which they could not comprehend the connection, made them take recourse to fables which gradually augmented to form a mythology that is much more loaded with monstrous circumstances than that of the ancient Greeks whose false gods, however dissolute they are represented,

are in no respect inferior to those of the Indies regarding obscenity, profanation, absurdities, and contradictions. (p. 462)

The Brahmans, while pretending to restore original religion, hid their pearl of truth under a heap of mythology drawn from various places and even put some biblical elements into the mix:

> To come back to the Brachmans, one must admit that their absurd religion in both its cult and its mythology is far from excluding the idea of the infinitely perfect Being; it presupposes it everywhere and puts the label of paganism on all religions that do not agree with this. Besides, this religion has the marks of great antiquity. One finds in it distinct traces of the Law of Moses and histories that have a visible connection with those reported by our Sacred Writ. (p. 496)

Thus, the people were fed a mixture of truth and lie that was so powerful that all of India got intoxicated. While "having nothing very certain in their histories and no fixed epochs for events" (p. 469), the Brahmans propagated ideas about multiple worlds and their great age that are the apex of absurdity (p. 467). The Gnanigöl, outraged by all this, produced books "that are read even by the common people who, though they feel and recognize that there is only one God, remain stupidly in their idolatry" (pp. 461–62). This explains the Gnanigöl's opposition to Brahman authority and the wide dispersion of their texts. They were determined to expose the secret that the Brahmans, who belong to only the second stage of the religious path, are exclusive keepers of the Vedas and use religion for their own advantage. By contrast, the Gnanigöl teachings and writings divulge the secret of the Veda, which contains "in explicit terms these sublime ideas about God" (p. 454).

La Croze's Sammanéens

But what was the role of the Sammanéens in all this? Who were they for La Croze? Based on Ziegenbalg's translation of the story of Vishnu's sixth transformation (which features the account of their extermination and displacement from India), La Croze adopted the view that the "two sects" of the Buddergöl and Sammanergöl share the same religion:

We will limit ourselves to report the sixth [transformation of Vishnu], which will throw some light on what we are seeking. It was in this apparition that Vishnu was born as a man called *Veggouddova Avatarum* and exterminated two sects that professed a pernicious religion, the *Buddergueuls* and the *Schammanergueuls*, that is to say, the worshippers of Budda and the Sammanéens whose religion was the same. . . . He [Vishnu alias *Veggouddova*] instructed twelve disciples and through them completely exterminated this religion. (pp. 497–98)

How did La Croze come to identify the Buddergöls as "worshippers of Budda"? Ziegenbalg never mentioned the founder's name in this form and appears to have been ignorant of the presence of his religion even in Ceylon. But La Croze was not only very versed in missionary literature but also in Europe's Greek and Latin literature. Based on Ziegenbalg, he wrote in accord with one of the alternatives discussed above (namely, that the Brahmans established their cult in India after the Sammanéens): "The Brahmans recognize that in Malabar their cult followed after that of a certain people that they treat as pagans and call the nation of Sammanéens" (p. 491). He continues:

It is thus with this idea in mind that we must approach the Sammanéens, the ancient inhabitants of India, whose religion is possibly not yet entirely destroyed, even though at present it is unknown in all lands on this side of the Ganges where only the religion of the Brahmins or Brachmanes is in use. This idea of the Sammanéens does not entirely conform with what Porphyry reports about them in his treatise on abstinence of animal flesh. It is true that he identifies the Brachmanes, but he gives them [the Brahmans and the Sammanéens] more or less the same law and the same religion. (p. 492)

But La Croze, having studied Bayle's 1702 article on the Brachmans and a dissertation by Fabricius[13] of 1703 that presented much information in Greek and Roman texts about the Brahmans (pp. 443–44), of course knew that Clement of Alexandria had distinguished "Sarmanes" and "Brachmanes" and had linked the former to Boutta. La Croze translated the Greek text as follows:

There are two kinds of Indian gymnosophists or barbarian philosophers. The first are called Sarmanes and the others Brachmanes. Those of the

Sarmanes, who are called hermits [Solitaires], do not live in towns and have no houses. They cover themselves with the bark of trees and nourish themselves from fruit. They drink only water from the palm of their hands. They do not marry, and live like Encratites.[14] They are the ones among the Indians who obey the commandments of *Boutta* whom they honor like a god because of the sanctity of his life. (p. 492)

La Croze comments that this "Boutta" of the "Sarmanes" must be the man who was called "Boudda" in St. Jerome's *Adversus Jovinianum* and several other books by ancient authors (pp. 492–93). From European antiquity La Croze cites information about India from Herodotus, Pausanias, Diodorus of Sicily, Porphyry, Strabo, Megasthenes, Tertullian, Clement of Alexandria, and St. Jerome. Megasthenes, the author of a book called *Indica*, who around 300 B.C.E. visited the Indian city of Pataliputra as an envoy, is today considered the most important ancient European informant about India, even though only fragments of *Indica* are preserved in the form of quotations and summaries by other Greek and Latin authors (de Jong 1987:13). His description of *śramaṇas* fits ascetic renouncers in general rather than Buddhist monks. The passage quoted by La Croze from Clement of Alexandria (c. 150–c. 215 C.E.) about Indians who follow the precepts of Boutta stems from the *Stromateis* (c. 200 C.E.; I.15.71).

It is possible that Clement got such information from his teacher Pantainos who, according to Eusebius of Caesarea, had traveled to India (p. 13). Other authors such as the Neoplatonist Porphyry (c. 234–c. 305) also tend to mention these "Sarmanes" but furnish little detail. Only St. Jerome (c. 342–420) alluded to legends about the Buddha's birth from the flank of a virgin (La Croze 1724:501). But even such sparse information, when combined with biographical elements of Xaca or Xekia (Shakyamuni)—for instance, from Chinese sources excerpted in the *Tratados* of Navarrete (1676)—convinced La Croze "that there is a manifest connection [between Xaca or Xekia] and St. Jerome's Boudda that at the same time proves the antiquity of the fables of the Indies" (p. 501).

This identification was a crucial corner piece in La Croze's puzzle. He noted that "it is difficult to assign a fixed epoch to this legislator" and that "the consulted authors are all at variance about this," but he detected some consensus that Boudda or Butta "precedes by several centuries the epoch that begins with the birth of our Lord" (pp. 501–2). With regard to the geographical origin of this "legislator," La Croze concluded on the basis of information furnished by missionaries from Siam, Laos, China, Japan, and Vietnam that he likely hailed from a kingdom in the central Indies (milieu des Indes). La Croze thus concluded that the Boudda of the Greeks and Romans, the Sommona-Codom of Southeast-Asian missionaries, the Xe-kia of the Chinese, and the Xaca of the Japanese (p. 502) all referred to the person worshipped by Ziegenbalg's Putters or Buddergöls.

He had read vast amounts of sources to come up with this educated guess. For Mideastern and Persian religions, he mainly relied on Barthélémy d'Herbelot (1697), Thomas Hyde (1700), and François Bernier (1671). His main sources about Indian and Ceylonese religions were Abraham Roger (1651), Bernier (1671), Philip Baldaeus (1672), Vincenzo Maria (1678), João Ribeyro (1701), François Catrou (1705), Jean Venant Bouchet (1702–3/1781), and Bartholomäus Ziegenbalg. But of particular importance for his conjectures about Buddhism were data about Southeast Asian religions from the likes of Christopher Borri (1631), Alexandre de Rhodes (1651), Giovanni Filippo Marini (1663), and Simon de la Loubère (1691), combined with information about the religions of Tibet, China, and Japan stemming mainly from António de Andrade (1626), Charles Maigrot, Domingo Navarrete (1676), Philippe Couplet (1687), Louis Lecomte (1696), and Dionysius Kao (1705).

As a reader of Navarrete's *Tratados* of 1676—which were firmly based on João Rodrigues's research—and much material on the conflict about the Chinese Rites, La Croze was well informed about the claim that the "legislator Boudda" or Fo, as the Chinese called him, taught two doctrines: an exoteric one for the common people and an esoteric one for the initiated. In the Latin translation of Alexander de Rhodes's *Catechismus* of 1651 (which was originally written in Vietnamese), he found the fascinating account of the son of an Indian king who married, retired into solitude after the birth of his only child, studied magic, and learned from demons "a doctrine to which he gave the name of *Thicca*,[15] which is nothing but a veritable atheism":

> When he began to insinuate to people this doctrine, which is entirely opposed to natural understanding [Lumieres naturelles], everybody took distance from him. Realizing this, he began on the advice of the demons of his teachers to envelop his doctrine in diverse fabulous narrations and to mix in the transmigration of souls and the cult of idols, suggesting to his disciples that they make him the principal object of worship, and tried to pass for the creator and preserver of heaven and earth. . . . His magic and fables served him with the [common] people to whom he

only taught the cult of idols and metempsychosis; whereas the doctrine of atheism was only revealed to his most cherished disciples. It is to them that he uttered that nothingness [le néant] is the cause of all beings as well as the end which awaits all. (La Croze 1724:503–4)

This theme of a twofold teaching—an exoteric idolatry with metempsychosis for the common people and a nihilistic atheism for the initiate—will be discussed in more detail in the next chapter. It clearly played a central role in La Croze's perception of "the idolatry of the Indies," since, in his scenario, the Sammanéens were identical with the Buddergöl whose founder Boudda taught such a twofold doctrine and had his followers missionize large swaths of Asia. La Croze's translated de Rhodes's conclusion of 1651 as follows:

Thus, the doctrine of this idolatrous sect is double. The exterior [doctrine] consists in the cult of idols and in a great number of ridiculous fables; but the interior one, which is most detestable, is a veritable atheism that gives reins to all sorts of crimes. It is this religion that the philosopher Confucius calls in his books the doctrine of the barbarians. (p. 504)

Of course, we have in the meantime learned that Confucius (551–479 B.C.E) did not know anything about the teachings of "Boudda" since this religion was only imported to China about four centuries after his death. But, as La Croze lamented, no chronology was available in his time that allowed putting Asian events into a decent order. Basing his view on his reading of Ziegenbalg, La Croze thought that the Buddergöl and Schammanergöl professed the same religion. They were the ones who had brought culture to India and were the major cause of the degradation of original monotheism. In La Croze's eyes, their religion was similar to that of the Brachmanes except for one crucial point: whereas the Brachmanes had maintained monotheism as an esoteric teaching hidden from the people, the Buddergöl/Schammanergöl had in the course of time become atheists.

The testimony of the ancient authors that I cited as well as that of the Indian Brahmins makes it certain that these Sammanéens practiced the same abstinence [of meat] as today's Indians and that they believed, like them, in the transmigration of souls. They also had their idols, and it does not seem at all that their religion differed from that of the Brachmanes except for an important subject: the knowledge of an infinitely perfect Being. (pp. 493–94)

Combining the information from Ziegenbalg and from many missionaries and travelers, La Croze thus concluded that the atheism of the Buddergöl/ Schammanergöl was their distinguishing characteristic:

> In effect, the kingdoms of Arekan, Pegu, Siam, Laos, and Cambodia, not to speak of Tonkin, Cochin China, China, and Japan, have a religion that is different from that of the Malabaris even though they agree on the doctrine of the transmigration of souls, the cult of idols, and some other superstitious opinions. But what I find singular is their absolute ignorance of the existence of God. With respect to the Siamese, whose religion is that of all the nations just mentioned, this is confirmed by the testimony of Mr. de la Loubére, one of the most judicious and learned travelers of our times. (pp. 499–500)

Simon de la Loubère (1691) had indeed written that "the Siamese have not the slightest idea resembling [Aristotle's prime mover] and are far from recognizing a creator God" and felt able to "state with assurance that the Siamese have no idea whatsoever of a God" (p. 500). According to La Croze, the atheism of the Buddergöl/Schammanergöl was "the principal reason why the Brahmins regarded the Sammanéens as pagans" (p. 500); and it also explains why they were, according to Ziegenbalg's sources, persecuted and finally driven out of India.

To sum up, La Croze's historical scenario featured an original pure monotheism with the Gnanigöl as heirs; an invasion of the Buddergöl/ Schammanergöl that introduced or strengthened idolatry and superstition and eventually degenerated into atheism; and a Brahmin reform movement that claimed to restore the ancient pure religion but in fact appropriated monotheism as a privileged secret teaching of the clergy while continuing to encourage idolatry, polytheism, and superstition among the people. With regard to "Hinduism," whose boundaries Ziegenbalg had sketched, La Croze's summary—built as it was on wrong assumptions of original monotheism and of an extremely old Gnanigöl tradition, a mistaken view of the Vedic tradition and of the content of the Vedas, wrong conjectures about Egyptian influence, and a tenuous chronology—did not advance beyond Ziegenbalg but rather represented a significant step backward.

Less prone to speculation and less interested in history, Ziegenbalg remained closer to his observations and to direct textual evidence. He limited his discussion to the Indian subcontinent and thus defined the geographical area in which "Malabar heathendom" was prevalent. But the pan-Asian perspective adopted by La Croze also had advantages since the studies it entailed led to a hypothesis about the religion of "the disciples of Boutta" that was influential throughout the eighteenth century. That his "conjectures" on this subject, as La Croze called them (p. 497), are partially based on Ziegenbalg's work on Hinduism (or, as he called it, Malabar heathendom) is clear. Ziegenbalg's and La Croze's discoveries of Hinduism and of Buddhism are intimately connected, and since La Croze summarized many findings of Ziegenbalg long before they were published, Europe's reading public first got informed about both in the same book, namely, La Croze's *History of Christianity of the Indies*.

Buddhism Avant la Lettre

Questions about the origin of a religion and its founder are naturally of central importance for any historical and doctrinal definition. La Croze's initial view was of course influenced by some predecessors in speculation about a pan-Asian religion. Probably most influential before Couplet was Athanasius KIRCHER (1601–80). If João Rodrigues had connected China's three religions (the religion of Shaka/Fo, Daoism, and Confucianism) to a common root in Chaldea, Kircher attempted to unearth the Egyptian roots of all Asian religions. Transmitted to India, this Egyptian affliction eventually infected the whole of Asia. This is why Kircher's section on Indian religion in his *China illustrata* (1667) bears the title: "Brahmin institutions and how an Egyptian superstition passed by means of the Brahmins to Persia, India, China, and Japan, the farthest kingdom of the East" (Kircher 1987:141).

Kircher imagined that a "crowd of priests and hieromants" from Egypt had in ancient times fled to India and "discovered that Hermes, Bacchus, and Osiris had preceded them there." Kircher's Egyptian connection explained why the Indians to this day venerate "Apis, or the cow" and believe in the Egyptian doctrine of "metempsychosis, or the transmigration of the soul" (p. 141). This "preposterous superstition" had infected the whole Orient by means of "an imposter known all over the East," namely, the Buddha. According to Kircher, this founder is known under different names in different countries: Rama in India, Xe Kian in China, Xaca in Japan, and Chiaga in Turkey (p. 141). All of Asia's cults thus had their roots in Egypt:

> There is no cult of the ancient Egyptians and their descendants which isn't followed today by our modern barbarians, who have changed the worship of sun and moon, or Isis and Osiris, into that of Foto and Chamis.[16] You can find Bacchus, Venus, Hercules, Aesculapius, Serapides, Anubides, and other similar Egyptian gods, whom they worship under various other names. (p. 121)

For Kircher, the religions of China and Japan also had Egyptian origins and replicated the Egyptian "two truths" dichotomy of exoteric idolatry (superstition for the common people) versus esoteric doctrines for the clerical elite. Laozi's Daoism "corresponds to the Egyptian common people and magi" (p. 123), while "Xekiao" (Buddhism) employs, as we have seen, both esoteric and exoteric teachings and teaches "Egyptian" metempsychosis or transmigration of souls. We note that in Kircher's scenario an impostor with the Buddha's biography was "the very sinful brahmin imbued with Pythagoreanism" and "the first creator and architect of the superstition" (p. 141).

According to Kircher the missionaries who transmitted the Buddha's creed from India to other parts of Asia were Brahmins. This meant that India was the sole Asian distribution center for the "preposterous superstition" that, in Kircher's view, is "not only found in the regions of India far and wide, but was also propagated to Cambodia, Tonchin, Laos, Concin China, as well as all of China and Japan" (p. 141). The biographical details of the "impostor" who from his Indian base "infected the whole Orient with his pestilent dogmas" (p. 142) leave no doubt about his identity: it is the very Xaca who was born in central India after his mother had a dream of a white elephant, etc., and whose disciples "can stop all activity to the point that no life remains" (p. 142).

> They add that when a man has made such intellectual progress, he falls into ecstasy and an unmoving stupor. Then finally he can be said to have arrived at the greatest possible happiness and he is said to be among the gods in the pagodas. (p. 142–43)

Kircher's erudite fantasies were very influential in promoting the idea of a single Asian idolatry radiating from India, of a founder figure preaching an exoteric and esoteric doctrine, and of a missionary dispersion by means of Indian priests ("Brahmins"). Though still very hazy in its dimensions, the religion of the man whom we now know as Buddha thus gained an Indian base and a pan-Asian projection. While there were bits and pieces of information accumulating from countries that we today associate with Buddhism (for example, reports from Tibet, beginning with Andrade [1626], or from Thailand), information from China drew the most attention in the seventeenth and early eighteenth centuries.

Couplet's Buddha

The essence of Jesuit knowledge about the religion of Foe (Ch. Fo, Buddha) in the second half of the seventeenth century is contained in the 106-page introduction of the famous *Confucius Sinarum philosophus* of 1687. Dedicated to King Louis XIV of France, this book—and in particular its introduction signed (though not wholly written) by the Jesuit Philippe Couplet (1623–93)—played a central role in the diffusion of knowledge about Far Eastern religions among Europe's educated class and created quite a stir. A review in the *Journal des Sçavans* of 1688 shows that it was especially Couplet's vision of the history of Chinese religions that attracted interest. The anonymous reviewer (who according to David Mungello [1989:289] was Pierre-Sylvain Régis) calculated on the basis of the chronological tables in Couplet's book that the Chinese empire had begun shortly after the deluge—provided that one use not the habitual Vulgata chronology but the longer one of the Septuaginta (Régis 1688:105). The reviewer summarized Couplet's argument about the history of Chinese religions as follows:

> Following this principle, Father Couplet holds that the first Chinese received the knowledge of the true God from Noah and named him Xanti [Ch. Shangdi, supreme ruler]. One must note that the first emperors of China lived as long as the [biblical] Patriarchs and that they therefore could easily transmit this knowledge to their descendants who preserved it for 2,761 years until the reign of Mim-ti [emperor Ming] . . . who through a bizarre adventure strangely altered it. (pp. 105–6)

This "bizarre adventure" was the introduction of Buddhism in China as related by Matteo Ricci, who had, with almost Voltairian guile, transformed the *Forty-Two Sections Sutra*'s story of Emperor Ming's embassy to India in search of Buddhism into a botched quest for Christianity.[17] In its course, the Chinese ambassadors supposedly stopped "on an island close to the Red Sea where the religion of *Foe* (this great and famous idolater of the East Indies) reigned" and ended up bringing Foe's idolatry instead of Christianity to China (p. 106). The religion of Foe or Fo was thus seen as the major cause for the loss of true monotheism in China. The role of the Jesuit missionaries, by implication, is analogous to that of Chumontou in the *Ezour-vedam*: it was their task to show how the true original religion of the natives had become disfigured and to prepare the ground for its restoration and perfection under the sign of the cross.

Couplet's pages about the Foe Kiao (Ch. *fojiao*, Buddhism) presented a summary of Jesuit knowledge to a large European public. This information was mainly gained from Japanese and Chinese sources, and the amount of detail (for example, about the life of the founder) leaves no doubt that some serious study had been going on. Apart from data about the founder of this religion of Foe (Buddha), the introduction furnishes information about its history, texts, geographical presence, and teaching. Since the doctrinal part will be discussed in the "Exoterica and Esoterica" section of Chapter 3, I will here summarize the rest (Couplet 1687:xxvii–xxxiv). According to Couplet, the religion of Foe originated in Central India around 1000 B.C.E. Its founder, Xe Kia (whom the Japanese call Xaca), was the son of an Indian king whose wife Maya saw a white elephant in a dream, gave birth to the boy through her right side, and died soon afterward. This happened in 1026 B.C.E.

Immediately after his birth, the boy took seven steps in every direction, pointed with one hand toward heaven and the other toward the earth, and said: "In heaven and on earth, I am the only one to be venerated" (p. xxviii). At age 17 he married three women and had a son named Lo heu lo (Rāhula). At age 19 he left his palace in order to do penance for causing his mother's death and practiced austerities with four *Jogues* (yogis); and at age 30 understood the essence of the first principle while in contemplation. At that moment "the disciple turned into Master and the man into God" (p. xxviii), and Foe began his teaching career, which was to last until his death at age 79. His teachings and miracles became widely known through many books and elegant works of art. He had as many as 80,000 disciples who missionized large parts of Asia. In China, where the religion arrived in the year 65 C.E., his followers are called "Sem" and "Ho xam" (Ch. *seng*, monk; *heshang*, reverend); in Tartary "Lama sem" (Ch. *lama seng*); in Siam "Talepoii"; and in Japan "Bonzii" (p. xxix). The religion of Foe thus spread all the way from Central India to Tibet and Tartary in the north, and Southeast Asia, China, and Japan in the east. According to Couplet, as many as 15,000 texts contain the doctrines of this religion, and the founder personally instructed his favorite disciple Mo o Kia ye (Mahākāśyapa) to preface all books containing his doctrine by the words "Ju xi ngo ven: Sic ego accepi" (Ch. *rushi wo wen*, thus I have heard) (p. xxx).

Foe also venerated a teacher called O-mi-to, who in Japanese is called "Amida." According to Couplet, O-mi-to is anterior to Foe and lived in the Bengal region of East India where the Chinese priests locate the Elysian Fields called *çim tu* (Ch. *jingdu*, Pure Land). To gain the favor of these two "monsters" and be pardoned for their sins, the Chinese constantly recite "O mi to, foe" (Ch. Omituofo, Amida Buddha). Apart from Foe and O-mi-to, the Chinese followers of Foe are said to also venerate Quon in pu sa (Ch. *Guanyin pusa*, Avalokiteśvara Bodhisattva) and "inferior gods" such as the Lo han (Ch. *luohan*, arhats).

Couplet's portrayal of Foe's doctrine begins with Foe's deathbed confession and the distinction between his long-held "exterior" teachings and the ultimate "interior" teachings (see next chapter). Foe's interior teaching, which is according to Couplet also propagated by the Indian gymnosophists, formed around 290 C.E. a Chinese sect called Vu guei Kiao (Ch. Wuwei jiao, the teaching of nonactivity).[18] A further link between India and China is the "contemplantium secta" (sect of meditators) founded by Ta mo (Ch. Damo, Bodhidharma), the twenty-eighth patriarch after Xaca, who meditated only on "that chimerical principle of his, *emptiness* and *nothingness* [*vacuum* & *nihil*]" and ended in the gutter of atheism (p. xxxiii).

The Pan-Asian Sect of Fo or Buddhum

Partly wrapped in Chinese terminology and mostly based on Chinese and Japanese sources, Couplet's introduction to *Confucius Sinarum philosophus* thus presented major features of Asia's dominant religion, its founder's biography, and its teachings while furnishing the names of priests in different countries and mentioning its large sacred literature, various sects, numerous elegant statues, and relics. The accuracy of a good part of this information shows how much information had already been accumulated, mainly from

Japanese and Chinese texts and informants, in the 130 years since the Jesuits' arrival in Japan in 1549.

Besides Couplet's book of 1687, two works published at the very end of the seventeenth century were of particular importance because they were whirled into the Chinese Rites controversy and because their information was extensively used in the 1702 edition of Bayle's *Dictionnaire historique et critique* and later compilations. The first of these works is Louis Daniel Lecomte's *Nouveaux mémoires sur l'état présent de la Chine* (1696); the second is Charles Le Gobien's *Histoire de l'edit de l'empereur de la Chine* (1698). Le Gobien's book was published both as a separate work and (in some editions) as volume 3 of Lecomte's *Nouveaux mémoires* (1698); but since it will play a major role in or Chapters 3 and 4 below, I will here only briefly discuss Lecomte's portrayal of the "religion of Fo."

Louis Daniel LECOMTE (1655–1728) was one of the French Jesuits who was sent by the French king to China, studied Chinese, and advocated the view that China's ancient religion had once been "the veritable religion" and that, even after its fall into the darkness of idolatry, China had for millennia safeguarded "the knowledge of the true God" while Europe and almost the entire rest of the world were mired "in error and corruption" (Lecomte 1696:2.118–19). This was one of the arguments that boosted the book's sales, led to its public condemnation, deepened the crisis of the Jesuit order, and effectively destroyed the brilliant prospects of its author. The fall into idolatry, according to Lecomte, was primarily due to two kinds of "superstition" that were introduced to China. The first was the teaching of "*Li-Laokun . . .* who lived before Confucius," a "monster" with a "pernicious doctrine" who nevertheless "wrote several useful books about virtue, the discarding of honors, the contempt for wealth, and that admirable solitude of the soul that removes us from the world in order to make us exclusively enter into ourselves" (p. 120).

After some more discussion of Laozi and Daoism, Lecomte turns to the second superstition. It "dominates China and is even more dangerous and universal than the first" and "worships as the only divinity of the world an idol called *Fo* or *Foë*" (p. 123). This religion was brought to China from India in 65 C.E. and eventually became "a monstrous assemblage of all sorts of errors" including "superstition, metempsychosis, idolatry, atheism" and so forth (pp. 123–24). Lecomte furnishes rather detailed information about its founder from "the kingdom of India" who is said to have lived "more than a thousand years before Jesus Christ," and he mentions that this man was first called Chékia but took the name Fo at age 30 after having been "suddenly seized, as if penetrated by the divinity who gave him omniscience" (p. 125). After that "moment in which he became God," he gained many disciples who infected the entire Indies with his pernicious doctrine. Lecomte locates this religion of Fo in China, Japan, Tartary, and Siam and provides the appellations of its clergy: "The Siamese called them *Talapoins*, the Tartars *Lamas* or *Lama-sem*, the Japanese *Bonzes*, and the Chinese *Hocham*" (p. 125). Just before his death, this "chimerical God," having preached idolatry throughout his life, "attempted to inspire atheism":

> Then he declared to his disciples that in all his discourses he had only spoken in enigmas; and that one would mislead oneself if one searched the first principle of things outside of nothingness [neant]. *It is from this nothingness*, he said, *that everything has come; and it is into nothingness that everything will fall back. That is the abyss where all our hopes end.* (pp. 125–26)

This ultimate teaching of Fo became the basis for "a particular sect of atheists among the bonzes;" but there were also those who maintained idolatry, and a third group "attempted to combine them by making up a body of doctrine where they taught a double law which they call the exterior law and the interior law" (p. 126). Lecomte thus clearly envisioned the religion of Fo as a major religion of Asia with an Indian founder, a history of nearly 3,000 years, several sects, and much clergy in countries from India to Japan. However, instead of the name "Buddha," which is today more familiar to us, Lecomte uses the Chinese words *Fo* (Buddha) or *Xekia* (Shakya). Unlike Couplet, he makes no mention of this sect's literature, even though it was well known since the sixteenth century that the Buddhists have a voluminous sacred literature. For example, Alessandro Valignano's Biography of Francis Xavier of the early 1580s had already associated numerous texts with Xaka's religion and had specifically mentioned the Lotus Sutra as the expression of Xaca's ultimate teachings (Valignano 1900:114).

In the second half of the seventeenth century, enough data about this religion and its founder had thus accumulated in the hands of some Jesuit missionaries to allow drawing conclusions based on the combination and comparison of information from India, Japan, China, Vietnam, Ceylon, Cambodia, Burma, Tibet, Tartary, and Siam. A good example is the work of Fernão de QUEYROZ (1617–88) who spent a total of fifty-three years in India.

Corresponding with fellow Jesuits in China and other parts of Asia, Queyroz gathered copious information about the founder of "the religious sect of Buddum" for the purpose of comparison (Queyroz 1930:122–41). His research, and in particular the comparison of Ceylonese data with a detailed summary (sent from Beijing by the Jesuit Tomé PEREYRA [1645–1708]) of a large Chinese collection of Buddha legends, convinced him that "the Buddhum of Ceylon, the Fô of China, the Xaca of Japan is the same as the Xekia of India, for the word Buddum is only an adapted name, and in Ceylon it means Saint by antonomasia" (p. 141).

With regard to the origin and identity of the religion of this "Buddhum," he noted that "this Sect has disappeared from many parts of India, where it began" (p. 141) and came to the correct conclusion that "the Ganezes of Ceylon, the Talpoys of Arracan, Peguy, Siam and other neighbouring Realms, as well as the Lamazes of Tartary agree with the Bonzes of China and Japan in the essentials of their sect and profession" (p. 140). Queyroz sharply distinguished these monks of Ceylon, Burma, Siam, Tartary, China, and Japan from the Indian "Bramanes" who are "the Priests of Idols in this Hindustan" and reside only "in the countries between the Indus and the Ganges as far as Mount Caucasus,[19] for beyond that they never crossed." Within this subcontinent the Bramanes are "the authors of all the idolatries that are practised" (p. 164). The Bramanes "never crossed the Ganges, nor have they anything to do where there are Ganezes, Talapoys, Bonzes or Lamas" (p. 171).

In the second half of the seventeenth century, Queyroz thus already distinguished the religion of the "Bramanes," which reigned only on the Indian subcontinent, from the religion of Buddhum/Fo/Xekia/Xaca prevalent in many other regions of South, Central, North, and East Asia. But on the question of the origin of the religion of the Bramanes, Queyroz was not better advised than many others; he explained that "Abraham and Sara are the same as Bramâ (who according to them is the first person of their false Trinity) and Sara Suati [Sarasvati]" (p. 143).

La Croze's Conjectures

The interesting studies and conclusions of Queyroz were only published in 1930, and their significance for the history of the Western discovery of Buddhism was noticed by Henri Bernard-Maître as late as 1941. By contrast, La

Croze's "conjectures" at the end of his sixth chapter were printed in 1724 and reached an international public. They concerned the religion of the Sammanéens in various parts of Asia. La Croze was fully aware that he could offer no more than "conjectures about this subject;" but he added that he found them "quite plausible [vrai-semblables]" and that one had to be content with this "until more exact knowledge of the books of these heathens will further clarify this subject" (p. 497). The only books that La Croze attributed to the Sammanéens, apart from scriptures purportedly written by Xaca's disciples on palm leaves (p. 506), were a few texts that Ziegenbalg had identified as being of Buddergöl or Sammanergöl authorship: a manual of Indian poetry, a poetic lexicon, and a book with moral principles (pp. 494–95). Today we know that these texts have little or nothing to do with Buddhism. However, based on Ziegenbalg who had conflated the Sammanergöl and Buddergöl creeds into a single religion, La Croze used Shaivite critiques of the Jains to characterize the teachings of the "disciples of Budda":

> These Sammanéens, disciples of Budda, blaspheme openly the religion of Vishnu and Ishvara [Shiva] and forced the Malabars to profess their [religion]. They neither apply red earth nor cow dung ash and do not at all observe the outer purification of the body through ablutions. Apart from having idols which they worship, they do not seem like a religion. This cannot mean anything other than that they neither knew nor worshiped the Lord of all beings. They regarded all men as equal and did not make any distinction between the different castes or tribes. They detested the theological books of the Brahmins and wanted that the world submit, willingly or by force, to their laws. They say that this religion neither resembled Mohammedanism nor Christianity. In a word, in their eyes this was an infamous and miserable sect. (p. 498)

Shaivite literature critical of the Jains along with Tamil Siddha texts, translated by Ziegenbalg into German and applied to the "disciples of Budda" by La Croze, thus gave rise in Europe to the persistent idea that this religion was fiercely opposed to the caste system and that this opposition had played a role in its extinction in India as well as its dispersion to other Asian countries. But most important for La Croze was the allegation, reported by Ziegenbalg, that for the monotheistic Indians the creed of the Sammanéens did "not seem like a religion." La Croze concluded that they were atheists and established the link between these Indian "atheists" and that of Buddhists as described by de Rhodes (1651; Vietnam), Navarrete (1676; China), and de la Loubère (1691; Thailand). He most trusted the latter two authors, and it was Navarrete (whose information in part relied on João Rodrigues's research) who furnished crucial data for La Croze's conjectures about the religion that we today call "Buddhism."

> The father Dominique Fernandez Navarrete, one of the most sincere and illustrious missionaries of the past century, speaks also in great length about this legislator of the Indies whose doctrine has spread for a very great number of years in the empires of China and Japan. I shall briefly report what he says about this in the second of his historical treatises about the Chinese empire. First he observes that the name of this impostor in China is Xe-Kia and in Japan Xaca . . . ; that his sect gained entry into the [Chinese] empire about sixty years after the birth of our Lord; that apart from China and Japan it has infected the kingdoms of Siam, Cambodia, Laos, Cochin China, Tonkin, and several other countries in North and South Asia [Indes] and that this false religion is thus far more widespread than that of the Mahommedans. (La Croze 1724:504–5)

With regard to the founder of this very large religion, La Croze was convinced that "Boudda, Sommona-Codom, and Xaca refer to one and the same person" (p. 502). Far from accepting a single account from China, La Croze examined reports and legends from different Asian countries with the understanding that information about Budda, Boutta, Budu, Boutta-varam, Xaca, Chaca, Xe-kia, Tcháou cà, Thicca, Sommona-Codom, Pouti Sat, Foë, and so on all relate to the same founder figure (pp. 499–513). He conjectured that this founder must have lived "several centuries before the birth of our Lord" and noted that many authors think he was "a native of a kingdom situated in the middle of the Indies" (p. 502). Apart from ancient India, the countries that La Croze associates with this religion are Ceylon, Burma (Arakan, Pegu), Siam, Laos, Cambodia, Vietnam (Tonkin, Cochin China), Tibet, Bhutan, Tartary (Mongolia, Siberia), China, and Japan (pp. 492–519). He thus felt justified in writing of a single "idolatry of the nations of the East Indies" (p. 513) and adduced the testimony of "Denys Kao, a Chinese Christian instructed by the Jesuits" for the conclusion that "the religion of the Bonzes of China is spread in all the kingdoms of Pegu, Laos, Siam, Cochin

China, Japan and Great Tartary," which includes Tibet whose Lamas "differ in few respects from the Bonzes of the Chinese" (p. 518).[20]

With regard to this religion of the "Sammanéens, the disciples of Budda," La Croze specified, partly based on Ziegenbalg, that it fought against the religion of Vishnu and Shiva and its customs, does not know God in spite of its veneration of idols, is opposed to castes, regards all men as equal, hates the theological books of the Brahmins, resembles neither Islam nor Christianity, and tries to convert people of other creeds (p. 498). Though this pan-Asian religion agrees with that of the Malabaris about "the doctrine of transmigration of souls, the cult of idols, and some other superstitious opinions," its "absolute ignorance of God's existence" was for La Croze the most decisive feature (p. 499). He found this atheism clearly expressed not only in the reports by de la Loubère, Borri, and de Rhodes (pp. 499–504) but also in the last words that the founder had reportedly uttered shortly before his death:

> During the more than forty years that I preached, I have never communicated my true feelings because I only revealed the outer and apparent meaning [sens exterieur & apparent] of my doctrine wrapped in diverse symbols. I saw all of this as falsities. Concerning the inner meaning that I always regarded as true, I presently declare that the first principle and the last end of beings is the primary matter [matiére prémiére], which is chaos or emptiness [le Cahos ou le Vuide] beyond which nothing is to be sought nor hoped. (pp. 505–6)

Apart from the founder, La Croze also mentions the Chinese idol Tamo [Bodhidharma], who had entered China from India "after the year 552" of the common era.[21] He argued that this was by no means the apostle Thomas, as some missionaries assumed, but rather a representative of the founder's inner doctrine who "made himself the chief of a branch of the sect of Foë that is called the Sect of the Meditators [Secte des Contemplatifs]" (p. 507). Tamo's chief accomplishment consisted in "sitting for nine years with his face toward the wall and contemplating nature or emptiness [la Nature ou le Vuide]" and thus to "annihilate himself in order to be put among the idols of his sect" (p. 507). While the exterior precepts of this religion are the same for "all the idolaters of the Indies, the Brahmins as well as the others," the initiates of the inner doctrine teach "that all creatures come from nothingness" and that they "return to nothingness" provided that they "practice contemplation and the most austere virtues, accompanied by a perfect detachment from the world" (p. 508).

For La Croze, this ideal of the inner teaching as described by missionaries to China and Japan shows "an exact conformity with the doctrine of the Siamese whose *Nireupan* [nirvāṇa] is identical to the annihilation that is the goal of the doctrine of Xaca" (p. 507). But La Croze was very aware of the lack of data:

> This is very difficult to understand because we do not sufficiently know what they mean by this word [nothingness]. They consider their nothingness [néant] as a kind of Being without understanding [entendement], without will, without strength, and without might, even though it is pure, subtle, uncreatable [*ingenerable*], infinite, incorruptible, and very perfect. It is this nothingness, they say, that one can attain in this life and thus procure for oneself through contemplation a very happy eternity. (p. 508)

Such descriptions of the founder's esoteric teaching suggested to La Croze that "due to the lack of understanding of the mysteries of this false religion, what is only a mystical annihilation similar to the *apathy* of the Stoic philosophers has been mistaken for a real annihilation" (p. 509). This hint of La Croze—which may have been inspired by Bayle (1702:2770)—was taken up and amplified, as we will see in Chapter 4, by Nicolas Fréret and Joseph de Guignes who interpreted the inner doctrine of the followers of Buddha as a kind of mystical monotheism.

Chapter 3

Diderot's Buddhist Brahmins

In the first volumes of the central monument of the French Enlightenment, the *Encyclopédie*, there are several articles about Asian religions that are either signed by or attributed to Denis DIDEROT (1713–84). The most important ones in the first volumes are entitled "ASIATIQUES. Philosophie des Asiatiques en général" (1751:1.752–55), "BRACHMANES" (1752:2.391), and "BRAMINES" (1752:2.393–94). Today, these articles have such a bad reputation that they are often criticized and held up for ridicule. For example, Wilhelm Halbfass wrote,

> In the article "Brachmanes," Diderot discusses what he calls "extrava-gances tout-à-fait incroyables," stating that the persons who had referred to the Brahmins as "sages" must have been even crazier than the Brah-mins themselves. The article entitled "Bramines" is essentially a sum-mary and in part literal paraphrase of the article "Brachmanes" contained in Bayle's *Dictionnaire historique et critique*; it also reproduces a mixup of Buddhism and Brahminism occurring in the original: citing the Jesuit Ch. LeGobien, Bayle described a Brahminic sect thought to be living in China as worshippers of the "God Fo." (Halbfass 1990:59)

Diderot's "inaccuracy and lack of originality" (p. 60), Halbfass argues, is evident in his use of "Bayle's and Le Gobien's portrayal of the Chinese 'Brahmins' and Buddhists" to conjure up a vision of "quietism" and love of "nothingness" among the Indians and thus to highlight "their desire to stu-pefy and mortify themselves" (p. 59). Halbfass cites the following passage from Diderot's article on the "Bramines" as an illustration:

They assert that the world is nothing but an illusion, a dream, a magic spell, and that the bodies, in order to be truly existent, have to cease existing in themselves, and to merge into nothingness, which due to its simplicity amounts to the perfection of all beings. They claim that saintliness consists in willing nothing, thinking nothing, feeling nothing. . . . This state is so much like a dream that it seems that a few grains of opium would sanctify a brahmin more surely than all his efforts. (pp. 59–60)

Diderot's only contribution in this passage, Halbfass contends, was to add to his paraphrase of Bayle the reference to opium; but even this was not original since this is "a motif which we find also in the *Essais de théodicée*, which Leibniz published in 1710" (p. 60). As is well known, this "opium" motif reappeared in the nineteenth century "among Hegel and other critics of Indian thought" (p. 60) and, broadened by Marx to apply to religion in general, found its way into the minds of hundreds of millions of twentieth-century communists: religion as opiate for the people. Halbfass could also have cited the very first sentence of Diderot's article, which precedes the given quotation and presents his "mixup of Buddhism and Brahminism" in a nutshell:

BRAMINES, *or* BRAMENES, *or* BRAMINS, *or* BRAMENS, . . . Sect of Indian philosophers anciently called *Brachmanes*. See BRACH-MANES. These are priests who principally revere three things: the god Fo, his law, and the books that contain their constitutions. (Diderot 1752:2.393)

Diderot here clearly defines the subjects of his article, the Brahmins, as priests of the "god Fo" who, as we have seen, was already in the seventeenth century often identified as Buddha. Diderot's Brahmins believe in this Fo, preach his doctrine (the dharma or law), and value the books that contain his teachings. Today we are able to identify these three items as the "three jewels" or "three treasures" that are ceaselessly evoked and pledged allegiance to by Buddhists of all nations. While the first two (Fo = Buddha and law = dharma) clearly evoke the first two treasures, the third treasure is now known to be the *sangha*, that is, the Buddhist community, rather than its sacred scriptures.

Historians of the European discovery of Buddhism, who tend to be rather unforgiving schoolmasters, of course also denounce Diderot's terrible "mixup." In 1952, Cardinal de Lubac used even stronger terms than Halbfass:

> Diderot makes himself the echo of such phantasmagoric science. The diverse articles of the *Encyclopédie* that touch on Buddhism (several of which are by Diderot himself) rest on some superficial readings without the slightest attempt at critique.[1] They range from 1751 to 1765 and are a bunch of hypotheses, gossip, and errors that are mutually contradictory. The Buddha, who is habitually named Xekia, or Xaca, or Siaka, supposedly is an African from Ethiopia (Diderot read the critical note of Abbé Banier about the text by Kaempfer and attempts to harmonize the two authors); or maybe he was a Jew—at any rate, he had knowledge of the books of Israel. . . . He supposedly founded, in Southern India, "the sect of Hylobians, the most savage of the gymnosophists" and is said to have written all of his exoteric doctrine on tree leaves. (de Lubac 2000:121–22)

Citing the beginning of Diderot's "Brahmin" article, de Lubac makes fun of Diderot's "sketchy comparatism" and of his claim that the Jewish kabbalists modeled their *ensoph* doctrine on the "emanatism of Xekia" (p. 122).

Here, instead of comparing and ridiculing information about Asian religions from many different *Encyclopédie* articles by Diderot and other authors, just three entries from the first two volumes will be analyzed: "ASIATIQUES. Philosophie des Asiatiques en général" (1751:1.752–55), "BRACHMANES" (1752:2.391), and "BRAMINES" (1752:2.393–94). They are likely to be from the pen of Diderot. At any rate, they present a mid-eighteenth-century view of Asian religions by an intelligent Frenchman who, while primarily relying on the work of Pierre Bayle (1702) and Johann Jacob Brucker (1742–44), made direct and indirect use of much of the information available in Europe at that time. Instead of the "monkey show" approach where historical views are held up for ridicule like chimpanzees dressed in human clothes who must show to the laughing public how far we have come along, this chapter will present the main points of Diderot's view of Asian religions in historical context. His "lack of originality," "sketchy comparatism," and especially his "mixup" of different religions are thus seen as worthy objects of study rather than ridiculous defects. Just as the island of Hokkaido ("Yeso") at the northern end of Japan was for a long time thought to be so gigantic as to stretch all the way to North America, the dimensions and confines of Asian religions were in Diderot's time still rather hazy. In this respect discoveries and explorations of religions are not so different from those of barely known lands. Even a century after Diderot's articles, the historical and doctrinal dimensions of Asian religions were still far from clear, and many boundaries that have since been drawn (for example, those dividing "shamanism" from "Buddhism" in Tibet or "folk religion" from "Daoism" in China) are so problematic that some professors of religious studies would love to wipe them off the map. With regard to the discovery of Asian religions, parading "false" ideas (for example, about the founder of Buddhism) is far easier than understanding why those ideas arose and realizing the fragility of present-day certitudes. As a matter of fact, two centuries of "scientific" study have utterly failed to produce a consensus even about the centuries in which Buddhism's founder lived, and skeptics who argue that he is just one more legend that took on flesh and bones are not easily refuted. Was not the life story of a popular Christian saint of the Middle Ages, St. Josaphat, derived from legends about the Buddha and unmasked as a pious fiction, even though some of "his" bones are to this day revered in Antwerp's St. Andries Church? In 1997 the church's friendly sacristan got me a ladder so I could see how the Buddha legend calcified (see Figure 4).

As we will see in the present and subsequent chapters, variants of Diderot's idea of a pan-Asian religion or philosophy were very popular in his time and should hardly be fodder for reproaches and "monkey show" treatment. Indeed, anybody who believed in the Old Testament account of the deluge and the dispersion of peoples after Babel was bound to favor monogenetic hypotheses and to presuppose common roots of possibly unrelated phenomena. The idea of a pan-Asian religion or doctrine—conceived either positively as an ancient theology or negatively as an ancient idolatry—was not only common throughout Diderot's century but dominant. It is a subject well worth exploring; after all, almost every chapter of this book shows that this was a far more influential factor in the birth of Orientalism than the much-evoked and blamed colonialism. This chapter will describe key features of Diderot's "philosophie asiatique" and dig into the past to expose some of its main roots. If the previous chapter showed how deeply intertwined the European discoveries of "Brahmanism" and Buddhism in the first quarter of the eighteenth century were, the present chapter will expand the field of view both backward toward the sixteenth and seventeenth centuries and forward to the mid-eighteenth century when Diderot compiled his first articles on Asian religions.

Figure 4. The bones of a legend: relics of Saint Josaphat (St. Andrieskerk, Antwerp; photo by Urs App).

Exoterica and Esoterica

We have seen in the previous chapters that the Jesuits of the Japan mission already began studying the Japanese varieties of Buddhism in the 1550s. This was not exactly a nineteenth-century philological workshop. In his letters from Yamaguchi of 1551, Cosme de TORRES (1510–70) distinguished several groups of Japanese heathens including worshipers of Shaka, Amida, and a sect called "Jenxus" (Jap. *Zen-shū*, Zen sect). According to Frater Cosme, who was the first European to mention this sect by name, Zen adepts teach in two ways [dos maneras]. The first is described as follows:

> One way says that there is no soul, and that when a man dies, everything dies, since they say that what has been created out of nothing [crió de nada] returns to nothing [se convierte en nada]. These are men of great meditation [grandes meditaçiones], and it is difficult to make them understand the law of God. It is quite a job [mucho trabajo] to refute them. (Schurhammer 1929:95)

According to Fr. Cosme's subsequent letter of October 20, 1551, these men held that "hell and punishment for the evil ones are not in another life but in this one" and "denied that there is a hell after a man dies" (p. 101). Numerous adepts of the Zen sect, both priests and laymen, informed the Jesuit missionaries that "there are no saints and that it is not necessary to search for a way [buscar su caminho] since what had come into existence from nothing could not but return to nothing [que de nada foi echo, não puede deixar de se comvertir em nadie]" (p. 99). When the missionaries tried to convince these representatives of Zen that "there is a principle that constitutes the origin of all other things," the Japanese are said to have replied:

> This [nothing] is a principle from which all things arise: men, animals, plants: every created thing has in itself this principle, and when men or animals die they return to the four elements, into that which they had been, and this principle returns to that which it is. This principle, they say, is neither good nor bad, knows neither glory nor punishment, neither dies nor lives, in a manner that it is a "no" [de manera que es hum nó]. (p. 99)

Such views uncannily resemble the "internal teaching" described in the seventeenth and eighteenth centuries, and they confirm that its principal features emerged in Japan when the first missionaries engaged in conversations with representatives of the Zen denomination who might have told told them about Bodhidharma's legendary responses to Emperor Wu ("Empty, nothing holy"; "no merit") and kept uttering the word "*mu*" (nothingness). In contrast to the inner teaching, the second manner of teaching described by Frater Cosme seems to accept an eternal soul and transmigration:

> There are others who say that souls [las animas] have existed and will exist forever and that with the death of the body each of the four elements returns to its own place, as does the soul that returns into what it was before it animated that body. Others say that, after the death of the body, the souls return to enter different bodies and thus ceaselessly are born and die again. (p. 95)

This teaching encapsulates essential elements of what later came to be known as the "exterior" teaching of Buddhism: an eternal soul and transmigration. Tutored by former Buddhist monks and knowledgeable laymen, the missionaries in the following decades gradually became more familiar with the sects, clergies, rituals, and doctrines of Japan's rich Buddhist tradition and learned of the distinction between an "outer" or provisional teaching for the common people (Jap. gonkyō) and an "inner" or true teaching (Jap. jikkyō). In the catechism of 1586, Alessandro VALIGNANO's entire presentation of doctrines and sects is based on the distinction between provisional (gon) and real (jitsu) teachings (Valignano 1586:4v).

Today we know that various forms of this "gon-jitsu" distinction played a major role in the history of Buddhism. During the first centuries of the common era, when the Indian religion took root in China, various classification schemes (Ch. panjiao) were created by the Chinese to bring order into a bewildering array of Buddhist doctrines and texts. Some made use of the Indian Buddhist "two-truths" scheme, which asserts that, apart from the absolute truth of the awakened, there is also a provisional truth designed to accommodate deluded beings and help them reach enlightenment. Others came to attach particular doctrines and texts to phases of the Buddha's life, and naturally those of one's preferred sect tended to be associated with particularly poignant events of the founder's life, such as the first sermon after his enlightenment or the ultimate teachings before passing away. Such schemes often employed, in one form or another, the distinction between a "provisional" (Jap. *gonkyō*) and "genuine" or "real" teaching (Jap. *jikkyō*), which is exactly what the Buddhist informers must have explained to Valignano and his fellow Jesuits. A related distinction is that between exoteric and esoteric teachings (Jap. *kengyō* and *mikkyō*) that was promoted, among others, by the famous founder of Japanese esoteric Buddhism, Kūkai (734–835; Abé 1999:9). But in the sixteenth century most of this was unknown. However, through the inclusion of Valignano's catechism in Antonio Possevino's *Bibliotheca selecta* of 1593, the distinction between provisional and real (or exoteric and esoteric) teachings and sects in Japan gained a foothold in Europe among Jesuits, their students, and some sections of Europe's educated class.

As early as the mid-sixteenth century, Jesuit missionaries also linked this distinction between exoteric and esoteric doctrines with phases of the Buddha's life. In 1551 Japanese Buddhists informed the Jesuit brother Juan Fernandez, who spoke some Japanese, that the founder of their religion, Shaka, "also wrote books so that they would pray to him and be saved." But at the age of 49 years, so Fernandez reported,[2] Shaka had suddenly changed his approach and confessed that "in the past he had been ignorant, which is why he wrote so much." Based on his own experience Shaka thereafter discouraged people from reading his old writings and advocated "meditation in order to learn about oneself and of one's end" (Schurhammer 1929:82). In the first comprehensive report about Buddhist sects and doctrines that reached the West (the *Sumario de los errores* of 1556), certain Buddhist texts were thus associated with specific sects, and Shaka was said to have dismissed his earlier writings: "They said that many people followed him and that he had 80,000 disciples. And ultimately, after having spent 44 years writing these scriptures, he said that nothing of that was true and that all was fombem [Jap. *hōben*, expedient means]" (Ruiz-de-Medina 1990:664).

However, Matteo RICCI's 1615 description of the sect of "*sciequia* or *omitofo*" (Shakya/Amitabha) and the corresponding Japanese teaching of "*sotoqui*" (Jap. *hotoke*, that is, buddhas) shows no trace of such a fundamental distinction between expedient and true teaching and exhibits little familiarity with Buddhism's "multitude of books" that, according to Ricci, "were either brought from the West or (which is more likely) composed in the Kingdom of China itself" (Ricci 1615:122). But the date of 65 C.E. from the preface of the *Forty-Two Sections Sutra*, along with its tale of the transfer of this religion from India to China and of the translation of its texts, became fixtures in virtually all subsequent Western accounts. This sutra was thus, long before de Guignes's 1756 translation (see Chapter 4), instrumental in attaching a founder's name (Fo/Buddha), a place of origin (India), a date of the first transmission to China (65 C.E.), a body of sacred scriptures including the sutra itself, and an eastward trajectory (from India to Siam, China, and Japan) for a large religion dominant in major parts of Asia. Ricci's account, as edited by Nicolas Trigault, was read all over Europe in schools and refectories and published in several languages. It was a work that opened up a whole new world for a surprisingly large public.

But after Ricci's death in 1610 and the publication of his view of Chinese religions by Trigault (1615), Ricci's critic João RODRIGUES (1561–1633) applied the distinction between exoteric and esoteric teachings more broadly to all three major religions of China and linked it to the ancient use of symbols in the Middle East and Egypt (see also Chapter 1). Rodrigues's view of a common root of Asia's major religions and his conviction that all of them used symbols to hide the real content of their teaching from the general public were influential in several respects. Chinese "idolatry" was not an amorphous mass but consisted of several well-defined creeds, each with its sacred scriptures, doctrines, and particular history. But if one dug deep enough, their common root could be exposed. For Rodrigues this common root was lodged in Mesopotamia and associated with Zoroaster and the evil habit of the elites to mislead the common people by hiding the true doctrine under a coat of symbols. Mainly because of his opposition to Ricci-style missionary strategy, Rodrigues's writings were suppressed. Some of them got buried in archives and may still lie there; others were plagiarized by ideological opponents (for instance, Rodrigues's writings on Asian history and geography by Martino Martini) and then possibly destroyed; and much of the rest, especially Rodrigues's letters and reports, were noted in their time but forgotten by posterity. But overall, Rodrigues's writings are a splendid example of the influence of underground sources. His reports about Chinese religions were widely read by Jesuits and other orders and formed, as the basis of Niccolò Longobardi's treatise, a core argument of the opponents of the Jesuits in the Chinese Rites controversy. In this form they came to play a crucial but hitherto overlooked role in the downfall and prohibition of the Jesuit order in the eighteenth century.

The Buddha's Deathbed Confession

Rodrigues's ideas and scholarship burrowed their way into the minds of other missionaries. One of them was the Milanese Cristoforo BORRI (1583–1632) who lived in Saigon from 1610 to 1623. His report about Cochinchina, published in 1631, gave the distinction between the exoteric and esoteric teachings of Buddhism a fateful twist. He reported that Xaca had immediately after his enlightenment written books about the esoteric teaching:

> Therefore returning home, he wrote several books and large volumes on this subject, entitling them, "Of Nothing;" wherein he taught that the things of this world, by reason of the duration and measure of time, are nothing; for though they had existence, said he, yet they would be nothing, nothing at present, and nothing in time to come, for the present being but a moment, was the same as nothing. (Pinkerton 1818:9.821)

He argued likewise about moral things, reducing everything to nothing. Then he gathered scholars, and the doctrine of nothing was spread all over the East. However, the Chinese were opposed to this doctrine and rejected it, whereupon Xaca "changed his mind, and retiring wrote several other great books, teaching that there was a real origin of all things, a lord of heaven, hell, immortality, and transmigration of souls from one body to another, better or worse, according to the merits or demerits of the person; though they do not forget to assign a sort of heaven and hell for the souls of departed, expressing the whole metaphorically under the names of things corporeal, and of the joys and sufferings of this world" (pp. 821–82). While the Chinese gladly received the "external," modified teaching of Xaca, the teaching of nothing also survived, for instance, in Japan in the dominant "gensiu" (Jap. *Zen-shū*, Zen sect) (p. 822). According to Borri, it was exactly this acceptance in Japan that had the Buddha explain on his deathbed that the doctrine of nothingness was his true teaching:

> The Japanese and others making so great account of this opinion of nothing, was the cause that when Xaca the author of it approached his death, calling together his disciples, he protested to them on the word of a dying man, that during the many years he had lived and studied, he had found nothing so true, nor any opinion so well grounded as was the sect of nothing; and though his second doctrine seemed to differ from it, yet they must look upon it as no contradiction or recantation, but rather a proof and confirmation of the first, though not in plain terms, yet by way of metaphors and parables, which might all be applied to the opinion of nothing, as would plainly appear by his books. (p. 822)

Of course, Borri's tale lacks all historical perspective and has the Buddha make decisions based on events (the introduction of Buddhism to China and Japan) that happened many centuries later. But for people who have no idea of the history of this religion, its attribution of motives to the founder must have sounded believable, and Borri's book was one of the early works on East Asia that was widely read and translated. This story, in my opinion, forms the kernel of the Buddha's "deathbed confession" tale. Borri appears to have spun it on the basis of information from Japan, from Rodrigues, and possibly also Vietnamese informants, in order to make sense of the different teachings of this religion whose founder is Xaca = Buddha. In the *Cathechismus* (sic) of Alexander de Rhodes, which was printed in Rome in 1651, the geographical references were removed, and the story appeared in a more biographical form where not the Chinese but Buddha's immediate disciples rejected the original doctrine:

> When he wanted to teach others this impious doctrine [of nothingness], so contrary to natural reason, they all abandoned him. Seeing this, he began, with the demons as his teachers, to teach another way filled with false stories in order to retain his disciples. He taught them the false doctrine of reincarnation, and at the same time taught the people the worship of idols, among whom he placed himself as their head, as if he were the creator and lord of heaven and earth. . . . Those who were more advanced in his impious doctrine were forbidden to divulge it to the public. . . . As to his closest disciples, he led them to the abyss of atheism, holding that nothingness is the origin of all things, and that at death all things return to nothingness as to their ultimate end. (Phan 1998:250)

This tale soon mutated in an ominous way that again had its roots in early reports from Japan. Instead of first teaching about emptiness and subsequently "accommodating" Chinese or Indian sensibilities in a manner that resembles the Jesuit mission strategy, the founder of Buddhism was exposed as a liar and fraud who never told anyone about his nihilism and for forty-nine years preached an "exterior" doctrine he did not believe in. This resounded throughout Europe, thanks to the megaphone of Couplet's 1687 introduction to *Confucius Sinarum Philosophus*, and found its way into works such as Louis Daniel Lecomte's *Nouveaux mémoires sur l'état présent de la Chine* (1696), Jean-Baptiste du Halde's *Description de la Chine* (1736), and scores of dictionaries, encyclopedias, travel accounts, and other books. Thus canonized, the story presented the Buddha as a fraud, liar, and coward who needed to be prodded by the cold breath of death to reveal his nihilism and even then dared to do so only to his closest and dearest disciples. It combined elements from Jesuit letters and reports from Japan (particularly those regarding the Zen sect), Valignano's catechism, Rodrigues's reports, and Borri's and de Rhodes's tales and molded them into an easily understood deathbed confession story that not only exposed the founder's profound character flaw but also furnished a simple classification scheme for variants of his religion. The founder's disciples, so the story went, after his death formed two factions, an esoteric and an exoteric one. Soon a third faction that combined both teachings got added (App 2008a:29) and took care of whatever would not fit into the first two categories.

At the beginning of the eighteenth century, it was especially the *Treatise on Some Points of the Religion of the Chinese* (written by Niccolò Longobardi in 1624–26) that created waves because it stood at the center of the Chinese Rites controversy. This internal Jesuit document, whose core consisted of Rodrigues's reports of the 1610s and 1620s, had been leaked and published in 1676 by the Dominican friar Domingo NAVARRETE (1618–89) and was read, among many other European intellectuals, by the philosopher Gottfried Leibniz (Leibniz 2002). Longobardi's treatise stated that the use of symbols "gave birth in all nations to two kinds of science: a true and secret one, and a false and public one" (Leibniz 2002:122). The first was only possessed by the learned and kept secret, while the second constituted "a false appearance of popular doctrine," a mirage that the people, attached as they are to the bark of words, "took for the true teaching" instead of recognizing it as a "gross shadow that disguises truth" (p. 122). Longobardi explained, following Rodrigues:

> The three sects of the Chinese entirely follow this kind of philosophizing. They have two kinds of doctrine: a secret one that they regard as true and that only the learned understand and teach encoded in figures; and the vulgar one which is a figure of the first and is regarded by the learned as false in the natural meaning of the words. (p. 122)

Longobardi also followed Rodrigues's lead in putting the three great Chinese religions in the evil transmission line by declaring them to be forms of atheism going back to "Zoroaster, the magus and prince of the Chaldeans" (pp. 128, 141).

Even opponents of Rodrigues such as Martino MARTINI (1614–61), who in 1651 traveled to Europe to defend Ricci's approach, drew information about Chinese religions from Rodrigues. In the introduction to his *Novus Atlas Sinensis* of 1655, Martini described the sect of Shakyamuni as follows:

The second sect is the idolatric one, called *Xekiao*. This pest infected China shortly after Christ's birth. It admits metempsychosis. It is of two kinds; one is internal and the other external. The latter [external or exoteric kind] teaches the worship of idols, portrays the transmigration of souls after death as a punishment for sins, and continually abstains from [eating] anything that lives. It is a ridiculous law that is disapproved of even by the clergy of these sectarians who consider it necessary to keep the ignorant people away from vice and to incite them to be virtuous. The internal [teaching of] metempsychosis is excellent and one of the best parts of moral philosophy since it regards the passions, those depraved inclinations of the soul, as emptiness [vacuitatem] and aims at victory over them. As long as this [victory] is not obtained, so they believe, the souls of those dominated by such feelings continue to migrate in the bodies of brute animals. [The inner teaching] does not believe in any reward or punishment after death, just a void [vacuum]. It asserts that there is no truth in this life unless it can be touched and that good and evil are just different viewpoints. (Martini 1665:8)

Athanasius KIRCHER's *China Illustrata* (1667) was even more instrumental in promoting the esoteric/exoteric divide. The chapter titled "Parallels Between Chinese, Japanese, and Tartar Idolatry" presented these two "manners" as the two main kinds of Japanese religion and confirms the divide's sixteenth-century Japanese mission roots and the close association of Zen with the esoteric doctrine. Kircher wrote:

Lest I seem to be asserting something only on my own authority, I will quote here some words of Fr. Ludwig Gusmann in his Spanish language account:There are many sects in Japan which have been, and still are, different from each other, but these can be reduced to two main ones. The first denies that there is any other life than that which we perceive with our senses and that there is any reward for good works or punishment for crimes which we do in the world except those we get while we live on the earth. Persons who profess this view are called Xenxus [Jap.

Zen-shū, Zen sect]. . . . As regards those who believe in an afterlife, there are two principal sects, and from these have come an infinite number of others. (Kircher 1987:131)

Like Rodrigues and Borri, Kircher used this division as a tool to bring order into East Asia's idolatries:

> Since the Japanese have borrowed their idolatrous religion from the Chinese, they have as great a variety of sects as the Chinese. These can be summarized under two headings. The first of these is those who deny an afterlife and who believe that there is no future punishment or reward for good works or evil. They lead an Epicurean life. This sect is called Xenxus [Jap. Zen-shū, Zen sect]. . . . The others, who believe in immortality of the soul and an afterlife, are similar to the Pythagoreans in their rites and ceremonies. Most of the Chinese sages follow this theory. They worship an idol by the name of Omyto, commonly called Amida. (p. 131)

This portrayal pitches, like the early Jesuit reports of 1551 mentioned above, the (esoteric) Zen adherents against the (exoteric) Pure Land worshipers of Amida and is thus an example of a practice that even today is rampant in academia, namely, the projection of Japanese distinctions on China.

Couplet's Atheist Contemplators

Two decades after Kircher, Philippe COUPLET (1623–1693) presented in the introduction to *Confucius Sinarum Philosophus* rather detailed information about Fo (whom he also calls *Xe kia* and *Xaca*) and Fo's religion. It is found in the introductory exposition that contains a very influential discussion of the content of Fo's doctrine (Couplet 1687:xxvii–xxix) that formed the focus of very detailed reviews in the most widely read European review journals. Couplet's views thus reached a surprisingly broad international readership. Major elements of it were cited, for example, in Bayle's famous "Spinoza" article of the *Dictionnaire historique et critique* (1702, vol. 3)—a main source of Diderot's article "Asiatiques" in the first volume of the *Encyclopédie* (1751). Couplet's portrayal[3] is a summary of Jesuit learning on the subject and forms a hinge between sixteenth- and seventeenth-century information (mainly from Japan, China, and Vietnam) and the eighteenth and nineteenth centuries. Among the items of information that stunned Europeans was the sheer size of the religion of Fo and of its sacred literature. According to Couplet, Fo was born in central India in 1026 B.C.E., preached for forty-nine years, and gained as many as 80,000 disciples. Couplet's list of clergy appellations from various countries suggests a gigantic area that includes Japan, China, Tartary, and Siam and a sacred literature amounting to 15,000 volumes (pp. xxix–xxx).

In the second half of the seventeenth century, stories of "expedient means" and of a "true" teaching hidden from the masses had already coagulated into the above-mentioned attractive narrative about the last teachings of Shakyamuni that was ceaselessly repeated. The version contained in Couplet's *Confucius Sinarum Philosophus* of 1687 was seminal. Pierre Bayle cited it, based on an extensive book review, in his article on Spinoza. This entry is one of the most widely read and discussed articles ever to appear in a dictionary. Bayle's readers learned, among other interesting things, that *Foe Kiao* (Ch. *Fojiao*, Buddhism) was established in China in the year 65 C.E. by royal authority and that its founder, Xe kia (Shakya), the son of an Indian king, had revealed his true teaching only shortly before his death:

> Having retired to the desert at the age of 19 and having put himself under the guidance of four gymnosophists to learn philosophy from them, he stayed under their tutelage until age 30 when, one day before dawn he contemplated the planet Venus, and this simple view suddenly gave him perfect knowledge of the first principle. Full of divine inspiration, or rather of pride and folly, he began to instruct people, had himself regarded as a God, and attracted as many as 80,000 disciples. . . . At the age of 79 years, when he felt close to death, he declared to his disciples that, during the forty years of his preaching, he had not told them the truth; that he had kept it hidden under the veil of metaphors and figures, but that it was now time to tell it to them. It is, said he, *that there is nothing to seek and nothing to pin one's hopes on, just emptiness* [le vuide] *and nothingness* [le néant], *which is the first principle of all things.* (Bayle 1702:2769, article "Spinoza")

The account of the Buddha's deathbed confession to his closest disciples (in which he called his earlier teachings untrue and only metaphorical) was used by Couplet as an introduction to his discussion of the "famous distinction of his doctrine into an *exterior* and *interior* one" (Couplet 1687:xxix). The *exte-*

rior doctrine is compared to the wooden scaffolding used for building an arch: though useful for the purpose of construction, it becomes useless and is removed as soon as the edifice is completed (p. xxx). According to Couplet, this doctrine has the following content:

> The main tenets [summa] of the *exterior* or provisional doctrine [supposititiae doctrinae] are that there is a real difference between good and evil, justice and injustice; that there is a future state with recompense and punishment and places for this; that happiness can be obtained by 32 figures and 80 qualities; that Fo or Xaca is a deity [numen] and the savior of mortals; that he was born for their sake out of compassion for their aberration from the way of salvation [via salutis]; that he has atoned for their sins; and that through his expiation they will attain salvation and rebirth in a happier world (pp. xxx–xxxi)

Couplet also mentions the five Buddhist precepts (no killing of living things, no theft, etc.) and six good works (donations to monks, etc.), as well as transmigration via six realms into innumerable forms, and so forth. Such features of the exterior doctrine tended to be augmented and elaborated by subsequent authors; for example, Diderot (1751:1.753–54) listed a total of fourteen points that were in part also drawn from more recent sources such as Engelbert Kaempfer's description of Japanese Buddhism (1729; see here below). The full acceptance by 1750 of the two-fold doctrine view is confirmed by this statement of Diderot:

> The Indians and the Chinese unanimously attest that this impostor had two sorts of doctrines: one designed for the people and the other a secret one that he only revealed to a few of his disciples. Le Comte, la Loubère, Bernier, and especially Kaempfer have notably informed us of the first which is called *exoteric*. (p. 753)

Diderot's account of the *interior* doctrine (1751:754), by contrast, differs so little from the one furnished by Couplet six decades earlier that it is a good summary of Couplet's view. Diderot described its essential points as follows:

1. Emptiness [le vuide] is the principle and end of all things.
2. It is where all humans have their origin and what they return to after death.

3. Everything that exists comes from this principle and returns to it after death; it is this principle that constitutes our soul and all elements. Therefore, all living, thinking, and feeling beings, regardless of their differences of capacities or shape, are neither different in essence nor distinct from their principle.

4. This principle is universal, admirable, pure, limpid, subtle, infinite; it can neither be born nor die nor dissolve.

5. This principle has neither virtue nor understanding [entendement] nor power nor any other similar attribute.

6. Its essence is to do nothing, think nothing, desire nothing.

7. He who wants to lead an innocent and happy life must make all efforts to become similar to his principle; that is, he must master or rather extinguish all his passions so that he will not be troubled or unsettled by anything.

8. He who attains this point of perfection will be absorbed in sublime contemplations without any use of his faculty of understanding, and he will enjoy the kind of divine repose that forms the apex of happiness.

9. When one reaches knowledge of this sublime doctrine, one must let others keep the exoteric[4] doctrine, or at least adopt it just for show. (Diderot 1751:754)[5]

We have seen that most of these points are firmly rooted in sixteenth-century missionary accounts of Japanese Buddhist doctrine where they were usually linked to the teachings of the Zen sect. This genealogy shows not only how important and long-lived the first impressions from Japan were but also how old information from the missions was instrumental in shaping more recent, secular sources (such as Kaempfer) that later found its way into eighteenth-century encyclopedias such as Diderot's and d'Alembert's *Encyclopédie*, which prided themselves for their critical review of source materials, their secular perspective, and their accuracy.

The Specter of Spinozism

Couplet's digest of the esoteric doctrine of Fo evoked an echo in Europe whose amplitude cannot be understood without taking into account the theological and philosophical climate of the late seventeenth century that

Paul Hazard (1961) labeled "the crisis of European conscience." Here we glance only at a single aspect of this "crisis," namely, the early reception of Spinoza's thought and its role in publicizing what was portrayed as the Buddha's "inner" doctrine. Since Spinoza's writings were still insufficiently known, the term "Spinozism" will be used to designate Spinoza's philosophy as it was perceived at the time. To my knowledge, the Swiss theologian and publicist Jean Le Clerc (1657–1736) was the first European to see a link between Spinozism and Fo's esoteric doctrine. In his extensive review of *Confucius sinarum philosophus* in the widely read *Bibliothèque universelle et historique* (1688) he boiled this doctrine down to three points:

> The inner doctrine—which one never divulges to ordinary people because of the need, as these philosophers say, to oblige them to stick to their duty through the fear of hell and similar stories—is indeed, according to them, the solid and genuine one. It consists in establishing as the principle and end of all things a certain *emptiness* [*vuide*] and a *real nothingness* [*néant réel*]. They say that [1] our first parents have come from this emptiness and return to it after death, and that the same applies to all humans: all dissolve into this principle at death; [2] that we along with all elements and creatures form part of this emptiness; [3] that therefore only a single and same substance exists which differs in individual beings only by virtue of the qualities or the interior configuration, like water that always remains water regardless of its form as snow, hail, rain, or ice. (Le Clerc 1788:348–9)

Immediately after this interesting summary, Le Clerc advises "those who would like to find out more about the philosophy of the Indians and the Chinese, which is not very different from the system of the Spinozists, if one can say that they have one" to inform themselves in the travel account of Bernier (p. 349). Le Clerc thus first triangulated the Buddha's "inner" doctrine with the information supplied by Prince Dara's pandit (as found in Bernier) and Spinozism. Since Spinozism was at the time equivalent to atheism and sympathizers risked their jobs or even their lives, this was an explosive charge. The origin and significance of this link would lead too deep into issues connected with the history of philosophy and will be discussed elsewhere, but in our immediate context it is of interest to note that replacing this "emptiness" by Spinoza's "substance" and "qualities or configuration" by "modification" suffices to arrive at Le Clerc's conclusion that the Buddha's inner doctrine is "not very different" from Spinozism. This line of argument was taken up and amplified by Bayle in the famous "Spinoza" and "Japan" articles of his *Dictionnaire* (1702). Thus the "inner" teaching of Buddhism with its Japanese Zen roots, the Sufi-Vedanta-Neoplatonic amalgam of Prince Dara as reported by Bernier, and the Spinozism that frightened Europe's churchgoers and theologians entered into a fateful alliance with tremendous repercussions. All of a sudden, much of Asia from Persia and India to China and Japan appeared as a gigantic motherland of atheism, and the philosophies of India and China became relevant to the burning questions and controversies of Europe. Bayle denounced the Buddha's teaching of a single substance with manifold configurations (Bayle 1702:3.2769; Couplet 1687:xxxi) and called it more absurd than Spinoza's philosophy:

> If it is monstrous to assert that plants, beasts, and men are really the same thing, and to ground such an opinion on the pretension that all particular beings are not distinct from their principle, it is even more monstrous to utter that this principle has no thought, no power, and no virtue at all. Yet this is what these philosophers say when they place the supreme perfection of that principle in its inaction and absolute repose. . . . Spinoza was not so absurd: the unitary substance admitted by him is always acting, always thinking; and not even his most general abstractions could enable him to divest it of action and thought. (Bayle 1702:3.2769)

Couplet shocked his European readers by asserting that this extremely widespread and ancient esoteric doctrine firmly rejects central Christian doctrines such as divine providence, a future state with reward and punishment, and an immortal soul and thus has also no place for a savior (1687:xxxii). Instead it advocates reaching happiness by "chimerical contemplations," and according to Couplet, it even formed a sect for this purpose. He calls this sect *Vu guei Kiao*, the sect of nonaction [nihil agentium secta]."[6] Founded about the year 290 C.E., this sect is said to be similar to the Indian gymnosophists (p. xxxii). In China it became so successful that even some of the most eminent men of the empire "adopted this insanity" and habitually "spent several hours without any movement of body and mind," declaring that such insensibility made them happier (pp. xxxii–xxxiii). As an illustration Couplet mentions the case of the twenty-eighth successor of Xaca, a man called Ta mo (Ch. Damo, Bodhidharma) who spent "a total of nine years facing a wall" and during the entire time "did nothing other than contemplate this chimerical principle of his, emptiness and nothingness [vacuum & nihil]" (p. xxxiii). For Couplet this "sect of the contemplators [contemplantium Secta]" was "engulfed in the most profound atheism" (p. xxxiii); but Bayle, who quoted some of Couplet's explanations and called it "the sect of idlers or do-nothings [la secte des oiseux ou des faineans]," wondered whether its doctrine of nothingness was correctly described. If these illustrious men of China really believed that "the nearer a man comes to the nature of tree trunk or a stone, the greater his progress and the more he is like the first principle into which he is to return," how did they conceive this principle of nothingness?

> I tend to believe that either one does not correctly express what these people understand by *Cum hiu* [Ch. *kongxu*, emptiness] or that their ideas are contradictory. Some would have these Chinese words signify *emptiness* and *nothingness* [*vuide* & *neant, vacuum & inane*] and have fought against this sect pretending that nothingness [le neant] is the principle of all beings. I cannot persuade myself that this captures the exact sense of the word nothingness, and I imagine that it means something like when people say that there is nothing in an empty suitcase. . . . I believe that by that word they meant more or less what the moderns call space [espace]. (Bayle 1702:3.2770)

Couplet's link of this originally Indian "interior" doctrine to a popular "sect of contemplators" in China and to Indian gymnosophists was much noted and cited, starting with Le Clerc (1688) and Bernier (1688). Was Ta mo [Bodhidharma], the twenty-eighth successor of the Indian founder of the esoteric doctrine, the transmitter of this Indian doctrine to China? And what texts were associated with this transmission? For Diderot, writing fifty years after Bayle, this esoteric teaching of the "Budda or Xekia" was not transmitted via texts but rather, as in the Buddha's deathbed confession scene, by word of mouth to a select few. If in China this Indian system had formed the basis of a famous sect of contemplators, so Diderot thought, it was "very likely" that in Japan it also "gave birth to a famous sect" (Diderot 1751:754). He was thinking of the Japanese Zen sect described by Engelbert Kaempfer:

> It teaches that there is only one principle of all things; that this principle is bright and luminous, incapable of accretion or diminution, without form, sovereign and perfect, wise, but without reason or intelligence,

resting in perfect inaction and supremely tranquil like a man whose attention is fixed on one thing without thinking of anything else. They also say that this principle is in all particular beings and communicates its essence in such a manner that they form the same thing with it and dissolve in it when they are destroyed. (p. 754)

By the mid-eighteenth century a vision of a twofold pan-Asian religious movement was thus well established. Much of the information about its doctrine—which purportedly represented the teachings of Fo alias Xaca alias Xekia alias Budda—was based on data and legends reported from Japan and China by Jesuit missionaries. Its inner doctrine was associated with sects of "contemplators" in both countries and linked to the deathbed instruction of an Indian founder figure (Fo, Shaka, Buddha) and to transmitter figures who in the first centuries of the common era brought this teaching from India to China (the Chinese ambassadors with the *Forty-Two Sections Sutra*; Bodhidharma). But the connection with Spinozism was not the only booster hurling Asia's "inner" doctrine into European consciousness. A second booster was its association with quietism, which was one more hot-button theme of seventeenth- and eighteenth-century theology, and a third the link with the Kabbala.

Bernier's Asian Mysticism

Kircher's *China Illustrata* (1667) chapter on "The Ridiculous Brahmin Religion and the Teachings About the Origin of Man" begins with the statement that "the brahmins take their origin according to the Indian writers from Cechian or Xaca" and ends with a passage that soon acquired fame throughout Europe as the essence of the Indian theory of creation:

They say that a spider is the first cause, and he created the world by spinning a web with the threads coming from his stomach. Then he formed the heavenly spheres and he rules everything until the end of the world, which he will cause by pulling back into himself all of the threads in his web. (Kircher 1987:145)

Kircher collected information about Asian religions from diverse sources, but the input of his fellow Jesuit Heinrich ROTH (1620–68), a native of

Figure 5. Kircher's Indo-Japanese divinities: Dainichi/Brahma (left) and
Amida (right).

Augsburg and longtime resident of India, was crucial. Roth was one of the
European missionaries who studied Sanskrit long before the British colonialists, and Kircher claimed that Roth "took these doctrines mainly from their
arcane books" (p. 147). Some of these doctrines sounded rather familiar to
those who had read about Fo's esoteric doctrine:

> They say the universal is the nature of that supreme being itself. The
> particular is nature divided by particles into the variety of things. From
> this they conclude that there can be no generic or specific distinction of
> created things, but that everything is one and the same being. The natu-
> ral universe is distinguished by particles, some of which may take the
> figure of a man, others a rock, and yet others a tree, and so on. They say
> that the matter worn by these particles is only a deception. (p. 148)

But Kircher's explanations were imbedded in such a plethora of disjointed
facts and arguments that many readers may have remembered little more

than the central narrative of an impostor called Xaca whose Brahmin missionaries spread from their base in India and eventually infected the whole of Asia with their pestilent idolatry.

In the year 1667 when Kircher's *China Illustrata* was published, another acquaintance of Fr. Roth, the French medical doctor and philosopher François BERNIER (1620–88) sent a long letter from Persia to Paris about "the superstitions, strange customs, and doctrines of the Indous or Gentiles of Hindoustan." Four years later, when this letter appeared in print as part of his *Travels in the Mogul Empire*,[7] Bernier was already a man whose fame reached far beyond the frontiers of his native France. From 1654 he had traveled in Asia, first in Palestine and Syria, then in Egypt, and he subsequently sojourned for no less than eight years in India (1659–67). After his 1659 arrival in Surat during the succession struggles of the sons of the Mogul rulers Shah Jahan, he was for a short time the medical doctor of the crown prince, Mohammed Dārā Shikūh (1615–59), the very man who commissioned and supervised in 1657 the Persian Upanishad translation whose Latin rendering Anquetil-Duperron was to publish under the title of *Oupnek'hat* in 1801 (see Chapter 7). After Prince Dara's execution (1659), Bernier worked at the court of a rich Indian named Daneshmend-khan and spent several years with one of India's most excellent scholars who had played a central role in Prince Dara's Upanishad translation project. Bernier reported,

> My Agah [lord], *Danechmend-kan*, partly from my solicitation and partly to gratify his own curiosity, took into his service one of the most celebrated *Pendets* in all the *Indies*, who had formerly belonged to the household of Dara, the eldest son of the King *Chah-Jehan*; and not only was this man my constant companion during a period of three years, but he also introduced me to the society of other learned *Pendets*, whom he attracted to the house. (Bernier 2005:324)

Prince Dara had been interested in Sufi mysticism since his youth and had authored several books about this subject (App 2007). For him the Upanishads represented the esoteric essence of the Vedas, and he argued that a Koran passage mentioning a "hidden book that none but the purified can grasp" (Quran 56:78) referred to the Upanishads. They represent God's original revelation as transmitted to initiates, which is why Dara gave his translation the title *Sirr-i akbar*, that is, the Great Secret.[8] Prince Dara's (and Bernier's) pandit, who had been instrumental in explaining this secret to Dara, was versed both in Sufism and Indian philosophy and spoke Persian. Bernier's Persian was so good that he could translate philosophical texts by René Descartes and Pierre Gassendi into that language. Though unable to read Sanskrit, he thus found himself in the enviable position of receiving first-hand information about the secret doctrine of the yogis and Sufis from one of the most learned Indians"

> The trance, and the means of enjoying it, form the grand Mysticism of the sect of the *Jauguis* [Yogis], as well as that of the *Soufys*. I call it Mysticism [Mystere], because they keep these things secret among themselves, and I should not have made so many discoveries had it not been for the aid of the *Pendet*, or *Indou* Doctor whom *Danechmend-kan* kept in his pay, and who dared not conceal anything from his patron; my *Agah*, moreover, was already acquainted with the doctrines of the *Soufys*. (Bernier 2005:320)

Europeans suspicious of the reports by missionaries and by uneducated travelers were understandably delighted to get more trustworthy and objective information from Bernier, the learned disciple of the philosopher Gassendi. To judge by the number of Bernier quotations and references in other books, it is clear that the data from Prince Dara's pandit elicited pronounced interest among European readers. In particular, the spider allegory that is mentioned in the Upanishads was frequently cited and is an example of the influence of native informants. Bernier wrote about "the secret of a grand cabal that has lately made great noise in Hindustan because certain *pandits* or Gentile doctors have used it to infect the minds of Dara and Sultan Sujah, the two elder sons of [Moghul emperor] Shah Jahan" (Bernier 1699:2.163). What kind of infection was this? It was the doctrine of "a world-soul, of which they want our souls and those of animals to be part" (p. 163). Bernier calls this "the almost universal doctrine of the *Gentile Pendets* of the *Indies*" and regards it as "the same doctrine which is held by the sect of the *Soufys* and the greater part of the learned men of *Persia* at the present day" (Bernier 2005:346).

> [They] pretend that God, or that supreme being whom they call *Achar* (immoveable, unchangeable), has not only produced life from his own substance, but also generally everything material or corporeal in the universe, and that this production is not formed simply after the manner of

efficient causes, but as a spider which produces a web from its own navel, and withdraws it at pleasure. The Creation then, say these visionary doctors, is nothing more than an extraction or extension of the individual substance of *God*, of those filaments which He draws from his own bowels; and, in like manner, destruction is merely the recalling of that divine substance and filaments into Himself. (p. 347)

Individual beings are thus not real, and "the whole world is, as it were, an illusory dream, inasmuch as all that variety which appears to our outward senses is but one only and the same thing, which is God Himself" (p. 347).

But apart from a Persian Sufi book entitled "*Goul-tchen-raz*, or Garden of Mysteries,"[9] Bernier could not name any textual sources containing this doctrine. The "extremely old" Indian *Beths* (Vedas) in "four sacred books" that according to the Indians were "given to them by God," and the *Purane*, which Bernier portrays as "an abridgment and interpretation of the Beds" (p. 335), were not available to him. He describes the Vedas as being "of great bulk" and "so scarce that my *Agah*, notwithstanding all his diligence, has not succeeded in purchasing a copy" (pp. 335–36). In this respect Bernier was dependent on Prince Dara's pandit and on Fr. Roth whose explanations were prominently featured in Kircher's *China illustrata*. Bernier rarely mentions regions of Asia to the east of India; but in 1688, shortly before his death, he read Couplet's *Confucius Sinarum Philosophus* (1687) and published a paper about the "Quietism of the Indies." In it he connects his Indian Yogis and Fakirs with Couplet's Chinese sect of contemplators and furnishes the following explanation of the "mystery of the cabal" that he had written about two decades earlier:

Among the different *Fakirs* or idolatrous religious men of the Indies, there are some that are commonly called *Yogis* which is something like saints, illumined ones, perfect ones, or men who are perfectly united with the sovereign Being, the first and general Principle of all things. . . . Above all they are engulfed in contemplation, and I say engulfed because they push themselves so much into it that they reportedly spend hours in ecstasy. Their outer senses seem without any activity, and they pretend to see the sovereign Being as a very bright and inexplicable light, with an inexpressible joy and satisfaction followed by contempt and complete detachment from the world. (Bernier 1688:47–48).

Bernier's explanations indicate that he regarded the doctrine of Sufis, Indian Yogis, and Fakirs as largely identical with that of Couplet's sect of contemplators:

> Their ancient books teach that this first principle of things is very admirable; that it is something very *pure*, in their own words, and *very clear* and *subtle*; that it is infinite; that it cannot be created [engendré] nor corrupted; that it is the perfection of all things, sovereign perfection; and, what needs to be noted, [that it is] in perfect repose and absolute inaction—in a word, in perfect quietism. (p. 48)

As in the familiar descriptions of the esoteric teaching of Shaka/Fo, this first principle is said to be without any action and understanding and so on. Perfection consists in becoming exactly like this principle through "continuous contemplation and victory over oneself" (p. 49). Once all human passions are extinct, there is no more torment, and "in the manner of an ecstatic, one is completely absorbed in profound contemplation" and achieves "divine repose or quietism, the happiest state to be hoped for" (p. 49). It is only logical that the Buddhist "bonzes" and the *Wuwei jiao* ("secta nihil agentium" or sect of do-nothings) of Couplet's preface are thus presented as the Far Eastern cousins of Bernier's Yogis and Fakirs. Bernier mentions Couplet's Ta-mo (Bodhidharma)—who brought this teaching from India to China and "looked at a wall for nine whole years"—as a perfect example of this "mental illness" (p. 50). However, this "illness" is found not only in Asia but also, though with less extravagance, in the West: for Bernier, all quietism is characterized by "this abyss of contemplation, this great inaction, this great union of our soul with God," whether it is professed by the Spanish divine Miguel de MOLINOS (1628–97), by the Sufis of Persia, or by "the Joguis of the Indies, the Bonzes of China, or the Talapois of Siam" (pp. 50–51).

In Bernier's reflections on quietism, we see the outlines of a mysticism that transcends East and West. It is likely that in this respect Bernier was inspired by Prince Dara via his pandit, which once more points to the crucial role of native informers in the genesis of modern Orientalism. But contrary to their exalted idea of universal esotericism, Bernier regarded the "quietisms" of East and West as similarly suspect. Though it "might be more a case of exaggerated devotion and of extravagance," he wrote, the idea of a world soul "approaches atheism" because it envisions "a corporal God, and therefore a divisible and corruptible one" (Bernier 1688:51). But Bernier's critique was instrumental in connecting the "inner teaching" of Fo/Shaka with the practices of Sufism and Indian ascetics and putting a pan-Asian "quietism" with Indian roots on the map. At the end of his life, Bernier used Couplet's presentation of Fo's "inner teaching" to characterize Indian Yogis and Sufi mystics, yet he remained unable to furnish any textual evidence from India other than what was decades ago included in the books of Henry Lord (1630) and Abraham Roger (1651).

Both in Diderot's article on "the philosophy of the Asians in general" and in that on the "Brahmins" Bernier plays a central role. The first cites Bernier's entire passage about emanation with the spider allegory (Diderot 1751:1.752) and identifies it not only with the teaching of "Persian Sufis whom he [Bernier] names *cabalistes*" but also with "the doctrine of the Pendets, heathen of the Indies" (p. 753) and "the doctrine of Xekia" whose esoteric teaching of "the origin of things through emanations from a first cause" also influenced Jewish kabbalists and their idea of "*En-soph* or the first infinite being which contains all things" and "distributes itself through emanation" (p. 754).

Burnet's Sapientia Orientalis

In 1792, barely four years after Bernier's seminal paper on quietism, a much-cited book with the intriguing title *Archæologiae philosophicæ: sive Doctrina antiqua de rerum originibus* appeared in England. Its author, Thomas BURNET (1635–1715), was famous for having written one of the great books about origins, namely, *The Sacred Theory of the Earth* (*Telluris theoria sacra*, 1680). In the *Sacred Theory* he proposed a stunning theory of earth formation that attempted to bridge his interpretation of the Bible's creation story and scientific knowledge. See Figure 6. Burnet explained in detail how our globe first coagulated from a mass of chaotic particles of matter into the shape of an egg, how it then gained a perfect spherical form, how a crust completely free of irregularities hardened on this structure, and how this crust was gradually baked by the action of the sun. He described the result of this process as follows:

> This smooth, perfect surface, over which the air was perennially calm, serene, and free of those disordinate movements that are caused by winds and the existence of mountains, coincides—all of it—with the terrestrial

Figure 6. The earth formation cycle of Burnet (1684).

paradise. This world was an inhabited world, for antediluvian humanity lived in it in simplicity, purity, and innocence. (trans. Rossi 1987:34–45)

Noah's flood played a central role in Burnet's theory since it completely changed the face of the earth and turned the ubiquitous paradise into the earth as we know it: a globe with seas, mountains, and valleys—"the image or picture of a great Ruine" and "a World lying in its rubbish" (Burnet 1694:193).[10]

If the *Sacred Theory* had tried to reconstruct the earth's golden age before the deluge by investigating the results of the deluge—for example, geological fallout or "rubbish" like mountains—Burnet's *Philosophical Archaeology* of 1692 attempted an analogous feat, namely, the reconstruction of the wisdom of paradise through the study of its vestiges in the religions and philosophies of the world. As a disciple of Ralph Cudworth, the author of *The True Intellectual System of the Universe* (1678), who had detected monotheism in just about any religion of the world (including atheism), Burnet was well informed about Egypt and the religions of European antiquity. He was dissatisfied with attempts (such as the one by Pierre-Daniel Huët) to regard all ancient religions as Bible rip offs; yet he also opposed the opinion that the religions of such countries as Egypt and India had arisen without any outside influence. Instead, Burnet opted for a common source of all ancient religions and philosophies and an orderly transmission process:

When we abandon these prejudices we must go back farther to search for the origin of barbaric philosophy. Farther than Moses and farther than Abraham: to the Flood and to Noah, the common father of the Jews and the Gentiles. . . . Why not believe that from this source, from this original man have descended to posterity, that is to say, to post-diluvian man, those principles of theology and philosophy that can be found among antico-barbarian peoples? (trans. Rossi 1987:39)

Since the "origin and seat of ancient wisdom" had to be traced back to "Noah's bosom, and from there to his sons and their descendants" (Burnet 1694:296), for Burnet "barbaric philosophy" had to form part of ur-wisdom and play a prominent role in his philosophical archaeology. According to him, remnants of such wisdom can be detected not only with the "Indians under whose name several ancient peoples are confusedly comprehended" (p. 297) but also with the Scyths in the North, the Celts and their druids in the

West (p. 298), and the Egyptians and Ethiopian gymnosophistae in the South (p. 300). But the religious vestiges of the Indies attracted Burnet's particular interest because "it was there that the postdiluvial men had their first seat and that the origins of mankind's wisdom and writing must be sought" (p. 302). This interest is also apparent in an appendix to Burnet's philosophical archaeology entitled *De Brachmanis hodiernis apud Indos, eorumque dogmatibus* ("On today's Brachmans in the Indies and their doctrines"), pp. 471–74.

One year after its first publication (1692), this appendix already appeared in an English translation by Charles Blount that publicized Burnet's argument that the modern Brachmins "descended from the ancient Race" as well as Burnet's view of the transmission of Noah's religion to various parts of Asia:

> Under the name of *Indies*, we here comprehend, besides the *Chineze* Empire, and Kingdom of *Indostan*, or Dominion of the Great *Mogul*, the Kingdoms of *Siam*, of the *Malabars*, of *Cochinchina*, of *Coromandel*, and whatever others are known to us in the *East*, that have in some measure shaken off their Barbarity. Now in each of these are a certain sort of Philosophers or Divines, and in the Kingdoms of *Indostan*, *Siam* and the other adjacent Parts, there are some who seem to be the Progeny of the ancient *Brachmins*, being different and distinguished from the rest of the People by their Manner and Way of Living, as well as by a Doctrin and Language wholly peculiar to themselves. (trans. Blount 1693:78)

These descendants of the ancient Brachmins are said to have "a certain Cabala, or Body of Learning," that is, a secret doctrine transmitted "from one to the other" that treats "of God, of the World, of the Beginning and Ending of Things, of the Periods of the World, of the Primitive State of Nature, together with its repeated Renovations" (trans. Blount 1693:78).

Focusing on "the Mogul's Kingdom call'd Indostan" that is "extremely large," Burnet honed in on its "Tribe or Order of Men, who bear the Title, and perform the Offices of Sages, Priests or Philosophers" (p. 79):

> They have a Language peculiar to themselves, which they call Hanscrit, or the pure Tongue; in this Language they have some very ancient Books, which they call Sacred, and say were given by God to the Great Prophet *Brahma*; as formerly the Law of the *Israelites* was to *Moses. Athan. Kircher* gives you an Alphabet of this *Brachmin's* Language, written by the Hand

of Father *Henry Roth*, who for several Years in the *Indies* apply'd himself to the learning of *Brachmins*. And in this they not only write and conceal their Divinity, but also their Opinions in Philosophy of all Kinds: besides the *metempsychosis*, and the *epochê empsychôn*, which are Opinions of a very ancient Date. (Burnet 1694:471–72; trans. Blount 1693:79–80)

The descendants of the ancient Brachmins in India and the surrounding Asian countries have a striking resemblance to Egyptian priests: like their Egyptian counterparts who encoded and concealed their monotheist doctrine in hieroglyphs, the Brachmins "conceal their Divinity" in a tightly guarded secret language (Sanscrit, or in Burnet's spelling Hanscrit). Furthermore, both clergies have particular doctrines regarding the soul and its transmigration—which form the core teachings associated by Burnet with the "oriental doctrine." But as an attentive reader of Kircher and Bernier, Burnet was also familiar with a second ancient, secret teaching of the Brachmins about the origin and the end of the world: "They likewise Philosophize after the manner of the Ancients, upon the Creation of the Universe, together with its end and Destruction; for they explain these Things by the Efflux or Emanation of all things from God, and by their Reflux or Restoration into him again: But this they propound in a Cabalistical Mythological way" (trans. Blount 1693:80). Burnet here refers to the allegory of the spider and its cosmic web as reported in Kircher and Bernier:

> For they feign a certain immense Spider to be the first Cause of all Things, and that she, with the Matter she exhausted out of her own Bowels, spun the Web of this whole Universe, and then disposed of it with a most wonderful Art: whilst she herself in the mean time sitting on the Top of her Work, feels, rules and governs the Motion of each part. At last, when she has sufficiently pleas'd and diverted her self in adorning and contemplating her own Web, she retracts the Threads she had unfolded, and swallows them up again into her self; whereby the whole Nature of Things created vanishes into nothing. (p. 80)

Noting that—provided that "taking off the fabulous Shell, we go to the Kernel"—this idea of emanation from and return to One does not differ much from the opinions of other ancients, Burnet encourages his readers to find out more about this "in *Henry Lord*, *F. Bernier*, and other Travellers, who have more diligently enquired into their Literature" (pp. 80–81). He also adduces the ideas of "*Siamese Brachmins*" about the end of the world through fire from Guy Tachard's *Relation of the voyage to Siam* (1687/1688) and notes their agreement with his theory:

> Tis really a most wonderful thing that a Nation half barbarous should have retained these Opinions from the very times of *Noah*: for they could not have arrived to a Knowledge of these things any other way, than by Tradition; nor could this Tradition flow from any other Spring, than *Noah*, and the Antediluvian Sages. (Burnet 1694:473; trans. Blount 1693:82)

Burnet identified several additional features of ancient oriental wisdom in the book of Abraham Roger (1651) and claimed that they confirm his theory:

> Now they affirm that there are several Worlds which do at one and the same time exist in divers Regions of the Universe: and that there are several successive ones; for that the same World is destroyed and renewed again according to certain Periods of Time. They say also that our Terrestrial World began by a certain Golden Age, and will perish by Fire. Lastly, they retain the Doctrin of the *Ovum Mundanum* comparing the World to an Egg; as did the ancients both *Greeks* and *Barbarians*. (Burnet 1694:473; trans. Blount 1693:83)

In China Burnet found a similar comparison of the world to an egg, but he doubted that the Chinese "derived their Philosophy of History from the *Brachmins*" even though they reportedly value Indian letters highly, regard the Indian's "secret Alphabet" as sacred and extremely ancient, and use it "to inscribe them on their idols" (trans. Blount 1693:84). However, Burnet lamented that much of the old glory of Asia was only found in secret teachings and ancient texts. Though "by Tradition from their Ancestours" there remain "some *Footsteps* of the most ancient Tenents" among Asia's "Modern *Pagans*," Burnet could not but "pitty the Eastern World" and lament that "the place which was the first habitation of wise men, and one day a most flourishing *Emporium* for Learning should for some ages past have been changed into a wretched Barbarity," leading him to pray to God that Europe "may not undergo the same Vicissitude" (pp. 85–86).

Essential facets of Burnet's notion of Oriental wisdom (*sapientia orientalis*) are the distinction of exoteric and esoteric knowledge and the use of a sacred language (in India: Sanskrit) for the latter; the progression from a golden age to degeneration and regeneration; emanation from oneness to multiplicity and the return of multiplicity to oneness; ancient revelation and its transmission; the notion of a world egg and cycles of creation and destruction of multiple worlds; and the idea of a world soul and of metempsychosis. In his view, the vestiges of this *sapientia orientalis* could serve as signposts for the reconstruction of antediluvial or early postdiluvial religion, an idea that reverberated in the writings of various eighteenth-century authors from John Toland and Andrew Ramsay to William Jones and Thomas Maurice.

Among the authors who amply quoted Burnet's *Philosophical Archaeology* were also Pierre Bayle and Johann Jakob Brucker, the two authors Diderot most heavily relied on when writing his articles on Asian religion in the first volumes of the *Encyclopédie*. Major features of Burnet's *sapientia orientalis*—the ideas of emanation, of a world soul, of transmigration, and of mystical annihilation and return to oneness—are all present in Diderot, who criticized some of them along the lines of intellectual heavyweights like Bayle and Johann Lorenz von Mosheim. Some critics tended, as we have observed, to emphasize the exclusive role of the Hebrews and to line up Asian religions on an axis of idolatry reaching from Egypt—which often was seen as the origin—via India to China and Japan. Others, by contrast, believed like Burnet that the Orient harbors genuine vestiges of primeval god-given wisdom and assumed a transmission of it not only to the Hebrews but also to other ancient people. This more inclusivist group included, as we have seen, many missionaries including Ricci, Bartholomäus Ziegenbalg, and the authors of the *Ezour-vedam* (see Chapter 7). Of course, they were, on another level, usually also exclusivists since they tended to believe in Christianity as the sole path to salvation. We will see in subsequent chapters that the idea of a "doctrina orientalis" or an "oriental system" played an important role in the genesis of modern Orientalism. These possible vestiges of humankind's oldest religion were deemed most important subjects of study, and such study necessitated the systematic study of ancient oriental languages and texts.

Diderot's Oriental Blend

As explained at the beginning of this chapter, Diderot's encyclopedia article on the "Bramines" (1751:2.393–94) portrays them as "priests of the god Fo" who "principally revere three things, the god Fo, his law, and the books containing their constitutions." His description of these priests combines characteristics of Fo's esoteric teaching (as reported by Japan and China missionaries) with facets of Indian religions, for example, the doctrines of emanation, cosmic illusion (*maya*), and ascetic quietism as described by Bernier. According to Diderot, the Brahmin priests of Fo "assert that the world is nothing but an illusion, a dream, a magic spell, and that the bodies, in order to be truly existent, have to cease existing in themselves, and to merge into nothingness, which due to its simplicity amounts to the perfection of all beings" (trans. Halbfass 1990:59–60). Thrown into the blender were also some lumps from missionary reports about Zen as well as the *Forty-Two Sections Sutra* (see next chapter), for example, the notion that "saintliness consists in willing nothing, thinking nothing, feeling nothing, and removing one's mind so far from any idea, even that of virtue, that the perfect quietude of the soul stays unaltered" (Diderot 1751:2.393).[11] Diderot's Brahmins pretend, as in Kircher, to have sprung from the head of the god Brahma, to possess "ancient books that they call *sacred*," and to have preserved the ancient language of these texts (p. 393). Diderot also associates these "Brahmin priests of Fo" with some of the doctrines that form the staple of descriptions of Indian religion since Henry Lord (1630) and Abraham Roger (1651). Under Diderot's label of *philosophie asiatique*, the readers of the *Encyclopédie* thus found a blend of "Asian" teachings and practices that were all associated with Brahmins who propagated the religion of Fo.

Such is the background of Diderot's famous "mixup." But what was the immediate source for his notion that the Brahmins are priests of Fo? It was Bayle's article on the Brachmanes that—apart from much information from Europe's classical sources (Bayle 1702:1.689–91)—furnishes the following information:

> The Brachmanes still subsist in the Orient. The third sect which is current among the Chinese can be called the Religion of the Brachmanes or Bramenes, and they give themselves this name. These are the priests who revere principally three things: the God Fo, his law, and the books containing his particular regulations. They have bizarre sentiments about nothingness and morals that show much conformity with the visions of our quietists. (p. 691)

Much of Diderot's "Oriental blend" philosophy was thus already present in Bayle's 1702 description of the Brachmanes who remained in India:

The report of Father Tachard shows that the Brachmanes or Bramines of Bengal lead a very austere life, walk barefoot and with uncovered head on the burning sand, and live from herbs alone. The Brachmanes of Hindostan have very ancient books that they call sacred and pretend that God gave to the great prophet Brahma. They preserve the language in which these books are written and make exclusive use of them in their theological and philosophical explanations. By such means they prevent the common people from knowing them. They believe in metempsychosis and eat no meat. They say that the production of the world consisted in that all things came out of God and that the universe will perish through the return of these things to their first origin. A spider serves as emblem to explain this opinion. (p. 692)

In turn, Bayle's description is reminiscent of one of his main sources, namely, Bernier's report of "the almost universal doctrine of the *Gentile Pendets* of the *Indies*" which is also "held by the sect of the *Soufys* and the greater part of the learned men of *Persia* at the present day" (Bernier 2005:346). However, based on information by Guy Tachard and Thomas Burnet, Bayle also located such Brachmanes or Brahmins in Thailand:

The Brachmanes of Siam believe that the first humans were taller than those of today and lived several centuries without any illness; that our earth will one day perish through fire; and that from its ashes another world will be born where there will be no sea and no vicissitudes of seasons but an eternal spring. (Bayle 1702:1.692)

At the beginning of the eighteenth century, the notion of an extremely large pan-Asiatic religion with exoteric and esoteric branches and with many local variations was apparently already well ensconced. But a religion with many millions of believers and with a huge clergy in India, China, and their surrounding countries obviously also had to have something like a bible. Bayle's Brahmins possess sacred scriptures in the ancient sacred language of India, Sanskrit, so it is a safe bet that by these scriptures Bayle meant the Vedas. These Vedas would therefore be the books containing the laws and particular regulations of Fo followed by the Brahmins of India, China, and other regions of Asia. For a European familiar with the transmission and translation history of the Bible, it would only be natural to assume that the Chinese Brahmin priests of Fo had translated the sacred scriptures of their religion into Chinese and would thus have Chinese translations of the Vedas. We will see in the next chapter that this is exactly what Joseph de Guignes proposed in the 1770s, and Chapter 7 will show an altogether surprising outgrowth of this same thought. But at the beginning of the eighteenth century, when Bayle wrote his article about the Brachmanes, so little was known about the Vedas and about China's Brahmin priests of Fo that such speculation was not yet possible.

Unlike Diderot, Bayle clearly identified his direct source of what modern scholars have called "the mixup": the *Histoire de l'edit de l'empereur de la Chine* (1698) by Charles LE GOBIEN (1671–1708).[12] Its unpaginated preface presents a brief description of the four "sects" of China: (1) ancient monotheism; (2) Neo-Confucianism; (3) "the religion of the *Brachmanes* or *Bramenes*"; and (4) "the religion of the Bonzes" (Daoism). What interests us here is China's third religion. Le Gobien's description of it begins in a way that should by now sound familiar:

> The third religion current among the Chinese is the religion of the *Brachmanes* or *Bramenes*, and they give it themselves this name. Because *Polomen*, [the word] they use, is the *Bramen* of the Indians that they could not pronounce and that they apparently travestied in their language. Nevertheless, they ordinarily call these false priests *Hochan* [Ch. *heshang*, Reverend], which signifies people united from various countries. These priests revere principally three things: the God Fo, his law, and the books containing their particular regulations. (Le Gobien 1698; unpaginated preface)

Le Gobien thus unequivocally identifies the Brahmans—or *Polomen*, as the Chinese call them—as priests of Fo and uses the very terms later adopted by his readers Bayle and Diderot.[13] Le Gobien reports that the enemies of these *Polomen*, the Neoconfucian philosophers of China, are particularly indignant that "these *Bramenes* maintain that the world is only an illusion, a dream, a semblance." In order truly to exist, they assert, one must cease to be oneself and "confound oneself with nothingness which by virtue of its simplicity represents the perfection of all Beings." Their morality is described as "even more outrageous than that of our Stoics":

> They push this apathy or indifference, to which they attribute all their sanctitude, so far that one must turn to stone or become a statue to

acquire perfection. Not only do they teach that the sage must not have any passion, but he may not even have any desire. Thus he must continually apply himself to will nothing, think of nothing, feel nothing, and to banish any idea of virtue and holiness so thoroughly from his mind that nothing in him is contrary to perfect quietude of the soul. (unpaginated preface)

Once this state is reached, so these Brahmin priests of Fo teach, one is no more subject to change and metempsychosis: "For him there is no more transmigration, no more vicissitude, no more fear of the future, because he is in the proper sense nothing; or, if one wants that he still is something, he is sage, perfect, happy—in a word, he is God and perfectly similar to the God *Fo*: which definitely is a bit crazy" (unpaginated preface).

In his article on "Asiatic philosophy," Diderot connected the teachings of the "Persian Sufis whom he [Bernier] names *cabalistes*," with those of "the Pendets, heathen of the Indies" and "the doctrine of Xekia." The latter's esoteric teaching of "the origin of things through emanations from a first cause," in turn, is said to have influenced Jewish kabbalists and their idea of "*En-soph* or the first infinite being which contains all things" and "distributes itself through emanation" (Diderot 1751:1.752–54).

Whether it was conceived as a vestige of ancient monotheism or a poisonous seed of paganism, around the beginning of the eighteenth century the idea of a pan-Asian doctrine linked to the founder figure Fo or Xaca had taken root in Europe. Sieur de la Créquinière's argument about Fo's profound influence even in the West is an early symptom of a reversal of traditional eurocentric scenarios: he explained in his *Agreement of the Customs of the East-Indians with those of the Jews* (1704),

'Tis pretended, that the *Cabala* has taken a great part of its Follies from the Philosophy of *Phoe*, which we mention'd in the Article of *Metempsychosis*: And in this confus'd Heap of *Rabbinism* and *Magick*, something is discover'd, that comes near to the Doctrine of the Learned *Chinese*, concerning Heaven and the Etherial Matter, into which *Phoe* said that the Souls were resolv'd, after their separation from the Body: For if this Philosopher believ'd, that our Souls are dispers'd in the Air, of which according to him they are Part, the *Cabalists* had no less strange *Idea*'s about the Matter of which the Heaven is fram'd; they believe this Matter to be animated, and pretend that the Queen of Heaven, *Regina Coeli*,

mention'd in *Jerem.* C. 44. is the Soul of this Material Heaven which
appears to our Eyes. 'Tis thought also, that the *Cabala* deriv'd many
things from *Plato*'s Philosophy, which is deduc'd from that of *Phoe.*
(Créquinière 1999:102–3)

Here Pythagoras is no more the teacher who introduces his Indian students to the idea of transmigration. Rather, the reader is bound to imagine
Pythagoras sitting at the feet of the Brahmin priests of Fo in India before
returning to Greece and imparting such wisdom to his fellow Greek philosophers. Créquinière, a traveler who had sojourned in India, in effect suggests
that Fo's religion not only conquered most of Asia but also infected some
movements in Judaism and Greek philosophy, thus turning even the divine
Plato, whose philosophy was blossoming anew among the Cambridge Plato-
nists, into a follower of Fo. This was just one of the early signs of a trend to
locate the origins of human culture and religion in India. It is exactly this
trend—boosted by the likes of Voltaire, Abbé Vincent Mignot, John Zephaniah Holwell, and Louis-Mathieu Langlès—that formed the soil for the "indomania" of the second half of the eighteenth and early nineteenth century.

Toland's Twofold Philosophy

Frank Manuel's chapter on the English deists' "two-fold philosophy" in his
thought-provoking study *The Eighteenth Century Confronts the Gods* (1959:65–
69) shows little awareness of the influence of missionary literature from Asia
but correctly describes the popularity of this idea:

> In one form or another the double-truth doctrine was entertained by
> episcopal worthies like Warburton, avowed pantheists like Toland, cau-
> tious philosophical sceptics like Hume, grand Deist lords like Boling-
> broke, abbés like Le Batteux, scholarly authors who specialized in the
> mystery cults like Sainte-Croix, that most outrageous materialist Dr. La
> Mettrie, the most popular orthodox scientific writer, Abbé Pluche, the
> revolutionary atheist Charles Dupuis. Wherever a sounding is made one
> comes upon the idea that there were always two pagan religions: gross
> polytheism, with human sacrifices, brute-worship, even cabbage-wor-
> ship, for the masses; secret monotheism, a religion of virtue, love, adora-
> tion of the First Cause, for an elite. (pp. 65–66)

Yet the material presented so far in this book indicates that the European discovery of Asian religions, and in particular the deeply intertwined discoveries of Hinduism and Buddhism, played a major role in the exploding popularity of such views. The earliest nonclassical source for this double-truth doctrine adduced by Frank Manuel is the Cambridge Platonist Ralph Cudworth who "in 1678 already described the simultaneous existence among the Egyptians, the Persians, and the Indians of a 'Vulgar and Fabulous Theory and an Arcane and Recondite Theology'"—a doctrine out of which "Toland made a program of action" (p. 67). But we have seen that Valignano's *Catechismus christianae fidei* of 1586 had already presented both the theory and a program of action; and one might argue that Renaissance writers like Marsilio Ficino and Giordano Bruno (who touted hermetic texts of "Egyptian" pedigree) had analogous agendas. Yet this does not diminish the validity of Manuel's point that what he calls "the twofold philosophy" or "the double-truth doctrine" played a central role in the deist movement and the eighteenth-century European perception of religion in general. In particular, Manuel highlighted the importance of John TOLAND (1670–1722), "a magnificent stylist whose pungent writings in Latin and translations from the English dominated the continental debate for more than a century" and who influenced such eighteenth-century luminaries as Voltaire and David Hume (p. 66). It is probably no mere coincidence that Toland's first extensive discussion of this theme occurs in his *Letters to Serena* (1704), a book that appeared while he was working on the English translation of La Créquinière's 1704 work. Toland did not subscribe to Créquinière's idea of Fo's role and the Indian origin of the notion of an immortal soul that led to the conception of transmigration. Rather, he advocated an Egypt-based scenario:

> Thus have I shown you, Madam, how this Opinion of the Souls Immortality, and the Consequences of the same, was introduc'd from the Egyptians among the Grecians, spread by the latter in their Colonys in Asia and Europe, and deliver'd to the Romans, who from the Greeks had their Religion and Laws. I mark'd the Progress of it among the Scythians, Germans, Gauls, and Britains. I have likewise prov'd how from Egypt, the Place of its Birth, it travel'd to the Chaldaeans and Indians, and from them over all the Eastern Parts of the World. (Toland 1704:52–53)

Toland's description of heathen legislators—who "did not believe it themselves" while teaching to common people that the wicked would be punished in the other life and the good rewarded—has a close match in ideas about Fo from the sixteenth, seventeenth, and eighteenth centuries. Indeed, Toland's description of Pythagoras's double teachings is eerily reminiscent of the Buddha's deathbed "confession":

> Pythagoras himself did not believe the Transmigration which has made him so famous to Posterity; for in the internal or secret Doctrin he meant no more than the eternal Revolution of Forms in Matter, those ceaseless Vicissitudes and Alterations, which turn every thing into all things, and all things into any thing, as Vegetables and Animals become part of us, we become part of them, and both become parts of a thousand other things in the Universe, earth turning into Water, Water into Air, Air into Aether, and so back again in Mixtures without End or Number. But in the external or popular Doctrin he impos'd on the Mob by an equivocal Expression, that *they shou'd become various kinds of Beasts after Death*, thereby to deter 'em the more effectually from Wickedness. (p. 57)

However, for Toland the origin of such doctrines still lay in Egypt rather than India. He proclaimed that he could "with very small pains . . . manifestly prove that in Egypt *Men had first, long before others, arriv'd at the various beginnings of Religions*" (p. 70) and outlined a genealogy of religion that proceeded from the roots of Egyptian superstition in the worship of the dead (p. 72) to the institution of priestcraft (p. 101), the invention of hell (p. 105), the cult of saints (p. 123), and various other customs that show "how almost in every corner of the world Religion and Truth cou'd be chang'd into Superstition and Priestcraft" (p. 129). The gist of Toland's deist genealogy of religion is, as he put it, "elegantly comprehended in those four Lines which are in everybody's mouth" (pp. 129–30):

> Natural Religion was easy first and plain,
> Tales made it Mystery, Offrings made it Gain;
> Sacrifices and Shows were at length prepar'd,
> The Priests ate Roast-meat, and the People star'd.

Kaempfer's Oriental Paganism

In the light of such Egypt-based or Egypt-related genealogies of religion, it is hardly surprising that the founder of Asian idolatry and propagator of transmigration and the twofold doctrine should eventually get a genuinely Egyptian pedigree. Athanasius Kircher's idea of an axis of idolatry linking Egyptian origins to a pan-Asiatic religion propagated by the India-based Xaka or Shaka (Shakyamuni Buddha) was particularly potent. Fifty years after Kircher and in spite of much more accurate conjectures about the religion of the followers of Buddha, Mathurin Veyssière de La Croze also had ideas about the Egyptian origin of this religion that resemble Kircher's. The same is true for another reader of Kircher who became one of Diderot's main sources, the German Engelbert KAEMPFER (1651–1716) who died eight years before La Croze's book was published. After his departure from Sweden in 1681 at age 30, the well-educated Kaempfer had honed his skills as an observer of Asian countries and cultures during stays of more than four years in Persia, six months in southwest India (1688), a year in Indonesia (1689–90), and one month in Siam (1690). In Siam, Kaempfer had the unique chance of observing Thai Buddhism immediately before embarking for Japan. Though his sojourn in Japan lasted only two years (September 1690 to October 1692) and was mostly spent confined to a trading post on the Dejima island off Nagasaki, Kaempfer was very successful in collecting information about the secluded country. Much of his extraordinarily detailed (and more often than not surprisingly accurate) information about Japan's religion and history stemmed from a very knowledgeable Japanese servant and interpreter, Imamura Gen'emon Eisei (Katagiri 1995, Van der Velde 1995). The role of Asian informants in Europe's budding Orientalism was absolutely crucial, and Imamura is only one figure in a long line of knowledgeable natives that include Ziegenbalg's Aleppa, Étienne Fourmont's Huang, and Prince Dara's/Bernier's Indian pandit. Imamura and some other Japanese collaborators supplied Kaempfer not only with oral information but also with a number of Japanese books; and since he knew little Japanese, he had them translate relevant portions into Dutch. Kaempfer's extant notebooks in the British Library show that translations and transliterations from Japanese sources were made with the utmost care and formed a solid basis for his redactions between his return to Europe in 1693 at age 42 and his death in 1716 at age 65.

   In 1694 Kaempfer submitted a dissertation at Leiden University and was awarded a doctorate, and in 1712 he published a long-awaited, richly illustrated 900-page work called *Amoenitates Exoticae*. In its preface he also mentions a finished manuscript about Japan, but after his death in 1716, that manuscript lay unpublished among his belongings. After its sale to the learned collector Hans Sloane in London, it was translated into English by a young Swiss doctor of philosophy, Johann Caspar Scheuchzer. Scheuchzer's qualifications, apart from his mastery of English, consisted in a famous naturalist father and a dissertation about, of all things, the biblical deluge. But he was a quick study, and his beautifully illustrated English translation of Kaempfer's Japan manuscript was published in 1727.[14] For half a century, all subsequent translations into other languages (including French and German) were based on this English version rather than Kaempfer's German manuscripts.[15] On the European continent the French version of 1729 was particularly influential; it not only deeply marked Diderot and his fellow encyclopedists but also Voltaire, Kant, Herder, and many other luminaries of the age of Enlightenment.

A thorough evaluation of Kaempfer's knowledge about Asian religions and his influence on European perceptions would necessitate a detailed comparison of the extant manuscript of his Japan work (British Library, Sloane 3060)[16] with various translations and editions and especially also with his notes and his Japanese textual sources (Imai 1982). This would be a worthy subject for a monograph. Here the focus will be on Kaempfer's impact on Diderot, an attentive reader of the French version of 1729. Kaempfer's opening chapter was of particular importance. Right at the beginning of his book, the doctor takes his description of Siamese religion as an occasion to present his views about the origin and character of "Oriental paganism" ("Orientalisches Heÿdenthumb"). In Scheuchzer's translation, however, Kaempfer's introductory chapter is preceded by an account from Kaempfer's diary of the journey from Batavia to Siam. Kaempfer's first translator thus took the liberty of creating a first chapter from extraneous materials and relegating Kaempfer's opening chapter, edited and with some added material,[17] to secondary status. Scheuchzer's habit of "improving" Kaempfer has made him the target of severe critique. The new English translation of Kaempfer's Japan book by the best informed of these critics, Beatrice Bodart-Bailey (1999), is generally more reliable than Scheuchzer's. But it introduced a new kind of tampering with Kaempfer's text that may be even more detrimental to the understanding of his view of Asian religions. Claiming that Kaempfer did not plan to include the opening chapter with his description of Siam in the Japan book and that this was Scheuchzer's idea (p. 34), Bodart-Bailey translated only a few lines. But there is no way around the fact that Kaempfer's extant manuscript at the British Library opens with the chapter on Siam (fols. 27r–45v) in which the author not only describes Thai Buddhism but also presents an overall vision of Asian religions that furnishes the context for his portrayal of

Japanese religions. Kaempfer's interest in origins and in the history of religions is also apparent in the first book's fifth chapter ("On the origin of the inhabitants") that includes the doctor's reflections on the origin of Japan's religions. Interestingly, that chapter was also considered unfit for translation by Bodart-Bailey who only rendered Kaempfer's tantalizing summary:

> Summarizing, we may say that in the first age of plurality after the Babylonian discord of minds and languages, at a time when the Greeks, Goths, Slaves, and Celts left for Europe, when others scattered and spread in Asia, while still others even entered America, the Japanese set out on their journey. Perhaps wandering for many years and suffering great deprivation, they finally reached this furthest corner of the earth. Therefore, according to their roots and earliest beginnings, the Japanese must be regarded as an independent nation, owing nothing to the Chinese with respect to their origins. Even though they adopted their code of conduct, liberal arts, and learning—as the Latin people did from the Greek—they never accepted a conqueror or hegemon from China or any other nation in the world. (Bodart-Bailey 1999:50)

Kaempfer's interesting argument that the Japanese do not stem from the Chinese and came directly from Babylon rests on two main pillars: language and religion. According to Kaempfer, language is "without dispute the most certain indicator of the origin of peoples" (British Library, Sloane 3060:74r–v); but religion comes as a close second. Due to Bodart-Bailey's misguided censorship, readers of English are even today forced to refer to Scheuchzer's translation of this chapter, which contains the following explanation about Japanese Shinto and Buddhism ("Bupo"):

> The old, and probably, original Religion of the Japanese, which is by them call'd Sintos,[18] and the Gods and Idols, worship'd by its adherents, Sin, and Came,[19] is peculiar only to this Empire, nor hath it ever been admitted of, nor their Gods acknowledged and worship'd, nor the religious way of life of the Japanese followed by the Chinese, or indeed any other heathen Nation. It was the only one establish'd in Japan during a succession of many ages. For the foreign pagan doctrine of Siaka, which the Japanese now call Bupo, or Budsdo,[20] and the Gods which it commands to worship, Buds and Fotoge,[21] tho' ever since its early beginnings it met with uncommon success, and speedily spread over the best part of

Asia, yet it was not introduc'd into Japan till sixty years after our Saviour's nativity under the reign of the Emperor Synnin, when it was brought over from Corea. (Kaempfer 1906:1.137)[22]

Leaving aside Kaempfer's confusion of Buddhism's legendary introduction to China around 60 C.E. (as described in the preface of the *Forty-Two Sections Sutra*) with its arrival in Japan, we note that Kaempfer contrasts Shinto, the "old, and probably, original Religion of the Japanese," with the "foreign pagan doctrine of Siaka," that is, Buddhism. Based on biblical authority, Kaempfer surmised that Shinto must be rooted in ancient Babylonian religion:

> If then our Japanese Colony did reach that part of the World, which Divine providence assign'd for their future abode, as soon as the Chinese, Tunquinese, and other neighbouring Nations did theirs, it must be suppos'd that they fortunately fell in with such a road, as could with safety and speed bring them to the Eastern extremities of Asia, from whence there is but a short passage over to Japan. In order therefore to trace out what road it is probable they took, we must consider the first Babylonians in the condition, they were in, after that dreadful confusion of Languages. (p. 139)

Kaempfer's opening chapter thus traces not only his own path to Japan but also that of the entire Japanese people and its religions. While warning that these were "conjectures, for as such only I deliver them" (p. 146), Kaempfer opted for an itinerary of the ancient Japanese from Mesopotamia through eastern Tartary and the Country of Jeso (which supposedly linked northern Japan's isles to the continent and possibly even to America).

At any rate, Kaempfer traced the Japanese people and their language straight to the biblical Babylon:

> The difficulty now remaining to be clear'd up, is, how, and from what parts of the world, to trace out their true original descent. In order to do this we must go up higher, and perhaps it is not inconsistent with reason, and the nature of things, to assert, that they are descended of the first Inhabitants of Babylon, and that the Japanese language is one of those, which Sacred Writs mention, that the all-wise Providence hath thought fit, by way of punishment and confusion, to infuse into the minds of the

vain builders of the Babylonian Tower. This at least seems to me the most probable conjecture, whatever way they went to Japan, or whatever time they spent upon this their first peregrination. (p. 138)

Japan's ancient Shinto religion was also given a Babylonian pedigree. Like the ancient Persians and other neighboring nations, the Chaldean denizens of the region around Babylon worshiped "the Luminaries of the Heavens, particularly the Sun, and the Fire, as being its Image" (p. 66).

> For as it cannot be suppos'd, that these sensible Nations liv'd without any Religion at all, like the brutal Hottentots, it is highly probable, that they rever'd the divine Omnipotence by worshiping, according to the Custom of the Chaldeans, the Sun, and other Luminaries of the Firmament, as such parts of the Creation, which most strike the outward senses, and fill the understanding with the admiration of their unconceivable proprieties. (p. 66)

Kaempfer also deemed it "probable" that the ancient Indians "had the same kind of worship with the neighbouring Chaldeans and Persians" (p. 66). If much of ancient Asia between Mesopotamia, India, and Japan "rever'd the divine Omnipotence" through sidereal worship and a symbolic fire cult, one must assume that Kaempfer thought it once was (at least to some degree) the home of a monotheist religion. However, about six centuries before Christ's birth another religion with roots in ancient Egypt began to sweep the continent. First India and then large parts of Asia including Tartary, Tibet, Burma, Siam, Laos, Cambodia, Vietnam, China, Korea, and Japan were invaded by this religion that Kaempfer calls "general paganism" (p. 63) or "Eastern Paganism" (p. 66). It "is to be distinguished" from the sun and fire worship of Chaldaea which has a semblance of monotheism" (p. 63) and has "two articles . . . which were most religiously maintained": "the Transmigration of Souls, and a Veneration for Cows, particularly for the holy Cow at Memphis, call'd Apis, or Serapis, which had divine honours paid her, and was serv'd by Priests" (p. 67):

> Both these Articles are still observed by the Asiatick Heathens, particularly those that inhabit the West-side of the Ganges; for no body there dares to kill the least and most noxious Insects, as being animated by some transmigrated human Soul; and the Cows, whose Souls they think

are by frequent transmigrations, as it were, deified, are serv'd and attended with great veneration, their Dung being burnt to ashes is turn'd
into holy Salve, their Urine serves for holy Water, the Image of a Cow
possesses a peculiar Chapel before their Temples, is every day honour'd
with fresh flowers, and hath sweet-scented oyl poured upon her. (p. 67)

Since Kaempfer had spent half a year in southwest India, he was familiar
with such customs and had also observed the veneration of human monsters
(such as Ganesha with his elephant head). But how had such "Egyptian"
forms of worship reached far-away India? As a careful reader of Athanasius
Kircher, Kaempfer was thoroughly familiar with the notion of a pagan axis
stretching from Egypt to Japan and also knew that Kircher's main culprit was
a man called Xaca. Furthermore, he had read in Kircher's *China illustrata*
(1667) that some Egyptian gods are worshipped all over Asia and that such
cults were brought to India after the invasion of Egypt by Cambyses:

> The statues of the gods were pounded into dust. The great obelisks were
> overthrown. Apis, the greatest Egyptian god, a sacred bull who was cared
> for in a certain enclosure, was killed by Cambyses himself. The whole
> crowd of priests and hieromants was cut to pieces or destroyed in the
> same fire that ruined their hieroglyphic monuments, or they were driven
> into exile. Since the land routes were filled with bands of the enemy who
> would not allow them safe passage, they finally made their way along the
> Arabian Gulf, which borders on Egypt, and so reached India, today
> called Hindustan. (Kircher 1987:141)

This is how "the doctrine of metempsychosis, or the transmigration of
souls from animal to animal, was first spread to the world by the Egyptians"
(p. 141). According to Kircher, the Egyptian priests and hieromants found in
their Indian exile "a very sinful Brahmin" who "was not content just to
spread the doctrine but even added to it so much that there is scarcely any
one who is able to describe the doctrine or to write about it." Kircher had
identified this person as the "imposter known all over the East" and explained that "the Indians called him Rama, the Chinese Xe Kian, the Japanese Xaca, and the Turks Chiaga" (p. 141). He reportedly had as many as
80,000 disciples who spread his noxious teachings all over Asia.

Thus prepared, Kaempfer saw during his sojourn in Siam many statues
of the founder of this huge religion. Noting his usual sitting posture with

crossed legs and particular positions of his hands, he had no doubt that this man—whom the Siamese call *Prah* (saint), *Prahpuditsau* (saint of high descent), *Sammana Khutama* (the Man without Passions), *Budha, Putha,* etc.—is identical with the divinity venerated in other parts of Asia under various names: *Budhum* in Ceylon; *Sacca,* or *Siaka, Fotoge,* or *Si Tsun* in Japan and China; and so on (p. 64). However, discrepancies regarding the period in which this founder lived led Kaempfer to conjecture that there must have been two such founder figures. The older figure, whom the Indians regard as an incarnation of the god Vishnu, was called Budhum or Budhá. Probably a mythological figure, as the dates of 100,000 or 20,000 years B.C.E. indicate, he is represented as a man with four arms sitting on a Tarate flower and "praising the supreme God ever since 21,639 years (reckoning from the present 1690 year of Christ)" (p. 65). The younger figure, on the other hand, is the "God *Prah,* or *Siaka,*" described in "whole Books full of the birth, life, and miracles" (p. 65).

Kaempfer explains how he came up with his innovative two-Buddha theory:

> I am at a loss how to reconcile these various and opposite accounts, which I have gather'd in the abovesaid Countries, unless by supposing, what I really think to be the true opinion, viz. that the Siamites and other Nations lying more Easterly have confounded a younger Teacher with Budhá and mistaken the former with the latter, which confusion of the Gods and their names is very frequent in the Histories of the Greeks and Egyptians; so that Prah or Siaka, is not the same with Budha, much less with Ram, or Rama, as he is call'd by Father Kircher in his Sina Illustra, the latter having appear'd many hundred thousand years before, but that he was some new Impostor who set up about five hundred years before Christ's nativity. (pp. 65–66)

Subsequent "two-Buddha" theories such as the one proposed by Agostino Giorgi in 1762 (App 2008a:18–20) also had the aim of reconciling discrepancies of dating and descriptions of the founder figure. Building on the erudite fantasies of Kircher and noting that the Thai date of the Buddha's birth matches exactly that of Cambyses's invasion of Egypt, Kaempfer transformed Kircher's sinful Brahmin Xaca into a curly-haired Memphis priest of the sixth century B.C.E. Fascinated by the dark color, curly hair, and "Egyptian" lotus base of the founder's statues, Kaempfer favored—against all Asian evidence pointing to Ceylon, India, or Siam—an African origin of the "younger" Buddha. If Giorgi's two Buddhas went on to confuse such eminent men as the Orientalist William Jones, the geographer Carl Ritter, and the philosopher G. W. F. Hegel, Kaempfer's pioneer version also had a brilliant career as it found its way into many publications[23] including the *Encyclopédie*.

Seduced by Kaempfer's "Egyptian" theory, Diderot summarized in his article on the philosophy of the Asiatics the four main points of Kaempfer's argument as follows:

1. The religion which the inhabitants of the Indies received from this legislator is very much connected with that of the ancient Egyptians because all these peoples represented their gods in the form of animals and monstrous humans.

2. The two principal dogmas of Egyptian religion were the transmigration of souls and the cult of Serapis whom they represented in the form of a bull or a cow. Now it is certain that these two dogmas also form the basis of the religion of the Asian nations. . . . What is remarkable is that the closer these barbarian nations are located to Egypt, the more they are attached to these two dogmas.

3. One finds with all these peoples of East Asia the majority of Egyptian divinities, though under different names.

4. What confirms Kaempfer's conjecture above all is that 536 years B.C. Cambyses the king of Persia invaded Egypt, killed Apis . . . and chased all the priests from the land. Now if one examines the chronology of the Siamese which begins with the death of Xekia, one sees that it coincides precisely with the time of Cambyses's expedition, which makes it very probable that Xekia got refuge with the Indians and taught them his Egyptian doctrine. (Diderot 1751:1.755)

Diderot was so utterly convinced by Kaempfer's arguments that he concluded that "there is no room whatsoever to doubt that Xekia was African and that he taught the Indians the dogmas he himself had drawn from Egypt" (p. 755). For Diderot as for Kircher and Kaempfer, the figure of Xaca/Xekia/Buddha thus became the very incarnation of Egyptian origins, complete with "frizzy hair like a negro" (Kaempfer 1729:33). In their view, the journey of this Memphis priest to India in the sixth century B.C.E. had a fatal effect on the religious landscape of Asia. Apart from introducing the ancient Indians (who originally worshiped God in the symbolic form of sun and stars) to the veneration of animals and the belief in transmigration, his fame led to the fatal mixup of the younger "Egyptian" Shaka with the older "Indian" Budha. It was this mixup that fueled the explosive growth of the religion that Kaempfer called "Oriental paganism"—the religion of Buddha. This religion took many different forms as it spread from its Indian base to other countries. Its clergy achieved dominance in large swaths of Asia: the Brahmans in India, the talapoins in Burma and Thailand, the lamas in Tartary, the bonzes in China and Japan, and so forth (Figure 7). Against this background, the first sentence of Kaempfer's description of Siamese religion and Asia's "general paganism" appears in a new light—as do Diderot's Brahmin priests of Fo:

> The Religion of these [Siamese] People is the Pagan Doctrine of the Brahmans, which ever since many Centuries hath been profess'd amongst all Nations from the River Indus to the extremity of the East, except that at the Court of the Grand Mogul, and in his great Cities, as also in Sumatra, Java, Celebes, and other neighboring Islands the Mahometism has gain'd so much ground, that it seems to prevail above it. This general Paganism (which is to be distinguished from the Religion of the old Persians worshipping the Sun, now almost extinct) tho' branch'd out into several Sects and Opinions, according to the various Customs, Languages and Interpretations, yet is of one and the same Origine. The Siamites represent the first Teacher of their Paganism in their Temples, in the figure of a Negro sitting, of a prodigious size, his hair curl'd, the skin black, but as it were out of respect gilt over, accompanied on each side by one of his chief Companions, as also before and round about him by the rest of his Apostles and Disciples, all of the same colour and most in the same posture. They believe according to the Brahmans, that the Deity dwelt in him, which he prov'd by his Doctrine, Way of Life, and Revelation. (Kaempfer 1906.1:62–63).

This conception of "Oriental paganism"—or, as we would call it today, "Buddhism"—laid out by Kaempfer in his opening chapter is thus crucial for an understanding of his view of Asian religions including those of Japan. Through his introductory reflections about the pan-Asiatic religion of Budha/ Siaka, he laid the groundwork for the understanding of Japan's "Budsdo, or Foreign Pagan Worship" in his Chapter 6:

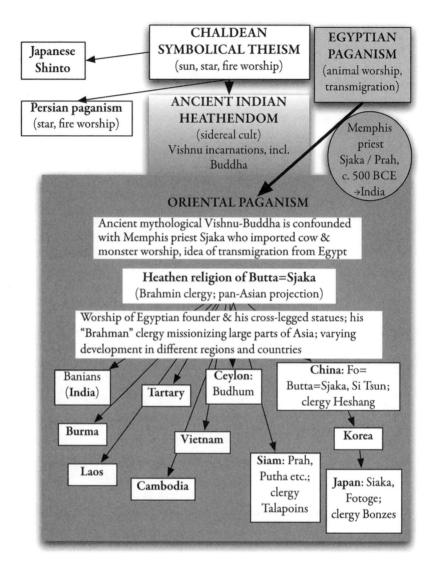

Figure 7. Engelbert Kaempfer's view of Asian religions (Urs App).

The origine of this religion, which quickly spread thro' most Asiatick Countries to the very extremities of the East, (not unlike the Indian Fig-tree, which propagates itself, and spreads far round, by sending down new roots from the extremities of its branches,) must be look'd for among the Brahmines. I have strong reasons to believe, both from the affinity of the name, and the very nature of this religion, that its author and founder is the very same person, whom the Brahmines call Budha, and believe to be an essential part of Wisthnu, or their Deity, who made its ninth appearance in the world under this name, and in the shape of this Man. The Chinese and Japanese call him Buds and Siaka. These two names indeed became in success of time a common Epithet of all Gods and Idols in general, the worship of whom was brought over from other Countries: sometimes also they were given to the Saints and great men, who preach'd them new doctrines. The common people in Siam, call him Prah Pudi Dsai, that is, the Holy Lord, and the learned among them, in their Pali or holy language, Sammona Khodum. The Peguans call him Sammana Khutama. (Kaempfer 1906:2.56–57)

Diderot's Pan-Asiatic Philosophy

Diderot made especially heavy use of Kaempfer's sixth chapter "On Budsdo or the foreign paganism and its founder in general." In its French translation, Diderot read that Budsdo "in its literal sense signifies the *way of the foreign idols*, i.e., *the manner to render a cult to the foreign idols*" (Kaempfer 1729:1.208). We have seen above that Diderot's presentation of the esoteric doctrine of the pan-Asiatic religion of "Budda or Xekia" was mainly based on sources stemming from sixteenth- and seventeenth-century Jesuit literature as presented by Bayle and Brucker. For the exoteric doctrine of the Brahmin priests of Fo, by contrast, he almost exclusively relied on Kaempfer's description of the Japanese "Budsdo" (Diderot 1751:1.753).

Some of Kaempfer's detailed information about this religion was based on Japanese books and chronicles such as the *Dai nihon ōdaiki*.[24] But Kaempfer also relied on reports of Japanese informers, personal observation, and the study of European sources after his return to Europe. An example is his biography of Buddhism's founder in which "Safen" (Jap. *zazen*, seated meditation) and "Satori" (Jap. *satori*, enlightenment) are mentioned. Kaempfer's description of the founder's teaching does not even mention the widely publicized legend of the founder's deathbed confession and the distinction between exoteric and esoteric teachings. Instead he related the Buddha's life as the Japanese knew it and drew a colorful portrait of the beliefs of popular Japanese Buddhism. His report about the Buddha's exoteric teachings was boiled down to fourteen points by Brucker, and as in the case of the esoteric teachings, Diderot translated Brucker's Latin synthesis of Kaempfer's explanations into French.[25]

Since no mention was made by Kaempfer of the famous "nothingness" from which everything comes and to which everything returns, Diderot assumed like Brucker that the Budsdo described by Kaempfer corresponds to the "exoteric" teaching of Budda or Xekia, the man who in the Indies "is regarded as the greatest philosopher ever" (Diderot 1751:1.753). Such teachings for the common people (pp. 753–74) begin with the notion that (1) there is a real difference between good and evil and that (2) the souls of men and animals are immortal. Once these souls are separated from their bodies after death, they (3) are rewarded or punished according to their actions. The place of rewards (4) is called "gokurakf" (Jap. *gokuraku*, paradise), and the rewards are proportional to the accumulated merits during one's lifetime (5). The governor of this place of delights is Amida, "the sole mediator who can obtain for men remission of sins and eternal life" (6).[26] Amida gives happiness to those who followed the law of Xekia (7). This law has five precepts that are "very famous in all of South and East Asia" (pp. 753–74): no taking of life, no theft, no incest, no lies, and no intoxication (8). The place of torment, on the other hand, is called "dsigokf" (Jap. *jigoku*, hell) where punishment is meted out according to the amount and kind of the evil deeds one committed (9). The governor and judge of these horrible prisons (10) is "Jemma O" (Jap. Emma ō, King Yama). Those who are tormented in hell can be helped by the prayers of the living and by sacrifices of the clergy addressed to Amida (11) who can to some degree diminish punishments and speed up the transmigration of souls into other bodies (12). Depending on the former deeds, souls can also transmigrate into animal bodies (13), and in the process of purification, they may eventually animate another human body and either grasp the chance of gaining eternal joy in paradise or undergo another cycle of punishment and transmigration (14).

In this light, Diderot's "mixup" of Brahmanism and Buddhism must be reevaluated. His portrait of the "Brahmin priests of Fo" represents an important phase in the European discovery of Buddhism in which some major features of this pan-Asiatic religion gradually emerged. They include information about its founder, his different datings in Southeast Asian and Sino-Japanese Buddhist traditions, clergy in various countries and their practices, some popular beliefs, and bits and pieces of Buddhist texts and philosophy (for example, the "emptiness" of Mahayana thought and the "no-thought" of Zen). Though the name of this religion was by no means fixed, Kaempfer's

"Budsdo" (or "Budso" in the French translation of 1729) soon became a convenient label. In Pierre-François-Xavier de Charlevoix's *History and General Description of Japan* (1736), the term "Budsoïstes" is already frequently used to refer to the adherents of this religion, for example, in the description of the "great pilgrimage of the Budsoïstes" (p. 119) or in the statement that the language of the prayers of this religion "seems older than the introduction of Budso in the empire but was adopted by the Budsoist ministers" (pp. 123–24). The enormous difference between the portrait of this religion in Charlevoix's *History of Christianity in the Empire of Japan* (1715)—written before the publication of the works of La Croze (1724) and Kaempfer (1727)—and his *History* of 1736 shows the great and immediate impact of these two works and the importance of La Croze and Kaempfer for the construction of its identity in the European mind.

Based on Ziegenbalg's data, La Croze had correctly concluded that the religion of the "disciples of Budda" that reigned in vast stretches of Asia was different from that of the "Brachmanes" and had vanished long ago from India. In this respect La Croze was far ahead of his time. The vast majority of other authors—for instance, Rodrigues, Kircher, Kaempfer, Charlevoix, and Diderot—were under the impression that the Buddha's religion was still dominant in India and that its clergy, the Brahmins, had from their Indian base missionized large parts of Asia. From their perspective, India's Brahmins were—regardless of their ultimate origin—simply the oldest representatives of a pan-Asiatic religion that in each region had taken on vastly different local coloring. Europeans had no trouble understanding what a difference even a few hundred leagues and a different language can make, and to them it was only natural that an extremely old religion would undergo fundamental changes over such vast time spans and geographical as well as cultural and linguistic chasms.

The described Western discovery of what we call "Buddhism" forms part of a long and complicated process that stretches into our time, and the assertion of some modern writers that European Orientalists "created" or "invented" Buddhism in the first half of the nineteenth century[27] is a problem of faulty optics rather than history. The case of Diderot shows once more that the retroprojection of modern knowledge (such as the strict separation of Buddhism from Hinduism) not only is unhelpful for the reconstruction of discovery processes but almost inevitably leads to the kind of "monkey show" treatment mentioned at the outset of this chapter. Diderot was only one of many eighteenth-century luminaries who regarded "Brahmanism" as a form of "oriental paganism" that has many elements congruent with what we today call "Buddhism." Diderot's view presents a snapshot of an important stage in the discovery process.

Of course, some of its aspects, for example, the speculation about Egyptian origins, seem misguided or even ridiculous from today's viewpoint. But in the historical context, this link made a lot of sense; and for us today the Buddha's multifaceted career in the West is, among other things, a looking glass into Europe's evolving worldview and the changing vision of its origins and identity at the intersection where biblical judaeomania and Enlightenment egyptomania met growing indomania. It also shows how many different observations, motivations, and ideas underlie a simple sentence such as Diderot's opening phrase of the "Brahmins" article. The same applies to the twofold doctrine that by the mid-eighteenth century had become the most prominent characteristic of a perceived pan-Asian religion. This rich religious and ideological background is also bound to remain invisible when looking through the coarse lens of preconceived ideas such as Edward Said's Orientalist "colonialism" or Western "exploitation."

In 1787, almost forty years after Diderot's early *Encyclopédie* articles, the German grandfather of Indomania, Johann Gottfried HERDER (1744–1803), surmised that the "Religion des Schaka" (Shakyamuni Buddha) is the largest religion on earth. Dominant in Tibet, Mongolia, and Manchuria, Herder saw it also extend far to the South and East:

> Also toward the South this religion is widespread; the names Sommona-Kodom, Schakscha-Tuba, Sangol-Muni, Schigemuni, Buddo, Fo, Schekia are all one with Schaka; thus this sacred monastic tradition . . . is found in Hindustan, Ceylon, Siam, Pegu, Tonkin and up to China, Korea, and Japan. (Herder 2002, 3/1:407)

Like Diderot, Herder thought that Brahmanism was a subform of the pan-Asiatic religion we now know as "Buddhism"; theirs was therefore less a "mixup" of two entities than an overestimation of the boundaries of *one* religion. That religion, regardless of its name ("Oriental paganism," "Budsoïsme," "Bupo," etc.) is usually traced back to a single founder (Buddha, Shakya, etc.), and its characteristics and geographical distribution leave no doubt that we are mainly dealing with the tradition that is today called "Buddhism." Herder's chapter on India—which exerted great influence on German Romanticism and romantic Orientalism—presents this view in an initial statement that used to puzzle researchers: "Even though the teaching of the Brahmans is nothing but a branch of the widespread religion that, from Tibet to Japan, has formed sects or governments . . ." (p. 411). Thinking that Herder's "Buddhism" and "Hinduism" correspond to the Buddhism and Hinduism we know today, the author of the only monograph on Herder's reception of Asian religions demonstrated how easy it is to get such things completely wrong: "When Herder expresses himself about the mythology and religion of the Indians, we do not get to hear anything about Buddhism. Rather, the subject is then Hinduism" (Faust 1977:152).

If anything, the reverse is true; like Diderot, Herder thought that the Buddha's religion adapted itself in every country to local circumstances and cultures and developed a vast variety of different forms and branches. The indophile Herder liked its "brahmanic" branch best:

> In contrast with all the sects of Fo that dominate the Eastern world of Asia, this [Brahmanic] one is the blossom; [it is] more learned, more humane, more useful, more noble than all the bonzes, lamas, and tala-poins. (Herder 2002, 3/1:415)

Diderot's view of Asian religions was thus neither an exception nor a careless mistake. Rather it reflects the growing consensus of many seventeenth- and eighteenth-century writers and researchers. Herder, for example, did not base his view on Diderot but on another influential Frenchman whom he had as a young man visited in Paris and whose numerous papers he wanted to see published in German translation: the famous orientalist Joseph de Guignes who is the protagonist of our next chapter.

Chapter 4

De Guignes's Chinese Vedas

The "invention," "discovery," or identification of major Asian religions (in particular, Hinduism and Buddhism) is often situated in the "longer" nineteenth century during which, as a recent book claims, "the Invention of World Religions" took place. Its author states that toward the end of the nineteenth century Buddhism "had only recently been recognized as 'the same' tradition existing in diverse regions of South, South-east, East, and Central Asia," and that until that time European observers had not "thought of these divergent rites and widely scattered institutions as constituting a single religion" (Masuzawa 2005:122). The discovery of Buddhism is characterized as being "from the beginning, in a somewhat literal and nontrivial sense, a textual construction," so much so that "one might say that Buddhism as such came to life, perhaps for the first time, in a European philological workshop" (p. 126). Such arguments are based on several assumptions that merit questioning. We have already seen that the emergence in the European mind of a pan-Asiatic religion (that we now readily identify as Buddhism) did not happen overnight in some nineteenth-century study. Such scenarios of a nineteenth-century "creation" of Buddhism grew on a soil fertilized by several biases. The "Indian" bias links the European discovery of Buddhism to India as Buddhism's country of origin, the "textual" bias to the study of Buddhist texts in Indian languages, and the "colonialist" bias posits that such discovery and study were primarily linked to colonial interests. This accounts for the exaggerated role of British "pioneers" in recent studies. Charles Allen's "men who discovered India's lost religion," for example, are without exception British colonialist "Sahibs" (Allen 2002). But even scholars with a much broader perspective suffer from similar biases. For example, J. W. de Jong's *Brief History of Buddhist Studies in Europe and America* (1997) fails to mention João Rodrigues (see our Chapter 1), La Croze (see Chapter 2), and the protagonist of the present chapter, Joseph de Guignes. Even the most informative study to date, Henri de Lubac's *La rencontre du bouddhisme et de l'Occident* (1952/2000), ignores that de Guignes's 1756 French rendering of the *Forty-Two Sections Sutra* was the first published translation in a Western language of a Buddhist sutra.

Related to these "Indian" and "Sanskrit" biases is one that pitches "science" against missionary "protoscience." It assumes that the onset of "modern" Orientalism in the first decades of the nineteenth century was a clean break from the "missionary" past. The pre-nineteenth-century discovery of Buddhism is thus divorced from its "scientific discovery," and the latter is portrayed as a "new start from almost nothing" (Droit 1997:29). Unlike the installation of a new operating system on a computer, which guarantees at least some continuity of data, Droit regards this new start as a total break with the past and generalizes: "It is a permanent feature of the West's relation with the doctrines of Buddhism that, in the very long run, information does not accumulate" (p. 29). For Droit, the decisive "new start" and thus Buddhism's "discovery in the proper sense" only happened "from the moment when the languages of its canonical scriptures were deciphered and the fundamental texts translated in a systematic manner" (p. 36). When did this happen, and what languages were in play? Droit explains:

> Now, even though Sanskrit had been known since the 1780s, the Buddhist treatises in Sanskrit were only discovered during the 1820s in Nepal by Brian Houghton Hodgson; Pali was only deciphered by Eugène Burnouf and Christian Lassen during the same period; and the Chinese Buddhist texts were only at this moment studied by Jean-Pierre Abel-Rémusat, who was soon followed by the Hungarian Alexander Csoma de Körös's study of Tibetan. (p. 36)

If such bias is combined with constructivism, the 1820s become the "turning point" that "led Europe from ignorance to knowledge" and the crucial moment when the word "Buddhism" and the "phenomenon itself" were simultaneously "born in the scholarly gaze" (p. 36). In contrast to such a clean-cut birth by Caesarian section in the lecture halls of state-sponsored Orientalist academia, we have seen that the discovery of a large Asian religion with a specific founder, history, geographical presence, body of teachings, and sacred texts was a rather messy and protracted event that began long before the moment in the 1820s when European scholars began to read Sanskrit and Pali Buddhist texts. Contrary to Droit's assertion, much information gradually accumulated over several centuries, and the permanent feature of the West's relation with Buddhism was that information, once it was collected or invented, was rarely forgotten but rather tended to be endlessly repeated and widely accepted. The above-mentioned story of the Buddha's deathbed confession is a perfect illustration of this phenomenon. Moreover, Buddhist texts were studied and even translated long before Sanskrit entered the picture. To mention just a few examples: in 1574 the Jesuit Japan missionaries Organtino Gnecchi-Soldo and Luis Frois devoted two hours per day to the study of the Chinese text of the *Lotus Sutra* under the guidance of a former Buddhist abbot and persisted for a whole year (Frois 1926:452); the first partial translation of a Buddhist text from Pali was published by Simon de la Loubère in 1691; Ippolito Desideri studied and translated Tibetan Buddhist texts in the early eighteenth century; and the first Buddhist sutra to be published in Europe, the *Forty-Two Sections Sutra*, was translated by de Guignes from the Chinese in the 1750s. All of this happened long before Europeans became aware of Buddhist Sanskrit texts.

The European obsession with origins and Bible-like canonical texts contributed to the bias for India, Sanskrit, and Pali. However—just like wars—discoveries happen as they actually do and not as one might wish they should; and it is a matter of historical fact that Sanskrit entered the stage rather late. But a fundamentalist obsession with "genuine" Buddhist "bibles" from India led from the late nineteenth century to the view that the Buddhisms of distant countries such Japan, China, and Tibet are "degenerate" and their texts incomparably inferior to those of mother India. It is as if researchers of Christianity would regard Roman Catholicism or Syriac orthodoxy as degenerate and inferior because they are removed from Christianity's Aramaic and Greek origins. When European missionaries ventured to Asia, Buddhism had long vanished from India and flourished in distant countries such as Mongolia, Japan, China, Tibet, Siam, Burma, Cambodia, Ceylon, Vietnam, and Laos. To no one's surprise, these were exactly the countries where the Europeans discovered Buddhism, and de Guignes is an excellent example for the impact of literature from such non-Indian countries. The discovery of long-vanished *Indian* Buddhism, by contrast, indeed happened to a large extent in the nineteenth-century "European philological workshop" (Masuzawa 2005:126). The present chapter will show, however, that prior to that there were "workshops" not manned by Sanskritists but rather by French missionaries and by academics who studied and translated Arabic and Chinese sources long before the first British colonialists began to dabble in Sanskrit.[1]

Fourmont's Dirty Little Secret

When Joseph DE GUIGNES (1721–1800) at the young age of fifteen was placed with Étienne FOURMONT (1683–1745), Fourmont enjoyed a great reputation as one of Europe's foremost specialists of classical as well as oriental languages. As an associate of Abbé Bignon (the man so eager to stock the Royal Library with Oriental texts), Fourmont had met a Chinese scholar called Arcadius HOANG (1679–1716) and had for a short while studied Chinese with him (Elisseeff 1985:133ff.; Abel-Rémusat 1829:I.260). In 1715 the thirty-two-year-old Fourmont was elected to the chair of Arabic at the Collège Royal. Hoang's death in 1716 did not diminish Fourmont's desire to learn Chinese, and in 1719 he followed Nicolas FRÉRET (1688–1749) in introducing Europe to the 214 Chinese radicals. This is one of the systems used by the Chinese to classify Chinese characters and to make finding them, be it in a dictionary or a printer's shop, easier and quicker.

Thanks to royal funding for his projected grammar and dictionaries, Fourmont had produced more than 100,000 Chinese character types. But in Fourmont's eyes the 214 radicals were far more than just a classification method. Naming them "clefs" (keys), he was convinced that they were meaningful building blocks that the ancient Chinese had used in constructing characters. For example, Fourmont thought that the first radical (—) is "the key of unity, or priority, and perfection" and that the second radical (|) signifies "growth" (Klaproth 1828:234). Starting with the 214 basic "keys," so Fourmont imagined, the ancient Chinese had combined them to form the tens of thousands of characters of the Chinese writing system. However, as Klaproth and others later pointed out, the Chinese writing system was not "formed from its origin after a general system"; rather, it had evolved gradually from "the necessity of inventing a sign to express some thing or some idea." The idea of classifying characters according to certain elements arose only much later and resulted in several systems with widely different numbers of radicals ranging from a few dozen to over 700 (Klaproth 1828:233–36).

Like many students of Chinese or Japanese, Fourmont had probably memorized characters by associating their elements with specific meanings. A German junior world champion in the memory sport, Christiane Stenger, employs a similar technique for remembering mathematical equations. Each element is assigned a concrete meaning; for example, the minus sign signifies "go backward" or "vomit," the letter A stands for "apple," the letter B for "bear," the letter C for "citrus fruit," and the mathematical root symbol for a root. Thus, "B minus C" is memorized by imagining a bear vomiting a citrus fruit, and "minus B plus the root of A square" may be pictured as a receding bear who stumbles over a root in which a square apple is embedded.

Stenger's technique, of course, has no connection whatsoever to understanding mathematical formulae, but Fourmont's "keys" can indeed be of help in understanding the meaning of some characters. While such infusion of meaning certainly helped Fourmont and his students Michel-Ange-André le Roux DESHAUTERAYES (1724–95) and de Guignes in their study of complicated Chinese characters, it also involved a serious misunderstanding. Stenger understood that bears and fruit were her imaginative creation in order to memorize mathematical formulae and would certainly not have graduated from high school if she had thought that her mathematics teacher wanted to tell her stories about apples and bears.

But *mutatis mutandis*, this was exactly Fourmont's mistake. Instead of simply accepting the 214 radicals as an artificial system for classifying Chinese characters and as a mnemonic aide, he was convinced that the radicals are a collection of primeval ideas that the Chinese used as a toolset to assemble ideograms representing objects and complex ideas. Fourmont thought that the ancient Chinese had embedded a little story in each character. As he and his disciples happily juggled with "keys," spun stories, and memorized their daily dose of Chinese characters, they did not have any inkling that this fundamentally mistaken view of the genesis of Chinese characters would one day form the root for a mistake of such proportions that it would put de Guignes's entire reputation in jeopardy.

Apart from a series of dictionaries that never came to fruition, Fourmont was also working on a Chinese grammar. He announced its completion in 1728, eight years before the arrival of de Guignes. The first part of this *Grammatica sinica* with Fourmont's presentation of the 214 "keys" and elements of pronunciation appeared in 1737. The second part, prepared for publication while de Guignes sat at his teacher's feet, contained the grammar proper as well as Fourmont's catalog of Chinese works in the Bibliothèque Royale and was published in 1742. When Fourmont presented the result to the king of France, he had de Guignes accompany him, and the king was so impressed by the twenty-one-year-old linguistic prodigy that he endowed him on the spot with a pension (Michaud 1857:18.126).

But de Guignes's teacher Fourmont had a dirty little secret. He had focused on learning and accumulating data about single Chinese characters, but his knowledge of the Chinese classical and vernacular language was simply not adequate for writing a grammar. By consequence, the man who had let the world know that a genius residing in Europe could master Chinese just as well as the China missionaries decided to plagiarize—what else?—the work of a missionary. No one found out about this until Jean-Pierre Abel-Rémusat in 1825 carefully compared the manuscript of the *Arte de la lengua mandarina* by the Spanish Franciscan Francisco Varo with Fourmont's Latin translation and found to his astonishment that Fourmont's ground-breaking *Grammatica sinica* was a translation of Varo's work (Abel-Rémusat 1829:2.298). In an "act of puerile vanity," Abel-Rémusat sadly concluded, Fourmont had appropriated Varo's entire text "almost without any change" while claiming that he had never seen it (1826:2.109).[2]

While de Guignes helped prepare this grammar for publication, Fourmont continued his research on chronology and the history of ancient peoples. During the seventeenth century, ancient Chinese historical sources had become an increasingly virulent threat to biblical chronology and, by extension, to biblical authority. As Fourmont's rival Fréret was busy butchering Isaac Newton's lovingly calculated chronology, de Guignes's teacher turned his full attention to the Chinese annals. These annals were in general regarded either as untrustworthy and thus inconsequential or as trustworthy and a threat to biblical authority. However, in a paper read on May 18, 1734, at the Royal Academy of Inscriptions, Fourmont declared with conviction that he could square the circle: the Chinese annals were trustworthy just because they confirmed the Bible. Dismissing Fréret's and Newton's nonbiblical Middle Eastern sources as "scattered scraps," he praised the Chinese annals to the sky as the only ancient record worth studying apart from the Bible (Fourmont 1740:507–8).

But Fourmont's lack of critical acumen is as evident in this paper as in his *Critical reflections on the histories of ancient peoples* of 1735 and the *Meditationes sinicae* of 1737. In the "avertissement" to the first volume of the *Critical reflections*, Fourmont mentions the question of an India traveler, Chevalier Didier, who had conversed with Brahmins and missionaries and came in frustration to Paris to seek Fourmont's opinion about an important question of origins: had Indian idolatry influenced Egyptian idolatry or vice versa?

Fourmont delivered his answer after nearly a thousand tedious pages full of chronological juggling:

> With regard to customs in general, since India is entirely Egyptian and *Osiris* led several descendants of Abraham there, we have the first cause of that resemblance of mores in those two nations; but with regard to the religion of the Indians, they only received it subsequently through commerce and through the colonies coming from Egypt. (Fourmont 1735:2.499)

For Fourmont the Old Testament was the sole reliable testimony of antediluvian times, and he argued that the reliability of other accounts decreases with increasing distance from the landing spot of Noah's ark. Only the Chinese, whose "language is the oldest of the universe," remain a riddle, as their antiquity "somehow rivals that of Genesis and has caused the most famous chronologists to change their system" (1735:1.lii). But would not China's "hieroglyphic" writing system also indicate Egyptian origins? Though Fourmont suspected an Egyptian origin of Chinese writing, he could not quite figure out the exact mechanism and transmission. He suspected that "Hermes, who passed for the inventor of letters" had not invented hieroglyphs but rather "*on one hand* more perfect hieroglyphic letters, which were brought to the Chinese who in turn repeatedly perfected theirs; and *on the other hand* alphabetic letters" (Fourmont 1735:2.500). These "more perfect hieroglyphs" that "seemingly existed with the Egyptian priests" are "quite similar to the Chinese characters of today" (p. 500).

Fourmont was studying whether there was any support for Kircher's hypothesis that the letters transmitted from Egypt to the Chinese were related to Coptic monosyllables (p. 503); but though he apparently did not find conclusive answers to such questions, the problem itself and Fourmont's basic direction (transmission from Egypt to China, some kind of more perfect hieroglyphs) must have been so firmly planted his student de Guignes's mind that it could grow into the root over which he later stumbled. Fourmont's often repeated view that Egypt's culture was not as old as that of countries closer to the landing spot of Noah's ark made it clear that those who regarded Egypt as the womb of all human culture were dead wrong and that China, in spite of its ancient culture, was a significant step removed from the true origins.

Though the Chinese had received their writing system and probably also the twin ideas that in his view "properly constitute Egyptianism"—the idea of metempsychosis and the adoration of animals and plants (p. 492)— Fourmont credited the Chinese with subsequent improvements also in this respect: "My studies have thus taught me that the Chinese were a wise people, the most ancient of all peoples, but the first also, though idolatrous, that rid itself of the mythological spirit" (Fourmont 1735:2.liv). This accounted for their excellent historiography and voluminous literature:

> I said that the Chinese Annals can be regarded as a respectable work. First of all, as everybody admits, for more than 3,500 years China has been populated, cultivated, and literate. Secondly, has it lacked authors as its people still read books, though few in number, written before Abraham? Thirdly, since few scholars know the Chinese books, let me here point out that the Chinese Annals are not bits and pieces of histories scattered here and there like the Latin and Greek histories which must be stitched together: they consist of at least 150 volumes that, without *hiatus* and the slightest interruption, present a sequence of 22 families which all reigned for 3, 4, 8, 10 centuries. (p. liv)

While Fourmont cobbled together hypotheses and conjectures, the Bible always formed the backdrop for his speculations about ancient history. A telling example is his critique of the Chinese historian OUYANG Xiu (1007–72), who argued that from the remote past, humans had always enjoyed roughly similar life spans. Lambasting this view as that of a "skeptic," Fourmont furnished the following argument as "proof" of the reliability of ancient Chinese histories:

> We who possess the sacred writ: must we not on the contrary admire the Chinese annals when they, just in the time period of Arphaxad, Saleh, Heber, Phaleg, Reü, Sarug, Nachor, Abraham, etc., present us with men who lived precisely the same number of years? Now if someone told us that *Sem* at the age of 550 years married one of his grand-grand-nieces in the fourteenth generation: who of us would express the slightest astonishment? . . . It is thus clear that all such objections are frivolous, and furthermore, that attacks against the Chinese annals on account of a circumstance [i.e., excessive longevity] which distinguishes them from all other books will actually tie them even more to Scripture and will be a sure means to increase their authority. (Fourmont 1740:514)

No comment is needed here. Immediately after Fourmont's death in 1745, the twenty-four-year-old Joseph de Guignes replaced his master as secretary interpreter of oriental languages at the Royal Library. It was the beginning of an illustrious career: royal censor and attaché to the *Journal des Sçavans* in 1752, member of the Académie des Inscriptions et Belles-Lettres in 1753, chair of Syriac at the Collège Royal from 1757 to 1773, *garde des antiques* at the Louvre in 1769, editor of the *Journal des Savants*, and other honors (Michaud 1857:18.127). De Guignes had, like his master Fourmont, a little problem. The pioneer Sinologists in Paris were simply unable to hold a candle to the China missionaries. Since 1727 Fourmont had been corresponding with the figurist China missionary Joseph Henry PRÉMARE (1666–1736), who, unlike Fourmont, was an accomplished Sinologist (see Chapter 5). Prémare was very liberal with his advice and sent, apart from numerous letters, his *Notitia linguae sinicae* to Fourmont in 1728. This was, in the words of Abel-Rémusat,

> neither a simple grammar, as the author too modestly calls it, nor a rhetoric, as Fourmont intimated; it is an almost complete treatise of literature in which Father Prémare not only included everything that he had collected about the usage of particles and grammatical rules of the Chinese but also a great number of observations about the style, particular expressions in ancient and common idiom, proverbs, most frequent patterns—and everything supported by a mass of examples cited from texts, translated and commented when necessary. (Abel-Rémusat 1829:2.269)

Prémare thus sent Fourmont his "most remarkable and important work," which was "without any doubt the best of all those that Europeans have hitherto[3] composed on these matters" (p. 269).

But instead of publishing this vastly superior work and making the life of European students of Chinese considerably easier, Fourmont compared it unfavorably to his own (partly plagiarized) product and had Prémare's masterpiece buried in the Royal Library, where it slept until Abel-Rémusat rediscovered it in the nineteenth century (pp. 269–73). However, Fourmont's two disciples Deshauterayes and de Guignes could profit from such works since Fourmont for years kept the entire China-related collection of the Royal Library at his home where the two disciples had their rooms; thus Prémare was naturally one of the Sinologists who influenced de Guignes.[4] So was

Antoine GAUBIL (1689–1759), whose reputation as a Sinologist was deservedly great.

But there is a third, extremely competent Jesuit Sinologist who remained in the shadows though his knowledge of Chinese far surpassed that of de Guignes and all other Europe-based early Sinologists (and, one might add, even many modern ones). His works suffered a fate resembling that of the man who was in many ways his predecessor, João Rodrigues (see Chapter 1) in that they were used but rarely credited. The man in question was Claude de VISDELOU (1656–1737), who spent twenty-four years in China (1685–1709) and twenty-eight years in India (1709–37). One can say without exaggeration that the famous Professor de Guignes owed this little-known missionary a substantial part of his fame—and this was *his* dirty little secret.

De Visdelou's Brahmins

The fact that the reader has already encountered one of de Visdelou's seminal ideas without realizing it is symptomatic. De Visdelou was the direct source of Le Gobien's "Brahmin followers of Fo" mixup that reached, as we have seen in the previous chapter, such a large European readership via Bayle's and Diderot's "Brachmanes" articles. After his arrival in China in 1685, the linguistically gifted Frenchman made such fast progress in learning Chinese that even China's crown prince was astonished. In a letter dated January 20, 1728, De Visdelou remembers a scene from the year 1790:

> When I was five years in China and had begun to devote myself to reading Chinese books for barely four years, emperor Kangxi ordered me and one of my companions to come from Canton to Beijing. We were directly led to the palace. The emperor was gravely ill, and we could not see him. The crown prince of the empire who conducted affairs in place of his father was told that a European had arrived who within four years had acquired knowledge of the canonical books and the classics. The prince soon appeared at the door asking where that foreigner was. Here he is, I answered, after I had prostrated in the manner of the land. The prince immediately ordered that a volume of the canonical book called *Shujing* be brought, i.e., the Canonical History. Opening it at random, he asked me to stand up and read it; I did so and explained it in the presence of several persons who accompanied the prince. Since the Chi-

nese have a high opinion of themselves and their products, the prince was in admiration and said the following words: "*Ta-ting*, i.e., he understands very well." The crown prince did not leave it at this verbal testimony but also wanted to provide an authentic attestation, written in Chinese characters on a piece of satin one *aune* in length and half an *aune* in width. It said: "We recognize that this man from Europe is loftier in intelligence [lumière] and in the knowledge of Chinese characters than the clouds floating above our heads, and that he is more profound in penetration and knowledge than the abyss on which we tread." (de Visdelou 1760:341–42)

Seven years after this incident, de Visdelou dictated a few pages about the religions of China to the visiting Mr. Basset in order to explain the background of a regional persecution of Christians. Basset's notes made their way to Paris and into the hands of Father Le Gobien who edited and used them as introduction to his book about the edict of tolerance issued by the Chinese emperor (1698) ,which was then used by Bayle and Diderot. Already the first few lines show the extent and character of Le Gobien's editorial interference. He was an inclusivist in the line of Matteo Ricci who shared the opinion of the vast majority of Jesuits that the ancient religion of China (and Confucianism as its successor) had venerated the true God. De Visdelou, by contrast, was one of the few dissenters in the line of João Rodrigues who thought that ancient Chinese religion and Confucianism were forms of atheism. Already the initial paragraphs of de Visdelou's report as taken down by Basset were heavily edited by Le Gobien and exhibit an immense difference of opinion. De Visdelou only discussed modern Confucianism, Buddhism, and Daoism and lost no word about an ancient Chinese monotheism. The latter was added by Le Gobien, who claimed that this ancient Confucianism was still extant with the Chinese emperor as head; see Table 5, where major differences are highlighted in gray.

Leaving aside the missionary's discussion of Neoconfucianism (de Visdelou's first and Le Gobien's second religion), we will here focus on the passages that for the first time provided support from the Chinese side for Kircher's idea that the Brahmins were the missionaries who brought Xaca's religion from India to China. Though Basset, who wrote down the text dictated by de Visdelou, appears to have left out a few words, the overall meaning of de Visdelou's statement is clear: it is *de Visdelou* who calls this "sect" that "has many names in China" by the name of "brachmanes of China." In the paren-

TABLE 5. CHINESE SECTS IN VISDELOU'S DICTATION TEXT AND LE GOBIEN

De Visdelou's dictation text (c. 1696)[a]	Le Gobien's published text (1698)
I cannot dispense myself from providing a general idea of the different sects of China. Without this one would not understand the thinking of the Viceroy who compares them among themselves and with the Christian religion. It is sufficiently known that there are three principal ones of which the first is that of the philosopher scholars (I mean the modern philosophers, not the ancient ones). The second one is that of the brachmanes, and the third that of the bonzes.	Since the history I write concerns only religion, I cannot dispense myself from providing to my reader a general idea of the different sects that are current in China. There are four principal ones.
	The first is of those who, less by a feeling of piety than by respect for the ancients, recognize in the world a superior spirit, eternal, almighty, and much like the one known in the first centuries of the monarchy as the Lord of Heaven. It must be admitted that the number of these veritable worshippers is not very great, even though the Emperor is their head and has often decclared that it was to God that he offered the sacrifices in the temples and not to those inferior and imaginary spirits with which the people is so ridiculously infatuated.
The first is the dominant one . . . [etc.]	The second is the dominant one . . . [etc.]
The second sect which I call that of the brachmanes of China (they themselves take this name. Because the name of polomen, which they give to themselves, is the Indian brahmen travestied as Chinese, [and] because [this religion] has really been brought from the Indies to China by the brachmanes.) It has many names in China.	The third sect current among the Chinese can be called the religion of the *Brachmanes* or *Bramenes*, and they themselves call it by that name. Because *Polo-men*, which is [the word] they use, is the *Bramen* of the Indians which they could not pronounce and that they apparently travestied in their language.

[a] English translation of text in *Archives de la Société des Missions Etrangères* (vol. 418:277–82) as reproduced in Timmermans 1998:578–88.

theses he adduces two reasons to justify his choice: (1) its representatives call themselves *polomen*, which is the Chinese pronunciation of *brahmin*; and (2) this religion was brought from the Indies to China by the *brachmanes*. Today we know that *boluomen seng* (Brahmin monk) was mainly used for Buddhist monks who had come from India to China and that on some occasions it served as a generic honorific for monks (as the Italian "monsignore" would flatter Catholic priests of any country). De Visdelou's choice to call Chinese Buddhism "the sect of the brachmanes of China" was not based on Chinese custom but rather on the Western idea, popular since the publication of Kircher's *China illustrata* (1667), that the religion of Xaca/Fo (that is, Buddhism) had been brought to China by Brahmins. In fact, after the parentheses explaining his reasons for this choice, de Visdelou clearly states that this religion "has many names in China" and that its priests are commonly called *hochan* (Ch. *heshang*, reverend) and not *polomen*. In Le Gobien's published text, de Visdelou's "I call" becomes "can be called," and de Visdelou's choice turns into an official nomenclature since "they themselves call it by this name." Under Le Gobien's pen, de Visdelou's "sect of the brachmanes of China" loses both the "of China" and its "many names" and turns straight into Brahmanism by becoming "the religion of the *Brachmanes* or *Bramenes*"—and there can be no doubt about this since "they themselves call it by that name." These changes might be regarded as minor, but they are not. As the explanations continue, de Visdelou keeps calling the priests of this religion by the name they use themselves, namely, *hochans*, whereas Le Gobien changed this into *Bramenes*.

This was not de Visdelou's (or Basset's?) only confusing sect name; he called his third religion (which we now call Daoism) the sect of the "bonzes," a term usually employed for Buddhist priests. Here, de Visdelou once more emphasizes that this is *his* choice rather than that of the Daoists, and in the first section of Table 6 he justifies this by pointing once more to the origin of the "sect" (which in this case is China).

De Visdelou's *hochans* are transformed by Le Gobien into *Bramenes*, and this choice of words contributed to the "mixup" that filled the critics of Bayle and Diderot with so much indignation. But Le Gobien's confusion is understandable. As the second section of Table 6 shows, de Visdelou seems to have held that the religion brought by *brachmanes* from India to China has priests called *hochan*, and that *hochan* from different countries venerate three identical treasures: Buddha, dharma, and "the rule of the brachmanes."

Like Rodriguez and Kircher, de Visdelou thus seems to have thought

TABLE 6. BRAHMANS IN VISDELOU'S DICTATION TEXT AND LE GOBIEN'S

The third sect which I have called that of the bonzes because it has its origin in China is ordinarily called the sect of the Taossée or the doctors of the law.	The fourth sect is that which is named the religion of the *Bonzes*; it has its origin in China and its priests call themselves commonly *Taossé*: which in Chinese means the doctors of the Law.
Their morals are quite in accord with those of the Epicureans. They bring back everything to indolence, which really is a half-hearted apathy; because they are not nearly as severe as the **hochans**.	Their morals seem hardly different from those of our Epicureans; they do not plunge man's spirit into that exaggerated indifference of the ***Bramenes*** but are content to banish the vehement desires and despondent passions.
The most common [name] one gives to these false priests is hochan, which signifies people reunited from various countries by the preference they give to three precious things which are the Fo, the law of Fo, and the rule of the brachmanes.	Nevertheless they ordinarily call these false priests *Hochan*, which signifies people reunited from various countries. These priests worship principally three things, the God *Fo*, his law, and the books containing their particular rules.

that the religion of Fo had been brought to China by Indian Brahmins and that the old "rule of the brachmanes" was still operative in China. But he neither mentioned a "God Fo" nor "books" containing "particular rules." Instead of simplifying things as he intended, Le Gobien added another layer of confusion. Hardly anybody had access to de Visdelou's dictation text or knew that de Visdelou was the source of this information. Bayle, Diderot, de Guignes and others could thus only refer to Le Gobien's description with its clear-cut identification of Indian Brahmanism with Fo, his law, and his "books." The identification of the religion of India's ancient Brachmanes with the religion of Fo in China, where it was imported by Brahmins (*polomen*), was the first seminal idea of de Visdelou that shaped de Guignes's outlook.

Huns from Shinar

Claude de Visdelou got much unattributed exposure in Paris when Le Gobien's book on the Chinese emperor's edict (whose introduction, as we have seen, is a heavy-handed edition of de Visdelou's dictated words about Chinese religions) became the joint subject of a hearing at the Sorbonne on July 1, 1700. One of the five propositions that was condemned on October 18 of the same year was from Le Gobien's *Histoire de l'édit de l'empereur de la Chine* (1698) and the rest from Lecomte's *Nouveaux mémoires sur l'état présent de la Chine* (whose 1698 edition also contained Le Gobien's book, as previously mentioned) and his *Lettre au duc du Maine sur les cérémonies de la Chine.* The central point of contention of all five condemned propositions is exactly the "first religion" that Le Gobien had added to de Visdelou's report. De Visdelou, like Rodrigues before him, was familiar enough with Chinese literature and religion to realize that Ricci's and his successors' monotheistic idealization of ancient Chinese religion and of classical Confucianism was a pipe dream. He was also staunchly opposed to Bouvet's, Prémare's, and Fouquet's attempts to somehow make the *Yijing* (Book of Changes), the *Daodejing* (Book of the Way and its Power), or other Chinese classics into a kind of Asian Old Testament where the Dao would appear as creator God and prophecies of lambs, sacrificed saviors, and virgin mothers abounded.

De Visdelou's opposition to such views and his willingness to furnish proofs from Chinese sources to those who fought such figurist and accommodationist fantasies eventually led to his consecration as a bishop, his ouster from China and the Jesuit order, and twenty-eight years of exile in southeast India. The French government did not allow him to return to France, and he was forced to spend the rest of his life (1709–37) in exile at the house of the French Franciscans in Pondicherry. There he used his large library of Chinese books to produce works, reports, and translations of rare quality. Unlike his colleagues in the China mission, he could devote almost all his time to study, and unlike the scholars in Paris scavenging his work, he had twenty-four years of China experience under his belt and was arguably the most competent Western Sinologist of his time. Like Fourmont (his junior by seventeen years) and later de Guignes, de Visdelou was able to use sources not only in the major European languages and Chinese but also in Arabic and Persian. He was thus perfectly positioned to correct and supplement the famous *Bibliothèque Orientale* of seventeenth-century Europe's foremost Orientalist, Barthélemy D'HERBELOT DE MOLAINVILLE (1625–95), one of de Guignes's eminent predecessors as holder of the chair of Syriac from 1692 to 1695. De Visdelou remarked that d'Herbelot's Turkic, Arabic, and Persian sources contained much information about Central and East Asia that was either incorrect or questionable, and he decided to "redress the Mahometan histories in what they falsely assert about China and Tartary" by furnishing alternative or supplementary information from Chinese sources.

The resulting work by de Visdelou, written at the beginning of the eighteenth century, only saw publication in 1779. De Visdelou gave it a title that almost says it all:

> Abbreviated history of Tartary, containing the origin of the people who appeared with verve in this vast land more than two thousand years ago; their religion, their manners, customs, wars, and the revolutions of their empires together with the chronological and genealogical sequence of their emperors; all of this preceded and followed by critical observations on several entries of the *Bibliothèque Orientale*. (1779:46)

His manuscript came in four tomes that—according to the geographer Jean-Baptiste Bourguignon d'Anville (1776:33)—were sent from Pondicherry to the Academician and economic historian Jean-Roland Mallet.

D'Anville, whose *New Atlas of China* appeared in the year of de Visdelou's death (1737), appreciated de Visdelou's manuscripts for their precious information about many places in Central and North Asia whose Chinese names de Visdelou had managed to identify and whose descriptions from Chinese sources he furnished and expertly translated.[5] D'Anville must have been particularly interested in de Visdelou's additions to d'Herbelot, his summary and translations from Chinese dynastic histories about the nations north and west of China, and his Latin translation of the history of the Mongols (Herbelot et al. 1779:4.333). If both the academician Mallet (who died in 1736) and d'Anville (member of the Academy of Inscriptions and Literature) had their hands on these precious manuscripts, it is likely that fellow Academy member Fourmont—at the time the only man in Paris reputed to be expert in both Arabic and Chinese—and/or his disciples de Guignes and Deshauterayes were also in the loop. Apart from his work on Tartary and the Mongols, de Visdelou had also sent an annotated translation of the *Shujing* (Classic of History; unpublished but used by Deshauterayes), an annotated translation of the eighth-century Nestorian stele of Xi'an (partly published by Voltaire's nephew Abbé Vincent Mignot in 1760), and a long letter about the *Yijing* or Book of Changes (used by Mignot in 1761–62 and published by de Guignes in 1770). De Visdelou's four-volume work on Tartary and the inserted manuscript with his annotated translation of the Nestorian stele somehow ended up in The Hague where Jean Neaulme, the well-known publisher of Voltaire and Rousseau, purchased them for 400 Dutch florins and communicated them to the bibliophile Prosper Marchand (c. 1675–1756) and others (Herbelot et al. 1779:4.iii).

Jean Neaulme resided in Paris between 1740 and 1750 (p. iv) and sought the advice of specialists regarding its publication. In the course of this examination, the inserted small manuscript containing Visdelou's expertly annotated translation of the Nestorian stele of Xian was also discovered. Neaulme asked several professors for advice (the names s'Gravensande and de Joncourt are mentioned, p. iii); and if anybody in Paris would be consulted for this prospective publication involving Chinese as well as Arabic and Persian, it would have been Fourmont or his disciples de Guignes and Deshauterayes. Abel-Rémusat[6] and others had long suspected that de Guignes had used de Visdelou's Tartar manuscript; but only in the summer of 2008 did I find the conclusive proof of this among the papers of Fourmont at the Bilbiothèque Nationale in Paris. The Fourmont dossier contains dozens of pages in de Guignes's hand, copied word for word from de Visdelou's Tartar manuscript. The notes contain references indicating that these copies from de Visdelou's manuscript were very voluminous.[7]

In 1751 de Guignes published a 24-page prospectus for a large work on the origin of the Huns and Turks (*Mémoire historique sur l'origine des Huns et des Turks, adressé à M. Tavenot*) whose central argument and methodology eerily resemble those of de Visdelou's manuscript on the Tartars. In various places in his manuscript, de Visdelou had advanced the idea that the Xiongnu, a horse-mounted nomad people of the steppe that had for many centuries invaded and threatened the Chinese empire, might correspond to the people known to Europe as "the Huns."[8] The first section of de Visdelou's *Abbreviated History of Tartary* in the same manuscript deals exactly with the empire of the Xiongnu and begins as follows:

> The *Toum-hou*, or Oriental Tartars, recognize as first father of their nation *Yen-yue*, son of the emperor of China named *Kao-sin* who began his reign 2,432 years before the Christian era. . . . The *Hioum-nou* or Occidental Tartars (which may be the *Huns* whom the Greeks called OΩ'N-NOI and the Romans *Hunni*) drew their origin from *Chun-vei*, son of a Chinese emperor of the *Hia* dynasty, which ended in the year 1767 before the Christian era. (Herbelot et al. 1779:48)

De Visdelou then goes on to cite at length Chinese historians about the Xiongnu and concludes that this people (which the Chinese eventually labeled *Hioum-nou* [Xiongnu]) "may be those who appeared in Europe in the fourth century under the name of *Huns*" (p. 51).

De Guignes's Visdelou-inspired view that the Xiongnu are identical with the Huns formed the basis of his 4-volume magnum opus: *Histoire générale des Huns, des Turcs, des Mogols, et des autres tartares occidentaux, & c. avant Jésus-Christ jusqu'à présent*. It was an immediate success and received praise from many eminent men including Edward Gibbon, the author of the *Decline and Fall of the Roman Empire*, who called it a "great history" and praised de Guignes for having "laid open new and important scenes in the history of mankind" (Pocock 2005:110). Such interest was understandable since the hitherto isolated islands of Chinese dynastic histories and the history of the late Roman Empire received a connecting link that showed the origins of Europe in a new, far more global light.

But where did the Chinese and the Huns ultimately come from? De Guignes addresses this question at the beginning of his second volume. Like his teacher Fourmont, de Guignes's vision of origins was thoroughly biblical: "Only Moses has in few words reported the sequence of generations before the deluge, and it is a fact worthy of mention that the histories of all nations stop in unison around the times that approach this great catastrophe" (de Guignes 1756:1.2.2). As the fictions of antiquity-obsessed Egyptians and Chaldeans had supposedly all vanished under the gaze of critical scholars like Fourmont, it was now de Guignes's turn to confirm that the histories of the Chinese "do not at all contradict the account of Moses" but rather "indirectly confirm it" (p. 2).

> The Huns do not seem less ancient than these famous people. They are mentioned in the history from the first beginnings of Chinese monarchy; they thus are part of those colonies that abandoned the plains of Shinar shortly after the deluge. One might be tempted to believe that these two nations [the Huns and the Chinese] stem from the same people. (p. 2)

Though de Guignes was reluctant to discuss topics without any base in some historical record, he developed a scenario that traced the course of the Chinese people from Shinar in Mesopotamia to Persia and along the Silk Road to China. Another colony turned north from Shinar toward Armenia where it split into a western and eastern branch. The first went on to form the ancient Europeans, whereas the second formed the Tartar nations including those that the Chinese from the Han period onward called *Hiong-nou* or

Huns (pp. 3–13). These Huns had reportedly established an empire as early as 1230 B.C.E. (p. 21), and de Guignes spent much of the rest of his four volumes tracing their fate.

In the nineteenth century, de Guignes's view of the identity of the Huns and their connections with the Mogols and Turks came under heavy fire and was no longer accepted. But de Visdelou's and de Guignes's conjecture of an initial identity has recently found unexpected support through the analysis of a few letters that Sir Aurel Stein dug out of the desert sand 55 miles west of Dunhuang. These "Sogdian Ancient letters" confirm "a long-suspected but never proven link between the Xiongnu of old Chinese sources and the Huns unleashed on Europe from 370," even though they "do not imply that the Huns of Europe or Central Asia *after* A. D. 350 are themselves descendants of the Xiongnu" (de la Vaissière 2004:22). On the other hand, the Bible-inspired scenario linking the Chinese and the Huns to the plains of Shinar was abandoned by its author de Guignes barely two years after publication. In 1758, just before the fourth and last volume of his *History of the Huns* went to press, de Guignes had the printer set the following stunning announcement on the last page of his work:

> At the beginning of the second part of the first volume of this work, I made some reflections about the origin of the Chinese. I then believed that these peoples came directly from the plains of Shinar. New researches oblige me to change my view and to beg the reader not to pay any attention to what is said about this subject in the first two or three pages. The Chinese are only a rather modern colony of the Egyptians. I have proved this in a paper read at the Academy. The Chinese characters are nothing more than monograms formed by Egyptian and Phoenician letters, and the first emperors of China are the ancient Kings of Thebes. This I intend to show in a separate work. (de Guignes 1758:4.518)

How could an author who had just finished his 4-volume magnum opus, erected on the reliability of Chinese annals, rip out its foundation on the last page? It was by no means only a problem of "the first two or three pages," as de Guignes suggested. If the Chinese were a "rather modern colony of the Egyptians," then central pillars of de Guignes's argument like "the Huns were not less ancient than the Chinese who knew them even before the Hia Dynasty, which began its reign in 2207 before Jesus Christ" (de Guignes 1756:1.2.16) or "the establishment of the empire of the Huns must be dated to the year 1230 before Jesus Christ" (p. 21), crumbled to dust. What in the world had happened?

De Guignes's Egyptian Enlightenment

Two major events had triggered this spectacular change of opinion. The first is not obvious unless one carefully reads de Guignes's response to a review of his first volumes in the *Mémoires de Trévoux*. De Guignes printed this letter to the editors just before the index at the end of the fourth volume of his *History of the Huns*, but it was written in 1757, that is, before de Guignes's "Egyptian enlightenment" of 1758. In this letter he criticizes "modern writers" who believe in the "authenticity of Chinese Annals and the Chinese Chronology" in order to attack that of the Bible (1758:4.347). De Guignes's main target is obvious since his name appears twice: Voltaire. Voltaire's *Essai sur les moeurs* first appeared in the year 1756, the very year that also saw publication of the first volumes of de Guignes's *Histoire des Huns*. The view of origins in these two works is indeed diametrically opposed. For de Guignes, everything has its roots in the plain where Noah's ark landed, whereas Voltaire began his work by making fun of such "oriental fables" and "vain ideas" that are "an insult to reason" and "suffocate what little we know about antiquity under a mass of forced conjectures" (Voltaire 1756:4–7). Arguing that the Jesuits themselves had confirmed by calculation of solar eclipses that the Chinese Annals were both old and reliable, Voltaire had begun his universal history with a chapter on China that stated that twenty-five centuries before Christ the Chinese already had a well-established empire (p. 11). De Guignes sharply criticized such enthusiasm that makes the Chinese empire "begin well before the deluge and possibly even before the epoch of creation" (de Guignes 1758:4.348). Insisting that "nothing is as uncertain as this kind of chronology" (p. 349), de Guignes went on to dismiss the historical value of the very sources on which his early history of the Huns and of the Chinese was based. He now held that Chinese annals delivered neither detailed nor reliable information and were mostly late works that are "barely more ancient that Herodotus . . . who flourished around 480 B.C.E." (p. 351):

> The Chou-king, which is the most ancient, contains only some haphazard events without chronology. The Tsou-chou, whose authority is contested by the Chinese themselves and that was composed around 300

B.C.E. is, as it were, no more than a chronological table. The Chun-tchieou of Confucius is only a very dry short chronology; and the Chi-pen is very short. That's all there is of Chinese sources. (p. 351)

As we have seen in Chapter 1, Voltaire was at this point still unsure whether he should assign the role of cradle of human civilization to China or to India. But his sarcastic dismissal of biblical history and his initial chapters on China and India—which relegated the Mediterranean cultural region and Israel to the also-rans—ruffled many feathers. Furthermore, Voltaire's argument that the constant inundations of the Nile must have prevented early settlement in Egypt (Voltaire 1756:30) was a provocation to the majority of the encyclopedists and the egyptophile antiquarians of the time. As the author of an entire volume of chronological tables (vol. 1) and a history that took Chinese chronology and annals very seriously, de Guignes had good reason to fear being instrumentalized by Bible-averse critics like Voltaire. While his letter at the end of the fourth volume was a brave attempt at preventing such misuse, it also risked throwing the baby out with the bath water.

But there was another, far more decisive event that led to de Guignes's radical change of mind. After reading the abstract of an April 1758 report by Abbé Jean-Jacques Barthélémy on the Phoenician alphabet, de Guignes decided "to work on the manner in which alphabetical letters could have formed" (de Guignes 1760:36). Having before him a table with Phoenician letters, de Guignes happened to glance at a Chinese dictionary with old forms of characters. The similarity of ancient Chinese character elements and Phoenician letters struck him so forcefully that he was soon convinced that not only the Chinese characters "but also the laws, form of government, the sovereign, the ministers governing under him, and the entire Empire were Egyptian; and that the entire ancient history of China was nothing other than the history of Egypt inserted before that of China proper" (p. 37). Utterly convinced of having made an epoch-making discovery, de Guignes on November 14, 1758, read a report to the public assembly of the Royal Academy of Inscriptions and Literature in Paris. In the following year he published an abstract of this report together with some older opinions about Egypto-Chinese connections along with part of Abbé Barthélémy's paper on Phoenician letters in form of a booklet with the title "Report in which one proves that the Chinese are an Egyptian colony" (de Guignes 1760). De Guignes argued, to the astonishment of missionaries and academics alike, that the Chinese had constructed their characters using a toolset of Phoenician letters. Unaware that these letters represent sounds, he explained, the Chinese interpreted them as elements of meaning or keys—that is, character radicals in Fourmont-style—and in this manner constructed myriads of characters with a hidden story they themselves could not grasp. It is here that, in Indiana Jones style, Professor de Guignes bursts upon the scene and discovers the hidden code.[9] If the first Chinese radical (according to Fourmont) "signifies unity among the Chinese," *aleph* has the same meaning for the people of the Middle East; and "for both groups it also signifies preeminence and the action of steering" (de Guignes 1760:61). Soon enough, de Guignes drew up a kind of Ur-alphabet that was "perhaps very analogous to the primitive alphabet of all nations" (pp. 61–62). This would of course be the kind of writing system used in the plains of Shinar before peoples and languages multiplied. "New combinations gave me new letters, and I saw my alphabet develop imperceptibly to my eyes" (p. 63).

But if the Chinese had adopted alphabetic letters as hieroglyphic elements of meaning, then there had to be a proof of the pudding: it had to be possible to disassemble Chinese characters and get Egyptian or Phoenician words.

> I began with the character by which the Chinese designate the word father [父]; and disregarding the sound which they give to this character, I found it composed of an I and of a D, and I read *Jad* or *Jod*. Now in the Coptic language which has preserved numerous Egyptian words, *Jod* meant father. (p. 64)

While de Guignes cobbled together Phoenician letters infused with some meaning, disassembled Chinese characters into radicals whose meaning was just as contrived, and used his linguistic skills and Fourmont-schooled acumen to connect the dots and lines, he marveled at the enormous consequences of his discovery: "a strange phenomenon for Chinese literature, for the history of ancient peoples a new order of things, and systems new and more conform to truth" (p. 67). Thus, an entirely new vista opened before the eyes of the historian:

> A people for a long sequence of centuries in possession of a language that it does not know; this language wrapped in traits that disfigure it and loaded with sounds that are foreign to it; an alphabetical script converted

into hieroglyphic signs; Egypt and Phoenicia linked by the most palpable connections; the letters, the languages, the annals of the most ancient nations linked in a sequence and all concurring in general harmony. (pp. 67–68)

Details such as when this supposed Egyptian colonization of China had taken place were only cursorily addressed, but de Guignes proposed the year 1122 B.C.E. as the date "when the Egyptian colony appears to have come to China" (pp. 76–77). It is clear that the defense of the biblical scenario and its chronology against the likes of Voltaire was a major motive of de Guignes's Orientalist tour de force:

What will become of the Chinese and the immense duration that they attribute to their empire, all those divisions in historical and uncertain mythical times, all those works aiming to establish their chronology, and all those fashioned to destroy it? And of all those proofs that one draws from them against the books of Moses, and all those systems produced to defend the testimony of this legislator? And of that precocious wisdom, that superiority in all things attributed to the Chinese? . . . All this disappears, and only a simple fact remains, namely, that the ancient savages of China, exactly like those of Greece, were cultivated by the Egyptians—but much later than them because China is much further away than Greece. (p. 79)

As De Guignes refined his argument and replaced the Phoenician alphabetical radicals by Egyptian hieroglyphic ones it became increasingly clear that his theories were intimately linked to the defense of Europe's Bible-based view of history. He was convinced that an antediluvial unitary language of humankind and a writing system to represent that language had once existed. In a paper read on Easter 1766 at the Royal Academy about "the method to arrive at reading and understanding Egyptian hieroglyphs," he explained in some detail his concept of the 214 "primitive ideas" that the Chinese use as radicals and his view of hieroglyphic and alphabetic elements (which had also considerably evolved since 1758):

These 214 keys are either used alone as a character to express a meaning or combined in various ways and then considered parts of a character of group. Each of these parts is the representation of a simple idea which,

united with two or three others, produces a word or another idea resulting from these simple ideas; that is to say, they form together a kind of
phrase which is like the definition of a more complex idea. One could
thus regard the 214 keys as the representation of the 214 simple and
primitive ideas of which the first humans made use and which they
combined in various ways to express other novel ideas as the need arose
(de Guignes 1770:13).

The first humans, de Guignes thus proposed, wrapped little Fourmont-
style stories in their hieroglyphs: the character for night, 夜, for example, "is
composed of three such keys that signify 'obscurity,' the 'action of covering,'
and 'man'"; literally rendered, "this means *the obscurity covering men*, a
phrase that perfectly expresses the idea of night" (p. 13). This kind of implicit
poetry, de Guignes suggested, is the ultimate source of the "oriental style"
(which at that time was *en vogue* as a research topic in Bible studies) and
accounts for the striking "poetic" similarities between various Asian languages.

According to de Guignes, this system of "hieroglyphic" writing was "that
of the first men and by consequence common to all those who remained
in the region where the Hebrew, Arabic, Syriac, Phoenician, and Egyptian
languages were in use" (p. 26). The Egyptians had a special status since they
had "cultivated the sciences earlier than other people, transmitted them to
other peoples, and instructed Moses in all their sciences" (pp. 26–27). "More
than any other people, the Egyptians had safeguarded the simplicity of this
ancient language which must have been that of the first humans" (p. 41).
They also passed on their "keys," which is why oriental languages, as seen in
Figure 8. "have preserved the roots of Egyptian words" (p. 29).

Other oriental languages inherited the characteristics of primeval speech
and writing via Egypt. De Guignes concluded:

I believe having sufficiently proved: 1. That the oriental languages, which
must be regarded only as dialects, are related to that of the Egyptians,
and that they all seem to have been formed from a mother language—
which apparently was that of the first humans—that the Egyptians had
preserved with the most care. 2. That the Chinese characters are the same
as the Egyptian ones, and by consequence, that one can succeed in reading and understanding these latter [Egyptian] ones. (pp. 46–47)

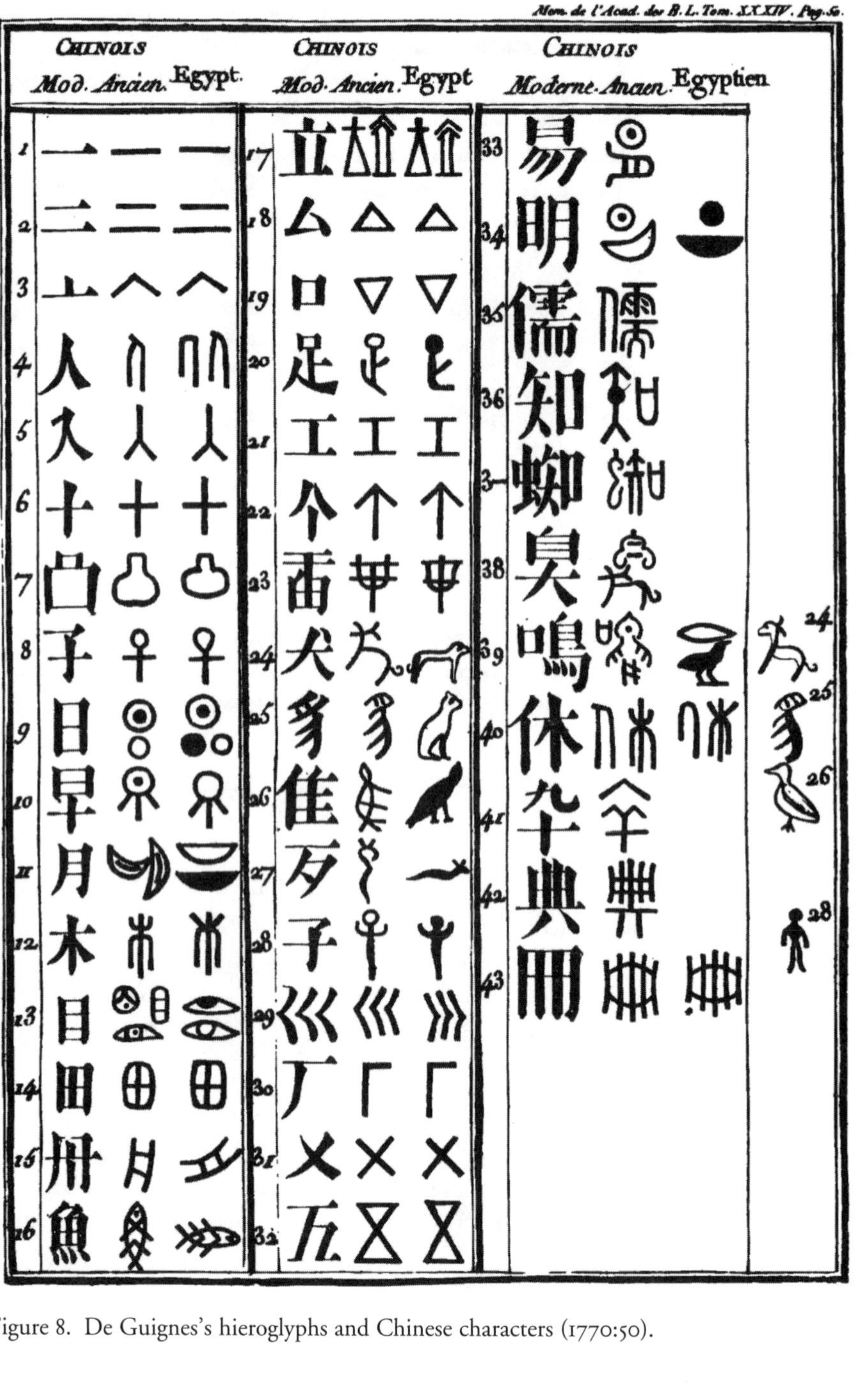

Figure 8. De Guignes's hieroglyphs and Chinese characters (1770:50).

De Guignes was aware that the verification and documentation of his discovery would necessitate decades of hard labor. The volumes furnishing the promised proofs never came to completion, but by and by, de Guignes addressed some of the major issues in separate papers. His 1759 bombshell had been severely taken to task, especially by his codisciple under Fourmont, Deshauterayes, most of whose twenty-three objections—published in the same year under the title of "Doubts about the dissertation of Mr. de Guignes about the Chinese"—de Guignes was incapable of invalidating. They included the observation that the depiction of objects and hieroglyphic writing must be older than alphabetic systems (Deshauterayes 1759:12–15);[10] that in spite of the Egyptian priests who supposedly carried the hieroglyph system to China, there is no trace of early Egyptian religion in China (pp. 16–18); and that the doctrine of metempsychosis was introduced to China from India in the year 65 C.E. and not from Egypt at some much earlier time (pp. 81–85).

The question of the relationship of Chinese religion to its supposed Egyptian origins was a central one. In 1775 de Guignes finally addressed it in a report, while admitting that this issue of religion was "the most difficult, the most important, and the least likely to furnish the kind of proofs I was looking for" (de Guignes 1781d:305). In spite of Jesuit speculation about ancient Chinese monotheism, little was known about ancient Chinese religion, and the exoteric/esoteric division in Chinese religion was not specific enough to allow a clear identification of Egyptian origins. Since the religion of Fo was excluded from discussion because of its non-Egyptian origin (see below), de Guignes had to fall back on the supposedly oldest Chinese book, the *Yijing*. Here he found himself once more in possession of an excellent analysis by de Visdelou (1770). But the similarities he came up with were less than impressive: Osiris and Yang, Isis and Yin, eight elements and trigrams, the conceptions of world soul and emanation, and an elaborate number system. He compared this with what is known about the doctrines of Pythagoras and quickly concluded that it was "borrowed from Egyptianisme, the source of Pythagorisme" (de Guignes 1781d:314). Similarities between the *Yijing* and Pythagorean numeric philosophy were seen as due to their common Egyptian source, and this short circuit allowed de Guignes to jump to the conclusion that it was "proven that one of the two nations borrowed its system from the other" (p. 314) and that "the Chinese—who hitherto were portrayed as an isolated people that drew nothing from other nations and who some even wanted to make into the cradle of sciences and arts—have borrowed everything from Egypt" (p. 345).

De Guignes's "Indian Religion"

It is interesting that in such discussions de Guignes did not mention one word about another focus of his interest, the religion of Fo. We have seen in previous chapters that Athanasius Kircher, Mathurin Veyssière de La Croze, and Engelbert Kaempfer all regarded its origin as Egyptian and that in the case of Kaempfer, whose writings de Guignes studied with much attention, the founder was even identified as an Egyptian priest from Memphis. It also would have been easy to expand La Croze's list of similarities between Egyptian religion and that of the Samanéens who followed Fo/Buddha. However, though inspired by La Croze's synthesis, de Guignes held a different view of this pan-Asian religion. This view will be explored in the remainder of this chapter based on the following pertinent publications by de Guignes:

1. The *Recherches sur les philosophes appelés Samanéens* ("Researches about the philosophers called Samanéens"). De Guignes read this paper to the Royal Academy in July 1753 and published it six years later (de Guignes 1759:770–804).
2. A section of the second volume of the *History of the Huns* containing de Guignes's pioneering translation of the *Forty-Two Sections Sutra* (de Guignes 1756:1B.223–37).
3. Three reports read in the course of 1776 to the Royal Academy under the title of *Sur la Religion Indienne, & sur les Livres fondamentaux de cette religion, qui ont été traduits de l'Indien en Chinois* ("On Indian religion and the basic texts of that religion that were translated from the Indian [idiom] into Chinese"). These were first published in 1781 (de Guignes 1781a, b, c).

What distinguishes de Guignes's research on the Samanéens from that of his predecessors is his use of Asian sources. We recall that La Croze's synthesis only mentioned a poetry lexicon, an ancient language book, and (with a question mark) the *Civavākkiyam* as "books of the Samanéens" (La Croze 1724:494–95). None of these texts is currently associated with Buddhism. By contrast, de Guignes from the outset based his view on two specific texts. He devoted the entire second part of his 1753 paper to their analysis and included partial translations from the Arabic and Chinese (de Guignes 1759:791–804). The first of these texts, the so-called *Anbertkend* (sometimes also spelled *Ambertkend*), is today known as the *Amrtakunda* (Pool of Nectar), a Hatha Yoga text of Indian origin that has nothing to do with Buddhism. Carl W. Ernst called it "one of the most unusual examples of cross-cultural encounter in the annals of the study of religion" on account of its complex synthesis of Indian, Islamic, gnostic, and Neoplatonic influences and the fact that no other literary source on yoga was so widely disseminated among Sufis (Ernst 1996:9–11). The use of this text by de Guignes is a hitherto unexplored facet of this interesting cross-cultural encounter. For him the *Anbertkend* was an important text of the so-called "Indian religion" that "contains the principles admitted by the *Yogis*, particularly those related to magic" (p. 791).[11] The second text discussed by de Guignes is presented as "the work of Fo himself that includes all the moral teachings he bequeathed to his disciples" (p. 791). While this second text is well known under the title *Forty-Two Sections Sutra* and is extant in Chinese, the *Anbertkend* or *Amrtakunda* is not exactly a household word. De Guignes described it as an Indian book that was "translated into the Persian language by the Imam Rokneddin Mohammed of Samarkand who had received it from a Brahmin called *Behergir* of the sect of the *Yogis*" and was subsequently translated into Arabic by Mohieddin-ben-al-arabi.[12] D'Herbelot's *Bibliothèque Orientale* features the following information under the heading "Anbertkend" (1697:114):

> Book of the Brachmans or Bramens which contains the religion and philosophy of the Indians; this word signifies the cistern where one draws the water of life. It is divided into fifty Beths or Treatises of which each has ten chapters. A Yogi or Indian dervish called Anbahoumatah, who converted to Islam, translated it from the Indian into Arabic under the title *Merat al mááni*, The Mirror of Intelligence; but though it was translated, this book cannot be understood without the help of a Bramen or Indian Doctor.

Four decades after d'Herbelot, Abbé Antoine BANIER (1673–1741) widely disseminated the idea that the four Vedas contain "all the sciences and all religious ceremonies" whereas the *Anbertkend* "contains the doctrines of the Indians" (Banier 1738:1.128–29). De Guignes also thought that "this book is not at all the *Vedam* of the Indians" but regarded it as "a work of the contemplative philosophers who, far from accepting the *Vedam*, reject it as useless based on the great perfection they believe to have attained" (de Guignes 1759:791–92). This description very much resembles the one given by Bartholomäus Ziegenbalg and La Croze of the Gnanigöl and their (Tamil Siddha) literature including the *Civavākkiyam*. According to de Guignes, the *Anbert-kend* is a "summary of the contemplatives of India" (p. 796) that advocates that "to become happy one must annihilate all one's passions, not let oneself be seduced by the senses, and be in the kind of universal apathy that is so much recommended in the book of *Fo*" (p. 793). Apart from this, the only apparent connection to Fo or Buddha is a mantra connected with the contemplation of the planet "*Boudah* or Mercury" (p. 800). The questions that thus need to be first addressed are why de Guignes regarded this Yogic text (of which he translated sample sections) as a scripture belonging to the tradition of the "philosophers called Samanéens;" what he meant by this term; and how he situated these "philosophers" within the religious universe of India and Asia as a whole.

Relying on several authors of European antiquity whose view of Indian religions La Croze had popularized, de Guignes accepted that in ancient India there were two main factions: the "ancient Brakhmanes," and the "Germanes, Sarmanes, or Samanéens" (p. 770). Supplementing the sparse information from Greek and Roman authors, de Guignes proposed to "make use of clarifications from Chinese and Arab authors in order to provide a more exact idea about the sect of the Samanéens by examining who their founder is, in which country it originated, and what doctrine he left to his disciples at his death" (p. 770). The information from ancient European authors led him to a view that fundamentally differs from that of La Croze. We recall that, based on information furnished by Ziegenbalg, La Croze saw Brahmanism and the religion of the Samanéens as rival religions that came into such conflict that the Samanéens or followers of Buddha were eventually driven from India to other countries of Asia. But de Guignes had a very different starting point:

> What I have reported based on the Greek and Latin writers compels me to believe that there is little difference between the Samanéens and the Brachmanes, or rather, that they are two sects of the same religion. In effect, one still finds in the Indies a crowd of Brachmanes who appear to have the same doctrine and live in the same manner [as the Samanéens described by Greek and Latin writers]; but those who resemble the ancient Samanéens most perfectly are the Talapoins of Siam: like them, they live retired in rich cloisters, have no personal possessions, and enjoy great reputation at court; but more austere ones exclusively live in woods

and forests, and there are also women under the direction of these Tala-poins. (p. 773)

De Guignes explains that in India there are still Brahmins who "hold a doctrine that is more or less similar to that of the Samanéens" (p. 775):

> If the name of Samanéen seems no more extant in this [southern] part of India [described by La Croze], one still finds the Yogis, the Vanapras-tas, the Sanjassis, and the Avadoutas which all go under the common denomination of Brahmins, and like the Samanéens they do not admit any difference between castes or tribes and still follow the precepts of Budda, the founder of the Samanéens. (p. 776)

But what is this religion of which the Brachmanes and the Samanéens supposedly constitute two separate sects? De Guignes simply calls it "the Indian religion" (*la religion Indienne*; p. 779). It is likely that de Guignes was also inspired by Johann Jacob Brucker's treatise on Asian philosophy (Brucker 1744:4B.804–26)[13] and by Nicolas FRÉRET (1688–1749), who had studied Chinese even before Fourmont and had read a paper in 1744 that advanced exactly this opinion (see the beginning of Chapter 7). Fréret asserted that "La religion indienne" is extremely widespread in Asia; reigning in India as "la religion des Brahmes," "Indian religion" has also conquered Tibet, Bhutan, China since the year 64 C.E., Vietnam, Laos, Cambodia, Siam, Burma, and so on (Fréret 1753:36). But while Fréret sought the doctrine of this religion in Diogo do Couto's description of the Vedas and combined it with some Bud-dhist elements, de Guignes decided to take the Buddhist track and identified the founder of his "religion Indienne" as Buddha who is venerated under various names in different countries of Asia.

> Several Arab authors who knew this personage name him *Boudasp* or *Boudasf.* Beidawi, the celebrated Persian historian, calls him *Schekmou-niberkan*, or simply *Schekmouni*; the Chinese *Tche-kia* or *Chekia-meouni*, which is the same name as the *Schek-mouni* of Beidawi; they give him also the name of *Fotéo* or *Foto*, which is an alteration of *phutta* or *butta*. But the name under which he is best known in all Chinese works is that of *Fo*, the diminutive of *Foto*. The Siamese name him *Prah-poudi-tchaou*, that is to say, the *Saint of high origin, Sammana-khutama, the man with-out passion*, and *phutta*. Mr. Hyde derives this name from the Persian

word *butt, idol*; and Mr. Leibniz believed that this legislator was identical with the *Wodin* of the Northern peoples. In the language of the Indians *Butta* or *Budda* signifies Mercury. (De Guignes 1759:776)

De Guignes furnished much detail about the life of this founder from Arabic and especially Chinese sources (pp. 785–87) and thought that a birth of around 1027 B.C.E (p. 778) appears more likely than an earlier date that might be due to a confusion of Buddha with Zoroaster (pp. 780, 785). He also included a short version of the Buddha's deathbed confession story but added a particular twist:

> When dying he said to those of his disciples who were most attached to him that until then he had only made use of parables and that he had hidden the truth under figurative and metaphorical expressions; his true opinion being that there is no other principle than emptiness and noth-ingness [le vuide & le néant], and that everything came out of nothing and would return to it. So, according to all missionaries, atheism seems to be the favorite principle of this philosopher; but a more attentive examination of the conduct of those who follow his doctrine and of the book which he has left to us does not allow our wholesale adoption of this opinion. (pp. 786–77)

De Guignes's subsequent explanations about the two sects produced by the last words of Fo—"*la doctrine extérieure* consisting in the cult of idols" and "*la doctrine intérieure* that adopted this emptiness and nothingness of which Fo had spoken at his death" (p. 787)—are key for understanding his "Indian religion."[14] This religion, founded by Buddha around 1000 B.C.E. in India (p. 778), has as its fundamental principle the "system of metempsy-chosis" (p. 779). This explains the fact that even founders of other religions came to be incorporated as apparitions of the Buddha. De Guignes had read in Chinese sources that there were many "Fo"; in Ma Duanlin's *Wenxian tongkao*, for example, he found a reference to "seven Fo" (p. 779). He mistak-enly thought that these were "authors of different religions that had succes-sively been destroyed" but correctly inferred that the name Fo is not necessarily referring to one person but can be used as a generic term. In India this founder was "said to be identical with the god Vishnu who, according to the fabled traditions of India, appeared ten times in the world, and whose tenth apparition was in the shape of the Buddha" (p. 786).

De Guignes located representatives of the two "sects" of this "Indian religion" founded by Buddha throughout Asia. In his view the particular doctrines and practices of "Indian religion" gradually changed as they adapted themselves to local circumstances and customs; and this accounts for the great variety of forms in diverse countries. In the *History of the Huns* de Guignes explained:

> One notices that the further the Samanéens were from their place of origin, the more they veered from the principles of their founder. The customs of the peoples to whom they taught their religion brought about great changes, and these Samanéens attached themselves more particularly to certain dogmas and certain religious practices that they judged to be more suitable to the peoples among which they lived. (de Guignes 1756:1B.235)

The two basic forms of his "Indian religion" are well characterized by the "exoteric" and "esoteric" labels.

> The adherents of the exterior doctrine are those whom we know more commonly under the name of *Brahmes*, of *Bonzes*, of *Lamas*, and of *Talapoins* who, always prostrated at the feet of their gods, think their happiness consists in holding the tail of a cow, worshipping *Brahma*, *Vishnu*, *Eswara* [Shiva] and 330 million inferior divinities, constructing temples in their honor, having a singular reverence for the water of the Ganges, and believing that after death their soul will receive punishment for its crimes in Hell or recompense of its virtues in Paradise. From there the soul continues, as a form of recompense or punishment, to animate the bodies of humans, animals and even plants, until it has reached the highest degree of purification and perfection to which the different transmigrations imperceptibly lead. It is only after having transmigrated through the bodies of several beings that it finally takes shelter in that of a Samanéen. (de Guignes 1759:787)

De Guignes's "Indian religion" has metempsychosis as its central tenet, and the Samanéens represent the ultimate stage of the purification process of souls. Like La Croze's Gnanigöls, de Guignes's Samanéens are no longer bound to the rituals, superstitious practices, and divinities of ordinary people and their clergy. In the manner of mystics, these adherents of the Buddha's esoteric teaching live in poverty and seclusion while devoting themselves entirely to the task of "contemplating God" and "becoming one" with him:

> They regard the rest of men as so many unfortunates who cannot reach the state of Samanéen unless they pass through all the degrees of metempsychosis. Thus, the true Samanéen or adherent of the interior doctrine, on account of having been born into the most perfect state, is no longer obliged to expiate the sins which have been washed away by previous transmigrations. He has no more need to go prostrate himself in a temple nor to direct his prayers to the gods worshipped by the people—gods who are but ministers to the great God of the Universe. Freed from all passions and exempt from all crime, the Samanéen only dies to rejoin this unique Divinity of which his soul was a detached part. They think that all souls together form the supreme being, that they exist in him in all eternity, that they emanate from him; yet that they can only be reunited with him after having purified themselves to the level they were at when they were first separated. (pp. 787–88)

This view of the Samanéens explains why de Guignes associated the *Anbertkend* with the Samanéens and why Herder, as mentioned at the end of Chapter 3, began the India section of his *Ideas for a Philosophy of the History of Humanity* with the phrase "Even though the teaching of the Brahmans is nothing but a branch of the widespread religion that, from Tibet to Japan, has formed sects or governments" (Herder 2002, 3/1:411). The Brahmans—joined by the Tibetan Lamas, Chinese and Japanese Bonzes, Siamese Talapoins, and possibly even the Siberian shamans—are seen as part of the exoteric clergy of the "Indian religion" of Buddha whose local variants with their multiform idolatry, polytheism, superstition, and ritualism stand in sharp contrast to the pure mysticism and resolute esoteric monotheism of the Samanéens.

Unlike La Croze who had theorized that the Samanéens of India turned into atheists and were mainly for this reason driven from India to surrounding countries, de Guignes depicted them as most ardent monotheists:

> According to their principles, this Supreme Being, the Being of all Beings, is from all eternity; he has no form whatsoever, is invisible, incomprehensible, and the origin of everything; he is the power, the wisdom, the knowledge, holiness, and truth itself; he is infinitely good, just, and

merciful; he has created all beings and preserves everything; because he himself is beyond any adoration, he cannot be represented by idols; yet his attributes—to which he allows a cult to be rendered—may be depicted. (de Guignes 1759:788)

We have already encountered similar monotheistic hymns in earlier chapters, and the amalgamation of much of Asia under the banner of a single religion made it as easy to find statements of "esoteric" monotheism as of "exoteric" polytheism. Similar to François Bernier's Sufis and Ziegenbalg's Gnanigöls, the Samanéens of de Guignes are portrayed as fervent monotheists of a mystic tendency who occupy themselves exclusively with meditation on the Supreme Being.

> For this reason the Samanéen is always busy contemplating him in his meditations and has no sign of an exterior cult; but he is not at the same time atheist, as the missionaries pretend, because he has the exclusive aim to snuff out in himself all passions in order to be ready to rejoin his God. Thus the emptiness and nothingness, the principles of the Samanéens, do not signify at all the destruction of the soul. Rather, they mean that we must annihilate all our senses, annihilate ourselves, in order to lose ourselves, as it were, in the bosom of the Divinity who has drawn all things out of nothing and who himself is not matter. (p. 788)

De Guignes's Samanéen mystics—like Ziegenbalg's Gnanigöls—regard gods like Brahma, Vishnu, and Shiva as vulgar representations of the attributes of the one and only creator God; but unfortunately, "the rest of the Indian religion, which is no more that of the Samanéens, is less susceptible to the grand ideas and profound meditations that form the entire cult of the disciples of *Budda*" (p. 789).

Though the boundaries of de Guignes's "Indian religion" are larger than those of the "Buddhism" that we know today, there are many fundamental correspondences. They include the name and biography of its founder; the religion's Indian origin; its expansion to various surrounding countries in Southeast, Central, and East Asia from the beginning of the common era; its existence in such places as Tibet, Mongolia, Siam, Cambodia, Burma, Ceylon, Vietnam, China, and Japan; the presence of marked local variations; its distinctive monastic culture; some its rituals; the appellations of its clergy in these countries; the existence of a sacred literature linked to the founder; and so forth. With regard to the doctrines of this religion, the fable of the Buddha's deathbed confession had created a fuzzy mold with enough space to accommodate various phenomena.

On the esoteric side of de Guignes's "Indian religion," the Zen monks of Japan were joined by such colorful company as Abraham Roger's Vanaprasthas, Bernier's Sufis and Yogis, and Ziegenbalg's Gnanigöls. On the exoteric side, the Bonzes of Japan and China were in the company of a motley crowd of Indian Brahmins, Tibetan Lamas, and Siamese Talapoins. In the doctrinal sphere not much solid information had been gained since the days of the sixteenth-century Japan mission when the elements of the Buddha's "deathbed confession" made their first appearance. Though the Jesuits in Japan and China had studied some Buddhist texts such as the Lotus Sutra, biographies of the Buddha, and collections of Zen sayings—and though Simon de la Loubère had published some excerpts that someone had translated from Buddhist texts in the Pali language—the purportedly very large literature of this "Indian religion" remained an enigma. Kircher's inclusion of Indian Brahmins and de Visdelou/Le Gobien's view of the *polemen* as adherents of Fo further blurred the picture. If Indian Yogis, Gnanigöls, and Tamil Siddhas were associated with the esoteric followers of Buddha, could it not be that the fabled Indian Vedas, too, formed part of the literature of the Samanéens?

This kind of haze lent itself to rampant speculation. For example, in a letter by Deshauterayes (de Guignes's co-disciple under Fourmont) to Anquetil-Duperron, the professor speculated that "this Budha or Phta could be the same as the founder of the Egyptian monarchy, the first to introduce among men the system of the transmigration of souls into animal bodies."[15] But Deshauterayes was acutely aware that only the study of Asian languages and the ability to read its sacred literature could bring change to the state of ignorance enveloping even the natives themselves: "It is in their books that one must find what one wants to know" (NAF 8872:71v). He thus urged his young disciple to study the Pali language, "which is the only language of the Indies that, apart from the Tibetan, I advise you strongly to learn because these are the languages of the learned through which you will make an abundant harvest" (p. 70v).

Barely one year after this letter, the first Buddhist sutra appeared in the French translation of de Guignes. In fact he had already included a rendering of the short preface of this Chinese text in the second part of his 1753 Samanéens paper (de Guignes 1759:802–3). His portrayal of the central doctrines of the Samanéens was primarily based on his reading of this text that, according to de Guignes, Fo had "left to us" (p. 787) and that supposedly laid out the essence of the doctrine of the Samanéens. It appears that de Guignes was the first European who by himself translated a Buddhist text from an Asian language and published it. This can be seen as another waystation toward the "new Orientalism" that Thomas Trautmann too narrowly associated with early students of Indian languages (1997:32–33) and Raymond Schwab with Anquetil-Duperron and the *Zend Avesta* (1950:25). The particular text that de Guignes translated from Chinese into French was held in high esteem throughout East Asia as the (reputedly) earliest of all Buddhist texts and as the first sacred scripture to be brought from India to China in the year 65 C.E. We have seen that thanks to this text this date stood like a fixed centerpiece among the ever shifting shards in the European kaleidoscope of Asian religions. What kind of text is this "Book of Fo"? Which version did de Guignes use for his pioneer translation? And how did he arrive at his monotheistic interpretation of its fundamental doctrine?

The *Forty-Two Sections Sutra*

De Guignes had a kind of Bible for all things Chinese. Whether he was writing about Chinese history or religion, on virtually every page he either refers to or quotes from the *Wenxian tongkao* (Comprehensive examination of literature) compiled by MA Duanlin (1245–1322). Published after twenty years of work in 1321, this masterpiece of Chinese historiography soon became indispensable because it provided thematically arranged extracts from a very wide range of other Chinese works. Students preparing for China's civil service examinations sometimes memorized Ma's chapter introductions, and missionaries and early Western Sinologists appreciated the giant work because it furnished so much (and so judiciously selected) textual material from original sources.

> One can say that this excellent work is by itself equivalent to an entire library and that even if Chinese literature would only consist of this work it would be worth the trouble to learn Chinese just to read this. It is not only about China that one would learn much but also a large part of Asia, and regarding everything that is most important and noteworthy about its religions, legislation, rural economics and politics, commerce, agriculture, natural history, history, physical geography, and ethnogra-

phy. One only has to choose the subject which one wants to study and then to translate what Ma Duanlin has to say about it. All the facts are reported and classified, all sources indicated, and all authorities cited and discussed. (Abel-Rémusat 1829:2.170)

This was the work that men like de Visdelou and de Guignes always seemed to have at hand; and some China missionaries only appeared to be so well read because they failed to mention that Ma Duanlin was the source of their quotations from so many Chinese works (p. 171). It was in the *Wenxian tongkao* that de Guignes found much of the material for his *History of the Huns*, and the influence of this collection was so great that Abel-Rémusat stated in 1829 that Ma Duanlin alone was at the origin "of the large part of positive knowledge that one has so far acquired in Europe about Chinese antiquity" (p. 171–72). While this may be a bit exaggerated in view of the translations of Chinese classics and histories of the seventeenth and eighteenth centuries, there is no doubt that for de Guignes this collection was of supreme importance. For example, fascicles 226 and 227 of Ma Duanlin's work, which deal with Buddhism and its literature, are the source of much of the solid information (as opposed to speculation) that de Guignes conveyed about this topic to his pan-European readership.

In the introduction to his Buddhism sections, Ma Duanlin recounts the traditional story about the dream of Emperor Ming of the Han dynasty (re. 58–75 C.E.) and the introduction of Buddhism to China. The emperor saw a spirit flying in his palace courtyard, was told that this had to do with an Indian sage called Buddha, and sent an embassy to India. Accompanied by two Indian monks, this embassy brought the *Forty-Two Sections Sutra* and a statue of the Buddha on a white horse back to China in 65 C.E. The famous White Horse Monastery (*Baimasi*) was built near the capital Chang'an (today's Xian) in order to store this precious text and China's first Buddha statue.

This is the story de Guignes was familiar with. But the more modern Sinologists led by Maspéro (1910) learned about it, the more this story turned out to be a classic foundation myth. Today we know that there is no evidence that such an embassy ever took place; that the oldest extant story of Emperor Ming's dream had a man as leader of the ambassadors who had lived two hundred years earlier; that Buddhism was introduced to China before the first century of the common era; that the first references to a White Horse Monastery date from the third century C.E.;[16] and of course, as is the rule with such myths, that striking details—such as the first Buddha image and the two Indian monks accompanying the white horse—enter the game suspiciously late (here in the fifth century).

While this tale of the introduction of Buddhism to China is today regarded as a legend without any historical basis, the *Forty-Two Sections Sutra* itself has a reasonable claim to antiquity. It is an exaggeration to say that "most scholars believe that the original *Scripture of Forty-Two Sections*, whatever its origins, was indeed in circulation during the earliest period of Buddhism in China" (Sharf 2002:418). One can only state with confidence that some of its maxims and sayings are documented from the second century onward and that some of the vocabulary of the text indicates (or wants to indicate) an origin in the first centuries C.E. The scholarly consensus in Japan holds that the text as we know it stems not from the first or second century but is a Chinese compilation dating from the fifth century C.E. that combined passages and sayings from a number of different Buddhist texts (Okabe 1967).

Twentieth-century research has also revealed that there are three major versions of this text (Okabe 1967). The first, included in the Korean Buddhist canon, appears to more or less closely reproduce the original fifth-century compilation and is here called "standard version." The version used by de Guignes, by contrast, first emerged around 800 C.E. and contains some sections that are strikingly different from the standard version. Figure 9 shows the genealogy of editions of the *Forty-Two Sections Sutra*.

Since exactly these modified sections (Yanagida 1955) are of central importance for de Guignes's interpretation of "Indian religion," a bit more information is needed here. The book entitled *Baolin zhuan* ("Treasure Forest Biographies") of 801—which was the first text to include the modified *Forty-Two Sections Sutra*—is known as a scripture of the Chan or Zen tradition of Chinese Buddhism. Rather than a separate "sect" in the ordinary sense, this was a typical reform movement involving Buddhist monks of a variety of different affiliations who had a particular interest in meditation[17] and wanted to link their reform to the founder's "original teaching." For this purpose, lineages of transmission were created out of whole cloth, and soon enough the founder Buddha was linked to his eighth-century Chinese "successors" by a direct line of Indian patriarchs at whose end stood Bodhidharma, the legendary figure who fulfills the role of transmitter and bridge between India and China. Needless to say, all this was a pious invention to legitimize and anchor the reform movement in the founder's "original"

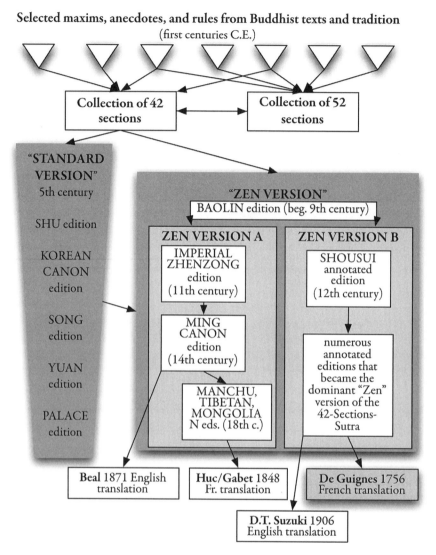

Selected maxims, anecdotes, and rules from Buddhist texts and tradition
(first centuries C.E.)

Collection of 42 sections

Collection of 52 sections

"STANDARD VERSION"
5th century

SHU edition

KOREAN CANON edition

SONG edition

YUAN edition

PALACE edition

"ZEN VERSION"
BAOLIN edition (beg. 9th century)

ZEN VERSION A

IMPERIAL ZHENZONG edition (11th century)

MING CANON edition (14th century)

MANCHU, TIBETAN, MONGOLIA N eds. (18th c.)

ZEN VERSION B

SHOUSUI annotated edition (12th century)

numerous annotated editions that became the dominant "Zen" version of the 42-Sections-Sutra

Beal 1871 English translation

Huc/Gabet 1848 Fr. translation

De Guignes 1756 French translation

D.T. Suzuki 1906 English translation

Figure 9. Stemma of major *Forty-Two Sections Sutra* editions (Urs App)

teaching that supposedly was transmitted "mind to mind" by an unbroken succession of enlightened teachers reaching back to the Buddha. According to this very creative story line, the Buddha once showed a flower to his assembly and only one member, his disciple Mahakashyapa, smiled. He thus became the first Indian "Zen" patriarch who had received the Buddha's formless transmission. Such transmission lineages had much evolved since their modest beginnings in genealogies of Buddhist masters of Kashmir and in Tiantai Buddhist lore. In the eighth century, Zen sympathizers tested a number of variants until, in the year 801, a model emerged that carried the day (Yampolsky 1967:47–50). This was the model of the *Baolin zhuan* featuring twenty-seven Indian patriarchs and the twenty-eighth patriarch Bodhidharma, the legendary founder of Zen whom Engelbert Kaempfer had depicted crossing the sea to China on a reed (see Figure 10 below).

The partially extant first chapter of this "Treasure Forest" text presented the biography of the founder, Shakyamuni Buddha, and this chapter contained the modified text of the *Forty-Two Sections Sutra.* The setting is, of course, significant: the sutra is uttered just after the Buddha's enlightenment and thus constitutes the founder's crucial first teaching. This alone was quite a daring innovation that turned a collection of maxims, anecdotes, and rules into a founder's oration. But the ninth-century editor of the *Baolin zhuan* went one significant step further. Not content faithfully to quote the conventional text of the sutra, he changed various sections and added passages that clearly reflected his own reformist "Zen" agenda. This method of putting words into the founder's mouth was and is, of course, popular in many religions; but in this case it was a particularly effective ploy. Not only did the Buddha now utter things that furthered the editor's sectarian agenda—and turned the text into a "sutra"—but he said these things in his very first speech after enlightenment! And this speech formed a text that was not just *any* text but the reputedly *first* and *oldest* text of Buddhism and for good measure also the first one to make its way to China and to be translated into Chinese! What better pedigree and vehicle for reformist teachings could one wish for?

The Zen movement as a whole was crowned with brilliant success, as Ma Duanlin's list of Buddhist literature in fascicle 227 of his work shows: more than one-third of the eighty-three listed texts are products of the Zen tradition (for example, the *Platform Sutra of the Sixth Patriarch, Blue Cliff Record*, and *Records of Linji*). The "Zen-ified" text of the *Forty-Two Sections Sutra,* too, was a smashing success. It became by far the most popular version of this sutra, was printed and reprinted with various commentaries, and in the Song period was even included as the first of the "three classics" (Ch. *sanjing*) of Buddhism.[18] A copy of it found its way into the Royal Library in Paris, and this is the text de Guignes set out to translate in the early 1750s.[19] It is worthy of note that it was exactly the most "Zen-ified" version of this text that served to introduce Europe to Buddhist sutras, that is, sermons purportedly uttered by the Buddha.[20]

The difference between the three major versions of the *Forty-Two Sections Sutra* is of great interest as it exhibits the motives of their respective editors. For example, the end of section nine of the standard version reads as follows:

> Feeding one billion saints is not as good as feeding one solitary buddha (*pratyekabudda*). Feeding ten billion solitary buddhas is not as good as **liberating one's parents in this life by means of the teaching of the three honored ones. To teach one hundred billion parents is not as good** as feeding one buddha, studying with the desire to attain buddha-hood, and aspiring to liberate all beings. But the merit of feeding a good man is [still] very great. It is better for a common man to be filial to his parents than for him to serve the spirits of Heaven and Earth, for **one's parents are the supreme spirits**. (Sharf 2002:424)

Whether one regards the portions of the text that are here emphasized by bold type as interpolations or not, their emphasis on filial piety clearly exhibits the Chinese character of this text and fits into the political climate of fifth-century China. The Imperial Zhenzong edition (Zen version A), which adopted a number of the "Zen" changes from the *Baolin zhuan*, leaves out part of the first phrase but also praises filial piety:

> Feeding one billion saints is not as good as feeding one solitary buddha (*pratyekabudda*). Feeding ten billion solitary buddhas is not as good as feeding one buddha, studying with the desire to attain buddhahood, and aspiring to liberate all beings. But the merit of feeding a good man is [still] very great. It is better for a common man to be filial to his parents than for him to serve the spirits of Heaven and Earth, **for one's parents are closest**.

For a religion whose clergy must "leave home" (ch. *chujia*) and effectively abandon parents and relatives in order to join the family of the monastic *sangha*, this call for filial piety may seem a little odd; but this kind of passage certainly helped fend off Confucian criticism about Buddhism's lack of filial piety. Compared to the standard edition, the "imperial" edition (Zen version A) effectively sidelined the issue and made it clear that "feeding one buddha, studying with the desire to attain buddhahood, and aspiring to liberate all beings" is the highest goal. The Shousui text (Zen version B), by contrast, mentions not one word about filial piety and advocates a rather different ideal:

> Feeding one billion saints is not as good as feeding one solitary buddha (*pratyekabudda*). Feeding ten billion solitary buddhas is not as good as feeding one of the buddhas of the three time periods. And feeding one hundred billion buddhas of the three time periods is not as good as feeding **someone who is without thought and without attachment, and has nothing to attain or prove.**

This goal reflects the agenda of the Zen sympathizer who edited the *Forty-Two Sections Sutra* around the turn of the ninth century and decided to put this novel teaching straight into the mouth of the newly enlightened Buddha. De Guignes, who used a "Zen version B" text, translated the part emphasized by bold type quite differently from my rendering above:

> One billion O-lo-han are inferior to someone who is in the degree of Pie-tchi-fo, and ten billion Pietchi-fo inferior to someone who has reached the degree of San-chi-tchu-fo. Finally, one hundred billion San-chi-tchu-fo are not comparable to **one who no more thinks, who does nothing, and who is in a complete insensibility of all things**. (de Guignes 1759:1.2.229)

This last passage played a crucial role in de Guignes's definition of the Samanéens and their ideal. He interpreted the different stages of perfection as stages of rebirth and purification. This conception lies at the heart of his view that the ideal Samanéens, who in the Zen version B text are credited with exactly such absence of discriminating thought and attachment, represent the ultimate stage of transmigration before union with the Supreme Being. Theirs is the "religion of annihilation" (la religion de l'anéantissement) de Guignes found at the very beginning of the Sutra text where the Buddha says, "He who abandons his father, his mother, and all his relatives in order to occupy himself with the knowledge of himself and to embrace the religion of annihilation is called Samanéen" (de Guignes 1759:1B.227).

The corresponding standard text defines the Samanéens as follows: "The Buddha said: Those who leave their families and their homes to practice the way are called *śramaṇas*." The Zen text version A and also version B used by

TABLE 7. SECTION OF DE GUIGNES'S *FORTY-TWO SECTIONS SUTRA* TRANSLATION

"Zen" version B (Shousui text)	English translation based on de Guignes (1756:1.2.228)	English translation based on the Chinese text (App)
出家沙門者、斷欲去愛。識自心源。達佛深理。悟無爲法。	A Samanéen, after having abandoned everything and smothered his passions, must always occupy himself with contemplating the sublime doctrine of Fo;	A "home-leaver" or śramaṇa cuts off all desire and frees himself from attachment, understands the source of his own heart-mind, attains the Buddha's profound principle, and awakens to the doctrine of *wu-wei*.
內無所得。外無所求。心不繫道。亦不結業。無念無作。非修非證。	then there is nothing to desire any more, his heart is no more bound, nothing touches him, and he thinks of nothing.	He has nothing to attain inside and nothing to search for outside; his heart-mind is not bound to the Way nor is he tied to karma. Free of thought and action, he has nothing to cultivate and nothing to prove.

de Guignes, by contrast, have: "The Buddha said: A home-leaver or śramaṇa **cuts off all desire and frees himself from attachment, understands the source of his own mind, attains the Buddha's profound principle, and awakens to the doctrine of** *wu-wei*." This "doctrine of *wu-wei*" (literally, "nonaction") was interpreted by de Guignes as "religion of annihilation."[21] It was thus exactly the eight-character-phrase 識心達本、解無爲法 ("know the mind / reach the source / understand the doctrine of *wu-wei*") that the Zen editor had slipped into the opening passage that inspired de Guignes to define the religion of the Samanéens as a "religion of annihilation." He found this ideal confirmed in other passages of his *Forty-Two Sections Sutra*. The second section, which is also exclusive to the Zen versions, is shown in Table 7.

De Guignes's translation in places reads more like a paraphrase; some phrases are left untranslated, and there is a very understandable ignorance of technical terminology. For example, de Guignes translates the text's "nor is he tied to karma" as "nothing touches him." The lack of specialized dictionaries and a tenuous grasp of classical Chinese grammar must have made translation not just a tedious but also a hazardous enterprise. So much more astonishing is the degree of confidence that de Guignes seemed to have in his skill as a translator and interpreter of Chinese texts.

The God of the Samanéens

An anonymous British reviewer once described de Guignes as a man who is "almost always wading through the clouds of philology, to snuff up conjectures."[22] He must have been thinking of de Guignes's theories about the Egyptian origin of the Chinese people or his conviction, built on a flimsy legend in Ma Duanlin's work, that Chinese Buddhist missionaries had discovered America in the fifth century C.E. (de Guignes 1761). But de Guignes's tendency to take some ambiguous drop of information and to wring earth-shattering torrents of conclusions from it is already in evidence in his very first translation from the *Forty-Two Sections Sutra*. His interpretation of the first word of the sutra's preface, as it happens, was just such a "cloud of philology," and the house of cards de Guignes built on this one-legged stool was of a truly astonishing scale. This was de Guignes's first attempt to come to terms with the content and history of the creed that he called "Indian religion" and to introduce the central and oldest text by this religion's founder, so it is no surprise that many readers and other authors were inspired.[23] De Guignes's mistranslation and misinterpretation of the first word of this preface thus not only set his own interpretation of Buddhism on the wrong footing but misled a generation of readers unable to read Chinese who naturally relied on de Guignes's "expertise."

Zen version B's short preface appears to have been authored by the editor of the *Baolin zhuan* around the turn of the ninth century. Since that editor wanted to portray the *Forty-Two Sections Sutra*—which he had so cleverly used as a host for his reformist "Zen" agenda—as the first sermon of the Buddha after his enlightenment, his "Zen Version B" text, of course, situated the action at the Deer Park in Saranath where the Buddha first taught (turned the dharma wheel of the Four Noble Truths); see Table 8.

De Guignes's translation of this preface makes one doubt his grasp of classical Chinese and confirms that he would hardly have been in a position to produce the translations in his *History of the Huns* without the constant help of de Visdelou's manuscripts. But translating such texts in mid-eighteenth-century Paris was an extremely difficult undertaking. Some reading of Buddhist texts would have quickly showed that "the world-honored one" is

TABLE 8. BEGINNING OF DE GUIGNES'S *FORTY-TWO SECTIONS SUTRA* PREFACE

Zen version B text	English translation based on de Guignes (1759:802–3)	English translation based on the Chinese text (App)
世尊成道已。作是思惟。離欲寂靜。是最為勝。	The veritable law of the adoration of *Chi* only consists in meditations, in the removal of one's passions, and in perfect apathy. The one who has reached the greatest perfection in this law,	When [Buddha] the World-honored One had attained the Way [buddhahood] he had the following thought: "To free oneself of desire and be calm is most excellent."
住大禪定。降諸魔道。於鹿野苑中。	after having lost himself in profound contemplations, can submit the spirits, go in the middle of deserts,	Absorbed in a great state of meditation [samadhi], he subdued all demonic ways, and while in the Deer Park
轉四諦法輪。度憍陳如等五人。	traverse the revolutions of the four *Ti*, meditate on the five famous philosophers and particularly on *Kiao-chin-ju*,	he revolved the Dharma wheel of the Four [Noble] Truths. He converted Kaudinya, etc., the five companions.
而證道果。	and finally pass through the different degrees of sanctity that one acquires by practicing the law.	and had them attain the fruit of the Way.

a very common epithet of the Buddha. But there were few such texts at hand, and the Chinese character dictionaries of the Royal Library (Leung 2002:196–97) as a rule did not list compounds. Still, the "subject-verb-past particle" structure should have suggested something like "XX having attained the Way . . ." rather than de Guignes's wayward "the veritable law of the adoration of *Chi* only consists in . . ." For de Guignes everything turned around this "adoration of *Chi*." In his view this "veritable law" consisted in "meditations, removal of one's passions, and in perfect apathy." Furthermore, de Guignes thought that this preface outlined a process through which those who practice this law "pass through the different degrees of sanctity" before reaching the greatest perfection, and used this as textual support for his conception of the Samanéens as the ultimate stage of the transmigration process. But ultimately de Guignes's interpretation hinged on the meaning of the first two characters that he translated as "adoration of *Chi*." The first character *chi* (which today is romanized as *shi*) usually means "century" or "world." But here it forms part of the compound *shizun*, which in Chinese Buddhist texts is one of the most common appellations of the Buddha. It literally means "the world-honored one" and is as common in Buddhist texts as in Christian texts the phrase "our savior" that, as everyone knows, refers to Jesus. Probably due to lack of exposure to Buddhist texts, de Guignes did not realize this and explained the meaning of the first character *chi* or *shi* as follows:

> *Chi*, in the Chinese language, means *century* and corresponds to the Arabic word *Alam*, which the translator of the *Anbertkend* employed in the same sense; it is thus the adoration of the century that is prescribed in both works. What *Masoudi* reports of the *Hazarouan-el-alam*, a duration of 36,000 years (or according to others 60,000 years) was adopted by the Brahmins and is the same as this *Chi* of the Chinese. This *Hazarouan* possessed the power over things and governed them all. In the Indian system, the *Chi* or *Hazarouan* corresponds perfectly to this *Eon* of the Valentinians who pretend that the perfect *Eon* resides in eternity in the highest heaven that can neither be seen nor named. They called it the first principle, the first father. (de Guignes 1759:803)

In support of this view, de Guignes here referred to the famous two-volume *Critical History of Mani and Manichaeism* (1734/1739) by Isaac de BEAUSOBRE (1659–1738). Citing St. Irenaeus, Beausobre had characterized this *Eon* of the Valentinians as "invisible, incomprehensible, eternal, and alone existing through itself" and as "God the Father" who is also called "*First* Father, *First* Principle, and *Profundity*" (Beausobre 1984:578). Following Beausobre, de Guignes stated that these Christian heretics "admitted a perfect *Eon*, the *Eon* of *Eons*," and concluded without further ado that exactly this *Eon* of *Eons* "is the *Chi* of the Samanéens" (de Guignes 1759:804). For de Guignes and his readers this appeared to be solid textual evidence in support of a monotheistic interpretation of esoteric Buddhism, an interpretation that some had already encountered in Brucker (1742–44:4B.821–22) or Fréret (1753; see Chapter 7).

De Guignes's 1753 paper on the Samanéens thus ended with a monotheistic bang. Three years later, in the *History of the Huns,* he spelled out some of the implications. After having once more laid out his view of the exoteric and esoteric followers of Fo and described the Samanéen as a person who "is free of all these passions, exempt of all impurity, and dies only to rejoin the unique divinity of which his soul was a detached part" (de Guignes 1756:1.2.225), de Guignes explains the Samanéen vision of God in a manner that echoes Brucker:

> This supreme Being is the principle of all things, he is from all eternity, invisible incomprehensible, almighty, sovereignly wise, good, just, merciful, and self-originated. He cannot be represented by any image; one cannot worship him because he is beyond any adoration, but one can depict his attributes and worship them. This is the beginning of the idolatric cult of the peoples of India. The Samanéen who is ever occupied with meditation on this great God, only seeks to annihilate himself in order to rejoin and lose himself in the bosom of the Divinity who has pulled all things out of nothing and is itself different from matter. This is the meaning that they give to emptiness and nothingness. (de Guignes 1756:1.2.226)

For de Guignes this sovereign Being, this "great God," is the one who in the "doctrine of the Samanéens or Philosophers has the Chinese name of *Chi*" (p. 226). This fact forms the core of de Guignes's conception of the real (monotheist) religion of Buddha. He even read a creator God into the last section of his 1756 translation of the *Forty-Two Sections Sutra*. That section contains a passage that compares the Buddha's "method of skilful means" (Ch. *fangbianmen*) to a magician's trick (視方便門, 如化寶聚). Like a magician in his own right, de Guignes pulled nothing less than the *creatio ex nihilo* out of this simple phrase. He translated it by "the creation of the universe that has been pulled from nothingness [I regard as] just the simple transformation of one thing into another" (p. 233).

After his translation of the *Forty-Two Sections Sutra*, de Guignes summarized his view of it as follows:

> I thought I had to report here the major part of this work that forms the basis of the entire religion of the Samanéens. Those who glance at it will only find a Christianity of the kind that the Christian heresiarchs of the first century taught after having mixed ideas from Pythagoras on metempsychosis with some other principles drawn from India. This book could be one of those false gospels that were current at the time. With the

exception of a few particular ideas, all the precepts that Fo conveys seem to be drawn from the gospel. (pp. 233–34)

De Guignes's misunderstanding and mistranslation not only confirmed his fixed idea of the monotheism of the Samanéens but also led to an entirely original assessment of the history of their religion. Without making any attempt to help his confused readers, de Guignes suggested that the purportedly oldest book of this religion was an apocryphal Christian gospel of gnostic tendency from the early first century C.E. In a paper read in the fall of 1753 he also argued—possibly inspired by de Visdelou's annotated translation of the Nestorian stele that repeatedly made the same point—that the Chinese had mixed up Nestorian Christians with Buddhists.[24] Not content with this narrow argument based on the text of the stele, he grew convinced that the Chinese mixup of Christianity with Foism happened on such a scale that they even "gave Jesus Christ the name of *Fo!*" (de Guignes 1764:810). In a sense, his theory about the *Forty-Two Sections Sutra* was a counterpart to the story line advanced by Ruggieri (Rule 1986:10) and Ricci that proposed that Emperor Ming's dream about a saint from the West had been about Jesus Christ and that the imperial embassy had mistakenly brought back the idolatry of Fo instead of the truth of Christianity. According to de Guignes, however, the Chinese ambassadors had imported a heretical kind of Christianity and fallen victim to the delusion that it was the religion of Fo.

But what about the origin of the religion of Fo around 1000 B.C.E. that de Guignes had found documented in so many Chinese and Arabic sources? Did he now believe that its exoteric and esoteric teachings were all from the common era? Where did Pythagoras learn about metempsychosis? What were those "other principles" from (presumably pre-Christian-era) India that were supposedly mixed in? Do the Vedas belong to this religion or are they older? In the 1750s de Guignes left these and many other questions unanswered; and when he revisited the theme two decades later, the Christian heresiarchs and the view of the *Forty-Two Sections Sutra* as an apocryphal gospel had vanished like a magician's doves and rabbits.

The History of Buddhism

In the two decades since the publication of his *History of the Huns*, de Guignes had continued to study Ma Duanlin's *Wenxian tongkao*. Much of the accurate information conveyed by the Frenchman in his three 1776 papers stemmed from its 226th and 227th fascicles. These papers contained an extraordinary amount of solid information about the history of Buddhism that may have been lost on those who were only interested in origins and the most ancient events. De Guignes hoped that many such people, especially indomaniacs, would study his findings, accept his view of the Vedas as relatively young texts (not much older than 1100 B.C.E.) and regain or fortify their faith in the accuracy of the biblical account.

With regard to the history of de Guignes's "Indian religion," which, as we now know, consisted mostly of Buddhism, comparatively little solid information had hitherto been available in Europe. Much of it concentrated on tales about the founder's biography, and few missionaries had actually studied Buddhist texts. It was all very confusing. But from the 1750s, many decades before Pali and Sanskrit sources came into play, the ability of a few Europeans to read Chinese opened up a new and abundant source of data, and for a while Fourmont's two disciples, Deshauterayes and de Guignes, were the sole pioneers in Europe able to exploit this treasure trove. As we will see in Chapter 7, Deshauterayes was confused by some ideas that de Visdelou had sent from Pondicherry to Fourmont. Deshauterayes eventually produced some translations from the Chinese that were posthumously published in 1825 and 1826 and influenced Arthur Schopenhauer (App 1998b), but in the eighteenth century he had very little impact and was sidelined by de Guignes.

For information on Buddhism and its history (which for him, of course, formed part of "Indian religion"), de Guignes profited mainly from Ma Duanlin's sections on Buddhism and from the famous travelogue by the Chinese monk Faxian (337–422), who had made a long pilgrimage via Central Asia to India. Such data transmitted by de Guignes had no equal in Europe until the appearance of studies by Jean-Pierre Abel-Rémusat and Eugène Burnouf half a century later. However, the accurate data contained in de Guignes's writings tended to be overshadowed by his spectacular (and spectacularly wrong) conclusions. Yet long sections of his three papers lay out, based on Ma Duanlin, how China had become familiar with Buddhism in the first centuries when Indian and Central Asian monks brought their sacred literature to China and helped translate it into Chinese.

Soon afterward, Chinese monks began to travel to Central Asia and then to India itself in search of Buddhist texts and relics. Some of these monks wrote travelogues that even today are considered precious sources of information about ancient India and Buddhism. Ma Duanlin described many important figures, events, and texts of Buddhism and provided an excellent survey of the history of Chinese Buddhism up to the thirteenth century. De Guignes's European readership thus could learn much about the Indian origin of the religion of Buddha; the life of its founder; the religion's early presence in Kashmir, Afghanistan, and Central Asia; its introduction into China; its famous missionaries, masters, and translators; its abundant sacred literature; some of its doctrines; its two main branches; its spread to Ceylon, Tibet, Mongolia, Southeast Asia, and Japan; and much else.

Almost sixty years before Abel-Rémusat's posthumous *Foe Koue Ki* (1836) and seventy years before Burnouf's justly famous *Introduction à l'histoire du Buddhisme Indien* (1844), the first shot at a presentation of the history of Buddhism was de Guignes's. Apart from details about famous Chinese India travelers such as Faxian and Xuanzang, many Indian or Central Asian monks who had sojourned in China were mentioned by de Guignes (Bodhiruci, Gunabhadra, Kumarajiva, etc.). For some of them even important translations into Chinese are listed; for example, the titles of no less than twenty-three texts translated by Kumarajiva are specified (de Guignes 1781b:40–41). The history of Buddhism in China was laid out in several phases: from the introduction of Buddhism in the first century to 419 (pp. 1–81); from 419 to 543 C.E. (pp. 82–111); from 544 to 698 C.E. (de Guignes 1781c:112–32); from 698 to 965 C.E. (pp. 132–63); and finally from 965 to 1648 C.E. (pp. 163–200). Accurate historical information mostly stems from Ma Duanlin and is sometimes reproduced in detail; for example, de Guignes reports that the important *Biographies of Eminent Monks* (Ch. *Gaoseng zhuan*) and its supplement contain information about 257 persons between the years 67 and 519 CE (1781b:109–10). But apart from a few texts including the *Forty-two Sections Sutra*, de Guignes enjoyed no access to Buddhist literature in Chinese and could thus not study the content of the texts that were listed with so much detail. The readers of these three papers, however, must have been very impressed by the wealth of Buddhism's sacred literature whose history in China went back to the first century of the common era.

The Battle Against Indomania

De Guignes's discoveries were invariably of a kind that stunned the public and seemed to provide answers to important questions. His Visdelou-inspired identification of the Xiongnu and the Huns (1751, 1756) established a hitherto unknown connection between Chinese, Mongol, Turkic, Persian, Arab, and European history and seemed to have solved the mystery of the Huns. His analysis of the *Forty-Two Sections Sutra* (1753–56) claimed to have uncovered a connection between early Christian heretics and the "Indian religion" that dominates large parts of Asia by portraying one of Asia's most famous religious texts as an apocryphal gospel. His sensational discovery of the Egyptian origin of the Chinese (1758) not only proposed to rewrite the history of much of Asia and to show ancient Chinese historical sources in a new light but also to furnish a comprehensive solution to the riddle of China's "hieroglyphic" writing system. His theory about a fifth-century voyage of Chinese Buddhist monks (1761) to a country named Fusang, built on a Chinese legend mentioned by Ma Duanlin, supposedly dethroned Columbus by a thousand years as discoverer of the Americas. If the public thought that five major discoveries in ten years were plenty and that the time had come to furnish solid evidence, it underestimated de Guignes's creative powers. He had one more ace up his sleeve, and once more it was Ma Duanlin who furnished much of the raw material on which the French professor built an impressive tower of speculation.

During the 1760s Europe's interest in India had grown exponentially through Voltaire's propaganda, Abbé Mignot's papers on the ancient philosophers of India,[25] and the supposedly very ancient texts of "Indian" origin that had made their way to Europe: Voltaire's *Ezour-vedam*, Holwell's *Chartah Bhade Shastah*, and Dow's *Shastabad*. By the early 1770s the major threat to biblical authority and chronology was no more China but India, so it comes as no surprise that de Guignes's last great endeavor was the debunking of India as cradle of all human culture. The title of three lectures held in 1776 at the Royal Academy of Inscriptions and Literature ("On the Indian religion and the fundamental texts of this religion that were translated from the Indian [idiom] into Chinese") indicates the direction of his effort. De Guignes explained:

> My principal aim in these researches is to demonstrate that the Chinese have not been cultivated by the Indians, to whom one pretends to attribute great antiquity, and that this sentiment [of great Indian antiquity] is only based on pure conjecture. They are a means that has for some time now been abused with too much impudence in order to establish a bunch of paradoxes because one does not consult the veritable sources

and abandons oneself too much to one's own imagination. (de Guignes 1781a:77.349–50).

De Guignes does not mention any names but we can infer that he mainly thought of Voltaire, Raynal, and Bailly:

The Ancients chastized the poets for having altered and corrupted history: we could address the same criticism to several writers who in recent times have set themselves up as *Historiens Philosophes*. Abandoning themselves to their imagination, they dare to invent and assume facts because they are ignorant of the sources. Overall, they are little versed in the study of antiquity and even less familiar with the art of criticism; they do not weigh the authorities; and they adopt without examination everything that seems to agree with their system. After having shaped the earth to their liking, they place on it the diverse tribes and arrange the cradle of science where they see fit. According to some, the sciences were born in India; according to others in Siberia near Selinginskoi and Lake Baikal, a region where nature seems numb and where the inhabitants were anciently plunged in the greatest barbarity. Such are the aberrations which the spirit of systematization [esprit de système] produces! . . . But all these hazardous assertions vanish when one examines history. (pp. 354–55)

Of course such assertions were only "hazardous" for someone attached to biblical chronology and the orthodox Christian ideology of history that held Europe in its grip for so many centuries. In the second half of the eighteenth century dissenters were no longer dragged before the inquisition and tortured by its henchmen until they confessed. But resistance to alternative views was still extremely strong and de Guignes, like many fellow pioneers of orientalism, was eager to build academic barricades in its defense. It is amazing how much orientalism as a discipline owes to religious motivations. In this case, the will to defend Europe's orthodox view of history resulted not only in a series of mind-boggling theories but also in Europe's first detailed (and, thanks to Ma Duanlin, largely accurate) description of large chunks of Buddhist history.

In his first 1776 presentation, de Guignes proposed to establish some basic facts about Indian history and religion, and in the second and third lectures he planned to trace "the history of this religion in China" and discuss "various Indian texts that were translated into Chinese" (p. 350). The most important first step consisted in proving that Indian religion was not as old as the indomaniacs claimed. This was not too difficult given that for de Guignes both "sects" of Indian religion came from the same founder, namely, Buddha. Though the dates of this figure vary in different sources (de Guignes mentions 688, 1027, and 1122 B.C.E; p. 361), they are not of overly great antiquity. Since "these Brahmins as well as the Samanéens follow the same doctrine of *Fo*" (p. 360), de Guignes found that their religion cannot be older than 1122 B.C.E. According to Ziegenbalg and La Croze, the Samanéens had first brought culture to India, and de Guignes read a confirmation of this in a Chinese author who wrote, "*Boudha*, after having examined the character of the Indians and adapting and rectifying it, succeeded in instructing and civilizing these people" (p. 372). All this led to de Guignes's conclusion that around 1100 B.C.E the Indians were still "nothing but barbarians and brigands" (p. 372) and that any notion of India as cradle of human civilization was pure fantasy.

Ma Duanlin and the Chinese travelogues also permitted de Guignes to trace the dissemination of this "Indian religion" founded by Buddha into various regions of Asia. Much of this information was new for European readers. De Guignes traced the religion's spread southward to Ceylon (p. 393), northward to Tibet and Tartary (p. 406), south-eastward to the whole region of Southeast Asia including some islands (p. 429), and eastward to China and Japan (p. 447). But fact and fiction were hard to disentangle. For example, de Guignes also claimed that in the year 966 C.E. India was still full of Samanéens and that only the name of their religion had disappeared from India, not its doctrine (p. 385). As confusing as the mass of data was, readers like Herder and Sainte-Croix had no trouble understanding de Guignes's overall notion of a huge pan-Asian religion of Indian origin that consisted of "interior" and "exterior" branches. In this vision the Samanéens represent the interior doctrine—a doctrine that, according to de Guignes, had survived not only in India but also in other countries.

The Chinese Vedas

In the 1750s de Guignes had only mentioned the Yogic *Anbertkend* and the *Forty-Two Sections Sutra* as representatives of the interior teaching and failed to mention the Vedas. But in the age of growing indomania, he could not avoid this discussion, and he prepared himself by reading everything in his reach about these elusive texts. In the 1760s the purported age of Indian texts had become the centerpiece of arguments by proponents of India as humanity's cradle of civilization. The Chinese annals, Voltaire's exaggerations about the age of the *Ezour-vedam*, and the even greater antiquity claimed by Holwell and Dow for their Indian texts were becoming serious challenges to biblical chronology and Mosaic authority. At the end of the decade, another supposedly very ancient Indian text turned up in Paris: the manuscript of the *Bhāgavata purāṇa* ("*Bagavadam*") translated by the South Indian Maridas Poullé. In 1772 de Guignes rode a first attack against the antiquity of Indian texts. Debunking all claims of antiquity of the *Bagavadam*, he showed that this supposedly extremely ancient text is at best 1,000 years old (de Guignes 1777:320). But de Guignes had bigger fish to fry. For the better part of his century, the reputation of the Vedas as the oldest texts of humankind had been slowly growing (see Chapters 5 and 6), and at the beginning of the 1770s, the interest in these texts had reached a first peak that prepared the ground for the claim in 1790 by Louis-Mathieu Langlès that the Old Testament's Pentateuch was a late imitation of the five Indian Vedas.[26] In the mid-1770s de Guignes felt exactly the same danger as Father Gaston Laurent Coeurdoux in Pondicherry (see Chapter 7); but instead of using Coeurdoux's method of linking India's famous seven penitents (*rishis*) to some descendant of Noah, de Guignes employed a secular historical approach involving no reliance on the Bible: he linked India's sacred literature to the Buddha. Drawing his data mainly from Jean-François Pons (letter of 1740; Pons 1781), and to some degree also from Abraham Roger (1651) and some additional authors who had discussed the Vedas, de Guignes projected his exoteric/esoteric divide on the sacred literature of India and divided it in two categories (see Table 9).

Though Father Calmette had sent the Vedas in the 1730s to Paris in Telugu script (see Chapter 7), nobody could read them. But had not the Brahmins or *polomen* brought their religion to China, and could the Vedas not have formed part of their baggage of sacred scriptures? Scouring through Ma Duanlin's account of the introduction of Buddhism to China, de Guignes kept encountering the terms "small vehicle" and "great vehicle." At the time it was, of course, not yet known that these "vehicles" designate the Hinayana (Ch. *xiaosheng*) and Mahayana (Ch. *dasheng*) branches of Buddhism. For de Guignes these two terms signified the religion's exoteric and esoteric branches: "From the earliest times of the establishment of this reli-

TABLE 9. INNER AND OUTER DOCTRINES ACCORDING TO DE GUIGNES

Inner (esoteric) Doctrine Religion of the Brachmanes/Samanéens	Outer (exoteric) Doctrine Religion of the people
• Main scriptures: the *four Vedas*. Rig- and Yajurveda mainly used in South India, Sama- and Atharvanaveda mainly used in North India	• Main scripture: *Dharma shastram*; by different authors
• does not contain ceremonies of popular religion but explain meditation, ascetic practices	• contains ceremonies, sacred rites of vulgar religion
• inner doctrines and practices of philosophers	• exterior practices of vulgar religion
• strictly monotheistic	• polytheistic; attributes of God are personified

gion, the opinions of the Buddha engendered two great sects. One was called *Ta-tching* and the other *Siao-tching*" (p. 370). He also learned from Ma Duanlin that the sacred scriptures of this religion did not stem from the Buddha himself:

> Buddha has written nothing; but after his death five hundred of his disciples, of which the principals were *Ta-ka-ye* or the great *Kia ye* and *Onan*, collected everything that he had taught, transcribed it, and formed a body of scriptures of it that they divided into twelve *Pou* or classes. The Japanese call these personages *Kasja-sonsja & Annan-sonsja*;[27] this last word seems to correspond to the Indian *Sanjassi*. (p. 370)

As long as de Guignes stuck to the data that he found neatly arranged and summarized in Ma Duanlin, he conveyed more or less what the Chinese tradition held to be true. Of course, this can be quite different from what scholars today believe; we now know that for several centuries after the Buddha's death there was no written tradition and that the Mahayana reform movement arose about half a millennium after the founder's death. But de Guignes was not content simply to translate Ma Duanlin and present the result as the view of an extremely well-read Chinese intellectual of the early fourteenth century. Instead he presented very interesting (and for Europe, absolutely new) information about the history and texts of Buddhism in a framework of speculation that gave it a sensational touch. The first mistake was, as we have seen, de Guignes's rejection of La Croze's view that Buddhism and Brahmanism were different religions; he preferred Kircher's "Brahmin" missionaries of Buddhism and Le Gobien's *polomen* who venerate the Buddha, the dharma, and Brahmanic scriptures. The second mistake was his uncritical acceptance of the Buddha's supposed "deathbed confession" (of which the Chinese sources known to him contained no trace) and the identification of Buddhism's smaller and larger vehicle with the exoteric and exoteric branch of de Guignes's "Indian religion." But the third mistake was perhaps even more spectacular: on the basis of a slight similarity of epithet, de Guignes concluded that Shakyamuni Buddha was identical with the purported redactor of the Vedas, Vyasa.

> This *Che-kia* or *Schaka* was the elder son of *Tcing fan*, King of the country called *Kia-goei-goei*; his mother was called *Yeou-hie*, and one recounts many fables about his birth. The name *Che kia* is, according to the Chinese, an Indian word that signifies *very good*, or *very compassionate* (*Meng-gin*); this is the same person whom Mr. Dow called *Beass-mouni* or *Beas the inspired* and whom the Indians, as he reports, regard as a prophet and philosopher who composed or rather collected the Vedas. (p. 363)

De Guignes's overall view of Indian sacred literature was mainly responsible for this mistake. It seduced him into identifying the "interior" doctrine and the Vedas with Mahayana doctrine and its texts. Starting with this idea, de Guignes soon detected evidence in support of his idea that the Vedas are scriptures of the Samanéens and thus of the followers of Buddha's "inner" or esoteric teaching. Once he had his stool standing on these seemingly solid feet, he piled more conjectures on it. In the absence of translations from the Vedas, he used the *Ezour-vedam* (see Chapter 7) as proof that the teaching of the Vedas and of the Samanéens are identical (p. 368): "The most perfect state taught by the Vedas, following the *Ezour-vedam*, is the same as that prescribed in the books of the Samanéens, which has me believe that these books are the same as the Vedas; it is a constant . . . that the doctrine is identical" (p. 369). The *Ezour-vedam*'s "total absence of passion in order to occupy oneself exclusively with the knowledge of God and the truth" is thus seen as matching the core teaching of the *Forty-Two Sections Sutra*. This suggested a link between the Vedas and the esoteric Buddhist scriptures that the *polomen* had brought to China and translated into Chinese. As mentioned above, de Guignes's main source about the Vedas was the famous letter by Father Pons of 1740 to which de Guignes refers time and again:

> It is obvious, according to these missionaries, that the four Vedas did not form a single unified textual corpus because they are not generally adopted [in both the north and south]. Still, they could not contain the ceremonies of the people because it is prohibited to communicate them; besides, they belong to the secret doctrine that does not admit any such ceremonies. In India there are two doctrines, an exterior one which is the religion of the people and an interior one which is that of the philosophers. There is also a rather general consensus that the *Adharvana-vedam*—to which Father Pons still gives the name of *Brahma vedam*—is lost. It was followed in the North of India whence this religion passed to China. (pp. 380–81)

The *Atharva-veda*—which was usually listed as the fourth veda and sometimes considered lost—was thus among the texts that the *polomen* had conceivably brought from India to China. De Guignes was impressed by the number of Indian books that, according to Ma Duanlin's *Wenxian tongkao*, had been imported in China and translated into Chinese. Ma Duanlin, of course, regarded these texts as Buddhist; but as we have seen, this religion had a rather different scope for de Guignes who identified the Buddha with Vyasa:

> Among the great number of Indian books that were translated into Chinese, there is one that is regarded as the basis of this Indian religion, and it carries the title of *Book of Brahma*. In China it is the most important book of this religion, and several translations and innumerable commentaries of it have been made. This book seems to me to be the *Brahma-vedam* that is lost in India; but I am tempted to believe, for reasons that I will develop below, that it must be different from the *Adharvana-vedam*. Consequently one can suspect that all the Vedas can be found in China. (de Guignes 1781a:77.381)

This stunning conjecture of de Guignes seemed confirmed by a story that he read in his second major source on Buddhism, a polyglot glossary of Buddhist terms that he cites as *Ou yin yun-tong* (de Guignes 1781b:78.25–28).

The story is about Zhu Shixing, the first Chinese monk to leave his country in quest of Buddhist scriptures (Zürcher 1959:1.61). In the year 260 C.E., Reverend Zhu and his group went to Khotan in Central Asia where they found the Sanskrit text of the *Prajñāpāramitā* scripture in 25,000 verses.

> These Samanéens stayed in Khotan until 282. When they prepared for departure, the inhabitants of Khotan who followed the doctrine of the *small Tching* [vehicle] were opposed to their departure and said to the King: *The Samanéeens of China want to have the books of the Brahmins.* (de Guignes 1781b:78.27).

De Guignes found this information noteworthy because it indicated that to communicate the *Prajñāpāramitā* scripture to the Chinese would signify "altering the true doctrine":

> You are the king of this land, they said, if you do not prevent them from taking along these books, the great Law will be destroyed because the Chinese are a deaf and blind people, and it will be your fault. (p. 27)

This is a legend of interest for the history of Buddhism since it indicates tensions between adherents of traditional (Hinayana) and reformist (Mahayana) branches of Buddhism. But for de Guignes, fixated as he was on his conception of "Indian religion," this seemed to be a conflict between adherents of the Buddha's "inner" and "outer" doctrines. Making the connection to the Indian Brahmins and the Vedas, de Guignes grew convinced that the Vedas contain the Buddha's secret doctrine and that this doctrine was well known in China through the Mahayana texts that had been translated into Chinese. He explained:

> The Indians have even today the same principles about their Vedas that they do not want to communicate to anybody. Not even all of them may read them since this privilege is reserved to the Brahmins, and those who do may not be involved in commerce. Also, they are not allowed to teach it to everybody without distinction. The people may not speak of it nor listen to others talk about it. So these books of the Indian religion must be guarded as a secret among a few elect ones. As to the text in question here, whose communication proved to be so difficult, could it be one of the *Vedas*? One would have [to have] the *Vedas* before one's eyes to decide

this question; but the text is portrayed as the basis and foundation of the entire secret doctrine. It seems likely that those in China who followed the Indian religion had to know finally the most hidden books of this religion and to possess them in China where a great number of Indians resided. (pp. 27–28)

In de Guignes's mind, an interesting story about tensions between Hinayana and Mahayana Buddhists in third-century Central Asia thus became a tale about the transmission of the scriptures of the esoteric branch of his "Indian religion," and the *Prajñāpāramitā* literature of early Mahayana Buddhism seemed to be the Vedas translated into Chinese. Scouring through Ma Duanlin's *Wenxian tongkao*, de Guignes found additional evidence to support this view. DHARMARAKṢA (c. 230–308), an important translator of Indian Buddhist texts, was said to have translated the same text (p. 30). Moreover, Ma Duanlin's list of twenty-three texts translated by the great Kuchean monk KUMARAJIVVA (344–413) featured several texts containing "puon-jo" (Ch. *ba-nruo*, Skt. *prajñā*; wisdom) in their title. In second place of this list, there was a text whose title attracted de Guignes's particular attention: the *Diamond Prajñāpāramitā Sutra*. *Prajñā pāramitā* (literally, perfection of wisdom) is one of the perfections of the Bodhisattva, and in East Asia the word *pārami* or *pāramitā* was often interpreted as "[means of] reaching the other shore." But for de Guignes the word *pārami* (from Skt. *parama*, the highest), which the Chinese read "boluomi" (in de Guignes's transcription "Polomi"), had a very different meaning, namely, "Brahma"! This mistranslation (p. 46) confirmed de Guignes's idea that certain Mahayana texts are Chinese translations of the Vedas:

Father Pons speaks of a Veda that he names *Adharvana vedam* or *Brahma vedam* whose doctrine was followed in the North of India. Since the Chinese book under discussion is called the *book of Brahma*, is one of the principal books of this religion, and was adopted in the north, it could be this *Brahma vedam* or the *Vedam of Brahma* that the missionary talks about. (pp. 46–47)

As he scanned the pages of Ma Duanlin for text titles that somehow resembled the names of Vedas—in particular, those of the Sama- and Atharvana-veda used in India's north where frequent communication with China was amply documented—de Guignes struck gold and wrote:

Before the year 479 . . . an Indian called *Kieou na po-to-lo* or *Kieou-na poutra* [Gunabhadra, 394–468] translated a work called *Leng-kia-king* [the *Laṅkāvatāra Sūtra*] in four books. It is said that *Leng-kia* is the name of a mountain where Fo [Buddha] meditated on the Law. *Leng-kia* is pronounced *Lang-ka* in the Tibetan dictionary; it is the name that the Indians give to the island of Ceylon, which is famous in Indian mythology. . . . In the Tang period seven other books [of this sutra] were translated, and it was called *Leng-kia O-po-to-lo pao king* [*Lengqie abatuo-luo baojing*], that is, the precious book called *O-po-to-lo* of *Leng-kia*. This name of *O-po-to-lo* resembles very much the word *Obatar*, which is the name of a Veda. (pp. 97–98)

The word "*O-po-to-lo*," whose Sanskrit equivalent *avatara* is well known to millions of gamers and moviegoers today, made de Guignes think of the Veda that is traditionally listed as the fourth and youngest, the Atharvana Veda. De Guignes must have been excited about this additional confirmation. Now not only the Diamond Sutra and the great Prajna-paramita Sutra were Vedic texts in disguise, but the supposedly lost fourth Veda—the very Veda, incidentally, as whose teacher Roberto de Nobili presented himself (see Chapter 7)—was also extant in China, where it was called *Lankavatara Sutra*!

Thus, de Guignes became convinced that the "religion established in China is still absolutely the same as that of India" (p. 57) and that the Chinese had translated and were using the Indian Vedas including the fourth Veda. They contain the inner doctrine of Buddha, and the practice of both its Chinese followers and all sects of Indian philosophers "begins with the meditation and contemplation of the Supreme Being and ends with a kind of identity where there is no more feeling nor will"—a perfection that can only be reached after many transmigrations (p. 50). This was a repetition of the idea that he had already gained from his very particular reading, to put it charitably, of the *Forty-Two Sections Sutra* in the early 1750s.

Why Did Bodhidharma Go from India to China?

Between the 1750s and the 1770s, de Guignes thus sought to find additional textual evidence for his pan-Asian religion of Indian origin with esoteric and exoteric branches. This search constituted, as we will also see in the next chapters, a powerful force that propelled traditional orientalism toward an ever more secularized modern form—a form able to dispassionately and competently investigate ancient sacred texts and monuments. The literature of the esoteric branch seemed increasingly voluminous to de Guignes who quoted various texts, from the *Anbertkend* (de Guignes 1781b:60) and a text excerpted by Dow, the *Neadirsen* (p. 63), to the so-called *Bequeathed Teachings of Buddha* (p. 61). The latter is an apocryphal Buddhist text grouped by a Zen monk of the Song dynasty with the "zen-ified" *Forty-Two Sections Sutra* and a text of his own Guishan lineage to form the so-called *Fozu sanjing*, the *Three Sutras of Buddha and Patriarch* (Ch. *Fozu sanjing*). These three were among the few Buddhist texts studied by de Guignes. Given his idea of the doctrine of the esoteric branc of "Indian religion," he paid much attention to the word *Chan* (Jap. *Zen*, literally, contemplation or meditation). Since the main informer Ma Duanlin was writing in the golden age of Chinese Zen, the word popped up everywhere in his Buddhism section and was contained in many titles of scriptures. De Guignes was intrigued by these "particular treatises related to contemplation" and remarked:

As we have seen, this doctrine is very much in fashion with the Indians. These contemplatives are penitents who live in greatest austerity, observe the most extraordinary practices, and maintain the most ridiculous body positions. Although I do not have these treatises and do not find them mentioned in the Chinese books [other than Ma Duanlin] that I can consult, I feel obliged to discuss this subject for a moment and explain what other works have to say about this. (pp. 64–65)

In his discussion, de Guignes throws all kinds of data from India and Tibet (from Giorgi's *Alphabetum Tibetanum*; p. 65) into the mix and quotes La Croze on the Gnanigöls and the *Anbertkend* as well as Dow on Yogic practices (pp. 69–70). Everything seemed to support his idea that these practitioners were trying hard to achieve total concentration on God (p. 70).

But this seemingly pure religion was not immune to change. Already in the 1750s, de Guignes had read about Fo's "three doctrines;" but at the time he believed them to be three religions of the seven *Fo* [Buddhas] of the past whom he saw as "foreign legislators":

Among the different religions that these *Fo* have established, there are three principal ones: 1. *Tchim-kiao*, the simple and natural religion;

2. *Siam-kiao*, the religion of idols; and 3. *Mo-kiao*, the posterior religion. (de Guignes 1759:779)

As his ability to read Chinese improved, de Guignes realized that Ma Duanlin had not written about three religions by foreign legislators but rather about three phases or epochs of the religion of Fo:

> One distinguishes in this religion of *Fo* three different epochs. In the first it was called *Tching-fa*, i.e., the *first Law*. According to a book which treats of these first times, this epoch began with the death of *Fo* or *Boudha* and lasted five hundred years. The second is called *Siang-fa*, the *Law of Figures* or *Images*. It lasted for 1000 years. The third is named *Mo-fa*, or the *last Law*, and it must last for 3000 years. As Boudha was born in 1027 or 1122 and lived 79 years, he died in 969 or 1043 B.C.E. That's when the first Law that lasted for 500 years began, and it must have ended in 469 or 543 B.C.E. (de Guignes 1781a:77.373)

De Guignes's reliance on Ma Duanlin had many benefits; in this instance he had more or less accurately grasped the Chinese conception of three periods of the dharma: (1) the period of the genuine dharma, Ch. *zhengfa*; (2) the period of the semblance dharma, Ch. *xiangfa*; and (3) that of the end of the dharma or law, Ch. *mofa*. But not surprisingly, he misinterpreted the first period as the pure monotheism of remote antiquity and the second period as the age of idolatry (p. 376). In this second period something happened that, unbeknownst to de Guignes, strangely resembles the fate of the *Forty-Two Sections Sutra*:

> It is likely that in the second [epoch, i.e., Xiangfa], which began around 470 or 544 B.C.E., people abandoned themselves increasingly to the cult of images. In that period they would compose books to explain the most ancient texts in conformity with the new cult; and it is not rare in such circumstances that the partisans of the new religion compose such [purportedly ancient] texts and attribute them to the first legislator. Later on, further books by unknown authors could have been attributed to him. The Indians, by the way, are quite used to attribute their religious texts to the Divinity. (pp. 376–77)

De Guignes saw this scheme of the Fo religion's three epochs as proof that "the Indian Religion has not always remained the same since its origin and is not as ancient as people pretend" (p. 374). The degeneration of relatively pure esoteric monotheism into idolatric cults was bad enough; but who was the culprit responsible for the further degradation that rang the bell for the final period of the Dharma?

Here we enter the treacherous territory of Indian religion's axis of evil. If the Vedas were seen as embodiments of the interior doctrine and of monotheism professed by philosophers who kept such teachings among themselves, de Guignes identified the *Dharma shastra* as their exoteric, vulgar counterpart:

> After the Vedas, the *Dharma-chastram* was composed, which contains the practices of the different sects, the rites of all kinds, the ceremonies and the laws for the administration of justice: there you have vulgar religion, in which all the attributes of the divinity were personified and the most absurd fables admitted. The people believe them and the philosophers teach them to the people even though they believe nothing of it and admit only a single God, the soul of the universe present everywhere. (p. 383)

Here the reader will hear a distinct echo of the Buddha's "deathbed confession" story that was endlessly repeated in Western sources. If the four Vedas with the inner doctrine of Indian religion had made their way to China disguised as the *Diamond Sutra* and other texts that we today associate with the Prajna paramita literature of Mahayana Buddhism, then the vulgar *Dharma shastra* had conceivably also been transmitted to China. After all, the panorama of Chinese religion—riddled as it was with superstitious practices—did not look all that rosy. According to the three-stage scheme, the last period of the true doctrine was said to have begun in the sixth century C.E. As de Guignes read the names of the major Buddhist figures of that century in Ma Duanlin's book, he came across a "Bodhidharma," an Indian "contemplative philosopher" (p. 106) who "had come to China with many books of contemplation" and had retired to a small temple where he "devoted himself entirely to contemplation with his face turned to a wall that he did not cease to stare at for nine years" (p. 107). If his name already suggested an association of this man with the *Dharma shastra*, his purported pivotal role in both India and in China was an additional hint. Was he the person who had perverted the "Indian religion" of China and launched the era of "*Mo-fa*, that is, the *end of the Law* which is to last for 3,000 years" (p. 112)?

I believe I can here conjecture that this [Bodhi-]*Darma* of whom I spoke is the author of this revolution [the beginning of the final phase of the Law]. In India there exists a book with the title *Darma Schastram* or *Dirm Schastram*, i.e., *Explication of Darma*; and the doctrine contained in this book is adopted by a great number of Indians. This *Darma* seems to have played a great role in India, and this authorizes me to regard him as the author of the change in religion. For the rest, this is only a conjecture that I propose, a conjecture that Indian history can confirm or destroy. (p. 113)

De Guignes was aware that he was stepping on slippery ground here; but the reputation of Bodhidharma as symbol of transmission was already firmly established. In fact he is a splendid example of a "person of memory" (Assmann 1998:9) who probably never existed in the flesh yet has had a large impact in history. Students of religion know all too well that invented personages and traditions can become so real that they can not only save many souls but also pack in enormous amounts of baggage.

By the Song dynasty, when Ma Duanlin wrote, the Zen tradition of Chinese Buddhism and its model of Ur-tradition had become so dominant that other schools of Buddhism and later even Daoist movements began to imitate its lineage trick. But it was not easy to invent such a colorful transmitter figure as Bodhidharma, who not only was credited with having brought the Buddha's original teaching from India to China floating on a reed and having sat for nine years facing a wall but even with having, as Kaempfer excitedly reported, cut off his eyelids to avoid falling asleep (see Figure 10). He threw them away—and behold, the next day two tea shrubs had grown at the exact spot where they had hit the ground. Thus Bodhidharma became the inventor and patron saint of tea . . . (Kaempfer 1906:218–19). In the Song period the "successors of Bodhidharma" began to use *koans* in their training, and an entire literature grew around these poignant "Zen presentations offered as a Zen challenge" (DeMartino 1983). One of the most famous *koans* features a simple question: "Why did the patriarch [Bodhidharma] go from India to China?" Twenty years ago, during a pleasant research group party, an aggressive Japanese university professor suddenly shouted this question in a shrill voice at Professor Seizan Yanagida. He calmly replied: "Watakushi no tame" ("Because of me").

Now we also know de Guignes's answer, as I interpret it: *Because Bodhidharma wanted to destroy genuine Indian religion in China and launch the*

Figure 10. Bodhidharma crossing the sea on a reed (Kaempfer 1906:221).

final age of the dharma by carrying the entire Dharma shastra, *packed with the exterior practices of vulgar religion, in his bulky robe as he crossed the sea on that slender reed!*

If the idea of a pan-Asian religion gradually took hold in European minds during the first half of the eighteenth century, the second half turned into a race to substantiate this idea and supply textual evidence for it. This was a task only orientalists could hope to tackle, and the chapters of this book present various facets of this endeavor that is so intimately connected with the birth of modern orientalism. Starting with de Guignes's translation of the *Forty-two Sections Sutra* in the early 1750s, texts that seemed to answer this need successively appeared, and most of them pointed to an Indian cradle. In 1761 it was Voltaire's *Ezour-vedam*, in 1767 Holwell's *Shastah*, in 1768 Dow's *Bedang Shaster* and *Neadirzin*, in 1771 Anquetil-Duperron's *Zend-Avesta*, in 1785 Wilkins's *Bhagvat-Geeta*, and so on until de Guignes's death in 1800. Despite an almost superhuman effort during half a century of orientalist research, de Guignes was unable to furnish conclusive textual evidence for his "Indian religion." But the search was launched, and passionate orientalists such as Anquetil-Duperron were ready to risk their lives to gain the prize that had eluded de Guignes.

Chapter 5

Ramsay's Ur-Tradition

When D. P. Walker wrote about "ancient theology" or *prisca theologia*, he firmly linked it to Christianity and Platonism (Walker 1972). On the first page of his book, Walker defined the term as follows:

> By the term "Ancient Theology" I mean a certain tradition of Christian apologetic theology which rests on misdated texts. Many of the early Fathers, in particular Lactantius, Clement of Alexandria and Eusebius, in their apologetic works directed against pagan philosophers, made use of supposedly very ancient texts: *Hermetica*, *Orphica*, Sibylline Prophecies, Pythagorean *Carmina Aurea*, etc., most of which in fact date from the first four centuries of our era. These texts, written by the Ancient Theologians Hermes Trismegistus, Orpheus, Pythagoras, were shown to contain vestiges of the true religion: monotheism, the Trinity, the creation of the world out of nothing through the Word, and so forth. It was from these that Plato took the religious truths to be found in his writings. (Walker 1972:1)

Walker described a revival of such "ancient theology" in the Renaissance and in "platonizing theologians from Ficino to Cudworth" who wanted to "integrate Platonism and Neoplatonism into Christianity, so that their own religious and philosophical beliefs might coincide" (p. 2). After the debunking of the genuineness and antiquity of the texts favored by these ancient theologians, the movement ought to have died; but Walker detected "a few isolated survivals" such as Athanasius Kircher, Pierre-Daniel Huët, and the Jesuit figurists of the French China mission (p. 194). For Walker the last Mohican of this movement, so to say, is Chevalier Andrew Michael RAMSAY

(1686–1743), whose views are described in the final chapter of *The Ancient Theology*. But seen through the lens of our concerns here, one could easily extend this line to various figures in this book, for example, Jean Calmette, John Zephaniah Holwell, Abbé Vincent Mignot, Abraham Hyacinthe Anquetil-Duperron, Guillaume Sainte-Croix, and also to William Jones (App 2009).

Ur-Traditions

To better understand such phenomena we have to go beyond the narrow confines of the Christian God and Platonism. There are many movements that link themselves to some kind of "original," "pure," "genuine" teaching, claim its authority, use it to criticize "degenerate" accretions, and attempt to legitimize their "reform" on its basis. Such links can take a variety of forms. In Chapter 4 we saw how in the eighth and ninth centuries the Buddhist reform movement known as Zen cooked up a lineage of "mind to mind" transmission with the aim of connecting the teaching of the religion's Indian founder figure, Buddha, with their own views. The tuned-up and misdated *Forty-Two Sections Sutra* that ended up impressing so many people, including its first European translator de Guignes, was one (of course unanticipated) outcome of this strategy. Such "Ur-tradition" movements, as I propose to call them, invariably create a "transmission" scenario of their "original" teaching or revelation; in the case of Zen this consisted in an elaborate invented genealogy with colorful transmission figures like Bodhidharma and "patriarchs" consisting mostly of pious legends. Such invented genealogies and transmissions are embodied in symbols and legends emphasizing the link between the "original" teaching and the movement's doctrine. "Genuine," "oldest" texts are naturally of central importance for such movements, since they tend to regard the purity of teaching as directly proportional to its closeness to origins.

A common characteristic of such "Ur-tradition" movements is a tripartite scheme of "golden age," "degeneration," and "regeneration." The raison d'être of such movements is the revival of a purportedly most ancient, genuine, "original" teaching after a long period of degeneration. Hence their need to define an "original" teaching, establish a line of its transmission, identify stages and kinds of degeneration, and present themselves as the agent of "regeneration" of the original "ancient" teaching. Such need often arises in a milieu of doctrinal rivalry or in a crisis, for example, when "new" religions or reform movements want to establish and legitimize themselves or when an established religion is threatened by powerful alternatives.

When young Christianity evolved from a Jewish reform movement and was accused of being a "new religion" and an invention, ancient connections were needed to provide legitimacy and add historical weight to the religion. The adoption of the Hebrew Bible as "Old Testament," grimly opposed by some early Christians, linked the young religion and its "New Testament" effectively to the very creation of the world, to paradise, and to the Ur-religion of the first humans in the golden age. Legends, texts, and symbols were created to illustrate this "Old-to-New" link. For example, the savior's cross on Golgotha had to get a pedigree connecting it to the Hebrew Bible's paradise tree; and the original sinner Adam's skull had to be brought via Noah's ark to Palestine in order to get buried on the very hill near Jerusalem where Adam's original sin eventually got expunged by the New Testament's "second Adam" on the cross (Figure 11). Theologians use the word "typology" for such attempts to discover Christian teachings or forebodings thereof in the Old Testament.

Similar links to an "oldest," "purest," and "original" teaching are abundant not only in the history of religions but also, for example, in freemasonry and various "esoteric" movements. They also tend to invent links to an original "founder," "ancient" teachings and texts, lineages, symbols of the original doctrine and its transmission, eminent transmitter figures ("patriarchs"), and so on; and they usually criticize the degeneration of exactly those original and pure teachings that they claim to resuscitate. In such schemes the most ancient texts, symbols, and objects naturally play important roles, particularly if they seem mysterious: pyramids, hieroglyphs, runic letters, ancient texts buried in caves, and divine revelations stored on golden tablets in heaven or in some American prophet's backyard . . .

In premodern Europe such "original" teachings were usually associated with Old Testament heroes who had the function of transmitters. A typical example that shows how various ancient religions were integrated in a genealogy linking them to primeval religion as well as its fulfillment in Christianity is Jacques Boulduc's *De Ecclesia ante legem* ("On the Church before the [Mosaic] Law") of 1626. Boulduc shows in a table how the extremely long lifespans of the patriarchs facilitated transmission: for example, Adam lived for 930 years and could instruct his descendants in person until his sixth-generation Ur-nephew Lamech, Noah's father, was fifty-six years old. Adam's son

Figure 11. Adam's skull underneath the cross. Collection of Drs. Valerio and Adriana Pozza, Padova, Italy.

Seth was 120 years old when the first priestly functions were instituted; 266 years old when his son Enos first offered prayers in a dedicated house; and 800 years old when he took over the supreme pontificate of the "church before the law" at Adam's untimely death (1630:148–49). In the second book, Boulduc shows that "all philosophers, both of Greece and of other regions, have their origin in the descendants of the prophet Noah" (p. 271) and includes in this transmission lineage even the "wise rather than malefic Persian magi [Magos Persas non maleficos, sed sapientes]," Egyptian prophets, Gallic druids, the "naked sages of India [Indis Gymnosophistae]," etc. (p. 273). Boulduc took special care to document through numerous quotations from ancient sources that the wise men who were variously called *Semai*, *Semni*, *Semanai*, *Semnothei*, and *Samanaei*[1] "all have their name from Noah's son Shem" and are therefore direct descendants of Noachic pure Ur-religion (p. 275). The same is true for the Brachmanes of India who were so closely associated with these *Samanaei* by St. Jerome (p. 277). Even "our Druids" worshipped "the only true God," believed "in the immortality of the soul" as well as "the resurrection of our bodies," and adored almost all the very God who "at some point in the future will become man through incarnation from a virgin" (pp. 278–79). The correct doctrinal linage of such descendants of Shem is guaranteed by the fact that "after the deluge, Shem brought the original religion of Enos's descendants to renewed blossom [reflorescere fecit]" (p. 280). Boulduc also paid special attention to Enoch, the sixth-generation descendant of Adam who could boast of having lived no less than 308 years in Adam's presence (pp. 148–49). This excellent patriarch, who at age 365 was prematurely removed from the eyes of the living and has been watching events ever since from his perch in the terrestrial or celestial paradise, had left behind "writings, that is, the book of Enoch, which contains nothing false or absurd" (p. 131). Noah had taken special care to "diligently preserve these writings of Enoch, placing them at the time of the deluge on the ark with no less solicitousness than the bones of Father Adam and some other patriarchs" (p. 138). Boulduc did not know where this famous Book of Enoch ended up, but some well-known passages in scripture specified that it conveyed important information about the activities of angels.

In the second half of the seventeenth century, textual criticism began to undermine the very foundation of such tales, namely, the text of the Old Testament and particularly of its first five books (the Pentateuch). These books had always been attributed to Moses and regarded as the world's oldest extant scripture. But in 1651 Thomas HOBBES (1588–1679) wrote in the third part of his *Leviathan* that the identity of "the original writers of the several Books of Holy Scripture" was not "made evident by any sufficient testimony of other history, which is the only proof of matter of fact" (Hobbes 1651:368). However, Hobbes did not deny that Moses had contributed some writings: "But though Moses did not compile those books entirely, and in the form we have them; yet he wrote all that which he is there said to have written" (p. 369). By contrast, Isaac LA PEYRÈRE (1596–1676)—who wrote earlier than Hobbes and influenced him though his book on the pre-Adamites appeared later—was far more radical in questioning whether Moses had in fact written any of the first five books of the Old Testament:

> I know not by what author it is found out, that the Pentateuch is *Moses* his own copy. It is so reported, but not believed by all. These Reasons make one believe, that those Five Books are not the Originals, but copied out by another. Because *Moses* is there read to have died. For how could *Moses* write after his death? (La Peyrère 1656:204–5).

La Peyrère's conclusion was shocking:

> I need not trouble the reader much further, to prove a thing in itself sufficiently evident, that the five first Books of the Bible were not written by Moses, as is thought. Nor need any one wonder after this, when he reads many things confus'd and out of order, obscure, deficient, many things omitted and misplaced, when they shall consider with themselves that they are a heap of Copie confusedly taken. (p. 208)

Such textual criticism[2] initiated "a chain of analyses that would end up transforming the evaluation of Scripture from a holy to a profane work" (Popkin 1987:73). Until La Peyrère, the Bible had always been regarded as a repository of divine revelation communicated by God (the "founder" figure) to a "transmitter" figure (in this case Moses). Unable to reconcile biblical chronology and events with newly discovered facts such as American "Indians" and Chinese historical records, La Peyrère came to the conclusion that the Bible contained not the history of all humankind but only that of a tiny group (namely, the Jews). His rejection of Moses' authorship, of course, also entailed doubts about the Bible's revelation status: if it was indeed revealed by God, then to whom? To a whole group of people whose notes were cut and pasted together to form a rather incoherent creation story with "many things confus'd and out of order"? At the end of the chain of events described by Popkin, the Bible was no longer "looked upon as Revelation from God, but as tales and beliefs of the primitive Hebrews, to be compared with the tales and beliefs of other Near Eastern groups" (p. 73), leading Thomas Paine to declare: "Take away from Genesis the belief that Moses was the author, on which only the strange belief that it is the word of God has stood, and there remains nothing of Genesis, but an anonymous book of stories, fables and traditionary or invented absurdities or downright lies" (Paine 1795:4).

But such loss of biblical authority was a gradual and painful process that frequently elicited the kind of apologetic intervention evoked by Walker in *The Ancient Theology*. I doubt that Walker would have gone as far as including the Bible among his pseudepigraphic and misdated texts. Yet if one views phenomena like the Reformation from the perspective of Ur-traditions, the biblical text appears as a (misdated) record of "original teaching" used by reformers like Calvin and Luther in their effort to discard "Romish" degenerations and to restore what they took to be the "genuine," "original" religion revealed by the "founder" God to "transmitters" from Adam and the antediluvian "patriarchs" to Noah, Abraham, Moses, and ultimately the authors of the New Testament. But this kind of Reformation was soon denounced as degenerate in its own right, for example, by the radical English deists who regarded "genuine" Christianity not as revealed to any particular Middle Eastern tribe but as engraved in every human heart. From this perspective, Christianity was—as Matthew TINDAL (1657–1733) in 1730 succinctly put it in the title of his famous bible of the Deists—exactly "as Old as Creation," and the holy Gospel was no more than "a Republication of the Religion of Nature" (Tindal 1995). While biblical answers became suspect and alternative creation narratives began to be culled from apparently far more ancient sacred texts, the search for humankind's origins, its "original" religion, and its oldest sacred scriptures had to begin again. In this "crisis of European consciousness,"[3] a number of men sought to anchor Europe's drifting worldview anew in the bedrock of remotest antiquity via a solid Ur-tradition chain. Among them was an Englishman who defended the Middle Eastern and biblical framework while dreaming of restoring Noah's pure religion (Isaac Newton); a Scotsman who determined that China offered better vestiges of the Ur-religion and wanted to reinterpret the Bible accordingly (Andrew Ramsay); and the Irish protagonist of the next chapter, John Zephaniah Holwell, who presented Europe with an Indian Old Testament that—he alleged—was so much older and better than Moses's patchwork that it could form the basis for the ultimate reformation of Christianity.

Newton's Noachide Religion

Isaac NEWTON (1642–1727) is, of course, known as one of the greatest scientists of all time, but his theological and chronological writings have become the focus of increasing attention. They amount to more than half a million words and are in great part still unpublished; but their study[4] points to a central "Ur-tradition" pattern in Newton's worldview. For example, modern specialists point out that "it can be shown how Newton regarded his natural philosophy as an integral part of a radical and comprehensive recovery of the true ancient religion, which had been revealed directly to man by God" (Gouk 1988:120); that Newton tried to prove "that his scientific work in the *Principia* was a rediscovery of the mystical philosophy which had passed to the Egyptians and the Greeks from the Jews" (Rattansi 1988:198); and that the great scientist "believed that alchemical writings preserved a secret knowledge which had been revealed by God" (Golinski 1988:158). Newton apparently saw himself as a *regenerator* of an *Ur-wisdom* that had been *encoded in symbols* and *transmitted* through dark and *degenerate ages* by a *line* of eminent men (*patriarchs*). The italicized words in this sentence are all elements of what I call Ur-traditions.

Newton developed such views over many decades but dared to discuss them only with a few close friends. But the last sentences of his famous *Opticks* let the reader catch a glimpse:

> If natural Philosophy in all its Parts, by pursuing this Method, shall at length be perfected, the Bounds of Moral Philosophy will be also enlarged. For so far as we can know by natural Philosophy what is the first Cause, what Power he has over us, and what Benefits we receive from him, so far our Duty towards him, as well as that towards one another, will appear to us by the Light of Nature. And no doubt, if the Worship of false Gods had not blinded the Heathen, their moral Philosophy would have gone farther than to the four Cardinal Virtues; and instead of teaching the Transmigration of Souls, and to worship the Sun and Moon, and dead Heroes, they would have taught us to worship our true Author and Benefactor, as their Ancestors did under the

Government of *Noah* and his Sons before they corrupted themselves. (Newton 1730:381–82).

This closing passage suggests that for Newton the religion of the "golden age" or Ur-religion was preserved by Noah and his sons who were thoroughly monotheistic. Far from being only the religion of the Hebrews, this Ur-religion reigned for a long time everywhere, even in Egypt (Westfall 1982:27). But these "blinded heathen" who had initially shared Noah's Ur-religion could barely remember the cardinal virtues because their religion at some point degenerated into the worship of false gods, objects of nature, and dead heroes and into the teaching of the transmigration of souls.

Newton had closely studied Thomas Burnet's *Archæologiæ philosophicæ* of 1692 (see Chapter 3), and though the outlines of his historico-theological system were already developed in 1692, Burnet's influence is unmistakable:

> Like Burnet, Newton regarded Noah, rather than Abraham or Moses, as the original source of the true religion and learning; consequently, he, too, argued that vestiges of truth could be found among the ancient Gentile peoples as well as that of the Jews since all were descendants of Noah and his sons. Both also shared the belief that modern philosophy was contributing to the recovery of ancient truths which had been distorted after Noah's death. (Gascoigne 1991:185)

Newton clearly thought that an initial divine revelation was the ultimate source of all religion, that this Ur-religion was once shared by all ancient peoples. Nevertheless, he sought to root his views firmly in the Old Testament narrative. Monogenesis and the universality of the great flood, for example, were nonnegotiable. Thus, all postdiluvial humans, gentiles and Hebrews alike, originally shared the religion transmitted by Noah and his sons, and vestiges of this religion could be found in all ancient cultures. Newton explained:

> From all of which it is manifest that a certain general tradition was conserved for a very long time among the Peoples about those things which were passed down most distinctly from Noah and the first men to Abraham and from Abraham to Moses. And hence we can also hope that a history of the times which followed immediately after the flood

can be deduced with some degree of truth from the traditions of Peoples. (Yahuda Ms. 16.2, f. 48; Westfall 1982:22–23)

But Newton did not go as far as taking Chinese chronology into account. He owned and studied Philippe Couplet's 1687 work that was discussed in the previous chapter yet grew convinced that the famous burning of books by Emperor Shih Huangdi in the third century B.C.E had reduced all ancient Chinese history to legend. In the New College Manuscript (I, fol. 80v) Newton wrote,

> And there are now no histories in China but what were written above 72 years of this conflagration. And therefore the story that Huan ti founded the monarchy of China 2697 years before Christ is a fable invented to make that Monarchy look ancient. The way of writing used by the Chinese was not fully invented before the days of Confucius the Chinese philosopher & he was born but 551 years before Christ & flourished only in one of the six old kingdoms into which China was then divided. (Manuel 1963:270)

Newton instead studied Middle Eastern chronologies and used them to defend the Bible as the most reliable source for remote antiquity. Moses had in his opinion originally written a history of creation, a book of the generations of Adam, and the book of the law. Though these oldest books "have long since been lost except what has been transcribed out of them in the Pentateuch now extant" and though the existing text of the Pentateuch was in his opinion redacted by Samuel rather than Moses (Manuel 1963:61), Newton remained firmly convinced that the first books of the Old Testament "are by far the oldest records now extant," that the Bible is the most authentic history of the world, and that the Kingdom of Israel was the first large-scale political society with all the attributes of civilization (p. 89).[5] Manetho of Heliopolis, Berosus the Chaldaean. and others had, like the Persian and Chinese historians, created extravagant chronologies that were infinitely less reliable and old. In a chapter of his *Chronology* dedicated to the Persian Empire, Newton wrote,

> We need not then wonder, that the Egyptians have made the kings in the first dynasty of their monarchy, that which was seated at Thebes in the days of David, Solomon, and Rehoboam, so very ancient and so

long-lived; since the Persians have done the like to their kings Adar and
Hazael, who reigned an hundred years after the death of Solomon, "worshipping them as gods, and boasting of their antiquity, and not knowing," saith Josephus, "that they were but modern." (Newton 1785:5.263)

Newton employed such chronologies that "magnified their antiquities so
exceedingly" (p. 263) in a manner that much resembled that of William Jones
a century later, namely, to confirm the biblical account and vindicate biblical
authority; but Jones was to use the even more hyperbolical Indian chronologies. Newton's final system appeared, as Frank Manuel put it, "as a eulogy of
Israel" and is evidence "for his central proposition that the Hebrews were the
most ancient civilized people" (Manuel 1963:97). Though the Bible bestows
greater antiquity on the Egyptian and Assyrian royal institutions than on the
tribes of Israel, Newton "was able to cling to his *idée fixe* throughout the
revision of the history of antiquity, both in the fragments and in the final
Chronology" (p. 99).

Newton's "ancient theology" was thus—unlike that of Ramsay and Holwell—still exclusively rooted in the Middle East and the Bible. Since events
before the biblical deluge remained hazy due to the fragmentary character of
the Pentateuch and the lack of reliable ancient pagan sources, Newton's history of religions really starts with Noah and his sons. His true religion "most
closely resembled that which prevailed at the time of Noah, immediately after
the Deluge, before the idolatry—which to Newton was the root of all evil
not only in religion but also in politics and even philosophy—began to corrupt it" (Gascoigne 1991:185). The symbol of this pure original religion is the
Temple of Solomon (Figure 12), which not only features the eternal flame on
a sacrificial altar at the center but also a geometrically precise representation
of the heliocentric solar system.

Newton's "prytanea," sacred cultic places around a perpetual fire, sym-
bolize God's original revelation and are at the source of the transmission
line.[6] Cults with prytanea were for Newton the most ancient of all cults.
According to him this religion with the sacred fire "seems to have been as
well the most universal as ye most ancient of all religions & to have spread
into all nations before other religions took place. There are many instances
of nations receiving other religions after this but none (that I know) of any
nation's receiving this after any other. Nor did ever any other religion w^{ch}
sprang up later become so general as this" (Westfall 1982:24).

This religion around the prytanea was professed by Noah and his sons.

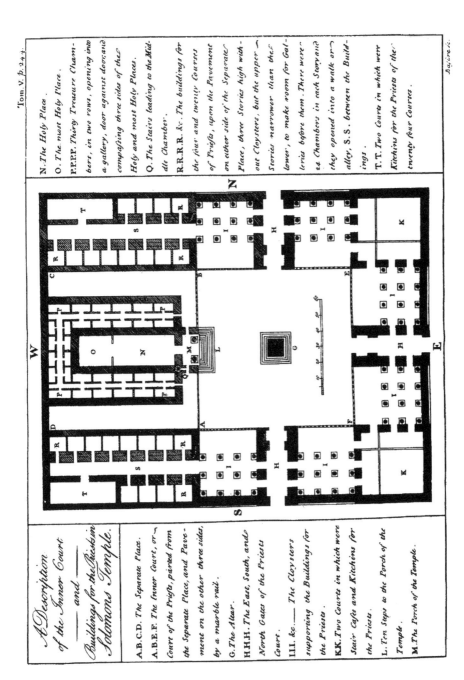

Figure 12. Newton's map of Solomon's temple (Newton 1785:5.244).

They spread "the true religion till yᵉ nations corrupted it" (p. 25). This first corruption consisted in forgetting that the symbols in the prytanea (for example, lamps symbolizing heavenly bodies around the central "solar" flame) are symbols, leading men to engage in sidereal worship. It is of interest to note that Newton's history of religion—and, I might add, Ur-traditions in general—are intimately linked to the encoding and decoding of symbols. Here the degeneration process begins with a misunderstanding of symbols; and this misunderstanding eventually leads to the worship of dead men and statues, the belief in the transmigration of souls, polytheism, the worship of animals, and other "Egyptian" inventions. In parallel with such religious degeneration, the false geocentric system took hold thanks to a late Egyptian, Ptolemy (pp. 25–26).

The first major postdiluvial regeneration was due to Moses who, according to Newton, "restored for a time the original true religion that was the common heritage of all mankind" (p. 26). But soon enough the degeneration process began anew, punctuated by calls of prophets for renewal, until Jesus came not to bring a new religion but rather to "restore the original true one" not solely for the Jews but for all mankind (p. 27). Soon enough, another round of degeneration set in with the Egyptian Athanasius, the doctrine of the Trinity, and Roman Catholic idolatry, which got worse and worse until the Reformation cleaned up some of the mess. But Protestantism and Anglicanism were not immune from corruption either, which is why Newton (who was adamantly opposed to the Trinity) felt the need to call—in a very muted voice and in heaps of unpublished notes and manuscripts—for one more restoration of true, pure, Noachic religion and wisdom.

Ramsay's Quest

In 1727, the very year of Newton's death and one year before his *Chronology of the Ancient Kingdoms Amended* was published, a bestseller by Andrew Michael RAMSAY (1686–1743) appeared on the market both in French and English: the *Travels of Cyrus* (*Les voyages de Cyrus*). It saw over thirty editions in English and French and was translated into German, Italian, Spanish, and Greek (Henderson 1952:109). The two volumes that Ramsay called his "Great work," however, *The Philosophical Principles of Natural and Revealed Religion Unfolded in a Geometrical Order*, only appeared posthumously in 1748 and 1749.

Ramsay grew up in modest circumstances in Ayr (Scotland), and after studying philosophy and theology at Glasgow and Edinburgh, he went to London in 1707 or 1708 to study mathematics with Nicolas Fatio de Duilliers (Walker 1972:234), a Swiss refugee who was perhaps Newton's most intimate friend and was well informed about Newton's unorthodox religious views. Newton's preference for the prophet Daniel is reflected in Ramsay's *Travels of Cyrus*. In the preface to the revised edition, Ramsay gave his readers the following key to his bestselling book:

> The Magi in Cyrus's time were fallen into a kind of atheism, like that of Spinoza; Zoroaster, Hermes and Pythagoras adored one sole Deity, but they were deists; Eleazar resembled the Socinians, who were for subjecting religion to philosophy; Daniel represents a perfect Christian, and the hero of this book a young prince, who began to be corrupted by the maxims of irreligion. In order to set him right, the different philosophers with whom he converses successively unfold to him new truths mixt with errors. Zoroaster confutes the mistakes of the Magi; Pythagoras those of Zoroaster; Eleazar those of Pythagoras; Daniel rejects those of all the others, and his doctrine is the only one which the author adopts. (Ramsay 1814:xvii)

Ramsay's goal was "to prove against the Atheists the existence of a Supreme Deity, who produced the world by his power and governs it by his wisdom," and he wanted to show "that the earliest opinions of the most knowing and civilized nations come nearer the truth than those of latter ages" (p. xiv). According to Ramsay, the "theology of the Orientals" was far purer than that of the Egyptians, Greeks, and Romans (pp. xiv–xv). If the most important point of *The Travels of Cyrus* was the demonstration that the primitive system of the world was monotheistic, Ramsay's second major objective was described as follows:

> The second point is to shew, in opposition to the Deists, that the principal doctrines of revealed religion, concerning the states of innocence, corruption and renovation, are as ancient as the world; that they were foundations of Noah's religion; that he transmitted them to his children; that these traditions were spread throughout all nations; that the Pagans disfigured, degraded, and obscured them by their absurd fictions; and

lastly, that these primitive truths have been no where preserved in their purity, except in the true religion. (pp. xv–xvi)

This passage presents in a nutshell some of the main elements of what I have called "Ur-tradition": an Ur-teaching from a founder (here God and his original revelation); an overall scheme of golden age/degeneration/regeneration; a transmission lineage of the Ur-teaching; pivotal transmission figures; and the linking of this Ur-doctrine to the religion of the proponent that purportedly regenerates the true original creed. For Ramsay as for Newton, Noah's religion seems to form a crucial juncture since he was the sole heir of antediluvial pure monotheism; and for both men the protagonist of the Hebrew Bible's Book of Daniel is another crucial "transmitter" figure. In his treatise on the prophecies of Daniel, Newton pointed out that already Ezekiel had joined "Daniel with Noah and Job, as most high in the favour of God" and that "Daniel was in the greatest credit amongst the Jews, till the reign of the Roman emperor Hadrian: and to reject his prophecies, is to reject the Christian religion" (Newton 1785:5.311).

If some protagonists of the Old Testament are so highly valued as transmitters of Ur-religion, the question of the text's reliability inevitably arises. Indeed, Newton's treatise "Upon the Prophecies of Daniel" begins with a chapter "Concerning the compilers of the books of the Old Testament" (pp. 297–305). In the second volume of his "Great work," Ramsay summarizes Newton's argument as follows:

1. Several great men, both of the Greek and Latin Church, of the Roman and Protestant communion, think as the famous Sir Isaac Newton, That we have lost some books wrote by the patriarchs, both before and after the deluge, concerning the creation, first origin and primitive history of the world; and that the book of Genesis preserved was rather a short extract, than an exact copy of these original patriarchal records. It is certain, as Sir Isaac remarks, that Scripture mentions, in different places, several books lost, such as "the book of the generations of Adam; the book of the wars of God; The books of Enoch" (see Sir Isaac Newton's observations upon Daniel, page 4 & 5). (Ramsay 1749:215)

Ramsay claims that he is not in a position "to decide such an important question" and has decided to "leave it to the decision of the learned," but his second point immediately shows that he accepted Newton's view:

2. If there be any truth in this conjecture, we must not be surprized, if the transitions from one subject to another be more rapid in the extracts preserved, than in the originals that are lost, and if many particular circumstances be omitted, that would have been very useful to illustrate several curious enquiries concerning the primitive creation and fall of angels and men, tho' they were not absolutely necessary to regulate our faith. (p. 216)

If the Old Testament contains only "extracts" of the whole story and its originals are "lost," are there any other, possibly more complete and reliable sources? The presentation of such sources was exactly the objective of the second volume of Ramsay's "Great work":

In the second part we shall show "That vestiges of all principal doctrines of the Christian religion are to be found in the monuments, writings, or mythologies of all nations, ages and religions; and that these vestiges are emanations of the primitive, antient, universal religion of mankind, transmitted from the beginning of the world by the Antidiluvians (sic) to the Postdiluvian patriarchs, and by them to their posterity that peopled the face of the earth." (Ramsay 1748.iv–v)

Ramsay's great quest was to collect all vestiges of the "original traditions of the patriarchal religion" from the writings of "the antient Hebrews, Chinese, Indians, Persians, Egyptians, Greeks and Romans," and he was convinced that even "among the ancient Gauls, Germans, Britons, and all other nations," one would "find vestiges of the same truths" if we would possess any "records left of their doctrines" because "all flowed from the same source" (Ramsay 1749:iv). But if the records of the "antient Hebrews" were only fragmentary, those of the Egyptians indecipherable, those of the Indians and Persians still largely unknown, and those of the Greeks and Romans too young, where could such vestiges of Ur-religion be found?

Before he enters this discussion, Ramsay clarifies the origin of his Urtradition and firmly links Adam's "perfect knowledge" to its regeneration through the Messiah:

According to the Mosaic accounts of the origin and propagation of mankind, the protoplast had a perfect knowledge of all the great principles of Natural and Revealed Religion. Adam created in a state of innocence,

before sin and passion had darkened his understanding, who conversed
with the Logos in paradise under a human form, must have had a perfect
knowledge of the Deity, and of the love we owed to him. Adam, after
the fall, could not but know the miserable state, into which he had
plunged himself, with all his posterity. Scripture assures us, and all di-
vines agree, that God, after having banished him from paradise, revealed
to him the sacrifice, sufferings, and triumphs of the Messiah. Thus Adam
must have had a perfect knowledge of all the great principles both of
Natural and Revealed Religion. (p. 8)

This quoted passage also sets the stage for Ramsay's "three states"
scheme (initial perfection, degeneration or fall, and regeneration). Next
comes the problem of a line of transmission of Adam's initial wisdom:

Yea, he [Adam] must not only have instructed his children then existent
in these sublime truths, but have given them orders to transmit the same
notions to their posterity. All the holy patriarchs must have done the
same, from generation to generation, till the deluge; when Noah, possessed with the same spirit, had, no doubt, the same care to hand down,
to succeeding ages, those essential truths. Now, since the holy patriarchs,
before and after the deluge, could and should have acted thus, it is sure
they did so. (p. 9)

But such direct transmission was risky, which is why even Ur-tradition
movements that emphasize "mind-to-mind" transmission tend to place their
trust in ancient texts:

It is no ways probable, that such a wise man as Noah, who was instructed
by, and conversed with the Logos, would have trusted to oral tradition
alone, for the preservation and transmission of these divine lights, and
sublime mysteries of faith to his posterity, and all the nations who were
to cover the face of the earth. He, no doubt, took care to have them
wrote in such characters as were then in use. All grant that the first way
of writing was by hieroglyphics. (p. 9)

Ramsay mentions the famous pillars of stone and clay that were, according to Flavius Josephus and numerous Old Testament pseudepigraphs, designed to withstand both water and fire, but he rejects the view that they

contained astronomical knowledge (p. 10). Rather, the symbolical characters on these pillars had the aim "to preserve and transmit to posterity some idea of the mysteries of religion" (p. 11). Here we have one more element of Ur-traditions: a code for the transmission of original doctrine. Ramsay thought that the inscriptions on the pillars were "Enochian or Noevian symbols" designed "to preserve the memory of these sacred truths" (p. 13). In this manner sacred texts were transmitted to all nations, thus forming a global written Ur-tradition:

> Thus the symbolical characters, images and representations of divine intellectual truths, were much the same in all nations. Of this we have uncontestable proofs, since the symbols of the Chinese are very oft the same with those wrote upon the Egyptian obelisks yet preserved: for all the Chinese characters are hieroglyphics. We find also, that the Gauls, Germans and Britains long before they were conquered by Julius Caesar, had much the same symbolical representations of their sacred mysteries and Deities, as the Egyptians, Greeks and Romans. (pp. 13–14)

Though these "Enochian or Noevian symbols" were "at first invented not to render religion mysterious, and cover it with an impenetrable veil, but, on the contrary, to render its sublime, intellectual, spiritual ideas sensible, visible and familiar to the vulgar," their true original sense was soon forgotten; "men attach'd themselves to the letter, and the signs, without understanding the spirit and the thing signified," and soon "the Pagans fell by degrees into gross idolatry and wild superstition" (pp. 14–15). Ramsay's story about the degeneration of the original religion continues very much like Newton's. Desire for power, greed, and priestcraft were some of the reasons why "the sacred, ancient and primitive symbols were degraded, obscured, misinterpreted, dismember'd, mangled and disfigured. The sacred became profane; the divine, human; and the most sublime truths were turn'd into wild fictions" (p. 16). Thus "the original sense was intirely perverted, the sign became the thing signified, and the reality was look'd upon as a symbol" (p. 19). Such degeneration took place not only in pagan nations but also with the Jews, and their claims of exclusive transmission form part of it:

> We must not however think, that the Pagans alone were guilty of these degradations, alterations and false explications of the sacred symbols and ancient traditions. As men are much the same in all nations, ages and

religions, and that human nature is an inexhaustible source of ignorance, self-love and cupidity, the members of the visible church both Jewish and Christian fell into far greater tho' very different abuses, and misinterpretations of ancient tradition, than the Pagans. Tho' the Jews had a law written not in a hieroglyphical style, but in vulgar language, yet they explain'd all the metaphorical descriptions of the divine nature and attributes in a literal sense, and form'd to themselves the idea of a partial, fantastic, furious, wrathful God who loved one nation only and hated all the rest. Because they were chosen to be the depositaries of the sacred oracles, and had the external means of salvation, they fancied that the God of the Israelites was not the God of the Gentiles; that he abandon'd all other nations to a total ignorance of his essence, and to inevitable damnation. (pp. 19–20)

Ramsay also included the Christians and declared at the beginning of his "Great work" that not only the Pagan mythologists who "adulterated by degrees the original traditions of the patriarchal religion" needed to be set straight but also the "Jewish rabbins, and then the Christian schoolmen" who "disfigured revealed religion, by many absurd opinions, popular errors, and wild fictions, which being neither founded in scripture, nor authorized by the consent of the universal church, ought not to pass for doctrines of faith" (Ramsay 1748:v). Ramsay obviously had a reformist agenda. But what did the "original" doctrine consist in? How could one hope to get some idea of Adam's "perfect knowledge" without access to (and understanding of) "Enochian or Noevian symbols"?

Noah's Chinese Heirs

When Ramsay wrote his books in the first half of the eighteenth century, a new avenue to humanity's past had opened up through the study of Chinese. Long before students of Sanskrit began to throw light on Indian antiquities, a number of pioneer Sinologists studied the Chinese "hieroglyphs" and tried to make sense of China's ancient texts. Though earlier books such as Juan Mendoza's *Historia . . . del gran reyno de la China* (1596), Matteo Ricci and Nicolas Trigault's *De Christiana Expeditione* (1615), and Alvaro Semedo's *Imperio de la China* (1642) had provided some enticing information about Chinese history, language, and religion, it was from the mid-seventeenth century that information about China's antiquity really began to sink in. In 1662, when Bishop Edward Stillingfleet wrote his *Origines sacrae* (Sacred Origins), he sensed that the defense of biblical authority entered a new phase. "The disesteem of the Scriptures," he wrote, "is the decay of religion" (Stillingfleet 1817:1.viii), and he mentioned threats from three main sides:

> The most popular pretences of the Atheists of our age, have been the irreconcileableness of the account of times in Scripture with that of the learned and ancient Heathen nations; the inconsistency of the belief of the Scriptures with the principles of reason; and the account which may be given of the origin of things, from principles of philosophy, without the Scriptures. These three therefore I have particularly set myself against, and directed against each of them several books. In the first, I have manifested that there is no ground of credibility in the account of ancient times, given by any Heathen nations, different from the Scriptures, which I have with so much care and diligence inquired into. (p. xiv)

The bishop's book shows that his scope was still limited to Egypt, Phoenicia, Chaldaea, and Greece; and after less than one hundred pages, he declared his proof complete that "there is no credibility in any of those Heathen histories" (p. 94). One thing that bothered Stillingfleet about these "Heathen histories" and other new discoveries was that the defense of Scripture became increasingly costly. He hoped that his book would silence men like Isaac La Peyrère who claimed to defend the Bible but ended up undermining it, and he prayed "that from thence we may hope to hear no more of men before Adam to salve the authority of the Scriptures by" (p. xiv).

But while the bishop wrote these words, a new and much less easily discounted threat had already ominously raised its head in two publications by a Jesuit: Martino MARTINI's *Novus Atlas Sinensis* (1655) and his *Sinicae historiae decas prima* (1658).[7] The potential of this threat may have dawned on some early readers when Gabriel DE MAGALHAES (1610–77) declared in 1668[8] that Chinese characters predated Egyptian hieroglyphs; but it was a noted English architect and amateur antiquarian who was among the first to have a sense of its implications.

John WEBB (1611–72), the close collaborator of Inigo Jones and coauthor (1655) as well as author (1665) of two works on Stonehenge, published a book in 1669 that attempted to prove that Chinese is the sole remnant of antediluvial human language and that the Chinese still use the antediluvial writing system. Writing many decades before Ramsay, Webb also mentions the engravings made by Seth or Enoch on the two pillars of brick and stone and thinks that they must have been written in humankind's original language. Based mainly on the Bible, Flavius Josephus, Walter Raleigh (1614), and Peter Heylin's *Cosmographie* (1652), Webb concludes "that *Noah* carried the *Primitive Language* into the Ark with him, and that it continued pure and uncorrupted amongst his succeeding generations until the *Confusion* of *Tongues* at *Babel*" (Webb 1678:17). Until the great flood the whole earth was therefore "*of one Language and one Lip*" (p. 17).

The arguments of Jan Gorp (Goropius Becanus; 1569:473) and Walter Raleigh (1614:144) convinced Webb that Noah's ark landed "in the confines of *Tartaria, Persia,* and *India,*" and he deemed it "very probable" that Noah "first inhabited *India*" before sending Nimrod and his followers to the Middle East (Webb 1678:20–21). He seconded Raleigh's opinion "that *India* was the first Planted and Peopled Countrey after the Flood" (p. 25). Instead of going to Shinar in Mesopotamia, Noah and his followers "sent out Colonies to the more remote parts of *Asia,* till at length they setled (sic) in the remotest CHINA" (p. 26). Webb held it "for a matter undeniable, that *the Plantation of India preceded that of Babel*" and inclined to believe "that all the Eastern parts of *Persia,* with CHINA, *and both the Indias, were peopled by such of the Sons of* Sem, *as went not with the rest to the Valley of Shinaar*" (p. 27).

Webb's scenario squarely contradicted the traditional narrative of the ark's landing on Mt. Ararat and the Mesopotamian epicenter of dispersion. Webb did not question the universality of the great flood, but his speculation about Noah's whereabouts after the flood (which the biblical account leaves unclear) led him to the conclusion that India and China were populated by the descendants of Noah and Shem and did not suffer from the disastrous confusion of tongues that befell the colonies that Noah had sent from India to the Middle East.

Rejecting Kircher's scenario of the Egyptian origins of Indian and Chinese religion, Webb maintained, based on Raleigh's calculation, that Noah's son Cham had founded his kingdom in Egypt 191 years after the flood (p. 30) and that the Egyptians did not flourish until the times of Moses (p. 31). By contrast, China was "in all probability . . . after the Flood first planted either by *Noah* himself, or some of the sons of *Sem*, before the remove *Shinaar*"; thus, the "Principles of Theology, amongst the *Chinois,* . . . could not proceed from the wicked and idolatrous race of accursed *Cham*, but from those ones that were, *de civitate Dei*, of the City of God" (p. 32). The Indians and Chinese "retained the PRIMITIVE Tongue, as having received it from *Noah*, and likewise carry the same with them to their several Plantations, in what part of the East soever they setled themselves" (p. 32).

Whereas other writers such as La Peyrère began to doubt the universality of the flood, Webb transformed the confusion of tongues into a local Mesopotamian event that could not have affected India and "its Plantations in the East" where the "Language of *Noah*" reigned without any change (pp. 33–34). Webb's intensive study of Martino Martini's *Novus Atlas Sinensis* (1655) and the *Sinicae historiae decas prima* (1658) convinced him, in the absence of evidence from India, that "*the Language of the Empire of CHINA, is, the PRIMITIVE Tongue, which was common to the whole World before the Flood*" (p. 44). Even the famous Isaac Vossius, so Webb claims, confirms that the Chinese "preserve a continued History compiled from their monuments, and annual exploits of four thousand five hundred yeares" and have "Writers . . . more antient than even *Moses* himself" (p. 48). Unlike the Indians and all other nations, the Chinese "have never been corrupted by intercourse with strangers" and have, "unknown indeed to other Nations," continued "enjoying to themselves their own felicity at pleasure" (p. 48). The great antiquity of this isolated people could not be doubted in view of the evidence furnished by secular as well as Jesuit experts:

> Whereby appears, that according to the vulgar *Aera*, which *Martinius* follows, and which makes from the Creation to the Flood of *Noah* one thousand six hundred fifty six years; and from thence to the coming of CHRIST into the World two thousand two hundred ninety four years; the Historical time of the *Chinois* begins several Ages, to wit, five hundred fifty three years before the Universal Deluge, computing to the year one thousand six hundred fifty eight: as *Vossius* doth. (p. 52)

Again relying on Martini, Webb argues that the only possible explanation of China's ancient and uninterrupted historical records is that "this extreme part of *Asia*, whereof we treat, was for certain inhabited before the flood" and that the family of Noah, which alone could know of antediluvian events, had indeed settled there and saved ancient records on the ark (p. 55). He even speculated that Noah had built his ark in China since "no Countrey in the habitable Earth could better furnish *Noah*, with all manner of conveniences, and every sort of materials proper for the building of such a Machine than *China*" (p. 71).

Apart from humankind's Ur-language, the Chinese had, of course, also safeguarded antediluvian Ur-religion: "But that of old, saith *Martinius*, the *Chinois* professed the true God from the Doctrine delivered them by *Noah*, there is no doubt to be made" (p. 88). The proof of this lies in the Chinese books where "this *Theology* of the *Chinois*, not by tradition, and a perpetual same" is found "successively written from Age to Age, ever since the universal Deluge, above seven hundred years before *Moses* was born" (p. 92). According to Webb's Jesuit sources, idolatry was unknown to the Chinese "till after the birth of CHRIST, when for many Ages preceding, the whole World had followed Idols"; but when idolatry was imported to China "in the sixty fifth year after CHRIST, infected by an *Indian* Philosopher that crept into *China*," it was of the very worst kind (p. 94).

Webb's conclusion from all this was that, absent any ancient information from India, "*China* is the most antient, and in all probability, was, the first planted Country of the World after the flood" and that there is "no doubt to be made" that the Chinese knowledge "in Divine matters, of the true God especially, was taught them by *Noah*" (p. 116). With regard to the antediluvian writing system that survived in China equally unscathed by events in the rest of the world, Webb was convinced that antediluvian books had survived the flood; some parts of the books of Enoch were reportedly "found after the flood in *Arabia Felix* . . . of which *Tertullian* affirmeth, that he had seen and read some whole pages" (p. 147). Regarding the Chinese "hieroglyphics," Webb found that their inventor "was *Fohius* their first Emperour, who according to the time that is given to the beginning of his reign might be contemporary with *Enos*" (p. 152).[9] But the language extant in China is even older—in fact, it must be "as antient, as the World itself and Mankind" (p. 162). All Chinese books are written in this "true ORIGINAL Language," whose characters "ever have been one and the same throughout their whole Empire" (p. 180). The characteristics of this language—picked up by Webb from Semedo, Martini, and Kircher—seemed to prove that Chinese is the language of paradise, which "perdures in its Antient purity without any change or alteration,"

> And I must not omit, that several books yet live amongst them, written in their first and original Hieroglyphicks, which still remaining in their Libraries, are understood by all their *Literati*, though they are no longer

used, except in some Inscriptions, and Seals instead of Coats of Arms. Among these sort of Books is extant one called *Yeking* of great Antiquity, as taking beginning with *Fohius*, and of as great esteem for the *Arcana* it contains. This Book seems much to confirm the opinion of those that would have the Inscription of *Persepolis* more antient than the flood. For, as *This* in *Persia* consists only in Triangles several wayes transversed: So *That* in *China* consists only of streight lines several wayes interrupted. It treats especially of Judicial Astrology, Politique Government; and occult Philosophy. (p. 190)

Such information and conclusions could not but interest Europe's "antiquarians," who were intrigued by the age, origin, and meaning of Mesopotamian cuneiform inscriptions, Egyptian hieroglyphs, the hexagrams of the *Yijing*, and the runic inscriptions of northern Europe. Were they all some kind of code from the dawn of time—a kind of Ur-shorthand—the key to which was exclusively preserved in that most mysterious and secluded of all ancient countries of the world, China?

The Search for the World's Oldest Text

Martino Martini began his *Sinicae historiae decas prima* of 1658—the first genuine history of China to appear in a European language[10]—with the reign of Fuxi (Fu Hsi; Webb's Fohius) from 2952 to 2838 B.C.E. According to the widely accepted chronology of Archbishop James USSHER (1581–1656), the creation of Adam had taken place in 4004 B.C.E and the great flood in 2349 B.C.E. The reign of Martini's Fuxi thus took place about six centuries before Noah's flood. The Jesuits in China had long been aware of this discrepancy and had in 1637 received permission to use a Septuagint-based alternative chronology whose flood occurred in 2957 B.C.E., five years before Fuxi began his reign (Mungello 1989:127). Martini was convinced that East Asia was inhabited before the time of Noah's flood, yet unlike John Webb, he "was willing to leave the problem unresolved" (p. 127) and thus stimulated a heated debate among chronologists and so-called antiquarians that continued well into the eighteenth century. Martini accepted the Chinese view that Fuxi had invented the trigrams and was fascinated by the sixty-four hexagrams that he associated with ancient mathematical knowledge and "a mystical philosophy similar to Pythagoras, but many centuries older" (Martini 1658:6).

Though the Chinese "use it today mainly for divination and sortilege and either ignore or neglect its genuine meaning" (p. 6), Martini regarded this system as a repository of ancient wisdom transmitted from patriarch to patriarch since the time of Noah. He thought that the *Yijing* was China's most ancient book and was convinced that Fuxi had invented the Chinese writing system that reminded him so much of the Egyptian hieroglyphs (p. 12) he had seen in the 1630s in Rome while studying under Athanasius Kircher.

Martini published his China atlas and history while traveling through Europe to drum up support for the accommodationist approach in the Jesuit mission, and during his stay in Rome (fall 1654 to January 1656), he gave his teacher much of the China-related information that ended up in Kircher's famous *China Illustrata* (1667).[11] But their view of Fuxi was completely at odds, and this difference is very significant. For Martini, Fuxi was a transmitter of "genuine meaning" and a great astronomer who had come to China some time before the confusion of tongues (Martini 1658:11). He was thus a member of the "good" transmission. Kircher, by contrast, followed Martini's informer João Rodrigues (who had first identified Fuxi with Zoroaster) in asserting that Fuxi was a descendant of Ham and therefore a member of the "evil" transmission (Kircher 1987:214).

The difference between Webb and Martini on one hand and Rodrigues and Kircher on the other does not just concern the burning question of Egyptian or Chinese anteriority (which evoked passionate discussions well into the nineteenth century). It also lies at the heart of the protracted dispute about the Jesuit "accommodation" policy and formed the crux of the famous controversy about Chinese Rites in Paris when the Sorbonne in 1700 condemned the following propositions:

1. China had knowledge of the true God more than two thousand years before Jesus Christ.
2. China had the honor of sacrificing to God in the most ancient temple in the world.
3. China has honored God in a manner that can serve as an example even to Christians.
4. China has practiced a morality as pure as its religion.
5. China had the faith, humility, the interior and exterior cult, the priesthood, the sacrifices, the saintliness, the miracles, the spirit of God, and the purest charity, which is the characteristic and the perfection of the genuine religion.

6. Of all the nations of the world, China has been the most constantly favored by the graces of God.[12]

The controversy reached enormous proportions because it did not just involve China but also India (where the toleration of "Malabarian Rites" by Roberto de Nobili and his successors was based on a similar notion of pure ancient monotheism) and ultimately even Europe's ancient religion and its druids. The two opposing views of China's first emperor were emblematic of two completely different views of the past. I have earlier called them "inclusive" and "exclusive," but even the "inclusive" view was in a sense exclusive since it also hijacked other people's histories and religions and embedded them in a fundamentally biblical scenario. For example, Webb's journey of Noah to China left the entire basic framework of the Old Testament narrative with its creator God, paradise, the Fall, the patriarchs, the deluge, and other biblical events intact and turned the Chinese into descendants of Noah. A metaphor from the commercial realm may be more to the point. What Webb, Martini, the China figurists, and Ramsay attempted can be called a "friendly takeover" whereas the approach of Rodrigues, Kircher, and the victors of the Rites controversy would constitute a "hostile takeover." The "hostile takeover" group usually made the Chinese descend from Noah's problem child Ham—the one who had mocked his drunken father—and regarded China's ancient religion not as noachic monotheism but as an evil concoction reeking of polytheism, idolatry, and superstition of Egyptian or Chaldean ancestry. The Sorbonne accusers of Louis Daniel Le Comte's and Charles Le Gobien's writings were of this persuasion, and so were the exclusivists in Rome, China, and India who adamantly opposed the approach of Ricci, de Nobili, and Ur-traditionalists of all colors. This "hostile takeover" group won in the rites controversy, and its victory not only led to the prohibition of publications by "friendly takeover" promoters but also became a factor in the expulsion of missionaries from China and the eventual dissolution of the Jesuit order (see Chapter 7). Moreover, as is documented in this book, it exerted a profound influence on the growth of Orientalism. But so did the opposing faction.

The proponents of a "friendly takeover" put the Chinese and their first emperor into the transmission line tethered to Noah and his good son Shem and believed that they were soundly monotheistic and fundamentally good. The hazards of this sort of friendly takeover are shown in the tragic fate of Li Zubo, a Chinese Christian who was executed in 1665 for having asserted in a treatise that biblical teachings were carried to China by early descendants of Adam and Eve, that China's founding father Fuxi was one of them, that biblical teachings had for many ages reigned in China, and that the old Chinese classics showed vestigial evidence of such teachings (Mungello 1989:93). Li wrote,

> The first Chinese really descended from the men of Judea who had come to the East from the West, and the Teaching of Heaven is therefore what they recalled. When they produced and reared their children and grand-children, they taught their households the traditions of the family, and this is the time when this teaching came to China. (trans. Rule 1986:99)

While Li's treatise pleased the "accommodationist" faction and his Jesuit mentors, who possibly had a hand in its redaction, it enraged seal-carrying shareholders of the Chinese empire like the official Yang Guangxian, who launched a formal accusation and succeeded in having the unfortunate Li Zubo executed.

It seems that Chinese officials regarded this not exactly as a "friendly" takeover of their past. Yet some decades later some of the most extremist proponents of this view were studying the *Yijing* with the emperor's consent right under the officials' noses in the precincts of Beijing's imperial palace. They were the Jesuit missionaries who are now commonly called "figurists," a label that alludes to both their interest in "figures" or symbols and their central typological enterprise, which consisted in finding the New (their Christianity) prefigured in the Old (the *Yijing* and the Chinese classics). In a letter to Étienne Fourmont, Father Prémare expressed the aim of this group and of his own work as follows:

> The ultimate and last goal to which I dedicate this *Notice* and all my other writings is to bring about, if I can, that the whole world realizes that the Christian religion is as old as the world, and that the God-Man was very certainly known to the man or men who invented the Chinese hieroglyphs and composed the *Jing*. (Abel-Rémusat 1829:2.266)[13]

The fact that Prémare included his *Notitia Linguae Sinicae*, the first comprehensive textbook of the Chinese language and of Chinese literature (Lundbæk 1991:64), in this dedication is significant: research of ancient Asian texts necessitated a thorough knowledge of language and literature, and it is certainly not by chance that the best Sinologists of the early eighteenth century were all deeply involved in the search for humankind's earliest religion, whether they promoted figurism (Bouvet, de Prémare, Foucquet) or eventually rejected it on the basis of intensive study (de Visdelou). Although the "hostile takeover" policy of the Catholic Church and the Jesuit order prevented them from publishing (and even openly discussing) the results of their research, the effort to identify, date, and understand ancient texts while making use of available native commentaries, dictionaries, reference works, and literati advice was a very important event in the history of Orientalism and opened many doors. It influenced, among many others, pioneer anthropologists like Lafitau, historians like Olof Dalin and Paul Henri Mallet, and of course also via Ramsay a number of eighteenth-century Orientalists such as Holwell (Chapter 6); Mignot, Anquetil-Duperron, and Sainte-Croix (Chapter 7); and William Jones (App 2009).

A new phase in the study of ancient Asian materials began in earnest at the end of the seventeenth century, around the time when Jean-Paul BIGNON (1662–1743) became president of the Académie des Sciences (1692), began his reform of the Academy of Sciences (1699), became director of the *Journal des Savants*, gave it its lasting form (1701), and reorganized Europe's largest library (the Royal Library in Paris that evolved into the Bibliothèque Nationale de France). It was Bignon who stacked the Collège Royal with instructors like Fourmont (Leung 2002:130); it was Bignon whom Father Bouvet wanted to get on board for his grand project of an academy in China (Collani 1989); it was Bignon who employed Huang, Fréret, and Fourmont to catalog Chinese books at the library and to produce Chinese grammars and dictionaries; it was Bignon who ordered Calmette and Pons to find and send the Vedas and other ancient Indian texts to Paris (see Chapter 6); and it was Bignon who supported Fourmont's expensive project of carving over 100,000 Chinese characters in Paris (Leung 2002). The conversion of major libraries into state institutions open to the public, which Bignon oversaw, was a development with an immense impact on the production and dissemination of knowledge, including knowledge about the Orient. So was the promotion of scholarly journals like the *Journal des Sçavans* (later renamed *Journal des Savants*) that featured reviews of books from all over Europe and fulfilled a central function in the pan-European "République des lettres".

Joachim BOUVET (1656–1730) first explained his figurist system in a letter to Bignon (dated September 15, 1705) that was originally intended for Leibniz (Collani 1989:26). Seeing features of Christianity prefigured in ancient (or seemingly ancient) sources was quite common throughout the history of Christianity, but Bouvet brought an amazing text into play:

> One will be forced to admit that the canonical books of China are the most ancient works of natural law that can today be found among the heathens and even among the believers, not even excepting the Pentateuch of Moses; that is true at least for the book *ye kim* [*Yijing*] which can with assurance be regarded as the most ancient work known in the world. (p. 39)

The "veritable author" of this book is, according to Bouvet, the "holy Patriarch Enoch whose works, according to Tertullian, were rejected by the Jews because they talked too clearly of the Messiah and the incarnation of a God who would himself come to expiate the world" (p. 39). While the Chinese people thought that Fuxi was the *Yijing*'s author and inventor of its hieroglyphs and ancient "mystical science" (p. 39), Bouvet was convinced that the Chinese had—like many other peoples—unknowingly adopted the antediluvian biblical patriarch Enoch as a founder figure:

> But we add and dare to affirm that this alleged founder of the Chinese monarchy is none other than he whom most ancient nations have recognized . . . as the founder not only of their laws and customs but also of their religion, sciences, ancient books, writing systems, and languages. Consequently the Fo-hi [Fuxi] of the Chinese, the Hermes or Mercury Trismegist of the Egyptians and Greeks, the Thot of the Alexandrians, the Idris or Adris of the Arabs, and the Enoch of the Hebrews are one and the same person who is revered by diverse nations under different names. (p. 42)

In this manner Bouvet attempted a friendly takeover of the remote antiquity of the world's ancient nations, and the two reputedly oldest ones—Egypt and China—both got a biblical pedigree. This was more elegant than Huët's attempt to hijack entire dynasties of gentile divinities by identifying them all as disguised members of Moses's family, but it was nevertheless a takeover of global proportions. Whoever authored the *Yijing*, it was the oldest extant book of the world and therefore of the greatest interest:

> In effect, in spite of its small volume and very simple figures, this work contains in a kind of natural, methodical, clear, and abbreviated algebra,

as it were, the principles of all sciences and forms, and a system of nature and religion. Following the very simple principles on which it is wholly based, one discovers in it all the mysteries of the hieroglyphs of Egypt and the entire economy of symbolic science of this ancient nation, invented by Enoch, the true Mercury. Who could, in the face of such a perfect affinity between China and Egypt in such an extraordinary type of doctrine . . . deny that this must have come to them from a common origin and that their first master must necessarily have been identical? (p. 46)

But who had brought this oldest book, the *Yijing*, to China? Since Bouvet was in the "friendly takeover" camp this task fell to Noah's good son Shem:

Indeed, Shem—who because of his rare piety and his seniority doubt-lessly succeeded to his father's sovereign dignity of priesthood and king-ship—inherited the treasure trove of sacred hieroglyphic books that Noah had saved from the waters of the deluge after having received them from Methusalem, the nephew of Enoch with whom he had spent several centuries. This holy patriarch [Shem] preserved through his wise and religious policy almost the entire lineage of Noah in the cult of God and in the faithful observance of the natural law until about the end of the fifth century after the deluge when the numerous descendants were divided by divine order into several colonies in order to populate the earth. (p. 47)

The tribe that populated China was, in Bouvet's scenario, "probably the most considerable of the colonies issued by Shem's family," and it was "only natural" that it received as heritage "from the very hands of Shem" some precious treasures: antique "vases, sacred texts, and most genuine hiero-glyphic sources that certainly included the *Yijing* and the other ancient books of China" (p. 47). Thus, the ancient treasures of Enoch came to be transmit-ted "via the hands of Noah and Shem to China" (p. 48). Since both the transmission and its content were so pure, it is hardly surprising that China was "since the beginning of her foundation in possession of his [Enoch's] sciences, his laws, and his religion in the highest degree of purity and perfec-tion" and has ever since safeguarded its canonical books "with the same attachment and the same respect as the Hebrews show for the sacred books of the Old Testament" (p. 48).

So far we have here an Ur-religion and Ur-science revealed by the founder (God) to a line of patriarchs, plus a secure transmission in the form of texts and symbols in canonical books that are substantially older than the Old Testament but go back to the same source. While the Chinese were thus living in purity and perfection, the Egyptians—instructed by Cham "who was as abhorred by men for his impiety as his elder brother [Shem] was admired"—learned "the detestable and conjectural [supposé] meaning of the hieroglyphs, the diabolical secrets of magic, and the sacrilegious rites of idolatry" that Cham had smuggled onto the ark of his father (p. 48). But unfortunately, the Chinese had in the course of time forgotten the true significance of the "hieroglyphs" of their Enochian science as preserved in the *Yijing*, and of true Noevian Ur-religion. It is here that Bouvet and his disciples had to step in as regenerators of Ur-religion with the ability to introduce the Chinese, starting with their emperor, to the "genuine" meaning of their canonical books, their ancient religion, and that oldest book of the world, which contained all this. For those who could read it, the *Yijing* proves—as Prémare put it—that "the Christian religion is as old as this world" and that the oldest Chinese texts contain "vestiges of the dogmas of Christianity" (Prémare 1878:9, 51).

At the beginning of his *Vestiges*, Prémare lists the essential prefigured doctrines:

> *The Principal Dogmas of the Christian Religion Rediscovered in the Ancient Chinese Books*
> The following is the plan of this work:
> 1. I will first explain different points necessary for understanding the book.
> 2. I will speak of God as *One* and *Trine*.
> 3. I will treat of the question of the state of *unspoiled and innocent Nature*.
> 4. Then of the state of *corrupted Nature*, and separately of the *rebellion* of Angels and the *fall* of Adam.
> 5. Of *restored Nature* through Jesus Christ. This point, with God's help, will be treated at length because of the importance of the subject and the abundance of material. (p. 22)

Bouvet and his disciples had, in spite of a number of differences, the same basic vision of Ur-tradition and shared the dream to show the Chinese and also Western skeptics that the world's oldest books contain vestiges of a primitive revelation, form part of the antediluvian patriarchal transmission, and constitute an Oldest Testament containing the encoded prefiguration of central doctrines of Christianity.

As the idea of Asian antiquity and ancient wisdom slowly took hold among Europe's cultured class, it also played a role in one of the famous controversies of the time: the struggle between the "ancients" and the "moderns." In 1690 Sir William TEMPLE (1628–99) wrote in *An Essay upon the Ancient and Modern Learning* that the Egyptians, who had the reputation of being the oldest civilization and the instructors of Moses, might themselves "have drawn much of their learning from the Indians" and explained:

> To strengthen this conjecture, of much learning being derived from such remote and ancient fountains as the Indies, and perhaps China; it may be asserted with great evidence, that though we know little of the antiquities of India, beyond Alexander's time, yet those of China are the oldest that any where pretend to any fair records; for these are agreed, by the missionary Jesuits, to extend so far above four thousand years, and with such appearance of clear and undeniable testimonies, that those religious men themselves, rather than question their truth, by finding them contrary to the vulgar chronology of the Scripture, are content to have recourse to that of the Septuagint, and thereby to salve the appearances in these records of the Chineses. (Temple 1814:3.455)

Sir William was aware that it "may look like a paradox, to deduce learning from regions accounted commonly so barbarous and rude" yet insisted that "whoever observes the account already given of the ancient Indian and Chinese learning and opinions, will easily find among them the seeds of all these Grecian productions and institutions": the transmigrations of souls, the four cardinal virtues, abstinence from all meats that had animal life, the eternity of matter with perpetual changes of form, the indolence of the body and tranquility of mind, the care of education from the birth of children, the austere temperance of diet, and so on (p. 457).

Ramsay and the Figurists

With the return to Europe of Foucquet in 1722 and his residence in Rome from 1723 until his death in 1741, the Chinese figurist message and the notion that there are extremely old Chinese scriptures got a somewhat broader exposure. Among Foucquet's interlocutors were Voltaire,[14] Saint-Simon, Montesquieu, Charles de Brosses, Étienne Fourmont, Joseph Spence, and Chevalier Ramsay (Witek 1982:308). Ramsay conversed with Foucquet in 1724, and Spence called him the "great friend of Foucquet" (pp. 310–14). During a lengthy talk, the former missionary confirmed that "the canonical Chinese books were truly more ancient than those of Moses" and that "their authors were unable to know these things except by the ancient tradition which should be recognized as having come from Adam through Seth and Enoch, who was the author of these books" (pp. 310–11). Foucquet must also have supplied Ramsay with some of his translations, as he certainly is the "gentleman of superior genius, who does not care to be mentioned" who allowed Ramsay to publish some "passages, which he translated himself out of some ancient Chinese books that have been brought into Europe" (Ramsay 1814:382–83). After citing some "ancient commentaries of the book Yking, i.e., the book of Changes" that "continually speak of a double heaven, a primitive and a posterior," Ramsay included two pages of quotations from these commentaries as well as Daoist classics in his *Of the Mythology of the Pagans* appended to the *Travels of Cyrus*. The texts supplied by Foucquet were chosen to prove that the Chinese knew a golden age of innocence ("former heaven"), an age of degradation ("latter heaven"), and also "an ancient tradition common to all nations that the middle god was not to expiate and put an end to crimes but by his own great sufferings" (pp. 383–85). It is very likely that Ramsay's basic scheme of a "primitive perfection of nature, its fall, and its restoration by a divine hero"—the scheme that he detected "in the mythologies of the Greeks, Egyptians, Persians, Indians, and Chinese"—was inspired by, or even stemmed from, "the superior genius" of Foucquet.

Prémare, who remained in China, read Ramsay's *Travels of Cyrus* in 1731 and expressed his elation of having found a kindred soul in a letter to Fourmont on August 27, 1731 (Lundbæk 1991:171). After this welcome discovery, Prémare began to exchange letters with Ramsay and supplied him with the best of his writings. Ramsay used so much of them in his "Great work" that Lundbæk called him "Prémare's editor" (p. 170).[15] This material radically changed Ramsay's view of the Bible. In the *Travels of Cyrus* he had acknowledged that some ancient peoples cannot be accused of having plagiarized Moses because "the Jews and their books were too long concealed in a corner of the earth, to be reasonably thought the primitive light of the Gentiles" and suggested that one "must go farther back even to the deluge" in order to

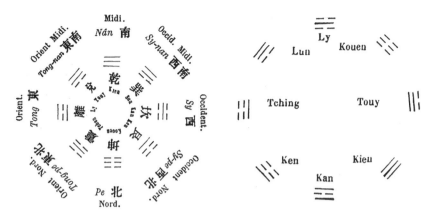

Figure 13. *Yijing* trigram charts (former and latter heaven) by Prémare (1878:79).

prove the essential correctness of the biblical account (Ramsay 1814:390–91). At the time Ramsay was still convinced that the truth of the three states (initial perfection, the fall, and salvation through a Messiah) "has been transmitted to us from age to age, from the time of the deluge till now, by an universal tradition; other nations have obscured and altered this tradition by their fables; it has been preserved in its purity no where but in the holy scriptures, the authority of which cannot be disputed with any shadow of reason" (p. 390).

In his posthumously published "Great work," however, Ramsay accepted Newton's conjecture that the book of Genesis is only a short extract of older, lost sources (Ramsay 1749:215–16), and he supplied so much information missing in the Bible that the description of "the rapid Mosaical narration" as "rather an abridgment, than a full detail of that great legislator's original writings" seems adequate. In the chapter on "the three states of degraded angelical nature," Ramsay finally states without ambiguity:

> As the book of Genesis is probably, but an extract and abridgment of the antidiluvian and Noevian traditions, concerning the creation, Moses, in his rapid narration, does not enter into any full description of the primitive state of the angelical world, nor so much as mention the fall of angels, which is only hinted at, by a transient word about the chaos. (p. 301)

Apart from missing information about the fall of angels, Ramsay was also concerned about the lack of Old Testament support for the Trinity, even though this must have been taught by the antediluvian patriarchs. Here, too, the Chinese transmission seemed more reliable:

> If the Noevian patriarchs taught the great mystery of the Trinity to their children; if this sublime truth was transmitted to their posterity by the different heads of the families that peopled the various countries of the earth; if the most ancient of all nations the Chinese have such plain vestiges of this sacred truth in their original books, is it surprising, if we find some traces of the same doctrine among the Chaldeans and Persians, both descended from the same source? (p. 124)

In this last of his works, Ramsay keeps coming back to "the Chinese, the most ancient of all nations now existent under a regular form of government, uninterrupted almost, since the first times after the universal deluge" (pp. 124, 274) and to their closeness to the Ur-tradition:

> As the Chinese are one of the most ancient people that inhabited the earth, and that were formed into a regular government soon after the deluge it is no wonder we find among them such venerable traces of the Noevian tradition. The nearer we approach to the origin of the world, the clearer is this tradition concerning a triplicity in the divine essence. We must not then be surprised, if we find some vestiges of the same truth in the following ages. The Chinese mythology, or rather theology, is a key to all the others less ancient, and more obscured by the succession of time. (p. 121)

Prémare's texts had convinced Ramsay that "the canonical books of China contain many scattered fragments of the ancient Noevian, yea, antidiluvian tradition concerning the sublimest mysteries of faith" (p. 181), and he was in awe of the new kind of Orientalist research performed by "some very learned and great men who have lived twenty, thirty and forty years in China, studied the language of the country, seen these original books, and read the ancient commentarys upon them" (p. 181). But how did Ramsay see their system? He boiled it down to seven points:

> 1. They pretend to demonstrate, that all the Chinese characters were originally hieroglyphics, as those wrote upon the Egyptian obelisks . . .
> 2. These ancient monuments, characters, symbols and hieroglyphics were

originally wrote upon pillars, or tables of stone and mettal, by some antidiluvian patriarch who foresaw the universal deluge, who knew the mysteries of religion, and who was desirous to preserve the memory of those sacred truths from shipwrack. 3. That tho' those hieroglyphical monuments may have been adulterated, interpolated and ill copied in succeeding ages, yet they still contain many vestiges of the most essential doctrines of our most holy faith, as of God and his three essential attributes; of the sacred Trinity; of the pre-existence, suffering and triumph of the Messiah, of the fall of angels and men; and of the true means of reunion to our great original. (p. 181)

The remaining four points deal with the Chinese's mistaken belief that they were the only people to possess this tradition because of their ignorance of Fuxi's identity with Enoch; the mixup of past and future because of the lack of conjugation; and their ignorance of the true meaning of the ancient hieroglyphs that constitutes, as with other peoples, the origin of mythologies:

The original hieroglyphics transported from nation to nation were by succession of time falsely translated, adulterated, or misunderstood, and the true sense of the ancient traditions, being at last forgot, every nation explained them differently according to their fancy, and applied them as fabulous facts that had already happened, or to fictitious heroes, that had once lived in their own country. Hence arose all the different mythologies of the Eastern and Western, of the Southern and Northern nations, where the ground and canvass is still the same, tho' the colourings and ornaments are different. (pp. 182–83)

These seven points that Ramsay attributes to the Chinese figurists had great repercussions in his work, since he consistently uses the translations of Father Prémare to render his demonstrations incontestable:

If these seven principles can be demonstrated, or at least proved in such a manner, as to render them not only possible and probable; but even, as uncontestable as any matters of fact can be, then we see, how some hints and vestiges of the same divine truths may, and must be found in all learned and religious nations, since they are so clear in the ancient monuments of China. (p. 183)

For orthodox readers who had followed Ramsay's religious itinerary from Protestant theology studies in Scotland into the arms of the Catholic Church and from there toward François FÉNELON (1651–1715), the French mystic Madame GUYON (1648–1717), and finally the Jesuit figurists, Ramsay's conclusions from all this must have been hard to swallow:

> The only objection that can be made, is, that if this system be true, then the five canonical books of China would contain clearer revelations concerning the mysteries of our holy religion, than the Pentateuch, or the five canonical books of Moses. (p. 183)

Ramsay lets this objection stand without further comment; and since he continues to adduce Chinese evidence for his arguments, the readers could not fail to understand his answer to this objection.

Thus, the *Yijing* and the other ancient "canonical" books of ancient China had their brief but poignant moment of fame. The study of Chinese sources and the Jesuit figurist obsession with Enoch's symbols left a permanent mark, as they directed Europe's attention to the study of the most ancient Oriental texts and played a crucial role in opening a new phase of Orientalist research. The French king opened the eighteenth century at Versailles with a display of Chinese fireworks, and half a century later Voltaire began his universal history with a chapter on China. But by then Voltaire was already guessing that India had an even older civilization than China. But let us now turn to some other Ur-teachings discovered by Ramsay: doctrines that influenced men like Holwell, the protagonist of the next chapter.

Angels, Souls, and the Origin of Evil

The problem of the origin of evil was basic both for the radical deists who refused to accept any divine revelation and for men like Ramsay and Holwell in whose systems vestiges of a divine revelation to our first forefathers were central. In the *Discourse upon the Theology and Mythology of the Pagans*, Ramsay points out that even without the help of revelation and "left to the light of their reason alone," men have always been shocked that evil could be "the work of a Being infinitely wise and powerful" and knew that "what is supremely good, could never produce any thing that was wicked or miserable" (Ramsay 1814:362).

From hence they concluded, that souls are not now what they were at first; that they are degraded, for some fault committed by them in a former state; that this life is a state of exile and expiation; and, in a word, that all beings are to be restored to their proper order. Tradition struck in with reason, and this tradition had spread over all nations certain opinions, which they held in common, with regard to the three states of the world, as I shall shew in this second part, which will be a sort of abridgment of the traditional doctrine of the ancients. (p. 362)

This "tradition" refers to the divine revelation transmitted from the earliest patriarchs whose vestiges are found among all ancient nations. The fact that it "strikes in with reason" is the overall theme of Ramsay's *Philosophical Principles of Natural and Revealed Religion*, which argues that supernatural revelation is not opposed to reason, as the deists argued, but rather in perfect accord with it.

There are but two possible ways of coming to the knowledge of truth, by natural evidence, or by supernatural revelation. Both are emanations of that sovereign wisdom which alone has the right to command our assent, and both are employed in this essay. Tho' natural light is not always sufficient to discover supernatural truths, yet revelation never contradicts reason. The former serves to exalt and ennoble, but never to degrade and extinguish the latter. (Ramsay 1748:iii)

One instance where man's "natural light" is not sufficient for the discovery of "supernatural truths" is the question of the origin of evil. When young Cyrus in Ramsay's *Travels of Cyrus* interviews Pythagoras about this, Pythagoras—who in Ramsay's portrait believes in an "infinite Being" that produced everything and is "only power, wisdom, and goodness"—ran through "all the different opinions of the philosophers," but the best of Greek philosophy could not satisfy Cyrus (Ramsay 1814:225, 230). Of all the opinions he had heard regarding the origin of evil, the only one that made sense was one proposed by some Hebrews (p. 230). This "solution" stemmed from the Kabbala and was explained to Prince Cyrus by an "allegorist" called Eleazar, "one of the great geniuses of his age," who was able to prove "that the religion of the Hebrews was not only the most ancient, but the most conformable to reason" (p. 290). This doctrine of "the Hebrew philosophers, concerning the three states of the world" is based on supernatural revelation

that never contradicts reason, and since the Hebrew transmission of revelation is so ancient and pure, Eleazar knows details of Ur-tradition that do not
necessarily appear in the vestiges of the heathens. According to him, God
first "created divers orders of intelligences to make them happy," but two
kinds of spirits "lost their happiness by their disloyalty" (pp. 290–91). The
cherubim of superior order did so by pride, rebelled, and their sphere of the
heavens "became a dark chaos" (p. 292). The less perfect *ischim* became too
attached to material objects and sensual pleasures and were punished less
severely because they sinned through weakness rather than through pride.
They were forced to be "souls which actually inhabit mortal bodies," and
when such a body dies they must occupy another (p. 292):

> The organic moulds of all human bodies were shut up in that of Adam,
> and the order of generation was established; each soul awakens in such a
> body, and in such time, place and circumstances, as suit best with the
> decrees of eternal wisdom. The earth changed its form, it was no longer
> a garden of delights, but a place of banishment and misery, where the
> continual war of the elements subjected men to diseases and death. This
> is the hidden meaning of the great Hebrew lawgiver, when he speaks of
> the terrestrial paradise and of the fall of our first parents, Adam does not
> represent a single man, but all mankind. (p. 292)

One can discuss whether this solution ought to have satisfied Ramsay's
Cyrus; but variations of it involving the preexistence of souls were well
known in Ramsay's time; in fact, they stretch from the days of Origen to
Henry MORE (1614–87) and to the Latter-day Saints knocking on our doors
today. In his book on *The Immortality of the Soul* (1662), Henry More not
only asserted that "the hypothesis of *Praeexistence* is more agreeable to Reason
than any other Hypothesis" and "has the suffrage of all Philosophers in all
Ages" but also that "the *Gymnosophists* of Aegypt, the Indian *Brachmans*, the
Persian *Magi*, and all the learned of the *Jews* were of this Opinion" (More
1662:110). Preexistence of souls assumes that people's souls "did once subsist
in some other state; where, in several manners and degrees, they forfeited the
favour of their Creatour" and were punished for their apostasy (p. 112). The
main benefits of the preexisting soul theory are that original sin is committed
by all souls and not just Adam; that nobody is, therefore, unjustly punished;
and that God is cleared of accusations of meanness. This also has implications
for the end of times when such souls are to be restituted to their original

state, and it can accommodate a measure of transmigration of souls among humans.

According to Ramsay, other peoples preserved vestiges of the same Ur-tradition. For example, Greek philosophers such as Pythagoras and Plato who "endeavored to re-establish the ancient theology of the Orientals" (Ramsay 1814:359) believed in the "very ancient doctrine, common to all the Asiatics," that "the souls of beasts are degraded spirits"; and their followers "thought the doctrine of transmigration less absurd" than believing that "the divine justice could inflict sufferings on intelligences that had never offended." These philosophers held that "none but the depraved souls were destined to such a transmigration, and that it would one day be at an end, when they were purified from their crimes" (pp. 364–65). Plato wrote that the souls "free themselves from the impurities of their terrestrial prison" and after death retire to "the first earth, where souls made their abode before their degradation." This means that our "second earth" was seen as a "low abyss" and a "prison" (pp. 366–67).

> When souls no longer make their felicity consist in the knowledge of truth, and when lower pleasures turn them off from the love of the supreme Essence, they are thrown into some planet, there to undergo expiatory punishments, till they are cured by their sufferings. These planets are consequently, according to Plato's notion, like hospitals or places instituted for the cure of distempered intelligences. (p. 371)

This was, according to Ramsay, "the system adopted by the heathen philosophers, whenever they attempted to explain the origin of evil," and Pythagoras "had learned the same doctrine among the Egyptians" (p. 372). The core doctrine of the Egyptians was thus another vestige of primeval revelation. Their belief was

> 1. That the world was created without any physical or moral evil, by a Being infinitely good. 2. That several genii abusing their liberty, fell into crimes, and thereby into misery. 3. That these genii must suffer expiatory punishments, till they are purified and restored to their first state. 4. That the god Orus, the son of Isis and Osiris, and who fights with the evil principle, is a subordinate deity, like Jupiter the conductor the son of Saturn. (p. 378)

The Persian doctrine is less well known "because we have lost the ancient books of the first Persians" (p. 379); but Ramsay was convinced that "the doctrine of the Persian magi is a sequel of the doctrine of the Indian Brachmans" (p. 380), and he had consulted "what has been translated of the Vedam, which is the sacred book of the modern Bramins." Though "its antiquity be not perhaps so great as it is affirmed to be, yet there is no denying that it contains the ancient traditions of those people, and of their philosophers" (p. 381). The Vedam of the Indians states

> that souls are eternal emanations from the divine Essence, or at least that they were produced long before the formation of the world; that they were originally in a state of purity, but having sinned, were thrown down into the bodies of men, or of beasts, according to their respective demerits; so that the body, where the soul resides, is a sort of dungeon or prison. (p. 382)

This quotation stems from Abraham Roger and will be discussed in the next chapter since it forms the core of Holwell's "Indian" text and of his conception of the world's oldest religion. This view of souls that existed before the formation of the world in a state of purity, sinned, and were imprisoned in the bodies of humans and animals was linked by the Indians with the concept of transmigration. Ramsay saw this confirmed by a quotation from Kircher's *China Illustrata* (1987:142–43): "Lastly, they hold that 'after a certain number of transmigrations, all souls shall be re-united to their origin, re-admitted into the company of the gods, and deified'" (Ramsay 1814:382). Ramsay expressed his surprise about finding such a clear formulation in the Indian Veda but saw this as a confirmation of Indian influence on Pythagoras:

> I should hardly have thought those traditions authentic, or have brought myself to trust to the translators of the Vedam, if this doctrine had not been perfectly agreeable to that of Pythagoras, which I gave an account of a little before. This philosopher taught the Greeks nothing but what be had learned from the Gymnosophists. (p. 382)

While Ramsay insisted—as a good Catholic should—that he was not defending such opinions, he acknowledged their efficacy in confounding "such philosophers as refuse to believe" (p. 390):

In all these systems we see that the ancient philosophers, in order to refute the objections of the impious concerning the origin and duration of evil, adopted the doctrine of the pre-existence of souls, and their final restoration. Several fathers of the church have maintained the first opinion, as the only philosophical way of explaining original sin; and Origen made use of the latter, to oppose the libertines of his time. (p. 390)

But by presenting such doctrines as vestiges of primeval revelation and linking them to "the foundation of our religion" (pp. 390–91) Ramsay gave them a tacit seal of approval. In his posthumously published "Great work," Ramsay's approval was open enough for David HUME (1711–76) to conclude in his *Natural History of Religion* (1757) that Ramsay, "having thus thrown himself out of all received sects of Christianity," was "obliged to advance a system of his own which is a kind of *Origenism*, and supposes the pre-existence of the souls both of men and beasts, and the eternal salvation and conversion of all men, beasts, and devils" (Hume 1976:86).

Hume was averse to Ramsay's basic view of initial perfection, gradual decline, and return to perfection. He saw monotheism not as the religion of Paradise but rather as the result of a long, hard slog from utter primitivity:

'Tis a matter of fact uncontestable, that about 1700 years ago all mankind were idolaters. The doubtful and sceptical principles of a few philosophers, or the theism, and that too not entirely pure, of one or two nations, form no objection worth regarding. Behold then the clear testimony of history. The farther we mount up into antiquity, the more do we find mankind plunged into idolatry. No marks, no symptoms of any more perfect religion. The most antient records of human race still present us with polytheism as the popular and established system. The north, the south, the east, the west, give their unanimous testimony to the same fact. What can be opposed to so full an evidence? (p. 26)

Ramsay's answer was, as Cudworth's before him: ancient textual evidence! But unlike Cudworth who had to dig for signs of Ur-monotheism in the Middle East and in Egypt, Ramsay had informants supplying him with ancient Chinese evidence. Nevertheless, Europe was gradually warming to the idea, promoted by Hume, of humankind's gradual rise from primitivity. This was diametrically opposed to Ramsay's notion of a decline from initial perfection. But both Ur-theologians of the Ramsay-type and believers in progress from primitivity of the Hume-type were interested in evidence— particularly ancient texts from Asia, since this continent was (at least in Europe and Asia itself) universally considered to be the cradle of civilization. The hunt for such evidence was a task made for Orientalists, and the next chapters will present some of the men who tried to rise to this challenge.

Chapter 6

Holwell's Religion of Paradise

An Internet search for John Zephaniah HOLWELL (1711–98) produces thousands of references, most of which contain the words "Black Hole." The back cover of Jan Dalley's *The Black Hole: Money, Myth and Empire* explains:

> The story of the Black Hole of Calcutta was once drilled into every
> British schoolchild: how in 1756 the Nawab of Bengal attacked Fort
> William and locked the survivors in a tiny cell, where over a hundred
> souls died in insufferable heat. British retribution was swift and merci-
> less, and led to much of India falling completely under colonial domina-
> tion.[1]

Dalley's book tells the story of this foundation myth of the British Empire, a myth that was "based on improbable exaggeration and half-truth" and
"helped justify the march of empire for two hundred years" (2007: back
cover). The reason Holwell is associated with this myth is that he was its
creator. When Holwell's account of the dreadful night in the Black Hole was
printed in 1758, it provoked scandal and horror. Fueled by numerous reprints,
the story soon became an event of mythic proportions, a symbol of the fall
of Calcutta and the beginning of empire that Dalley lines up with the likes
of the Boston Tea Party and the Battle of Wounded Knee (2007:199). According to Hartmann (1946:195) this story was "about as well-known in the En-
glish-speaking world as the fact that Napoleon was Emperor of France"; but
the fact that this statement occurs in a paper titled "A Case Study in the
Perpetuation of Error" points to the raging controversy about the "Question
of Holwell's Veracity," as J. H. Little put it in the title of his influential 1915
article. Having examined Holwell's original Black Hole report line by line,

Little arrived at the conclusion that the whole episode was a gigantic hoax. Hartmann summarized Little's observations as follows:

> Specifically, Little shows that Holwell (1) fabricated a speech and fathered it on the Nawab Alivardi Khan; (2) brought false charges against the British puppet ruler of Bengal, the Nawab Mir Jafar, accusing him of massacring persons all of whom were later shown to be alive . . . (3) forged a whole book and called it a translation from the ancient sacred writings of the Hindus. (Hartmann 1946:196)

Hartmann defended Holwell against the last accusation by portraying him as a possible victim of fraud rather than a forger:

> This last might be defended on Holwell's behalf if we assume him to have been victimized by some Brahmin or pundit who enjoyed pulling a foreigner's leg; but certainly the first two cases have a brazen political significance also possessed by the similar story of the Black Hole. (pp. 196–97)

The book that Holwell (according to Little) forged and sold as a translation from the ancient sacred writings of the Hindus was the very *Chartah Bhade Shastah* that Voltaire from 1769 onward so stridently promoted as monotheism's oldest testament (see Chapter 1). Is there any evidence that Holwell's *Chartah Bhade Shastah* is a brazen forgery? Some modern historians and Indologists have tried to identify the text translated by Holwell, thereby absolving him of the charge of having invented the whole text. For example, A. Leslie Willson thought that Holwell had adapted a genuine Indian text:

> John Z. Holwell (1711–1798), a former governor of Bengal and a survivor of the famed Black Hole of Calcutta, gives an account of his favorable impression of the religious and moral precepts of India. Because of his acquaintance with one of the holy books of the Hindus (the Sanskrit *Satapatha-brâhmana*, called the *Chartah Bhade* in Holwell's adaptation), he believed he discerned a great influence of Indic culture upon other lands in ancient times. The more familiar he became with the Sanskrit work, the more clearly he claimed to see that the mythology as well as the cosmogony of the Egyptians, the Greeks, and the Romans was borrowed from the teachings of the Brahmans contained in the *Satapatha-*

brâhmana. Even the extreme rituals of Hindu worship and the classification of Indic gods found their way West, although extremely falsified and truncated. (Willson 1964:24)

Based on the authority of Johannes Grundmann (1900:71), Willson claimed that Holwell's source, the *Śatapatha-Brāhmaṇa*, was later lost (p. 24). In *The British Discovery of Hinduism in the Eighteenth Century*, P. J. Marshall argued that "judging by the words which he reproduces, Holwell must have made his translation out of a Hindustani version" but added that "the original of Holwell's *Shastah* cannot be identified" (Marshall 1970:46). Marshall, who took the trouble of annotating Holwell's *Shastah* text, thus seems to have regarded it not as a literary hoax or an invention but as a translation of a genuine Indian text, albeit not from Sanskrit but from a Hindustani original. More recent research has questioned earlier opinions but otherwise hardly advanced matters.

In the introduction to the 2000 reprint of Holwell's text, M. J. Franklin calls the *Shastah* text "a text which must remain rather dubious as Holwell asserted it covered all doctrine, and no independent record of such a work exists" (Holwell 2000:xiii). Franklin and other recent authors all rely on Thomas Trautmann's excellent study *Aryans and British India*, which found that Holwell's book "contains what purport to be translations from a mysterious ancient Hindu text, *Chartah Bhade Shastah* (Sanskrit, *Catur Veda Śāstra*), a work not heard of since" (1997:30). Trautmann characterized Holwell's "supposed translations of the supposed ancient *Shaster*" as "obscure and dubious" (p. 33), his Indian sources as "not otherwise known, before or since," and the details of his account as "confusing" (p. 68). Thus, his valiant attempt to identify Holwell's Indian sources[2] ended with a sigh: "It is all rather murky and more than a little suspicious" (pp. 68–69).

According to his obituary in the *Asiatic Annual Register* for 1799 (1801:25–30), John Zephaniah Holwell was born in Dublin on September 17, 1711. At age 12 the intelligent boy won a prize for classical learning but was soon sent by his father as a merchant apprentice to Holland, where he learned Dutch and French. Before he turned eighteen, he became a surgeon's apprentice in England, and at age twenty he embarked as a surgeon's mate on a ship sailing to Bengal. As surgeon of a frigate of the East India Company, he soon was on the way to the Persian Gulf and studied Arabic, and on his return to Calcutta he also learned some Portuguese and Hindi. At the young age of twenty-three, he was appointed surgeon-major, and after another trip to the

Gulf he could speak Arabic "with tolerable fluency" (p. 27). During his residence in Dacca, he was "indefatigable in improving himself in the Moorish and Hinduee tongues" and began "his researches into the Hindû theology" (p. 27). Back in Calcutta, he quickly rose through the ranks; at age 29 he was appointed assistant surgeon to the hospital, and in 1746 (age 35), he became principal physician and surgeon to the presidency of the Company. In 1747 and 1748, he was successively elected mayor of the corporation. In the winter of 1749/50, he returned for the first time from India to England. It was for health reasons, and while recuperating, he enjoyed the leisure "to arrange his materials on the theology and doctrines of the ancient and modern Brahmans." Only after his return to India did he become acquainted "with the *Chartah Bhade* of *Bramah*," of which he claims to have translated a considerable part (Holwell 1765:3). During the sack of Calcutta when the Black Hole incident took place, Holwell allegedly lost both the Indian manuscripts of the *Chartah Bhade Shastah* and his English translation.

After this incident Holwell had to sail back to Europe for the second time, and this time he used his sojourn to publish the famous Black Hole narrative (1758). Upon his return to India, he became governor of Bengal for a few months but was soon replaced. During the last eight months of his long stay in India, he was "freed from the plagues of government" and reassumed his researches into Indian religion "with tolerable success" when "some manuscripts" happened to be "recovered by an unforeseen and extraordinary event" (p. 4), which Holwell never explained. In 1761, at age 50, he returned to England for the third and final time and lived there for almost four leisurely decades until his death in 1798 at the age of 87. Of particular interest among the books published during these decades are the three volumes of *Interesting historical events, relative to the provinces of Bengal, and the empire of Indostan* (1765, 1767, 1771) and his *Dissertations on the Origin, Nature, and Pursuits, of Intelligent Beings, and on Divine Providence, Religion, and Religious Worship* of 1786.

Indian Paradises

In order to understand Holwell's pursuit and intention, one needs to examine not only the second volume of his *Interesting historical events* (1767), which contains the *Chartah Bhade Shastah* "translation" with his commentary, but also the first and third volumes. The title page of the first volume (1765) indicates that Holwell had from the outset planned a three-part work of which the first was to present the historical events of India during the first half of the eighteenth century, the second "the mythology and cosmogony, fasts and festivals of the Gentoos, followers of the Shastah," and the third "a dissertation on the metempsychosis." In the first volume (published in 1765 and revised in 1766), there is an easily overlooked account that is crucial for understanding both the "Question of Holwell's Veracity" and the character of his *Chartah Bhade*. Modern scholars paid no attention to it, but Voltaire highlighted this sensational report by Holwell in chapter 35 of his *Fragmens sur l'Inde* under the heading "Portrait of a singular people in India" (Voltaire 1774:212–16). Voltaire wrote:

> Among so much desolation a region of India has enjoyed profound peace; and in the midst of the horrible moral depravation, it has preserved the purity of its ancient morality. It is the country of Bishnapore or Vishnapore. Mr. Holwell, who has travelled through it, says that it is situated in north-west Bengal and that it takes sixty days of travel to traverse it. (p. 212)

Quickly calculating the approximate size of this blessed territory, Voltaire concluded that "it would be much larger than France" (p. 212), and exhibited some of his much-evoked "complete trust" in Holwell by accusing him of "some exaggeration" (p. 212). But Voltaire did not exclude the possibility that it was someone else's fault, for example, "a printing error, which is all too common in books" (p. 212). Instead of double-checking the number in his copy of Holwell's book (which on p. 197 has "sixteen days" rather than "sixty"), Voltaire proceeded to correct Holwell:

> We had better believe that the author meant [it takes] sixty days [to walk] around the territory, which would result in 100 [French] miles of diameter. [The country] yields 3.5 million rupees per year to its sovereign, which corresponds to 8,200,000 pounds. This revenue does not seem proportionate to the surface of the territory. (pp. 212–13)

Feigning astonishment, Voltaire adds: "What is even more surprising is that Bishnapore is not at all found on our maps" (p. 212). Could Holwell have invented this country? Of course not! "It is not permitted to believe that a state employee of known probity would have wanted to get the better of simple people. He would be too guilty and too easily refuted" (p. 212). When reporting biblical events that defy logic, Voltaire often cut the discussion short with a sarcastic exhortation to his readers to stop worrying about reason and to embrace faith. Here he "consoles" readers who are surprised that this blissful country is not found on any map with the tongue-in-cheek remark: "The reader will be even more pleasantly surprised that this country is inhabited by the most gentle, the most just, the most hospitable, and the most generous people that have ever rendered our earth worthy of heaven" (p. 213).

Today we know that Bisnapore (Bishnupur) is located only 130 kilometers northwest of Calcutta (Kolkata). The city is famous for its terracotta craft and Baluchari sarees made of tussar silk and was for almost a thousand years the capital of the Malla kings of Mallabhum. But Holwell's report carries a far more paradisiacal perfume. The country that he reportedly visited is portrayed as the happiest in the world. It is protected from surrounding regions by an ingenious system of waterways and lock gates that gives the reigning Rajah the "power to overflow his country, and drown any enemy that comes against him." Holwell, ever the sly and devoted colonial administrator, suggests that the British could avoid an invasion and easily bring the country to its knees through an export blockade that would oblige the Rajah to pay the British as much as two million rupees per annum (Holwell 1766:1.197–98). But, of course, this was just an innocent idea and by no means a call for the colonialization of paradise:

> But in truth, it would be almost cruelty to molest these happy people;
> for in this district, are the only vestiges of the beauty, purity, piety,
> regularity, equity, and strictness of the ancient *Indostan* government.
> Here the property, as well as the liberty of the people, are inviolate. Here,
> no robberies are heard of, either private or public. (p. 198)

When a foreigner such as Holwell enters this country, he "becomes the immediate care of the government; which allots him guards without any expence, to conduct him from stage to stage: and these are accountable for the safety and accommodation of his person and effects" (p. 198). Goods are duly recorded, certified, and transported free of charge. "In this form, the traveller is passed through the country; and if he *only passes*, he is not suffered to be at any expence for food, accommodation, or carriage for his merchandize or baggage" (p. 199). Furthermore, the people of Bisnapore are totally honest:

> If any thing is lost in this district; for instance, a bag of money, or other valuable; the person who finds it, hangs it up on the next tree, and gives notice to the nearest Chowkey or place of guard; the officer of which, orders immediate publication of the same by beat of tomtom, or drum. (p. 199)

The country is graced by 360 magnificent pagodas erected by the Rajah and his ancestors, and the cows are venerated to such a degree that if one suffers violent death, the whole city or village remains in mourning and fasts for three days; nobody is allowed to displace him- or herself, and all must perform the expiations prescribed by the very *Chartah Bhade Shastah* whose existence and content Holwell herewith first announced to the world (pp. 199–200).

The country described by Holwell is a carefully delimited territory within whose boundaries time seems to have stood still since the proclamation of the *Chartah Bhade Shastah* several thousand years ago. Its elaborate water management system with lock gates and canals offers total protection from the dangers of the outside world, and within its boundaries perfect honesty, piety, purity, morality, tolerance, liberty, generosity, and prosperity reign since time immemorial. Surely some of Holwell's and Voltaire's readers must have asked themselves why—given the free transport, food, accommodation, and even health care for visitors—Mr. Holwell was the only person ever to transmit the good news about this paradisiacal enclave at Calcutta's doorstep. Is it too farfetched to think that Holwell endowed Bisnapore with its ideal characteristics in order to prepare the ground for the *Chartah Bhade Shastah* in the second volume of his *Interesting events*? If a real country with a real economy existed—a country whose religion was strictly based on the *Chartah Bhade Shastah* and whose rites had followed this text to the letter for millennia—then the existence of this ancient sacred text could not be subject to doubt, could it?

Of course, Holwell was not the first person to imagine a paradise in or near India; medieval world maps are full of interesting information about it. In the year 883, about eight hundred years before Holwell wrote about Bisnapore, a Jew by the name of Eldad ha-Dani ("Eldad of the tribe of Dan") showed up in Tunisia.[3] Presenting himself as a member of one of the ten lost tribes of Israel (which according to Eldad continued to flourish in Havilah), he told the local Jews a story that could have been written by Holwell. Beyond the boundaries of the known world, somewhere in Asia, he claimed, four tribes of the "sons of Moses" continue to lead pure lives protected by a river of rolling stones and sand called Sambatyon, and their laws and texts remain unchanged since antiquity.[4] Their Talmud is written in the purest Hebrew, and their children never die as long as the parents are alive. Eldad supported his own credibility by an impressive genealogy stretching back to Dan, the son of Jacob. Eldad's tales provoked an inquiry addressed to the rabbinical academy in Sura, Babylon; and while not much is known about the further fate of Eldad, his story pops up here and there in medieval manuscripts. Eventually, the inquiry triggered by his account and the response it received were printed in Mantua in 1480 (Wasserstein 1996:215).

About three centuries after Eldad, in 1122, a story with many similar elements began to make the rounds in Europe, and its protagonist ended up as a prominent feature on numerous illustrated world maps. It was the tale of John, archbishop of India, who had reportedly traveled to Constantinople and Rome. Patriarch John was said to be the guardian of the shrine of St. Thomas, the favorite disciple of Jesus; and through his Indian capital, so the story went, flow the "pure waters of the Physon, one of the rivers of Paradise, which gives to the world outside most precious gold and jewels, whence the regions of India are extremely rich" (Hamilton 1996:173).

In 1145, Otto von Freising also heard of "a certain John, king and priest, who lived in the extreme east beyond Armenia and Persia." He reportedly was of the race of the very Magi who had come to worship the infant Christ at Bethlehem (p. 174). Otto first connected Prester John with the Magi and with Archbishop John, and soon after the completion of his *History* in 1157 three corpses exhumed in a church in Milan were identified as the bodies of the Three Magi (pp. 180–81). These relics were solemnly transported to the Cologne cathedral in 1164 and became objects of a religious cult (p. 183). It is around this time that a letter signed by a Prester John began to circulate in western Europe. In his letter Prester John portrays himself as the extremely rich and powerful ruler of the Three Indies, whose subjects include the Ten Lost Tribes beyond the river Sambatyon. Prester John claims to live very close to Paradise and emphasizes that he guards the grave of St. Thomas, the apostle of Jesus.

Though the country described in Prester John's letter is richer and far larger than Holwell's Bisnapore, it is also extremely hospitable and its inhabitants are perfectly moral: "There are no robbers among us; no sycophant finds a place here, and there is no miserliness" (Zarncke 1996:83). As in Holwell's Bisnapore, "nobody lies, nor can anybody lie" (p. 84). All inhabitants of Prester John's country "follow the truth and love one another;" there is "no adulterer in the land, and there is no vice" (p. 84).

The Prester John story became so widely known that the famous patriarch became a fixture on medieval world maps as well as a major motivation for the exploration of Asia (from the thirteenth century) and Africa (from the fifteenth century).[5]

Another layer in the archaeology of Holwell's Indian paradise can be found in the famous *Travels of Sir John Mandeville* of the fourteenth century, a book that fascinated countless readers and travelers as well as researchers.[6] Mandeville's "isle of Bragman"—like Prester John's Indies, Eldad's land beyond the Sambatyon, and Holwell's Bisnapore—is a marvelous land. Its inhabitants, though not Christians, "by natural instinct or law . . . live a commendable life, are folk of great virtue, flying away from all sins and vices and malice" (Moseley 1983:178). The still unidentified Mandeville, who habitually calls countries "isles," described a great many of them in his *Travels*. But the country of the "Bragmans" (Brachmans, Brahmins) is by far the most excellent:

> This isle these people live in is called the Isle of Bragman; and some men call it the Land of Faith. Through it runs a great river, which is called Thebe. Generally all the men of that isle and of other isles nearby are more trustworthy and more righteous than men in other countries. In this land are no thieves, no murderers, no prostitutes, no liars, no beggars; they are men as pure in conversation and as clean in living as if they were men of religion. And since they are such true and good folk, in their country there is never thunder and lightning, hail nor snow, nor any other storms and bad weather; there is no hunger, no pestilence, no war, nor any other common tribulations among them, as there are among us because of our sins. And therefore it seems that God loves them well and is well pleased by their manner of life and their faith. (p. 178)

Of course, the antediluvian patriarchs of the Old Testament who lived many years before Abraham and Moses were not yet Jews blessed with the special covenant with God, something only conferred finally after the Exodus from Egypt at Mt. Sinai, much less Christians. But the virtues of these antediluvians were so great that they enjoyed extremely long life spans. Mandeville's Bragmans, too, though ignorant of God's commandments as conveyed to Moses, are said to "keep the Ten Commandments" (p. 178) and enjoy the benefits:

> They believe in God who made all things, and worship Him with all their power; all earthly things they set at nought. They live so temperately and soberly in meat and drink that they are the longest-lived people in the world; and many of them die simply of age, when their vital force runs out. (p. 178)

Like Holwell's inhabitants of Bisnapore, they are a people without greed and want; all "goods, movable and immovable, are common to every man," and their wealth consists in peace, concord, and the love of their neighbor. Other countries in the vicinity of the land of the Bragmans for the most part also follow their customs while "living innocently in love and charity each with another." Almost like Adam and Eve in paradise before they sinned, these people "go always naked" and suffer no needs (p. 179).

> And even if these people do not have the articles of our faith, nevertheless I believe that because of their good faith that they have by nature, and their good intent, God loves them well and is well pleased by their manner of life, as He was with Job, who was a pagan, yet nevertheless his deeds were as acceptable to God as those of His loyal servants. (p. 180)

Mandeville's naked people are extremely ancient and have "many prophets among them" since antiquity. Already "three thousand years and more before the time of His Incarnation," they predicted the birth of Christ; but they have not yet learned of "the manner of His Passion" (p. 180). These regions that evoke paradise and antediluvian times form part of the empire of Prester John. Mandeville explains: "This Emperor Prester John is a Christian, and so is the greater part of his land, even if they do not have all the articles of the faith as clearly as we do. Nevertheless they believe in God as Father, Son and Holy Ghost; they are a very devout people, faithful to each other, and there is neither fraud nor guile among them" (p. 169). In Prester John's land, there are many marvels and close by, behind a vast sea of gravel and sand, are "great mountains, from which flows a large river that comes from Paradise" (p. 169).

The lands described by Eldad, Prester John, Mandeville, and Holwell share some characteristics that invite exploration. The first concerns the fact that all are associated with "India" and the vicinity of earthly paradise. In the Genesis account (2.8 ff.) God, immediately after having formed Adam from the dust of the ground, "planted a garden eastward of Eden" and put Adam there. He equipped this garden with trees "pleasant to the sight, and good for food," as well as the tree of life at the center of the garden and the tree of knowledge of good and evil. The story continues:

> And a river went out of Eden to water the garden; and from thence it was parted, and became into four heads. The name of the first is Pishon: that is it which compasseth the whole land of Havilah, where there is gold; and the gold of that land is good: there is bdellium and the onyx stone. (Genesis 2.10–12)

The locations of this "land of Havilah" and the river Pishon (or Phison) are unclear, but the other rivers are better known. The second river, Gihon, "compasseth the whole land of Ethiopia," the third (Hiddekel) "goeth to the east of Assyria," and the fourth river is identified as the Euphrates (Genesis 2.13–14). In his *Antiquities*, written toward the end of the first century C.E., the Jewish historian Flavius Josephus for the first time identified the enigmatic first river of paradise as the Ganges river and the fourth river (Gihon or Geon) as the Nile:

> Now the garden was watered by one river, which ran round about the whole earth, and was parted into four parts. And Phison, which denotes a *Multitude*, running into India, makes its exit into the sea, and is by the Greeks called *Ganges*. . . . Geon runs through Egypt, and denotes the river which arises from the opposite quarter to us, which the Greeks call *Nile*. (trans. Whiston 1906:2)

The location of the "garden in Eden" (*gan b'Eden*), from which Adam was eventually expelled, is specified in Genesis 2.8 as *miqedem*, which has both a spatial ("away to the East") and a temporal ("from before the beginning") connotation. Accordingly, the translators of the Septuagint, the *Vetus Latina*, and the English Authorized Version rendered it by words denoting "eastward" (Gr. *kata anatolas*, Lat. *in oriente*), while the Vulgate prefers "a principio" and thus the temporal connotation (Scafi 2006:35). But the association of the earthly paradise and enigmatic land of Havilah with the Orient, and in particular with India, was boosted by Flavius Josephus and a number of Church fathers who identified it with the Ganges valley (p. 35) where, nota bene, Holwell located his paradisiacal Bisnapore.

For the Christian theologian AUGUSTINE of Hippo (354–430), too, Pishon was the Ganges River and Gihon the Nile, and his verdict that these rivers "are true rivers, not just figurative expressions without a corresponding reality in the literal sense" hastened the demise of other theories as to the identity of the Pishon and Gihon (p. 46). In the seventh century, ISIDOR of Seville (d. 636) described in his *Etymologiae* the earthly paradise among the regions of Asia as a place that was neither hot nor cold but always temperate (Grimm 1977:77–78). Isidor also enriched the old tradition of allegorical interpretations of paradise. If paradise symbolized the Christian Church, he argued, the paradise river stood for Christ and its four arms for the four gospels (p. 78).

The allegorical view of paradise as the symbol of the Church, watered by four rivers or gospels and accessed by baptism, had first been advanced by Thascius Caelius CYPRIANUS (d. 258) and became quite successful in Carolingian Bible exegesis (pp. 45–46). The *Commemoratio Geneseos*, a very interesting Irish compilation of the late eighth century, identified the Pishon with the Indus river and interpreted Genesis's "compasseth the whole land of Havilah" as "runs through Havilah" while specifying that "this land is situated at the confines of India and Parthia" (p. 87). The *Commemoratio* also associates the Pishon with the evangelist "John who is full of the Holy Ghost," and the gold of Havilah with "the divine nature of God [diuinitas dei] which John wrote so much about" (p. 87).

Such Bible commentaries helped to establish an association of paradise with the name "John," with India, and with a mighty Indian river. Until the end of the fifteenth century, many medieval world maps depicted paradise somewhere in or near India (Knefelkamp 1986:87–92), and travelers like Giovanni MARIGNOLLI of the fourteenth or Columbus of the fifteenth century were absolutely convinced that they were close to the earthly paradise.

Their view that paradise itself was not accessible does not signify that for them "earthly paradise . . . was in a sense *nowhere*," as Scafi (2006:242) argues. When Marignolli met Buddhist monks at the foot of Adam's Peak in Ceylon, he noted that they "call themselves sons of Adam" and reports their

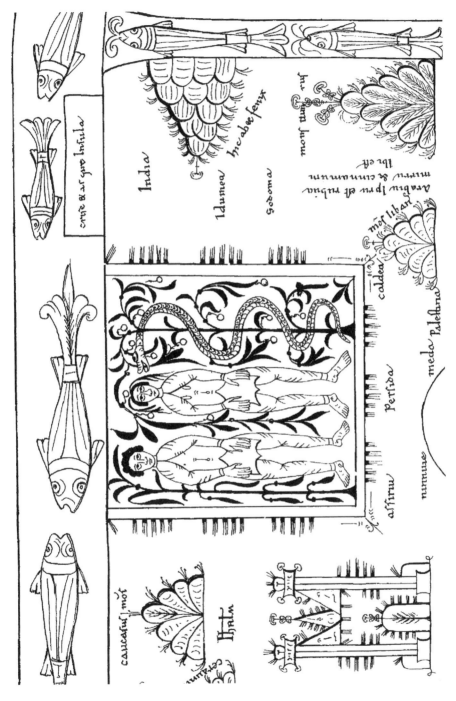

Figure 14. Paradise near India at Eastern extremity of Osma world map (Santarem 1849).

claim that "Cain was born in Ceylon." According to Marignolli, these monks lead a "veritably holy life following a religion whose founder, in their opinion, is the patriarch Enoch, the inventor of prayer, and which is professed also by the Brachmans" (Meinert 1820:85). No wonder that the missionary felt close to paradise. Did these monks not refrain from eating meat "because Adam, before the deluge, did not eat any," and did they not worship a tree, claiming that this custom stemmed "from Adam who, in their words, expected future salvation from its wood" (p. 86)?[27] Marignolli also reports about his arrival "by sea to Ceylon, to the glorious mountain opposite paradise which, as the indigens say according to the tradition of their fathers, is found at forty Italian miles' distance—so [near] that one hears the noise of the water falling from the source of paradise" (p. 77)—and was proud to have visited Adam's house "built from large marble plates without plaster," which featured "a door at the center that he [Adam] built with his own hands" (pp. 80–81). A pond full of jewels was reportedly fed by the source of paradise opposite the mountain, and Marignolli boasted of having tasted the delicious fruit of the paradise (banana) tree, whose leaves Adam and Eve had used to cover their private parts (pp. 81–83).

This paradise mythology was very influential and far reaching, and it shows itself sometimes in perhaps unexpected domains. Christopher COLUMBUS (1451–1506), a man who was very familiar with maps and had once made a living of their trade, also thought that he approached the earthly paradise on his third voyage. While he cruised near the estuary of the Orinoco in Venezuela, he firmly believed he had finally reached the mouth of a paradise river.

> Holy Scripture testifies that Our Lord made the earthly Paradise in which he placed the Tree of Life. From it there flowed four main rivers: the Ganges in India, the Tigris and the Euphrates in Asia, which cut through a mountain range and form Mesopotamia and flow into Persia, and the Nile, which rises in Ethiopia and flows into the sea at Alexandria. I do not find and have never found any Greek or Latin writings which definitely state the worldly situation of the earthly Paradise, nor have I seen any world map which establishes its position except by deduction. (Columbus 1969:220–21)

Since Columbus knew that the earth is round and that he was far away from Africa and Mesopotamia, he apparently thought that he was in the

"Indies" and noted the unanimity of "St Isidor, Bede, Strabo, the Master of Scholastic History [Petrus Comestor], St Ambrose and Scotus and all learned theologians" that "the earthly Paradise is in the East" (p. 221). Columbus clearly imagined himself near the Ganges and the Indian Paradise.

> I do not hold that the earthly Paradise has the form of a rugged moun-
> tain, as it is shown in pictures, but that it lies at the summit of what I
> have described as the stalk of a pear, and that by gradually approaching
> it one begins, while still at a great distance, to climb towards it. As I have
> said, I do not believe that anyone can ascend to the top. I do believe,
> however, that, distant though it is, these waters may flow from there to
> this place which I have reached, and form this lake. All this provides
> great evidence of the earthly Paradise, because the situation agrees with
> the beliefs of those holy and wise theologians and all the signs strongly
> accord with this idea. (pp. 221–22)

Who would have thought that the "Indian" fantasies of Flavius Josephus, Augustine, and the medieval theologians and cartographers in their wake would one day play a role in the discovery of the Americas? But while Columbus was looking forward to exploring the East Indies and enriching himself with the gold and jewels promised by the Bible commentators, the heyday of the "Indian" Paradise on world maps was coming to a close. In 1449, Aeneas Silvius PICCOLOMINI (1405–64; Pope Pius II from 1458–64) had already come to doubt the identification of the Gihon with the Nile (Scafi 2006:197), and soon the learned Augustinus STEUCHUS (1496–1549) argued that Pishon and Gihon had nothing to do with the Ganges and Nile since Havilah and Cush were not located in India and Ethiopia but in Mesopotamia and Arabia (p. 263).

Subsequently, the location of earthly paradise became unhinged and drifted for a time; Guillaume Postel, for example, first located it in the Moluccas, the home of the paradise birds (Postel 1553a), but subsequently made a U-turn and placed it near the North Pole (Secret 1985:304–5). Though arguing that the entire earth had once been paradise, Postel's contemporary Jan Gorp (Goropius Becanus) of Antwerp believed that Adam had lived in India (Gorp 1569:483, 508) and that Noah's ark had landed not on Mt. Ararat but on the highest mountains of the Indian Caucasus, that is, near Mt. Imaus in the mountain range that we now call the Himalaya (p. 473). In his *History of the World* of 1614, Sir Walter Raleigh called this view "of all his conjectures the most probable" (1829.2.243); and around the end of the seventeenth century, some physical theories related to the deluge and the formation of the earth also revived Gorp's idea that the entire earth had initially been paradise (Burnet 1694). However, around the turn of the eighteenth century most specialists of biblical exegesis tended to place earthly paradise somewhere near the Holy Land.

Paradise and Reform

While the physical paradise had found a more or less stable abode in the Middle East, the search for the religion of paradise entered a period of chaos. Textual criticism of the Bible increasingly threatened scripture's claims to antiquity and authenticity; Moses's ancient "Egyptian" background was explored; and gradually texts from far-away China and India that purportedly were much older than the Old Testament entered the picture.

In contrast to physical and historical interpretations, some allegorical or spiritual (*spiritaliter*) Bible commentaries likened the lands in the vicinity of the Ganges to the holy Church, its gold to the genuine conception of monotheism, and the four cardinal virtues and foundational gospels to the four paradise rivers (Grimm 1977:87). The land of the Ganges was thus associated with the pure original teaching of Christianity, and Christianity in turn with humankind's first religion that was personally revealed by God to Adam before the Fall. Indeed, the view of "India" as a motherland of original teachings is a characteristic that links the reports by or about Eldad, Prester John, Mandeville, Prince Dara, Holwell, and Voltaire. They all portray pure original teachings and practices that survived in or near India: Eldad of the original Judaism of the sons of Moses, Prester John of the Ur-Christianity of St. Thomas, Mandeville of the seemingly antediluvian monotheism of the Bragmans, Prince Dara of Ur-Islam, Voltaire of Ur-deism, and Holwell of the Ur-religion. Characteristically, each author also had a particular reform agenda that is apparent or implicit in the critique of the reigning religion as degenerate compared to "Indian" teachings and practices.

The example of Mandeville's *Travels* is quite instructive. The pilgrimage motif that forms the setting for his entire tale is really "a metaphor for the life of man on earth as a journey to the Heavenly Jerusalem"—but this promised land can only be reached if Christians reform themselves (Moseley 1983:23). Interestingly, the model for this reform is found not in Rome or the

Holy Land but rather in far-away India. This region in the vicinity of the earthly paradise and its extremely ancient religion are held up as a mirror by Mandeville to make his Christian readers blush in shame. Prester John, the guardian of the shrine of Jesus's favorite disciple, managed to keep original Christianity pure and heads an ideal Christian state where even the empire's heathen live in ways that Christians should imitate.

Mandeville's description of non-Christian religions, particularly those of the regions near paradise, thus has a definite "Ambrosian" character and very much resembles Voltaire's use of the *Ezour-vedam* and Holwell's *Shastah* (see Chapter 1). Like St. Ambrose's Brachmanes (Bysshe 1665), Eldad's Ur-Jews, Voltaire's Indian Ur-deists, Holwell's Vishnaporians, and Prester John's prototype Christians, the heathens and Christians of Mandeville's India have the mission of encouraging European Christians to reflect upon themselves and to reform their religion according to the "Indian" ideal. In each case, the model is the respective Ur-tradition—appropriately set in the vicinity of paradise—which forms both the point of departure and the ultimate goal. This goal can typically be reached by a "regeneration of the original creed" that entails eliminating degenerate accretions and stripping religion down to its bare Ur-form.

Rehabilitation Station Earth

As we have seen in Chapter 4, the three-step scheme of golden age/degeneration/regeneration and return to the golden age formed the backbone of Andrew Ramsay's book *The Travels of Cyrus*, first published in French and English in 1727. It was a smashing success; a Dublin print of 1728 is already marked as fourth edition (Ramsay 2002:7). One of its readers in London may have been a London liveryman[8] whose *Oration*, published in 1733, caught Holwell's attention at an early stage and influenced him so profoundly that he "candidly confessed" in the third volume of his *Interesting historical events* that the "well grounded" yet "bold assertions of Mr. *John Ilive*"[9] had given him the "first hints":

> [It was Mr. Ilive's bold yet well grounded assertions] from whom we candidly confess we took our first hints, and became a thorough convert to his hypothesis, upon finding on enquiry, and the exertion of our own reason, that it was built on the first divine revelation that had been

graciously delivered to man, to wit, THE CHARTAH BHADE OF BRAMAH; although it is very plain Mr. Ilive was ignorant of the doctrine of the Metempsychosis, by confining his conceptions only to the angelic fall, man's being the apostate angels, and that this earth was the only hell; passing over in silence the rest of the *animal creation*. (Holwell 1771:3.143)

Jacob ILIVE (1705–63) was a printer, owner of a foundry, and religious publicist who in 1729 wrote down a speech, read it several times to his mother, and was obliged by his mother's testamentary request to proclaim it in public. Ilive went a bit further; after his mother's death in 1733, he read it twice in public and then printed it in annotated form. Later he rented Carpenters' Hall and lectured there about "The religion of Nature" (Wilson 1808:2.291). His *Oration* of 1733, which so deeply influenced Holwell, addresses several themes of interest to deists such as the origin of evil, original sin, eternal punishment, and the reliability of Moses's Pentateuch. Ilive offered more or less creative solutions to all of the above. Moses was for him not only a typical representative of "priestcraft" but one who began his career with a vicious murder. "I observe, that for the Truth of this, we have only *Moses's ipse dixit*, and I think a Man may chuse whether he will believe a Murderer" (Ilive 1733:37). Moses not only commanded people to steal and cheat but he also contrived "a great Murder, yea, a Massacre" while lying to his people as he told them that "the Lord God of Israel" had ordered "to slay every Man his Brother, and every Man his Neighbour" (p. 42). Ilive regarded the author of the Pentateuch as far from inspired:

What is to be understood by delivering Laws as the Result of Divine Appointment, if hereby is not meant, that *Moses* had for every Law and Ordinance he instituted not received miraculously and immediately the Command of the Great God of Heaven, but delivered them to the *Jews* only as (what he thought) agreeable to the Mind of God. (p. 41)

Ilive was not content with the Reformation either and described how the first reformers "glossed away the Christian truths":

In the first Article they say God is without Body, Parts, or Passions: in the second they sware, that God the Son has Body and Parts now in

Heaven. In the third, that he went down into Hell, i.e. into the Centre of the Earth, or a distinct Creation from the Earth, I suppose is meant. Article Six they do not insert here, that the Books of the Old Testament were written by the Inspiration of the Holy Ghost, but they dub all the Stories contained in them for Truth. In Article seven, they are not *Jews*; but because the Old Testament would be necessary to back Christianity, they say, therefore, it is to be held in respect. In the ninth they establish three Creeds at once: in two of them this absurd Doctrine, the Resurrection of the Body, or Flesh. It is too tedious to go through them all. (pp. 43–44)

Ilive was clearly planning a more thorough reform of Christianity and was not happy with the Pentateuch. He felt that Moses had not explained who we are and why we are here in "the Place we now inhabit" (p. 9). Inspired by the notions that there is a plurality of worlds, that our world was created long after a more perfect one, and that souls preexisted, Ilive came up with a scenario that could very well have been inspired by Ramsay's *Discourse upon the Theology and Mythology of the Pagans* at the end of the *Travels of Cyrus*. The *Discourse* contains almost all the central elements of Ilive's system and appeared in 1727, exactly two years before Ilive apparently wrote his text, in the city of London where Ilive happened to earn his living in the printing business. As we have seen in the previous chapter, Ramsay had traced in the kabbala and various ancient cultures the idea that angels had fallen from their state of perfection and were exiled; that they formed the souls of beings on planets that are like hospitals or prisons for these fallen higher intelligences; that they were there imprisoned in the bodies of men; and that they had to migrate from one body to another until their purification was complete and the return to their initial state of perfection possible. This was the central theme of Ramsay's *Of the Mythology of the Pagans* where it was presented as "a very ancient doctrine, common to all the Asiatics, from whom Pythagoras and Plato derived it" (Ramsay 1814:384–85). The idea had also played an important role in early Church heresiology since it was one of the main accusations leveled against Origenes (c. 185–254).[10]

Ramsay called this "the doctrine of transmigration," and its features of "a first earth" where "souls made their abode before their degradation, the "terrestrial prison" where they are confined, and the divine plan for their rehabilitation in order to regain their original state (pp. 366–67) form the very fabric of Ilive's system that so inspired Holwell. It is a classic golden age/ degeneration/regeneration scenario proposed by people intent on reforming the degenerate Christian religion and defending ideal Christianity against "all the Atheists" including "*Spinoza, Hobbes, Toland,* &c." (Ilive 1733:25). The task was to show that the world was "created for the Good and Benefit" and that its evils (ignorance, wars, cruelty, illness, etc.) are not due to the creator God's sadism but are part and parcel of his compassionate rehabilitation plan for fallen angels. Since "there has not been given as yet any real satisfactory Reason for the Creation of the World," Ilive (and in his wake, Holwell) attempted to furnish exactly that: an improved creation story. While Holwell eventually cobbled together an "Indian" one and presented it as a better (and older) Old Testament, Ilive relied mostly on inspired interpretations of New Testament passages.[11]

Ilive's creation story begins long before Adam enjoyed paradise. "Many years, as we compute Time, before the Creation of Man," God "thought fit to reveal the Eternal Word, his Equal, unto the Angels" (p. 10). While two thirds of them "were chanting forth their Halleluja's," another third were "seized with Anger and Pride" and rebelled (pp. 11–12). Soon there was war in heaven, and the rebels were cast "into this very Globe . . . which we now inhabit, before its Formation out of Chaos" (p. 15). At that time the earth was just a "Place of Darkness, and great Confusion, a rude Wilderness, an indigested Lump of Matter." The matter "out of which this World was formed, was prae-existent to the Formation of the Earth, and to the Creation of Man," and this dark chaotic world "was a Dungeon for the Punishment of the Lapsed Angels, and the Place of their Residence" (p. 26). After about 6,000 years of such confinement in chaos, "God began the Formation of the World" (p. 16) as we know it. Whereas for Milton this formation of the second world was designed to repopulate heaven by giving men on earth the chance to join the diminished number of good angels in heaven (Milton 2001:163; book 7, verses 150–60), Ilive regarded it as an act of divine compassion with the aim of giving the banished angels a chance for rehabilitation. Our planet earth, therefore, is, as it were, a rehabilitation center for rebel angels, and the bodies of men are "little Places of Confinement for the Reception of the apostate Angels" within this gigantic facility (Ilive 1733:23). Contrary to Holwell's assertion (1771:3.143), transmigration is clearly part of Ilive's design since rehabilitation and purification can take a very long time: "The Reader is desired to observe, that I suppose the Revolutions of these Angels in Bodies, and that they may have actuated or assumed Bodies many times since the Creation, in order for their Punishment, Probation and Reconciliation" (Ilive 1733:24).

In Ilive's narrative, human souls are thus fallen angels who must atone for past rebellious acts in small prison cells (our bodies) within a facility (the earth) that was created for the very purpose of punishing and rehabilitating them. One might say that our earth resembles a giant Guantanamo Bay prison camp, which during the administration of U.S. president George W. Bush was established as a facility tailor-made to house evil spirits (terrorists) brought in by "extraordinary rendition." The delinquents were incarcerated without the possibility of appeal since they were considered outlaws undeserving of the ordinary course of justice. The worst offenders were subjected to the trademark "Guantanamo frequent flier program" in which prisoners were constantly moved from cell to cell after short periods of sleep. In terms of our metaphor, they had to undergo seemingly endless transmigration from body to body and feel lucky if they got to inhabit a better cell for a little while. The final goal of this grueling regime was atonement, rehabilitation, and eventual release; but since this was a realm without habeas corpus rights, the best the prisoners could do was to follow the rules in order to accumulate expiation points. Regaining their original status and returning home, however, possibly necessitated an almost endless sequence of transmigrations.

Holwell's Delinquent Angels

In the *Historical events*, Holwell makes a great effort to convey the impression that his entire system is based on the *Chartah Bhade Shastah of Bramah* and that he is no more than a translator and commentator of an ancient text who intends "to rescue from error and oblivion the ancient religion of Hindostan"[12] and to "vindicate" it "not by labored apologies, but by a simple display of their primitive theology."[13] Following Holwell's candid confession that he took his "first hints" from Ilive and "became a thorough convert to his hypothesis," one would expect him to acknowledge that he subsequently found a similar system in the *Shastah*. Instead, Holwell makes the startling claim (1771:3.143) that Ilive's system "was built on the first divine revelation that had been graciously delivered to man, to wit, THE CHARTAH BHADE OF BRAMAH"!

Not only Egyptian religion and the Pythagorean system but even Ilive's ideas are thus supposedly based on an ancient Indian text whose two manuscripts Holwell claims to have bought very dearly and thereafter lost in the sack of Calcutta:

> It is well known that at the capture of *Calcutta*, A.D. 1756, I lost many curious *Gentoo* manuscripts, and among them two very correct and valuable copies of the *Gentoo Shastah*. They were procured by me with so much trouble and expence, that even the commissioners of the restitution, though not at all disposed to favour me, allowed me two thousand *Madras* rupees in recompense for this particular loss; but the most irreparable damage I suffered under this head of grievances, was a translation I made of a considerable part of the *Shastah*, which had cost me eighteen months hard labour: as that work opened upon me, I distinctly saw, that the *Mythology*, as well as the *Cosmogony* of the *Egyptians, Greeks* and *Romans*, were borrowed from the doctrines of the *Bramins*, contained in this book; even to the copying their exteriors of worship, and the distribution of their idols, though grossly mutilated and adulterated. (Holwell 1765:1.3–4)

If Holwell had spent no less than eighteen months of "hard labor" to translate a "considerable part" of the *Shastah*, then one must assume that he had bought a text of gigantic proportions. The manuscripts that he owned and translated were, he says, lost in 1756. However, he claims to have recovered "some manuscripts . . . by an unforeseen and extraordinary event" that allowed him to publish his translation; but though he tantalizingly adds that he "possibly" may "recite" this wondrous recovery afterward (p. 4), he never explained himself, and nobody has ever seen an original manuscript. One is reminded of James Macpherson's phantom *Ossian* manuscripts that excited the curiosity of an entire generation of Europeans after the publication of their English "translation" in 1761. But though there are some striking similarities one notes a major difference: Macpherson's Ossian was very prolix compared to Holwell's Brahma. Holwell's entire translation from the *Shastah* amounts to a skimpy 531 lines, printed in large type on narrow pages with very conspicuous quotation marks at the beginning of each line. In fact, there was so little substance that Edmund Burke decided to include Holwell's entire translation in his *Annual Register* book review (1767:310–16), and it fit neatly on six and a half pages!

This means that the "unforeseen and extraordinary event," which Holwell never explained, yielded very little material. Moreover, over 80 percent

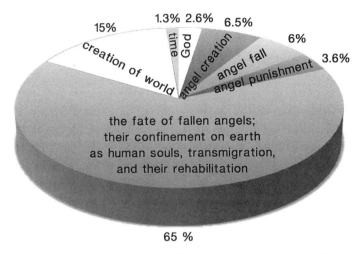

15% — creation of world

1.3% — time

2.6% — God

6.5% — angel creation

6% — angel fall

3.6% — angel punishment

the fate of fallen angels; their confinement on earth as human souls, transmigration, and their rehabilitation

65 %

Figure 15. Chapter theme percentages of Holwell's *Shastah* translation (Urs App).

of the translated text deals with the fate of angels: their creation, their fall, their punishment, and of course their incarceration on "rehab station" earth. A single section entitled "The Mitigation of the Punishment of the delinquent Debtah, and their final Sentence" (Holwell 1767:2.47–59)—which basically replicates Jacob Ilive's argument spiced up with some Indian terminology—constitutes no less than two thirds of Holwell's *Shastah* translation; see Figure 15. This is the section that explains the core of Holwell's system, namely, that human bodies host the souls of rebellious angels; that the earth was created as a rehabilitation facility in which these souls could purify themselves in successive existences; that transmigration is part of this rehabilitation process; and that vegetarianism is obligatory for the obvious angelic reason

Table 10 shows that the volume of Holwell's commentaries on sections translated from the *Shastah* is similarly lopsided.

The thematic analysis of Holwell's *Shastah* fragments indicates that the *Shastah* author's interests strangely resemble those of Ilive and that the possibility of an ancient Indian origin seems remote. But does the content of Holwell's text—which purportedly "is as ancient, at least, as any written body of divinity that was ever produced in the world" (Holwell 1767:2.5)—support such doubts about the *Shastah*'s authorship? Let us examine the first section of Holwell's translation, which is shown in Figure 16.

While an ancient Indian inspired by Brahma might have had other ideas,

TABLE 10. TEXT PERCENTAGES IN HOLWELL'S TRANSLATIONS PER THEME

Part	Lines of "translation"	% of total	Theme	Pages of commentary	% of total
1.1	14	2.6	God & attributes	3	4.9
1.2	35	6.5	creation of angels	5	8.2
1.3	31	6.0	fall of angels	0	0.0
1.4	20	3.6	punishment angels	1	1.6
1.5	343	65	fate of angels	41	67.2
2.8	81	15	creation of world	7	11.5
?	7	1.3	computing time	4	6.6
Total	531			61	

a European would quite naturally tend to have a catechism begin with an affirmation of monotheism and a creator God. The very first sentence of the *Shastah* already points toward an author familiar with Christian theology. Holwell seems to have vacillated on how to formulate this crucial initial statement that echoes God's first commandment to Moses. The text cited in Burke's review in the *Annual Register for the Year 1766* (1767:310) must stem from the galley proofs and begins with "God is the one that ever was" in place of the final version's "God is ONE." If Holwell's Indian text—which was written in Hindi, as his note suggests—contained the words *ek* (one) and *hamesha* (always), then "the one that ever was" or "the eternal one" seem just fine. So why did Holwell at the last minute decided to change his initial translation (which did not need a note) to "God is ONE" and to banish the literal translation into a note? Did a unitarian friend who read the proofs suggest this, or did Holwell try to "improve" the text Voltaire-style? At any rate, the published text begins with a strong statement against trinitarianism.

That this God rules all creation by "general providence resulting from first determined and fixed principles" again points to an author familiar with eighteenth-century theological controversies. Moreover: what ancient Indian author would have thought of prohibiting research about the laws by which God governs? Here, too, one has reason to suspect the interference of a certain eighteenth-century author who was opposed to scientific research into the laws of nature. It so happens that Holwell had exactly this attitude. Pointing out that Solomon had called the "pursuits of mankind, in search of *knowledge, arts,* and *sciences* . . . all futile and *vain*," Holwell called it a Christian reformer's duty "to prevent the misapplication of time, expence, and talents, which might be employed for better purposes" (1786:45). Of

SECT. I.

" Of God and his Attributes.

" God is One *. — Creator of all that
" is.—God is like a perfect sphere,
" without beginning or end.—God rules
" and governs all creation by a general
" providence resulting from first deter-
" mined and fixed principles.——Thou
" shalt not make enquiry into the ef-
" fence and nature of the exiftence of
" the ETERNAL ONE, nor, by what laws
" he governs.—An enquiry into either,
" is vain, and criminal.—It is enough,
" that day by day, and night by night,
" thou feeft in his works; his *wisdom*,
" *power*, and his *mercy*. —— Benefit
" thereby."

* *Ekhummefha*, litterally, *the . one that ever . was* ;
which we tranflate, *the eternal one*.

BOOK I. SECT. I.

" *Of God and his attributes.*"

" G OD is the one that ever
   was, creator of all that
is.—God is like a perfect fphere,
without beginning or end.—God
rules and governs all creation by a
general providence refulting from
firft determined and fixed principles.——Thou fhalt not make inquiry into the effence and nature
of the exiftence of the ETERNAL
ONE, nor by what laws he governs.——An inquiry into either
is vain, and criminal.——It is
enough, that day by day, and
night by night, thou feeft in his
works, his *wifdom, power*, and his
mercy.——Benefit thereby."

Figure 16. First section of Holwell's *Shastah* in review and published versions.

what significance is it, he asks (p. 46), "to know whether our globe stands still, or has a daily rotation from East and West?" This might sound strange coming from a man who had traveled so much at sea, but Holwell offered an explanation in tune with Brahmah's will:

> It is highly improbable, that when the DEITY planted the different regions of this globe with the fallen spirits, or intelligent beings, his design was, they should ever have communication with each other; his placing the expanded and occasionally tempestuous ocean between them exhibits an incontestable proof to the contrary. But in this as in every thing else, man has counteracted his wise and benevolent intentions. (pp. 49–50)

The first lines of the *Shastah* thus already strongly indicate European authorship. Another example suggesting an eighteenth-century author is the crucial passage in Section 2, titled "The Creation of Angelic Beings."

> The ETERNAL ONE willed.—And they were.—He formed them in part of his own essence; capable of perfection, but with the powers of imperfection; both depending on their voluntary election. (Holwell 1767:2.35)

In his commentary Holwell explains that this passage is related to the problem of "free will" and "the origin, and existence of *moral evil*" (p. 39). Here he openly joins the fray and attacks authors "who have been driven to very strange conclusions on this subject" and even "thought it necessary to form an apology in defence of their Creator, for the admission of moral evil into the world" (p. 39). One of the culprits is Soame Jenyns's *A Free Inquiry into the Nature and Origin of Evil* whose fourth edition appeared in 1761 just after Holwell's final return to England. Holwell quotes from Jenyns's book and then contrasts it with the *Shastah*'s solution that is, in his eyes, by far the best to date:

> How much more rational and sublime [than such eighteenth-century apologies is] the text of *Bramah*, which supposes the Deity's voluntary creation, or permission of evil; for the exaltation of a race of beings, whose *goodness* as free agents could not have existed without being endued with the contrasted or opposite powers of doing *evil*. (p. 41)

Though Holwell gives all the credit to his *Shastah*, this was an ingenious if somewhat circular solution that both Ilive and Ramsay had proposed.

Whoever authored the *Shastah*, it certainly addressed problems of utmost interest not to any ancient Indian author but rather to a certain eighteenth-century Englishman familiar with Indian religion as well as the theological controversies of his time. Is it not noteworthy that Holwell seems to have recuperated only *Shastah* sections that deal exactly with the questions he felt passionate about? One gets the distinct feeling that he was considerably more than just a translator of "Bramah's" ancient text, and as one reads on, the signs pointing to Holwell multiply. Section 4 of the *Shastah* begins with the words: "The eternal ONE, whose omniscience, prescience and influence, extended to all things, except the actions of beings, which he had *created free*" (p. 44). In his remarks Holwell points out that this section begins "by denying the prescience of God touching the actions of free agents" and that "the *Bramins* defend this dogma by alleging, his prescience in this case, is utterly repugnant and contradictory to the very nature and essence of free agency, which on such terms could not have existed" (p. 46). Whatever these *Bramins* may have explained to Holwell, here it is old Bramah himself who seems to react to the attacks of seventeenth- and eighteenth-century deist writers, and it is striking how familiar he is not only with Indian religion but also—as his omniscience and prescience would have one expect—with eighteenth-century Europe's theological controversies!

Holwellian Contradictions

It is certain that during his long stay in India Holwell had conversed with many Indians about their religions. He severely criticized Western authors who "have (either from their own fertile inventions, or from mis-information, or rather from want of a competent knowledge in the language of the nation) misrepresented" the Indians' religious tenet (pp. 4–5). Holwell was proud of having studied the language and to have had "various conferences with many of the most learned and ingenious, amongst the laity of the *Koyt*," the tribe of writers,[14] as well as "other *Casts*, who are often better versed in the doctrines of their *Shastah* than the common run of the *Bramins* themselves" (p. 21). Holwell also mentions a "judicious *Bramin* of the *Battezaar* tribe, the tribe . . . usually employed in expounding the *Shastahs*" who explained images to him (p. 113). It is from such Indians that Holwell claims to have learned about the origin of his text.[15] But the origin and other aspects of this text are clouded by a number of strange contradictions. On one hand, Holwell openly admitted that his idea of "the antiquity of the scriptures"— namely, that the *Shastah* of *Bramah* "is as ancient, at least, as any written body of divinity that was ever produced in the world"—is based upon "our conjecture and belief" (p. 5) and emphasized that the ideas of the Brahmins are not very trustworthy and that they led to conjectures rather than historical facts:

> Without reposing an implicit confidence in the relations the *Bramins* give of the antiquity of their scriptures; we will with our readers indulgence, humbly offer a few conjectures that have swayed us into a belief and conclusion, that the original tenets of *Bramah* are most ancient; that they are truly original, and not copied from any system of theology, that has ever been promulged to, or obtruded upon the belief of mankind: what weight our conjectures may have with the curious . . . we readily submit to those, whose genius, learning and capacity in researches of this kind, are much superior to our own. (p. 23)

On the other hand, Holwell presented an elaborate scheme of the origin of Indian sacred literature with precise dates: it was precisely "4866 years ago" (3100 B.C.E.) that the Almighty decided to have his sentence for the delinquent angels "digested into *a body of written laws* for their guidance" and ordered Bramah, "a being from the first rank of angels . . . destined for the eastern part of this globe," to transmit God's "terms and conditions" to the "delinquents" (pp. 11–12). Bramah "assumed the human form," translated God's sentence from "*Debtah Nagur* (literally, the language of angels)" into "the *Sanscrît*, a language then universally known throughout *Indostan*." This oldest book of the world "was preached to the delinquents, as the only terms of their salvation and restoration" and is known as "*the Chartah Bhade Shastah of Bramah* (literally, the *four scriptures of divine words of the mighty spirit*)" (p. 12). This was the text that Holwell claimed to have found, translated, lost, found again in fragments, translated again, and finally published in 1767. Since Holwell's text titles are a bit confusing—he claims at the bottom of the same page that *Bhade* means "a written book"—I will call this first Sanskrit scripture from 3,100 B.C.E. "Text I."

For a thousand years Text I remained untouched and many delinquent angels were saved by its teachings; but in 2100 B.C.E. some commentators wrote a paraphrase called *Chatah Bhade of Bramah* or "the *six scriptures of the mighty spirit*" and began to "veil in mysteries the simple doctrines of *Bramah*" (pp. 12–13). The product of these commentators, Text II, consisted of Text I plus comments.

Again five hundred years later, in 1600 B.C.E., a second exposition swelled "the Gentoo scriptures to eighteen books"; this was Text III, called "*Aughtorrah Bhade Shastah, or the eighteen books of divine words*" (pp. 14–15). In Text III the original scripture of Bramah, Text I, "was in a manner sunk and alluded to only" and "a multitude of ceremonials, and exteriour modes of worship, were instituted," while the laity was "precluded from the knowledge of their original scriptures" and "had a new system of faith broached unto them, which their ancestors were utterly strangers to" (p. 14).

Text III "produced a schism amongst the *Gentoo's*, who until this period had followed one profession of faith throughout the vast empire of *Indostan*" (p. 14). But now the Brahmins of South India formed a scripture of their own, "*the Viedam of Brummah*, or *divine words of the mighty spirit*" (Text IV: p. 14). The southerners claimed that their *Viedam* (= Veda) was based on Text I; but in reality they had, like the authors of Text III, included all kinds of new things and even "departed from that chastity of manners" still preserved in Text III.

While the southerners based their religion on the *Viedam* (Text IV), the northerners continued to use the *Aughtorrah Bhade Shastah* (Text III):

> The *Aughtorrah Bhade Shastah*, has been invariably followed by the *Gentoos* inhabiting from the mouth of the *Ganges* to the *Indus*, for the last three thousand three hundred and sixty six years. This precisely fixes the commencement of the *Gentoo mythology*, which until the publication of that *Bhade*, had no existence amongst them. (p. 18)

Having read about Holwell's "conjecture" and "belief," the reader is astonished to find such a precisely dated genealogy of the sacred scriptures of India. To ensure that the reader understands that this is not Holwell's personal "conjecture" and "belief," every line of this 12-page history (pp. 9–21) begins with a quotation mark. But who said or wrote all this, including what was just quoted about the precise beginning of *Gentoo mythology*? Holwell calls it a "recital" that he had heard "from many of these [learned *Bramins*]"—which must signify that these twelve pages, in spite of no less than 329 conspicuous quotation marks, present no quotation at all but rather a kind of summary of things that Holwell had heard at various times from a variety of people.

However, in Europe, Holwell's fake precision had a great impact. In the second volume of his *Interesting historical events* (1767), Holwell delivered extended "quotations" from numerous "learned among the *Bramins*" (p. 9) who hitherto had hardly discussed such things with foreigners; he ostensibly translated parts of the world's most ancient book; he declared that this text was much older and more authentic than the Veda that the Europeans had coveted for so long; he explained the origin and unity of Indian religion (the religion of the *Gentoos* or, as we would say today, the Hindus); he furnished precise dates for a "schism" that had set the religion of the South against that of the North; and he asserted that his *Shastah* was the one and only original revelation that God had granted to the ancient Indians. Holwell's "conjecture and belief" seemed to have vanished underneath a giant heap of certified facts.

Another contradiction that strikes the reader concerns the story Holwell weaves around the transmission of his *Shastah* text. On one hand, he claims that this text was extremely rare and hard to find; hence, the high price he had to pay for the acquisition of the two manuscripts lost in 1756, the failure of acquiring a replacement after that, and the miraculous (though unexplained) recovery of just a few fragments. On the other hand, the *Shastah* text seems to have been rather well transmitted. Holwell claims to have had not just one but two complete copies in the early 1750s and insisted that it was from recovered fragments of this original text that he translated the chapter on the fate of the delinquent angels (which forms 65 percent of the entire translation).[16] Furthermore, Text I could not have been rare since it was also included in Text II and to some extent in Text III, which both "derive their authority and essence, in the bosom of every *Gentoo*, from the *Chartah Bhade* of *Bramah*" (p. 29), and could easily be consulted when the need arose:

> It is no uncommon thing, for a *Gentoo*, upon any point of conscience, or any important emergency in his affairs or conduct, to reject the decision of the *Chatah* [Text II] and *Aughtorrah Bhades* [Text III], and to procure, no matter at what expence, the decision of the *Chartah Bhade* [Text I], expounded in the *Sanscrît*. (p. 29)

Those who included Text I in Text II, commented on it, and eventually produced Text III—"some *Goseyns* and *Battezaaz Bramins*"—obviously also had access to Text I (p. 13):

Thus the original, plain, pure, and simple tenets of the *Chartah Bhade* of *Bramah* (fifteen hundred years after its first promulgation) became by degrees utterly lost; except, to three or four *Goseyn* families, who at this day are only capable of reading, and expounding it, from the *Sanscrît* character; to these may be added a few others of the tribe of the *Battee-zaaz Bramins*, who can read and expound from the *Chatah Bhade* [Text II], which still preserved the text of the original, as before remarked. (p. 15)

Also blessed with access to Text I were apparently "many of the most learned and ingenuous, amongst the laity of the *Koyt*, and other *Casts*, who are often better versed in the doctrines of their *Shastah* than the common run of the *Bramins* themselves" (p. 21). Furthermore, as mentioned at the beginning of this chapter, Holwell reported that there existed an entire country near Calcutta whose religion had forever been based on Text I and that had preserved paradisiacal purity! And just before the end of his second volume, Holwell mentions another group who intimately knows Text I and seems also on course to paradise:

> The *remnant* of *Bramins* (whom we have before excepted) who seclude themselves from the communications of the busy world, in a philosophic, and religious retirement, and strictly pursue the tenets and true spirit of the *Chartah Bhade of Bramah*, we may with equal truth and justice pronounce, *are the purest models of genuine piety that now exist, or can be found on the face of the earth.* (p. 152)

Yet another contradiction concerns the language of Text I. Holwell stated that his text first existed in the language of angels[17] and was then translated and promulgated in Sanskrit. He accused missionaries as well as "modern authors . . . chiefly of the *Romish* communion" of having presented "the mythology of the venerable ancient *Bramins* on so slender a foundation as a few insignificant literal translations of the *Viedam*" that were not even "made from the book itself, but from unconnected scraps and bits, picked up here and there by hearsay from *Hindoos*, probably as ignorant as themselves" (Holwell 1765:1.6). Holwell, by contrast, was using the unadulterated original *Shastah* text rather than the degenerate southern "Viedam," and his thirty-year sojourn in Bengal (p. 3) had supposedly equipped him to deal with this original text. Holwell never claimed openly to have studied Sanskrit, but the reader of his account gets the impression, as Voltaire did, that Holwell knew Sanskrit since he was able to translate the ancient text and labored for many months to produce not only a literal translation but one that even took the diction and style of the original into account. But it is evident that Holwell never studied Sanskrit and that the Indian words he quotes from Text I are not Sanskrit.

There are also many unanswered questions concerning Holwell's recovery of some fragments of the *Shastah* that ought to have taken place before his return to England in 1761. A comparison of Holwell's announcement in 1765 with the actual content of the 1767 volume seems to indicate that, in 1765, Holwell was not yet planning to include any translations from the *Shastah* except for the creation account. The 1765 announcement only mentioned "A summary view of the fundamental, religious tenets of the *Gentoos*, followers of the *Shastah*" and "A short account, from the *Shastah*, of the creation of the *worlds*, or universe" (p. 15). The latter became in 1767 the eighth section of the *Shastah*'s second book (1767:2.106–10). Why did Holwell in his first volume (on whose title page the second and third parts were already announced) not lose a single word about the literal translations he was about to publish from the world's oldest text? Did Holwell decide around 1766 to transform his "summary view of the fundamental religious tenets of the *Gentoos*" into "translations"? The content of the *Shastah* texts as well as their style, inspired as they seem by Milton's *Paradise Lost*, Salomon Gessner's *Death of Abel* (1761), and James "Ossian" Macpherson's *Fragments of Ancient Poetry* (1760), also point in that direction. Are all those hundreds of quotation marks signs of a bad conscience?

Contradictions pertaining to Holwell's (and Ilive's) system will go unmentioned here, except for one related to the salvation of fish that was pointed out in a delightful passage by Julius Mickle who noted many suspicious facets of Holwell's text:

> Nature has made almost the whole creation of fishes to feed upon each other. Their purgation therefore is only a mock trial; for, according to Mr. H[olwell] whatever being destroys a mortal body must begin its transmigrations anew; and thus the spirits of the fishes would be just where they were, though millions of the four Jogues [*yugas*; world ages] were repeated. Mr. H. is at great pains to solve the reason why the fishes were not drowned at the general deluge, when every other species of animals suffered death. The only reason for it, he says, is that they were

more favoured of God, as more innocent. Why then are these less guilty spirits united to bodies whose natural instinct precludes them the very possibility of salvation? (Mickle 1798:190)

The Shastah and the Vedas

A further contradiction concerns the discrepancy between Holwell's and the standard Indian view of Vedas and Shastras. To contemporaries like Voltaire or Anquetil-Duperron, Holwell's presentation of sacred Indian literature— delivered purportedly in the words of learned Indian informers—seemed impressive. Holwell apparently set the beginning of the last world age (and thus the promulgation of Text I in Sanskrit) at 3100 B.C.E.,[18] but nobody knows how he came up with a 1000-year golden age until Text II and another 500 years until Text III. The descriptions of the four corpora of Indian sacred scriptures by Holwell's "learned *Bramins*" seem to stem, in spite of their 329 quotation marks, from a non-Indian source since Indians of all stripes always regarded the four Vedas as their basic sacred scriptures and Shastras as commentarial literature.[19] This is also what European reports since the sixteenth century had affirmed (Caland 1918), and it is why Abbé Bignon urged Father Calmette to acquire and send the four Vedas to Paris and not some Shastras. So where did Holwell get this idea that the Vedas are late and degenerated scriptures, a mere shadow of the far older *Shastah* of *Bramah*?

Holwell boasted that he had "studiously perused all that has been written of the empire of *Indostan*, both as to its ancient, as well as more modern state" but added that what he had read was "all very defective, fallacious, and unsatisfactory to an inquisitive searcher after truth" (Holwell 1765:1.5). However, in the meantime we may have learned not to take every word of Holwell as gospel. He occasionally cited Ramsay's *Travels of Cyrus*, which contained an interesting passage about Indian religion that could not fail to inspire him. Ramsay reported that the Veda states

> that souls are eternal emanations from the divine Essence, or at least that they were produced long before the formation of the world; that they were originally in a state of purity, but having sinned, were thrown down into the bodies of men, or of beasts, according to their respective demerits; so that the body, where the soul resides, is a sort of dungeon or prison. (Ramsay 1814:382)

Ramsay attributed this passage to Abraham Roger's *De Open-Deure tot het verborgen Heydendom* (The Open Door to the Hidden Paganism), whose French translation (1670) he had consulted. In the preface to that edition, translator Thomas La Grue particularly emphasized "what was also clearly a motif with Roger himself: that the Indians did indeed possess a pristine and natural knowledge of God, but that it had decayed almost completely into superstition as a result of moral lapses" (Halbfass 1990:46–47). But Holwell, a good reader of Dutch, could consult Roger's original edition of 1651.[20] There Roger called the Indian *Dewetaes* (Skt. *devatas*; Indian guardian spirits or protective divinities) "Engelen" or angels (Roger 1915:108). But here we are primarily interested in Roger's description of the *Vedam*, which for him is the Indian's book of laws containing "everything that they must believe as well as all the ceremonies they must perform" (p. 20).

> This *Vedam* consists of four parts; the first part is called *Roggowedam*; the second *Issourewedam*; the third *Samawedam*; and the fourth *Adderawa-nawedam*. The first part deals with the first cause, the *materia prima* [eerste materie], the angels, the souls, the recompense of good and pun-ishment of evil, the generation of creatures and their corruption, the nature of sin, how it can be absolved, how this can be achieved, and to what end. (p. 21)

After a brief explanation of the content of the second to fourth Vedas, Roger states that conflicts of Vedic interpretation generated a literature of commentaries called *Iastra* (Skt. *śāstra*), "that is, the explanations about the *Vedam*" (p. 22). As Willem Caland has shown in detail (1918),[21] Roger's source for such information was Diogo do Couto's *Decada Quinta da Asia* of 1612. Couto's account of the content of the Vedas was in turn, as Schurham-mer (1977:2.612–20) proved, plagiarized from an account by the Augustinian brother Agostinho de Azevedo's *Estado da India e aonde tem o seu principio* of 1603, a report prepared in the 1580s for King Philip III of Portugal, which "includes an original summary of Hindu religion, from Shaiva Sanskrit and Tamil texts" (Rubiés 2000:315). The question as to what exactly Azevedo's sources were still awaits clarification in spite of Caland's speculations (1918:309–10); but here we will concentrate on Couto whose report about sacred Indian literature, unlike Azevedo's, was used by Holwell who could handle Portuguese. Couto's report of 1612 describes Indian sacred literature as follows:

TABLE 11. Do Couto's Vedas and Holwell's Sacred Scriptures of India

Couto		Holwell (1767)
4 Vedas	I	4 scriptures of divine words of the mighty spirit (*Chartah Bhade Shastah of Bramah*)
6 Xastras	II	6 scriptures of the mighty spirit (*Chatah Bhade of Bramah*)
18 Puranas	III	18 books of divine words (*Aughtorrah Bhade Shastah*)
28 Agamon	IV	Divine words of the mighty spirit (*Viedam of Brummah*)

They possess many books in their Latin, which they call Geredaom, and which contain everything they have to believe and all ceremonies they have to perform. These books are divided in bodies, members, and articulations. The fundamental texts are those they call Vedas which form four parts, and these again form fifty-two in the following manner: Six that they call Xastra which are the bodies; eighteen they call Purana which are the members; and twenty-eight called Agamon which are the articulations. (Couto 1612:125r)

The numbers four, six, and eighteen first made me think that Holwell's weird history of Indian sacred literature might be modeled on Couto's report. As we have seen, Holwell also mentioned four textual bodies. The number of scriptures of the first three bodies thus correspond exactly to Couto's, as shown in Table 11.

Holwell's wild potpourri of *Bhade* (which would be the Vedas), *Shastah* (which would be, as Roger indicates, commentaries), and *Viedam* has confused many readers.[22] Trautmann commented that *Chartah Bhade Shastah* of Bramah "would be something like *Catur Veda Śāstra* in Sanskrit, an odd title since it combines two classes of Sanskrit literature that are distinct, Veda and Śāstra" (1997:68), and he complains, "Holwell does not seem to understand that his *Bhade* is the same word as his *Viedam*, the one under a Bengali pronunciation, the other a Tamil one" (p. 69). At any rate, Holwell garnished such information with a plethora of quotation marks and presented it as the opinion of knowledgeable Indians. But it is abundantly clear that no knowledgeable Indian would ever have said anything remotely similar. Rather, Holwell once again used Western information as a basis for a house of cards. Calling the *Viedam* "a corruption" of his *Shastah*, Holwell asserted that it was only used in the South "by the *Gentoos* of the *Mallabar* and *Cormandel* coasts: and also by those of the Island of Ceylon" (Holwell 1767:2.11–12) and claimed that only his Text I contained the genuine teaching of antiquity:

> Enough has been said, to shew that the genuine tenets of *Bramah*, are to be found only in the *Chartah Bhade* [Text I]; and as all who have wrote on this subject, have received their information from crude, inconsistent reports, chiefly taken from the *Aughtorrah Bhade*, and the *Viedam*; it is no wonder that the religion of the *Gentoos*, has been traduced, by some, as utterly unintelligible; and by others, as monstrous, absurd, and disgraceful to humanity:—our design is to rescue these ancient people, from those imputations; in order to which we shall proceed, without further introduction or preface, to investigate the original scriptures, as contained in the *Chartah Bhade*. (pp. 29–30)

In particular, Holwell attacked the Dutch pastor Philip BALDAEUS (1632–72) for having "given a laborious translation of the *Viedam*" and having claimed that the part that "treated of God, and the origin of the universe, or visible words" was lost. Baldaeus had indeed written that "the first of these [Vedam] Books treated of God, and of the Origin and Beginning of the Universe" and that "the loss of this first Part is highly lamented by the *Brahmans*" (Baldaeus 1732:891. Holwell accused Baldaeus of a double error: first, of "alleging the part lost" even though "both the *Viedam*, and *Shastah*, are elaborate on the subject . . . and fix not only the period of its creation but also its precise age, and term of duration"; and second, of lamenting "a loss they never sustained" (p. 32). He must have preferred Couto's description of the Veda's content:

> To better understand these [*Vedáos*] we will briefly distinguish all of them. The first part of the four fundamental texts treats of the first cause, the first matter [materia prima], the angels, the souls, the recompense of good, the punishment of evil, the generation of creatures, their corruption, what sin is, how one can attain remission and be absolved, and why. The second part treats of the regents and how they exert dominion over all things. The third part is all about moral doctrine, advice exhorting to virtue and obliging to avoid vice, and also for monastic and political life, i.e., active and contemplative life. The fourth part treats of

TABLE 12. CONTENTS OF DO COUTO'S FIRST VEDA AND THE FIRST BOOK OF HOLWELL'S *SHASTAH*

Couto's first Veda in Decada Quinta *(1612:125r)*	*First book of Holwell's* Shastah *(1767:30)*
first cause, materia prima	God and his attributes
angels	creation of angelic beings
souls (of angels in human bodies)	lapse of angelic beings
punishment / recompense	punishment, mitigation
remission, absolution	final sentence leading to remission

temple ceremonies, offerings, and their festivals; and also about enchantment, witchcraft, divination, and the art of magic since they are much taken by this kind of thing. (Couto 1612:125r)

The comparison of this description with Holwell's summary (1767:30) of the contents of his *Shastah* (see Table 12) shows that they are also quite a good match. This common inspiration may explain another contradiction in Holwell's portrayal of Indian sacred literature, namely, why—in spite of his rantings against the Veda as a late and degenerate text—Holwell claimed that both his *Shastah* (Text I) and the *Viedam* (Text IV) were "originally *one*":

Both these books [the *Viedam* and *Shastah*] contain the institutes of their respective religions and worships,[23] often couched under allegory and fable; as well as the history of their ancient Rajahs and Princes—their antiquity is contended for by the partisans of each—but the similitude of their *names, idols,* and a great part of their worship, leaves little room to doubt, nay plainly evinces, that both these scriptures were originally *one*. (Holwell 1765:1.12)

If Couto's summary of Veda content does not seem overly concerned with angels, the more detailed explanations (Couto 1612:125v) provide details that were certainly of great interest to a man so thoroughly converted to Jacob Ilive's system as Holwell. Couto wrote that Indian manuals of theology portray God as first cause and as "a pure, incorporal, infinite spirit, endowed with all might, all knowledge, and all truth" who "is everywhere, which is why they call him Xarues Zibarú which signifies creator of all" (p. 125v). According to Couto, the first Veda then describes three kinds of angels: the good angels that remain in heaven with God; the delinquent angels who must go through rehabilitation imprisoned in human bodies on earth; and the angels shut in hell. It furthermore treats of the immortality of souls and their transmigration during the rehabilitation process on earth: "They believe that the souls are immortal; but they think that a sinner's soul at death passes into the body of some living being where it continues purification until it merits rising to heaven" (p. 125v). Couto goes into considerable detail about the meaning of transmigration and its deep connection with the punishment of evil and recompense of good: the souls of the worst sinners transmigrate after death into the most terrible animals, and those of the good into an ever better body. In this way they can purify themselves and atone until they become ready to regain their original state before the fall (pp. 125v–126r).

The Making of an Ur-Text

One can imagine how delighted Holwell must have been to find such stunning similarities between the description of India's ancient religious texts and Ilive's vision. But the doctrines that had been translated or summarized from old texts by the likes of Roger, Baldaeus, and the Catholic missionaries showed little similarity with this. All of it seemed "very defective, fallacious, and unsatisfactory" to Holwell, in fact, no more than "unconnected scraps and bits, picked up here and there by hearsay" from ignorant *Hindoos* rather than solid "literal translations" (Holwell 1765:1.5–6). Hence the need to "rescue" this distant nation "from the gross conceptions entertained of them by the multitude" (p. 9) and "to vindicate them" by "a simple display of their primitive theology" (Holwell 1767: Dedication). Disgusted by all these misunderstandings and misrepresentations (1767.2:4), converted by Ilive's theory of delinquent angels, and possibly already fascinated by Ramsay's vision of Ur-tradition, Holwell collected materials about the *Gentoo* religion and "on his departure from Bengal in the year 1750 imagined himself well informed in the *Gentoo* religion" about which he had learned through "conversations with the *Bramins* of those *Bhades* who were near" (pp. 63–64). He had already thought of writing a book about this but did not find the time (p. 64). Given the fact that he already had such a plan, it is likely that during his stays in Europe he also collected relevant Western literature about India and its religions. If he was not already acquainted with Ramsay and Couto before, he must have studied them after his return to India in 1751 and as a result gained a rather precise idea of what he was looking for. If Holwell was trying to find the Vedas, he was not alone; but Couto's description of the first Veda, which seemed so similar to Ilive's ideas, certainly brought more motivation and focus to his search. He knew that he was looking for an extremely ancient scripture treating of God, the creation story, angels and their fall, the immortality of souls, the purification of delinquent angels in human bodies, transmigration, the punishment of evil and reward of good, and remission and salvation.

What could happen when a wealthy foreigner was trying to locate such information in old Indian texts is exemplified by the case of Francis WILFORD (1761?–1822), a respected member of the Asiatic Society of Bengal who lived in India four decades after the sack of Calcutta rang in the British Empire. Unlike Holwell, Wilford had studied Sanskrit. He was intent on proving on the basis of Indian texts that India and Egypt had from ancient times been in close contact and that their religions came from a common source. Since that source was, of course, ultimately Noah's ark, Wilford had Indian assistants look for a precise set of topics: the deluge, the name of Noah and his sons, and so forth. Like Holwell some decades before him, Wilford had to tell a learned Indian what he was looking for "as a clue to guide him," and for several years he faithfully translated what this Indian guru gave him. But suddenly he detected that he had fallen victim to fraud:

> In order to avoid the trouble of consulting books, he conceived the idea of framing legends from what he recollected from the *Puránas*, and from what he had picked up in conversation with me. As he was exceedingly well read in the *Puránas*, and other similar books . . . it was an easy task for him; and he studied to introduce as much truth as he could, to obviate the danger of immediate detection. . . . His forgeries were of three kinds; in the first there was only a word or two altered; in the second were such legends as had undergone a more material alteration; and in the third all those which he had written from memory. (Wilford 1805:251)

The output of this Indian expert was quite astonishing, and the most famous example shows what good remuneration, a sense of what the customer is looking for, and skill in composition can achieve. The learned Indian composed a story "which in nine Sanskrit verses . . . reprises the story of Noah, his three sons, and the curse of Ham" and convinced no less a man than William Jones that Noah and his three sons figured in genuine Indian *Purāṇas* (Trautmann 1997:90–91). Wilford described how his Indian teacher proceeded in this case:

> It is a legend of the greatest importance, and said to be extracted from the *Padma*. It contains the history of NOAH and his three sons, and is written in a masterly style. But unfortunately there is not a word of it to be found in that *Purána*. It is, however, mentioned, though in less explicit terms, in many *Puránas*, and the pandit took particular care in pointing out to me several passages which confirmed, more or less, this interesting legend. Of these I took little notice, as his extract appeared more explicit and satisfactory. (Wilford 1805:254)

Since Wilford had told his pandit exactly what he was looking for, the forger produced an ingenious narrative that presented elements of the story of Noah and his sons in an Indian dress and included some surprising details such as "the legend about the intoxication of NOAH" which, as Wilford now realized, "is from what my pandit picked up in conversation with me" (p. 254). In all, this man "composed no less than 12,000 brand new Puranic *ślokas*—about half the length of the *Rāmāyaṇa!*—and inserted them into manuscripts of the *Skanda* and *Brahmānda Purāṇa*" (Trautmann 1997:92). This was a fraud committed on a man who was far more learned than Holwell; the texts were in Sanskrit, not Hindi; and the source texts could be verified.

In Holwell's case, there is always the possibility that his description of Veda content led some knowledgeable Indian to the very texts that Azevedo had used for the description that Couto plagiarized and Roger and others then used. Caland (1918:49–50) concluded on the basis of the book titles mentioned by Couto that these texts were Śaivite Agamas; but an able Indologist would need to substantiate this not just by titles but by contents. While it is possible that similar texts in Hindi were sold to Holwell, I think that the likelihood of a fraud is greater. If Holwell, ready as he was to spend almost any amount of money on this text after the 1756 loss, could not manage to recuperate more than a few fragments—or, more likely, nothing at all—one would think that the people who sold it to him in the first place had produced only two slightly different manuscripts and, having sold them to Holwell, were in no position to repeat that feat. If Holwell's text had been available to various people, then someone would probably have sold it to him, especially given the fact that for a while he was governor of Bengal and certainly did not lack the means to get what he wanted.

But who could have forged such a text? Since Holwell remarked that members of the tribe of writers "are often better versed in the doctrines of their *Shastah* than the common run of the *Bramin* themselves" (Holwell 1767:2.21) and that "a few others of the tribe of the *Batteezaaz Bramins* . . . can read and expound from the *Chatah Bhade* [Text II], which still preserved the text of the original [Text I]" (p. 15), the culprit(s) might have come from either or both of these groups.

Whether Holwell ever recovered fragments of his text (Holwell 1765:1.4) is also subject to doubt. If in 1766 he really had parts of his text at hand, then why did he not show them to anyone or have a sample page printed in his book? And why did he not mention in 1765, when he listed the second volume's prospective content, that it would contain genuine translations from the world's oldest text? Faced with this golden opportunity to get more people to read and buy his work, he only announced "a summary view of the *fundamental*, religious tenets of the *Gentoos*" and "a short account, from the *Shastah*, of the creation of the *worlds*, or universe" (Holwell 1765:1.15). If one takes him at his word, then in 1765 he still planned to publish only summaries and a single "short account" drawn from the *Shastah*. This "account" now forms the "creation" chapter that barely amounts to four and a half small pages of "translation" (Holwell 1767:2.106–10).

But to furnish only summaries of the world's oldest text rather than translations would have pleased neither Holwell's publisher nor his readers. I think that this is why Holwell must have decided to recast his "summary views" of the *Shastah* into "translation" form framed in convincing quotation marks. This might have happened in 1766. A sign of hasty conversion are phrases that would fit a summary but sound odd in a direct quotation. For example, "a being from the first rank of angels was destined for the eastern part of this globe" (p. 11) is perfect for a summary written by a Westerner but is a strange statement for an Indian to make: "eastern" in relation to where? The same applies for the phrase that is presented as another quotation from an Indian: "This precisely fixes the commencement of the *Gentoo* mythology, which, until the publication of that *Bhade*, had no existence amongst them" (p. 18)—an odd statement coming from a "Gentoo" since he would have to say "us" rather than "them," even assuming some self-consciousness as a "Hindu," something likewise highly unlikely in an ancient text.

Other contradictions that were mentioned above also seem explainable by Holwellian authorship in the mid-1760s. The content of the *Shastah* fragments that Holwell supposedly recuperated reflect his intense interests of the period, which he embedded in the *Shastah* text and his comments. Both have a unitarian and anti-deist, mid-eighteenth-century flavor. The *Shastah*'s God needed to be one and not three-in-one or "the one that ever was." He had to be all-creative, of course, and too just to punish innocent babies; and thoughts like "original sin" would not even cross his mind. He needed to be omniscient and equipped with perfect providence—except for those purposefully ignored free-will acts that eventually put the delinquent angels into their rehab camp on earth. He needed to be almighty yet leave a little space for angels to rebel. He needed to be so absolutely good that he created earth out of compassion for those delinquent angels whose rebellion he had allowed. And he had to refrain from eternal punishment and guarantee a good and just final outcome for everyone. The core issue was, of course, the origin of evil, and the *Shastah* text trumpets Jacob Ilive's "delinquent angel" solution. As shown in the pie graph in Figure 15, even the volume of "translated" text and of Holwell's comments reflects this agenda. Other solutions to the theodicy problem are rejected both via the *Shastah* text with its purported authority and by Holwell's comments, which openly criticize and reject alternative models.

Apart from Ilive's and Ramsay's works, a 1762 book by Capel BERROW (1715–82) appears to have been used in the composition of the "Shastah" text and its commentary. Its title describes the author's intention well: *A Pre-existent Lapse of Human Souls Demonstrated from Reason; shewn to be the Opinion of the most eminent Writers of Antiquity, Sacred and Profane: Proved to be the Ground-work likewise of the Gospel Dispensation; And the Medium through which many material Topics, relative thereto, are set in a clear, rational, and consistent Light.* In 1771, Holwell wrote about this work:

> An ingenious, speculative, and learned divine of our church, published, in the year 1762, a treatise, entitled, "A Pre-existent Lapse of Human Souls, &c." This truly valuable performance relieves us from much labor in the prosecution of our work, as it confirms, *from our own scriptures,* many leading and essential points of the Metempsychosis, as, the existence of angels, their rebellion, their expulsion from their blessed abodes,

the coeval creation of the angelic and human spirits, and the association of the latter with the former in their apostacy; that their situation on earth is a state of *degradation* and *probation* for that lapse, and that *original sin* is not that which is erroneously imputed to us from *Adam*, but springs from a much higher source, *viz.* the *pre-existent* lapse of the (human) spirit from its primeval purity. (Holwell 1771:3.37–38)

It seems to me that Holwell italicized "*from our own scriptures*" for a good reason: he had, as both his *Shastah* text and commentary show, the same objective as Berrow except for one thing: he wanted to confirm all this not *from our own scriptures*, that is, the Bible, but from a much older *Indian Bible* that he portrayed as the oldest testament of divine revelation to humanity. One cannot doubt Holwell's conviction since he seems to have held fast to these exact beliefs until the end of his life and published about little else in the decades following his return from India. His conviction seems to have been sufficiently solid to propel the transformation of reminiscences from a lost text into oa "translation," the invention of a suitable pedigree for this text, and its canonization as the oldest text of the world. It seems like a classic case of Ur-tradition, complete with a grossly misdated, dubious sacred text; a fake translation; an invented life of transmission; and a reform motive that is explained in Holwell's essay on metempsychosis of 1771 and his dissertations on angels and divine providence of 1786.

Back to Indian Eden

But why would Holwell present his obsession with angels and their fate in the form of the world's most ancient text? Because he intended, like other proponents of an Ur-tradition system with reform ambitions, "to *revive* and *reestablish* the *primitive truths* which constituted the ground-work of the first universal religion, at the period of the creation of the material worlds and man" (Holwell 1771:3.52). This restoration of Ur-religion obliged him, so he explained, to strip the religions of India as well as Judaism and Christianity "of all disguise, mystery, and fable" and to examine them not "under the guise in which they now appear before us, but as they really were at their first promulgation" (p. 52).

For of all the theologic systems that have been broached to mankind, we think we are well supported in marking these [three religions] alone as

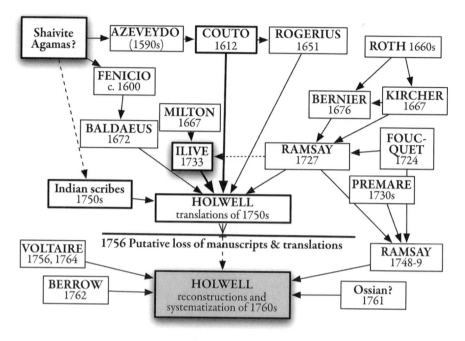

Figure 17. Genesis of Holwell's Chartah Bhade Shastah of Bramah (Urs App).

true originals; but our benevolent view extends even farther, and we flatter ourselves (however chimerical it may appear) mankind may be restored again to that *one unerring original faith*, from which, by undue influence in every age of the world, they have unhappily swerved: we are convinced, if they consulted their present and future felicity, they would fly to embrace a rational hypothesis, that leads to such a blessed issue. (Holwell 1771:3.52–53)

The "one unerring original faith" was, of course, contained in the text that Holwell presented as the world's oldest written document and the earliest and purest divine revelation to humanity. This is a classic case of a reformer's Ur-tradition. Naturally, the events from before the creation of the earth and the adventures of angels could not have been communicated in any other way than by divine revelation; and God's earliest revelation had taken place in India where "the *primitive truths* [were] revealed by a gracious God to man, in the early days of his creation, at a time when it may be reasonably presumed he retained a lively sense of his soul's former transgression" (p. 5). What followed this golden age is a sad history of degeneration:

That these are the only *primitive truths* necessary to man's salvation, and restoration, appears from hence, that they have, from the earliest records of time to this day, remained more or less *the stock* upon which the blindness, or wickedness of man has engrafted very extravagant, un-profitable, as well as unintelligible doctrines, to delude their fellow-crea-tures, and seduce them from a strict adherence to, and reliance on, those *primitive truths only.* (pp. 5–6)

Holwell's "primitive truths" are, as we would expect, the fundamental principles shared by all peoples because they spring from a common source. The "concurring testimony of all mankind" (or universal consent) is thus an essential part of the argument, as in Ramsay; but Holwell has—partly due to his conversion to Jacob Ilive's creed—a somewhat different set of *primitive truths* from Ramsay's. He enumerates a total of thirteen of them, starting with the creator God and ending with the ministration of angels in human affairs. They can be arranged in four categories: (1) God and his attributes; (2) angels, their fall, expulsion, evil leader, and influence; (3) man, his immor-tal angelic soul, and his life in the rehabilitation facility earth; and (4) the existence of a golden age followed by degeneration, an intermediate state after death for punishment, the necessity of a mediator, and final restoration (pp. 4–5).

But why did this first revelation happen in India and not, say, in Judaea? Because, according to Holwell, the *Gentoos* of India and not the Hebrews were God's chosen people!

If the mission of *Moses* contained a *spiritual*, as well as *temporal* allusion to the salvation of the *Hebrews*, and the spiritual sense was hidden from them, it was then indeed imperfect, and the *Gentoos* seem to have been *the chosen people of God*, in place of the *Israelites*; for to them was revealed by Bramah, with God's permission, not only the *real state and condition of man*, but his doctrines also taught, the existence of *One Eternal God*, and *temporal* as well as *future* rewards and punishments. (p. 20)

But since God cannot be allowed to be so blatantly partial, he also gra-ciously provided special revelations to two other groups:

The religions which manifestly carry the divine stamp of God, are, first, that which *Bramah* was appointed to declare to the ancient *Hindoos*;

secondly that law which *Moses* was destined to deliver to the ancient
Hebrews; and thirdly, that with *Christ* was delegated to preach to the
latter *Jews* and *Gentiles*, or the *Pagan* world. These, and these only, bear
the signature of divine origin. (p. 50)

Sadly, all such dispensations inevitably fall prey to degeneration through
priestcraft. If in India the Brahmins had presided over a drawn-out degradation process leading to the blatant idolatry and superstition reigning there
now, the Christian dispensation was also "utterly mutilated and defaced since
the ascension," so much so "that Christ himself, when he descends again on
earth, will disown it" (p. 51). Like Newton, Holwell was a unitarian and
deplored the trinitarian heresy promoted by Athanasius along with the per-
versions of genuine Christianity by the "primitive fathers of the church" who
"may with more propriety be stiled *the destroyers*, than *the fathers*" of the
church (p. 8). Even Moses' dispensation needed to be reinterpreted:

> When we attentively peruse *Moses's* detail of the *creation and fall of man*,
> we find it clogged with too many incomprehensible difficulties to gain
> our belief, that that consummate legislator ever intended it should be
> understood in a literal sense . . . and so we hope to prove that his detail
> of *the fall of man* was *typical only* of the angelic fall. (p. 10)

For Holwell the basis for a correct interpretation of the Mosaic account
of the fall of man was, of course, the *Shastah* of the Indians who are "*as a
nation*, more ancient than any other" (p. 14). As usual, antiquity was closely
linked to purity of transmission:

> It has been well remarked that the nearer we approach to the origin of
> nations the more pure we shall find their Theology, and the reason of
> things speaks the justness of the remark; because *the period* when the
> angelic spirits were doomed to take upon them mortal forms was doubt-
> less the origin of all nations; and at that time, as the nature of their
> transgression and the terms of their restoration, were fresh upon their
> memories, their Theology was pure, universal and unerring; professing
> *one universal faith*, which they had as we say from the mouth of GOD
> himself. (p. 44)

That there was once an age when "all nations had but *one system of
Theology*" is proven by the "uniform concurrence of all people touching the

primitive truths," and it is an entirely "logical supposition" that there is "*one faith* at the origin of all nations" that reigned in the "*terrestrial golden age*" (p. 44). In support of his view that "the religion of *Bramah* is the *most ancient, and consequently the *most pure*," Holwell also cited the opinions of Ramsay and James Howell (p. 43). Sir James HOWELL (1594–1666) had written in a letter dated August 25, 1635, that Diodorus Siculus made Egypt "thrice older than we do" since he claimed that the Egyptians "had a Religion and Kings" as much as "eighteen thousand years" ago and deduced their philosophy and science from even older sources:

> Yet for matter of Philosophy and Science, he [the *Egyptian*] had it from the *Chaldean*, he from the *Gymnosophists*, and *Brachmans* of *India*, which Country, as she is the next neighbour to the rising Sun, in reference to this side of the Hemisphere, so the beams of learning did first enlighten her. (Howell 1705:305).

Holwell liked to cite such support for the antiquity of the Indians. He was among the pioneers of the idea that the system "of most ancient worship" was Indian and that elements of this system were pilfered by the Egyptians:

> If we grant that it is probable the rest of the world adopted the doctrine of the Metempsychosis from the *Egyptians*, after *they* had stolen it from the *Gentoo* Bramins, and imposed it as their own, we grant a circumstance which is not clearly proved;—but another circumstance is pretty evident; and will be subsequently proved, that, at the time they stole this doctrine, they also purloined other fundamentals of the *Chartah Bhade Shastah*, namely, *the unity of the Godhead, the immortality of the soul, a general and particular Providence, and a future state of rewards and punishments.* (Holwell 1771:3.16)

If Bishop Huët had suggested that all other peoples had plagiarized Moses, Holwell now made a similar claim in favor of the Indians: even the teachers of Moses, the ancient Egyptians, had stolen their wisdom from the Indians—and the text they used was, of course, the very *Shastah* whose fragments Holwell exclusively presented to the world. That Pythagoras also "took the doctrine of the *Metempsychosis* from the *Bramins* is not disputed," and Holwell reports that when the philosopher passed through Persia, he "is said (with probability of truth) to have held many conferences with *Zoroaster*, on the doctrines of the *Bramins*" (Holwell 1767:2.27). Thus, not only the Egyptians and Jacob Ilive were inspired by the ancient teachings of the *Shastah* but also the Greeks and the Persians:

> They had so long, and intensely thought, and reasoned on the *divine nature*, and the *cause of evil*; that the portion of divine nature they possessed, seemed utterly impaired, and bewildered, as soon as they began to form their crude principles into a *system*;—they appear to have preserved the basis and out-lines of *Bramah's Shastah*, on which (probably in conjunction with the *Persian* and *Egyptian* Magi) they raised an aerial superstructure, wild and incomprehensible! and labored to propagate an unintelligible jargon of divinity, which neither themselves, nor any mortal since their time, could explain, or reduce to the level of human understanding. (pp. 27–28)

Old nations were thus all tributary of "the *primitive truths* of *Bramah* . . . *viz.* the unity of the Godhead, the Metempsychosis, and its concomitant essential doctrines, the angelic origin, and immortality of the human soul, and its present and future state of rewards and punishments, &c." (Holwell 1771:3.14). The whole truth and all religions of remote antiquity thus seemed to rest on the single pole of the *Shastah*, and this pole was firmly and exclusively placed in the hand of John Zephaniah Holwell.

Holwell and Voltaire

Holwell was an avid reader of Voltaire and knew French well. He was not only familiar with Voltaire's attack on Bishop William Warburton (Holwell 1771:3.21) and on the credibility of Moses (pp. 21–22) but also with his mockery of angels (in the *Dictionnaire philosophique* of 1764) and his endeavor "to laugh religion out of countenance" (p. 32). It would be strange indeed if after his return from India Holwell had not also been reading Voltaire's *Essai sur les moeurs* (1756/1761) or his *Philosophie de l'histoire* (1765) that made exactly the kind of interesting claims about Indian antiquity that Holwell was searching for in such places as Sir James Howell's letters and Giovanni Marana et al.'s *Letters writ by a Turkish spy* (1723; Holwell 1771:3.156–57).

From the mid-1750s on, Voltaire's cradle of humanity was moving with increasing fanfare from Judaea toward India. As explained in Chapter 1, from the early 1760s, Voltaire's fight against the Hebrew antiquity and the Judeo-Christian monopoly got increasingly armed with "Indian" weaponry. Not the Jews but the far older Indians, whose sacred texts were plagiarized by Moses and the Jewish prophets, had to be consulted about origins. In spite of the fundamental differences between the two men's outlooks and religious convictions, Voltaire's and Holwell's "Indian campaigns" had surprisingly similar aims that fit the "Ur-tradition" pattern. Both were trying to prod degenerate European Christians to return to a purer creed whose oldest expression was found in some grossly misdated text whose Indian origin was, to say the least, highly questionable. Both infused these texts with their particular agenda, edited them at will, and published only the parts that served their campaign. Both were ardent proponents of India as humanity's most ancient civilization, and both fought against the notion that the Hebrews were God's only chosen people. Both Voltaire and Holwell sought proofs for universal consent about a unitary and just creator God, the punishment of evil and reward for good, and a future state. Both were incensed about the degeneration brought about by clergy and their false conception of God as someone to be influenced and bribed; both were outraged by radical atheists and materialists; and both saw universal reason and consent as the touchstone for truth.

Voltaire, who had first touted the *Ezour-vedam* to some friends as the world's oldest text, was elated to find in Holwell's *Shastah* a text with a precise date of origin: 3100 B.C.E. (Holwell 1767:10)—at any rate, long before Moses. After learning about Holwell's *Shastah* through Edmund Burke's review in the *Annual Register* for 1766, Voltaire wrote in 1767 to a friend: "It is proven that the Indians have written books since five thousand years ago" (Hawley 1974:146). Soon afterward he encountered his third major India source, Alexander Dow's *History of Hindostan* of 1768 (translated into French the following year), which also contained mostly apocryphal texts; but for Voltaire, the *Ezour-vedam* and Holwell's work remained the most important Indian sources (p. 147). From the first references to Indian theology in the additions to his *Essai sur les moeurs* onward, Voltaire used Indian texts to suit his agenda; and this agenda happened to be congruent with the tenor of both the *Ezour-vedam* and Holwell's work: all aimed at the regeneration of an ancient, purer monotheism. Thus, Voltaire teamed up with the *Ezour-Vedam*'s Chumontou and the *Shastah*'s Brahma (and willy-nilly also with their true authors). Of course his view of Christianity and angels was very different from both, as his scathing summary of the history of Christianity in the *Philosophical Dictionary* shows:

> The Christian religion is based on the fall of the angels. Those who revolted were precipitated from the spheres they inhabited to hell at the center of the earth and became devils. A devil tempted Eve in the form of a serpent and damned humankind. Jesus came to buy back humankind and triumph over the devil who still tempts us. However, this fundamental tradition is only found in the apocryphal book of Enoch, and even there in a manner that is very different from the received tradition. (Voltaire 1994:64–65)

Though Voltaire appreciated Holwell's delivery of a new weapon for his Indian campaign, it is clear that he did not take it seriously. As explained at the end of Chapter 1, Voltaire laughed about the *Shastah* story and regarded it as one of those "novels [romans] about the origin of evil" whose "extreme merit" is that "there never was a commandment that one must believe them" (Voltaire 1894:29.203). In the *Fragmens sur l'Inde* of 1774 Voltaire included a chapter about "the established ancient philosophical mythology and the principal dogmas of the ancient brachmanes about the origin of evil" (Voltaire 1774:148–58) that presents Holwell's narrative and shows how other peoples including the Jews have filched the angels, their fall, and other elements from ancient India. Angels were originally Indian *deoutas*; and the devil's original name was "neither Lucifer nor Beelzebub nor satan" but rather Holwell's "*Moisasor* who was the chief of a band of rebels" who was thrown with his followers in the vast *ondéra* prison and imprisoned "for millions of *monontour* . . . which are periods of 426 million years" (p. 156). Voltaire interprets Holwell's tale of the fate of the fallen angels as the Indian invention of purgatory (which the Egyptians and Christians later imitated): "With us, God did not yet pardon the devil; but with the Indians *Moisasor* and his band obtained their grace after one *monontour*. Thus their *ondéra* prison was, as a matter of fact, only a purgatory" (p. 156). Then Voltaire presents a brief summary of Holwell's narrative that is graced by the amusing title "Angels transformed into cows" in the margins. Thus, the *Shastah's* elaborate cosmogony and theodicy are reduced to a few sentences delivered in Voltaire's deadpan manner:

> So God created the earth and populated it with animals. He had the delinquents brought there and lightened their punishment. They were

first changed into cows. It is since then that the cows are so sacred in the Indian peninsula and that the pious of the region do not eat any animal. Afterwards the penitent angels were changed into men and divided into four castes. As culprits, they brought into this world the germ of vices; as punished ones, they brought the principle of all physical ills. There we have the origin of good and evil. (pp. 156–57)

Voltaire derided Holwell's core arguments about the origin of evil and God's limited liability because he gave the angels freedom of will. With regard to the latter, he remarked:

This enormous abuse of liberty, this revolt of God's favorites against their master, has the potential to dazzle; but it does not solve the problem because one could always ask why God gave to his favorites the power to offend? Why did he not force them into a happy incapacity to do evil? It is demonstrated that this difficulty is insoluble. (p. 153)

Regarding the *Shastah*'s explanation of the origin of evil, Voltaire was sarcastic:

One could possibly reproach to this system that the animals who have not sinned are as unfortunate as we are, that they devour each other and are eaten by all humans except for the brahmins. This would be a feeble objection from the times when there were still Cartesians. We will not discuss here the disputes of Indian theologians about this origin of evil. Priests have disputed everywhere; but one has to admit that the quarrels of the brahmins were always peaceful. (p. 157)

The whole explanation of the origin of evil that Holwell poured into his *Shastah* received Voltaire's damning praise as "ingenious" yet good only for "idiots":

Philosophers might be surprised that geometers and inventors of so many arts concocted a system of religion that, though ingenious, is nevertheless so unreasonable. We could reply that they had to deal with idiots [imbéciles]; and that the priests of Chaldea, Persia, Egypt, Greece, and Rome never came up with a system that was either better construed or more plausible. (p. 157)

No wonder that Voltaire did not lose as single word about the third volume of Holwell's work that presents some of the theories behind his system and spells out some of its implications.

The Holwellian Restoration

Michael John Franklin has called Holwell's contrast between "contemporary, complicated and degenerated Hindu custom and ritual and the purity of an original monotheism . . . characteristic of the deistic position of many of the eighteenth-century British pioneers of Indology, including Alexander Dow and, to a lesser extent, many of the Asiatic Society members, such as Wilkins and Jones" (Holwell 2000:xv). But was Holwell a deist? He defended himself against people who, on account of his analysis of Christianity's degeneration, "unjustly" accused him "of *Deism*, according to the common acceptation of the phrase" (Holwell 1771:3.90) and explained:

> But as we think we have as indisputable a right as Dr. *Clarke* or others, to extend or give *a new* signification to the word *Deist*, so we pronounce, that a man may, with strict propriety, be *an orthodox Christian Deist*; that is, that he may, *consistently*, have a firm faith in *the unity of the Godhead, and in the pure and original doctrines of Christ*. In this sense alone we glory in avowing ourself—A CHRISTIAN DEIST. (p. 91)

Holwell's "deism" is certainly of a very particular kind. While he adopted many objections against Christianity that were aired by deists, his (and Ilive's) system was of a kind that would enrage deists, as it was completely based on events known only through revelation. The tale of the first creation, the angels, their fall, the creation of rehabilitation station earth, and so forth can only be known with divine help:

> To a notion so universal in the first times, we think ourselves warranted in giving the title of a primitive truth; which must have had unerring fact, and a divine revelation for its source and foundation, as well as the other primitive truths of the rebellion, fall, and punishment of part of the angelic host, under the instigation and leading of an arch apostate of the first rank; hence the *Moisasoor* of the Bramins; the *Arimanius* of the

Persians; the *Typhon* of the *Egyptians*, Greeks &c. and the *Satan* of the Christians. (pp. 40–41)

Though human reason can accept such explanations as more logical than alternative scenarios, one ultimately has to accept them as revealed. Deists usually rejected such special revelations, whether they were made to the Hebrews or the Indians; but for Ur-tradition movements, they are the life blood since their raison d'être is the restoration of "primitive truths" or original teachings that, to be restored, had to be known through some kind of transmission. This is exactly the role Holwell cut out for himself:

> God forbid it should be thought, from the tenor of these our disquisitions, that, with *Hobbes, Tindal, Bolingbroke*, and others, our intent is to sap the foundation, or injure the root of Christianity. Candor and benevolence avert from us so uncharitable and ill-grounded an imputation! On the contrary, our sole aim is to *restore* its purity and vigor, by having those luxuriant injurious branches and shoots lopped off and pruned, which have so obviously obstructed, stinted, and prevented its natural, universal growth and progress; and as we have assumed to ourselves the title of *the reformed church*, by judiciously and piously abjuring *some* of the impious, idolatrous extravagances and tenets of the church of *Rome*, let us boldly, *in the cause of God and his supremacy, uniformly* deserve the character we have assumed.

Holwell's reformist "Christian deism" may thus better be called an Indo-Christian Ur-tradition. Restoring Christianity's "purity and vigor" was for Holwell tightly linked to the "primitive truths," and these truths were only insufficiently explained in the Old Testament.

> From all that has hitherto been advanced . . . three most important truths may be clearly gathered. Imprimis, that the FIRST and LAST revelation of God's will, that is to say, the *Hindoo* and the *Christian* dispensation, are the most perfect that have been promulged to offending man; secondly, that the FIRST was to a moral certainty the original doctrines, and terms of restoration, delivered from God himself by the mouth of his first created BIRMAH to mankind at their first creation in the *form of man*; and that, after many successive ages in sin, and every kind of wickedness, GOD, in his tender mercy, reminded mankind of *their true state*

and nature, of their *original sin*; and by the descent of BRAMAH, gave to the *Hindoos the first written* manifestation of his will, which (by the common fate of all oral traditions), had most probably, from various causes, been effaced from their minds and memories: Thirdly, that every intermediate system of religion in the world between that of BRAMAH and CHRIST are corruptly branched from the *former*, as is to demonstration evident, from their being founded on, and partaking of, with more or less purity those *primitive truths*. (p. 71)

With this *coup de grâce* the Mosaic dispensation was discarded as a corrupt derivate of the older Indian one, and as a result Holwell's *Shastah* became officially the ultimate Old Testament of Christianity. This also meant that it had to form the basis for any true restoration since it alone contains "the original doctrines, and terms of restoration" that God himself revealed to the Indians and took care to preserve in Holwell's *Shastah* (p. 71). Even the mission of Christ became a confirmation of the *Shastah*'s original doctrines:

The above, we think, will suffice to prove, that the *mission of Christ* is the strongest confirmation of the authenticity and divine origin of the *Chartah Bhade Shastah of Bramah*; and that they *both* contain all *the great primitive truths* in their original purity that constituted *the first and original religion*; and that the very ancient scriptures now under our consideration, exhibit also the strongest conviction of the truth of the celestial origin of *Christ's* mission. (pp. 74–75)

The portrayal of the *Shastah* as the basis for a thorough reformation of Christianity is not simply a by-product of having found an ancient Indian text but rather a result of Holwell's religious restoration project that included the production of an Old Testament that was more compatible with Ilive's, Berrow's, and Holwell's views. It is thus a mistake to assume that Holwell first translated the *Shastah* and subsequently developed increasingly strange interpretations, as Franklin suggests:

In the third volume of *Interesting Historical Events*, published in 1771, his speculation became more confident; Hinduism encapsulated "to a moral certainty the original doctrines, and terms of restoration, delivered by God himself from the mouth of his first created Birmah to mankind at his first creation of man." The Hindu scriptures not only completed the

Biblical revelation, but eclipsed it in priority and comprehensiveness; indeed, in the words of Trautmann, "By the end of the book Holwell has completely rewritten Christianity with the help of Hinduism," in the construction of a species of pre-Mosaic deism. (Holwell 2000:xv)

According to the scenario proposed in this chapter, the course of events was exactly inverse. Holwell's "speculation" was present from the beginning and essentially consisted in Jacob Ilive's new creation story (involving multiple worlds, angels, their fall, and their rehabilitation on planet earth) and his particular interpretation of Christianity. The Indian part of the story began when Holwell detected, inspired by Ilive's theory and possibly prodded by Ramsay's *Travels of Cyrus* and Abraham Roger's short version of Couto, a similar scenario in Western descriptions of the first Veda and set out to find this text. "Rewriting Christianity" was thus in my opinion not the *outcome* of a long process but rather its *starting point*; and Holwell's "Hindu scriptures" did not result in a rewriting of Christianity, but the rewriting of Christianity resulted in the creation of Holwell's "Hindu scriptures" that had to serve as an "improved," "older," "Indian" Old Testament.

In his third volume of 1771, Holwell delivered what he had already announced on the title page of the 1765 volume: his interpretation of transmigration ("A DISSERTATION on the METEMPSYCHOSIS, commonly, though erroneously, called the PYTHAGOREAN Doctrine"). In 1765 he had already announced that this volume would contain "A dissertation on the *Gentoo* doctrine of *metempsychosis*; improperly called *Pythagorean*, by all who have wrote on this subject, hitherto so little understood" (Holwell 1765:1.15). Ilive had not discussed delinquent angel souls in animals. But in India, transmigration or metempsychosis involves all animal bodies, and what Holwell read in Lord (1630), Roger (1651), Kircher (1667), Baldaeus (1762), and other sources about Indian religion was chock-full of transmigration stories that feature animals, for example, the famous incarnation of Vishnu into a boar (which Chumontou denounced in the *Ezour-vedam*). This was Holwell's extension of Ilive's system, and it was, of course, already firmly embedded both in Holwell's *Shastah* and his commentary of 1767.

What was new in the third volume of 1771 was Holwell's explicit identification of Christ as the *Birmah*—which is not at all heterodox if one accepts the congruence of the old (Indian) and new (Christian) dispensation:

This being premised, it is no violence to faith, if we believe that *Birmah* and *Christ* is one and the same individual coelestial being, the first begotten of the Father, who has most probably appeared at *different* periods of time, in *distant* parts of the earth, under *various* mortal forms of humanity, and denominations: thus we may very rationally conceive, that it was by the mouth of *Christ* (stiled *Birmah* by the easterns), that God delivered the *great primitive truths* to man at his creation, as infallible guides for his conduct and *restoration*: but the purity of *these truths* being effaced by time, and the industrious influence of *Satan*, assisted by the natural unhappy bent of the human soul to evil, it became necessary that they should be given on *record* to a nation that was most probably at that period much more extensive than we can at present form any idea of; and it appears as near to demonstration as a circumstance of this nature can admit of, that it was owing to this *divine revelation* delivered *to them*, that this people acquired so justly that early reputation for wisdom and theology, which the whole learned world has ascribed to them: but this by the bye. (pp. 80–81)

Thus, the messages of the *Shastah* and of Christ merge, and the task of a true reformer of Christianity is shown to consist in restoring "*once more* the true spirit of those *primitive truths*, which were, as the *first* and *last* grace of GOD, delivered . . . originally by BIRMAH, and subsequently by CHRIST, *the one and the same individual, first begotten by the Father* (p. 90). The "*pure original doctrines of Christ*" were thus first recorded in the *Shastah*, and it is "in this sense alone" that Holwell glories in avowing himself to be "A CHRISTIAN DEIST" (p. 91)!

Holwell's conception of Christ is not a creation of the late 1760s or early 1770s; rather, its groundwork is carefully laid in his introduction to the *Shastah* (1767:2.6–8) and must have been an old conviction of his. The identity of Birmah and Christ also ensures that the creation story of the *Shastah* is far more divine than that of Moses: unlike the Pentateuch it is "clogged with no difficulties, *no ludicrous unintelligible circumstances* or *inconsistencies*" (p. 114)—at least, in Holwell's eyes, who must have known it best.

Holwell's view of metempsychosis, too, was deeply rooted in the old convictions that he had expressed in the *Shastah* and its commentary. He held that both animal and human bodies are prison cells for delinquent angels. The difference is that animal bodies are cells reserved for punishment, while human bodies are transition cells with the possibility of eventual release:

In the *first* it [the delinquent angel] may be said to be in *a close prison*, and in the last, a prisoner more *at large*, and capable of working out its full and *final liberty*; a privilege it cannot obtain by issuing from the mortal brute form, which is destined to be its state of *punishment* and *purgation*, as before observed, and that of *man only*, its state of *trial* and *probation*. (p. 142)

In support of this idea, Holwell cited Berrow's opinion that "every organized body, as well in the brute as in the rational" can be "an allotted *temporary* prison for a *pre-delinquent* soul" and that this is "*an hypothesis, than which there cannot I think be one more rational*" (p. 125). In short, the souls of animals are also delinquent angels since "every brute is animated with *a soul* identical to *his* [man's] *own*"; therefore, God's command "*Thou shalt do No murder*" must also apply to animals (p. 148).

Since the dire state of our world could not be entirely explained by the delinquent angel story, Holwell was forced to posit another fall and degeneration, this time on earth. This fall happened when man began to slaughter and devour animals, which is "*one of the great roots of physical and moral evil in the world*" (p. 154). It entailed "a train of monstrous, unnatural, violent, and consequently ungovernable passions, . . . lusts of every kind and species, ambition, avarice, envy, hatred, and malice &c." (p. 161) and was all the result of a ruse of *Moisasoor* or *Satan* (p. 162). In conjunction with the ingestion of alcohol, all kinds of moral evils came to dominate the world; and only man's return "to his natural, primitive, simple aliments" can make his passions subside (p. 168). By contrast vegetarianism, as practiced in India, offers "a well-grounded hope of the renewal and restoration of the *primitive age*, of purity and holiness" (p. 169).

But Holwell also saw other problems in rehab station earth, for example, commerce, "that *bane* (falsely called the cement) of mankind" that leads "to invasions, fraud, and blood" (p. 169), and priests who set the example of "killing and eating the rational brute creation, and guzzling vinous, &c. potations" (p. 171). The thorough reform envisaged by Holwell was multifaceted and threatened to affect many unsuspecting citizens:

Lawyers, and their mischievous train of retainers, will have no employment.—Physicians and their coadjutors, upon the restoration of the human body to its original nature, will, in the second generation at least, have no friendly disease for their support.—Wine-merchants, distillers, brewers, vintners, dealers in spiritous liquors, cooks, (those dangerous instruments of luxury, disease and death) and butchers, &c. will all be turned a-drift, and be forced to seek for other means of subsistence. When we become, *bona fide*, Christians, the art and destructive practice of war would cease to be the bane of mankind, and the inoffensive brute creation; and a numerous race of able-bodied beings, who have hitherto been employed only to work out the perdition of the species, would contribute to their support and maintenance, by being employed in the cultivation of the lands of the state they belong to; a work they would most certainly prefer to the trade of spilling the blood of their fellow-creatures, *they know not why*, or in support of the tyranny and wanton ambition of others. (pp. 207–8)

Holwell's mission to "rescue the originally untainted manners, and religious worship of a very ancient people from gross misrepresentation" (1767 Dedication) was thus at the same time a mission to rescue Christianity and lead it back to the pure primitive truths as formulated in the *Shastah*. Holwell's third volume ends with his reform advice for Great Britain and Ireland and their "clergy of every denomination" (pp. 214ff.), his proposal for the abolition of the Athanasian and Nicene Creeds, and the correction of the Apostolic Creed (p. 221). While it remains unclear how mere "prison reforms" would affect God's eternal jurisdiction and the restoration of angels to their original home, the *Shastah*-based reforms proposed by Holwell would certainly ameliorate the situation on rehabilitation station earth in general and the British Isles in particular:

On the whole, we should become a new people: by quick gradations the pure spirit of *Christ's* doctrines would take root in our hearts; *power* would no longer constitute the *rule of justice*; the *primitive truths* and the *primitive age* would be restored; mankind, who has from that period hitherto been, by nature, principle, and practice, *very devils*, would revert to a perfect sense of their original dignity and angelic source, and no longer disgrace it; all jarring sects would be reconciled; peace and harmony would return to the earth; an effectual stop would be put to the carnage of man and brute; and *all united*, would produce *a sure and happy transmigration to eternity.*—GREAT BRITAIN AND IRELAND would blaze out as *the torch of righteousness* to all the world; her nations would prosper; her people be happy; their *pious flame* would be *caught* by their neighboring states, and from thence be spread over the face of the whole earth; and THE KINGDOM OF SATAN WOULD BE NO MORE. (pp. 222–23)

Fifteen years after the publication of the third volume of his *Interesting events*, Holwell gave his dwindling readership some additional advice. Although he had in his *Shastah* carefully formulated that God "governs creation only by a *general* providence resulting from first determined and fixed principles" (Holwell 1767:2.31) and had thus excluded any teaching of *particular* providence from the oldest divine revelation, there were still stubborn people who held this stupid opinion.

The Shastah Eclipsed by Hymns

The 1786 *Dissertations on the origin, nature, and pursuits of intelligent beings, and on divine providence, religion, and religious worship* begins with an apology for the "variations of sentiment . . . when contrasted with earlier productions submitted to the public eye," and these variations are explained by the "increase of years, experience, observation, and (we hope!) just reflection" (Holwell 1786:6). The most striking change is that Holwell never once mentions the *Shastah* by name. The first section quotes "the *most ancient Scripture*; at least, as far as our imperfect records tell" (p. 7).

This remark about "imperfect records" is very interesting and might confirm my hypothesis about the redaction of the text. Holwell's quotation reproduces the beginning of the second section of the *Shastah*, which deals with God's creation of the angels and features the memorable words: "These beings then, were not. The Eternal One willed, and they were; He formed them in part of his own essence capable of perfection, but with the powers of imperfection, both dependant on their voluntary election" (pp. 7–8). This was an absolutely central passage for Holwell's theory of free will and the origin of evil, and he had quoted it many times as their textual basis and proof. From 1767 onward, this passage was always presented as a literal translation from the *Shastah* with quotation marks at the beginning of every line, and this is the manner in which it is also reproduced almost twenty years later in his last book. But in the entire book this is the only *Shastah* quotation—and it is introduced by specifying that "the words and sentiments of the *most ancient Scripture*" are not based on God's Indian revelation but rather Holwell's "imperfect records"! If this crucial *Shastah* passage was based on Holwell's "imperfect records," was there *any* part of his *Shastah* that was *not* based on such "imperfect records"? In his last book, Holwell avoids further quotations from the *Shastah* and keeps using words like "presumption," "conviction," and "hypothesis":

> It has been for some time evident to the reader, that our chain of reasoning [about delinquent angels on probation] is founded on the presumption and full conviction, that the *souls* or *spirits*, animating every mortal organised form, are the identical apostate angels; but should any stumble at this pleasing, flattering, comfortable hypothesis, they are at liberty to reject it; as our essential arguments are equally applicable to *all*, considered as rational beings only. (p. 12)

What would a Christian say if a priest said that he or she was "at liberty to reject" the Bible? It appears that toward the end of his life Holwell had more or less abandoned his *Shastah*. While holding fast to all essential elements of his theory, he keeps saying things like "even if we totally give up this hypothesis as merely ideal" (p. 14), "according with our hypothesis" (p. 17), and "it is most consistent with reason and probability" (p. 23). What had happened to the *Shastah*? Had Holwell seen a copy of the first publication of a Sanskrit classic, Wilkins's *The Bhagvat-Geeta, or Dialogues of Kreeshna and Arjoon* that appeared in 1785, just when Holwell was working on his last book? Or had he buckled under the weight of criticism of his theories?

At any rate, in his 1786 book Holwell once more presented an outline of his system, which had little changed since he poured it into the *Shastah* on the basis of his "imperfect records." But Holwell's reform mission, very much apparent in the *Shastah* and its commentary, was alive and well. He confessed that his "former labours tended to establish the sacred doctrine of the UNITY and SUPREMACY of the GODHEAD which . . . the liturgy and worship of every Christian Church palpably opposed and discountenanced" but reassured his readers that he did not "wish the abolition of churches, the priesthood, or religious worship" but rather "to see them all reduced to such as standard as may do honour to God, and be consistent with reason, true piety, and propriety" (p. 70). Claiming to be "of no particular sect whatsoever, but an adorer of One God, in *spirit* and *truth*, and an humble follower and subscriber to the *unadulterated* precepts and doctrines of CHRIST" (p. 72), Holwell now surprised his readers with yet another theodicy and declared "without reserve . . . that all the evils with which mankind has been pestered in all ages, sprung from an undue *pre-eminence, power*, and *emoluments* . . . granted to the priest-hood" (pp. 75–76).

Accordingly, his first propositions for reform were that "the dignified Clergy under every denomination, be divested of all Rank, Precedence, and Title, in the Church and State" and that "all endowments of whatsoever kind, annexed to Cathedrals, Churches, Chapels, and Colleges, be seques-tered, *restored*, and appropriated to the relief of the exigencies of the state, and heave burdens of the people" (pp. 79–80). All ordinations and degrees, too, should be abolished and "a considerable reduction shall be made in the number of churches" (pp. 80–81). Only one incumbent per church should remain on a fixed salary, and sacked priests should get a retirement fee (pp. 81–83). The liturgy, being "incompatible with the true Christian religion, as dictated by its founder," should be totally reformed and no adoration whatso-ever offered to Christ: adoration "is *only* due to *his* God, and *our* God, to *his* Father, and *our* Father, which is in heaven" (pp. 91–93). The Lord's Supper may still be held, but all elements that "manifestly impeached the UNITY of the GODHEAD" (such as blasphemously calling Christ "God of God, Light of Light, very God of very God") must be removed (pp. 98–99). Making "the innocent and immaculate Christ . . . the scape-goat for the remission of sins and salvation" would no more be permitted, and neither would spilling blood in his name (p. 100).

In this manner Holwell revised the sacraments and denounced the ab-surdities of established liturgies that are just more proofs that we are "*the very apostate angelic beings* that are transmigrating through all animated organised mortal forms" (p. 119). Holwell's reform was designed to "work a happy change in favour of the miserable brute creation, who are looked upon and treated as mere material machines" rather than as "two children born of the same parents" (p. 120). "*Sacred musick*" would still be allowed in churches during Holwell's New Liturgy "conducted in the Cathedral stile" (pp. 121–22), and the remaining clergy should receive new uniforms: "We wish to see the *dismal black* banished, the officiating vestments of the Doctors in Divin-ity sumptuously ornamented, and their common habit *purple*, distinguished as the *uniform* of the Church; which colour should be prohibited to all other ranks" (p. 123).

The last section of Holwell's last book even proposes "A new liturgy; or, form of common prayer" in which, for example, the Lord's Prayer is prefaced by a hymn that identifies the faithful as delinquent angels:

To the Lord our God
Belongeth mercy and forgiveness,
Although we have *rebelled* against him;
Neither have we obeyed
The voice of the LORD our God,
To walk in his laws, which he left before us.

Holwell also included rhymed angelic anthems and choruses, for example, the chorus:

THE Lord descended from above,
And bow'd the heavens so high;
And underneath his feet he cast
The darkness of the sky.

On cherubs and on cherubims
Full royally he rode:
And on the wings of mighty winds
Came flying all abroad.

Thus Holwell fought until the end of his life for a worthy cause: the restoration of the religion of paradise. The crusade had officially begun with the publication of the *Shastah*, which in more than one sense came straight from paradise. But Holwell's mission as a reformer changed little over the years. In 1786 his aim was still identical to that which twenty years earlier he had so skillfully woven into the oldest revelation from India, the sacred scripture of his crusade:

to defend the honour and dignity of our Creator, from a fatal *misconception*: to expose the fallacy, inadequacy, and inconsistency, of all Christian religious worship: to extricate mankind from the superstitious, abject slavery they have for ages groaned under, to a *tribe* of their own species; to arraign the folly and inutility of what are called arts and sciences, and to stimulate the genius, study, and abilities of men, to more worthy and useful pursuits: to relieve the present and future exigencies of the state, and heavy burdens of the people, by a most equitable and necessary measure: and finally, to institute a form of worship more worthy of our God, and of ourselves. (pp. 147–48)

The Invention of Hinduism

In academic circles the debate about the "invention" of "Hinduism" has been so fashionable in recent times that Donald S. Lopez found that "one of the ways that scholars of Hinduism may be distinguished from experts on other religions at the annual meeting of the American Academy of Religion is by their overdeveloped pectoral muscles, grown large from tracing quotation marks in the air whenever they have mentioned 'Hinduism' over the past ten years" (2000:832). One name that is remarkably absent in this discussion is that of Holwell, himself a master of quotation marks. For example, Brian K. Pennington's 2005 book *Was Hinduism Invented? Britons, Indians, and the Colonial Construction of Religion* postulates that "a seismic shift" in the British perception of Hindu religions traditions happened "sometime between 1789 and 1832" yet does not mention Holwell even once. Holwell's name is equally notable for its absence in Richard King's *Orientalism and Religion* of 1999. Will Sweetman's otherwise interesting study *Mapping Hinduism: "Hinduism" and the Study of Indian Religions, 1600–1776* does not even list Holwell's three-volume *Interesting historical events* (1765–71) in its bibliography. However, he mentions that the Cambridge University library copy of a 1779 reedition of its second and third volumes carries on its spine the inscription "Holwell's Gentooism" (Sweetman 2003:56); that Holwell had a role in making "Gentoo" a common term to refer to the non-Muslim population of India (p. 80); and that the concept of "a unified pan-Indian religion" was already "firmly established by the 1770s, when 'Holwell's Gentooism' appeared," whereas the word "Hindooism" was first used in 1787 (p. 163). Though Sweetman does not claim a causal connection between this "Gentooism" or "Hindooism" and the geographical "conception of India as a region," he finds that the "concept of 'Hinduism' and the concept of 'India' in its modern sense, are coeval" (p. 163).

The question whether Hinduism was invented or discovered may posit a false alternative. R. N. Dandekar argued that

> Hinduism can hardly be called a religion at all in the popularly understood sense of the term. Unlike most religions, Hinduism does not regard the concept of god as being central to it. Hinduism is not a system of theology—it does not make any dogmatic affirmation regarding the nature of god. . . . Similarly, Hinduism does not venerate any particular person as its sole prophet or as its founder. It does not also recognize any

particular book as its absolutely authoritative scripture. Further, Hinduism does not insist on any particular religious practice as being obligatory, nor does it accept any doctrine as dogma. Hinduism can also not be identified with a specific moral code. Hinduism, as a religion, does not convey any definite or unitary idea. (Dandekar 1971:237; quoted in Sweetman 2003:33)

Whether one agrees with all of this or not, it is clear that at some point in history exactly these characteristics were projected on the dominant religion of the Indians and that this is how "Gentooism" or "Hinduism" as a "religion in the popularly understood sense" was invented. Its inventor, I propose, is Mr. John Zephaniah Holwell, and the year of this invention is 1766 when Holwell wrote his second volume. This was indeed a creative act and not just a discovery of something that was there for all to see and understand. In this sense—and for Holwell—it is therefore appropriate to speak of a "creation" or "invention" of Hinduism. It only was a far more creative creation than even constructivists could have dreamed.

For *this* kind of religion one needs, as Dandekar rightly says, an authoritative *scripture*—and what could be more authoritative than Holwell's *Shastah*, delivered by God personally and first promulgated exactly in 3100 B.C.E.? Then one needs a *god*—Holwell's creative "God is ONE" at the very beginning of the Shastah who was thoughtfully equipped with an urge to reveal himself and limited liability. Furthermore, a decent religion needs an excellent *founder*—Holwell's "spirit or essence of God," *Birmah*, who "descended to the delinquent angels, and made known unto them the mercy and immutable sentence, that God their creator had pronounced and registered against them" (Holwell 1767:10). This constituted another essential element, namely, that of *transmission*. *Birmah* transmitted the divine sentence to *Bramah* who descended to *Indostan* and translated it into Sanskrit to form the very text that Holwell claimed to have partially translated (p. 12). This *Birmah* is, *nota bene*, the Indian or rather Holwellian preexistent incarnation of Christ.

Dandekar also did not mention that it is absolutely crucial for such a religion to have the longest possible *history*. Previous researchers of Indian religion soon got so lost in the millions of years of Indian world ages and scores of unknown sacred scriptures that they were unable to find a foothold that somehow related to accepted chronology. But Holwell invented one, and we should not underestimate the impact of this invention. For decades, the date of the *Shastah* was a pillar of "Indian" chronology, and the neat succession of Text I (3100 B.C.E.), Text II (2100), Text III (1600) and the dating of the Veda after 1600 B.C.E. were a novelty that stunned even European specialists (for example, Anquetil-Duperron, as explained in the next chapter). Additionally, Holwell's simple four-step genealogy of Indian sacred literature also seemed to explain important regional, doctrinal, and historical differences, for example, the variations between the North and South that were due to a schism invented by Holwell.

Then there is, of course, the *dogma* question for which Holwell, inspired by Ilive and Couto, found a brilliantly simple solution, namely, the delinquent angel story wedded to transmigration. This was, as we have seen in Chapter 5, already touted by Ramsay as the very essence of "pagan mythology" and a core element of God's original revelation. Of course, this dogma needed to be revealed and transmitted, and this was the aim of Holwell's *Shastah* including its "translation." The question that bugged Ilive so much and that he did not find answered in the Old Testament, namely, who we are and why we are here, was answered in dogmatic and systematic fashion in the *Shastah*: we are delinquent angels incarcerated in mortal bodies and live in a giant penitentiary called earth in order to atone for our past rebellion, and as we go through countless transmigrations we might earn the right to return to our original heavenly homeland.

With regard to *practice*, vegetarianism and the cult of cows (which were both linked to delinquent angels and their rehabilitation on earth) were central; but the *Shastah* also contains other precepts such as the abstinence from alcoholic drinks that, one would assume, should promote the kind of peace and tranquility that reigns in Holwell's idyllic Bisnapore.

Another important topic that Dandekar failed to mention is the question of *origins*. Any religion that hopes to give a direction to people's lives must teach in one way or another where we come from, where we are, and where we are bound; and the answer to the first of these questions is usually decisive for the whole enterprise. S. N. Balagangadhara has defined religion as "an explanatorily intelligible account of the Cosmos and itself" and concluded that "Indian traditions could not possibly be religions because the issue of the origin of the world cannot properly be raised there" (1994:384, 398; quoted in Sweetman 2003:37). Regardless of the validity of this definition and its application to "Hinduism," one notes that Holwell and his *Shastah* delivered exactly the kind of content that would turn this "Indian tradition" into a "religion" that, in Holwell, is usually called "Gentooism" but soon became known as "Hindooism."

Holwell's portrait of "Gentooism" was so powerful and influential[24] exactly *because* it was an invention, and an essentially *European* one at that. It did not really need to take Indian history, cultic diversity, philosophy, textual problems, and so on into account and did not get lost in details and mazes with thousands of divinities because it was built on a preconceived idea that guaranteed a unified, compact design. Everything turned around God and the creation, fall, and restoration of angels, and that is exactly what the *Shastah* is all about. Holwell's influence was boosted by the free publicity that his book received courtesy of Voltaire and by its translation into French (1768) and then into German (1778). It is true that readers of Voltaire with a sense of humor will not overlook the sarcasm of some of his remarks about Holwell's scheme; yet, as was pointed out in Chapter 1, a consensus that Voltaire had promoted the *Ezour-vedam* and Holwell's *Shastah* in good faith reigned until today even among specialists. Now it appears that both men propagated a custom-made Hinduism to support their reformist ideology. Though their aims were at odds, Voltaire's crusade boosted Holwell's and vice-versa, and their exaggerated claims of Indian antiquity and portraits of "Indian" religion significantly influenced the European perception of the origin of culture and religion. An example of such influence is Herder who, dissatisfied with Dow, raved in 1772 about Holwell's *Shastah* (Faust 1977:146) and soon introduced Brahmins as guides to humanity's origins—a move that some decades later inspired a generation of German romantics. Through their inventive campaigns and sensationalist presentation of supposedly ancient "Indian" texts, Holwell and Voltaire almost single-handedly created the basis for Indomania.[25]

Chapter 7

Anquetil-Duperron's Search for the True Vedas

In 1762, after his return from India, Abraham Hyacinthe Anquetil-Duper-ron (1731–1805) wrote to one of his former classmates at a Jansenist seminary in Utrecht, Holland:

> To deepen the understanding of the history of ancient peoples, to elabo-rate the revolutions which peoples and languages undergo, to visit re-gions unknown to the rest of the people where art has preserved the character of the first ages: you will perhaps remember, with distress and sighing about my follies, that these subjects have always been the focus of my attention. (Schwab 1934:18)

From his youth, Anquetil-Duperron's interest in the world's first ages was connected to a deep religiosity that put him on the path to priesthood. It is probably during his theological studies at the Sorbonne that young Anquetil-Duperron wrote a manuscript of about a hundred pages that is now part of his dossier at the Bibliothèque Nationale in Paris.[1] It is titled "Le Parfait théologien" (The Perfect Theologian), but the word "Parfait" is doubly struck through. The title is emblematic for Anquetil-Duperron's career; and the manuscript, ignored even by Anquetil-Duperron's biographers,[2] merits a look.

The ~~Perfect~~ Theologian

Anquetil-Duperron starts out by insisting that theology is "a science like philosophy" but must, unlike philosophy, stay within the limits circumscribed by "a genuine revelation, the mysteries of religion, and several dogmas transmitted to us by apostolic tradition," which form the bedrock that no one is allowed to question (p. 369r). Since natural religion is also a subject of philosophy, the proper realm of theology is that of revelation (p. 371r). Yet the idea that people have of theology is far too narrow, and Anquetil-Duperron wants in this manuscript to show how broad and deep theology must be. Chapter 3 is titled "That a theologian must be almost universal" and argues that, faced with many pretended revelations, a theologian must be equipped to judge their claims. This indicates the need for knowledge of several languages in order to read the original texts; of history to understand their context; of geography to understand their setting; and of poetry to appreciate their style. "All such knowledge thus forms part of theology" (p. 373v). Furthermore, a real theologian should know not only the Old and New Testaments and all related languages but everything ever divinely revealed and transmitted (p. 375r). He must also question Old Testament authorship:

> Is Moses really the first of all writers, as has been asserted by some fathers? If that was the case, where did he get his creation story and deluge story and even the Abraham story from? Did he prophesy the past, as a monk has recently argued? Or has he only reported things that were known in his time and that he could have learned from the tradition of the patriarchs because of the long lifespan of the first humans, as the majority of authors think? But who can say if there were not other historians before Moses, and earlier books? (p. 381v)

A theologian worth the name has to go to the bottom of all these questions, research all opinions and sources ancient and modern, and must especially "discover the systems of Chaldaea, Phoenicia, and Egypt" (p. 393r). Another "thorny question" that "requires infinite caution" is that of Paradise and Adam's sin:

> What is this delicious garden of which we are told? Where was it? What has become of it? 1. Was it on the moon or in the air, as some fathers have believed? 2. Was it exclusively spiritual or corporeal, or both together as St. John Damascene thought? 3. Was it in the Orient? In Syria? In Armenia? Or close to India [vers le mogol], where one ordinarily places it? 4. Or was it the entire habitable earth, as some theologians have asserted? 5. How can one reconcile what Genesis says about these

four rivers [of paradise] with geography as it is now known? 6. Could the location have changed? What proofs are there of that? 7. If there is no proof: must one take recourse to parables? (p. 393v)

Such is the kind of questions over which young Anquetil-Duperron pondered. He asked himself why Moses put this narration of Adam's sin in the book of Genesis, why the angels rebelled, whether the deluge was universal, and other pressing questions (pp. 394r–v). A perfect theologian must go beyond the biblical text and learn about the histories of other peoples, including the Greeks and the Chinese, and about their religions and arts (p. 407r). With regard to languages, a theologian ought to master not only standard Hebrew and rabbinical Hebrew but also Greek, Syriac, Arabic, and Ethiopian (pp. 414v–41v), and he should also study the histories and philosophies of these peoples. After dozens of pages filled with such *desiderata*, Anquetil-Duperron begins to deal with the critical analysis of concrete texts, but this is where the manuscript abruptly ends (p. 481r).

Anquetil-Duperron's early manuscript already shows his interest in ancient textual sources and his boundless thirst for knowledge, and it defines the field of revelation as his working area. The task the young man had set for himself seems daunting, but his search for genuine ancient records of God's earliest revelations was to carry him far beyond the Middle East and become a drawn-out quest for the Indian Vedas that lasted from his youth to his death in 1805. His last publication—a posthumously published annotated translation of Father Paulinus a Sancto Bartholomaeo's *Viaggio alle Indie orientali* (Voyage to the East Indies, 1796) that appeared in 1808—shows the end point of Anquetil-Duperron's theological journey of a lifetime. Taking issue with Paulinus's statement that the *Ezour-vedam* was "composed by a missionary and falsely attributed to the brahmins" and that the Indians' conception of Brahma, Vishnu, and Shiva clearly shows "the materialism of the Indians" and their pagan philosophy (Paulinus a Sancto Bartholomaeo 1796:66), Anquetil-Duperron vigorously defended the *Ezour-vedam*'s genuineness ("a donkey can deny more than a philosopher can prove"[3]) as well as the orthodoxy of the Indian trinity:

The missionary [Paulinus] keeps forgetting that by his comparisons with the false Orpheus, the fake oracles of Zoroaster, Hermes, and the Egyptians he gives an air of falsity to the Indian dogmas. . . . It is no surprise that one finds the *trinity* in Plato, with the Egyptians, and possibly with the Pythagoreans: the earliest sages, the philosophers, have always been careful to preserve and meditate on the ancient truths. In the *Oupnek'hat* one finds the supreme Being, his word, his spirit. (Paulinus a Sancto Bartholomaeo 1808:3.419)

Anquetil-Duperron wrote that until Paulinus "makes positively known" who the author of the *Ezour-vedam* was "one cannot trust his magisterial assertions regarding erudition about India" (p. 120). But by the time this challenge was published, both Anquetil-Duperron (d. 1805) and Paulinus (d. 1806) were dead. In the meantime, several authors have faced that challenge, but so far the debate has ended inconclusively. The last word came from Ludo Rocher who, in his 1984 monograph on the *Ezour-vedam*, offers much interesting information but ends the discussion of authorship not with a culprit but with a list of suspects:

The question who the French Jesuit author of the EzV [*Ezour-vedam*] was we can only speculate on. Calmette was very much involved in the search for the Vedas; Mosac is a definite possibility; there may by some truth to Maudave's information on Martin; there is no way of verifying the references to de Villette and Bouchet. The author of the EzV may be one of these, but he may also be one of their many more or less well-known confreres. In the present state of our knowledge, we cannot go any further than that. (Rocher 1984:60)

In this chapter I will take up Anquetil-Duperron's challenge and offer my answer on the backdrop of a broader sequence of events: the European discovery of India's oldest sacred literature. How did Anquetil-Duperron come to regard the *Ezour-vedam* as genuine; and why could he, an ardent Christian, call Vedic texts "orthodox"?

Approaching the Vedas

Theological questions very much like those posed by young Anquetil-Duperron were *the* major motivation for the study of ancient languages and histories, and as textual critique and conflicts between secular (Chinese, Egyptian, etc.) and sacred (biblical) history stirred up debates in Europe, the study of ancient oriental languages and texts became increasingly important. Books possibly older than the Pentateuch were of special interest.

As we have seen, rumors circulated about the book of Enoch, which for a long time was regarded as possibly the oldest book in the world. It was coveted by eminent European intellectuals such as Reuchlin, Peiresc, and Kircher (Schmidt 1922) and stimulated the study of Ethiopian. Then the Jesuit figurists in China identified Enoch with Fuxi and the *Yijing* seemed for a while to be the world's oldest book. Its study stimulated the study of ancient Chinese texts and produced a number of excellent Sinologists like Prémare, Visdelou, Foucquet, and Gaubil.

India was also associated with Enoch's book since 1553 when Guillaume Postel suggested in *De originibus* that "treasures of antediluvian books" stored in India could include "the work of Enoch" (Postel 1553b:72). But scriptures of Indian rather than mideastern origin were also mentioned among the world's oldest. Henry Lord's 1630 book stated in the introduction that God gave *Brammon* "a Booke, containing the forme of diuine Worshippe and Religion" (p. 5). Since this divine work (which *Brammon* took to the East, "the most noble part of the world") reportedly was transmitted in the first world age, it must have been the world's oldest book; but it was lost at the end of the first *yuga*. In the second world age, after the great flood, God again "communicated Religion to the world" in "a book of theirs called the SHASTER, which is to them as their Bible, containing the grounds of their Religion in a written word" and was delivered "out of the cloud into the hand of *Bremaw*" (Lord 1630: Introduction). Lord's *Shaster* is said to consist of three tracts—a book of precepts, the ceremonial law, and the observations of castes (p. 40)—of which Lord translated some parts garnished with his (mostly critical) comments. But this information got relatively little publicity in Europe.[4] The same author's "The Religion of the Persees" described the religion of the Parsees in India, who have a "Booke, deliuered to Zertoost [Zarathustra], and by him published to the Persians or Persees" (p. 27) and furnished translations of some extracts. Lord's two thin volumes, which are often bound together, deal exactly with the two major areas of Anquetil-Duperron's work more than a century later: his research on the oldest texts of Persian origin found in India's Parsee community at Surat and his work on ancient India's religious literature.

For people in search of the world's oldest books, India's mysterious Vedas had a particular attraction, even though—or perhaps because—information about them often consisted of little more than the names of its four parts and the assertion of great antiquity. Agostinho de Azevedo's report about the Vedas and Shastras of India found its way into Johannes Lucena's *Historia da Vida do Padre Francisco de Xavier* (1600) and Diogo do Couto's *Decada Quinta da Asia* (1612), and from there into other works including Holwell's (see Chapter 6). The report in the *Livro da Seita dos Indios Orientais* by the Jesuit Giacomo Fenicio from the early seventeenth century was plagiarized by Baldaeus (1672) and also got some publicity. However, both Fenicio's and Azevedo's data were based not on the Vedas but on other texts.[5]

In the seventeenth century, bits and pieces of information about the Vedas from Heinrich Roth/Kircher, François Bernier, Jean Baptiste Tavernier, and others were floating around, and even Johann Joachim MÜLLER's (1661–1733) (in)famous *De tribus impostoribus* contained a passage about them. The false date of 1598 on the original printed edition of these *Three Impostors*[6] led some researchers[6] to conclude that this book contained the earliest Western mention of the four Vedas; but Winfried Schröder has proved that the book is by Müller and was written almost a century later, in 1688 (Müller 1999; Mulsow 2002:119). Müller had been involved in oriental studies, and his Veda passage shows beautifully how competition by alternative revelations and older texts could be used to destabilize Christianity, whether in jest—as seems to have been his intention—or in earnest, as his readers understood it. Müller's passage about the Vedas occurs in the context of an attack on Christianity on the basis of competing revelations that form the basis of the sacred scriptures of the "three impostors" Moses, Jesus, and Mohammed:

> By a special revelation? Who are you to say this? Good God! What a hotchpotch of revelations! Do you rely on the oracles of the heathen? Already antiquity laughed about this. How about the testimony of your priests? I offer you others who contradict them. Hold a debate: but who will be the judge? And what will be the outcome of the controversy? You cite the writings of Moses, of the prophets, and of the apostles? The Koran will be held against you which on the basis of the ultimate revelation calls them corrupt; and its author boasts of having cut by divine miraculous intervention the corruptions and quarrels of the Christians with his sword, like Moses those of the heathens. (Österreichische Nationalbibliothek Wien, Cod. 19540, pp. 8–9)

After this argument of mutually contradictory absolute truth claims—which was already advanced in the thirteenth century by Roger Bacon in the context of his discussion of the religious debates in front of the great Khan—Müller brings up the delicate topic of chronology, which was much discussed after Martino Martini's publications of the 1650s:

Indeed, Mohammed subjugated Palestine by force, as had Moses, and both were guided by great miracles. And their followers oppose you, as do the Veda and the collections of the Brachmans that date from 14,000 years ago, to say nothing of the Chinese. You, who hide yourself in this corner of Europe dismiss these religions and deny their validity, and you are right to do so; but the others negate yours with the same ease. (p. 9)

This kind of "foreign" perspective was also adopted by the author of the *Letters by a Turkish Spy* which will be quoted below, and in the eighteenth century it was quite fashionable and used, for example, by Montesquieu in his *Lettres Persanes* and by Voltaire in many writings. Instead of making the "older-is-better" argument, however, Müller immediately undercuts the authority of even the oldest scriptures of the world:

And what miracle could not convince men if [they are so credulous as to believe] that the world has been born from a scorpion's egg, that the earth is carried on the head of a bull, and that the ultimate basis of things would be formed from the three Vedas if some jealous son of the Gods had not stolen the first three volumes? Our people would laugh about this, and this would be another argument for them in support of the soundness of their religion, even if it has no basis except in the brains of their priests. Besides, from where did they get those enormous amounts of scriptures, packed with lies, about the heathen gods? (p. 9)

At the end of the seventeenth century, the reputation of the Vedas and of Sanskrit for great antiquity was also reflected in the much-read *Letters writ by a Turkish Spy*, whose eight volumes were reprinted many times. The third volume contains the following observation that Holwell, among others, adduced in support of his idea of humanity's origin in India (Holwell 1771:3.157):

But that seems very strange which thou relatest, of a certain *Language* among the *Indians*, which is not vulgarly spoken; but that all their *Books* of *Theology*, and *Pandects* of their *Laws*, the *Records* of their *Nation*, and the *Treatises* of *Human Arts* and *Sciences* are written in it. And that this *Language* is taught in their *Schools, Colleges,* and *Academies,* even as *Latin* is among the *Christians.* I cannot enough admire at this; for, where and when was this *Language* spoken? How came it to be difus'd? There seems to be a Mystery in it, that none of their *Brachmans* can give any other Account of this, save, That it is the *Language,* wherein *God* gave, to the *first Creature* he made, the *four Books* of the *Law*: which according to their *Chronology,* was above Thirty Million Years ago. (Marana et al. 1723:3.171–72)

These "four Books of the Law" are of course the four Vedas. The continuation of this "Turkish Spy" letter beautifully shows the subversive potential of such news from the Orient at the end of the seventeenth century:

I tell thee, my dear Brother, this News has started some odd Notions in my Mind: For when I consider, That this *Language,* as thou sayest, Has nothing in it common with the *Indian* that is now spoken nor with any other *Language* of *Asia,* or the World; and yet, that it is a copious and regular *Language,* learne'd by *Grammar,* like the other *material Languages*; and that, in this *obsolete Language* Books are written, wherein it is asserted, That the *World* is so many Millions of Years old; I could almost turn *Pythagorean,* and believe, The *World* to be within a *Minute* of *Eternal.* And, where would be the Absurdity? Since *God* had equally the same infinite Power, Wisdom and Goodness, from all *Eternity,* as he had Five or Six thousand Years ago. What should hinder him then from exerting these *divine Attributes* sooner? What should retard him from drawing forth this glorious *Fabrick* earlier, from the *Womb* of *Nothing*? Suffer thy Imagination to start backwards, as far as thou canst, even to Millions of Ages, and yet thou canst not conceive a Time, wherein this fair unmeasurable *Expanse* was not stretch'd out. As if *Nature* her self had engraven on our Intellects, this *Record* of the *Worlds* untraceable *Antiquity,* in that our strongest, swiftest Thoughts, are far too weak and slow, to follow time back to its endless Origin." (p. 172)

De Nobili's Vedic Restoration Project

Since access to the Vedas was nearly impossible, most of the information about their content was pure fantasy. We have seen in the chapter on Holwell how easy it was to be misled by speculation. But a few missionaries (whose writings were mostly doomed to sleep in archives for several centuries) were in a position to consult vedic texts or question learned informants. The Jesuit Roberto DE NOBILI (1577–1656) obtained direct access to some Vedas from his teacher, a Telugu Brahmin called Shivadharma. He wrote that the four traditional Vedas are "little more than disorderly congeries of various opinions bearing partly on divine, partly on human subjects, a jumble where religious and civil precepts are miscellaneously put together" (Rubiés 2000:338). Having been told in 1608 that the fourth Veda was no longer extant, the missionary decided to proclaim himself "teacher of the fourth, lost Veda which deals with the question of salvation" (Županov 1999:116). De Nobili apparently believed, like his contemporary Matteo Ricci in China, that though original pure monotheism had degenerated into idolatry, vestiges of the original religion survived and could serve to regenerate the ancient creed under the sign of the Cross. After his failed experiment with Buddhist robes (see Chapter 1), Ricci adopted the dress of a Confucian scholar, asserted that the Chinese had anciently been pure monotheists, and proclaimed Christianity to be the fulfillment of the doctrines found in ancient Chinese texts. A few years later, Ricci's compatriot de Nobili presented himself in India as an ascetic "sannayasi from the North" and "restorer of 'a lost spiritual Veda'" (Rubiés 2000:339) who hailed from faraway Rome where the Ur-tradition had been best preserved. In his *Relação annual* for the year 1608, Fernão Guerreiro wrote on a similar line that he was studying Brahmin letters to present his Christian message as a restoration of the spiritual Veda, the true original religion of all countries, including India whose adulterated vestiges were the religions of Vishnu, Brahma, and Shiva (p. 344).

For de Nobili, the word "Veda" signified the spiritual law revealed by God. He called himself a teacher of *Satyavedam*, that is, the true revealed law, who had studied philosophy and this very law in Rome. He maintained that his was exactly the same law that "by God's order had been taught in earlier times by Saṃnyāsins" in India (Bachmann 1972:154). De Nobili thus had come to India to restore *satyavedam* and to bring back, as the title of his didactic Sanskrit poem says, "The Essence of True Revelation [satyavedam]" (Castets 1935:40). De Nobili's description of the traditional Indian Vedas clearly shows that he did not regard them as "genuine Vedas" or genuine divine revelations. That de Nobili was for a long time suspected of being the author of the *Ezour-vedam* is understandable because in that text Chumontou has fundamentally the same role as de Nobili: he exposes the degenerate accretions of the reigning clergy's "Veda," represented by the traditional Veda compiler Biache (Vyāsa), in order to teach them about *satyavedam*, the divine Ur-revelation whose correct transmission he represents against the degenerate transmission in the Vedas of the Brahmins. This "genuine Veda" had once upon a time been brought to India, but subsequently the Indians had forgotten it and instituted the false Veda that is now religiously followed. The common aim of de Nobili and of Chumontou was the restoration of the true, most ancient divine revelation (Veda) and the denunciation of the false, degenerated Veda that the Brahmins now call their own.

In the wake of Ricci in China and de Nobili in India, the desire to find and study ancient texts and to acquire the necessary linguistic skills to handle them was increasing both among China and India missionaries, and this desire was clearly linked to the idea of a common Ur-tradition and its local vestiges that could be put to use for "accommodation" or, as I prefer to call it, "friendly takeover." What we have observed in other chapters, namely, that religion is deeply linked to the beginnings of the systematic study of oriental languages and literatures, clearly also applies to India; and if such study produced wondrous Egyptian (Kircher) and Chinese figurist flowers in the seventeenth and early eighteenth centuries, the heyday of India in this respect was yet to come.

Calmette's Veda Purchase

At the beginning of the eighteenth century, Europeans in search of humanity's oldest texts received some enticing news in letters by Jesuit missionaries in India. For example, on January 30, 1709, Pierre de la Lane wrote in a letter that Indians are idolaters but also have some books that prove "that they had antiently a pretty distinct Knowledge of the true God." The missionary went on to quote the beginning of the *Panjangan* almanac that, as we saw in Chapter 1, was among the earliest materials that impressed Voltaire about India (Pomeau 1995:161). In John Lockman's English translation of 1743, this passage reads as follows:

> I worship that Being who is not subject to Change and Disquietude; that Being whose Nature is indivisible; that Being whose Simplicity admits of no Composition with respect to Qualities; that Being who is the Origin and Cause of all Beings, and surpasses 'em all in Excellency;

that Being who is the Support of the Universe, and the Source of the triple Power." (Lockman 1743:2.377–78)

Father de la Lane wrote that the majority of Indian books are works of poetry and that "the Poets of the Country have, by their Fictions, imperceptibly obliterated the Ideas of the Deity in the Minds of these Nations" (p. 378). But India also has far older books, especially the Veda:[7]

> As the oldest Books, which contained a purer Doctrine, were writ in a very antient Language, they were insensibly neglected, and at last the Use of that Tongue was quite laid aside. This is certain, with regard to their sacred Book called the *Vedam*, which is not now understood by their *Literati*; they only reading and learning some Passages of it by Heart; and these they repeat with a mysterious Tone of Voice, the better to impose upon the Vulgar. (pp. 378–79)

Such mystery, antiquity, and potential orthodoxy whetted the appetite of Europeans with an interest in origins and ancient religion. After Abbé Jean-Paul Bignon had been nominated to the post of director of the Royal Library in 1719 and of the special library at the Louvre in 1720 (Leung 2002:130), he gave orders to acquire the Vedas. But this was easier said than done. In 1730 a young and linguistically gifted Jesuit by the name of Jean CALMETTE (1693–1740), who had joined the Jesuit India mission in 1726, wrote about the difficulties:

> Those who for thirty years have written that the *Vedam* cannot be found were not completely wrong: there was not enough money to find them. Many people, missionaries, and laymen, have spent money for nothing and were left empty-handed when they thought they would get every- thing. Less than six years ago [in 1726] two missionaries, one in Bengal and the other one here [in Carnate], were duped. Mr. Didier, the royal engineer, gave sixty rupees for a book that was supposed to be the *Vedam* on the order of Father Pons, the superior of [the Jesuit mission of] Ben- gal. (Bach 1847:441)

But in the same letter Calmette announced that he was certain of having found the genuine Vedas:

The *Vedams* found here have clarified issues regarding other books. They had been considered so impossible to find that in Pondicherry many people could not believe that it was the genuine *Vedam*, and I was asked if I had thoroughly examined it. But the investigations I have made leave no doubt whatsoever; and I continue to examine them every day when scholars or young brahmins who learn the *Vedam* in the schools of the land come to see me and I make them recite it. I even recite together with them what I have learned from some text's beginning or from other places. It is the *Vedam*; there is no more doubt about this. (p. 441)

Calmette achieved this success thanks to a Brahmin who was a secret Christian, and in 1731 he reported having acquired all four Vedas, including the fourth that de Nobili had thought lost (p. 442). In 1732, Father le Gac mailed to Paris two Vedas written in Telugu letters on palm leaves, and the copying of the remaining two was ongoing (p. 442). From the early 1730s Father Calmette devoted himself intensively to the study of the Vedas and wrote on January 24, 1733:

Since the King has made the decision to form an Oriental library, Abbé Bignon has graced us with the honor of relying on us for research of Indian books. We are already benefiting much from this for the advancement of religion; having acquired by these means the essential books which are like the arsenal of paganism, we extract from it the weapons to combat the doctors of idolatry, and the weapons that hurt them the most are their own philosophy, their theology, and especially the four *Vedam* which contain the law of the brahmins and which India since time immemorial possesses and regards as the sacred book: the book whose authority is irrefragable and which derived from God himself. (Le Gobien 1781:13.394)

The opponents in this combat were mainly Brahmins who considered the Europeans worse than outcasts. Calmette explained: "Nothing is here more contrary to [our Christian] religion than the caste of *brahmins*. It is they who seduce India and make all these peoples hate the name of Christian" (p. 362). The label *Prangui*, which the Indians first gave to the Portuguese and with which "those who are ignorant about the different nations composing our colony designate all Europeans" (p. 347), was a major problem from the beginning of the mission, and the Jesuits' Sannyasi attire and "Brahmin from the North" identity were in part designed to avoid such ostracism. The fight against the Brahmin "ministers of the devil" who "never cease to pursue their plan to ruin both our church and the Christians who depend on it" (p. 363) is featured prominently in Calmette's letters, and it is clear that the Frenchman meant business when he spoke about stocking up an arsenal of weapons especially from the four Vedas for combating these doctors of idolatry.

The preparation consisted in the intensive study of Sanskrit and a survey of India's sacred literature, in particular, of the Vedas. Of course, Calmette was eager to find any possible allusion to Jesus and major events of the Old and New Testaments. He searched for textual traces of the deluge and asked himself whether Vishnu is Jesus, if *Chambelam* means Bethlehem, and if the Brahmins stem from the race of Abraham (pp. 379–85). But the study of Sanskrit was also useful for disputing with Brahmins and scholars:

> Up to now we have had little dealings with this kind of scholars; but since they noticed that we understand their books of science and their *Samouscroutam* [Sanskrit] language, they begin to approach us, and because they are intelligent and have principles, they follow us better than the others in dispute and agree more readily to the truth when they have nothing solid to oppose it. (p. 396)

Naturally, Calmette profited from the experience of other missionaries who had mastered difficult languages and were interested in antiquity, for example, Claude de Visdelou who resided in Pondicherry for three decades and was very familiar with missionary tactics and methods in China.[8] But even more important, in 1733 a learned fellow Jesuit by the name of Jean-François PONS (1698–1751) had joined Calmette in the Carnate mission. Pons and Calmette came from the same town of Rodez in southern France, had both joined the Jesuit novitiate in Toulouse, were both sent to India, and were both studying Sanskrit. Pons had arrived in India two years prior to Calmette, in 1724, and spent his first four years in the Carnate region. It was Pons who had tried to buy a copy of the Veda for 60 rupees in 1726, only to find out that he had fallen victim to a scam. From 1728 to 1733, he was superior of the Bengal mission, and it is during this time that he studied Sanskrit. As superior in Chandernagor he became an important channel for the European discovery of India's literature. He spent on behalf of Abbé Bignon and the Royal Library in Paris a total of 1,779 rupees for researchers, copyists, and manuscripts in Sanskrit and Persian. They included the Mahabharata in 17 volumes, 24 volumes of Puranas, 31 volumes about philology, 22 volumes about history and mythology, 7 volumes about astronomy and astrology, and 8 volumes of poems, among other acquisitions (Castets 1935:47). Though Pons was Calmette's junior by five years, he was thus more experienced and knowledgeable than his countryman when he joined the Carnate mission for a second time in 1733, and the two gifted missionaries could combine their efforts.

In 1735 Calmette described some of the benefits of the study of Sanskrit and the Vedas for his mission:

> Ever since their *Vedam*, which contains their sacred books, has been in our hands, we have extracted texts suitable for convincing them of the fundamental truths that ruin idolatry; because the unity of God, the characteristics of the true God, salvation, and reprobation are in the *Vedam*; but the truths that are found in this book are only sprinkled like gold dust on piles of dirt; because the rest consists in the principle of all Indian sects, and maybe the details of all errors that make up their body of doctrines. (Le Gobien 1781:13.437)

Vedic Talking Points and Broken Teeth

From the early 1730s Calmette thus collected—probably with the help of knowledgeable Indians and later of Pons—examples of "fundamental truths" as well as "details of all errors" from the Vedas. This was the first systematic effort by Europeans to study such a mass of ancient Indian texts; and it was not an easy task because the language of these texts proved to be so difficult that even most Indians were at a loss:

> What is surprising is that the majority of those who are its depositaries do not understand its meaning because it is written in a very ancient language, and the *Samouscroutam* [Sanskrit], which is as familiar to the scholars as Latin is among us, is not yet sufficient [for understanding] unless aided by a commentary both for the thought and for the words. It is called the *Maha Bachiam*, the great commentary.[9] Those who make that kind of book their study are first-rate scholars among them. (p. 395)

At the time there were only six active Jesuit missionaries in the whole Carnate region around Pondicherry (p. 391), but they were assisted by many more Indian catechists who were essential for the mission. The missionaries could not personally go to some regions because of Brahmin opposition and other reasons, and to preach there was a main task of these catechists. Calmette's objective in studying the Vedas was not a translation of any part of them. That would definitely have been impossible after just a few years of study, even with the help of Pons. The language of these texts, particularly that of earlier Vedas, was a tough nut to crack even for learned Indians. In a letter dated September 16, 1737, Calmette wrote to Father René Joseph de Tournemine in Paris:

> I think like you, reverend father, that it would have been appropriate to consult original texts of Indian religion with more care; but we did not have these books at hand until now, and for a long time they were considered impossible to find, especially the principal ones which are the four *Vedan*. It was only five or six years ago that, due to [the establishment of] an oriental library system for the King, I was asked to do research about Indian books that could form part of it. I then made discoveries that are important for [our] Religion, and among these I count the four *Vedan* or sacred books. But these books, which even the most able doctors only half understand and which a brahmin would not dare to explain to us for fear of a scandal in his caste, are written in a language for which *Samscroutam* [Sanskrit], the language of the learned, does not yet provide the key because they are written in a more ancient language. These books, I say, are in more than one way sealed for us. (Le Gobien 1781:14.6)

But Calmette tried his hand at composing some verses in Sanskrit and wrote on December 20, 1737, after a bout of fever that had hindered his study of Sanskrit: "I could not help composing a few verses in this language, in the style of controversy, to oppose them to those poured forth by the Indians" (Castets 1935:40). Calmette was inspired by de Nobili's writings that were stored at the Pondicherry mission and seems to have partly copied and rearranged de Nobili's *Sattia Véda Sanghiragham* (Essence of genuine revelation) (p. 40), whose title expresses exactly the idea that seems to have influenced Calmette so profoundly: the notion of a true Veda (*satya veda*).

Unlike de Nobili who had thought that the fourth Veda was lost and had presented himself as the guru who brought at least its teaching back to

India, Calmette had also bought the fourth Veda[10] and found that it was far more readable and therefore of somewhat later origin:

> There are texts that are explained in their theology books: some are intelligible for a reader of Sanskrit, particularly those that are from the last books of the *Vedan*, which by the difference of language and style are known to be more than five centuries younger than the earlier ones. (Le Gobien 1781:14.6)

Even if the Vedas remained for the most part a sealed book for Calmette and Pons, they could make a survey of their contents and pick out certain topics, stories, and quotations that could be used as talking points in debates and serve as "weapons" in the missionary "arsenal." One goal of such a collection of "truth" and "error" passages drawn from the Veda was their use in public disputes against Brahmins. A favorite tactic mentioned by Calmette is the following:

> Another way of controversy is to establish the truth and unity of God by definitions or propositions drawn from the *Vedam*. Since this book is among them of the highest authority, they do not fail to admit this. Following this, it is very easy to reject the plurality of gods. Now if they reply that this plurality is found in the *Vedam*, which is true, it is confirmed that there is a manifest contradiction in their law as it does not accord with itself. (Le Gobien 1781:13.438)

Calmette described various dispute strategies that are based on the knowledge of the Vedas and address themes such as the concept of a world soul, punishment in hell, and reward in paradise. (pp. 445–50).

Like de Nobili, Calmette thought that the word "Veda" referred to the divinely revealed "word of God" and explained: "I translated the word *Vedam* by divine scriptures [divines Ecritures] because when I asked some brahmins what they understood by *Vedam*, they told me that for them it means the word of God" (p. 384). But if this was God's revelation, then it had been incredibly corrupted. The best proof of this was that Calmette had to look so hard for those little specks of gold. The more he studied the clearer it must have become to him that de Nobili had been right in concluding that the Indian Veda was far removed from the "genuine Veda" or *satya vedam*, that is, the divine revelation to the first patriarchs. That true Veda had been disfigured in India and needed to be restored to its ancient glory. It is for this purpose that Calmette collected both the specks of gold and the worst symptoms of degeneration in the Veda. In the quoted example, the unity and goodness of God were first confirmed on the basis of Vedic passages and then contrasted with very human failings and even crimes of Indian gods like Shiva and Vishnu. In this manner an inner contradiction of the Veda could be exposed, and the opponents in the debate who could not deny the accuracy of the quotations from the Vedas could be caught in a no-win, "heads I win, tails you lose" type of situation.

Such tactics thus required intensive study of Indian sacred scriptures. Since the Indian catechists were almost never from the Brahmin caste, they were at best familiar with some puranic literature but certainly not with the Vedas. But since they most often had to conduct the debates, the quotations from the Vedas and talking points had to be set in writing; and because the disputes were held in front of ordinary people, such texts and quotations needed to be in Telugu rather than Sanskrit. In the *Edifying and curious letters* there are many examples of disputes involving catechists; but one of them is of particular interest here since it features a catechist who used exactly the kind of text that could have resulted from Calmette's "talking points" effort. The letter by Father Saignes is dated June 3, 1736, a couple of years after the acquisition and copying of the Vedas, and it stems from the very region in which Calmette worked:

> A brahmin, the intendant of the prince, passed through a village of his dependency and saw several persons assembled around one of my catechists who explained the Christian law to them. He stopped, called him, and asked him who he was, of what caste, what job he had, and what the book which he held in his hand was about. When the catechist had answered these questions, the brahmin took the book and read it. He just hit upon a passage which said that the gods of the land are no more than feeble men. "That's a rare teaching," said the brahmin, "and I would like you to try to prove that to me." "Sir," replied the catechist, "that will not be difficult if you order me to do so." "If that's all you need then I order you," rejoined the brahmin. The catechist began to recite two or three events from the life of *Vishnu*, which were theft, murder, and adultery. The brahmin wanted to change the topic [détourner le discours]; but the catechist would not let him and pressed on even more. The brahmin realized too late that he had become caught in a

dispute without paying attention to his status as a brahmin; and not knowing how to extricate himself honorably from this affair, he flew into a violent rage against the Christian law. "Law of *Pranguis*," he said, "law of miserable *Parias*, infamous law." "Permit me to say this," said the catechist, "the law is without stain: the sun is equally worshipped [adoré] by the brahmins and the *Parias*, and it must not be called the sun of the *Parias* even though they worship it just as the brahmins do." This comparison enraged the brahmin even more and he had no other response than to hit the catechist several times with his stick. He also hit him on the mouth and shattered all his teeth, and he had him chased out of the village like a *Parias*, prohibiting him ever to come there again and ordering the villagers to never give him shelter. (Le Gobien 1781:14.29–30).

Father Saignes wrote that this catechist "explained the Christian law" to his local audience and that for this purpose he used a "book" that one could practically open at random and hit upon a passage that says that "the gods of the land are no more than feeble men." Was this a *praeparatio evangelica* type of work that denounces the reigning local religion (see Chapter 1) in order to prepare the people for the Good News of the Christians? At any rate, it must have been a book in Telugu whose content stemmed from the Carnate missionaries who intensively studied the local religion and prepared such materials for the catechists. All this would seem to point to Father Calmette and Father Pons who at that very time (in the mid-1730s) and in that very region devoted much time to the study of the sacred scriptures of India.

We do not know what book the catechist read, but to my knowledge, the only extant text that would fit the missionary's description is the *Ezour-vedam*. A Telugu translation of this text must have existed since both Anquetil-Duperron's and Voltaire's *Ezour-vedam* manuscripts contain the following passage:

Biache. I would now be interested in knowing the names of the different countries inhabited by people and the differences among them. You have told me about heaven and hell. Give me a brief description of the earth which brings me up to date on all the different countries that are inhabited.

Chumontou responding to the question tells him the names of the different countries he knew and marks their location for him. Those interested can find them on the other page in the Telegoa language.[11]

Apart from indicating that the *Ezour-vedam*'s original French text had been translated into Telugu and was illustrated with a map, this passage is also extremely significant because it shows that the *Ezour-vedam* was designed for use by missionaries or catechists in the region where Telugu is spoken. It is one of two passages in the book that betrays the book's intended use. The target audience must have spoken Telugu, and the content of the map must have conveyed not classical Indian geography but rather a more correct and modern vision of the world and its countries. World maps played an important role in the Christian mission since the vast advantage in knowledge they embodied could boost the claim of expertise about other unknown regions such as heaven and hell. Ricci's world maps created quite a sensation in China but I ignore if seventeenth-century world maps from the Indian missions are extant in some Indian or Roman archives.

Thus a Telugu version of the *Ezour-vedam* could very well have been in the hands of that catechist. Opening the *Ezour-vedam* at random, one may indeed hit upon some passage that could enrage a Brahmin. For example,

> Are you stupid enough to overlook even what is right there before your eyes? What you say about the inhabitants of the air is completely insane! How can beings born of a man and a woman and therefore with a body like us live in the air and keep afloat? . . . There is only one god, and there has never been any other; this god is not born from *Kochiopo*, and those who are born from him were never gods. They are all simply men, composed of a body and a soul like us. If they were gods, they would not be numerous, one would not have seen them getting born, and they would not be subject to death. (Rocher 1984:161–62)

There are many other pages in the *Ezour-vedam* that more or less fit the missionary's description, but the following example may suffice to make the point: "I will not stop, however, to repeat and tell you that *Brahma* is no God at all, that *Vishnu* is no God either, and neither are *Indra* and all the others on whom you lavish this name; and *Shiva*, finally, is no God either, and even less the *lingam*" (p. 180).

The speaker of these words in the *Ezour-vedam*, Chumontou, uses a method that strangely resembles Calmette's: "in order to instruct people and save them," Chumontou examines common features of Indian religion such as the "different incarnations" of its gods and "refutes them through the words of the *Vedan*" (p. 135)—the very "weapons" that, according to Calmette who was proud of this method, hurt the Brahmins most. But there is another feature that links Calmette to the *Ezour-vedam* and the other texts found by Francis Ellis in 1816 among the remains of the Jesuit library at Pondicherry: his overall view of the Vedas.

True and False Vedas

Ludo Rocher has pointed out that for many Europeans the word *Vēdam* (which is Veda pronounced the Tamil way) signified the sacred scripture or Bible of the Indians. La Croze, for example, defined it as "a collection of ancient sacred books of the Brachmans" that "has among these idolaters the same authority the Holy Scripture has among us" (Rocher 1984:65). However, for Paulinus a Sancto Bartholomaeo, the word "Veda" "does not signify exclusively a sacred book but implies in general as much as a *sacred law*, whether observed by Indians or other nations" (p. 65). Of course, Paulinus famously (and wrongly) argued that "the Vedas" do not exist as a specific set of ancient Indian scriptures and that the Indians call many texts, even non-Indian ones, "Vedas." But modern southern Indian usage agrees with Paulinus's view about the word, as the entries in the University of Madras *Tamil Lexicon* cited by Rocher (1984:65) show:

vētam	1. The Vēdas; 2. The Jaina scriptures; 3. The Bible; . . .
vēta-k-kāran	Christian (the only meaning!)
vēta-pustakam	1. The Vēdas; 2. The Bible.
vēta-vākkiyam	1. Vedic text; 2. Gospel truth.
vēta-vākkiyānam	1. Commentaries on the Vēdas; 2. Expounding the Bible.

As mentioned above, Calmette defined the word "Veda" as "divine scriptures [divines Ecritures]" and explained this use in a letter of the year 1730, which is when he got hold of the Vedas (Le Gobien 1781:13.384). But in order to understand how the author of the *Ezour-vedam* understood this word, we need to examine its use in the *Ezour-vedam* and in the notes published by those researchers who saw the originals of the other Pondicherry

Vedas before they vanished in the 1930s (Rocher 1984:75). In the *Ezour-vedam*'s first book, the fourth chapter is titled "Of the Vedams," and it is here that we can find the best expression of the *Ezour-vedam* author's overall view of the Vedas. In this chapter, Biache asks Chumontou how the *Védams* have come to humankind and who its authors are. Chumontou's explanation begins as follows:

> At the outset, God dictated them [the *Védams*] to the first man, and ordered that he communicate them to the other men so that they might learn in that way to do good and avoid evil. These are the names that one gave to them: the first is called *Rik*, the second *Chama*, the third *Zozur*, and the fourth *Adorbo*. (Sainte-Croix 1778:1.200)[12]

Though the first man was in the *Ezour-vedam*'s previous chapter called Adimo ("*Adimo* is the name of the first man to come from the hands of God," p. 195), we readily identify him as Adam. Instead of letting Biache ask immediately about the fate of these *Védams*, the *Ezour-vedam*'s author makes him first inquire about the origin of evil.

> *Biache.* One sees that on earth vice as well as virtue reign; God, who is author of all things, is thus the author of both; at least that's what I thought until now. But how could this God, whose goodness is his essence, create vice? That's a problem that weighs on me and that I cannot resolve.
> *Chumontou.* You're wrong about that; God never created vice. He cannot be its author; and this God, who is wisdom and holiness itself, was author of nothing but virtue. He has given us his law in which he prescribes to us what we have to do. Sin is a transgression of this law and is expressly prohibited by this very law. Our bad inclinations have made us transgress God's law. From that [transgression] the first sin was born, and once the first sin was committed it entailed many others. (pp. 201–2)

The (Christian) reader will find this association of the first man with the first sin natural, but the *Ezour-vedam*'s author used it ingeniously to create the basis for his transmission scenario of the Vedas. Thanks to evil and sin, God's original divine revelation (the *Védams* he dictated to Adimo) could get into the wrong hands:

Biache. You've told me the names of the *Védams* that God communicated to the first man. Tell me now to whom the first man communicated them in turn?

Chumontou. The most virtuous children were the first to whom he communicated them, because they were the only ones who could appreciate them [prendre goût]. Sinners into whose hands these sacred books fell have abused and corrupted them, going so far as to have them serve as foundation for their fables and musings [rêveries]. That's what you yourself have done. (pp. 202–3)

This conversation leaves no doubt that the author of the *Ezour-vedam* thought that the Indians and their purported Veda author Vyāsa (Biache) used a corrupt version of the original divine revelation. In other words, what the Indians and Vyāsa consider to be the *true* Veda is in reality a degenerate *imitation* Veda. For Chumontou (who speaks for the *Ezour-vedam*'s author), the true Veda maintained its purity only in a single transmission line. A long time ago, this line had also reigned in India, and the "teachers" in the *Ezour-vedam* as well as the other Pondicherry Vedas represent this correct transmission.

By contrast, the "pupils" such as Biache (Vyāsa) are transmitters of the corrupted tradition. Their Veda is thus for the most part degenerate, though its original pure source is still apparent in a few vestiges of genuine revealed truth. In the words of Calmette's 1735 letter, the Vedas in use by the Indian Brahmins are a "pile of dirt" since they contain "the principle of all Indian sects, and maybe the details of all errors that make up their body of doctrines"; but they also contain a few "specks of gold" (Le Gobien 1781:13.437). These specks could be used to highlight how degraded the original pure teaching has become. They could thus be used as a weapon for "the advancement of [our Christian] religion," which, of course, is the crown of the *genuine* transmission line. Calmette's view of the *Vedam* appears to be strikingly similar to both de Nobili's and Chumontou's.

To return to the *Ezour-vedam*'s chapter on the Vedas, like a Catholic priest in a confessional, Chumontou now sternly reproaches Biache for having "abused and corrupted" the sacred books:

That's what you yourself have done, but you've promised me that you won't do it anymore. It's only on this condition, remember, that I will continue to teach you the *Védam,* and you will only be in a position to profit from this [teaching] if you renounce these gross errors. (Sainte-Croix 1778:1.203)

With this the stage is set for the final question and answer of the *Védam* chapter. It concerns the genuine Veda transmission:

> *Biache.* I will not be satisfied if you do not tell me the names of those to whom the *Védams* were entrusted for the first time, or who were its first authors.
> *Chumontou. Poilo* was the author of the *Rik-Védam*; *Zomeni* of the *Chama-Védam*; *Chumontou* of the *Ezour-Védam*; and finally, *Onguiro* composed the *Adorbo-Védam*. Each of them communicated it to his children and made them learn it. And those [children] in turn communicated them to their descendants. That is how they have come down to us. (pp. 203–5)

What is important to keep in mind here is the fundamental narrative of the Pondicherry Vedas. It sets a pure, "teacher" transmission line of divine revelation against a degenerate "pupil" transmission line. Both teachers and pupils, of course, had to be Indian and not foreign *Pranguis*. Famous "pupils" were desirable, and authors of the Vedas or other sacred scriptures were an optimal choice. It is true that the author of the *Ezour-vedam* was far less knowledgeable and consistent than modern Indologists would wish, but in exchange, he was very systematic in his black-and-white vision. For him the objective was not the satisfaction of some scholar or Brahmin but rather the hammering in of a basic message conveyed to the people in the Telugu language by catechists. Each time the "teacher" insists on something, the famous "pupil" has to admit his error and promise to be a good boy from now on. The obvious objective was to pave the way for the "true Veda" and for conversion, and pupil Biache in the *Ezour-vedam* demonstrates what the desired outcome was: the rejection of his traditional creed and sacred scriptures, the confession of his sins, a place at his teacher's feet, and the permission to ask questions about the *true* transmission of God's teachings. For the author of the *Ezour-vedam*, the true Veda had to open the door for the Good News, the "science of salvation" at whose sight those suffering from bad transmission disease (especially the authors of the Indian Vedas) were to cry out: "Adoration to the Supreme Being! We have hitherto lived in ignorance, but you have now, great God, put us into the hands of the science of salvation!"

(p. 205). It was pure *praeparatio evangelica*. But not all Indians reacted so enthusiastically, as the unfortunate catechist who read from his book about the degeneration of Indian religion had to learn the hard way.

Enhanced Genealogies

The problem of how to present a new religion as the origin of an older one is ubiquitous in Ur-tradition movements. Early Christianity had this problem in an acute form, and eminent early Christians such as Eusebius of Caesarea, Lactantius, and Augustine struggled with it. All three were among the favorite authors of missionaries since they faced similar problems in defining the relationship of their "new" religion to far older ones. The example of Eusebius is particularly illuminating and pertinent because he is also the source of much ancient information about Indian religion that was carefully studied by the missionaries. Eusebius created a scheme that made sure that Christianity was both oldest and newest. The studies of Jean Sirinelli (1961) and especially Jörg Ulrich (1999) show that Eusebius did this by portraying his religion not only as a reform of Judaism, which of course it was, but also as the pure transmission of a pre-Judaic original monotheism. In this scheme, Judaism was seen as an increasingly degenerate successor to the religion of a number of "just ones" that included Enoch and Abraham. These just men had received the correct transmission of the original divine revelation. On the other hand, there was, due to the fall, also a kind of Ur-atheism (Sirinelli 1961:170–207) that developed into various well-known forms of ancient religion: astral cults, hero worship and divination, polytheism, and so on. But the central argument of Eusebius was that of a bifurcated transmission of original divine revelation. On the "pure" transmission side were not as usual Moses and Judaism but rather a more ancient line of "patriarchs" who had received divine revelation straight from the founder God via Adam.

In this manner, Christianity could, so to speak, jump the line and appear as a reform of Judaism and its ancestor. This was a truly ingenious scheme that Eusebius had worked out in intricate detail in one of the greatest displays of erudition of antiquity: his *Praeparatio evangelica*. This huge, early fourth-century work of preparation for the Good News is without any doubt the highest peak of early Christian apologetics, and it was supplemented by the *Demonstratio evangelica* and Eusebius's Church history (*Historia ecclesiastica*), which made him the founder of this field (Winkelmann 1991). For Jesuits, and even more for Jesuits dispatched to the missions, the *Praeparatio evangelica* was a must-read.

A very similar scheme, I believe, was adopted by the author of the *Ezour-vedam* and the other Pondicherry Vedas and helps explain a difficulty many commentators have felt. Julien Bach and Senator Lanjuinais put it this way:

> What embarrassed the critics a bit was that the author of the *Pseudo-Vēdas* spoke of the four *Vēdas* of the brahmins to refute them; he described their origin and even gave the names of their authors. "It is something inexplicable," said M. Lanjuinais, "that the missionary [who wrote the *Ezour-vedam*] did not shy away from inserting in his work what could convict him of his imposture." (Bach 1848:63)

Based on Christianity's direct link to the pure transmission of God's original teaching, Eusebius had called Christianity *verus Israel*, the true Israel (Ulrich 1999:119); so could the *Ezour-vedam*'s author not call Christianity the *vera India*? In the *Ezour-vedam*'s scheme of things, the authors of the "true Veda" transmission would belong to the "just men" lineage that jumps straight to Christianity, whereas the Brahmins with their Vedas would suffer gradual degeneration, just like Eusebius's Jews with their Old Testament. In Figure 18 this Indian component is indicated by dashed lines; the rectangle would represent Hinduism, which in this perspective is a form of degenerated monotheism similar to Judaism in Eusebius's scheme.

The overall character of the *Ezour-vedam* as *praeparatio evangelica* is similar to that of Eusebius's eponymous work since its aim is to refute the other religions as degenerate transmissions and to link one's own religion to the correct transmission of the original, pure doctrine. For Eusebius the pre-Judaic "just men" and Hebrews had to take the role of patriarchs of the correct transmission line. But the author of the *Ezour-vedam* could not risk inserting *Pranguis* anywhere along the path. He had to get his patriarchs, whether he liked it or not, from the pool of Indian "just men" rather than biblical patriarchs; and this was a problem that must have bugged him as much as it irritated Western readers who found these Indian patriarchs "inexplicable."

The Anti-Vedic Vedas

In 1816, Francis Ellis found in Pondicherry a total of eight manuscripts (including the *Ezour-vedam*) among the remains of the old Jesuit library. His

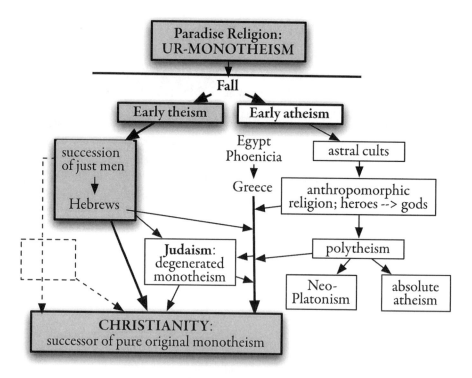

Figure 18. Christianity's transmission line in Eusebius of Caesarea (Urs App).

description of these texts, published in 1822, was fortunately rather detailed and must be used here because the texts from the old Jesuit library that Ellis saw have all vanished. The last person to hold the Pondicherry texts in his hands appears to be the Jesuit Castets who examined them some time before 1935 (Rocher 1984:75). All we thus have at our disposal today are the *Ezour-vedam* manuscripts at the Bibliothèque Nationale in Paris and a number of descriptions of other "Pondicherry Veda" texts (see below) by Ellis and others.[13]

These texts all employ the same basic scheme popular in mission literature: a conversation between a teacher and a pupil (Ellis 1822:43). As in the *Ezour-vedam,* the teacher figure represents the "cult of the genuine God" and the pupil the degenerate cult (p. 14). The teachers criticize the pupil's degenerate religion and urge a return to the faith of even earlier times. Both the style and content of these texts seem designed for easy memorization by catechists and maximum impact in debates and recitation before a public that needed to be convinced and prepared for the real Good News. The role of the Pondicherry Vedas was to prepare the ground by denouncing the reigning religion and undermining its claim to genuine transmission of divinely revealed teachings. This implied of course a frontal attack on the Vedas and its traditional guardians.

Once more, the comparison with Eusebius is helpful. He saw the exclusivity of Judaism and its sacred scripture as a symptom of degeneration, and Christianity as a liberation from such limits: it is a law for *all* peoples, not just for a small group or caste.

> First of all, Christ is for Eusebius the *telos* [goal] of the law because he abolishes exactly those limitations that were inherent in the Jewish law: in Christ, the revelation of the divine will to save is directed at all mankind, not just at the Jews; and [it is directed] at the entire earth, not just at the narrow confines of Palestine. (Ulrich 1999:155)

Chumontou makes a similar argument. While deploring the "evils with which the earth is inundated in this unfortunate century," he regards it as more fortunate than past ones; and though Chumontou is supposedly speaking in the distant past, we hear through his mouth very distinctly the voice of a desperately optimistic French missionary in eighteenth-century India:

> If in the first centuries virtue was easier to achieve, there were also more demands than today. Each profession, each caste was subject to particular ceremonies which are [now] abolished and no more in use. There were particular places, temples, and designated persons to offer sacrifices and carry out the other principal functions of religion. Only they could perform this. It would have been a crime for anybody else to interfere. Today one is no more subjugated to all this. Every person that has piety can carry out the functions of religion, and one can do this at any time and place. Furthermore, in the first centuries one could not teach the *Vedan* to the Choutres [Śūdra] and the general population; it would even have been a sin to do this. Now one can do this without fear and scruples. It is on account of this that this century has some advantage over earlier ones. (Rocher 1984:171–72)

A Brahmin would immediately understand that this was a frontal attack on his religion, caste, and the Veda; and the editor of the *Ezour-vedam*'s printed edition wrote in a note: "All that the author reports here can only apply to

TABLE 13. PROTAGONISTS OF THE PONDICHERRY VEDAS AND THEIR TRANSMISSION
LINES

Veda transmission	1st Veda (Rik; Ṛg)	2nd Veda (Chama; Sāma)	3rd Veda (Ezour/ Zozur; Yajur)	4th Veda (Adorbo; Atharva)
Genuine (teacher)	Poilo/ Poilapado	Zoimeni	Chumontou (Sumanta)	Otri/Atri
Degenerate (pupil)	Narada	Naraion (Narayana)	Biache (Vyasa)	Ongira (Angiras)

the times after the Mahommedan invasions and proves that his work is not
of great antiquity" (Sainte-Croix 1778:2.81). Sainte-Croix could have gone a
bit further, but he still clung to the belief that the *Ezour-vedam* was a translation of an Indian text.

The Pondicherry Vedas

Having thus gotten a taste of the genuinely anti-Vedic spirit of these "true
Vedas," it is time to look at the *Ezour-vedam*'s sister texts. Ellis's 1822 descriptions of the Pondicherry Vedas permit establishing the arrangement of the
heroes and villains in the axes of the genuine and the corrupt transmission of
divine revelation shown in Table 13.

Since the *Ezour-vedam* and its content were already to some degree
discussed in Chapter 1, I will here focus on Ellis's description of the fifth
Pondicherry manuscript. It contained the Pondicherry *Chama Vedam*, traditionally the second Veda (*Sāma*), and features in the first section Zoimeni as
teacher and Naraion as disciple. Naraion can only be Nārāyaṇa or Narayan,
that is, the god Vishnu. So much for name recognition of the disciple! But
in several parts of this text, the roles are reversed (p. 24), which may be a
symptom of the author's "Indian patriarch" problem. According to Ellis, this
fifth manuscript contained in the margins on the French side a sequence of
abstracts that appear to be either the grid on which the author constructed
his text or its summary by an astute reader or copyist. These comments are
extremely interesting because they so clearly express intentions that often
remain hidden in a finished text; but in this case, the finished text is lost, and
we only possess these notes as recorded by Ellis. They begin as follows.

Book I. Chapter 1. Contains the introduction [exorde] of the whole work, the aim of ZOIMENI in composing it.—Dedication of his book to the Supreme Being—character of the genuine guru and his functions.
Chapter 2. Contains a grand idea of God and his attributes and refutes the false idea that the false *Vedas* give of the divinity. Summary of the creation of the world.
Chapter 3. Treats of the imaginary [fabuleuse] creation of the false *Vedas*, undertakes their refutation. It then treats of the virtue of those who are able and unable to read the *Vedam*.
Chapter 4. Speaks of the true God and of the cult that must be given to him—in establishing the cult of the true God he condemns the cult which Naraion wants people to give to *Vishnu* and *Shiva*. (Ellis 1822:14)

Like the *Ezour-vedam*, this text also sets a "false *Veda*" transmission against the genuine one. The "false *Vedas*" convey a false idea of God, his attributes, and his cult, while the true Vedas explain the correct conception of these things. Chapter 3 is about the origin and transmission of both true and false Vedas and may also have discussed the caste restrictions regarding the reading and recitation of their "false" Veda in contrast with the "true" Veda that is open for all. This effort to undermine the authority of the Indian Vedas (and thus also that of the Brahmins) was sure to enrage Indian clergy, who must have been astonished by this kind of brazen hijack attempt by outcaste Johnny-come-latelies who had no idea of the Vedas. For the missionary author and the "teacher" of this text, on the other hand, the genuine tradition was now coming back to India, the cult of the true God was about to be restored, and the reigning cults of Vishnu and Shiva were on their way to extinction.

The *Chama Vedam*'s second book starts by digging deeply into what Calmette called "dirt":

Book II. Chapter 1. Speaks of five mythical [fabuleuses] opinions of creation: the first called Padmokolpo, attributed to VICHNOU; the second into the tortoise; the third into the pig; the fourth into GONECH; the fifth into the goddess BIROZA; then the second creation, attributed to the tortoise, of the deluge, of the metamorphosis of the Supreme Being into the tortoise, of the creation of a maiden whom the tortoise marries . . . [additional details omitted here but not in Ellis, p. 15]

Chapter 2. Includes the refutation of the preceding [chapter]—beautiful idea of God drawn from the true *Vedam*.

Chapter 3. Contains the continuation of the metamorphosis of the Supreme Being in a tortoise; it includes the system of total and partial metamorphoses, that is to say that comprise the entire divinity; a system that one will find well developed in the *Odorbo Bedo* or fourth *Véd*, a book which treats of this *ex professo*, refutation of this system—beautiful character of the true god. ZOIMENI makes in this chapter NARAION the author of the false *Chama Véd*, essential remark. (pp. 15–16)

Indian creation myths, incarnations, and metamorphoses of the "false" *Chama Véd* whose author is Naraion are contrasted with the pure gold of the *true Vedam*. This *true Vedam* is understood as the true "word of God," as Calmette had heard his Indian experts explain, and this is laid down in the genuine *Chama Véd* that is none other than this second Pondicherry Veda! The third book of the *Chama Vedam* continues to expose the creation myths of Brahma and Shiva in order to refute them on the basis of the true revelation tradition as laid down in the Pondicherry Vedas.

Book III. Chapter 1. Contains the creation attributed to the boar, it is BRAMMA or the Supreme Being under the name of CHIB which metamorphoses itself into a boar; and Parvati his wife into a sow to withdraw and sustain the earth, description of the place where CHIB lived.
Chapter 2. Contains the refutation of the precedent.
Chapter 3. Contains the description of the creation brought about by the Boar God, the substance of this creation is found in the body of the true *Ezour Véd*.
Chapter 4. Is the refutation of the precedent. (p. 16)

The "true *Ezour Véd.*" clearly refers to the Pondicherry text of the *Ezourvedam* containing the creation account that is here alluded to (Rocher 1984:133). If there still was any doubt whether the author or commentator really identified the "true Vedam" as the Pondicherry Vedas, it is here resolved. The whole configuration and content of these Pondicherry Vedas make Rocher's idea that *"Ezour* stands for *Y-ezus,* i.e. Jesus" (p. 66) very unlikely and shows that it was not de Guignes who invented the identification of the *Ezour-vedam* with the third Veda.

The fourth and final book introduces a theme that will play a role later in this chapter, namely, emanation.

> **Book IV.** Chapter 1. Contains the marriage of Chib the Supreme Being[,] the birth of his son Gonech, the loss of his head, which Chib substituted with that of an elephant and the beginning of the creation attributed to Gonech.
> *Chapter 2.* Is the refutation of the fables of the preceding.
> *Chapter 3.* Speaks of the manner in which Gonech made the 3 worlds with his 3 eyes: [. . . details . . .] This chapter ends with the two opinions about the nature of the soul [;] the first want it to be immortal, without principle and subjected to the Gounalous and that it reunites and identifies itself with God at the time of deluge, that is to say, at the end of each age; the second that it [the soul] is mortal and that it is compared to God what the reflection of the sun on water is to the sun.
> *Chapter 4.* Is the refutation of the precedent. Zoimeni author of the true *Chama Vêdam* combats as false the system which makes the soul an emanation of God, that unites itself with God at the end of each age; system that *Onguira*, author of the true *Odorbo Bédo*, appears to adopt as one can see at that place.
> N. Evident Proof that the true *Chama Vêdam* and the true *Odorbana Vêdam* have not come from the same hand and that the Brame who has communicated them is not their author. (Ellis 1822:16–17)

The final note by the author or annotator of the *Chama Vedam* is hard to figure out but seems to be part of an attempt to justify the missionary's choice of "true Veda" authors. It is a pity that the manuscript is lost because this would throw light into a shady corner.

The Authorship of the Pondicherry Vedas

Ludo Rocher (1984:28–52, 57–60) has extensively discussed previous opinions about the *Ezour-vedam*'s authorship, and there is no need to repeat this here. In most contributions, questions about the regional pronunciation of Sanskrit terms and regional information indicating either southern or Bengal origin play central roles. Often the Sanskrit translations and even the fate of the *Ezour-vedam* in Europe form part of the discussion of authorship. But we need to keep the issues separate.

First, the *Ezour-vedam* and its sister texts were created by one or several French missionaries, but as far as we know these missionaries did not have a European public in mind. Based on our analysis, we must conclude that these texts were written for an Indian audience. For a European readership, the link of ancient Indian figures in the texts to antediluvian patriarchs or to Noah and his sons would have been obligatory; but in the *Ezour-vedam* and its sister texts, such *Prangui* connections had to be avoided at all cost—a clear indicator of the intended public. Some confusion about the identities of the Indian patriarchs suggests that this was no easy task. This first phase is the only truly relevant one for the authorship question. One must be careful not to muddle the issue by confusing the question of authorship with issues such as who later added Sanskrit translations, who gave the text to Maudave, who transcribed Indian words in certain ways, and other considerations.

Second, since the *Ezour-vedam*'s original target public was speaking Telugu, Sanskrit translations must have been made later when some missionaries—possibly but not necessarily including the author of the original French text—decided to try to render some of the French text into as good a Sanskrit as they could manage. This individual or group of individuals may have studied Sanskrit in different regions of India, which helps explain the mixed transliterations,[14] and these individuals may also have edited the original French text to some extent. Every copyist could modify the text, as the three extant manuscripts of the *Ezour-vedam* show. Since we have no way of knowing how many times and by whom these texts were copied or edited, all we can do is speculate. We may never know what the intentions of the Sanskrit translator(s) were; it may just have been a pastime of some retired missionary Sanskritists like Pons or Antoine Mozac. At any rate, there is no indication whatsoever that these Sanskrit translation drafts were ever intended for public consumption; otherwise, they would have been corrected with the help of an Indian Sanskritist and properly edited. The second production stage, therefore, involves editing and copying of the French text and adding Sanskrit translation exercises on the facing pages of some texts.

Third, two of these texts (the *Ezour-vedam* and Voltaire's *Cormo-veidam*) may have undergone some clean-up editing (for example, eliminating passages like the "Telugu place name" remark in the Harlay manuscript) before being sent to Europe. The *Ezour-vedam*, which today is the only extant Pondicherry Veda, reached Europe in several somewhat different manuscript versions and

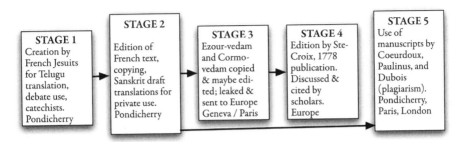

Figure 19. Stages of *Ezour-vedam* creation and dissemination (Urs App).

thus entered, with the significant help of Voltaire and then Sainte-Croix, a new career stage. This issue was to some degree discussed in Chapter 1.

Fourth, the *Ezour-vedam* was edited by the Baron of Sainte-Croix on the basis of Voltaire's and Anquetil-Duperron's manuscripts and published in 1778 as "the first original work published to date on the religious and philo-sophical dogmas of the Indians" (Sainte-Croix 1778:1.xii). Sainte-Croix's vi-sion of the text and its authorship will be discussed below.

Fifth, the manuscripts of the Pondicherry Vedas (and possibly additional notes and related study materials) were from 1770 onward used and plagia-rized by several persons and ended up directly and indirectly influencing the nineteenth-century image of Indian religion.

As explained above, the question of authorship of the French text con-cerns only the first of the stages shown in Figure 19. The author worked in the environment of the Malabar mission where Telugu was the target lan-guage. What he had in mind was not producing a fake Veda translation because he was inspired by La Croze's wish to see a European-language trans-lation of the Vedas (Rocher 1984:73), nor did he have any intention of com-mitting a literary forgery and a "religious imposition without parallel" (Ellis 1822:1). Rather, a missionary had the idea to create such texts for the educa-tion and conversion of heathens and designed a format that made them easy to memorize and use for missionaries and catechists and, of course, also easy to understand by the native audience who must for the most part have been illiterate. There were no Voltaires sitting at the catechists' feet in those villages near Pondicherry. The main point of these entertaining repartees was to prepare Indians for instruction in Christianity by undermining their trust in the native religion and its clergy and squarely attacking the authority of the Veda by calling it "false." This meant digging up much "dirt" about the indecent adventures of Indian gods and goddesses, gods turning into boars, and the like; but other educational content was also mixed in, for example, how to construct a water clock from a simple copper tube (Sainte-Croix 1778:1.267) and, as we have seen, geography lessons. This was part of instruction in the tradition of the "genuine Vedas." At this stage, nothing could have been further from the author's mind than an elaborate plan to mislead a generation of budding Orientalists in Europe about India's ancient religion. His focus on undermining the Vedas and on conveying information to natives who knew little of the world is all too evident.

Among all the letter-writing Jesuit missionaries active in India in the late seventeenth and early eighteenth centuries hitherto mentioned as possible authors of the *Ezour-vedam*, there is no one who comes even close to matching the profile of Jean Calmette with regard to motivation, eagerness, and ability to study Indian religions from primary materials; determination to use such materials as "weapons" in disputes; activity in the Telugu-speaking area; inspiration by de Nobili's conception of *satya vedam*; and other characteristics described above. Calmette has been on the authorship shortlist since Julien Bach's perceptive articles of 1847 and 1848 that were less concerned with linguistic issues than with questions of motivation and content. In his 1868 book, Bach summarized his argument as follows:

> If we accept with the missionary that Indian superstitions derive from primitive traditions altered by ignorance or their taste for fables, and we give the term *Veda* its real meaning *revelation*, we have the entire work of the missionary in a nutshell: there was a Veda, a primitive revelation, and its tradition spread as far as India; but you, brahmans, have corrupted the Veda by mistakes of all kinds. I shall destroy these mistakes. (Bach 1868:23; trans. Rocher 1984:44)

Calmette also found support for his view from a witness whom we will meet again later in this chapter: the famous Abbé Jean-Antoine Dubois. Bach reported:

> What I said above made me suspicious not only that the Ezour-Védam is a French work but also that Calmette was its author. To acquire certitude I thought of contacting the person in Paris who had to be most familiar with the question. I said to myself that the venerable Abbé Dubois—who had spent forty years as a missionary in India, lived with the

last remaining Jesuits, and stayed in Pondicherry—had without any doubt seen these odd manuscripts that created such a brouhaha. I went to see him and asked him, without telling him my opinion, if he knew the author of the Ezour-védam.—It is Father Calmette, he said immediately. But, he added, several missionaries have had a hand in it. (Bach 1868:23)

Actually, Abbé Dubois was far more familiar with these Pondicherry materials than Father Bach could imagine. Rocher noted shortly before his book on the *Ezour-vedam* went to press that "long passages in the EzV [*Ezour-vedam*] correspond to Dubois' text" and that "these correspondences, even in Dubois' French version, are never verbatim, but too close to be accidental" (1984:87). In the meantime, Sylvia Murr (1987) has shown that Dubois systematically plagiarized the writings of Father Gaston Laurent Coeurdoux that he had found in the remains of the Jesuit mission library at Pondicherry; and we know that the Pondicherry Vedas were also there. So the conclusion that Dubois also plagiarized these manuscripts is not difficult to draw. This also means that, in Julien Bach's time, there was nobody in the world who knew these manuscripts better than Dubois—yet Bach who questioned him had no idea of this fact. Dubois's opinion was thus incomparably more informed than that of Anquetil-Duperron and others who did not even know that several texts of the kind existed.

Bach's opinion convinced numerous library catalogers, but in the twentieth century, Julien Vinson rejected Calmette's authorship mainly with arguments related to Bengali transliterations and the fate of the text in Europe (Vinson 1902:293), which, as noted above, need to be separated from the authorship question. The objections of Castets (1935:40), too, are related to his idea that the *Ezour-vedam* must be of Bengali origin because of the transliterations. Additionally, Castets claims that "one can find nothing in this unpublished correspondence of Father Calmette that reminds one the slightest bit [de près ou de loin] of the famous *Ezour Védam*" (p. 40). But the letters by Calmette quoted by Castets actually offer excellent support for Calmette's admiration for and inspiration by de Nobili, and we have seen that this inspiration ties in very well with Calmette's published letters as well as the general trend of the Pondicherry Vedas. Objections by other people that were listed by Rocher (1984:45) are equally beside the point, and one must conclude that—unless one would like to have a single-author manuscript with no further interference by others—so far not a single objection to Calmette's authorship has merit.

Now if other missionaries "had a hand in it," as Dubois put it, who was he thinking of? There is an interesting passage in the *Ezour-vedam* that can provide a hint. For some reason the text's author wanted to educate the Telugu-speaking audience not just about the construction of a simple water-clock and the geography of our earth but also about other religions, such as that of the evil "Baudistes":

> *Chumantou*: . . . The most criminal of all are those called Baudistes. They are really abominable people who are so impious and blasphemous as to seek to destroy and annihilate even the idea of divinity.
> *Biach*: Tell me, Sir, what are these Baudistes?
> *Chumantou*: The Baudistes are dominant in different countries. Their system is to not recognize any purely spiritual substance and no god except for themselves, which is the greatest and most horrible of all crimes. (Rocher 1984:171)

The author of these lines is likely to have read La Croze's book of 1724 that contained, as discussed in Chapter 2, an early synthesis of information about Buddhism and argued mainly on the basis of Ziegenbalg's and La Loubère's information that Buddhism was a religion founded by an Indian man called Boudda who is called by various other names depending on the country, for example, "Fo" or "Foto" in China. This religion was long ago eradicated in India because of its atheism but found its way to various Asian countries including Siam, Tibet, China, and Japan. But the remark that the Baudistes do not recognize any purely spiritual substance is not found in La Croze and must come from another source. Now we have another very short description of this religion that stems from the very region in which the Pondicherry Vedas must have been written. It is by Father Pons who was from 1733 to 1740 with Calmette a member of the Malabar mission (Castets 1935:47) and had studied Sanskrit in the Bengal region. In this famous letter of November 23, 1740, about Sanskrit and Indian philosophy, Pons wrote:

> The Bauddistes, whose doctrine of metempsychosis has been universally adopted, are accused of atheism and admit only our senses as principles of our knowledge. Boudda is the *Photo* revered by the people of China,

TABLE 14. SIMILARITIES IN THE VIEW OF BUDDHISM IN THE *EZOUR-VEDAM*
AND PONS'S LETTER

Theme	Ezour-vedam *on Buddhism*	*Pons on Buddhism*
atheism	recognize no god except for themselves, seek to annihilate even idea of divinity	accused of atheism
sensualism	do not recognize purely spiritual substance	admit only senses as principles of knowledge
presence	dominant in different countries	China, Tibet, Japan (Lamas and Bonzes)
founder	—(no point to explain this to Indians?)	Boudda = Photo
metempsychosis	—(too trite for Indians?)	doctrine of metempsychosis universally adopted

and the Bauddistes are of the sect of the Bonzes and Lamas. (Le Gobien 1781:14.79)

The very brief remarks about this religion in the *Ezour-vedam* and in this letter could be miles apart, given that so little was known about it at the time. But in spite of their extreme brevity, they show a similar vision, as shown in Table 14.

Pons and Calmette, who came from the same little town of Rodez in southern France, had both been eager to find the Vedas, and both collaborated closely with Abbé Bignon in procuring precious Indian books for the Royal Library in Paris. In the 1730s, these two men were the only missionaries in the region capable of studying the Vedas and related texts, and it would be strange indeed if they had not worked together. After Calmette died in 1739 in Pondicherry, Pons was for a decade busy in Karikal (1740–50), but he returned to Pondicherry in 1750, more than a year before his death (1751). He was by then retired, and it is conceivable that he used his leisure to try his hand not only at reading Sanskrit, as he had done for a quarter-century, but also at practising his writing. What better texts to try his hand at translating than his friend Calmette's Pondicherry Vedas? I agree with Castets that Father Pons, the author of a treatise on Sanskrit prosody who had been both a superior in the Bengal mission from 1728 to 1733 and a longtime resident of the Malabar mission in the South, may have "distracted himself, reduced by his age and his tiring work, to forced leisure at the siege of the Pondicherry mission" (Castets 1935:46); but instead of just annotating the Pondicherry Vedas, I think he may have employed his great talents, instead of on the eighteenth-century equivalent of crossword puzzles, for some active mind-sport that resulted in fragmentary, unrevised, unsystematic translations of Calmette's French texts into Sanskrit—translations that were full of mistakes, as is to be expected of someone who reads a language but never writes it. It is hard to imagine that such jottings were designed for mission use or for public consumption. Pons's interest in the real Vedas was limited, as a letter written in 1740 just after the death of Calmette shows:

> The four *Vedan* or *Bed* are, according to them, of divine authority: one has them in Arabic at the Royal Library; accordingly the brahmins are divided in four sects of which each has its own law. *Roukou Vedan* or, according to the Hindustani pronunciation, *Recbed*, and the *Ya-jourvedam* are the most followed on the Indian subcontinent between the seas, and the *Samavedan* and *Latharvana* or *Brahmavedam* in the North. The *Vedan* contain the theology of the brahmins; and the ancient *Pouranam* or poems the popular theology. The *Vedan*, as far as I can judge by the little I have seen of it, are nothing but a collection of different superstitious and often diabolical practices of the ancient *Richi*, penitents, or *Mouni*, or anachorets. Everything, even the gods, is subjected to the intrinsic power of sacrifices and *Mantram*; these are sacred formulae they use to consecrate, offer, invoke, etc. I was surprised to find the following: *ôm Sântih, Sântih, Santih, harih.* You surely know that the letter or syllable *ôm* contains the Trinity in Unity; the rest is the literal translation of *Sanctus, Sanctus, Sanctus, Dominus.* Harih is a name of God which signifies Abductor. (Le Gobien 1781:14.75)

Editors and Copyists of the *Ezour-vedam*

With regard to the time of origin of the Pondicherry Vedas, Ellis reported: "At the end of this manuscript [No. 7] are two dates on a slip of paper, on which the concluding lines of the translation are written, one is 'Année 1732,' the other 'Année 1751'" (1822:27). Castets, who was the last man to see the Pondicherry Vedas, wrote that in 1923 when he first examined these manuscripts, the slip of paper documented by Ellis had disappeared (1935:33) but commented:

> These two dates are interesting in several respects. The second one shows that the *Védams* from No. 3 to No. 8 existed in collected and translated form before 1751, as the watermark of 1742 on the paper already suffi- ciently indicated. We do not talk about the numbers 1 and 2 which were probably much anterior to these latter ones and represented only copies of unknown originals that were evidently written by the French mission- aries themselves. Furthermore, these two dates which were written by the annotator of the whole collection, seemed to interest him personally and, by their conjunction, evoke in him emotions of contrast between the interest that he had for these *Védams*, or at least some of them, in 1732, and that which his critical inspection of the same inspired in 1751. (Castets 1935:34)

This sounds a bit too emotional, but neither this emotionality nor Castets's absurd conclusion that the Pondicherry Vedas were translations of the forged Vedas bought in 1726 by Pons (p. 46) should distract us from his valuable first-hand observations. He noted that the first two manuscripts— the *Ezour-vedam* (whose original title, *Zozur Bédo*, was crossed out in red ink and replaced by *Ezour Védam*, p. 11) and the *Zozochi Kormo Béd* (which in Castet's opinion was the *Kormo Védam* described by Voltaire; p. 13)— appeared to be much older than the others and must have been copies of even older originals. Manuscripts 3–8, on the other hand, appeared to be from a later date and were written on paper with a 1742 watermark. In the year 1732, Calmette was in the midst of studying the newly acquired Vedas, and I speculate that the first number on Ellis's slip of paper may refer to the year when Calmette wrote the first texts. By 1735 or 1736, the time of the "broken teeth" event, some texts could well have existed in a Telugu version. After his transfer back to the Malabar mission in 1733, Father Pons might well have collaborated, if the *Ezour-vedam*'s Buddhism passage is a sign; and this would explain some Bengali influence on pronunciation and also the inclusion of information that suggests an author familiar with that region. After Calmette's death in 1739, Pons could have worked on other texts by Calmette and annotated them (if Castets's guess is correct).

I would rather hypothesize that Pons found these texts again on his return to Pondicherry in 1750 and spent his last year reworking them and brushing up his Sanskrit. But possibly other fathers with some knowledge of Sanskrit like Calmette and Mozac also tried their hand at that. The second date noted on that slip of paper, 1751, is the year at whose end Pons died. By this time, all the Pondicherry Vedas probably existed, possibly with partial Sanskrit translations. This does not mean that they remained unchanged because Father Mozac, as we will see below, had—apart from copying the whole corpus—also added some revisions, and the copying of manuscripts must have continued. The first *Ezour-vedam* to be brought to Europe was, according to Rocher (1984:86), present in the Harlay Collection by 1755. If this is correct, then only two or three years passed between Pons's death and the arrival of the first *Ezour-vedam* manuscript in France.

To what degree the manuscript was edited (possibly with the removal of Sanskrit translations and tell-tale signs of its original target public, one of which—the one with the map—was overlooked) must remain unknown until the vanished Pondicherry Vedas make their reappearance. But I would guess that it must have been an inside job by one of the members of the Jesuit mission who looked through the Pondicherry Vedas after Pons's death and between 1752 and circa 1754 prepared two of them, the *Ezour-vedam* and its *Oupo-vedam*, the *Cormo-vedam*, for recycled use on a different target public. It is interesting and perhaps significant that this should have happened exactly when the first volumes of the *Encyclopédie* appeared in France (from 1751). Was a senior person in the mission, for example, its superior Lavaur or Father Coeurdoux, sufficiently concerned to give the go-ahead for refurbishing these two texts and their recycled use as weapons—only this time against the skeptics and atheists who were about to take over the French information industry? Would this help in convincing them about the existence of original monotheism in ancient India? And might it be an effective weapon against the continuing critique of Malabar Rites?

The rite problem was intimately linked to the idea of original pure monotheism, to the presence of its vestiges in ancient cultures, and to the kind of transmission scheme invented by Eusebius that the Pondicherry Veda's author had adapted for Indian use. If the most ancient religion of India was so excellent and the Ur-transmission of divine revelation to India proven, then it should certainly not be problematic to let the Indians continue performing some of their ancient rites, should it? The papal bull *Omnium sollicitudinum* of 1744 had once more confirmed the exclusivist hard line of the Vatican, which gradually grew into a threat not only to the Jesuit mission in the Malabar region but to the Jesuit order as a whole. It was a situation of crisis because thousands of Indian Christians began to return to

TABLE 15. PERIODIZATION OF THE CAREER OF THE PONDICHERRY VEDAS

Stage 1	Stage 2	Stage 3	Stage 4	Stage 5
Creation of French texts; Telugu translations for local use 1732–39 Calmette	Edition of French texts; annotation; Sanskrit pages 1739–51 Pons; later Mozac?	Edition of *Ezour-* and *Cormo-vedam* for Western use; leaking c. 1752–54 Coeurdoux?	Western dissemination of *Ezour-vedam.* Printed edition. Mozac copying, translating 1760s/70s c. 1755–78 Voltaire, Ste. Croix Mozac, Coeurdoux	Western reaction, doubts, controversy. Plagiarism. Discovery in Pondicherry 1778–1825 Dubois, Ellis

their native creed right at the moment when the foundations of the Jesuit order were shaking. During the 1750s, this pressure was building up, and in 1760, there was the first major earthquake: the dissolution of the Portuguese Jesuit mission in India and repatriation of all its missionaries (Launay 1898:I.cxxii). Four years later, King Louis XV signed an edict that ordered "that the Jesuit order shall no more exist in France" (p. 12), and in 1773, the papal bull *Dominus ac Redemptor* dissolved the entire Jesuit order.

In the 1750s, time seemed to be running out: the Jesuit mission team was losing the game in India, and the Christian side in Europe began to crumble under the onslaught of rampant secularism, skepticism, and outright atheism. Was the leaking of the *Ezour-vedam*, to use an American sports metaphor, a Hail-Mary pass? It might well have been. On the other hand, one cannot exclude the possibility that some missionary talked to a countryman in Pondicherry and casually mentioned manuscripts he had found in Father Pons's room, making the Frenchman so curious that he had to lend him a manuscript or two for perusal at home, whereupon the manuscript was copied without permission and sent to Europe as a curiosity. Be this as it may, in the scenario I propose here (see Table 15), there are five different stages that each have their listed main actor but certainly also various co-stars.that go unmentioned.

Zoroastrian Victory from the Jaws of Vedic Defeat

After Anquetil-Duperron's return from India following a five-year stay, he wrote a detailed report about his voyage that was published in abbreviated form in 1762 in French and the following year in English under the title of "A brief account of a voyage to India, undertaken by M. Anquetil du Perron, to discover and translate the works attributed to Zoroaster."[15] The *Annual Report* hails Anquetil-Duperron's journey for the purpose "of extending the bounds of virtue and learning" and calls the Frenchman, who "in so small a period, and in such circumstances, could learn so many languages, utterly unconnected with those already known in Europe, and copy and translate so many books written in them," "a true virtuoso, who braves every danger and difficulty in order to promote useful knowledge, and to increase the materials of speculation in the learned world" (Anquetil-Duperron 1787b:103). However, his chief hagiographer, Raymond Schwab, discerned a rather different heroic enterprise:

> If Voltaire wanted from Asia—in bad faith really—arguments against the fabricators of revelation, Anquetil hoped—blindly, for that matter—to draw from it materials for the confirmation of the dogma, because he was one of those believers in whose eyes the image of the world is divided in two halves, Christians and idolaters. However, the idolaters appeared to him like unconscious depositaries of a tradition that had come from Israel and that was to be recovered. What he wanted to snatch from the Hindus were "the oldest monuments of religion." He went to Asia to seek scientific proof of the primacy of the Chosen People and of the biblical genealogies: but it so happened that his investigations suddenly opened the way to a critique of the books accepted as revealed. (Schwab 1934:4)

We have seen that long before Anquetil-Duperron's trip to India, his early manuscript "Le Parfait Théologien" already showed signs of such critique. Schwab also accepted Anquetil-Duperron's basic narrative about the primary aim of his journey to India as stated in the title of the 1762 report: "to discover and translate the works attributed to Zoroaster."

> In 1754, I happened to see a fragment of the *Vendidad Sade*, which had been sent from England to M. Fourmont,[16] and I immediately resolved to enrich my country with that singular work. I formed a design of translating it, and of going with that view to learn the ancient Persic in Guzarate or Kirman; an undertaking which would necessarily enlarge the ideas I had already conceived, concerning the origin of languages, and

the several changes to which they are subject, and probably throw a light upon Oriental antiquity, which was unknown to the Greeks and Romans. (Anquetil-Duperron 1787b:104)

This narrative became gospel. While the *Encyclopaedia Iranica* does not mention dramatic details such as that his only baggage was a small knapsack with "two handkerchiefs, two shirts, a pair of stockings, a mathematics case, a Hebrew Bible, and a copy of Montaigne" and that he left France on a prisoner ship almost like in a scene from *Manon Lescaut* (Schwab 1934:23–24), it conveys the essence of the myth as historical fact:

> After distinguishing himself in classical studies, Anquetil-Duperron went to Holland to study Oriental languages, especially Arabic, with the Jansenists exiled at Amersfoort. Back in Paris, he was appointed to the Bibliothèque du Roi (now the Bibliothèque Nationale). In 1754, he was shown a few lines copied from a fragment of the Avesta brought in 1723 to the Bodleian Library, Oxford, by Richard Colbe. He decided to go to India to retrieve the sacred book, which Colbert, Louis XIV's minister, had ordered Father J. F. Pétis de la Croix, a Capuchin, to bring back from Iran without success. In order to hasten his departure he enrolled as a soldier in the Compagnie des Indes and walked all the way to Lorient on the Atlantic in the company of recruits from Parisian prisons. But before embarking on 7 February 1755 he received an allowance of 500 pounds from the Bibliothèque and thus was able to travel as a free passenger. (Duchesne-Guillemin 1987:2.100–101)

However, I found that Anquetil-Duperron already planned to go to India around the end of 1753—that is, no less than eighteen months before his departure and before he ever saw the Avesta fragment. He told Abbé Jean-Baptiste Ladvocat "at the beginning of 1754 about the voyage that I counted on making to India," and the Abbé then showed the young man the reports of the Danish missionaries of Tranquebar (Anquetil-Duperron 1771:I.2. ccccxcix).[17] This account contradicts Anquetil-Duperron's self-publicized myth that he made this decision in 1754 "on the spot [sur le champ]" (Anquetil-Duperron 1771:I.1.vi).

In the first report after his return from India (1762), he wrote of embarking in 1755 "with a resolution of bringing back the laws of Zoroaster and the Bramins" (p. 105) and added that, before leaving France, he promised "to make myself master of the religious institutions of all Asia" (p. 107). This did not mean that he would study them all, but rather that he would study their common basis: the Vedas. And for this he needed to know Sanskrit:

> There is a Samskretam of different ages, and I was desirous of having examples of it thro' all its variations, that I might fix the language in which all the books which are held sacred in that part of Asia which reaches from Persia to China are written. (p. 107)

This gives us a sense of the true objective of Anquetil-Duperron's India adventure. The books that are "held sacred" in most of Asia, from Persia to India and China, and are written in Sanskrit are certainly no Zoroastrian texts. By piecing together information from Anquetil-Duperron's travelogues and letters, one gains the distinct impression that the acquisition and study of the Vedas rather than of Zoroastrian texts was his primary objective and that he later mischaracterized his objectives in order to be seen as having achieved the exact goal that he had proposed. His travelogue is rich in information that disproves the reprioritized narrative that became part of his standard biography. At the very beginning of his stay in Pondicherry, he had the following plan: "After having become familiar with Persian, I wanted to go educate myself in the Malabar region, visit the Brahmes, and learn the Samskretan at some famous pagoda" (p. xxvi). In February 1756, half a year after his arrival in Pondicherry, Anquetil-Duperron was intent on "living from milk, rice, and vegetables in order to be able to afford from my savings the purchase of books and payment of Brahmes of which I planned to become the disciple" (pp. xxix–xxx). He also wanted to devote himself "more freely to the study of Indian books" (p. xxxi) and decided for this reason to travel to the Bengal region. In April 1756 he arrived in Chandernagor, fell ill, and remained for several months in the hospital built by the Jesuit Antoine Mozac, the very man who (probably after joining the Malabar mission) copied all the Pondicherry Vedas. Father Mozac told Anquetil-Duperron about the nearby city of Cassimbazar where he had studied Sanskrit and where several Brahmins resided. Anquetil-Duperron hoped to "stay there for an extended period without too many expenses" (p. xxxviii). But his illness was so grave that he had to remain in the Jesuit hospital until the fall of 1756.

Now more than a year had passed since his arrival in India, and Anquetil-Duperron seriously "thought about renouncing my projects and embracing the priesthood to which I always had been inclined"; even becoming a Jesuit was an option because the order's activity "corresponded sufficiently to the plan for whose execution I had come to India" (p. xxxix). In March 1757, he was still in Chandernagor; around this time he got news from a Frenchman in Surate that the Parsee doctors had "the books of Zoroaster" and were willing to explain it" to Anquetil-Duperron and to teach him the ancient languages (p. xl). Chandernagor being under attack and war in the air, Anquetil-Duperron made a trip to Cassimbazar but "did not find affairs in the state that I had expected" (p. xlii). His passport mentioned his "project in Benares" (p. L)—which was, of course, to study Sanskrit and translate the Vedas—but due to the war, this was impossible. It is only at this point that Anquetil-Duperron, fearing for his life and having lost most of his possessions, decided to travel to Surat via Pondicherry to study Zoroastrian texts (p. xlix). This course of events suggests that the principal objective of his voyage to India was not the acquisition and translation of Zoroastrian texts but the acquisition and translation of the Vedas. Not the Zoroastrian texts but the Vedas seemed to be the key to "all the religious institutions of Asia." But why was young Anquetil-Duperron so convinced that the Vedas contained "the sacred laws of all of Asia" (Anquetil-Duperron 1771:1.2.ccclxiv)?

Fréret, de Visdelou, and Deshauterayes

Through his employment at the Royal Library, before his India journey, Anquetil-Duperron came into contact not only with Deshauterayes, who showed him the famous Avesta fragment, but also with Fourmont's other disciple Joseph de Guignes. In the year 1753, at whose end Anquetil-Duperron decided to go to India to study Sanskrit and the Vedas—and thus to acquire the key to the sacred laws that anciently reigned in all lands between Persia, India, and China—there were several events of importance for Paris orientalists. One was de Guignes's presentation on July 24 at the Royal Academy about the Samanéens. De Guignes claimed that the Brachmanes and the Samanéens were in fact two sects of one religion that he called "la religion Indienne" (the Indian religion). This religion had metempsychosis as its central tenet and regarded the Samanéens as the ultimate stage of purification (see Chapter 4). But de Guignes left open many questions regarding the history of this religion and its relationship to the Vedas.

The idea of an Indian religion reigning in most of Asia was, as we have seen, rather old. But it had gained new relevance through Johann Jacob

Brucker's multi-volume history of philosophy (Brucker 1742–44) and through the ideas of an erstwhile rival of de Guignes's and Deshauterayes's teacher Fourmont. This man was Nicolas FRÉRET (1688–1749), famous as the first Frenchman in Paris to study Chinese and even more as an expert on chronology and ancient history.[18] In the last years of his life, Fréret showed acute interest not only in the chronologies of Asia but also in their religions, and on February 7, 1744, he presented some findings to the Royal Academy that he planned to include in a book. But this book never appeared, and four years after Fréret's death, a summary of his 1744 presentation was published under the title of "Researches on the religious and philosophical traditions of the Indians, to serve as preparation for the examination of their chronology" (Fréret 1753:34). Fréret not only thought, like many others, that "the Indian religion is very widespread in the Orient" but also spoke of two major branches. The first branch is "the religion of the Brahmes which encompasses almost all ancient inhabitants of the lands between the Indus and the Ganges," and the second branch consists of the religion "dominating the region to the North and East of the Ganges" as far as Tibet and Bhutan. This second branch of Indian religion is the one that "the Chinese have adopted in the year 64 of the Christian era and is also dominant in Japan" as well as Vietnam, Laos, Cambodia, Burma, and other Asian countries (p. 36).

Fréret's second branch of "Indian religion" clearly refers to what we today call Buddhism, and in his 1744 presentation to the Academy, he emphasized the importance of scientific research and language study to gain a better understanding of this religion that appeared to be the largest in the world. Like de Guignes a decade later, Fréret sought to associate specific sacred texts with this "branch." Instead of the *Anbertkend* and the *Forty-Two Sections Sutra* that de Guignes in the 1750s was to regard as foundational for this widespread branch of Indian religion, Fréret opted for the Vedas. Since the Vedas were not available to him, he relied—like Holwell after him—on the report about their content in the sixth book of the *Decada Quinta* of do Couto (see Chapter 6). Fréret quoted do Couto's assertion that Indian religion has a creator God named *Scharoües Zibari*, who is surrounded by pure spirits who contemplate him (p. 38). Unlike Holwell who interpreted Couto's good spirits as angels serving God, however, Fréret connected them with the quietist notion of supreme beatitude. In his view this state corresponds to "what the Siamese call *Niveupan*, the Peguans *Niban*, the Japanese *Safene*, and the Chinese *Coung-hiou*" (p. 38).[19]

Fréret thus relied on the reports by Couto, Roger, and Baldaeus for the first "branch of Indian religion"—the one that dominates the Indian subcontinent—and the descriptions by de la Loubère, Pierre Bayle, La Croze, and others for the other "branch" that dominated most of the rest of Asia. He weaved all this into his portrait of a gigantic religion that worships God in the form of Vishnu. Since he had read that Buddha is an incarnation of Vishnu, which marks the beginning of the fourth world age, the link between these two branches seemed obvious. Fréret explained:

> We omit here all that concerns the eight previous apparitions of *Vishnu* that do not belong to the present historical period. In the ninth [apparition] which belongs to our age, he came on earth in human form. In the Indies and on the island of Ceylon he is called *Boudhé* or *Boudhan*; in Siam *Ponti-tchaou* which is the same as *Sommonacodon*, translated in de la Loubère's report as *Talapoin of the woods*. In China he is called *Po* or *Fo* or according to Portuguese orthography *Foé*, and sometimes *Chékia* or *Chaka*. The Japanese honor him under the title of *Amida*;[20] this is throughout Vishnu under different names. (p. 44)

Fréret's report that was published in 1753, the year of Anquetil-Duperron's decision to travel to India, presented this "Indian religion" as "an extremely ancient system in the Indies" that radiated far toward East and West. He saw clear traces of it in the system of Pythagoras, and even "Plato adopted a part of Indian ideas." They also found their way into Christianity through Origen who "pretended to adapt them to Christianity" (p. 45). Fréret was convinced that "the Indian religion, like all the others, had at its origin the primary truths that are generally known by all men and that form the body of natural revelation that is as old as the universe" (p. 45). This view of "Indian religion" was surprisingly long-lived and influential. For example, in 1777, the huge *Dictionary of Classical Authors* furnished under the heading "The religion of the Indians" exclusively information from Fréret's summary, adopting it almost word for word (Sabbathier 1777:22.241–26).

But Fréret's vision also deeply influenced de Guignes, Deshauterayes, and young Anquetil-Duperron. From Fréret's viewpoint, there was nothing more urgent than the study of the Vedas. They had to contain not only the basis of the subcontinental "branch" of India's religion but also the second branch that we now call Buddhism. The Vedas were thus most likely to furnish the "key" that young Anquetil-Duperron had in mind when he wrote of making himself "master of the religious institutions of all Asia" through the study of ancient Sanskrit texts (Anquetil-Duperron 1787b:107). Exactly because he, like Fréret and de Guignes, thought that the religious traditions of the Indian subcontinent and most other Asian countries had the same "Indian" root, he thought of China as a possible avenue for information about it. Unable to gain access to the Vedas even after four years in India, Anquetil-Duperron planned to travel via Tibet to China where he hoped to find ancient Indian texts that the Brahmins or *polomen* might have brought there.[21] So he wrote two letters to the Jesuit Antoine Gaubil in Peking (who had been recommended to him by Deshauterayes) to inquire about this. Though Anquetil-Duperron's letters are no longer extant, Gaubil's response forms part of Anquetil-Duperron's manuscript dossier at the Bibliothèque Nationale in Paris:[22]

> I have received five days ago the letter that you made me the honor of writing from Goa on 20 March of 1758, [but] I have not received the one you said you wrote from Pondicherry. The polomen or brahmes came to China from the Indies more than 1600 years ago. More than 1300 years ago several Chinese put them into Chinese characters and in a Chinese language. What they learned from the polomen about the religion, astronomy, geometry, etc.—these books are lost, and what remains consists only of a few truncated and confused fragments. The Chinese bonzes then took care to translate into Chinese the Indian doctrine, and in their prayer books, etc., they transcribed in Chinese characters many terms and phrases that nobody understands.[23] . . . If you execute your plan to come to China by way of Tartary, you will have quite some expenses to incur, quite some obstacles to overcome, and more than once you will be in need of heroic patience. Add to this many life-threatening dangers.

To judge from Father Gaubil's letter, Anquetil-Duperron was discouraged by Brahmin unwillingness to teach foreigners Sanskrit and was intent on finding materials in Chinese for the study of Sanskrit and ancient Indian doctrine. But Gaubil informed him in a postscript: "Even if in the past the Chinese have learned the rules of the Sanscroudang [Sanskrit] by way of the polomen, one does not find these books at all, and I do not believe that there is someone who would have read such [books]."

Thus, Athanasius Kircher's and Claude de Visdelou's ideas of Brahmin missionaries in the Far East teamed up with Fréret's two-branched Asian monotheism to form a powerful motive for the search for ancient texts of "Indian" religion in countries other than India. But there was yet another hidden avenue of de Visdelou's influence on Anquetil-Duperron. On October 8, 1755, his mentor Deshauterayes wrote a long letter to India to inform the young man about several issues of interest.[24] He sent Anquetil-Duperron a reading list of literature about Indian religion (NAF 8872:70r) in which he particularly recommended books by Abraham Roger and La Croze. With regard to languages, Deshauterayes insisted that "one must learn the language of a people of which one wants to speak and critically read its writings" (p. 73r) and recommended the study of the "Baly [Pali] language which is the only language of the Indies, along with the Tibetan, that I strongly exhort you to learn" (p. 70v). Deshauterayes had told Anquetil-Duperron before his departure for India about an unpublished paper about the Samanéens that he had written. In the letter, Deshauterayes informs his protégé about some of its content. One passage in particular attracted my attention when I first read it. Deshauterayes informs Anquetil-Duperron that the Samanéens are monotheists worshipping a God called *Aruguen* and teach everywhere moral virtues and the transmigration of souls:

> The God *Aruguen* whom they worship has given the Vedam, which is why he is called *adi Veden* the legislator, and *Vêda-niden*, the Lord of the Law. These titles are also atrributed to Vichnou by his devotees; but there is nothing surprising about this because, for the Indians, the ninth incarnation of *Vishnu* was in *Boudha*, and *Boudha*, I believe, is not different from *Aruguen*. One still gives to this God Aruguen the epithet of *Siva cadigu'irveiven*, that is, *Lord of the glory of God Shiva*, and that of *Puten* which I believe derived from the term *Boudha*. (p. 70v)

Deshauterayes had a very similar argument printed more than twenty years later in 1778:

> *Arugen*, the god of the *Samanes*, is the same as *Boudha*; he has given the divine law of the *Védam*, and this is why he is called *Adi-vèden*, the first legislator, *Vêda-niden*, the lord of the law; titles which are also attributed to *Vichenou* by his devotees, which is not surprising because, according to the Indians, *Vichenou* in his ninth incarnation became *Boudha*, and *Boudha* seems not at all different from *Aruguen*. (Mailla 1778:5.52)

These "Samanes" who believe in Buddha = Aruguen appear to be monotheists of the purest kind whose religion is very ancient. The following passage
is not in the letter of 1755 but clarifies Deshauterayes's view of these pure
ancient monotheists:

> The *Samanes* are probably as ancient in the Indies as the *Brahmes* and
> have left many monuments of their genius, had a religion which was not
> different from that of the *Gymnosophistes* and knowledge of an infinitely
> perfect being that they called *Aruguen* and to whom they gave the most
> excellent attributes. They call him god of virtue, pure, infinite, eternal
> god, immovable, very wise god, very kind, very powerful, etc. They add
> that he reigned happily in the heavens in the shadow of a tree *Asôgu* or
> *Pindi*. Since the *Samanes* completely neglected the cult of other gods in
> favor of *Aruguen*, they were usually called *Aruguer;* but those among
> them who distinguished themselves through their spirituality and the
> sanctity of their life were called *Sâraner.* (p. 51)

Deshauterayes clearly thought that the sectarians of Buddha are monotheists; that they are no different from Vaishnavas; that the Veda is their
sacred scripture; and that the Veda is a thoroughly monotheist text revealed
by the god Buddha = Vishnu = Aruguen. I kept wondering where Deshauterayes got these ideas and words like *Adi-vèden* from, until in the summer of
2008, I went through the papers of a De Guignes folder[25] at the Bibliothèque
Nationale. Someone wrote in small letters on the cover sheet: "These papers
were mixed with those of Fourmont. One can, on account of the handwriting
and their content, attribute more or less all of them to De Guignes." Only
the first sheet is dated "3 May 1754"; it is an introduction to the history
of the Samanéens. On page 4 begins a long document titled "Letter from
Pondicherry. On the Sammaneens" which on page 7v has the following familiar passage:

> The God Aruguen worshiped by the Sammanéens is also called Puten.
> One gives him also the epithet of *Siva cadigu 'irveivem,* that is, Lord of
> the glory of God Chiven. They say that this God Aruguen gave the
> divine Law or Vêdam: that is why he is called *Âdi vèden,* that is first
> legislator, and *vêdaniden,* the Lord of the Law: yet it is true that these
> names are also given to Vichnou by his devotees.

Deshauterayes letter to Anquetil	Copy of Pondicherry letter
Boudha	*Budda*

Figure 20. Handwriting comparison of NAF 8872 and NAF 279.

The dossier contains a fragment of one more letter from Pondicherry (pp. 11r–12v), and the content of both letters indicates that there must have been a total of three letters written by a French-speaking missionary in Pondicherry. The first letter cites La Croze and was thus written after 1724. The third letter cites Engelbert Kaempfer and was thus written after 1729. The writer could read Chinese (he cites Ma Duanlin and various Chinese texts) and was familiar with Indian terminology. He also knew southern Indian literature and criticized a text dating by the Danish missionaries. And, of course, the writer of the letters resided in Pondicherry in the early 1730s, just around the time when Calmette wrote the *Ezour-vedam*. Given these data, the only author I can think of is Claude de Visdelou, who died in Pondicherry in 1737. The letters were thus probably sent to Paris between 1730 and 1737. The addressee is unknown (he is once called "mon cher Osman"), but there is little doubt that the precise references to Chinese texts were meant for Fourmont and that someone had copied parts or all of these letters. The copied first letter and part of the third letter somehow ended up in Fourmont's files at the Bibliothèque Nationale, and later someone decided that they are from de Guignes, which is why they ended up in his dossier (NAF no. 279).

However, a handwriting comparison (see Figure 20) shows that the copyist of these letters from Pondicherry was Deshauterayes and not de Guignes.[26] Deshauterayes' quotations from de Visdelou's letters in his missive to Anquetil-Duperron show, as does his note in de Mailla's history, that he was just as good as his rival de Guignes and their teacher Fourmont at plagiarizing the writings of missionaries. Having copied these Pondicherry letters, Deshauterayes used parts of them in his letter to Anquetil-Duperron as if these were his own findings, adding "I believe" and "I concluded," etc., to de Visdelou's text! He also asked Anquetil-Duperron to find out some things that he found intriguing in de Visdelou's letters, for example, the identity of the Parajacechatam sect that supposedly destroyed the sect of the Sammanéens in India

(NAF no. 8872:72). The Pondicherry of the 1730s was a truly amazing hub of information!

Abbé Mignot's Blueprint

On March 14, 1762, Anquetil-Duperron returned to Paris after a stay of nearly six years in India, and the next day he deposited his manuscripts at the Royal Library. In June his report appeared in the *Journal des Sçavans*, and he became an instant celebrity. The title of his report indicated that he had gone to India "to discover and translate the works attributed to Zoroaster." At age 31, Anquetil-Duperron was hailed in the *Annual Register* as a "a true virtuoso" who braved "every danger" for the sole purpose of increasing "the materials of speculation in the learned world" (Anquetil-Duperron 1787b:103). Just after the publication of his report, he was invited to a dinner where he saw de Guignes again and also met a guest who had the distinction of being Voltaire's nephew and a very erudite man: Abbé Vincent MIGNOT. That very month Mignot was reading his fourth paper on the ancient philosophers of India at a session of the Royal Academy, and there can be no doubt that Anquetil-Duperron attended it. Mignot had read the three earlier papers while Anquetil-Duperron was preparing for his return or was on his way back to Europe.

Mignot's first paper, read on February 27, 1761, had dealt mainly with the question of whether the Egyptians had influenced the Indians or vice versa. Mignot concluded that Buddha, who is considered the father of Indian philosophy, lived about 1000 B.C.E. and that this makes his religion too ancient to have been influenced by Greeks or Egyptians (Mignot 1768:81–113). The second paper, read on June 2 of the same year, showed that features of Indian religion that were considered to be of Egyptian origin (transmigration, lingam and cow cult, and such) could be explained without Egyptian influence and that La Croze's and Kaempfer's ideas about the Egyptian origin of Buddha's religion were built on sand because the association of Buddha and Mercury with Wednesday is much younger than they had believed (pp. 114–52). The third paper rejected early Egyptian influence on India by arguing that there simply was no commercial or other link between the two countries at such an early point (pp. 153–211).

For someone like Anquetil-Duperron who did not believe in the theories of Egyptian origins that were so fashionable among collaborators of the *En-*

cyclopédie, these three papers (which he might have read only in 1768 when they were printed together with numbers 4 and 5) were less interesting than the last two of Mignot's lectures that he could actually attend. Mignot continued to discount early Egyptian influence on India. In the fourth paper, read on June 15, 1762, he mainly sought to show the differences—all in India's favor—between a number of Indian and Egyptian religious doctrines. With respect to strict monotheism, for example, Mignot regarded the Indians as far superior to the Egyptians. Citing do Couto, La Croze, François Bernier, and also Indians' letters to Ziegenbalg, Mignot found that even the "successors of the ancient Brachmanes are intimately persuaded about the unity of God"; and so is "the sect of *Gnanigueuls* who are regarded as the sages and saints of India." They reject openly the "cult of idols and all superstitious practices of the nation in order to worship only God whom they call the *being of beings*" (p. 219). The Buddha, too, was called upon for the support of Indian monotheism:

> It is to express this perfect simplicity of God that Budda, the author of Indian philosophy, when he explained his true feelings to his dearest disciples, told them that the principle and end of all things was emptiness or nothingness [le vide ou le néant]; this nothingness or this emptiness was, according to his doctrine, a real being [un être réel] because he gave it attributes and taught that it was admirable, pure, infinite, and the principle and perfection of all beings. By calling it *empty* or *nothing* [vide ou néant] he adapted himself to the conventions of common people [vulgaire grossier] who use the term "nothing" for anything that has no coarse parts, does not fall, or is not perceived by its senses. The disciples of these philosophers, who remained faithfully attached to the doctrine of their master, recognize until today that God is a pure spirit and an infinite immaterial intelligence; this is how they put it in the comprehensive theology that was given in Couto, the continuator of Barros; and in one of their books entitled *Panjangam*, which is their almanach, one reads this prayer: I adore this being whose nature is indivisible, and whose simplicity does not admit any composition of qualities. (pp. 224–25)

The five papers Mignot read at the Royal Academy, and particularly the fourth and fifth whose presentation Anquetil-Duperron could attend in person, were almost like a blueprint for Anquetil-Duperron's further work on

India. Both men were convinced that India and its Vedas had preserved the most complete vestiges of man's Ur-religion, opposed the encyclopedists's ideas of Egyptian origin, and somehow wanted to build their Indian Ur-religion on the bedrock of the main events and chronology described in the book of Genesis. In the "triangle of origin narratives," the biblical corner was still dominant and very crowded. In exchange, the Egyptian corner could boast of some famous names of intellectuals and encyclopedists. The Indian corner was at this point still almost empty, but in the 1760s, the situation began to change. Merely four decades later, Friedrich Schlegel was to write enthusiastically in a letter: "alles, alles stammt aus Indien, ohne Ausnahme" [Everything, everything comes from India, without exception]" (Schlegel 1864:3.329). The *Ezour-vedam*'s deposition at the Royal Library, Voltaire's 1761 edition of the *Essai sur les moeurs* with its stunning vista of an Indian origin of civilization, Abbé Mignot's India papers with their monotheistic Buddha, and Anquetil-Duperron's return from India all seemed to ring in a new era. Long before the beginning of the European colonial domination of India, "Indian religion" was seen as a pan-Asian phenomenon with "Brahmanic" and "Buddhist" branches. Diderot and many others thought it had Egyptian roots and associated it with polytheism, idolatry, atheism, materialism, or fatalism. But a second major line of interpretation was gathering steam in the 1750s and 1760s. Inspired by Brucker,[27] Fréret, de Guignes, and Mignot, it interpreted even the Buddha's "inner" teaching of emptiness and nothingness as a (possibly degraded) vestige of ancient monotheism and identified Asia's dominant "Indian religion" with humankind's universal, god-given ancient theology. At the beginning of the nineteenth century this became one of the core ideas of the indomaniac Romantic age in which Anquetil-Duperron's translations played a key role. But in the 1760s, when Voltaire and Holwell peddled their "proofs" of ancient Indian monotheism, this second line of interpretation was still in its infancy.

The Holwell Shock

What bothered both Mignot and Anquetil-Duperron was that there were descriptions of the Vedas but hardly any translated material. Instead of being able to quote the Vedas themselves, Mignot had to rely on bits and pieces from do Couto, Jesuit letters, communications by Danish missionaries, Roger, La Croze, and, of course, the newly arrived *Ezour-vedam*. But this text was no Veda either but rather a commentary by someone who criticized the Vedas. On August 27 of 1766, Anquetil-Duperron received a visit of Antoine Court de Gébelin from Geneva who told him about another copy of the *Ezour-vedam* brought back from Pondicherry by a Mr. Tessier (Rocher 1984:8). From this manuscript, Anquetil-Duperron made his own copy and noted that it had a chapter at the end that was missing in Voltaire's copy. In the margins of his copy, he made several remarks that are signs of frustration. He would have liked to see Vedic quotations; but instead of citing textual authority, Chumontou keeps appealing to reason. One of Anquetil-Duperron's comments reads:

> This is how the Br[ahman] Chumontou proceeds. Later in this treatise he refutes the legends told by Biache, either because they are contrary to good sense, or because they are not found in the ancient books, and he provides a moralistic explanation for those that are based on facts which he agrees to. However, these legends are accepted throughout India (see Abrah. Roger), and Chumontou does no more than confront them with the doubts of a philosopher which cannot be held to represent the religion of India. To prove that they are, he ought to combat authority by authority. (Rocher 1984:8–9)

But soon afterward, in 1767, a sensational translation of an ancient Indian text arrived in France: Holwell's *Shastah*. It created quite a stir and was almost immediately publicized by Voltaire and published in French (1768). A major reason for the commotion was its introduction, which presented a four-stage genealogy of India's sacred literature, claimed that the "Vedam" was used only in southern India, and called it a late and degenerate source that was absolutely inferior both in age and quality to the *Shastah* presented and translated by Holwell (see Chapter 6). The matter bothered Anquetil-Duperron so much that he bought a second copy of the French edition of Holwell's book and sent it to Father Antoine MOZAC (1704–c.1784) in India asking for his opinion. In his parcel he also included the Royal Academy volume containing Abbé Mignot's five papers.

Anquetil-Duperron was full of big questions, but in his letter to Gaston Laurent COEURDOUX (1691–1779) that was included in the same package, he played down their scope: "I would like to ask you two small clarifications about matters that you surely know perfectly. The first is about the nature of the *Paraparavastou*, the supreme Being, the first cause in Indian theology;

and the second concerns the nature, origin, and antiquity of the *Vedams*, or *Vedes*, *Beids*. We would be very interested in seeing what you have collected about this" (Anquetil-Duperron 1808:672). His letter to Fr. Mozac, who had studied Sanskrit and given Anquetil-Duperron advice about this while he was for many months at the mission hospital at Chandernagor, was more explicit. Since his stay at Chandernagor, he had never contacted Mozac again, but now, eleven years later, he was desperate: everything he thought he knew about the Vedas had been torpedoed by Holwell's stunning assertions.

Holwell had, in fact, been second in command at Cassimbazar, the very city where Mozac had studied Sanskrit and where Anquetil-Duperron had wanted to follow in Mozac's footsteps. There was this strange link between the fate of Holwell, who apparently had managed to learn from the Brahmins at Cassimbazar, Mozac who had studied Sanskrit there, and Anquetil-Duperron, who had wanted to do the same but ended up having to embrace what really was his second choice, namely, the study of Zoroastrian texts. "It seems that his plan is to elevate the Indian religion above all other known religions," he wrote to Mozac about Holwell, "and if his work presents some exceptions in favor of Christianity, one sees well that they are only due to the author's profession of this religion" (p. 675). Anquetil-Duperron had carefully compared the French translation to the English original and noted some translation mistakes in the margins of the copy he sent to Father Mozac. He also sent a list of contradictions that he had noted: Holwell's claim that this religion is purely monotheistic, while the text contains numerous examples of polytheism; various problems in the relationship of God and the Trimurti; strange contradictions with regard to Holwell's angels; the list goes on (pp. 675–76). Anquetil-Duperron's most urgent questions, however, concerned the relationship between Holwell's *Shastah* and the Vedas:

> The fourth point that strikes me as particular about M. Holwell is that he reports, based on the words of Brahmes, about the origin of the *Vedam* which he makes younger by 1,500 years than the *Chartah Bhade Shastahs* of Brahma. First of all, it seems to me that one should have written *schastra* and not *schastah*. In malabar *schastiram*, in telougou *schastram* signify *science, doctrine*; and under this name is comprised what is in the *Vedam*. Second, the author distinguishes the *Bhades* from the *Vedam*; yet I find nothing in the books at my disposal that authorizes this distinction. (p. 677)

Anquetil-Duperron had never heard that the Vedas are only used in the south and the Shastah in the north and wondered how this was compatible with the description of the Vedas by do Couto (p. 677). Another doubt he presented to Father Mozac concerned Holwell's angels. Noting that do Couto had also described the second class of higher intelligences as prisoners in bodies that are on earth for purification, he asked Mozac, "Are these ideas about metempsychosis taken from ancient books of the Indians? Is what the author says about the fall of the angels and the apparitions of good genies on earth really found in the text that he calls the *Schartah Bhade* of *Bramah*?" (p. 678).

Anquetil-Duperron also felt that Holwell's ideas about metempsychosis were contradicted by Indian animal sacrifices. To make sure that Father Mozac's reply would cover his major doubts, he added a summary at the end with the title "Questions to clarify":

1. About the first principle recognized by the Indians; about *Bram, Birmah*; the allegorical explanations, etc.
2. On the origin and the nature of the *Vèdes* or *Bhades* or *Vedams*;
3. On the fall of the angels, the origin of metempsychosis, and the [origin of] the custom obliging women to burn themselves, etc.
4. About bloody sacrifices in use or not with the Indians; the Sanskrit dictionary mentions sacrificial horses. (p. 680)

These were indeed good questions, but Father Mozac never responded. While Anquetil-Duperron finished his *Zend Avesta* translation and prepared it for publication, two other works with translations of Indian texts came to his attention: Dow's *History of Hindostan* (1768) and the manuscript of Maridas Poullé's *Bagavadam* translation that he could borrow for two or three days in 1770 (Anquetil-Duperron 1787a:2.64).

In February 1771, Coeurdoux at last responded with a gentle criticism of Abbé Mignot's idealization of Indian religion and his misunderstanding of the lingam cult and wrote that Abbé Mignot might profit from "following in the footsteps of another scholar and spending a few years in India" while promising, should he do that, to show him "the unity of God and the great event of the deluge in the Indian books" (Anquetil-Duperron 1808:49.681–82). He also responded to Anquetil-Duperron's central question about the Vedas:

I must now respond to your questions about the *Vedams*. We name them in Telugu and in the Samscroutane script of this region, *Sâma vedam*, *Ezour vedam*, *Roug vedam*, *Adharvana vedam*. Several people say that this last *Vedam* is lost; I believe nothing of it. It is, one is assured, a book of *magic*; and this sort of books least of all gets lost in a heathen country where there are people everywhere who play themselves up as magicians. I saw a book of magic secrets that began with the first lines of the *Adharvana vedam*; but there was nothing more . . . There are Brahmes of every *Vedam*, and each knows of which *Vedam* he is. Does it seem possible that those of the fourth could have permitted theirs to get lost? (pp. 684–85)

But now Coeurdoux added two remarks that not only confounded Anquetil-Duperron but puzzled many readers, including this writer:

I will add here what I have heard Father Calmette—who knew the samscroutam [Sanskrit] and had much studied the books of Indian science—utter more than once: that the true *Vedam* [le vrai *Vedam*] is of such an ancient samscroutam that it is almost unintelligible, and that what one cites is of the *Vedantam*, that is, of introductions and commentaries that were made of the *Vedam*. In effect, in a famous prayer named *gaïtrì*, one understands only the word *savitourou*, the sun. (p. 685)

But it is the remark that immediately follows that led to accusations of lies and deception. Since this is a crucial passage, I quote also its original French:

D'un autre côté, le P. Mosac, qui n'a pas moins étudié la langue Samscroutane, prétend avoir découvert le vrai *Vedam*. Il le fait postérieur à la gentilité Indienne, dont il est la réfutation détaillée. Cet ouvrage a pour auteur un vrai philosophe ennemi du polythéisme, tel que toute la terre en eut long-temps après le déluge. Ce vaste ouvrage a été traduit par le P. Mosac; et quel trésor pour vous, s'il vouloit vous le communiquer.

On the other hand, the Father Mosac, who has studied the Samscroutane language not less [than Father Calmette], pretends to have discovered the true *Vedam*. He makes it posterior to Indian heathendom, of which it is a detailed refutation. This work has as its author a true philosopher and enemy of polytheism of the kind that the whole earth had for a long time after the deluge. This vast work has been translated by Fr. Mosac;

and what treasure [would it be] for you if he were willing to communicate it to you! (p. 685)

Coeurdoux's juxtaposition of two "true" Vedas is breathtaking. He clearly takes the side of Fr. Calmette, who talked about the difficulty of the Veda's language and about its *Vedanta* commentaries. The second "true" Veda, by contrast, seems to be genuine only for Father Mozac who *pretends* to have discovered it and *makes it* posterior to heathendom. Yet Coeurdoux lauds Mozac's Veda author as *a true philosopher* and *enemy of polytheism* and calls it a *vast work* that Father Mozac has *already translated*.

Anquetil-Duperron, who added some comments on other pages of this letter, did not write anything in the margins of this page. But in the printed version of 1808, he explained in a note, "This work must be the *Ezourvedam*" and added a reference to his *Zend Avesta* (where he first quoted the *Ezourvedam*) and to the printed edition by Sainte-Croix of 1778.

It is clear that Coeurdoux, who had attentively studied Mignot's articles and provided some detailed criticisms, knew that the *Ezour-vedam* was in the Royal Library in Paris and that it was now used and cited by academics like Mignot. What he probably did not know was that Voltaire had sent it there; Mignot had mentioned only the librarian's name. This remark about Mozac's Veda was not in answer to any question, since Anquetil-Duperron had written nothing in his letters about the *Ezour-vedam*. Coeurdoux clearly was in the loop about the content of Mozac's Veda because he knows that it is "a detailed refutation" of Indian heathendom written by "a true philosopher and enemy of polytheism." We must therefore assume that the reason why Coeurdoux even mentioned Mozac's Veda and described it in a way that would immediately point to the *Ezour-vedam* was linked to his knowledge that the *Ezour-vedam* was making waves in educated Paris.

Had Coeurdoux known at this point that it was being used by Voltaire for his anti-Christian propaganda campaign, he would very likely have kept mum; he could have mentioned some information about the real Vedas and left it at that. But he decided, for some intriguing reason, to advertise Mozac's Vedas in such a manner that Anquetil-Duperron was certain to associate it with the *Ezour-vedam*. Not only that: he wanted Anquetill-Duperron to think that it is a genuine, though later text than the Veda described by Calmette and that it forms part of a different *Vedam*. There is no doubt that he must have anticipated that this unsolicited remark about a "vast work" in the generous hands of a missionary (who for many months had taken care of

Anquetil-Duperron at the Chandernagor hospital and almost drew him into the Jesuit fold) would provoke the curiosity of the researcher who, as Coeurdoux knew, had been passionately chasing after the Vedas for years. There was no doubt that Anquetil-Duperron's next letter would bring a demand for this "vast work" that Coeurdoux dangled so conspicuously in front of the seeker of Ur-monotheism.

This is exactly what happened. In his reply of February 8, 1772, Anquetil-Duperron wrote again to Coeurdoux because Mozac never responded, and he made an attempt at flattering the silent father:

> Even though the Father Mosac has not honored me with his response, I do not doubt for a minute of his friendship for me and that the communicative character that I know him to have will cause him to share with us his important research on the languages, the history, and the mythology of North India. We wait, among other works by this erudite missionary, for the translation of what he calls the *true Vedam*, which includes the refutation of polytheism. We count on Father Mosac to join the original to his translation and to accompany this *precious treasure*, as you justly call it, with critical discussions of the nature, author, and age of this *Vedam*, the country in which it was composed, and the regions where it is the law in preference to the four *Vedas* accepted on the Malabar coast, Coromandel, the Gujarat, etc. (p. 688)

Anquetil-Duperron also made a connection that Coeurdoux might not have anticipated: he suspected that the *Vedam* of Father Mozac was the corpus of texts that contained Holwell's *Shastah*!

> Father Mosac has worked in Bengal, like Mr. Holwell; the one close to *Cassimbazar* and the other in *Cassimbazar* itself. Both speak of a *Vedam* or *Bhade* that is different from the four that we know: the *Bengal* and the neighboring countries seem the only regions of Hindostan where this *Vedam* is current. (p. 688)

But no amount of pleading could budge Father Mozac who never responded with a single word and did not even thank Anquetill-Duperron for the books he kept sending at great expense. Coeurdoux explained this silence as follows:

> I have read to Father Mozac the part of your letter which regards him. My eloquence, combined with yours, has been useless to persuade him to communicate his vast and erudite collections. (p. 690)

This was the last word Anquetil-Duperron heard from the Pondicherry missionary about this question; after this, he never received another letter.

Coeurdoux's Missing Link

The question why Coeurdoux advertised Mozac's Veda is intriguing, and it is linked to another mysterious manuscript that Hans Rothschild, the owner of the Amsterdam bookshop Antiqua, sold in 1954 to the India Office Library in London. The manuscript is now in the Asia, Pacific and Africa Collections of the British Library (APAC: Mss Eur D 22). In her fascinating two-volume study and edition of this 1987 manuscript, Sylvia Murr proved that its content stems from Father Coeurdoux and that a similar manuscript must have been plagiarized by Abbé Dubois for his famous book *Description of the Character, Manners, and Customs of the People of India* (1817). In the nineteenth century, Dubois's book became a classic about Indian religions and dominated the public image in the West for many decades, and Murr's discovery showed how information gathered by missionaries in the eighteenth century was still very much in use in the nineteenth. Here we are only interested in a small part of her fascinating story. The manuscript is in the handwriting of a French artillery officer named Desvaulx. The young man, accused of having traveled without permission and neglected his duties in India, had to return to Paris in 1777 to explain his case and justify his actions. When he showed up before the authorities, he produced this manuscript and claimed that he had not been idly traveling but had spent much of his time doing research on Indian customs and religion. Whatever the plan was, it seems to have gone awry and the manuscript, which was written in Pondicherry around 1775–76, left no trace until it resurfaced through unknown avenues in Amsterdam and was bought by the India Office half a century ago.

Since this manuscript contains entire parts that are virtually identical with texts that Coeurdoux had included in letters to Anquetil-Duperron, there is no doubt that Desvaulx's manuscript, though written in the officer's hand, consists of material authored by Coeurdoux that was modified and shortened by the officer. One of the intriguing questions raised by this is whether Coeurdoux, whose eyesight was deteriorating to the point of blindness, had used Desvaulx as his secretary and planned to have his work published in France, or whether he wanted Desvaulx to publish the book under Desvaulx's name. Murr (1987:2.50) thinks that Desvaulx could not have used

Coeurdoux's work without the missionary's approval. But did Coeurdoux want Desvaulx to copy and publish his original manuscript? Or did he "consent to let him abbreviate and modify it" (p. 50) in view of a goal that both agreed upon, namely, the defense of Christianity? Murr thinks it more likely that Coeurdoux and Desvaulx worked as author and secretary and that abbreviations and modifications were made with Coeurdoux's blessing (p. 51). Still, the question remains: did Coeurdoux also agree to modifications clearly designed to erase traces of authorship that were incompatible with Desvaulx's stay in India—for example, the elimination of earlier dates and of events in towns that Desvaulx had never visited? This would mean that Coeurdoux consented to publication of his writings under Desvaulx's name—in other words, a leak of his work for a good cause without implicating his name.

And this possibility is exactly what made me first think that Coeurdoux could have leaked not just this manuscript but also another one: the *Ezour-vedam*. Both texts were slipped into Europe to be published by someone not associated with the Pondicherry Jesuits; both were relatively carefully edited to erase traces of original authorship and purpose; and both were directed at Europeans who undermine Christianity—deists like Voltaire, for example. Voltaire was read in Pondicherry: after all, Maudave had studied Voltaire's 1756 edition of the *Essai sur les moeurs* in India. Murr speculates that there could be a causal connection between the arrival of Desvaulx in Pondicherry at the end of 1772 and the abrupt end of Coeurdoux's correspondence with Anquetil-Duperron in October of that year. In her opinion, Desvaulx "substituted himself for Anquetil-Duperron, Jansenist and academician, who was suspected of furnishing to Voltaire and to the Encyclopedia scientific informations that were then utilized against the Church and its institutions" (p. 53).

But I think there is a less convoluted explanation that involves another leak, namely, that of the *Ezour-vedam*. When Coeurdoux wrote his advertisement for Mozac's Veda—which implied the genuineness of the texts in spite of their younger age and praised them as "great treasures"—he probably was not yet aware of Voltaire's perversion of the *Ezour-vedam*. But Desvaulx, whom Murr describes as an ardent defender of Christianity and the Bible, must have informed Coeurdoux and Mozac after his arrival in the fall of 1772 about the latest brouhaha in France: Baron d'Holbach's *System of Nature*, rampant skepticism and atheism in the salons of Paris, and, of course, Voltaire's "Indian campaign," which must have confounded the missionaries. Both Coeurdoux and Mozac knew perfectly that the Pondicherry Vedas were authored by Jesuit missionaries; after all, the handwriting of these texts was, according to Henry Hosten, certifiably that of Mozac. According to my hypothesis, what happened was the following: Coeurdoux, for reasons described above, in the early 1750s either leaked the *Ezour-vedam* himself or authorized it in order to confound European doubters with a "proof" of ancient Indian monotheism and possibly also to support or justify Jesuit mission methods. He thought it would be a kind of vaccine against skepticism and atheism. But in 1772 he learned that the vaccine not only did not prevent the disease but actually helped spread it. Indomania with its inflated world ages and idealization of Indian Ur-religion was infectious, and it rapidly appeared as a threat to biblical authority. Coeurdoux, of course, could not imagine that less than twenty years later Langlès would openly declare that the Pentateuch was plagiarized from the Vedas; but he might have seen such horror scenarios in his nightmares. The main threat was that the biblical narrative, and in particular the story of the flood,[28] would be undermined by alternative scenarios that would show the Old Testament to be a record of local events and—even worse—show God as a local divinity propped up by a local myth. The *Ezour-vedam*, from that perspective, had indeed a certain nocuous potential because, due to its origin as a non-*Prangui* missionary tool, it tried to keep things Indian and did not feature any link to the biblical line of patriarchs. Even Adimo, the Adam of the *Ezour-vedam*, was Indian, as Voltaire remarked with much glee before accusing the Jews of having plagiarized their creation story from Indian sources.

But unmasking the *Ezour-vedam* was out of the question. The last thing the Jesuits needed in their dire straits[29] was an indictment for forgery of ancient Indian texts. So Coeurdoux decided to encode the truth in those two paragraphs that have caused reactions ranging from consternation to outrage. I will now cite them once more and try to decode them. First of all, the Pondicherry Veda's real author, Calmette, needed to be protected, and this was best done by citing him (and not Pons or someone else) as the one who told the truth about the true Vedas:

> I will add here what I have heard Father Calmette—who knew the samscroutam [Sanskrit] and had much studied the books of Indian science—utter more than once: that the true *Vedam* [le vrai *Vedam*] is of such an ancient samscroutam that it is almost unintelligible, and that what one cites is of the *Vedantam*, that is, of introductions and commentaries that were made of the *Vedam*. In effect, in a famous prayer named *gaïtrì*, one

TABLE 16. FATHER COEURDOUX'S TRUTHFULNESS CONFIRMED

On the other hand, the Father Mosac, who has studied the Samscroutane language not less [than Father Calmette], pretends to have discovered the true *Vedam*.	Calmette is out of the game since he represents the *real* "true *Vedam*" which is difficult to read and ancient. But Mozac is also an expert of Sanskrit; which *suggests* (without stating it and thus lying) that the texts he *pretends* to have discovered must be Indian. Coeurdoux does not say that Calmette really discovered them, which would also be a lie.
He makes it posterior to Indian heathendom, of which it is a detailed refutation.	This also has the appearance of truth and is Coeurdoux's way of telling Anquetil that the *Ezour-vedam* is part of this body of texts. The content of the Pondicherry Vedas is described accurately. Coeurdoux knows it.
This work has as its author a true philosopher and enemy of polytheism of the kind that the whole earth had for a long time after the deluge.	This "true philosopher" is not named, but Coeurdoux knows that his name is Jean Calmette, S. J. He was a true enemy of polytheism who forged weapons against it (such as the Pondicherry Vedas) and, like all missionaries, belongs to those numerous men involved in this fight since the deluge.
This vast work	This signals to Anquetil that the *Ezour-vedam* is part of a larger body of texts, which is true.
has been translated by Father Mosac;	Coeurdoux only says that Mozac "translated" this vast work, not from what language. Only for those who (unlike Anquetil) know that Mozac translated from French to Sanskrit this is a true statement.
and what treasure [would it be] for you if he were willing to communicate it to you!	This tells Anquetil how extremely valuable these texts are (always tacitly including, of course, the *Ezour-vedam*). Coeurdoux knows very well that Mozac will not send them; thus he adds the big IF.

understands only the word *savitourou*, the sun. (Anquetil-Duperron 1808:49.685)

The next paragraph on the same page contains the tricky part and is dissected in Table 16 where the left column contains Coeurdoux's statement and the right my interpretation of it.

Having skillfully encoded the truth and proclaimed both the genuine and the Jesuit Vedas "true," Coeurdoux turned to the crux of the problem that was partly responsible for the mess: the need to establish a solid link between Noah's ark and ancient India, thus filling in some of the dotted lines in the Eusebius-related graph above (Fig. 18). This was one of those friendly takeover attempts that the famous forger ANNIUS of Viterbo (c. 1432–1502) had brought into fashion in Europe. Thanks to Annius, the invented founder of France, "Francus," got a pedigree that linked him to Japhet (Asher 1993), and a "Tuisco" with a long beard became Germany's mythical founder (Hutter 2000). In a sense this was an antidote to a virus contained in the *Ezour-vedam* that Voltaire's incubator had set loose. It was not the *Ezour-vedam* itself that was the problem, only the missing link that Voltaire had so cunningly exploited.

The link to the biblical transmission line was thus the appropriate antidote, and it was administered to Europe in two doses: first via Anquetil-Duperron and via the Academy to Abbé Mignot and the learned society of Paris, and second to a larger public through Desvaulx's book. The first dose reached its target and strengthened Anquetil-Duperron's (and Sainte-Croix's) belief that the *Ezour-vedam* is a genuine Indian text that was possibly a bit mangled in the translation and copying process. The second dose, however, was for some reason a dud; Desvaulx might have guessed that such a publication would raise questions that he could never answer; or his distracted superior said, "I shall have a look at it" and forgot to put it even into the administration files; or someone from Desvaulx's family sold the manuscript—who knows? At any rate, it ended up in Amsterdam, and its neat handwriting can now be admired at the British Library. But a larger dose of the antidote remained in Pondicherry: Coeurdoux's complete manuscript. It was first extensively used by Paulinus a Sancto Bartholomaeo and then plagiarized in its entirety by Abbé Dubois. Dubois, the very man who had introduced smallpox vaccination in southern India, was an ideal host who succeeded not only in introducing Coeurdoux's antidote to readers of English and French but in inoculating an entire generation through insertion into the textbooks and university classrooms of nineteenth-century Europe.

Father Coeurdoux's dose for Anquetil-Duperron consisted, apart from that bit of encoded truth, in a small treatise that also is contained "except for six words and some commas" in Chapter 46 of the Desvaulx manuscript and in Dubois (Murr 1987:2.30). It is a convincing proof that Coeurdoux was the author of the Desvaulx manuscript. The theme of Coeurdoux's treatise is exactly that missing link between Noah's ark and the earliest Indians. He makes them migrate from the plains of Shinar via the mountains in the north to India and lets the Indians descend from Noah's son Japhet. This is said to have happened at the beginning of the fourth *yuga*, which was within the chronological safety margin of the Septuagint's flood, and the patriarchs chosen for transmission of Noah's religion are "seven penitents" who are India's seven *rishis*:

> The epoch of the beginning of this new age is exactly the end of the deluge, very distinctly marked in all Indian books. It destroyed all men except the seven famous penitents of India with their wives. Some [sources] add *Manouvou*, of whom I have already spoken and who appears to be Noah himself. They escaped the universal ruin by means of a ship whose builder was *Vishnu* himself. I do not believe that one finds the universal deluge more clearly attested to in the diverse authors of antiquity from almost all nations who have mentioned this great event, nor in a more similar manner to the recital of Moses. (Anquetil-Duperron 1808:49.693)

This is the antidote designed for the *Ezour-vedam*'s soft spot that Voltaire had exploited, and by extension for the entire indomaniac vision of India as the cradle of civilization. Coeurdoux's Indian history *confirms* biblical history, and his portrayal of Indian religion exposes those of Voltaire and Holwell as completely baseless. The seven *rishis* of India are the country's ancient legislators and, as descendants of Noah's son Japhet, they guarantee that Ur-monotheism reached India long before the reigning polytheistic cults developed. This treatise thus reinforces the vision of a monotheistic pre-Vedic religion that forms the core of the *Ezour-vedam* and of Chumontou's teaching. Far from rejecting the *Ezour-vedam*, Coeurdoux sees its author Calmette as an excellent philosopher and as a fighter in true postdiluvian tradition against polytheism. But Coeurdoux was directing his attack not only at Voltaire. He was possibly even more concerned about Holwell, whose work, as we have seen, he also received courtesy of Anquetil-Duperron. Holwell had built his edifice almost entirely on an Indian basis and presented fragments of an Indian Old Testament that seemed designed to replace the Pentateuch. But Coeurdoux's reaction is not as dismissive as Joseph Priestley's *Comparison of the Institutions of Moses with those of the Hindoos and other Ancient Nations* two decades later (1799). At the end of the century, Priestley was already reacting against rampant indomania supported by the first translations of Sanskrit texts, especially Charles Wilkins's *Bhagavad gita* of 1785, and he saw no room whatsoever for a friendly takeover. By contrast, Coeurdoux tried to integrate India gently into his sacred history and to find "a gangway between the universal history of Bossuet and the Indians," as Murr (1987:2.173) put it. But his ultimate intention in releasing these materials certainly was the defense of biblical authority; and he was right in sensing, like Priestley, that both Voltaire's and Holwell's ventures were in the final analysis direct attacks on the Bible. As the fate of the *Ezour-vedam* shows, India had become much more than an exotic working field of missionaries. It was on the best way to turn into a battleground where not only the Jesuit order was at risk but the entire biblical basis of Christianity. And this danger seemed real. In 1771, the Swiss librarian Jean-Rodolphe SINNER von Ballaigues (1730–87) adduced all available "primary" sources he knew (Lord's *Shaster*, Roger, the *Ezour-vedam*, Holwell's *Shastah*, Dow's *History of Hindostan*, Hyde's *Historia religionis veterum persarum*) to prove that "the most part of the dogmas taught in the mysteries of the Egyptians and the Greeks appear to be drawn from the theology of the ancient Brachmanes of India" and to show "how these dogmas have passed from the Orient to Egypt and from there to Europe until the northern countries, and that it is very probable that the Purgatory of St. Patrick in Ireland is a vestige of this doctrine" (Sinner 1771:135–36)!

Sainte-Croix's Buddhist Veda

To the relief of Voltaire's many fans in Europe who had read about this text for almost two decades, the year of the writer's death finally saw the *Ezour-vedam* appear in print. Once again Switzerland was the stage of *Ezour-vedam* promotion. Voltaire's Indian campaign headquarters had been at Ferney near Geneva, and now the *Ezour-vedam* was printed in Yverdon in 1778. It was a long-awaited work, and its German translation appeared the following year in the Swiss capital of Berne. The preface to this German edition (Ith 1779:22) divulged the identity of the unnamed editor, Guillaume E. J. G. de Cleremont-Lodeven, baron de SAINTE-CROIX (1746–1809). The Bernese philosopher Johann ITH (1747–1813), who translated the text from the French, hailed this publication as a milestone:

> We expect full light from the publication of primary sources of Indian religion that are found in various European libraries, but particularly from the great number stored at the Royal Library of France. Such a

work we present to the German public through this translation of the *Ezour-Vedam* (pp. 13–16).

The *Monthly Review* (Griffiths 1780:500–505) struck a similar tone and compared the *Ezour-vedam* favorably to the publications by Roger (1651), Dow (1768), and Holwell (1765–71):

> The relations of *Rogers*, however interesting, have only for their object the popular religion of India: the accounts of *Dow* and *Holwell* contain, indeed, the most ingenious explications of the Indian fables, which they allegorize into a pure and rational series of theological doctrines; but these explications are destitute of sufficient authority; they seem to have been the inventions of certain Brahmins, who were ashamed of their absurd mythology; and they are contradicted by the commentaries and explications of others. It is only a translation, of the canonical books of Indians (of which, many extol the wisdom and antiquity, without knowing much about them) that can fix our ideas on this subject. (pp. 500–501)

Finally, the time seemed to have arrived when not just speculations but real translations from primary sources became available. The *Monthly Review* informed its many readers that Baron de Sainte-Croix had made a first step by publishing a translation "made by a Brahmin of Benares, who was a correspondent of that Academy [the Royal Academy of Inscriptions in Paris]" whose manuscript, a gift of Voltaire to the king's library, had been compared and supplemented "from another copy of the same translation, made by M. *Anquetil du Perron*, from one in the possession of the nephew of M. Barthelemy" (p. 501). But the title page of the *Ezour-vedam* only states that the book "contains the exposition of the religious and philosophical opinions of the Indians, translated from the *Samscretan* by a Brahmin." On page ix, this translator is identified by Sainte-Croix as the "*grand-prêtre ou archi-brame de la pagode de Cheringham*," but the English reviewer promoted him to the status of correspondent of the illustrious Royal Academy in Paris. Not even Voltaire would have dared to go that far; he left it at "correspondent of the French Compagnie des Indes." Ith, who published the German translation, was skeptical about Sainte-Croix's claim and noted that it depends "almost entirely on the reputation of such an unreliable writer as *Voltaire*" (Ith 1779:25–26). But Sainte-Croix had apparently discussed this with Anquetil-Duperron and assured Ith that he was personally convinced of the text's authenticity (pp. 26–27). Regarding Ith's doubts about the francophone Indian translator, Sainte-Croix informed him that, according to Anquetil-Duperron's opinion, the office of correspondent of the French Compagnie des Indes was not incompatible with the position of chief Brahman (pp. 27–28). Coeurdoux's antidote was effective.

Sainte-Croix begins his two-volume edition of the *Ezour-vedam* with some remarks about previous work on Indian religion that show his familiarity with most of the available literature in European languages. He criticized "Holwell and Dow who, penetrated by admiration for the philosophy of the Brames and zealous defenders of the purity of their dogmas, published interesting excerpts of some Shasters that they believed to be sacred and authentic" (Sainte-Croix 1778:1.vi). Sainte-Croix, by contrast, could proudly present the *Ezour-vedam*, "the first original work published until today about the religious and philosophical dogmas of the Indians" (p. xii).

His "Preliminary observations" open with the following declaration of faith:

> Theism has been the primitive religion of humankind. The progressive march of polytheism would suggest this truth even if other facts were not demonstrating it. With the Indians, as with all other peoples on earth, one perceives, behind fables and fictions of the most bizarre kind, a cult that was pure in its origin and corrupted in its course. (pp. 13–14)

This statement already presents the *Ezour-vedam*'s content in a nutshell since, as we have seen, the teacher Chumontou stands for the pure monotheism of the origin, and his interlocutor Biache for the bizarre cult into which it degenerated. Sainte-Croix was perfectly in tune with Calmette on this basic point. In no less than 160 introductory pages, Sainte-Croix then presents his vision of the origin and history of Indian religion. This is his attempt to synthesize an enormous amount of often contradictory information about Indian religion and fashion a coherent story line that explains the history and content of Chumontou's and Biache's teachings, while addressing the question of the text's authorship.

Sainte-Croix was fundamentally in accord with de Guignes, whose papers on Indian religion, which were published in 1781, he was able partially to consult in manuscript form (pp. 52–53, 59). Rejecting Mignot's opinions, Sainte-Croix followed La Croze and de Guignes in discerning Egyptian influence on India (pp. 32–34). He did not mention the biblical narrative of the deluge or the dispersion of people even once. Nevertheless, the region north of Mesopotamia, where according to tradition the ark landed, had (as later in William Jones) a special role (App 2009). It is in Ariana and Bactria, that is, in the region linking Persia to India, that he located the cradle of two groups, "members of one family," which had migrated to India (Sainte-Croix 1778:1.45). The first to arrive were "the brachmanes who seemed to have made their principal residence near the Ganges and in the adjoining mountains" where some of their descendants have maintained their independence to this day in a "district to the west of *Burdwam*" (pp. 46–47). Sainte-Croix's source for this country "governed by the ancient laws" is, the reader might have guessed it, the ideal country around Bisnapore (see Chapter 6) from Holwell's first volume (p. 47).

The second group that came from Ariana via Bactria to India were the Samanéens, whose founder was "without any doubt Boutta or Budda" (pp. 47–48) and whose religion stretches from that region all across Asia to Japan (pp. 55–56). Sainte-Croix mentions many countries including Ceylon, Siam, Tibet, China, Korea, Japan, and Mongolia where the religion of Budda now reigns; and he thought, following La Croze, that they had brought literacy to India. They also "showed great disdain for the cult of *Vishnu* and *Shiva* and did not want to subject themselves to the ancient Indianism which they sought to destroy" (p. 70). They fought against the superstitions and polytheism that had disfigured the once pure patriarchal religion. These valiant reformers who wanted to reestablish original monotheism were unjustly accused "by the ignorant and fanatic priests that were then the brachmanes" of being "philosophers of atheism, gross idolaters, and worshippers of their master Budda" (pp. 71–72). Eventually, as reported by Ziegenbalg via La Croze, the Brachmanes even "made a horrible massacre of the unfortunate Baudistes" (p. 72), whereupon some of them carried their religion to other countries in Asia.

If for La Croze the Buddhists had turned into atheists, the roles were here reversed: for Sainte-Croix the Brachmanes had become degenerate polytheists, whereas the Buddhists had preserved their original monotheism. This was based on Brucker's interpretation of esoteric Buddhist doctrine as a kind of mystical monotheism, de Guignes's assertion of the monotheism of the Samanéens (supported by his mistaken translation of the term "world-honored one" at the beginning of the *Forty-Two Sections Sutra*), Fréret's conception of a monotheism professed by both the Buddhist and Brahmanic "sects of Indian religion," and Mignot's monotheistic interpretation of Buddhist emptiness. Convinced by such views, Sainte-Croix believed that the Buddha's esoteric doctrine, a monotheism of the purest kind, had also survived in India:

> In spite of the efforts of the brames and the feeling of horror that they wanted to inculcate for the Baudistes or Samanéens, several books of these philosophers are still respectfully preserved on the Malabar coast, and the different coasts of India have, if we may dare to say so, shared their doctrine. The *Ganigueuls*, the *Wanaprasthas*, the *Avadoutas*, the *Jogis* and the *Saniassis* have adopted the manner of living of the Baudistes and openly profess the majority of their dogmas. (pp. 76–77)

Since the Baudistes or Samanéens brought literacy to India, they were, of course, also the authors of the sacred scriptures of India:

> The first books of the Samanéens were with great likelihood written in this [Sanskrit] language. We know that the sectarians of Budda, who sometime after the birth of Jesus Christ went to China, took along a book which explained their principles in a language and characters that differed from those of the Chinese. Three hundred years passed before the bonzes translated the doctrine of the Indians into Chinese. (pp. 108–9)

Sainte-Croix had picked up such information from de Guignes's still-unpublished manuscripts whose content was described in Chapter 4. He criticized that, instead of translating the most ancient Indian texts, Holwell and Dow had presented the systems of the sects of their informants rather than "the doctrine of the ancient books" (p. 139). The ancient doctrine and books he referred to were brought by the Samanéens from Ariana to India where they were safeguarded by small groups of strictly monotheistic philosophers like the Gnanigöls or Ganigueuls (see Chapter 2).

> Everywhere in the *Ezour-vedam*, we find the principal articles of the doctrine of the Ganigueuls which we will discuss, and consequently one cannot doubt that a philosopher of this sect has composed this work. In it, a man enveloped by the gloom of idolatry reports, under the name of Biache, the most accredited fables of India and exposes the entire system of popular theology of his country. (p. 146)

By contrast, Chumontou represents for Sainte-Croix the true original monotheism transmitted by the Samanéens to the Ganigueuls. In this way the Tamil Siddhas identified by Ziegenbalg as Gnanigöls (see Chapter 2) became—at least in Sainte-Croix's scenario that was heavily inspired by de Guignes yet unpublished "Chinese Veda" papers—successors of the Buddha's strict monotheism whose teaching is preserved . . . you have guessed it . . . in the *Ezour-vedam*!

> Responding to the questions of Biache, the Ganigueul philosopher [Chumontou] explains his doctrine about the unity of God, creation, the nature of the soul, the dogma of punishment and recompense in a future state, the cult appropriate for the supreme Being, the duties of all classes [états], and so forth. Particularly those [duties] of the contemplatives attract Chumontou's attention; and in this respect his principles entirely conform with those of the Samanéens and the ancient sectarians of Budda. (pp. 147–48)

Of course, Sainte-Croix does not fail to refer here to the two texts that de Guignes had associated with the Samanéens: "the extract from the *Anbertkend*" and "the translation of the work attributed to Fo, or Budda"—the *Forty-Two Sections Sutra* in de Guignes's *History of the Huns* (see Chapter 4). Though the attentive reader might suspect he or she is hallucinating, there is no doubt—based on what we have learned about all this in Chapters 2, 4, and 7—that Fr. Calmette, who through his *Ezour-vedam* authorship had already shed his black Jesuit attire for an Indian disguise and a Brahmin tuft of hair, thanks to Sainte-Croix now appears before us with the shaved pate of a Buddhist monk who is indoctrinating us about the mystical meaning of the ultimate teaching of the Buddha: God's emptiness!

The *Ezour-vedam*'s Amazing Career

In sum, the *Ezour-vedam* is one of the most interesting and revelatory documents of nascent Orientalism. Created by European residents of India who pioneered the study of the Vedas, it is an extraordinary window to diverse premodern views of Asian religions and a mirror of Europeans' anxieties, hopes, passions, and obsessions as they struggled to understand their own origin and worldview. After humble beginnings as mission material for catechetes in South India, it soon became obsolete Some missionary must have decided to give it a second lease on life and a new mission in the struggle against European deists, skeptics, and atheists by letting French laymen make copies of it. After its arrival in France this mission backfired when Voltaire turned the text into a weapon against Judeo-Christianity and for his brand of deism. In defense, Coeurdoux attempted to link the text via the seven rishis to the biblical patriarchs. But Mignot and Anquetil-Duperron saw it as a testament of Ziegenbalg's monotheistic Gnanigöls. Sainte-Croix concurred but regarded these Gnanigöls as representatives of the ancient esoteric doctrine of Buddhism that in his view was a mystical form of Ur-monotheism. Soon enough, various doubters raised their voices and called the text a fake or "Pseudo-Veda." In the nineteenth and twentieth centuries, this opinion prevailed, and the Jesuits were accused of a heinous act. Now, however, the text is about to acquire a new valuation as a fascinating record of the early Western study of Indian scriptures, a testament to the diversity and extreme changes characterizing eighteenth-century European views of Asian religions, and a showcase for the twisted fate of religious texts. The biography of the *Ezour-vedam* presents us with a sequence of events that even a novelist might have trouble imagining: the mystical marriage of a wrongly translated, pieced-together, fifth-century Chinese Buddhist text, tuned up and put into the Buddha's mouth by an eighth-century Chinese Zen master, with the fake—yet oh so true!—Yajur Veda (*Ezour-vedam*) authored by a French Jesuit calling himself Sumantu who criticizes the Veda and whom Sainte-Croix portrayed as a Gnanigöl heir of the Buddha's deathbed teaching of God's emptiness. The mind-boggling fate of this text deserves a place of honor in the history-of-ideas hall of fame and is a perfect embodiment of a bon mot of the great researcher of Zen to whom this book is dedicated, the late Seizan Yanagida: "Fact is fiction, and fiction is fact" (App 2008b:7).

The Perfect Theology

In December 1776, Anquetil-Duperron received a package from India sent by his friend colonel Jean-Baptiste Le Gentil, the French envoy at Oudh (Awadh). It contained a voluminous Persian manuscript entitled *Sirr-i akbar*, the Great Secret. While reading its preface, Anquetil-Duperron already sensed that his search for the Veda, that most ancient record of divine revelation and master key to the "Indian religion" that had conquered Asia, was

TABLE 17. ANQUETIL'S DRAFT TRANSLATION OF PART OF PRINCE DARA'S
OUPNEK'HAT PREFACE

Anquetil's draft French translation (Bibliothèque Nationale, NAF 8857, fols. 4–5)	English translation of Anquetil's draft French translation (App)	English translation by Hasrat from the Persian (de Bary 1958:440)
Après la certitude de ces degrés (de cela), il a été scu que dans cette secte ancienne, avant tous les Livres celestes quatre Livres celestes qui (sont) le *Ragbeid* et le *Djedjèr Beid*, et le *Sam Beid*, et l'*Athrban Beid*, aux Prophetes de ce tems que le plus grand d'eux est *Brahma* qui est Adam choisi de Dieu, sur lequel soit le salut, avec tous les preceptes de conduite: et ce sens est paraissant de ces livres mêmes.	After the certitude of these degrees (of that), it was known that in this ancient sect, before all the heavenly books, four heavenly books which (are) the *Ragbeid,* and the *Djedjèr Beid,* and the *Sam Beid,* and the *Athrban Beid,* to the prophets of this time that the greatest of them is *Brahma* who is *Adam* chosen by God, on whom be salvation, with all the precepts of conduct: and this meaning is apparent from these books themselves.	And after verifications of these circumstances, it appeared that among this most ancient people, of all their heavenly books, which are the *Rig Veda,* the *Yajur Veda,* the *Sama Veda,* and the *Atharva Veda,* together with a number of ordinances, descended upon the prophets of those times, the most ancient of whom was Brahman or Adam, on whom be the peace of God, this purport is manifest from these books.
Et l'essentiel (la partie la plus pure, la substance) de ces quatre livres, tous les secrets de conduite (religieuse) et la meditation sur l'unité pure y sont renfermés, et on le nomme *Oupnek'hat.*	And the essence (the purest part, the substance) of these four books, all the secrets of (religious) conduct and the meditation on the pure unity are included in it, and it is called *Oupnek'hat.*	And the *summum bonum* of these four books, which contain all the secrets of the Path and the contemplative exercises of pure monotheism, are called the *Upanekhats* [Upanishads].

coming to an end. He translated the Persian preface by Prince Dara (see Chapter 3), written in 1657, word for word to make sure that he did not miss anything. It brought the confirmation that the book's fifty Upanishads contain the very essence of the Vedas.

The first two columns of Table 17 provide a taste of Anquetil-Duperron's style. His Latin has been called cryptic and impossible to understand, but sometimes it is clearer than his French in these translations, whose grammar sometimes has even native speakers scratching their heads. The Latin summary of this preface made the central point of this preface much clearer: after having studied the three celestial books (the Books of Moses, the Psalms of David, and the Evangile of Christ), Prince Dara found the four Vedas, which he saw as God's earliest revelation to Brahma (who is identical with Adam). These four Vedas contain the truth of unity (*unitatis veritas*), and their essence (*cremor*) is found in the book called *Oupnek'hat*, the Upanishads (Anquetil-Duperron 1801:7).[30] Anquetil-Duperron first announced his discovery in a 1778 book on Oriental legislation:

> Schahdjehan [Shah Jahan, 1592–1666], son of Djehanguir [Jahangir, 1569–1627] permits all religions as long as they serve the growth of his empire. Dara Shako [Mohammed Dārā Shikūh, 1615–59], the eldest son of Shahdjehan, shows publicly his indifference for Islam. In Delhi in 1656, this prince has brahmins of Benares translate the *Oupnekat*, a Sanskrit work whose name signifies *The Word that must not be enounced* (the secret that must not be revealed). This work is the essence of the four Vedas. It presents in 51 sections the complete system of Indian theology of which the result is the unity of the supreme Being [premier Etre] whose perfections and personified operations have the name of the principal Indian divinities, and the reunion [réunion] of the entire nature with this first Agent. I plan to publish as soon as possible the translation of this important work which I received in 1776 from North Bengal from Mr. Gentil, Chevalier of St. Louis and Captain of cavalry in the service of France. This work appears for the first time in Europe; no traveler has mentioned it until now. (Anquetil-Duperron 1778:21)

Nine years later, on March 18, 1787, he finished his French translation of all fifty Upanishads with the exclamation "oum oum oum oum oum," and the revision of the entire 862-page manuscript took him until July 3.[31] In the same year, he inserted his translation "into barbaric French" of four Upanishads into a book on Indian geography with the excuse that it would offer the reader "a break from the course of the Ganges" at Benares, the city of philosophers (Anquetil-Duperron 1787a:2.297). The translation's title clearly shows what the Persian Upanishads of Prince Dara represented for him: "The Basis of Indian Theology, drawn from the Vedas" (p. 297). Anquetil-Duperron's first four Upanishads of 1787 appeared in German translation in 1791 in a book published in Zürich by an anonymous editor; I suspect that it was the very Johann Ith who in 1779 had already proved his interest in Asian religions by translating Sainte-Croix's *Ezour-vedam* into German. They were contained in Europe's first collection of religious texts from the "Indian religion" that Fréret, de Guignes, Diderot, and numerous other authors had described, which was the very religion in search of whose key Anquetil-Duperron had gone to India.

The editor's emphasis of the need to present to the public not so much interpretations but rather translations of primary sources was a sign of a new age, while his view that his "Indian religion" is "about the same with the peoples hither and yonder the Ganges" (Anon., *Sammlung asiatischer Original-Schriften*, 1791:xiii) marks the end of a period. This Zurich collection appeared just before the effect of the first volumes of the *Asiatick Researches* on the European continent began. The editor planned a series of volumes with "original scriptures of Asia" and even suggested publishing these texts also in their original languages by using print shops in London for Sanskrit, Paris for Persian, and Berlin for Tamil texts (p. x). But probably because of the Orientalist revolution triggered by the work of the British in India (see Chapter 8), only one volume of the planned collection ever appeared under the title *Indische Schriften* (Indian Scriptures). In conformity with the editor's conception of "Indian religion," we find in this interesting volume German translations of Maridas Poullé's *Bagavadam* (pp. 1–216); La Loubère's *Life of Tewetat* and his Buddhist monastic rules "Patimuk" (pp. 217–56);[32] de Guignes's "Book of Fo" (the *Forty-Two Sections Sutra*; pp. 257–68)[33] and his summary of the *Anbertkend* (pp. 361–76); Anquetil-Duperron's four Upanishads (pp. 269–316); the *Dirm Schaster* and *Neadirsen* by Dow (pp. 389–410); the *Schastah-Bhade* by Holwell (pp. 419–32); Henry Lord's *Schaster* (pp. 433–52); and some additional materials, including text translations from the Danish India mission (pp. 453–94).

The editor of this Swiss book was a bit skeptical about Anquetil-Duperron's claims that the Upanishads represent the essence of the Vedas, and he commented that the words of the "four Bedes" [Vedas] seem only to be cited sporadically; but he gave Anquetil-Duperron the benefit of the doubt by stating that "if it is as [Anquetil-Duperron says], these *Upnekhat* will be doubly important because part of the content of the Vedas will then be no more subject to doubt" (pp. xiv–xv). For Anquetil-Duperron, by contrast, no doubt was possible; and he saw his view reinforced by comparing the "system" he had discovered in Prince Dārā's Upanishads with the first European translation from a classical Sanskrit text: Charles Wilkins's *The Bhagvat-Geeta, or Dialogues of Kreeshna and Arjoon* (1785). Anquetil-Duperron had received a copy of it just before delivering his 1787 manuscript with the four Upanishads to press and decided to add an "Appendix about the Bhagvat Ghita" in which he asserts that Wilkins has not quite understood the true import of the text he translated (Anquetil-Duperron 1787a:571).

Anquetil-Duperron subsequently decided to translate the whole book into cryptic Latin. In some sense, this brings home to Europeans the exclusivity of the ancient Sanskrit text in India; after all, this book was a *secretum tegendum* and not food for *hoi polloi*! This is reflected in its esoteric mix of languages where cryptic Latin is explained by Greek: "Nomen Dei semper (ἀεὶ) in ore Brahmanum, et *propriâ linguâ*, ἰδία φονῇ, id est, samskreticè pronunciatum, est *Oum*" (The name of God always in the mouth of the Brahmins, and pronounced in their own language, their own voice, in Sanskrit, is *Oum*) (Anquetil-Duperron 1801:1.cv). But the content of this explanation is also emblematic: both for Anquetil-Duperron and for Prince Dara, the *Oupnek'hat*'s theology is the true message of Oum = Allah = God to humankind, his first and most perfect revelation to Brahma = Adam as recorded in the world's oldest book, the Veda, whose essence they happened to hold in their hands. It is a record of God's Ur-message whose traces are found in all ancient sacred texts. In his introduction to the *Oupnek'hat*, Anquetil-Duperron therefore stresses that "the very same dogma of a single parent of the universe and unique spiritual principle" is described "clearly and transparently" in "the books of Solomon, the ancient Chinese *Kims* [Ch. *jing*, classics], the sacred *Beids* [Vedas] of the Indians, and the *Zend-avesta* of the Persians" (p. viii).[34]

This is why, in his defense of the genuineness of the *Ezour-vedam* at the very end of his life, Anquetil-Duperron insisted that "in the *Oupnek'hat* one finds the supreme Being, his word, his spirit" (1808:3.419). Even if he had not become the perfect theologian and had to strike through the word "perfect" from the dream of his youth, he had been blessed to find the oldest extant record of God's revelation, the "doctrina orientalis" par excellence, the perfect theology, his religion. OUM!

Chapter 8

Volney's Revolutions

"Orientalism" has been portrayed by Edward SAID in his eponymous book, first published in 1979, as a very influential, state-sponsored, essentially imperialist and colonialist enterprise. For Said, the Orientalist ideology was rooted in eighteenth-century secularization that threatened the traditional Christian European worldview. That worldview had been reigning for many centuries and was based on the "Biblical framework." Said held that "modern Orientalism derives from secularizing elements in eighteenth-century European culture" (1979:120) and pointed out the all-important role that the discovery of Oriental religions and languages played in the birth of Orientalism:

> One, the expansion of the Orient further east geographically and further back temporally loosened, even dissolved, the Biblical framework considerably. Reference points were no longer Christianity and Judaism, with their fairly modest calendars and maps, but India, China, Japan, and Sumer, Buddhism, Sanskrit, Zoroastrianism, and Manu. (p. 120)

I quite agree with this. Curiously, though, only Islam—which had the least potential of loosening or dissolving the biblical framework because it made itself use of it—plays a role in Said's argument. The European discovery of other Asian religions is strangely absent: Zoroastrianism and Brahmanism are only briefly mentioned in the context of Anquetil-Duperron's studies (p. 76), Hinduism not at all, Confucius once in the context of Fénelon (p. 69), and Buddhism twice more, but (as in the quotation above) only as part of uncommented lists (pp. 232, 259). Focusing on political power and imperialist strategy rather than the power of religious ideology, Said was not in a position to answer how the "loosening" of the biblical framework was connected to the discovery of Asian religions and the genesis of modern Orientalism.

Robert IRWIN (2006:294) rightly criticized the "newly restrictive sense" that Said gave to the term Orientalism: "those who travelled, studied or wrote about the Arab world." Nevertheless, he declared himself "happy to accept this somewhat arbitrary delimitation of the subject matter" for the very convenient reason that "it is the history of Western studies of Islam, Arabic and Arab history and culture that interests me most" (p. 6). It is thus hardly surprising that non-Islamic oriental religions are as little discussed in Irwin's book-length study about Orientalism as in Said's. For example, Buddhism—Asia's most widespread religion—is only once mentioned in passing, and the religions of Asia's most populous nations, India and China, play no role at all. While accusing Said of hating "religion in all its forms," harboring "anti-religious prejudice," and failing "properly to engage with the Christian motivations of the majority of pre-twentieth-century Orientalists" (p. 294), Irwin's portrayal of Anquetil-Duperron and of William Jones shows an almost Saidian lack of insight into religious motivations: Anquetil-Duperron's striking religiosity is completely ignored in favor of his "anti-imperialism" (pp. 125–26), and treatment of Jones's religious motivations is limited to Irwin's cursory remarks to the effect that Jones "hoped to find evidence in India for the Flood of Genesis" and had a "somewhat archaic and confused" ethnology in which "Greeks, Indians, Chinese, Japanese, Mexicans and Peruvians all descended from Noah's son, Ham" (p. 124).

Furthermore, Irwin criticizes Said for attributing far too much importance to Orientalism. In Irwin's view the "heyday of institutional Orientalism only arrived in the second half of the twentieth century." Before that time, Orientalism was a relatively insignificant affair given that its exponents, according to Irwin, usually were just "individual scholars, often lonely and eccentric men" driven by curiosity rather than colonialist and imperialist rapacity. This is reflected in the title of the original English edition of Irwin's book: "For Lust of Knowing."[1] Irwin's Orientalists, "always few in number and rarely famous figures," were at best influential in literary, historical, theological, cultural, and, of course, oriental studies (p. 5) but had hardly any impact outside the literary world. For the most part they were just a bunch of relatively isolated "dabblers, obsessives, evangelists, freethinkers, madmen, charlatans, pedants, romantics" driven not by grand imperialist dreams but by "many competing agendas and styles of thought" (p. 7).

This final chapter examines a member of this eccentric crowd, Constantin François de Chasseboeuf VOLNEY (1757–1820), whose life span extends a bit beyond the period covered in this book. In Said's eyes, Volney was one of the most prominent "orthodox Orientalist authorities" (1979: 38) whose travel account (*Voyage en Syrie et en Egypte*, 1785–87) and reflections on the Turkish war (*Considérations sur la guerre actuelle des Turcs*, 1788) constituted "effective texts to be used by any European wishing to win in the Orient." Said thus saw Volney as a major instigator of Napoleon's imperialist invasion of Egypt (p. 81). Being "canonically hostile to Islam as a religion," the "canny Frenchman" (p. 81) was not engaged in some haphazard "innocent scholarly endeavor." Rather, as an archetypal exponent of "Orientalism as an accomplice to empire" (p. 333), he was fit to join William Jones near the top of Said's Orientalist blacklist.[2]

Said's critic Irwin, by astonishing contrast, portrays Volney as an Orientalist sharply critical of the collusion of religion and political tyranny and as one of the leading spokesmen *against* the French plan to invade Egypt. Irwin argues against Said that Volney was not just an opponent of Islam but of all religions, particularly of Christianity. Unlike Said, Irwin also mentions Volney's most influential book, *The Ruins*, which was published during the French Revolution in 1791. According to Irwin, "everybody read this book. It was a bestseller and the talk of the salons, spas and gaming rooms. Even Frankenstein's monster read it" (2006:135). But instead of enlightening the curious reader about this startling exception to Irwin's rule of little-read Orientalist dabblings—after all, Volney's *Ruins* was among the most-read books of the revolutionary period and a smashing success by any standard—Irwin complains that "no one reads *Les Ruines* nowadays. It is quite hard going" (p. 135). In fact, to keep our gaze on the period when attention spans were a bit longer and passions stronger, Volney's book rapidly caught the attention of a large public, and already in 1792 an anonymous English translation was published in London. Another sign of strong interest is that excerpts of the bestseller were printed in the form of broadsides and pamphlets from late 1792 on. The full English text was also widely available in pocket-sized, undated editions (Weir 2003:48). According to E. P. Thompson, the book was "more positive and challenging, and perhaps as influential, in English radical history as Paine's *Age of Reason*," and during the mid-1790s "the cognoscenti of the London Corresponding Society—master craftsmen, shopkeepers, engravers, hosiers, printers—carried [*The Ruins*] around with them in their pockets (Weir 2003:48). Among such craftsmen was young William Blake, one of the myriad readers influenced by Volney (pp. 48–55). Prominent statesmen were also among the admirers of the book, for example, Volney's friend Thomas Jefferson who, before his election as president of the United States of America, was so inspired by *The Ruins* that he took the time to translate no less than twenty of its twenty-four chapters into English and invited Volney to stay at Monticello (Chinard 1923).

According to Irwin, the key question addressed in Volney's *Ruins* is "why the East was so impoverished and backward compared to the West," and a large part of Volney's answer consisted in the "prevalence of despotism in the East" (2006:135). Irwin does not mention the central role of religion in Volney's revolutionary analysis. While both Said and Irwin failed to remark on the centrality of religious tyranny and of the power of religious ideology in Volney's argument, eighteenth- and nineteenth-century readers certainly did not overlook this. Religion as humankind's most fundamental value system and primary source of conflicts plays a central role in *The Ruins*; in fact, more than half of its total volume is taken up by the famous Orientalist's fascinating survey of the world's religions and his revolutionary analysis of the origin and genealogy of religious ideas.

Holbach's System of Nature

In 1780, the twenty-three-year-old Volney began to follow courses in Arabic given by Professor Deshauterayes of the Collège Royal. His teacher was known as a dogged opponent of de Guignes's farfetched theories about the Egyptian origin of the Chinese, and he also produced some translations and studies of Buddhism-related materials from Chinese.[3] Volney also frequented the salon of Madame Helvétius, the widow of the famous naturalist and freethinker Claude-Adrien HELVÉTIUS (1717–71). In her salon, the word "atheism"—which Bernhardus Varenius had 130 years earlier smuggled into his survey of religions—had an entirely different, confident ring. Some Paris salons were teeming with skeptics, agnostics, and atheists, and the house of Madame Helvétius was their favorite hangout. Their bible was a two-volume book of 1770 titled *Le système de la nature* that had appeared in London under the name of "Mirabaud, perpetual secretary and one of the forty members of the Académie Française." The name of the eminent Jean-Baptiste DE MIRABAUD (1675–1760)—who had been in his tomb for a decade when this book was supposedly written—was only a shield to protect the book's real author: the notorious materialist and radical Paul-Henri Dietrich, Baron D'HOLBACH

(1723–1789). Holbach also happened to be a frequent visitor of Madame Helvétius's salon and became a dominating influence on young Volney.

Religion was, of course, a fashionable topic of conversation, as was the information about savages in various parts of the world that posed a continuing challenge to champions of the Bible. However, as Whiston and Lafitau and many others had proved, an author could bend the biblical narrative to a considerable degree without necessarily running the risk of being burned at the stake. In his pioneer study on the cult of fetish divinities (*Du Culte des Dieux fétiches*, 1760), Charles de BROSSES (1709–77) had achieved the feat of marrying primitive Africans to biblical perfection by arguing that primitive cults (such as African fetishism) only arose after the disappearence of original monotheism:

> The human race had first received from God the immediate instructions adapted to the intelligence with which his goodness had equipped the humans. It is so surprising to see them subsequently fallen in a state of brute stupidity that one can hardly avoid regarding this as a just and supernatural punishment for being guilty of having forgotten the beneficial hand that had created them. (de Brosses 1760:15)

Only God's "immediate instructions," that is, divine revelation, could explain primeval monotheism since "the human spirit could not have found in itself what led it immediately to the pure principles of theism" (p. 207). De Brosses thus held that "all peoples began with correct notions of an intellectual religion that they later corrupted with the most stupid idolatries" (pp. 195–96). Looking back at the history of humanity from his perch at the apex of French academia, de Brosses saw increasing darkness and blindness pointing to an ancient common polytheism: "The most ancient memory of these people always presents polytheism as the common and ubiquitous system" (p. 204). But such common polytheism was not really the primeval human religion; rather, it was only the result of the biblical deluge: "One sees that the arts of primitive times were lost, that previously gained knowledge was buried under the waters, and that almost everywhere a pure state of barbarity reigned: natural effects of such a general and powerful revolution" (p. 204). Not unlike Giambattista VICO (1668–1744) in his *Scienza nuova*, de Brosses thus used the deluge as a means of marrying a secular scenario of primitivity and progress to the Christian scenario that ran exactly in the opposite direction, that is, from initial perfection to such degradation that divine intervention in the form of Jesus's incarnation became necessary.

This was a far cry from the radicalism of Baron d'Holbach, who turned this scheme of initial perfection and subsequent degeneration not just on its head but attempted to reduce it to rubble. For Holbach there was neither a paradise at the beginning of history nor a creator God; in fact, there was no beginning at all since some form of matter infused with energy had always existed and will always exist (Holbach 1770:1.26). "Had one observed nature without prejudice," he wrote, "one would have been convinced for ages that matter acts by its own force and has no need of any exterior impulsion to set it in motion" (1.22–23). Holbach thus frontally attacked the very foundation of the three Abrahamic religions:

> Those who admit a cause exterior to matter are obliged to believe that this cause produced all the movement in this matter by giving it existence. This supposition is based on another, namely, that matter could begin to exist—a hypothesis that until this moment has never been demonstrated by valid proofs. The summoning out of nothing, or *creation*, is no more than a word which cannot give us any idea of the formation of the universe; it has no meaning upon which the mind can rely. The notion becomes even more obscure when the creation or formation of matter is attributed to a *spiritual* being, that is, a being which has no analogy and no connection whatsoever with matter. (1.25–26)

Following Epicurus and Lucretius, Holbach's "nature" is eternal and inherently energetic (2:172). Instead of creation, he sees only transformations of the existing into different forms, "a transmigration, an exchange, a continuous circulation of the molecules of matter" (1:33). It is thus the inherent movement of matter, not some God, that accounts for production, growth, and alteration. From the formation of rocks inside the earth to that of suns and from the oyster to man, there is "a continuous progression, a perpetual chain of combinations and movements resulting in beings that differ among themselves only by the variety of their constituent elements and the combinations and proportions of these elements which give rise to infinitely diverse ways of existing and acting" (1.39). All constituents of the universe follow the order of nature; what may appear to be a disorder, for example, death, is in fact only a transition and a new combination of elements.[4] For Holbach, everything is bound to matter infused with energy:

An *intelligent* being is a being that thinks, wills, and acts to achieve a goal. Now in order to think, will, and act as we do there is a need for organs and a goal that resembles ours. So, to say that nature is governed by an intelligence is to pretend that she is governed by a being equipped with organs, given that without organs there can be no perception, no idea, no intuition, no thought, no will, no plan, and no action. (1.66)

To speak of God or divinity or creation is thus only a sign of the ignorance of nature's energy; and man, supposedly the goal of creation, is only one of nature's myriad and fleeting transformations. He is an integral part of nature obeying its universal laws of cause and effect and of self-preservation by attraction of the favorable and repulsion of the unfavorable (1:45–46). Nine decades before Charles Darwin, Holbach was not yet able to clarify man's origin and to determine whether he "has always been what he is" or "was obliged to pass through an infinity of successive developments" (1.80); due to lack of reliable data, Holbach left the question open while taking issue with the notion that man is the crown of creation:

Let us then conclude that man has no reason at all to regard himself as a privileged being in nature; he is subject to the same vicissitudes as all her other productions. His pretended prerogatives are based on an error. If he elevates himself by imagination above the globe that he inhabits and looks down upon his own species with an impartial eye, he will see that man, like every tree producing fruit in consequence of its species, acts by virtue of his particular energy and produces fruits—actions, works—that are equally necessary. He will feel that the illusion that makes him favor himself arises from being simultaneously spectator and part of the universe. He will recognize that the idea of preeminence which he attaches to his being has no other basis than his self-interest and the predilection he has in favor of himself. (1.88–89)

But for Holbach such egoism is only natural since the goal of man, like that of nature as a whole, is self-preservation and well-being (1.133); and the realization that this goal necessitates cooperation with others and involves the happiness of others forms the basis of morality, law, politics, and education (1.139–47). In this manner Holbach attacked not only the cosmological and religious authority of the Judeo-Christian tradition and other forms of theism but also their exclusive claim to morality. Instead of commandments revealed on Mt. Sinai, Mosaic law, Confucian maxims, Christian catechisms, or Herbert's five common notions, Holbach proposed a universal natural basis of morality:

> If man, according to his nature, is forced to desire his well-being, he is forced to love the means leading to it; it would be useless and perhaps unjust to demand that a man should be virtuous if he could only become so by rendering himself miserable. As soon as vice renders him happy, he must love vice; and if he sees inutility honored and crime rewarded, what interest would he find in working toward the happiness of his fellow creatures or restraining the fury of his passions? (1.151)

It is thus not through revealed scriptures and commandments from above that man's morality is assured but through self-interest that is healthy and informed enough to encompass fellow beings and the outside world. Gaining true ideas, that is, ideas based on nature and not imagination, is, according to Holbach, the only remedy for the ills of man (1:351). But from where do those ills originate in the first place? From illusions and false ideas; for "as soon as man's mind is filled with false ideas and dangerous opinions, his whole conduct tends to become a long chain of errors and depraved actions" (1.151). And since religion and its representatives, according to Holbach, concentrate on fostering such false ideas, they must be identified as the source of man's evils:

> If we consult experience, we will see that it is in illusions and sacred opinions that we must search out the true source of that multitude of evils which almost everywhere overwhelms mankind. The ignorance of natural causes created the gods for him; imposture rendered them terrible to him; these fatal ideas haunted him without rendering him better; made him tremble without any benefit; filled his mind with chimeras; hindered the progress of his reason; and prevented him from seeking his happiness. (1.339)

The role of priestcraft in this perversion of nature was most objectionable to Holbach, and like the English deists, he loved describing the fatal results of the clergy's deception in the most graphic terms:

> His fears rendered him the slave of those who deceived him under the pretext of his welfare; he committed evil when told that his gods de-

manded crimes; he lived in misfortune because they made him believe that the gods had condemned him to be miserable. He never dared to throw off his chains because he was given to understand that stupidity, the renunciation of reason, sloth of mind, and abjection of his soul were the sure means of obtaining eternal felicity. (1.339)

The importance of the subject of religion to Holbach is highlighted by the fact that he devoted the entire second volume of his *System of Nature* to it. Instead of primitive monotheism, Holbach saw a gradual development of religious cults and offered the following genealogy of monotheism:

The first theology of man was to fear and adore the elements themselves, material and coarse objects; then he extended his reverence to the agents that he imagined to preside over these elements: to powerful spirits, inferior spirits, heroes, or to men endowed with great qualities. While thinking about this, he believed he would simplify things by putting the whole of nature under the rule of a single agent, a sovereign intelligence, a spirit, a universal soul that set this nature and its parts in motion. Recurring from cause to cause, the mortals ended up seeing nothing at all, and it is in this obscurity that they placed their God. In this dark abyss their feverish imagination went on and on churning out chimeras which they will be smitten with until their knowledge of nature shall disabuse them of the phantoms that they have for so long adored in vain. (2.16)

For Holbach, theistic religion was a giant mistake; accordingly, he filled page after page of the second volume with the diagnosis of its origin, characteristics, and disastrous effects. Whether humanity had forever been on this globe or constituted a recent invention of nature that arose after one of nature's periodical revolutions: a look at the origin of various nations convinced Holbach that, contrary to the mosaic narrative, primitivity and savagery always marked the beginning (2.31). In this point he fully agreed with David Hume's analysis that was briefly mentioned in Chapter 5.

In contrast to Volney's *Ruins*, Holbach's *System of Nature* focuses on the Judeo-Christian tradition and its champions and rarely mentions other religions. Its argument aims at generality but betrays its theistically parochial nature by statements such as "all religions of the world show us God as an absolute ruler" (2.113); "all religions of the world posit a God continually occupied with rebuilding, repairing, undoing, rectifying his marvelous works" (2.115); "the thinkers of all centuries and all nations quarrel without respite . . . about the attributes and qualities of a God that they have in vain occupied themselves with" (2.191); and "all nations recognize an evil sovereign God" (2.236). At any rate, what people call religion was for Holbach nothing but superstition:

> By the admission even of the theologians, mankind is without *religion*; it only has *superstitions*. According to them, superstition *is a badly understood and unreasonable cult of the deity*: or else *a cult offered to a false divinity*. But where is a people or a clergy that agrees that its divinity is false and its cult unreasonable? How can one decide who is right and who is wrong? (2.291)

Only someone who freed himself of such superstition could be called truly religious; and that is exactly what Holbach understood by atheism.

> What is really an *atheist*? It is a man who destroys the pernicious chimeras of humankind to lead the people back to nature, to experience, to reason. It is a thinker who has meditated matter, its energy, its characteristics and manners of action, and has no need of imagining ideal powers to explain the phenomena of the universe and the workings of nature. (2.320)

This was the kind of provocative discourse that evoked passionate discussions at Madame Helvétius's salon frequented by Volney and his friends. There is no doubt that Holbach's Epicurean view of nature and his radical vision of religion exerted a strong influence on Volney. But his focus on the Abrahamic religions prevented him from furnishing a panorama of religion that was truly global in scope. This was an opening for Volney. If Holbach had delivered his diagnosis in the *System of Nature* (1770) and presented a therapy in his *Catéchisme de la nature* (1790), Volney offered the former in *The Ruins* (1791) and the latter in his *Natural law or the catechism of the French people* (1793).

The Council of Religions

In the opening scene of Volney's *The Ruins*, the narrator is caught in a religious mood while contemplating the ruins of Palmyra:

The solitariness of the situation, the serenity of evening, and the grandeur of the scene, impressed my mind with religious thoughtfulness. The view of an illustrious city deserted, the remembrance of past times, their comparison with the present state of things, all combined to raise my heart to a strain of sublime meditations. I sat down on the base of a column; and there, my elbow on my knee, and my head resting on my hand, sometimes turning my eyes towards the desert, and sometimes fixing them on the ruins, I fell into a profound reverie. (Volney 1796:5)

Why had this city of Palmyra and the whole region been so prosperous while the *"unbelieving* people" inhabited them: "the Phenician, offering human sacrifices to Moloch," the Chaldaean "prostrating himself before a serpent," the Persian "worshipper of fire," and the city's "adorers of the sun and stars, who erected so many monuments of affluence and luxury"? And why was it now, as it lay in the hands of "the elect of Heaven" and "children of the prophets"—Christians, Muslims, and Jews—in poverty and decay, bereft of God's "gifts and miracles" (pp. 9–10)? Was this due to some malediction, or was it decreed by the "incomprehensible judgments" of "a mysterious God" (p. 13)? Lost in such gloomy thoughts, the narrator suddenly becomes aware of a "pale apparition, enveloped in an immense drapery, similar to what spectres are painted when issuing out of the tombs." It begins to talk to him in "a hollow voice, in grave and solemn accents" (p. 14) and promises, "I will display to your view this truth of which you are in pursuit; I will show to your reason the knowledge which you desire; I will reveal to you the wisdom of the tombs, and the science of the ages" (p. 25).

Carried aloft on the wing of this apparition, the man suddenly sees the world from an entirely different viewpoint: "Under my feet, floating in empty space, a globe similar to that of the moon" (p. 25). Volney's narrator thus learns to see our planet, its peoples, their political systems, and their religions from a global perspective. The apparition explains to him that the first human beings had, in a "savage and barbarous state," been driven by "inordinate desire of accumulation" that brought with it "rapine, violence, and murder" (p. 61). In its innumerable disguises, this "spirit of rapacity" had been "the perpetual scourge of nations" and the hotbed of political as well as religious despotism and tyranny (p. 63). Political and religious oppression are portrayed as closely related: in the state of political oppression, people fell into despair and were so terrified by calamities that they "referred the causes of them to superior and invisible powers: because they had tyrants upon earth, they supposed there to be tyrants in heaven; and superstition came in aid to aggravate the disasters of nations" (p. 73). Volney's narrator thus understands the origin of those "gloomy and misanthropic systems of religion, which painted the gods malignant and envious like human despots" (p. 73), and he mentions some of the means by which the priests, those "sacred impostors," took "advantage of the credulity of the ignorant" (p. 64):

> In the secrecy of temples, and behind the veil of altars, they have made the Gods speak and act; have delivered oracles, worked pretended miracles, ordered sacrifices, imposed offerings, prescribed endowments; and, under the name of *theocracy* and *religion*, the State has been tormented by the passions of the priests. (p. 64)

Religious impostors also took advantage of man's wishful thinking: frustrated by unfulfilled hopes and lack of happiness, man "formed to himself another country, an asylum, where, out of the reach of tyrants, he should regain all his rights." (p. 74)

> Smitten with his imaginary world, man despised the world of nature: for chimerical hopes he neglected the reality. He no longer considered his life but as a fatiguing journey, a painful dream; his body as a prison that withheld him from his felicity; the earth as a place of exile and pilgrimage, which he disdained to cultivate. (p. 74)

Whether man projected such chimerical hopes onto a future life in the yonder or on an imagined past "which is merely the discoloration of his chagrin" (p. 106), his illusion tended to increase the baleful effects of "ignorance, superstition and fanaticism" whose continuous power is apparent in the smoke that Volney's narrator sees rising high above the battlefields of Asia where Turkish Muslims battle Christian Muscovites (pp. 77–83). Now the narrator begins to understand the basic mechanism of the deceit of humankind: impostors "who have pretended that God made man in his own image" yet in reality "made God in theirs." Ascribing him their weaknesses, errors, and vices, they pretend to be in the confidence of God and to be able to change his behavior (pp. 84–85). Instituting observances such as the Jewish sabbath, the Persian cult of fire, the Indian repetition of the word *Aûm*, or the Muslim's ablutions (pp. 85–86), this "race of impostors" (p. 85) claims that the impartial God preferred a single sect of a single religion—namely, theirs—and withheld knowledge of his will to all except the prophet of their creed. It is exactly this kind of exclusive claim to absolute truth that contradicts and condemns all rival claims that, according to Volney, need to be abolished in a revolution that proclaims "equality, liberty, and justice" (p. 139).

Volney's readership could harbor no doubt that *The Ruins* was a revolutionary manifesto. If his subsequent booklet *La loi naturelle, ou principes physiques de la morale* (The Natural Law, or Physical Principles of Morality) of 1793 attempted to lay out a course of therapy, *The Ruins* offered the diagnosis of the ailment. Both civil and religious tyrants had much to fear from the trinity of revolutionary values:

> What a swarm of evils, cried they, are included in these three words! If all men are equal, where is our exclusive right to honours and power? If all men are, or ought to be free, what becomes of our slaves, our vassals, our property? If all are equal in a civil capacity, where are our privileges of birth and succession, and what becomes of nobility? If all are equal before God, where will be the need for mediators, and what is to become of priesthood? Ah! let us accomplish without a moment's delay the destruction of a germ so prolific and contagious! (Volney 1796:142)

In chapters 19 to 21 of *The Ruins*,[5] Volney did his best to nurture this contagious germ of equality and freedom. He chose to do so by a confrontation of the religious opinions of humankind in a council of the chiefs of nations and representatives of religions. It is designed to "dissipate the illusion of evil habits and prejudice" (p. 144) and have the impartial light of truth enlighten all peoples of the world.

> Let us terminate to day the long combat of error: let us establish between it and truth a solemn contest: let us call in men of every nation to assist us in the judgment: let us convoke a general assembly of the world; let them be judges in their own cause; and in the successive trial of every system, let no champion and no argument be wanting to the side of prejudice or of reason. (p. 145)

No sooner had the inhabitants of the earth gathered, agreed to "banish all tyranny and discord," and enthusiastically chanted the words *"equality, justice, union"* than the major source of conflict became apparent:

Every nation assumed exclusive pretensions, and claimed the preference
for its own opinions and code. "You are in error," said the parties pointing at each other; "we alone are in possession of reason and truth; ours
is the true law, the genuine rule of justice and right, the sole means of
happiness and perfection; all other men are either blind or rebellious."
(pp. 151–52)

The demolition of such unproven claims to exclusive possession of truth is
exactly the aim of Volney's chapters 20 ("Investigation of Truth") and 21
("Problem of Religious Contradictions"). He has representatives of each religion explain the central doctrines; but no sooner has each group laid out its
tenets than its assumptions are severely criticized by representatives of other
faiths.

In the thirteenth century, Roger Bacon had, in imitation of the Great
Khan's open debate of religions, adopted a similar scheme of competitive
argument: but he had too quickly declared victory for the Christians on the
grounds that "philosophy" is in perfect accord with such doctrines as the
"blessed Trinity, Christ, and the Blessed Virgin, creation of the world, angels,
souls, judgment to come, life eternal, resurrection of the body, punishment
in hell, and the like" (Bacon 1928:2.807). Obviously, the Jews, Muslims, and
idolaters had no chance against such impeccable logic. Predictably, Bacon's
argument culminated in his assertion that perfectly illustrates the attitude
criticized by Volney: because "Christ is God, which is not true of Mahomet
and Moses according to the testimony of even Jews and Saracens, it is evident
that he alone is the perfect lawgiver, and that there should be no comparison
of Moses and Mahomet or of any one else with him" (2.814).

Volney, by contrast, lets a mass of "worshippers of Jesus" acknowledge
using the same books as the Muslims and believing in "a first man, who lost
the whole human race by eating an apple." Though the Christian also professes faith in a single God, he "proceeds to divide him into three persons,
making each an entire and complete God" (Volney 1796:158). He believes in
an omnipresent God but nevertheless is adamant that "this Being, who fills
the universe, reduced himself to the stature and form of a man, and assumed
material, perishable, and limited organs, without ceasing to be immaterial,
eternal, and infinite" (p. 159). Not only that, the Christians are extremely
divided among themselves and dispute almost everything regarding God's
essence, mode of acting, and attributes (p. 159); hence, Christianity's "innumerable sects, of which two or three hundred have already perished, and

three or four hundred others still exist." In Volney's universal assembly, the large Christian delegation is led by a Roman faction in "absurd and discordant" attire, followed by adherents of the Greek pontiff who dispute Roman legitimacy, Lutherans and Calvinists who accept the authority of neither, and an exotic crowd of sectarians: "the Nestorians, the Eutycheans, the Jacobites, the Iconoclasts, the Anabaptists, the Presbyterians, the Wiclifites, the Osiandrins, the Manicheans, the Pietists, the Adamites, the Enthusiasts, the Quakers, the Weepers, together with a hundred others," all "hating each other in the name of the God of peace" (p. 161) and convinced of their exclusive claim to truth, even if that means perpetrating or suffering persecution.

Volney's portraits of other religions are hardly more flattering. The Jews insist on being God's favorite people "whose perfection consists in the cutting off of a morsel of their flesh" yet reduce their almost total insignificance in terms of numbers ("this atom of people that in the ocean of mankind is but a small wave") even more by acrid dispute about fundamental tenets among its two principal sects (pp. 162–63). The disciples of Zoroaster, now feeble and dispersed, will, as soon as they pick up the broken pieces of their creed, begin to dispute anew "the literal and allegorical senses" of "the combats of Ormuz, God of light, and Ahrimanes, God of darkness" as well as good and evil genii and "the resurrection of the body, or the soul, or both" (p. 164). The Indians worship gods like "Brama, who, though the Creator of the universe, has neither followers nor temples" and is "reduced to serve as a pedestal to the Lingam" (p. 165), or "Vichenou, who, though preserver of the universe, has passed a part of his life in malevolent actions" (p. 166)—not to speak of the Indian people's "multitude of Gods, male, female, and hermaphrodite, related to and connected with the three principal, who pass their lives in intestine war, and are in this respect imitated by their worshippers" (p. 167). The believers in the God "Budd" who worship him under many different names in numerous Asian countries—Volney mentions China, Japan, Ceylon, Laos, Burma, Thailand, Tibet, and Siberia—disagree about the necessary rites and ceremonies, are divided about "the dogmas of their interior and their public doctrines," and quarrel about the preeminence of incarnations of their God in Tibet and Siberia (p. 168). Volney also mentions other religions such as Japanese Shinto (p. 168), Confucianism (p. 169), the religions of the Tartars and other Siberians (pp. 169–170), and those of the "sooty inhabitants of Africa, who, while they worship their *Fetiches*, entertain the same opinions" as the shamans of Siberia (p. 170). But the picture is the same everywhere: the world's religions are an ideal breeding ground for division and conflict.

Like Varenius, Volney also has a special category in his lineup: people without any desire to join the colorful club of religions. However, unlike some of Varenius's atheists, they do not belong to the civilized nations:

> In fine, there are a hundred other savage nations, who, entertaining none of these ideas of civilized countries respecting God, the soul, and a future state, exercise no species of worship, and yet are not less favoured with the gifts of nature, in the irreligion to which nature has destined them. (p. 171)

With this reminder of the narrator's initial question why Palmyra flourished when governed by heathen and fell into ruin while in the hands of God's faithful, Volney turns to the analysis of some of the major contradictions in the discussed religions. Rival claims of monopolies of divine revelation, proof of their truth via miracles and martyrdom, unique records of divine communication, and so on quickly show that there can be no common ground as long as everybody insists that his religion "is the only true and infallible doctrine" (p. 173). A revolution is called for.

Volney's Three Revolutions

Volney's *Ruins* is obviously a composite book consisting of segments that had been written separately and for different purposes. The initial ode and introductory section may stem from 1787 or earlier; in fact, the preface and the last page of Volney's 1787 travelogue already announce *The Ruins*. The body of the book can, I think, be associated with three revolutions that Volney was intimately involved in.

1. The Political Revolution

During the time of the book's composition, Volney became a major player in the French Revolution. He published political pamphlets, became a member of the commission for the study of the revolutionary constitution, and worked as an influential legislator (Gaulmier 1959:65–111). His political and revolutionary interests are reflected in the titles of chapters 5 ("Condition of Man in the Universe"), 6 ("Original State of Man"), 7 ("Principles of Society"), 8 ("Source of the Evils of Society"), 9 ("Origin of Government and Laws"), 10 ("General Causes of the Prosperity of Ancient States"), 11 ("General Causes of the Revolutions and Ruin of Ancient States"), 12 ("Lessons Taught by Ancient, Repeated in Modern Times"), 13 ("Will the Human Race Be Ever in a Better Condition Than at Present?"), 14 ("Grand Obstacle to Improvement"), 15 ("New Age"), 16 ("A Free and Legislative People"), 17 ("Universal Basis of All Right and All Law"), and finally chapter 18 ("Consternation and Conspiracy of Tyrants"), which ends with the convocation of a general assembly of religions. This entire group of chapters is related to Volney's political and legislative activities during the French Revolution and appears to have been written between the revolution's first climax in 1789 when Volney became member of the representative assembly of the three estates (États généraux) and 1790 when he was elected to the influential position of secretary of the National Constituent Assembly.

2. The Religious Revolution

The work of eighteenth-century luminaries like Pierre Bayle, Voltaire, the French encyclopedists, Buffon, Hume, Helvétius, Holbach, and Charles-François Dupuis contributed to the erosion of biblical authority and helped in creating a revolutionary picture of religions, their origin, and their role. Christianity and its Jewish parent came to be seen as peculiar varieties of Mediterranean religions and their scriptures as repositories of local myths that were not only younger but also in many ways inferior to their Asian competitors (see Chapter 1). Our quick survey has already shown how modern Volney's conception of religion appears in comparison even with that of Holbach. *The Ruins* marks a decisive stage in what W. C. Smith has called the "reification" of religion—a stage in which even the deist attachment to a creator God evaporated and Christianity lost its incomparability. It now became an object of impartial study as an exemplar of "religion in general" (Smith 1991:43–49) whose sacred scriptures and doctrines, just like those of any other cult, had to undergo critical scrutiny and comparison. Thus, Volney's assembly of religions had to begin with the agreement to "seek truth, as if none of us had possession of it" (Volney 1796:172).

It has recently been claimed that the "construction of 'religion' and 'religions' as global, cross-cultural objects of study has been part of a wider historical process of western imperialism, colonialism, and neocolonialism" (Fitzgerald 2000:8) and that the origin of modern comparative religions or the science of religion can be located between 1859 and 1869 (Sharpe 1986:27).

Fitzgerald's point that much of the field of "religious studies" is still theology in disguise is valid; but it helps to investigate such issues in a broader historical and cultural context.[6] Volney's *Ruins* and the other case studies of this book illustrate both the complexity of processes at work and the very limited usefulness of bumper sticker labels such as "western imperialism" and "colonialism."

In the second half of the eighteenth century, Europe's confrontation with an increasingly complex world and an exploding history triggered an extraordinary amount of thought about the origin of things. Academies held essay contests about the origin of inequality among men (inspiring Jean-Jacques Rousseau's first philosophical work in 1755) or the origin of language (won by J. G. Herder in 1772); among European historians and philosophers, it became fashion to inquire about the origins of just about anything. For example, in 1758, Antoine-Yves Goguet published three volumes of his thoughts *On the origin of laws, the arts, and sciences and their progress among the ancients*; in 1773, the first volume of Antoine Court de Gébelin's 9-volume set of studies on the primeval world appeared; in 1777, Jean-Sylvain Bailly published his letters to Voltaire about the origin of sciences and their Asian inventors; and in 1781, Dupuis offered to the public his analysis on the origin of star constellations, which had such a profound impact on Volney and his *Ruins*.

In this environment, it was only natural that the origin of religion should also be a question of great interest. Volney addressed it in Chapter 22 of *The Ruins* ("Origin and Genealogy of Religious Ideas") which is disproportionately large (13 subsections). Chapter 22 appears to have been written as a separate essay under the influence of Holbach, Helvétius, and Dupuis before 1787. It fits awkwardly into the narrative; it seems as if a drab professor of religious studies took over the speaker's podium to lecture the representatives of the world's religions on his pet theory about the origin of religions. He is only occasionally interrupted by representatives of the world's religions muttering a few words of protest when one of the pillars of their faith gets reduced to astrological hocus pocus.

In spite of such stylistic problems, Volney's ideas about the origin of religions and of religious ideas are of great interest. Like David HUME's (1711–76) account in *The Natural History of Religion* (1757) and the second volume of Holbach's *Système de la nature* (1770), Volney's history of religion begins with an "original barbarous state of mankind" (Volney 1796:224). He explains:

If you take a retrospect of the whole history of the spirit of religion, you will find, that in its origin it had no other author than the sensations and wants of man: that the idea of God had no other type, no other model, than that of physical powers, material existences, operating good or evil, by impressions of pleasure or pain on sensible beings. You will find that in the formation of every system, this spirit of religion pursued the same track, and was uniform in its proceedings; that in all, the dogma never failed to represent, under the name of God, the operations of nature and the passions and prejudices of man; that in all, morality had for its sole end, desire of happiness and aversion to pain. (p. 295)

In stark contrast to the usual perfection-fall-redemption scheme of Christian theologians, Volney's genealogy of religions traces humanity's tortuous path from total primitivity toward advanced theistic superstition and religious despotism—a state that cries out for a revolution and a new catechism for the citizen. The Ruins is the manifesto for this revolution, and Volney's catechism (which he called the "second part" of The Ruins) proposes a "geometry of morals" that reduces God's role to the provision of natural law (Volney 1826:1.253).

Volney thus offers a rather bleak vision of the nature and history of religion. The Ruins's representative of "those who had made the origin and genealogy of religious ideas their peculiar study" (p. 297) regards the entire history of religion as "merely that of the fallibility and uncertainty of the human mind, which, placed in a world that it does not comprehend, is yet desirous of solving the enigma" (pp. 295–96). Thus, ignorant men invent causes, suppose ends, build systems, and create "chimeras of heterogeneous and contradictory beings," losing themselves "in a labyrinth of torments and delusions" while "ever dreaming of wisdom and happiness" (p. 296).

Volney's view of Christianity, which radicalizes Dupuis's outlook, has a particularly revolutionary tint. The title of the longest subsection of Volney's genealogy of religious ideas, section 13, ominously reads "Christianity, or the allegorical worship of the Sun, under the cabalistical names of *Chris-en* or *Christ*, and *Yés-us* or *Jesus*" (p. 283). Volney not only reduces major elements of Christian dogma to features of sidereal worship but declares that the Savior himself, Jesus of Nazareth, represents a solar myth and must thus be regarded as a mythological rather than a historical figure. The Christians may have faith in their Son of God, "this restorer of the divine or celestial nature" who

TABLE 18. PHASES IN THE GENESIS OF VOLNEY'S *RUINS*

Sequence 1791 edition	Ruins *Part*	*Chapter*	*Pages*	*Notes pages*	*Note density*
Before 1785– ca. 1787	Ode, introduction	1–3	vii–32 (38 pp.)	8	ca. 21% of text
Prob. before 1788 events	Genealogy of religions	22	218–296 (78 pp.)	34.5	ca. 44% of text
ca. 1789–90	Revolution-related	5–18	33–145 (112 pp.)	8	ca. 7% of text
ca. 1790–91	Assembly of religions	19–21	146–217 (71 pp.)	14.5	ca. 20% of text
ca. 1790–91	Geography; notes & revisions	4, 22, etc.			

in his infancy led "a mean, humble, obscure, and indigent life," but Volney's professor mercilessly demythologizes their belief:

> By which was meant, that the winter sun was humbled, depressed below the horizon, and that this first period of his four ages, or the seasons, was a period of obscurity and indigence, of fasting and privation. (p. 292)

3. The Orientalist Revolution

As mentioned above, Volney's essay on the origin and genealogy of religious ideas (chapter 22 of *The Ruins*) appears to have been written earlier than chapters 19, 20, and 21 on the assembly of religions. In his 1791 preface (1796:iii), Volney notes that he had formed the plan of *The Ruins* "nearly ten years ago," around the time of his travels in the Middle East (December 1782 to April 1785) and that his work was already "in some forwardness when the events of 1788 in France interrupted it" (p. iii). Such information, along with data gained from the analysis of Volney's sources, discrepancies in style, annotation density, and content of specific parts of *The Ruins* (shown in Table 18) suggests the genealogy of the text.

Of special interest in our context are some important discrepancies in Volney's view of Asian religions between the earlier "Genealogy of religions" (chapter 22) and the later "Assembly of religions" (chapters 19–21). They mainly concern his abandonment of Egypt as the geographical location of humanity's cradle. This is a symptom of a revolution that involved, as we have seen, a deepening crisis of biblical authority and new scenarios for humankind's origin based on the study of Asian antiquities and texts. Since the mid-seventeenth century, questions about the authenticity of the Bible and particularly its first chapters by the likes of Isaac LA PEYRÈRE (1596–1676) and Baruch SPINOZA (1632–77) grew louder; and in 1753, four years before Volney's birth, the Frenchman Jean ASTRUC (1684–1766) presented a detailed analysis of the glaring inconsistencies pointing to multiple authors and textual layers of the Pentateuch. The growing realization that the Pentateuch was a local myth of origin rather than a universal history went hand in hand with the study of Asian texts whose claim to antiquity seemed formidable. Alternative narratives of origin began to be explored, and many of them were based on reputedly very ancient Oriental sources. *The Ruins* was written at an important juncture of this revolution, and its layers reflect three distinct phases.

The *earliest layer*, Volney's "genealogy of religions" (chapter 22), still shows little influence of contemporary scholarship on non-Islamic Asian religions. It cites only three, rather dated, sources: Kircher's *Oedipus Aegyptiacus* (1654), Hyde's *Historia religionis veterum parsarum* (1700), and Beausobre's *Histoire critique de Manichée et du manicheïsme* (1734).

The *second layer* (the "assembly of religions" section, chapters 19–21), by contrast, refers to more recent sources. Apart from Engelbert Kaempfer's study of Siamese and Japanese religions (1729) Volney here cites the history of the Huns by de Guignes (1756), Giorgi's *Alphabetum Tibetanum* (1762), Holwell's *Interesting historical events* (1765–71), Mailla's *History of China* (1777–83), the *Ezour vedam* (1778), and Sonnerat's voyages (1782). Volney certainly also used Dow's *History of Hindostan* and materials by his compatriot Anquetil-Duperron but pointedly included no reference to them. At the time of writing *The Ruins*, Volney must have heard that the first two volumes of the *Asiatick Researches* were published in Calcutta in 1788 and 1790. However, he had not yet gained access to this new source, which was to ring in a new phase of the European discovery of Asia's religions. Apart from the first published translation of a genuine Indian classic, Charles Wilkins's *Bhagvat Geeta* (1785), Volney may also have consulted Francis Gladwin's *Asiatic Miscellany*.[7] But *The Ruins* was published just before the *Asiatick Researches* and other new English sources became available on the European continent. Volney wrote,

Scarcely even is the Asiatic Miscellany known in Europe, and a man must be very learned in oriental antiquity before he so much as hears of the Jones's, the Wilkins's and the Halhed's, &c. As to the sacred books of the Hindoos, all that are yet in our hands are the Bhagvat Geeta, the Ezour-Vedam, the Bagavadam, and certain fragments of the Chastres printed at the end of the Bhagvat Geeta. These books are in Indostan what the Old and New Testament are in Christendom, the Koran in Turkey, the Sad-der and the Zendavesta among the Parses, &c. (p. 351)

The *third layer* consists of the changes that Volney made to *The Ruins* between 1816 and his death in 1820. They were incorporated in the version published as part of his collected works in 1826. Volney mainly eliminated notes that had become outdated, revised old notes, and added new ones that exhibit his continued research on Asian religions and growing interest in Buddhism. The changes in Volney's view of this religion, which will be discussed below, represent significant signposts of the third major revolution that took place in Volney's lifetime: the revolution triggered and sustained by the work of orientalists and the beginnings of organized, state-supported Orientalism.

Renaissances and Origins

The first phase of the Orientalist revolution that, as was shown in Chapter 1, saw India gradually move to center stage, shows surprising parallels to aspects of the Italian Renaissance three centuries earlier. The Italian Renaissance had also been inspired by antiquity and obsessed with origins, and the hermetic texts—supposedly the world's most ancient works by Hermes Trismegistos, the inventor of writing—were naturally of great interest. In 1460, while Marsilio FICINO (1433–99) was translating the books of another major inspiration of the Renaissance, Plato, his sponsor Cosimo de Medici convinced him to render the hermetic texts into Latin first. Ficino's translation was finished in 1463 and published in 1471 under the title of *Pimander*. Ficino's preface called Hermes Trismegistos "the first theologian" and "the first philosopher who turned from natural and mathematical subjects to the contemplation of the divine" and situates him at the beginning of a line of esoteric transmission leading to Pythagoras and Plato (Ebeling 2005:92).

Already in the sixteenth century doubts were aired about the authenticity of the *Pimander* (pp. 130–31), but even in the early 1700s when it became common knowledge that these texts were for the most part products of the first Christian centuries (Nock and Festugière 1960), the hermetic renaissance continued in the writings of men like Kircher and Ralph Cudworth as well as the arcane doctrines of Rosicrucians, alchemists, and freemasons.

In the second half of the eighteenth century, a very similar mechanism was at work: Europeans were once more confronting the Orient and were in search of their identity and origin. But this time the Orient was—thanks to many missionaries, travelers, traders, and scholars—much larger and more diverse. As more information about the world and its peoples accumulated and the biblical narrative gradually lost credibility, humanity's past seemed murkier than ever. The French encyclopedists "kept repeating that all the sciences, all the arts, all human wisdom had been invented in Egypt," and they often linked their view of Egypt as the cradle of humanity to a portrayal of the Hebrews as "a gross, brutal, uncultivated, unlearned people" (Hubert 1923:42). However, thanks in part to Voltaire's provocative publications (see Chapter 1), during the 1760s and 1770s India became the new focus of interest in the search for beginnings. Could the Vedas and other ancient texts of India throw a ray of light into the darkness of antiquity?

It is obvious that the "oriental renaissance" of the nineteenth century described by Schwab (1950) had roots that stretched deep into the eighteenth-century orientalist revolution with its decisive turn toward India and "Indian" texts. The authenticity and age of these texts were as vastly overestimated as those of the hermetic texts during the Italian Renaissance three centuries earlier. Both renaissances began with a phase of intensive discovery of remote antiquity that was riddled with mistaken assumptions, questionable sources, farfetched conclusions, and claims that today seem utterly ridiculous; yet both produced an explosion of interest in ancient history, art, languages and texts that ended up working wonders for art, philology, and the humanities in general.[8] Works like Sinner's *Metempsychosis* of 1771, Raynal's *Histoire philosophique* of 1773, Voltaire's *Fragmens sur l'Inde* of 1774, Herder's *Ideen* (1784–91), and Volney's *Ruins* of 1791 mark a crucial phase of excited discovery preceding the arrival of the first copies of *Asiatick Researches* on the European continent. As the works just mentioned illustrate, this was a period when the cradle of humanity made a decisive move from the Eastern Mediterranean region toward India and the Himalayas. Here we will focus on a particularly poignant reflection of this process in Volney's *Ruins*: the evolution of the French Orientalist's image of Buddhism.

Volney's image of Buddhism evolved in three phases. The first phase is reflected in the early "genealogy of religions" section of *The Ruins* (Chapter 22) written before the French Revolution. In this first phase, Volney saw Buddhism as an offshoot of Egyptian cults. In the second phase, the "assembly of religions" section of *The Ruins* (chapters 19–21), Buddhism is portrayed as a pan-Asian religion with a variety of exoteric and esoteric teachings expounded by representatives of various countries. The third phase, stretching over a quarter-century from Volney's 1795 public lectures to his revisions of *The Ruins* before his death in 1820, is characterized by his study of new information by British Orientalists and new theories about the identity and history of Buddhism.

From Egyptian Buddhism to Oriental Paganism

In the initial phase, as reflected in the "genealogy of religions" section of *The Ruins*, all religions including those of Asia still are firmly rooted in Egypt:

> And this, O nations of India, Japan, Siam, Thibet, and China, is the theology, which, invented by the Egyptians, has been transmitted down and preserved among yourselves, in the pictures you give of Brama, Beddou, Sommanacodom, and Omito.[9] (Volney 1796:271)

However, this view of a connection at the root did not imply identity of the branches. As we have seen in previous chapters, in the seventeenth and eighteenth centuries the idea of an Egyptian "root" gave a feeling of unity to Asian "branches" that is missing from today's perspective; but this should not be occasion to commit what Montesquieu called the cardinal sin of the historian, namely, to project modern knowledge on the past.

In this section, Volney's description of Buddhism follows that of Zoroastrianism, which "revived and moralized among the Medes and Bactrians the whole Egyptian system of Osiris, under the names of Ormuzd and Ahrimanes," and "only consecrated the already existing reveries of the mystic system" (p. 281). In this respect, "Budoism, or the religion of the Samaneans," appeared to be very similar:

> In the same rank must be included the promulgators of the sepulchral doctrine of the Samaneans, who, on the basis of the metempsychosis,

raised the misanthropic system of self-renunciation and denial, who, lay-
ing it down as a principle, that the body is only a prison where the soul
lives in impure confinement; that life is but a dream, an illusion, and the
world a place of passage to another country, to a life without end; placed
virtue and perfection in absolute insensibility, in the abnegation of physical organs, in the annihilation of being: whence resulted the fasts, penances, macerations, solitude, contemplations, and all the deplorable
practices of the mad-headed Anchorets (sic). (p. 282)[10]

"Brahminism," which is discussed immediately after this critical portrait
of "Budoism," is "of the same cast" since its founders only refined Zoroaster's dualism into a "trinity in unity" of Brahma, Shiva, and Vishnu (pp.
282–83). These sections on Buddhism and Brahmanism are followed by Volney's discussion of Christianity (pp. 283–96), which characterizes the religion
as an allegorical worship of the sun and equally links it to Egypt. Volney's
genealogy of religions section (chapter 22 of *The Ruins*) clearly shows that at
this stage he regarded all major religions as developments of ancient Egyptian
cults.

The chapter's separate sections about "Budoism" and "Braminism"
show that Volney distinguished these two religions. In the second phase,
reflected in the "assembly of religions" section (chapters 19–21), this distinction gains profile. Here he clearly identifies "Budoism" as a single creed
holding sway over many Asian countries from Tibet to Japan. It reportedly
centers on "one God, who, under various names, is acknowledged by the
nations of the East." They all "agree as to most points of his history" and
celebrate events of his life while fundamentally disagreeing on doctrines and
practices" (pp. 167–68). Though Volney does not yet use the modern spelling
of this religion's name, the appellations of its "God" leave no doubt as to its
identity:

The Chinese worship him under the name of *Fôt*; the Japanese denomi-
nate him *Budso*; the inhabitants of Ceylon, *Beddhou*; the people of Laos,
Chekia; the Peguan, *Phta*; the Siamese, *Sommona-Kodom*; the people of
Thibet, *Budd* and *La*; all of them agree as to most points of his history;
they celebrate his penitence, his sufferings, his fasts, his functions of
mediator and expiator, the enmity of another God his adversary, the
combats of that adversary and his defeat. (pp. 167–68)

Volney's Buddhism

In Volney's time, the reification of religion took on a whole new dimension
when the incomparability of Christianity gradually waned. As Christianity
became just another religion and its sacred scriptures came to be seen as
examples of Middle Eastern mythography and legend formation, the mechanisms operative in the formation and history of religions gathered interest.
Volney's chapter 22 on the origin and genealogy of religious ideas is firmly
rooted in Charles-François DUPUIS's (1742–1809) new theory that sought to
explain "the origin of all cults" (Dupuis 1781, 1795).

> All the theological dogmas respecting the origin of the world, the nature
> of God, the revelation of his laws, the manifestation of his person, are
> but recitals of astronomical facts, figurative and emblematical narratives
> of the motion and influence of the heavenly bodies. (Volney 1796:223)

The origin of religious ideas lies thus not in a divine "miraculous revelation
of an invisible world" (p. 223) but rather in human observation of nature and
primitive ways of understanding and representing it. Human beginnings were
not blessed with divine wisdom; rather, as all histories and legends proved,
man was savage in an "original barbarous state" (pp. 224, 357) and only
gradually "learned from repeated trials the use of his organs" (p. 226). Only
after "a long career in the night of history" did he begin to "perceive his
subjection to forces superior to his own and independent of his will," such
as the sun, fire, wind, and water (pp. 226–27). Volney traced the process of
man's gradual rise, his representation of the incomprehensible powers of nature through emblems and hieroglyphs, the origin of religious specialists, the
beginnings of agriculture, the development of a system of astronomy and
almanacs, and eventually the idea of gods as physical beings (pp. 227–35).
Like Dupuis, he rejected the Bible-based chronology and voted for significantly longer time spans, as well as Egyptian roots of astronomy and organized religion:

> Should it be asked at what epoch this system took birth, we shall answer,
> supported by the authority of the monuments of astronomy itself, that
> its principles can be traced back with certainty to a period of nearly
> seventeen thousand years. Should we farther be asked to what people or
> nation it ought to be attributed, we shall reply, that those self-same

monuments, seconded by unanimous tradition, attribute it to the first tribes of Egypt. (p. 235)

When Volney wrote his genealogy of religious ideas in the 1780s, he still criticized Jean-Sylvain Bailly for placing the cradle of humanity somewhere in Siberia (p. 361). For him, the first humans needed a place "in the vicinity of the tropic, equally free from the rains of the equator, and the fogs of the north" (p. 235). At that time Volney did not doubt that it was "upon the distant shores of the Nile, and among a nation of sable complexion, that the complex system of the worship of the stars, as connected with the produce of the soil and the labours of agriculture, was constructed" (p. 236). It was also in Egypt "at a period anterior to the positive recitals of history" (p. 278) that the "complex power of Nature, in her two principal operations of production and destruction" was first projected into a "chimerical and abstract being," a development that Volney regarded as "a true delirium of the mind beyond the power of reason at all to comprehend" (p. 277). The ideas of an immortal soul and of transmigration were also linked to this notion of a power of nature or world soul (p. 273), and Egypt thus appeared as the mother of the world's major religions: "Such, O Indians, Budsoists, Christians, Mussulmans, was the origin of all your ideas of the spirituality of the soul!" (p. 277). Combining ideas from Maimonides's *Guide for the Perplexed* about early Sabean sidereal worship with the genealogies of Dupuis and Holbach, Volney envisioned a large tree of religions with Egyptian roots. His genealogy features separate sections for five major branches of this tree: the religions of Moses and Zoroaster, "Budoism," "Braminism, or the Indian system," and "Christianity, or the allegorical worship of the Sun."

One of humankind's imagined divine beings was Volney's Buddha. While the "genealogy of religions" section had little to say of his "sepulchral doctrine of the Samaneans" that regards the body as a prison and life as a dream (p. 282), the "assembly of religions" chapters and especially its notes present a later, much more elaborate layer of Volney's views. As mentioned above, that second layer reflects his views in 1791 after he had studied a range of new sources about Asian religions, and it represents a marked advance over the view expressed in the earlier "genealogy of religions" section of *The Ruins*. In the "assembly of religions" section (chapters 19–21) that represents the second layer, Buddhism is presented as a pan-Asian religion deeply split by "the dogmas of their interior and their public doctrine" (p. 168). Volney identifies this religion via its central figure of worship and through the similarity of the founder's biographical details in various countries. He locates Buddhism in China, Japan, Ceylon, Laos, Pegu (Burma), Thailand (Siam), Tibet, and Tartary (pp. 167–69). If Jesus was for Volney a mythological rather than a historical figure, the same was true of the founder of Buddhism. He associates him with Kircher's "orphic egg" (p. 270; Kircher 1654:2.205):

> The original name of this God is *Baits*, which in Hebrew signifies an egg. The Arabs pronounce in *Baidh*, giving to the *dh* an emphatic sound which makes it approach to *dz*. (p. 345)

According to Volney (who transposed an idea of Henry Lord, Kircher and La Croze into a different key), the "world egg" cosmogony was a major element of Egyptian influence on Asia. During the discussions in the assembly of religions, Volney has a "Lama of Thibet" explain this cosmogony. Volney drew its first part from de Guignes's *History of the Huns* (1756:1/ 2.225–26):

> "In the beginning," said he [the Lama of Thibet], "there was one God, self-existent, who passed through a whole eternity, absorbed in the contemplation of his own reflections, ere he determined to manifest those perfections to created beings, when he produced the matter of the world." (Volney 1796:205)

The next part of the Lama's account in *The Ruins* stems from Henry Lord's cosmogony of the Banians (1630:2), which, as Volney notes (1796:352), is said to be of Egyptian origin:

> The four elements, at their production, lay in a state of mingled confusion, till he breathed upon the face of the waters, and they immediately became an immense bubble, shaped like an egg, which when complete became the vault or globe of the heavens in which the world is inclosed. (p. 205)

Volney's Tibetan Lama asserts that "God, the source of motion" gave each living being "as a living soul a portion of his substance" that never perishes but "merely changes its form and mould as it passes successively into different bodies" (p. 205). He informs the assembly that God's "greatest and most solemn incarnation was three thousand years ago, in the province of Cassimere, under the name of Fôt or Beddou, for the purpose of teaching the doctrine of self-denial and self-annihilation" (p. 206). The Lama then reads some excerpts from de Guignes's translation of the *Forty-Two Sections Sutra* to the representatives of the world's religions (pp. 207–8). Volney's notes leave no doubt that he regarded this founder to be a mythological figure like Zoroaster: "The eastern writers in general agree in placing the birth of *Bedou* 1027 years before Jesus Christ, which makes him the cotemporary (sic) of Zoroaster, with whom, in my opinion, they confound him" (p. 353).

Based on a variety of ancient sources and stretching de Guignes's argument, Volney saw Zoroaster as identical with the mythical Egyptian Hermes—which brings also *Bedou* into the Egyptian fold and is "supported" by a another deathbed confession story:

> It is certain that his [Hermes's] doctrine notoriously existed at that epoch: it is found entire in that of Orpheus, Pythagoras, and the Indian gymnosophists. . . . If, as is the case, the doctrine of Pythagoras and that of Orpheus are of Egyptian origin, that of Bedou goes back to the common source; and in reality the Egyptian priests recite that Hermes, as he was dying, said: "I have hitherto lived an exile from my country, to which I now return. Weep not for me, I ascend to the celestial abode, where each of you will follow in his turn: there God is: this life is only death." (p. 353)

Additionally, the much-cited coincidence that the day in the middle of the week was associated with Hermes and Buddha (as an avatar of Vishnu) quickly led Volney to the expected conclusion:

> Such was the profession of faith of the Samaneans, the sectaries of Orpheus, and the Pythagoreans. Farther, Hermes is no other than Bedou himself; for among the Indians, Chinese, Lamas, &c. the planet Mercury, and the corresponding day of the week (Wednesday) bear the name of Bedou: and this accounts for his being placed in the rank of mythological beings, and discovers the illusion of his pretended existence as a man, since it is evident that Mercury was not a human being, but the Genius or Decan. . . . Now Bedou and Hermes being the same names, it is manifest of what antiquity is the system ascribed to the former. (pp. 353–54)

Inspired by a suggestion of de Guignes, Volney also drew another group into the circle: the shamans of "Tartary, China, and India" who are famous for their mortifications. Their system "is the same as that of the sectaries of Orpheus, of the Essenians, of the ancient Anchorets of Persia and the whole Eastern country" (p. 354). Out of this potent ancient Oriental matrix grew the entire sacred literature:

> That is to say, pious romances formed out of the sacred legends of the Mysteries of Mithra, Ceres, Isis, &c.; from whence are equally derived the books of the Hindoos and the Bonzes. Our missionaries have long remarked a striking resemblance between those books and the Gospels. M. Wilkins expressly mentions it in a note in the Bhagvat-Geeta. All agree that Krisna, Fôt, and Jesus, have the same characteristic features; but religious prejudice has stood in the way of drawing from this circumstance the proper and natural inference. To time and reason must it be left to display the truth. (p. 356)

The inference, of course, was that they are all branches of the same myth, as Dupuis had so eloquently suggested. Sacred literature had little religious appeal for Volney, and recent translations from ancient Persian and Sanskrit such as Anquetil-Duperron's *Zend Avesta* (1771), the *Ezour-vedam* (1778), Wilkins's *Bhagvat Geeta* (1785), and the *Bagavadam* (1788) did not impress him:

> When I have taken an extensive survey of their contents, I have sometimes asked myself, what should be the loss to the human race if a new Omar condemned them to the flames; and unable to discover any mischief that would ensue, I call the imaginary chest that contains them, the box of Pandora. (p. 351)

As his catechism for the citizen shows, Volney had a rather different idea of religion. But like other Europeans studied in this book, he also projected his own religion on ancient Asia and chose to put at least part of it into the mouth of Buddhist monks. When the participants in *The Ruins*'s council of religions fail to come to a common understanding after protracted discussions and presentations, "a groupe of Chinese Chamans, and Talapoins of Siam came forward, pretending that they could easily adjust every difference, and produce in the assembly a uniformity of opinion" (pp. 209–10). They explained that they had an elegant way of accounting for differences by calling them "exterior" and could overcome such differences by recourse to an underlying "esoteric" core. Volney explains in a note:

> The Budsoists have two doctrines, the one public and ostensible, the other interior and secret, precisely like the Egyptian priests. It may be asked, why this distinction? It is, that as the public doctrine recommends offerings, expiations, endowments, &c. the priests find their profit in teaching it to the people; whereas the other, teaching the vanity of worldly things, and attended with no lucre, it is thought proper to make it known only to adepts. (p. 356)

Volney, the revolutionary sworn to equality and fraternity—and the author of a new law expropriating the French Church—could not but harshly criticize this tactic: "Can the teachers and followers of this religion, be better classed than under the heads of knavery and credulity?" But in his narrative he needed representatives from somewhere to present an atheist viewpoint to the assembly; and who was better equipped for this delicate task than the "Chinese Chamans, and Talapoins of Siam," the supposed experts of the Buddha's secret doctrine? The triangular connection between "esoteric" Buddhists, ancient atheists like Epicurus and Lucretius, and modern thinkers accused of the same vice—particularly Spinoza—had long been made by the likes of Jean Le Clerc (1657–1736) and Pierre BAYLE (1647–1706). In *The Ruins*, Volney thus decided to use these Chinese and Siamese Buddhists as stand-ins for Holbach and himself. He has them explain:

> The soul is merely the vital principle resulting from the properties of matter, and the action of the elements in bodies, in which they create a spontaneous movement. To suppose that this result of organization, which is born with it, developed with it, sleeps with it, continues to exist when organization is no more, is a romance that may be pleasing enough, but that is certainly chimerical. God himself is nothing more than the principal mover, the occult power diffused through every thing that has being, the sum of its laws and its properties, the animating principle, in a word, the soul of the universe; which, by reason of the infinite diversity of its connections and operations, considered sometimes as simple and sometimes as multiple, sometimes as active and sometimes as passive,

has ever presented to the human mind an insolvable enigma. (Volney 1796:211)

In this way these Buddhists become advocates of a God that very much resembles that of Volney's work of 1793, the *Catechism of the Citizen*, which he regarded as the second part of *The Ruins*. Its first precept is the belief in a natural law inherent in the existence of things, and the second advocates the faith that this law "comes without mediation from God and is presented by him to each human being" (Volney 1826:1.253). This unmediated law becomes apparent when one "meditates on the properties and attributes of each being, the admirable order and harmony of their movements" and thus arrives at the realization that "a *supreme agent* exists, a *universal* and *identical* engine, which is designated by the name of GOD" (1.257). Volney instructs the revolutionary citizen that "the partisans of *natural law* [les sectateurs de *la loi naturelle*] are by no means atheists: "On the contrary, they have stronger and more noble ideas about the divinity than the majority of other people" (1.257). The esoteric Chinese and Siamese monks of *The Ruins* couch their doctrine in a somewhat different terminology, but there is no doubt that they represent Volney and some of his radical friends when they say,

> What we can comprehend with the greatest perspicuity is, that matter does not perish; that it possesses essential properties, by which the world is governed in a mode similar to that of a living and organised being; that, with respect to man, the knowledge of its laws is what constitutes his wisdom; that in their observance consist virtue and merit; and evil, sin, vice, in the ignorance and violation of them; that happiness and misfortune are the respective result of this observance or neglect, by the same necessity that occasions light substances to ascend, heavy ones to fall, and by a fatality of causes and effects, the chain of which extends from the smallest atom to the stars of greatest magnitude and elevation. (Volney 1796:211–12)

Whereas William Jones detected his favorite brand of mystical Neoplatonism in the writings of Kayvanites, Sufis, and Vedantins and came to regard their teachings as vestiges of the purest and oldest monotheism expressed in Vedic prayers (App 2009), Volney found some of the basic precepts of his own revolutionary catechism in the giant heap of superstition that the world calls its religious systems.

Exploding Horizons

When in the mid-1790s his reduced duties as a revolutionary lawmaker left Volney more time for study and he gained access to the first volumes of *Asiatick Researches*, he realized that he had still been caught in a rather parochial, Bible-influenced and Mediterranean-centered view of origins. In his second public lecture of 1795, the newly elected history professor of the École Normale criticized the so-called *universal histories* for being partial histories of some peoples and families.

> Our European classics wanted to speak to us only of the *Greeks, Romans,* and *Jews*: because we are, if not the descendants, then at least the heirs of these peoples with regard to the civil and religious laws, language, sciences, territory; which makes it apparent to me that history has not yet been treated with the universality that is needed. (Volney 1825:7.8–9)

Volney criticized Goguet for having based his famous study about the origin of jurisdiction, the arts, and the sciences (1758) on the events of the Bible's book of *Genesis* and for having failed to realize that Judaism was based on a far older cult. Readers familiar with the arguments of *The Ruins* would now expect to hear a rehash of Volney's ideas about Egyptian origins. But between 1791 and 1795, one more revolution had taken place, and Volney's numerous students at the École Normale must have been stunned to learn that Judaism's roots were to be found not in Egypt but in "a Druidic and Tartar cult, which at the time was observed from the pillars of Hercules to China—a cult which is none other than the system of *buddisme*, that is, the ancient and modern *lamaisme* whose seat has since then been in Tibet, the home of the Brachmanes reputed throughout antiquity to have been the fathers of Asian theology" (Volney 1825:7.99)!

What in the world had happened to Egypt? Volney had "followed the English writers," the experts on India, into "the profundities of the history of mankind" (7:109) and had also learned to better appreciate the ideas of Jean-Sylvain Bailly (see Chapter 5), which he now found filled with "critical acumen" and "profundity" (7.99). Based on the researches of these writers, a new and more universal view of history was called for:

> One used to only occupy oneself with the Greeks and Romans, following slavishly a narrow and exclusive method which relates everything to the

system of a small people of Asia [the Jews] that was unknown in antiquity, and to the system of Herodotus whose scope is infinitely narrow; one wanted to see only Egypt, Greece, and Italy, as if the universe consisted of this small domain; and as if the history of these minor peoples were something other than a feeble and late branch of history of all mankind. (7.108–9)

This sounds like something Voltaire could have uttered half a century earlier; but times had changed. In 1790, the Orientalist Louis-Mathieu LANGLÈS (1763–1824) dared to state in print that, in his opinion, the Pentateuch was "an abridgment of Egyptian books, the original of which still exists in India, where literature was cultivated long before Egypt was made habitable by the labour of men" (Langlès 1790a:15; trans. Priestley 1799:4). The scientist and unitarian theologian Joseph Priestley, was motivated by this statement and by Dupuis's system to read everything available on Indian religion, and to write *A Comparison of the Institutions of Moses with those of the Hindoos and other Ancient Nations; with remarks on Mr. Dupuis's Origin of all Religions* (1799). He was shocked to learn that it had become acceptable to propose openly in Paris that biblical authority was irrelevant—and be rewarded for it with the directorship of the newly founded École Spéciale des Langues Orientales Vivantes! The choice of Langlès was highly significant since he was not only a fierce critic of biblical authority but also a staunch advocate of Indian origins who in 1790 had published the following proclamation which is proof of Voltaire's influence on orientalists:

May I be permitted to support a system that Mr *de Voltaire* conceived before me, and with which I have become thoroughly acquainted not only by reading the works of this great writer but also by my study of Greek and oriental authors. I believe like him that the Chinese and the Egyptians are the pupils of the Indians who went to learn their sciences and arts from them. Thus I am not at all surprised that scholars of most profound erudition regarded the Chinese as an Egyptian colony. The conformities between these two people could inspire an idea of such a system and thus does not seem at all unreasonable. But by going a few steps further these scholars could have avoided the objections their opinion evoked: what was needed was the assignment of a common origin to the Chinese and the Egyptians through which the connections between these two people explain themselves very naturally. India, situated between China and Egypt, must have been the origin of the knowledge transmitted to both of these regions. (Langlès 1790a:iv)

As director of Europe's first school of modern Orientalism and curator of Europe's most important collection of oriental manuscripts, Langlès became one of the heralds of modern Orientalism, who made the first Sanskrit lessons in Europe by Alexander Hamilton possible, helped Friedrich Schlegel make a start in Persian and Indian studies, managed the translation project of the first volumes of *Asiatick Researches* into French, collaborated with Hamilton on the catalogization of Oriental manuscripts for the National Library, and did much more. A new age of Orientalism was dawning whose founding manifestos were the first volumes of *Asiatick Researches* and their translator Langlès's address to the French National Assembly about "The Importance of Oriental Languages for the Extension of Commerce and the Progress of Letters and Sciences" (Langlès 1790b). In this pamphlet Langlès tried to convince the deputies of France's national assembly that "the Orientals were knowledgeable and civilized long before we managed to escape from the sad state of nature or rather of barbarity" (Langlès 1790b:6) and that the Europeans "owe these [Oriental] peoples our principal notions of science, philosophy, and the basic part of our religious system" (p. 7).

Lauding the efforts of other European nations in the study of oriental languages and literatures and evoking the advantages this might also bring in terms of commerce, Langlès proposed the establishment of chairs of Arabic, Turkish, and Persian in Paris and Marseille, whose occupants should "give public lectures of four or five hours every morning" (p. 16). Langlès's dream did not immediately come true, but an important part of his vision was realized before France's colonialist ambitions broadened. After the Special School of Living Oriental Languages (which Langlès administrated and where he taught Persian) was founded by decree of the National Convention in 1795, the chair of oriental languages at the Collège de France was divided into a chair of Persian (Sylvestre de Sacy, 1806) and one of Turkish (Jean-Daniel Kieffer), and soon enough Europe's first chairs in Sanskrit (Antoine Leonard de Chézy) and Chinese (Jean-Pierre Abel-Rémusat) were created (1814).

In his efforts to promote bible-independent Orientalism, Langlès could count on the support of Volney. Instead of trying to locate the biblical paradise and attempting to trace the paths of Noah's descendants in the manner of William Jones or Thomas Maurice, Volney drew a picture of enormous migrations of "Scythian hordes" covering the gigantic landmass "from the sources of the *Ganges* and the *Sanpou* to the islands of Denmark and Great Britain" (Volney 1825:7.109). His view of the human past had literally exploded. Now it was no more focused on tiny Egypt and its secretive clergy. Instead, a vast panorama had opened up thanks to "another revolution which is taking its course" (7.110):

> [One needs to examine] the religious systems of *bramisme*, the even more ancient *lamisme* or *buddhisme*, and finally all the events of a period which presents to us the ancient continent, covered from the frontiers of Spain to the limits of Tartary by a single forest and peopled by one and the same kind of savage nomads that we know under the names of Celts, Germans, Cimbri, Scythians, and Massagetes. When one delves into these profundities following the English writers who have introduced to us the sacred books of the Indians, the Vedas, the Puranas, the Shastras; when one studies the antiquities of Tibet and of Tartary with Georgi, Pallas, and Stralhemberg and those of Germany and Scandinavia with Hornius, Elichman, Jablonski, Marcow, Gebhard, and Ihre, one will be convinced that we have barely opened the mine of ancient history and that within a century all of our Greco-Roman compilations, all those supposedly universal histories of Rollin, Bossuet, Fleury, etc., must be redone from scratch. Not even their arguments will remain because the facts on which they are based are false or altered. (7.109–10)

This revolution, prepared by the likes of Voltaire, Mignot, and Holwell—and subsequently boosted by some members of the Asiatic Society of Bengal as well as Langlès—had apparently caught up with Volney by 1795. Instead of ancient Egypt, which suddenly almost vanished from his discourse, another mysterious land of origins began to glitter on the oriental horizon:

> *Tibet* or Bud-Tan, *the land of Budd,* is the ancient home of the Brachmanes; since Alexander's times these Brachmanes or gymnosophists were the most learned and venerated caste of the peoples of the Indies; their capital *Lah-sa* and *Poutala* is the most ancient pilgrimage site of Asia; from time immemorial crowds of Scythian hordes or Getes went there; today their races, which survive under the name of Tatars, have preserved their dogmas and rites. (7.117).[11]

Orientalism and European Identity

Volney's enlarged perspective shows the profound effect exerted by the study of the Orient on the reevaluation of European identity. His Mediterranean-centered perspective began to give way to a much larger Eurasian vision. This was only a foretaste of a process in which nineteenth-century academic Orientalism was to play a central role. The similarity of major European languages to Sanskrit had been discussed in Paris since the late 1760s, when Abbé Barthélemy of the Academy asked Father Coeurdoux for his opinion about the question "why there are in the Samskroutane language so many words that it shares with Latin and Greek" (Anquetil-Duperron 1808:659). In the 1790s, the yearly discourses of William Jones in the first volumes of the *Asiatick Researches* (App 2009) provoked renewed and broader discussions about this question which had serious implications for European identity since Sanskrit was held to be far older than Latin and Greek. In 1795 Volney began to wonder if "the ancient language of India, *Sanscrit*, was not the primitive dialect of Tibet and India, and the stock of many dialects of the Mideast," and he expressed his desire to learn more about the genealogy of the Chinese and Malay languages (7.118). He was passionate about using the study and comparison of languages to penetrate the fog of early history and showed increasing interest in ancient India. Volney was one of the rare residents of continental Europe to become a member of the exclusive Asiatic Society of Bengal (Gaulmier 1951:485); and when fellow member Alexander Hamilton came to Paris in 1802, it was of course Senator Volney who assisted him in various ways (R. Rocher 1968:37–38). At the time, Hamilton was the only person in Europe capable of teaching Sanskrit, and Volney was among the chosen few instructed by him (pp. 54–55). He was interested in Indian religion and translated William Jones's first English rendering of an Upanishad into French.[12]

The third layer of Volney's view of Buddhism in *The Ruins* consists of notes he had eliminated, corrected, augmented, or added between 1816 and his death in 1820. These changes strikingly exhibit the effects of the onset of modern Orientalism and indicate Volney's new focus. The comparison of languages, a field he had a particular interest in, pointed increasingly to an Indo-European mother tongue; and the presence of an equally old primitive mother-religion ("old Buddhism" or shamanism) in the same region of Himalaya/Caucasus was a fertile soil for speculation. In this respect, too, Volney felt indebted to British researchers:

Only since a few years does one begin to have exact notions of the doctrine of Boudd and his various sects: for these notions we are obliged to the English scholars who, as their nation subjugates the peoples of India, study their religions and customs in order to make them known. The work entitled *Asiatick Researches* is a precious collection in this regard: one finds in volume 6, p. 163, and volume 7, pp. 32 and 399, three instructive papers on the *Boudistes* of *Ceylon*, *Burma*, and *Ava*. Furthermore, an anonymous author who appears to have meditated on this subject has published, in the *Asiatick Journal* of January 1816 and the following months until May, letters that make one wish for more detailed explanations. (Volney 1826:1.314–15)

At the time of Volney's death in 1820, such detailed explanations had not yet come forth; the newly elected professors of Sanskrit and Chinese in Paris were still gearing up for the difficult task of debunking some of the outrageous claims advanced by German, French, and English indomaniacs (as well as their critics) through research about the history and doctrines of Buddhism. Such research was to be no more based on flights of imagination but rather on solid evidence gained through the study of Asian texts and monuments. Some of Volney's amendments to his notes in *The Ruins* concern newly available information on ancient Indian texts, particularly the Vedas. Volney explains, "Since the year 1788, the English scholars in India exploit a mine of literature of which no one had an idea in Europe and which proves that the Indian civilization goes back to very remote antiquity" (1:318). Interestingly, Volney's notes show virtually no colonialist and imperialist interest; the man was obsessed with the question of origins and with the notion that the eurocentric view of history had to be replaced by a more global perspective.

This change of perspective was of course a gradual process which is far from finished even today. It is intimately connected to European identity, and the questions it involved—for example those about the origin of European languages, peoples, and religions—were considered important enough to warrant the establishment of university chairs occupied by orientalists capable of providing reliable answers. Before his death, when the first of these professors were already active in Paris, Volney was especially curious about the religion brought from Asia to Europe by "Odin or Voden, who is the divinity presented under diverse names such as Budd, Bedda, Boutta, Fôt, and Taut who is Mercury, as preserved in the Wednesday of the Nordic people which is called vonsdag and vodendag, the day of Voden or Wedn with the English" (Volney 1825:7.117).

But the public's worldview and historical outlook did not change as swiftly as the young revolutionary had once hoped. In 1813 Volney was still trying to educate the stubborn Christian faithful of France. He pored over the Bible, compared its chronological fantasies with those of other peoples, and wondered how in the world such a small and insignificant people in forlorn Palestine had managed to mislead so many people for so long. In his *New researches on ancient history* (1813–14), he bored his dwindling readership with detailed analyses of sources whose value he denigrated and with conclusions that Voltaire had long ago presented with much more passion, wit, and style. But Volney once more confirmed one of the cardinal tenets of modern Orientalism:

> The result of all these data is evidence that the books of the Jewish people have no right to dominate the annals of other nations nor exclusively to inform us of remote antiquity. They have only the merit of furnishing means of instruction that are subject to the same drawbacks and rules of critique as those of other peoples; and it was wrong to attempt, as was done until now, to make their system the benchmark of all others. (unnumbered final page of Volney 1825, vol. 5)

In the years before his death, while studying Asia's most widespread religion, whose representatives he had used in *The Ruins* to present his own radical ideas, Volney added numerous notes. It is striking that hardly a trace is left of Moses and the Egyptians. Instead we read about the importance of the Scyths in ancient history and their relationship to Bailly's *peuple instituteur*, about lamas and shamans, about the history of Buddhism, and about that strange and fascinating trinity: the Buddha of India, Hermes of Egypt, and Wotan of Europe. Volney's researches on ancient history had begun in his youth with the study of biblical and Greek chronology; but since those days, all horizons had exploded. Reflecting on the revolution of the past decades, the Orientalist mused toward the end of his life:

> The more one penetrated, in the last thirty or forty years, into the secret sciences and especially into the astronomy and cosmogony of the modern Asian peoples—the Hindus, the Chinese, the Burmese, etc.—the more one became convinced of the affinity of their doctrine with that of the

ancient people mentioned above [Bailly's *peuple instituteur*]; one could even say that in those places it has been transmitted more completely in certain respects, and more purely than with us, because it has not been so altered by anthropomorphic innovations which have warped everything. (5.184)

For a while, Volney was possibly the most politically active and influential Orientalist of his time, and his status as a senator and familiarity with Napoleon put him in a unique position to link Orientalism with emerging colonial and imperialist power. But it appears that he mainly promoted the scientific study of the Orient (particularly of its religions and languages) and that these activities were not driven by political or economic motives but rather by his rebellion against biblical authority coupled with a genuine curiosity about the history of humankind, its religions, and its languages. Such questions, which automatically signaled mistrust of the biblical narrative, were gradually becoming domains of state-sponsored research beyond the reach of biblical studies and Christian theology. Between Volney's publication of *The Ruins* in 1791 and his death in 1820, modern Orientalism had gained a first institutional foothold.[13] In 1791 the Benaras Hindu College was founded, in 1795 the École des Langues Orientales Vivantes in Paris, in 1800 Fort William College in Calcutta, in 1805 the East India College of Haileybury near London and chairs of Persian and Turkish at the Collège de France, in 1814 Europe's first university chairs in Sanskrit and Chinese at the Collège de France, and in 1818 the first Sanskrit courses at a German university (University of Bonn; A. W. Schlegel). The year of Volney's death saw the first issue of Schlegel's *Indische Bibliothek*, and in the following year the first Oriental society in Europe was founded: the Société Asiatique in Paris (1821). The first number of its journal, the *Journal asiatique*, appeared in 1822; and 1824, the year of Langlès's death, saw the foundation of the Royal Asiatic Society of Great Britain and Ireland. Volney would have been delighted with these clear signs of the institutionalization of modern orientalism. It is only fitting that in his testament he dedicated part of his fortune to the promotion of exactly the kind of research that these institutions and their journals represented.[14]

Synoptic List of Protagonists in This Book

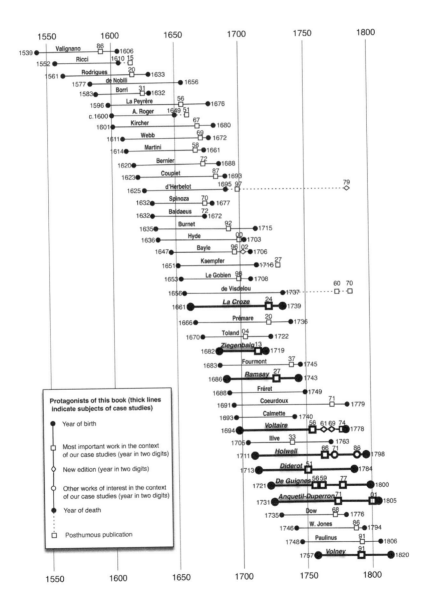

Protagonists of this book (thick lines indicate subjects of case studies)

● Year of birth

□ Most important work in the context of our case studies (year in two digits)

◇ New edition (year in two digits)

○ Other works of interest in the context of our case studies (year in two digits)

● Year of death

□ Posthumous publication

Notes

PREFACE

1. Urs App, "William Jones's Ancient Theology," *Sino-Platonic Papers* 191 (July 2009).

2. Needless to say, these translations are limited to materials connected to the included case studies. Translations from a substantially broader range of sources will appear separately in a Reader of source materials pertaining to the European discovery of Asian religions.

INTRODUCTION

1. Most prominent among them were the Jesuit Roberto de Nobili, who in the early seventeenth century applied Ricci's ideas to Indian religion, and the Dutchman Abraham Roger, who relied on Brahmin informers and wrote an influential manuscript on South Indian religion that was posthumously published in 1651 in edited and amplified form.

CHAPTER 1. VOLTAIRE'S VEDA

1. In *Orientalism*, Edward Said mentions only briefly that Voltaire was interested in the Orient because he wanted to make the Bible more unbelievable (1994:76), and Robert Irwin's *For Lust of Knowing* discards the theme after a brief discussion of Voltaire's contradictory treatment of Islam's prophet (2006:117).

2. This story is told in detail in App 1997a, b, 1998a.

3. See the original text, transcription, and commentary along with the Latin, Portuguese, and English translations of the entire document in App 1997a:232–39.

4. The complete Portuguese manuscript is in the Biblioteca Nazionale Roma, Fondo Gesuitico 1482, no. 33; transcribed in Ruiz-de-Medina 1990:655–67. An Italian version that is slightly shorter has the number 1384, no. 7, in the same Fondo Gesuitico. For other versions and translations, see Ruiz-de-Medina 1990:654.

5. A detailed history of this misconception is in preparation. Roger-Pol Droit's *The*

Cult of Nothingness: The Philosophers and the Buddha (2003) ignores its Japanese origin and interesting history but illustrates its remarkable staying power and great influence even in the nineteenth century—another proof, if any were needed, of the survival of certain fixed ideas from the missionary era in the age of modern Orientalism.

6. See also the "Exoterica and Esoterica" section at the beginning of Chapter 3.

7. Ruggieri was a very good friend of Possevino, the republisher of Valignano's catechism; see Ricci 1942:136.

8. See the Chinese text in table IX, Ricci 1942:195. Pasquale d'Elia's "sanitized" Italian translation is found on p. 194 of the same edition.

9. Jesuit archives, Rome, Jap-Sin, 9, ff. 263–64; table XII in Ricci 1942:201. The Pure Land of East Asian Buddhism is traditionally located in the West. The text of both inscriptions is by Wang Pan, the local Chinese prefect.

10. The original document is preserved in Rome (Archivio Romano della Compagnia di Gesù, Jap-Sin., 9, ff. 263–64) and is reproduced in Ricci 1942:1.200. The handwriting is here transcribed and slightly rearranged. The Chinese characters of the original appear to stem from the hand of a native (possibly Wang Pan, the prefect of Shaoqing who donated the plates).

11. D'Elia (Ricci 1942:199) supplemented Ruggieri's howler by proposing the equally misleading "gente venuta dalla santa terra del ponente" (people who have come from the Holy Land in the West), which effectively transforms the Buddhist Pure Land into Palestine!

12. For the West, Rodrigues used Sebastião Barradas's *Commentaria in concordiam et historiam evangelicam* (Coimbra, 1599–1611) and Benito Pereira's *Commentariorum et disputationum in genesim* (Rome, 1591–99). See Doi 1955:853.

13. Paper inscribed with Japanese notes of such lectures on Japanese religions (which went into great detail about Buddhist doctrine) was used for the lining of a folding screen that was sent to Europe in the late sixteenth century. The texts of this so-called Evora screen (Port. *Biombo de Evora*; Jap. *Ebora byōbu*) provide a fascinating glimpse into the sixteenth-century study of Buddhism. See Ebisawa 1963 and Itō 2000.

14. This appraisal stands in marked contrast to the caricature of Rodrigues by Paul A. Rule (1986:74–77), who failed to grasp the influence of forty years of Jesuit mission in Japan on the fledgling China mission and on the perception of Asian religions including Confucianism. In Rule's opinion Rodrigues, who spent thirty-three years in Japan and twenty-three years in China, suffered from a "lack of discrimination between the cultures of East Asia" (p. 75)!

15. Martini made extensive use of Rodrigues's materials. For example, the beginning of Martini's preface to his *Atlas of the Far East* (Martini 1655:1) is inspired by the first chapter of Rodrigues's *História da Igreja do Japão* (Rodrigues 1954:14ff.)

16. For more information about this important treatise, its history, and its influence see Leibniz 2002:8–9.

17. Rodrigues saw parallels to Chaldean divination in the *yin* (darkness) and *yang* (brightness) and the whole and broken lines, trigrams, hexagrams, and charts of the *Yijing* (Book of Changes), whose commentary was traditionally attributed to Confucius.

18. These were the beliefs of the two opposing camps in the so-called "Malabar Rites" controversy that began around 1610 and extended well into Voltaire's time. See Županov 1999.

19. See my view of *Ezour-vedam* authorship in Chapter 7.

20. The kernel of the story, the Chinese embassy to India in 64 or 65 C.E. that resulted in the foundation of the first Chinese Buddhist monastery (the White-Horse monastery or Baimasi in Xian), is a legend with no known historical basis. It is contained in the preface of the *Forty-Two Sections Sutra*—the text that the returning embassy supposedly brought to the Chinese capital on a white horse. See Chapter 4. For differences between Trigault's edition and Ricci's original text see d'Elia 1942:1.121–24.

21. On p. 36 of the 1761 version of the *Essai sur les moeurs*, Voltaire suggests having met Foucquet in person: "Father Fouquet (sic), a Jesuit who lived 25 years in China and returned as an ennemi of the Jesuits, told me several times that in China there were very few atheist philosophers."

22. Genesis 5 portrays Enoch as the seventh patriarch after Adam and gives him a life span of 365 years. At age 300, he begat Methuselah, Noah's grandfather, and afterward he had the unheardof honor of "walking with God." Saint Enoch's day in the Roman martyrologue is January 3. In Christianity, he is revered as an archetype of the heathen who attains salvation; see Daniélou 1956:55–72. See also Chapter 5.

23. See also Chapter 2.

24. Johann Arnold Kanne, with Joseph Görres and Friedrich Creuzer one of Germany's major romantic mythologists, produced a mirror image of Huët's reasoning. In his *Erste Urkunden der Geschichte oder allgemeine Mythologie,* Kanne asserts that the major "historical" figures of the Bible originated in the Orient: Abraham came from Brahma (Kanne 1808:120), Esau from Ahriman/Ormuzd, Jacob from Typhon/Osiris (p. 320), and so on.

25. Torrey (1967:98) argues that internal evidence related to the Woolston miracles would "fix the date of the *Sermon des cinquante* after November, 1761." However, the manuscript has been attested since 1752 and circulated for ten years until its publication after the Calas affair in 1762 (carrying the false date of 1749). See Trousson et al. 1994:216.

26. Translations from Voltaire's *Essai* are based on the Beuchot edition of 1828 in four volumes and, when necessary, from earlier editions. The comparison of various layers of the *Essai* has shown that René Pomeau's "critical" edition often fails to indicate even important changes. This added phrase, for example, is not marked by Pomeau (Pomeau 1963:1.214).

27. In his *Fragmens sur l'Inde* of 1774 (p. 44), Voltaire cites this passage and sets it against the Father's assertion in the same letter that "one cannot doubt that the Brames are truly idolaters since they venerate foreign gods."

28. See Sweetman (2004) for information about different versions of this letter. For Ziegenbalg's view of Indian religions, see Chapter 2 below.

29. Parā-para-vasttu = Skt. parāparavastu: "divine substance." According to Ziegenbalg (who begins his *Genealogy of Malabar Divinities* with this term). this is the "Ens Supremum or the supreme divine being" (Jeyaraj 2003:29, 373).

30. Voltaire uses a remark by La Croze not about the Vedas but about a passage quoted from the *Lettres édifiantes et curieuses*: "These sublime ideas of God are contained in explicit terms in the Vedam, which is the ancient book of their Law" (La Croze 1724:454).

31. It is likely that Maudave believed that his French texts were translations of the Veda. See Rocher 1984:81–83 for speculation about Maudave's source.

32. These prayers are found in Sainte-Croix 1778:1.323–27. In Voltaire's manuscript (Bibliothèque Nationale, Nouvelles Acquisitions Françaises no. 452), they are on p. 14r.

33. Manuscript no. 1765 of the Musée d'Histoire Naturelle in Paris contains part of a letter by Maudave to Voltaire on the lingam cult (pp. 117r–125v). Cf. Rocher 1984:48.

34. Since Maudave gave Voltaire his own copy with handwritten remarks, it is likely that Maudave did not make a clean copy of the manuscript for Voltaire as he had offered. That he was ready to part with his (presumably) only manuscript may be another indicator of his lack of appreciation of the text.

35. On August 27, 1766, Anquetil-Duperron received a visit of Court de Gebelin from Geneva who had received a copy of the *Ezour-Vedam* through the offices of Mr. Tessier from Pondicherry. This manuscript was later copied for Anquetil-Duperron and is now found in the Bibliothèque Nationale in Paris (Fonds Anquetil-Duperron, Nouvelles Acquisitions Françaises no. 8876). More information about this and a third variant manuscript of the *Ezour-Vedam* (the Harlay copy) is found in Rocher 1984:8, 74–89.

36. At one place in his *Ezour-Vedam* manuscript, which he lent to Sainte-Croix for preparing the printed edition, Anquetil-Duperron wrote in the margin: "This is a European speaking here" (Rocher 1984:59). Like Maudave, Anquetil-Duperron believed that such questionable passages were probably added by the translator.

37. This corresponds to *ñāṉikaḷ*, plural of *ñāṉi*; Skt. *jñānin*: "a wise one, one with higher knowledge" (Ziegenbalg 2003:391). See also La Croze 1724:451 and Chapter 2 below.

38. Even at the beginning of the nineteenth century, Anquetil-Duperron still regarded the text as authentic (1808:1.120) and included it among his sources in the *Oupnek'hat* (1.xviii). See Chapter 2. Even Lamennais still regarded the *Ezour-Vedam* as a reliable source and gives copious quotations of it (Lamennais 1836:242–46, 271, 300–301).

39. Seringham is situated on an island in the Kaveri River near Tiruchirapalli (Trichinopolis) at the southern extremity of the Indian subcontinent. Robertson (1791:283) wrote that the "Pagoda of Seringham" received large amounts of money from pilgrims to support the Brahmins inhabiting the pagoda who, together with their families, "formerly composed a multitude not less than forty thousand souls."

40. See, for example, Richard King's treatment in *Orientalism and Religion*, which consists of a brief discussion of Voltaire's vigorous promotion of the "spurious *Ezourvedam*, a Jesuit work purporting to be a French translation of a Hindu Veda" (1999:121), in order to demonstrate "the subtlety and superiority of Indian thought in comparison to a decadent Christianity" (p. 202).

41. Chapter 4 of the 1761 *Essai* (Voltaire 1761:53–57). The corresponding passages are

found in Sainte-Croix 1778:1.188–89, 189–96, 201–2, 208–10, 222–27, 235–40, 284, 308–9. References are given to the version published by Sainte-Croix because it corresponds more closely to Voltaire's manuscript than the Harlay text transcribed in Rocher 1984.

42. Voltaire expressed his opposition to such theories in the introduction to the 1761 *Essai* (p. 11): "Therefore one must not conclude that the whole earth was for a long time [covered by the] sea because several regions of the globe suffered this fate."

43. In the *Philosophie de l'histoire* of 1765 (see Voltaire 1969), Voltaire describes this text as "a ritual of all ancient rites of the brachmanes . . . translated by a Brahmin" and shows that he regarded the two manuscripts as a set of texts that "in truth is not the *Veidam* itself but a summary of the opinions and rites contained in this law" (p. 149). The *Ezour-Vedam* presumably contains the opinions and the *Cormo-Vedam* the rites. See also Chapter 6 below.

44. A letter by Voltaire to Mr. Thiériot (Ferney, January 21, 1761) refers to the book *De moribus brachmanorum*, which traditionally is attributed to St. Ambrose of Milan. This letter shows that Voltaire did not appreciate this book: "Received the small royal [library] book *de Moribus brachmanorum*. I am more confirmed than ever in my opinion that rare books are only rare because they are bad; I only exclude certain books of philosophy that are only read by sages, that the fools do not understand, and that the fools persecute" (Voltaire 1828:6.27).

45. From 1760 to 1778 (which was the year of Sainte-Croix's publication of the *Ezour-Vedam* and of Voltaire's death), only a small group of people including Voltaire, Court de Gebelin, Anquetil-Duperron, Sainte-Croix, and visitors to the Royal Library in Paris had access to *Ezour-Vedam* manuscripts. The general public thus had no way of verifying Voltaire's claims.

46. The "nephew" and his uncle are among the most hilarious false identities created by Voltaire in order to evade persecution and arrest. He had attributed his famous *Philosophie de l'histoire* of 1765 to an "Abbé Bazin." The abbé's nephew had supposedly found the manuscript after his uncle's death and decided to publish it. When the critics reprimanded Voltaire (whom they quickly identified as the real author), the invented nephew wrote a blistering defense of his invented uncle and even furnished biographical details for Abbé Bazin, thus giving him an interesting job: imperial interpreter for Chinese at the Czar's court in St. Petersburg!

47. Sainte-Croix 1778:1.189, 269, 316, and 2.13.

48. See note 13 above.

49. See Chapter 7. Anquetil-Duperron commented "plus negaret asinus, quam probaret philosophus" [an ass can deny more than a philosopher can prove] (Anquetil-Duperron 1808:3.120), and Anquetil's friend Sylvestre de Sacy specifically criticized Paulinus's view of the *Ezour-Vedam* as a catechism: "This book, directed against the idolatrous cult of the Indians, would be—whatever the learned missionary [Paulinus] might say—a very strange catechism of the Christian religion indeed" (Sainte-Croix 1817:68).

50. The term "indomania" was used by Trautmann, who analyzed some British exponents (1997:62–98).

51. In 1769 this work was incorporated into Voltaire's *Essai* as a book-length introduction. See Voltaire 1969:59.79–81.

52. This theory formed the basis of Bailly's theory of the Siberian origins of humanity that he discussed with Voltaire in a series of letters from 1775 to 1776 (Bailly 1777). See below.

53. Voltaire apparently neither owned nor consulted this French translation.

54. This refers to the three-volume treatise on the conformities of St. Francis with Jesus Christ by Father Valentin Marée (1658–60).

55. It is unclear to what Veidam Voltaire refers here. It could be to the *Cormo-veidam* or to translations he found in Baldaeus (1672).

56. See Chapter 6 for additional critical comments by Voltaire about Holwell's book.

57. For this text and William Jones's view of it, see App 2009.

58. See Chapter 8 for Langlès's description of Voltaire's influence on him.

CHAPTER 2. ZIEGENBALG'S AND LA CROZE'S DISCOVERIES

1. As Jan Assmann (2001) pointed out, metempsychosis or transmigration of souls, as commonly understood, was mistakenly associated with classical Egyptian religion.

2. This catalog was first published in 1880 by W. Germann (Ziegenbalg and Germann 1880:1–20, 62–94). A slightly shorter list of Ziegenbalg's *Verzeichnis der Malabarischen Bücher* is extant at the British Library (Sloane 3014). See Sweetman 2003:106.

3. These are the four Vedas: Ṛg, Yajur, Sāma, and Atharva.

4. Such influence, as documented in App 2008a and in this book, contradicts Jeyaraj's remark (2003:315) that La Croze's excerpts from Ziegenbalg's work had little impact, as well as arguments such as that by Dharampal-Frick (2004:127) to the effect that the belated publication of Ziegenbalg's books caused his work to be "largely unknown" in the eighteenth century.

5. Such passages were translated by La Croze into French (1724:452–53) and made their way into many books all over Europe. See the quotations by Voltaire in Chapter 1.

6. Ziegenbalg's *Genealogie der Malabarischen Götter* of 1713 was first published anonymously in 1791 under the title *Beschreibung der Religion und heiligen Gebräuche der malabarischen Hindous, nach Bemerkungen in Hindostan gesammelt*. His *Malabarisches Heidenthum* of 1711 first appeared in the edition of Willem Caland in 1926.

7. Tiru-valluvar (Holy Valluva) is the author of a famous didactic treatise on ethics titled *Tiru-k-kural* that consists of holy (*tiru*) short verse (*kural*). See Jeyaraj 2003:386–87, who lists several translations that usually contain the word "Kural" in the title.

8. *Nīti-cāram* (Skt. *nīti-sāra*), "Quintessence of *savoir vivre*," is also a didactic treatise on ethics (Jeyaraj 2003:424–25).

9. *Ñāna-veṇpa* is the title of an otherwise unknown didactic poem in the verse form of Veṇpā about wisdom (Tamil *ñāṉam*, Skt. *jñāna*). This is one of the three *nīti śāstras* whose translation Ziegenbalg finished in 1708. This translation was first published under the title *Nidi Wunpa*, edited by Willem Caland (1930:9–50).

10. La Croze filled several pages with quotations from this text (1724:456–59); he usually refers to it as "Le Livre Tchiva Vaikkium."

11. "Buddergöl" is Ziegenbalg's transcription of *puttarkaḷ*, the plural of puttar (Skt. *buddha*). "Buddergöl" thus designates followers of the one who attained *budd* or awakening, that is, Shakyamuni Buddha. See Jieyaraj 2003:377.

12. "Schammanergöl" is Ziegenbalg's transcription of *camaṇarkaḷ*, the plural of camaṇar (Skt. śramana).

13. La Croze only mentions that this "Dissertation" was published in 1703 in Hamburg in quarto format (p. 444). Even Brucker was unable to locate it (1736:7.1065). La Croze probably meant Johann Albert Fabricius's *Dissertatio de controversiis cum atheis & gentilibus* [Dissertation about the controversies with atheists and heathens] of 1703 that appeared in 1704 as part of the *Consideratio variarum controversiarum cum Atheis, Gentilibus, Iudaeis, Mahumedanis, Socinianis, Anabaptistis, Pontificiis et Reformatis*.

14. La Croze explains in a note (p. 492) that these are sectarians of Tatian, the disciple of Justin Martyr.

15. Thicca is the abbreviated form of the Vietnamese Thích-ca Mâu-ni (Skt. *śākyamuni*, Pali *sakkamuni*) and thus corresponds to the Chinese Xe-kia (Shejia) and the Japanese Xaca (Shaka).

16. Kircher's Foto refers to the Chinese Fotuo (Buddha) or possibly, given its pairing with the Japanese gods (*kami*), to the Japanese Fotoke (= *hotoke*, Buddha) in the old transliteration used by the Jesuit Japan missionaries.

17. This Chinese Buddhist text, about which more will be said in Chapters 3 and 4, had a preface containing the story of Emperor Ming of the Han's dream of a golden statue in the West, his dispatch of an embassy to India, and its return to China in 65 C.E. with (supposedly) the oldest Buddhist text, the *Forty-Two Sections Sutra*. This text and its tale of the introduction of Buddhism from India to China in 65 C.E. played an extraordinary role both in East Asian Buddhism and its Western discovery.

18. Since Couplet and his collaborators were rather well informed about Chinese history and expressly mention the date 290 C.E., it is unlikely that they referred to the Chinese sect of this name (Ch. Wuwei jiao 無為教), which was established by Luo Qing 羅清 (1443–1527).

19. Before the nineteenth century, "Caucasus" often referred to the Himalaya range as a whole or to parts of it.

20. Kao's interesting report about Chinese religion states that "the Idolatrous Worship and Religion of the *Bonzi's* is spread over all *East-India*, thro' the Kingdoms of *Pegu*, *Laos*, *Siam*, *Cochinchina*, *Japan*, and all over *Tartary*" (Kao 1705:170). See also Chapter 3.

21. For very contrasting views of this founder figure of Chan/Zen Buddhism, see also Chapter 4.

CHAPTER 3. DIDEROT'S BUDDHIST BRAHMINS

1. In a note, de Lubac lists only the authors mentioned by Diderot (Le Comte, La Loubère, Bernier, Kaempfer, Tissanier, Tavernier, and the *Dictionary* of Moreri) and fails to identify the main sources of Diderot's argument, which will be analyzed below.

2. This is one of the numerous mistakes in Fernandez's report that show his limited understanding both of Japanese and of Buddhism. For example, Fernandez claimed that Shaka was born when he was seven years old (possibly a misunderstanding of the seven steps the child made). Here, 49 years must refer not to the Buddha's age but rather to the duration of his teaching activity (from age 30 until his death at 79).

3. See also Chapter 2 above.

4. In this article of the *Encyclopédie*, the printer several times set "esoteric" instead of "exoteric"; the introduction of the twofold doctrine of Xekia (1.753) has, for example, "exotérique ou intérieure," which clearly is a mistake. Here, too, the text's "esotérique" is a mistake. The gist here, as in the old tale of Cristoforo Borri (Borri 1631:822), is that someone who has understood the esoteric teaching should nevertheless let the people follow the exoteric one.

5. This list is an almost literal translation by Diderot of the Latin summary by Brucker of Couplet's argument (1742–44:4B.820). However, Diderot abbreviated Brucker's last point that reads: "Those who reached [the goal] of this philosophy will leave to others the exoteric doctrine while conforming to it externally; but internally they will dedicate themselves to this mystical and beatific philosophy" (p. 822).

6. Ch. *Wuwei jiao*, that is, the teaching of nonaction. In early Chinese Buddhism, the term *wuwei* was also used as an equivalent of *nirvana*, and "the doctrine of *wuwei*" could thus simply mean "Buddhism" or, if the date of 290 C.E. is taken seriously, as a reference to early Chinese Mahayana Buddhism. See also Chapter 2, note 18.

7. Bernier's account was first published in 1670 under the title *Histoire de la dernière révolution des Etats du Grand Mogol*, 2 vols. (Paris: Claude Barbin). The letter of October 4, 1667, to Monsieur Chapelin was first included in the *Suite des Mémoires du sieur Bernier sur l'empire du Grand Mogol* of 1671 (Paris: Claude Barbin, 1:1–137). The letter appeared in English translation in 1672 and was soon also published in Dutch (1672), German (1672–73), and Italian (1675). See Bernier 2005:xxiii–xxx.

8. Anquetil rendered this as "Secretum tegendum," the secret to be safeguarded in silence. See Chapter 7 and my forthcoming book on the genesis of Schopenhauer's philosophy.

9. This is the *Gulshan-I Raz* (The Rose Garden of Mysteries) of Mahmoud al-Karim Shabistari, written in 1317, one of the great classics of Sufi literature.

10. Burnet's depiction of the earth formation cycle (Figure 6) shows smooth paradise as the rightmost sphere, followed by the earth covered by water with the ark in the middle, and (at the bottom) the postdiluvial world with continents, seas, and mountains.

11. This view of saintliness inspired, as mentioned above, Diderot's famous remark that the ideal state of such quietism "resembles sleep so much that it seems that a few grains of *opium* would sanctify a *brahmin* far more surely than all his efforts" (Diderot 1751:2.393).

12. As mentioned above, this book was also included as volume 3 in some post-1696 editions of Lecomte's *Nouveaux mémoires sur l'état présent de la Chine*. Le Gobien is also noted as the editor of the first few volumes of the famous collection of Jesuit letters

published under the title of *Lettres édifiantes et curieuses*. On his activities as editor, see Timmermans (2002:145–47, 155–220).

13. See Chapter 4 for Le Gobien's source and his manipulative use of it.

14. This means that Kaempfer and La Croze (whose theories on Buddhism appeared in 1724) developed their Egypt-related conjectures independently.

15. The most influential German version before Dohm's edition of 1777 was a re-translation of Scheuchzer's English version that appeared as volume 4 of the German version of Jean-Baptiste du Halde's China work (Kaempfer 1749).

16. Kaempfer's manuscripts are cited, like other manuscripts in this book, by folio number. See the excellent critical edition by Wolfgang Michel and Barend J. Terwiel (2001).

17. For omissions, additions, and alterations by Scheuchzer, see Bodart-Bailey 1990.

18. "Sintos" stands for Jap. *shintō*, the way of the gods.

19. *Shin* and *kami* are the Chinese-style and Japanese-style readings of the character 神, which stands for "god" or "gods."

20. "Bupo" is Kaempfer's reading of Jap. *buppō* (Buddha dharma) and "Budsdo" refers to Jap. *butsudō* (the Way of the Buddha, Buddhism).

21. "Buds" and "Fotoge" stand for Jap. *butsu* 佛 (Buddha) and the Japanese reading of the same character, *hotoke* (Buddha).

22. The *Nihon shoki* dates the introduction of Buddhism in Japan to the year 552.

23. See App 2008a for some examples.

24. See Imai 1982 and Katagiri 1995:43, who shows a page from this text and its translation in Kaempfer's notebook.

25. Brucker 1742–44:4B.817–19. This is a good example of the very international nature of information flow. The Frenchman Diderot translated a Latin summary by Brucker, a German historian of philosophy, of the English translation by the Swiss Scheuchzer of information from a German manuscript by Kaempfer, who worked for the Dutch and got such data from Japanese informers.

26. Diderot here specifies that "some Indians and Chinese attribute this [capacity of remission] to *Xekia* himself" (p. 753).

27. Among the proponents of this mirage are Almond 1988:11 and Droit 1997:36, as well as Faure 1998:17 and Lenoir 1999:90.

CHAPTER 4. DE GUIGNES'S CHINESE VEDAS

1. The Buddhist materials translated from Pali that are found in Simon de la Loubère's book of 1691 were given to him in translated form, presumably in French (1691:1.421). The translator is unknown.

2. Leung (2002:230–33) defends Fourmont to a certain extent by saying that he added Chinese characters to Varo's transcriptions; but even she could not pardon the fact that Fourmont based his work on a manuscript that he claimed to have been ignorant of.

3. By "hitherto" Abel-Rémusat meant not just "before Prémare" but rather "before 1829."

4. Later, de Guignes published Prémare's treatise on Chinese mythology (with the editor's "corrections" and various omissions) as an introduction to Gaubil's translation of the *Shujing* or *Classic of History*, one of the five ancient classics of China (de Guignes 1770). To its detriment, de Guignes also heavily edited and "corrected" Gaubil's excellent work.

5. D'Anville mentions having had de Visdelou's manuscripts "in his hands for a long time" (1776:24) and wrote, "The manuscripts I mentioned are the work of an erudite and virtuous missionary, Father de Visdelou, who died as bishop of Claudiopolis at Pondicherry. He had sent them to Mr. Malet of the Académie Française who had studied under him. Half an hour of looking at them were sufficient for me to realize their merit and to ask a friend to have access, and at that very instant he gave them to me" (pp. 33–34).

6. Abel-Rémusat wrote about de Guignes's use of de Visdelou's manuscript: "There are nevertheless reasons to think that it was not unknown to de Guignes to whom it could serve as a first guide to decypher the Annals of China, and to whom it must have at least suggested the idea of the research that gave value to his *History of the Huns*. The subject of both works is identical in many places; the same sources are used, and the work of P. Visdelou is much earlier than the first essay that de Guignes published under the title *Letter to M. Tannevot*. This is not an accusation of plagiarism directed against the erudite academician: he certainly consulted the originals. But this remark aims at elucidating how he could arrive at understanding them and drawing from them much more extensive extracts." (Abel-Rémusat 1829:2.247–48)

7. I found these notes in a collection of papers entitled "Fourmont l'aîné XXXIV Dissertations sur la Chine" (Bibliothèque Nationale, Nouvelles Acquisitions Françaises no. 8977:205–41). A note pasted on p. 205 by a librarian states that these fragments have no name of author but that they could be from de Visdelou who wrote on the same subject in the supplement to d'Herbelot. The person writing this did not notice that these notes were copied by de Guignes and reproduce pages and pages of de Visdelou's text almost word for word.

8. The first of these instances is near the beginning of de Visdelou's manuscript: "The Hioum-nou—which are, I believe, the Huns" (Visdelou 1779:18).

9. It is likely that both Fourmont and de Guignes were inspired by the *Museum Sinicum* of T. S. Bayer (1694–1738). This interesting book, an English translation of whose preface has been published in a study on Bayer by Knud Lundbæk (1986), was Europe's pioneer work about the Chinese language. Bayer's central achievement, in his own view, was the identification of nine "elementary characters" (which really are strokes) on which all Chinese characters are based. Bayer thought that each of these elements has a specific meaning: "First there are some very simple characters, single strokes, which, however, all mean something. Frome these the other characters are composed, gradually and step by step" (trans. Lundbæk 1986:115).

10. This led to de Guignes's hieroglyphic overhaul of 1766 in which the Phoenician

NOTES TO PAGES 215–227 493

alphabetic keys of 1758 are relegated to secondary importance and ideographic elements are regarded as the oldest units of writing.

11. According to d'Herbelot this manuscript was labeled no. 815 at the Royal library (Herbelot 1777:2.608) The text of Indian origin, which is lost, was first translated into Arabic and from there into Persian and Ottoman Turkish. A Persian translation in turn served as basis for a translation into Urdu. One of the Persian translations, titled *The Ocean of Life*, is by Muhammad Ghawth. It not only introduces, or rather translates, teachings and practices of Indian Nath yogis into a Sufi framework but also mixes in Gnostic and Persian illuministic elements (Ernst 1996, 2003, 2005).

12. The Royal library possessed the Persian translation whose author is given as Qazi Rukn ud-Din of Samarkand (d. 1218). According to a possibly fictitious account (Ernst 1996:9–10), Qazi stayed in Bengal for six years (1210–1216) and studied with a Brahmin convert to Islam with whose help he translated the *Amrtakunda* from Sanskrit into Persian. De Guignes summarized its content and translated parts of the fourth and seventh chapters (1759:791–801).

13. The analysis of this Latin treatise and appraisal of Brucker's influence would require a separate case study. Brucker had already advanced similar ideas in the seventh volume of his German history of philosophy (Brucker 1736:1044–1204).

14. As explained in the "Esoterica and Exoterica" section of Chapter 3, the classification of Asian religions into exoteric "idolatry" and esoteric "atheism" factions has its roots in sixteenth-century Japan and was applied to Chinese and other ancient religions by João Rodrigues who identified them as belonging to a single Hamitic lineage.

15. Letter of October 8, 1755. Bibliothèque Nationale, Nouvelles Acquisitions Françaises, Fonds Anquetil-Duperron no. 8872:72r. I recently discovered that several of the speculations aired by Deshauterayes in this letter were copied or adopted from de Visdelou's third Pondicherry letter (Nouvelles acquisitions françaises no. 279:11r–12v) titled "Lettre de Pondicheri. Dissertation concernant la Doctrine de Pythagore et le rapport qu'elle a avec celle de Boudha."

16. Palumbo (2003:200) has shown that in a comparatively short period between the end of the third and the mid-fourth century references to several monasteries named "White Horse" emerged; the oldest are those of Chang'an and Luoyang (c. 285 C.E.).

17. This movement's Chinese (*Chan*), Japanese (*Zen*) and Korean (*Son*) names all stem from the Sanskrit *dhyana* ("meditation" or "concentration") which the Chinese first transliterated as *chan-na*.

18. These "three classics," edited and commented by Zen Master Shousui 守遂 (1072–1147), are the Zen version B of the *Forty-Two Sections Sutra* (presented as the Buddha's first sermon after enlightenment), the *Sutra of the Buddha's Bequeathed Teachings* (presented as his last sermon), and the *Admonitions of Zen Master Guishan*.

19. The copy used by de Guignes in the Royal Library is today labeled Chinois 6149 (Bibliothèque Nationale, Paris); my thanks to Nathalie Monnet of the Bibliothèque Nationale for helping me identify it. Chinois 6149 contains the *Shousui* version commented by the prolific late Ming master Zhixu 智旭 (1599–1655) and corresponds to the text of the *Manji Zokuzōkyō* (*Xuzangjing*), vol. 37, no. 670.

20. D. T. Suzuki's Zen master, Shaku Sōen, also chose this text to introduce Americans to Buddhism (Suzuki 1906).

21. Since, as noted before, in early Chinese Buddhism the term *wu-wei* was used as translation of the Sanskrit term *nirvana*, the Chinese phrase in question here could accordingly be translated as "A home-leaver or *śramaṇa* . . . attains the Buddha's profound principle and awakens to the doctrine of nirvana."

22. The *Monthly Review; or, Literary Journal* 50 (1778): 540.

23. In particular, Agostino Giorgi (1711–97), the author of the *Alphabetum Tibetanum* (1762), got caught up in de Guignes's haeresiarch/manichean scenario and piled numerous additional conjectures on it (Giorgi 1762, vol. 1). See also the discussion of Sainte-Croix's vision of the *Ezour-vedam* in Chapter 7 below.

24. The Nestorian stele of Xian was erected in 781 by members of the Assyrian Church of the East (usually referred to as the Nestorian Church). It was discovered in the early seventeenth century and reproduced in several Jesuit publications including Athanasius Kircher's *China Illustrata* (1667). In the seventeenth and eighteenth centuries its authenticity was the subject of a protracted controversy. By far the best translation was by de Visdelou. Its manuscript ended up in Paris and was used by Voltaire's nephew, Abbé Mignot, for an article in the *Journal des Sçavans* of 1760 (Mignot 1760). Since the Abbé was on friendly terms with de Guignes, it is quite possible that he also read it and that therefore this idea of de Guignes was also inspired by de Visdelou.

25. Voltaire's nephew Abbé Vincent Mignot presented his papers in 1761 and 1762 to the assembly of the Royal Academy, but they first appeared in print in 1768. See Chapter 7.

26. Langlès applauded the "system that Voltaire conceived before me and of which I became convinced" (Langlès 1790a:iv) and concluded, "I thus regard the Pentateuch as the summary of Egyptian books of which the originals still exist in India where literature was cultivated long before Egypt became habitable through the labors of man" (pp. xiv–xvi).

27. The figures in question here are Mahākāśyapa (Jap. *Kasho*) and Ānanda (Jap. *Anan*). De Guignes found the Japanese names in Kaempfer. The "sonja" after these names signifies "revered person," something like "Saint . . . ," and is not related to *sannyasi*.

CHAPTER 5. RAMSAY'S UR-TRADITION

1. A century later they became the Samanéens or Sammanéens of La Croze and de Guignes.

2. See the expert description by Richard Popkin in his book about La Peyrère (1987) and in *The History of Scepticism* (2003).

3. This is the title of Paul Hazard's literally epoch-making 1961 book.

4. In particular, the books of Frank Manuel (1963, 1974), the essays in Force and Popkin (1990, 1999), the studies by McGuire and Rattansi (1966–67), Westfall (1982), and

Gascoigne (1991) as well as the essays in Fauvel et al. (1988) have been helpful for this section.

5. See Chapter 1 of Newton's *Observations upon the Prophecies*, entitled "Introduction concerning the Compilers of the books of the Old Testament" (Newton 1785:5.297–305).

6. A parallel is found, for example, in the Zen tradition whose histories are commonly called "transmissions of the lamp" or "transmissions of the flame" (Ch. *chuandeng*). Newton's "flame transmission" also involved the field of science, where "prophet" figures like Pythagoras transmitted the flame of original wisdom as well as true religion and knowledge of God's creation.

7. See the volume of essays on Martini edited by Malek and Zingerle (2000).

8. The manuscript by the Portuguese Jesuit Gabriel de Magalhaes (or Magaillans) entitled *Doze excellencias da China* of 1668 was partly burned, but the remaining parts were translated and annotated by Claude Bernou and published in 1688 in French under the title of *Nouvelle relation de la Chine*. It is a sign of keen European interest that an English translation by John Ogilby appeared in the same year. See Mungello 1989:91–105; the remark about the antiquity of Chinese characters is cited on p. 96.

9. "Fohius" is Fuxi, the legendary Chinese culture hero. Enos or Enosh is the son of Seth and thus the grandson of Adam who, according to the Old Testament, lived to the ripe age of 905 years (Gen. 5:6–11; Luke 3:38).

10. Mungello 1989:125. Collani calls it "the first printed and continuous history of China from the beginnings to the birth of Christ" and discusses Mendoza's earlier report (2000:149–150).

11. However, Martini also borrowed from Kircher's works, for example, most of the information in his *Atlas* about the Nestorian Monument of Xian. See Mungello 1989:138.

12. See the French list of objections in Pinot 1971:98, and the English translation of the entire accusation sent by the directors of the Foreign Missions of Paris to Pope Innocent XII in Rossi 1987:141–42.

13. For another translation of this passage, see Lundbæk 1991:61.

14. Foucquet met Voltaire in Paris shortly after his return from China in 1722 or early 1723 (Witek 1982:309).

15. Lundbæk compared Prémare's *Selectae quaedam vestigia* . . . with Ramsay's *Philosophical Principles* and found that "there can be no doubt that Ramsay was working with a copy or large extracts of a copy of Prémare's major Figurist work at his elbow" (1991:174).

CHAPTER 6. HOLWELL'S RELIGION OF PARADISE

1. Dalley's bibliography (2007: 214–16) lists a selection of the enormous literature about this episode.

2. Trautmann could only discern "a confused reference, one supposes, to the four Vedas," an "entirely obscure" text, and a third source that, judging not by content but "from the number, should be the eighteen major Purāṇas" (1997:68–69).

3. This paragraph about Eldad is based on Wasserstein 1996. D. H. Müller 1892 listed almost twenty versions of the Eldad story. See also Ullendorf and Beckingham 1982:15–16, 153–59; and Parfitt 2003:9–12 on the connection with the myth of Israel's ten lost tribes.

4. Sons of Moses separated by a river that cannot be traversed also occur in Rabbinic literature and Flavius Josephus; see Ullendorf and Beckingham 1982:154–55.

5. Out of the enormous multilingual Prester John literature one might mention, apart from the text editions in Zarncke (1996) and Wagner (2000): Rachewiltz (1972), Silverberg (1972), Knefelkamp (1986), Pirenne (1992), Beckingham and Hamilton (1996), and Bejczy (2001).

6. For a critical edition of the original old French text, see Deluz 2000; for various source texts and an annotated English translation, Letts 1953; for a modern English translation, Moseley 1983; and for a modern French translation with extensive notes, Walter 1997.

7. Marignolli was, of course, familiar with legends linking the paradise tree (from which Eve plucked the forbidden fruit) with the tree forming the Christian savior's cross through which original sin was expunged. The Buddhist monks observed by Marignolli, by contrast, acted on the basis of another legend that has the Buddha reach enlightenment under a species of fig tree ("Bo" tree or *ficus religiosus*), but Marignolli obviously did not know this.

8. Liverymen were Livery Company members with the exclusive right of voting in the election of the Lord Mayor of the City of London. Ilive dedicated his *Oration* to John Barber, the Lord Mayor of London (Ilive 1733:iii–iv).

9. This is a slip of the pen; the man's name was Jacob Ilive.

10. See the presentation of the Origenian heresy and major judgments condemning it in Crispo 1594:82–100, 130–59.

11. Ilive's *Oration* is an interpretation of John 14.2: "In my Father's House, are many Mansions, I go to prepare a Place for you" (Ilive 1733:1), which was inspired by Thomas Burnet's thoughts about the same passage in *A Treatise Concerning the State of Departed Souls* (1730:319). Burnet's book was originally published in 1720 as *De statu mortuorum et resurgentium liber* and seems to have been quite popular since reprints and corrected editions of the English translation appeared in 1733, 1737, and 1739.

12. This is the formulation Holwell chose in his dedication of the third volume (1771) of his work to the Duke of Northumberland.

13. Dedication of the second volume (1767). In this dedication Holwell also states that his intention is "to rescue the originally untainted manners, and religious worship of a very ancient people from gross misrepresentation."

14. These are the scribes of the Kāyastha or Kayasth scribal caste who can be Brahmin and Kshatriya.

15. I am looking forward to David Lorenzen's publication of Marco della Tomba's manuscript review of the French translation of Holwell's first and second volumes (announced in Lorenzen 2006:196–97). Della Tomba had unique knowledge of Cassimbazar, the city where Holwell was second in command just before della Tomba arrived.

16. Holwell calls it "almost a litteral translation from the *Chartah Bhade of Bramah*" and claims to have made a great effort to reproduce "the sublime stile and diction of the original" (Holwell 1767:2.60).

17. Holwell interprets the Sanskrit word *deva* as "angel" and apparently thought that the *devanāgarī* script (which is used, among others, for Sanskrit and Hindi) was an angelic language.

18. This was the widely used date for the beginning of the present world age.

19. However, Monier Monier-Williams explains that the term *śāstra* can be used for "any book or treatise, especially any religious or scientific treatise, any sacred book or composition of divine authority"—even the Veda (Sweetman 2003:72).

20. The first edition of 1651 contained Roger's text with notes that stem from the hands of Jacobus Scerperus (d. 1678) and/or a Leyden professor (Lach and Van Kley 1998:3.2.1030) who embellished the report about the Vedas with references to hermetic literature, Neoplatonism, and typical Ur-tradition fare such as Agostino Steuco's classic *De perenni philosophia* of 1540 (Roger 1663:222–25).

21. My thanks to Jonathan Silk and Thomas Cruijsen for sending me a copy of Caland's study.

22. To make things even more intractable, Holwell explained that "*Viedam*, in the *Mallabar* language signifies the same as *Shastah* in the *Sanscrît*, viz. divine words—*and sometimes, the words of God*" (1767:2.15).

23. The 1766 edition has "religion and worship" in the singular (p. 12).

24. In spite of numerous critiques, Holwell's "translation" of the *Shastah* and his "history" of Indian sacred literature were still copiously used in the nineteenth century. For example, Holwell's theories play a central role in the conceptual framework of Polier's two tomes on Indian mythology (1809), and the integrity of Holwell's *Shastah* was passionately defended as late as 1832 by Windischmann: "Even the strictest examination of his writings does not allow us to harbor any doubts about Holwell's fidelity and honesty concerning the truthfulness of his communications . . . Holwell has definitely neither invented nor modified the essence of the *content* of his source text [Urkunde]." (1832:616–17)

25. I originally planned to include a case study about a romantic indomaniac. But this phenomenon, which reaches well into the nineteenth century, is of such amplitude, complexity, and interest that it deserves and requires a separate book-length study.

CHAPTER 7. ANQUETIL'S SEARCH FOR THE TRUE VEDAS

1. Nouvelles Acquisitions Françaises 8858, Fonds Anquetil-Duperron, 367v–461r.

2. The pioneering biography is by Raymond Schwab (1934); there is a recent but bad one by Jacques Anquetil (2005). See also Kieffer (1983) and Stroppetti (1986).

3. Anquetil-Duperron 1808:3.120: "*plùs negaret asinus, quàm probaret philosophus.*"

4. For an analysis of this book and its reception, see Sweetman 2003:64–88.

5. See Willem Caland's *De Ontdekkingsgeschiedenis van den Veda* (1918) for details and some reproductions of early Portuguese, Dutch, and Italian passages about the Veda.

6. See, for example, Charpentier 1922, the article "Vedas" in Henry Yule's *Hobson-Jobson* (1903), and Caland 1918:264.

7. In an earlier letter of the year 1705, the same priest had already stated that the "book of the law" written in "Samouscroudam [Sanskrit], which is the language of the learned," is the book that the Indians "esteem most highly," even though "there is no one among them who understands it" (Le Gobien 1781–83:15.335).

8. De Visdelou may very well be the "ecclesiastic missionary from China who had come to Pondicherry" mentioned by Calmette (Le Gobien 1781:13.397).

9. This refers to the *Mahābhāṣya* ("great commentary") a second-century B.C.E. work on Sanskrit grammar attributed to Patañjali.

10. In his letter of September 17, 1735, Calmette describes this Veda as "The *Adarvanam*, which is the fourth *Vedam*, and teaches the secret of applying magic" (Le Gobien 1781:13.420).

11. The emphasis via bold type is mine. My translation follows Anquetil-Duperron's manuscript of the *Ezour-vedam* (Bibliothèque Nationale, NAF 8876, p. 45r): "Chum. pour satisfaire à la demande lui dit les noms des differens pays qu'il connoissoit, et lui en marque la situation. Les curieux les trouvent dans l'autre page en langue *Telegoa*." Voltaire's manuscript (NAF 452, p. 25r) has the identical text except for different orthography and an additional comma. The Harlay manuscript (Fonds Français 19117; transcribed in Rocher 1984:186) does not feature the highlighted sentence; probably its copyist, who also wrote in a much more careful hand than those of the other two manuscripts, noticed that this sentence does not make sense without the corresponding page that must have featured a map with place names in Telugu. It is unlikely that such a sentence would be added by a Western copyist; rather it would be a candidate for elimination, as happened in the case of the Harlay manuscript. Therefore, it almost certainly was found in the original French *Ezour-vedam* manuscript.

12. My translation is based on the French text given in Sainte-Croix. The Harlay manuscript version has in this chapter few significant differences and is reproduced in Rocher 1984:113–15. These four Vedas are today usually transliterated as Ṛg (= Rig), Sāma (= Chama), Yajur (= Zozur or Ezour), and Atharva (= Adorbo).

13. For a detailed account of such discussions and bibliographic references, see Rocher 1984.

14. In previous research on the *Ezour-vedam*, the question of authorship often hinged on the issue of the pronunciation of Sanskrit words transcribed in the text. But since both northern Indian (Bengali) and southern Indian pronunciations were involved, the issue remained complex. My argument here is that this issue is not connected with the question of original but rather concerns later stages of the production process.

15. The two parts of this report were published in French in the *Journal des Sçavans* for the year 1762 (June, pp. 413–29; July, pp. 474–500). The partial English translation appeared in the *Annual Register* for the year 1762 (pp. 103–29). References will be to its fifth edition, published in 1787.

16. The French original specifies that Anquetil-Duperron "had the occasion to see at Mr. Leroux Deshauterayes' place four sheets of the *Vendidad Sadé* that had been sent from England to Mr. Fourmont" (Anquetil-Duperron 1762a:419).

17. This must have been the three-volume French edition of Niecamp (1745) that contained, among many other interesting topics, a section about "The Vedam, Sacred Book" (Niecamp 1745:1.107) along with information about the *Nianigoëls*, the "Indian philosophers" who are said to "recognize only the one true God and reject all idolatric cults" (pp. 115–16).

18. Fréret had not only devastatingly criticized Newton's chronology but also approved that of Andrew Ramsay's *Travels of Cyrus* in a letter that Ramsay proudly included (from the second edition) as an appendix to his bestseller.

19. *Niveupan* and *Niban* refer to nirvana, *Safene* to sitting meditation (Jap. *zazen*), and *Coung-hiou* to emptiness (Ch. *kongxu*).

20. Amitābha (Jap. Amida) Buddha is the principal buddha of the Pure Land tradition of Buddhism but plays an important role in Mahayana Buddhism in general.

21. In Chapter 4 we noted how important the *polomen* (Chinese for Brahmins) were for the creation of the impression that Brahmanism had been imported to China and that what we today call Chinese Buddhism is really a branch of the Brahmins' religion.

22. Nouvelles Acquisitions Françaises, Fonds Anquetil-Duperron no. 8872:85r. This letter from Peking is dated September 2, 1758, and marked as received by Anquetil-Duperron on July 19, 1759.

23. Here Gaubil appears to refer to *dhāranī*, magical spells mostly of Indian (Sanskrit) origin that often have no meaning in classical Chinese.

24. This letter is in the Fonds Anquetil-Duperron at the Bibliothèque Nationale in Paris, Nouvelles Acquisitions Françaises no. 8872, pp. 70r–73v. It has been transcribed with numerous inaccuracies and lacunae in Stroppetti 1986:13–25.

25. Bibliothèque Nationale Paris, De Guignes Papiers divers, Nouvelles Acquisitons Françaises no. 279.

26. The difference in spelling in Figure 20 is irrelevant because "Boudha" is Deshauterayes's normal spelling, while "Budda" is de Visdelou's whose letter Deshauterayes copied.

27. The role of Johann Jacob Brucker and others in this development is deeply connected with premodern European views of Oriental philosophy and will be explored elsewhere.

28. Coeurdoux's offer to show Abbé Mignot proof in Indian scriptures for the universal deluge had the same aim (Anquetil-Duperron 1808:49.682).

29. The order was dissolved less than one year after Coeurdoux's last letter to Anquetil-Duperron when Pope Clemens XIV issued his bull *Dominus ac Redemptor* (July 21, 1773).

30. In the Latin translation of the Persian text of Prince Dārā's preface (Anquetil-Duperron 1801:4), he uses "pure unification [unificationi purae]" instead of "unity [unitatis]."

31. NAF 8857:862.

32. As mentioned in Chapter 2, these were the first translations from Buddhist texts to appear in Europe (Loubère 1691).

33. This was the first Buddhist "sutra" to be printed in Europe (de Guignes 1756). See Chapters 2 and 4.

34. "Eâdem animi libertate fruens, Libros Salomonis, antiquos Sinarum *Kims*, sacros Indorum *Beids*, Persarum *Zend-avesta* perlegas, idem dogma, unicum Universitatis parentem, unicum principium spirituale invenies, in illis clarè et pellucidè, uti veritatis fonti convenit, traditum" (Anquetil 1801:viii).

CHAPTER 8. VOLNEY'S REVOLUTIONS

1. The title of the American edition (*Dangerous Knowledge*) undermines this central argument of the author. My references are to the English edition.

2. The Australian academic Keith Windschuttle pointed out that Volney constituted the crown jewel of Said's argument: "In fact, Said's whole attempt to identify Oriental Studies as a cause of imperialism does not deserve to be taken seriously. The only plausible connection he establishes between Oriental scholarship and imperialism is the example of the Comte de Volney, who wrote two travel books on Syria and Egypt in the 1780s suggesting that the decaying rule of the Ottoman Empire in those countries made them ripe for political change. Napoleon used Volney's arguments to justify his brief, ill-fated expedition to Egypt in 1798, though Volney himself was an opponent of French involvement there." (Windschuttle, January 1999)

3. As mentioned in Chapter 4, much of Deshauterayes's work did not make it into print; but some of his early studies and translations of Chinese Buddhism were posthumously published in 1825 ("Recherches sur la croyance et la doctrine des disciples de Fo," Deshauterayes 1825; and the sequel published in the same year) and stimulated Arthur Schopenhauer's interest in Buddhism (App 1998b). Some of Deshauterayes's translations from Chinese annals appeared in Goguet (1758, 3:313–46).

4. This kind of argument has a long history both in the East and the West; in Europe, beautiful expressions of it are found, for example, in Lucretius's famous philosophical poem *De rerum natura* (On the Nature of Things; first century B.C.E.) and in Giordano Bruno's *Spaccio de la bestia trionfante* (The expulsion of the triumphant beast) of 1584.

5. Chapters 19 to 24 of *The Ruins* make up over half the book's volume.

6. Chapter 23 of Volney's *Ruins* is an interesting example of a face-off between a representative of the budding field of religious studies and theologians of various creeds written in 1790, long before Max Müller was born. It begins as follows: "Thus spoke the orator, in the name of those who had made the origin and genealogy of religious ideas their peculiar study. The theologians of the different systems now expressed their opinions of this discourse."

7. The first two volumes of this collection appeared in Calcutta in 1785 and 1786

and were in the early days sometimes mistaken for *Asiatick Researches*, edited by William Jones. In Europe, Gladwin's first two volumes of *Asiatick Miscellany* were soon made available in a reprint (London: J. Wallis, 1787). It contained under the heading "Asiatic Poems and Tales" also William Jones's hymns to Camdeo (pp. 1–6), Narayena (pp. 7–14), and Sereswaty (pp. 30–39).

8. Though the mechanisms show similarities, I am by no means claiming that the phenomena that Schwab describes as "renaissance orientale" added up to a renaissance in the customary sense.

9. "Beddou" and "Sommanacodom" were common names of the Buddha in seventeenth- and eighteenth-century sources, usually in association with Ceylon, Thailand, and Burma. Omito is the Chinese pronunciation of Amitābha Buddha (Ch. *Omito-fo*, Jap. *Amida-butsu*). About the European identity of this figure in Volney's time, see App (2008a).

10. Volney's main source here is La Loubère's work on Siam (1691:1.392–95), an English translation of which had appeared already in 1693.

11. Similar information, partly inspired by Bailly's theories, convinced Kant around the same time of the Tibetan origin of all culture. See App 2008a:5–22.

12. In his *Considérations sur l'origine*, Agricole Joseph de Fortia d'Urban reproduced Volney's entire translation with "slight changes" (1807:309–14). Volney's interest in Sanskrit and other Indian languages is also documented in receipts (sent at the end of 1805 to Langlès at the Department of Oriental Manuscripts of the French National Library) of an Indian manuscript and a grammar (R. Rocher 1968:55).

13. For facets of this interesting Europe-wide process, whose description would fill several more tomes, see Schwab 1950 and more recent studies such as Mangold 2004, Polaschegg 2005, Lardinois 2007, and Rabault-Feuerhahn 2008.

14. Volney donated 2,400 francs to the Institut de France to encourage improvement and application of his alphabetic transcription method for Asian languages. In accordance with his will, a yearly "Volney Prize" was given to outstanding works in that domain; but in 1835 the scope was considerably broadened to include historical and comparative linguistics. See Leopold and Leclant 1999.

Bibliography

Manuscript Sources

- Archives de la Société des Missions Etrangères, Paris. Vol. 418, pp. 277–82 (transcription of manuscript notes of a conversation with Claude de Visdelou). Reproduced in Timmermans 1998:578–88.
- Archivio Romano della Compagnia di Gesù (ARSI), Rome. Jap-Sin., 9, ff. 263–64 (door-plates for the Jesuit church and residence in Zhaoqing of Fathers Ruggieri and Ricci; transcribed and rearranged in this volume, Figure 1).
- Biblioteca Nazionale Roma.: Fondo Gesuitico 1482, no. 33 ("Sumario de los errores"). See the transcription in Ruiz-de-Medina 1990:655–67.
- Biblioteca Nazionale Roma: Fondo Gesuitico 1384, no. 7 (slightly shorter, Italian version of the "Sumario de los errores").
- Bibliothèque Nationale, Paris: De Guignes Papiers divers, Nouvelles Acquisitons Françaises no. 279 (notes from a manuscript by de Visdelou in the handwriting of Deshauterayes).
- Bibliothèque Nationale, Paris: Fonds Anquetil-Duperron, Nouvelles Acquisitions Françaises no. 8857 (Anquetil-Duperron's French translation of the *Oupnek'hat*).
- Bibliothèque Nationale, Paris: Fonds Anquetil-Duperron, Nouvelles Acquisitions Françaises no. 8858, pp. 367v–461r (Anquetil-Duperron: "Le Parfait théologien").
- Bibliothèque Nationale, Paris: Fonds Anquetil-Duperron, Nouvelles Acquisitions Françaises no. 8872, p. 85r (letter by Father Gaubil to Anquetil-Duperron dated Peking, September 2, 1758 and marked as received by Anquetil-Duperron on July 19, 1759).
- Bibliothèque Nationale, Paris: Fonds Anquetil-Duperron, Nouvelles Acquisitions Françaises no. 8876 (Anquetil's copy of an *Ezour-vedam* manuscript of Court de Gebelin from Geneva who had received it through the offices of Mr. Tessier from Pondicherry).
- Bibliothèque Nationale, Paris: Fonds Français 19117 (Harlay manuscript of the *Ezour-vedam*; transcribed in Rocher 1984).
- Bibliothèque Nationale, Paris: Nouvelles Acquisitions Françaises no. 279, pp. 11r–12v ("Lettre de Pondicheri. Dissertation concernant la Doctrine de Pythagore et le rapport qu'elle a avec celle de Boudha" in the handwriting of Deshauterayes).
- Bibliothèque Nationale, Paris: Nouvelles Acquisitions Françaises no. 452 (*Ezour-vedam*;

copy Maudave presented to Voltaire and Voltaire donated to the Royal Library in 1761)

- Bibliothèque Nationale, Paris: Nouvelles Acquisitions Françaises no. 8977, pp. 205–41: "Fourmont l'ainé XXXIV Dissertations sur la Chine" (notes in the handwriting of Joseph de Guignes from a manuscript of de Visdelou that later was published in the supplement to d'Herbelot's *Bibliothèque orientale* [de Visdelou and Garland 1779]).
- Bibliothèque Nationale, Paris: Nouvelles Acquisitions Françaises no. 8872, pp. 70r–73v (letter by Deshauterayes to Anquetil-Duperron dated Paris, October 8, 1755). See the transcription with numerous inaccuracies and lacunae in Stroppetti 1986:13–25.
- Bibliothèque Nationale, Paris: Nouvelles Acquisitions Françaises no. 22335, pp. 156–80 (Deshauterayes, "Histoire de Fo ou Boudha" in manuscript collection *Mélanges sur l'Histoire d'Afrique, d'Asie et d'Amérique*).
- British Library, London. Asia, Pacific and Africa Collections (APAC). Mss Eur D 22 (Desvaulx manuscript). See edition in Murr 1987, vol. 1.
- British Library, London. Ms. Sloane 3060 (Engelbert Kaempfer's Siam and Japan manuscript)
- Musée d'Histoire Naturelle, Paris. Manuscript no. 1765, pp. 117r–125v (partial copy of a letter by Maudave to Voltaire on the Lingam cult)
- Österreichische Nationalbibliothek Wien. Cod. 19540: *De imposturis Religionum breve Compendium* (by Johann Joachim Müller). See the critical edition by Winfried Schröder: *De imposturis religionum (de tribus impostoribus) = Von den Betrügereyen der Religionen. Dokumente.* Stuttgart: Frommann-Holzboog, 1999.

PRINTED SOURCES

Aarsleff, Hans. *The Study of Language in England, 1780–1860.* Princeton, N.J.: Princeton University Press, 1967.

Abé, Ryūichi. *The Weaving of Mantra: Kūkai and the Construction of Esoteric Buddhist Discourse.* New York: Columbia University Press, 1999.

Abel-Rémusat, Jean-Pierre. *Mélanges asiatiques: ou Choix de morceaux de critique et de mémoires relatifs aux religions, aux sciences, aux coutumes, à l'histoire et à la géographie des nations orientales.* Paris: Dondey-Dupré, 1826.

———. *Nouveaux mélanges asiatiques:* ou Recueil de morceaux de critique et de mémoires. 2 vols. Paris: Librairie Orientale de Dondry-Dupré, 1829.

———. *Foe Koue Ki.* Paris: Imprimerie Royale, 1836.

Allen, Charles. *The Buddha and the Sahibs: The Men Who Discovered India's Lost Religion.* London: John Murray, 2002.

Almond, Philip C. *The British Discovery of Buddhism.* Cambridge: Cambridge University Press, 1988.

Andrade, António de. *Novo descobrimento do Gram Cathayo, ou Reinos de Tibet, pello Padre Antonio de Andrade da Companhia de IESU, Portuguez, no Anno de 1624.* Lisboa: Mattheus Pinheiro, 1626.

Anon. *Siebende Continuation des Berichts derer Königl. Dänischen Missionarien zu Tranquebar in Ost-Indien.* Halle: Francke, 1714a.

———. *Der Malabarischen Correspondentz anderer Theil.* Halle: Francke, 1714b.

———. *Elfte Continuation des Berichts derer Königl. Dänischen Missionarien zu Tranquebar in Ost-Indien: Der Malabarischen Correspondentz anderer Theil.* Halle: Francke, 1717.

Anon. (Ith, Johann?). *Sammlung asiatischer Original-Schriften. Indische Schriften.* Zürich: Ziegler und Söhne, 1791.

Anquetil, Jacques. *Anquetil-Duperron: premier orientaliste français.* Paris: Presses de la Renaissance, 2005.

Anquetil-Duperron, Abraham Hyacinthe. Correspondance avec le ministre Bertin, Camus, Leroux-Deshauterayes, le P. Gaubil, Gentil (1758–1802). In Bibliothèque Nationale: Nouvelles Acquisitions Françaises, Fonds Anquetil-Duperron, 228. Paris, 1758–1802.

———. "Relation abrégée du voyage que M. Anquetil Du Perron a fait dans l'Inde pour la recherche & la Traduction des ouvrages attribués à Zoroastre." *Journal des Sçavans* (1762a): 413–29.

———. "Suite du voyage que M. Anquetil Du Perron. Liste des Manuscrits qui dans l'Inde & dans le Kirman sont attribués à Zoroastre, & des ouvrages qui ont rapport à la Religion des Parsses, déposés à la Bibliothèque du Roi, le 15 Mars 1762." *Journal des Sçavans* (1762b): 474–500.

———. Correspondance avec le Père Coeurdoux (1768–1773). In Bibliothèque Nationale: Nouvelles Acquisitions Françaises, Fonds Anquetil-Duperron, 55. Paris, 1768–73.

———. *Zend-Avesta, Ouvrage de Zoroastre.* Paris: Tilliard, 1771.

———. *Zend-Avesta, Zoroasters lebendiges Wort.* Translated by J. F. Kleuker. Riga, 1776–77.

———. *Législation orientale.* Amsterdam: Marc Michel Rey, 1778.

———. "Considérations philosophiques, historiques et géographiques sur les deux mondes, 1re partie." In Bibliothèque Nationale: Nouvelles Acquisitions Françaises, Fonds Anquetil-Duperron, 237. Paris, 1780.

———. "Oupnek'hat, traduit littéralement du persan, mêlé du samskrétam." In Bibliothèque Nationale: Nouvelles Acquisitions Françaises, Fonds Anquetil-Duperron, 866. Paris, 1786.

———. "Des Recherches historiques & géographiques sur l'Inde, & la Description du Cours du Gange & du Gagra, avec une très grande Carte." In *Description historique et géographique de l'Inde,* edited by Jean Bernoulli. Berlin: Pierre Bourdeaux, 1787a.

———. "A brief account of a voyage to India, undertaken by M. Anquetil du Perron." In *The Annual Register or a View of the History, Politics, and Literature of the Year 1762,* 103–29. London: J. Dodsley, 1787b.

———. "Vier Upnekhat, aus dem Samskrutamischen Buche die Upnekhat." In *Sammlung asiatischer Original-Schriften. Indische Schriften,* 269–315. Zürich: Ziegler und Söhne, 1791.

———. *L'Inde en rapport avec l'Europe.* 2 vols. Paris: Lesguillez Frères, 1798.

———. *Oupnek'hat (id est, secretum tegendum).* 2 vols. Argentorati: Levrault, 1801.

———. *Catalogue des Livres de M. A. H. Anquetil-Duperron*. Paris: Veuve Tilliard et Fils, 1805.

———. "Le premier fleuve de l'Inde, le Gange; selon les anciens, expliqué par le Gange, selon les modernes." *Mémoires de Littérature tirés des Registres des l'Académie Royale des Inscriptions & Belles Lettres* 49 (1808): 512–712.

———. *Voyage en Inde, 1754–1762: relation de voyage en préliminaire à la traduction du Zend-Avesta*. Edited by Jean Deloche, Manonmani Filliozat, and Pierre-Sylvain Filliozat. Paris: Maisonneuve et Larose & École Française d'Extrême-Orient, 1997.

———. "Tableau des quatre dynasties des rois de Perse: Dispute théologique entre une assemblée de théologiens musulmans et un Destour, 9 feuillets." In Bibliothèque Nationale: Nouvelles Acquisitions Françaises, Fonds Anquetil-Duperron, 9. Paris, n.d.

Anville, Jean-Baptiste Bourguignon d'. *Mémoire de M. d'Anville, Premier Géographe du Roi, sur la Chine*. Pékin/Paris: Chez l'auteur, aux Galeries du Louvre, 1776.

App, Urs. "St. Francis Xavier's Discovery of Japanese Buddhism. Part 1: Before the Arrival in Japan, 1547–1549." *Eastern Buddhist* 30, no. 1 (1997a): 53–78. "Part 2: From Kagoshima to Yamaguchi, 1549–1551." *Eastern Buddhist* 30, no. 2 (1997b): 214–44. "Part 3: From Yamaguchi to India, 1551–1552." *Eastern Buddhist* 31, no. 1 (1998a): 40–71.

———. "Schopenhauers Begegnung mit dem Buddhismus." *Schopenhauer-Jahrbuch* 79 (1998b): 35–58.

———. "Schopenhauer's Initial Encounter with Indian Thought." *Schopenhauer-Jahrbuch* 87 (2006): 35–76.

———. "How Amida Got into the Upanishads: An Orientalist's Nightmare." In *Essays on East Asian Religion and Culture*, edited by Christian Wittern and Lishan Shi, 11–33. Kyoto: Editorial Committee for the Festschrift in Honour of Nishiwaki Tsuneki, 2007.

———. "The Tibet of Philosophers: Kant, Hegel, and Schopenhauer." In *Images of Tibet in the 19th and 20th Centuries*, edited by Monica Esposito, 11–70. Paris: École Française d'Extrême-Orient, 2008a.

———. "Yanagida Seizan's Last Word." In *Yanagida Seizan sensei tsuitō bunshū*, edited by Yanagida Seizan sensei tsuitō bunshū kankōkai, 5–8. Kyoto: Zenbunka kenkyūjō, 2008b.

———. "William Jones's Ancient Theology." *Sino-Platonic Papers* no. 191 (July 2009):1–125.

Aronson, Alex. *Europe Looks at India: A Study in Cultural Relations*. Bombay: Hind Kitabs, 1946.

Asher, R. E. *National Myths in Renaissance France: Francus, Samothes and the Druids*. Edinburgh: Edinburgh University Press, 1993.

Assmann, Jan. *Moses the Egyptian: The Memory of Egypt in Western Monotheism*. Cambridge, Mass.: Harvard University Press, 1998.

———. *Tod und Jenseits im alten Ägypten*. München: C.H. Beck, 2001.

Astruc, Jean. *Conjectures sur les mémoires originaux dont il paroit que Moyse s'est servi pour composer le livre de la Genese: Avec des remarques, qui appuient ou qui éclaircissent ces conjectures*. Bruxelles: Fricx, 1753.

Bach, Julien. "Notice sur la première découverte des Védas." *Annales de philosophie chrétienne* 3, no. 18 (1847): 434–43.

———. "Notice sur l'Ezour-Vedam et sur les autres Pseudo-Védas." *Annales de philosophie chrétienne* 3, no. 19 (1848): 59–67.

———. *Le Père Calmette et les missionnaires indianistes.* Paris: Joseph Albanel, 1868.

Bachmann, Peter R. *Roberto Nobili, 1577–1656: ein missionsgeschichtlicher Beitrag zum christlichen Dialog mit Hinduismus.* Roma: Institutum historicum S. I., 1972.

Bacon, Roger. *The Opus Majus of Roger Bacon.* 2 vols. Philadelphia: University of Pennsylvania Press, 1928.

———. *Rogeri Baconis Moralis Philosophia.* Edited by Eugenio Massa. Zürich: Thesaurus Mundi, 1953.

———. *The "Opus Majus" of Roger Bacon.* Edited by John Henry Bridges. 2 vols. Frankfurt am Main: Minerva, 1964.

Bailly, Jean Sylvain. *Histoire de l'astronomie ancienne.* 2 vols. Paris: Debure, 1775.

———. *Lettres sur l'origine des sciences, et sur celle des peuples de l'Asie.* Paris: Debure, 1777.

———. *Lettres sur l'Atlantide de Platon et sur l'ancienne histoire de l'Asie.* London: E. Elmesly, 1779.

———. *Histoire de l'astronomie ancienne.* 2nd ed. Paris: Debure, 1781.

———. *Traité de l'astronomie indienne et orientale, ouvrage qui peut servir de suite à l'Histoire de l'astronomie ancienne.* Paris: Debure l'aîné, 1787.

Balagangadhara, S. N. *"The Heathen in his Blindness . . . ": Asia, the West and the Dynamic of Religion.* Leiden: Brill, 1994.

Baldaeus, Philip. *Naauwkeurige beschryvinge van Malabar en Choromandel, der zelver aangrenzende ryken, en het machtige eyland Ceylon.* Amsterdam: J.J. van Waesberge, 1672.

———. "A True and Exact Description of the Most Celebrated East-India coasts of Malabar and Coromandel as also of the Isle of Ceylon." In *A Collection of Voyages and Travels,* edited by Awnsham Churchill and John Churchill. London: Henry Lintot, 1732. Reprint, New Delhi: Asian Educational Services, 2000.

Banier, Antoine. *La mythologie et les fables expliquées par l'histoire.* Paris: Briasson, 1738.

Bary, William Theodore de. *Sources of Indian Tradition.* New York: Columbia University Press, 1958.

Batchelor, Stephen. *The Awakening of the West: The Encounter of Buddhism and Western Culture.* Berkeley, Calif.: Parallax Press, 1994.

Bayle, Pierre. *Dictionnaire historique et critique.* 2nd ed. 3 vols. Rotterdam: R. Leers, 1702.

Beal, Samuel. *A Catena of Buddhist Scriptures from the Chinese.* London: Trübner, 1871.

Beausobre, Isaac de. *Histoire critique de Manichée et du manichéisme.* 2 vols. Amsterdam: J.F. Bernard, 1734. Reprint, Leipzig: Zentralantiquariat der Deutschen Demokratischen Republik, 1970; New York: Garland, 1984.

Beckingham, Charles F., and Bernard Hamilton. *Prester John, the Mongols and the Ten Lost Tribes.* Aldershot: Variorum, 1996.

Bejczy, István Pieter. *La lettre du prêtre Jean. Une utopie médiévale.* Paris: Imago, 2001.

Bergen, Christian Gustav. *Herrn Bartholomäi Ziegenbalgs und Herrn Heinrich Plütscho,*

Kön. Dänischer Missionariorum, Brieffe. 3rd ed. Pirna: Georg Balthasar Ludewig, 1708.

Berkeley, George. *A Treatise concerning the Principles of Human Knowledge. Part I, etc.* Dublin: Jeremy Pepyat, 1710.

———. *A Treatise Concerning the Principles of Human Knowledge.* Edited by Jonathan Dancy. Oxford: Oxford University Press, 1998.

Bernard-Maître, Henri S.J. "Hinâyâna indien et Mahâyâna japonais: Comment l'Occident a-t-il découvert le Bouddhisme?" *Monumenta Nipponica* 4 (1941): 284–89.

Bernier, François. *Suite des mémoires du Sr. Bernier sur l'empire du Grand Mogol.* 2 vols. Paris: Claude Barbin, 1671.

———. "Mémoire sur le Quietisme des Indes." In *Histoire des Ouvrages des Sçavans,* 47–52. Rotterdam: Reinier Leers, 1688.

———. *Voyages de François Bernier, docteur en médecine de la Faculté de Montpellier: contenant la description des États du Grand Mogol, de l'Indoustan, du Royaume de Cachemire, etc.* 1st ed. 2 vols. Amsterdam: Paul Marret, 1699.

———. *Travels in the Mogul Empire, AD 1656–1668.* Translated by Archibald Constable. Delhi: DK Publishers, 2005.

Berrow, Capel. *A Pre-existent Lapse of Human Souls Demonstrated from Reason.* London: J. Whiston and B. White, 1762.

Blount, Charles. *The Oracles of Reason.* London, 1693. Reprint, London: Routledge, 1995.

Bodart-Bailey, Beatrice. "Preliminary Report on the Manuscripts of Engelbert Kaempfer in the British Library." In *British Library Occasional Papers 11,* edited by Yu-Ying Brown, 21–39. 1990.

———. *Kaempfer's Japan: Tokugawa Culture Observed.* Honolulu: University of Hawai'i Press, 1999.

Borri, Christopher. *Relatione della nuova missione delli PP. della Compagnia di Giesu, al Regno della Cocincina.* Roma: Francesco Corbelletti, 1631.

Bossuet, Jacques Bénigne. *Discours sur l'histoire universelle à Monseigneur le Dauphin.* Paris: Sebastien Mabre-Cramoisy, 1681.

Bouchet, Jean Venant. "Lettre du Père Bouchet, de la Compagnie de Jésus, Missionnaire de Maduré, & Supérieur de la nouvelle Mission de Carnate, à Monseigneur l'ancien Evêque d'Avranches." In *Lettres édifiantes et curieuses, écrites des missions étrangères,* edited by Charles Le Gobien. Vol. 12, 5–42, 170–255. Paris: G. Merigot, 1781.

Bougeant, Guillaume-Hyacinthe. *Amusement philosophique sur le langage des bestes.* Paris: Gissey, 1739.

Boulduc, Jacques. *De Ecclesia Ante Legem.* 2nd ed. Paris: Joseph Cottereau, 1630.

Bourdon, Léon. *La Compagnie de Jésus et le Japon, 1547–1570.* Lisboa/Paris: Fondation Calouste Gulbenkian/Centre Culturel Portugais, 1993.

Brerewood, Edward. *Enquiries touching the Diversity of Languages and Religions through the Chief Parts of the World.* London: John Bill, 1614.

Brosses, Charles de. *Du culte des dieux fétiches.* [Paris], 1760.

Brucker, Johann Jacob. *Kurtze Fragen aus der philosophischen Historie, von Christi Geburt biß auf unsere Zeiten.* Ulm: Daniel Bartholomäi und Sohn. Vol 7. 1736.

———. *Historia critica philosophiae*. Leipzig: Christoph Breitkopf, 1742–44.

Bryant, Jacob. *Observations and Inquiries relating to various parts of Ancient History*. Cambridge: T. & J. Merrill, 1767.

———. *A New System, or, an Analysis of Ancient Mythology*. London: T. Payne, 1774–76.

———. *A Treatise upon the Authenticity of the Scriptures, and the Truth of the Christian religion*. London: T. Cadell & P. Elmsly, 1792.

Burke, Edmund. "Review of Holwell: Interesting historical events relative to the provinces of Bengal, and the empire of Indostan. Part II." *Annual Register, or a view of the History, Politics, and Literature for the Year 1766* (1767): 306–19.

Burnet, Thomas. *Archæologi;ae philosophicæ: sive Doctrina antiqua de rerum originibus*. London: R. Norton, 1692.

———. *Telluris theoria sacra, Originem & Mutationes Generales Orbis Nostri, Quas aut jam subiit, aut olim subiturus est, complectens. Accedunt Archæologi;ae philosophicæ, sive Doctrina Antiqua de Rerum Originibus*. Amsterdam: J. Wolters, 1694.

———. *De statu mortuorum et resurgentium liber*. London, 1720.

———. *A Treatise Concerning the State of Departed Souls, Before, and At, and After the Resurrection*. London: John Hooke, 1730.

———. *Doctrina antiqua de rerum originibus; or, An Inquiry into the Doctrine of the Philosophers of all Nations concerning the Original of the World*. Translated by Mr. Mead and Mr. Foxton. London, 1736.

Burnouf, Eugène. *Introduction à l'histoire du Buddhisme Indien*. Paris: Imprimerie Royale, 1844.

Buswell, Robert. *The Formation of Ch'an Ideology in China and Korea: The "Vajrasamadhi-Sutra," a Buddhist Apocryphon*. Princeton, N.J.: Princeton University Press, 1989.

Bysshe, Edward. *Palladiou Peri ton tes Indias ethnon kai ton Bragmanon (graece): De gentibus Indiae et Bragmanibus (et) S. Ambrosius De moribus Brachmanorum (et) Anonymus De Bragmanibus. Quorum priorum et postremum nunc primum in lucem protulit ex Bibliotheca Regia Edoardus Bissaeus*. London: T. Roycroft, 1665.

Caland, Willem. *De Ontdekkingsgeschiedenis van den Veda*. Amsterdam: Johannes Müller, 1918.

Cannon, Garland Hampton. *Sir William Jones: A Bibliography of Primary and Secondary Sources*. Amsterdam Studies in the Theory and History of Linguistic Science, Series 5, Library and Information Sources in Linguistics 7. Amsterdam: J. Benjamins, 1979.

Castets, Jean. *L'Ezour védam de Voltaire et les pseudo-védams de Pondichéry. Voltaire et la mystification de l'Ezour Védam. Découverte des Pseudo-Védas de Pondichéry*. Pondichéry: Imprimerie Moderne, 1935.

Catrou, François. *Histoire générale de l'Empire du Mogol, depuis sa fondation. Sur les Mémoires Portugais de M. Manouchi, Vénitien*. La Haye: De Voys, 1708.

———. *History of the Mogul Dynasty in India*. London: J.M. Richardson, 1826.

Charlevoix, Pierre-François-Xavier de. *Histoire de l'établissement, des progrès et de la décadence du christianisme dans l'Empire du Japon*. Roven: Pierre le Boucher, 1715.

———. *Histoire et description generale du Japon*. 2 vols. Paris: P. Giffart, 1736.

Charpentier, Jarl. "Quelques observations sur l'Ezour-Védam et son auteur." *Journal Asiatique* Series 11, vol. 20 (1922): 136–46.

Chinard, Gilbert. *Volney et l'Amérique, d'après des documents inédits et sa correspondance avec Jefferson.* Baltimore: Johns Hopkins Press, 1923.

Coeurdoux, Gaston Laurent. "Des sciences des Brahmes solitaires, et de l'époque du déluge." *Mémoires de Littérature tirés des Registres de l'Académie Royale des Inscriptions & Belles Lettres* 49 (1808): 692–95.

Colebrooke, Henry Thomas. "On the Religious Ceremonies of the HINDUS, and of the BRÁHMENS especially. Essay I." *Asiatick Researches* 5 (1799): 345–68.

———. "On the Religious Ceremonies of the HINDUS, and of the BRÁHMENS especially. Essay II." *Asiatick Researches* 7 (1801): 232–311.

———. "On the Védas, or Sacred Writings of the Hindus." *Asiatick Researches* 8 (1808): 377–498.

Collani, Claudia von. *Die Figuristen in der Chinamission, Würzburger Sino-Japonica Band 8.* Frankfurt a. M./Bern: Lang, 1981.

———. *P. Joachim Bouvet S.J. Sein Leben und sein Werk.* Nettetal: Steyler, 1985.

———. *Eine wissenschafliche Akademie für China, Studia Leibnitiana.* Stuttgart: Franz Steiner, 1989.

———. "Theologie und Chronologie in Martinis 'Sinicae Historiae Decas Prima' (1658)." In *Martino Martini S.J. (1614–1661) und die Chinamission im 17. Jahrhundert,* edited by Roman Malek and Arnold Zingerle, 147–83. Sankt Augustin: Institut Monumenta Serica, 2000.

Columbus, Christopher. *The Four Voyages of Christopher Columbus.* Translated by J. M. Cohen. London: Penguin, 1969.

Cooper, Michael. "Rodrigues in China. The Letters of João Rodrigues, 1611–1633." In Tadao Doi, *Kokugoshi e no michi,* vol. 2, 355–231. Tokyo: Sanshodo, 1981.

———. *Rodrigues the Interpreter.* New York: Weatherhill, 1994.

Couplet, Philippe. *Confucius Sinarum Philosophus: Sive, scientia sinensis latine exposita.* Paris: D. Horthemels, 1687.

Court de Gébelin, Antoine. *Monde primitif.* 9 vols. Paris: Auteur, 1773.

Couto, Diogo do. *Década Quinta da Asia.* Lisbon: Pedro Crasbeeck, 1612. Reprint, Coimbra: Biblioteca da Universidade, 1936.

Couto, Diogo do, and Marcus de Jong. *Década Quinta da "Ásia": Texte inédit, publié d'après un manuscrit de la bibliothèque de l'université de Leyde.* Coimbra: Biblioteca da Universidade, 1936.

Créquinière, Sieur de la. *Conformité des coutumes des Indiens orientaux, avec celles des Juifs & des autres peuples de l'Antiquité.* Bruxelles: de Backer, 1704.

———. *The Agreement of the Customs of the East-Indians, With those of the Jews, And other ancient People.* Translated by John Toland. London: W. Davis, 1705. Reprint, New York: AMS Press, 1999.

Creuzer, Friedrich. *Idee und Probe alter Symbolik.* Bad Cannstadt: Frommann, 1969.

Crispo, Battista. *De ethnicis philosophis caute legendis.* Rome: Zannetti, 1594.

Croze, Mathurin Veyssière de la. *Histoire du Christianisme des Indes*. The Hague: Vaillant & N. Prevost, 1724.

——. *Abbildung des Indianischen Christen-Staats*. Translated by Georg Christian Bohnstedt. Halle: Johann Adam Spörl, 1727.

Cudworth, Ralph. *The True Intellectual System of the Universe*. 2 vols. London: Richard Royston, 1678. Reprint New York: Garland, 1978.

Cummins, J. S. *A Question of Rites: Friar Domingo Navarrete and the Jesuits in China*. Aldershot: Scolar Press, 1993.

Dalin, Olof. *Geschichte des Reiches Schweden*. Translated by Johann Carl Dähnert. Greifswald: J. Struck, 1756–63.

Dalley, Jan. *The Black Hole: Money, Myth and Empire*. London: Penguin, 2007.

Dandekar, R. N. "Hinduism." In *Historia Religionum: Handbook for the History of Religions*, edited by C. Jouko Bleeker and Geo Widengren, 237–43. Leiden: Brill, 1971.

Daniélou, Jean. *Les saints "payens" de l'Ancien Testament*. Paris: Seuil, 1956.

Davy, William, and Joseph White. *Institutes political and military*. Oxford: Clarendon Press, 1783. Reprint, Delhi: Idarah-i Adabiyat-i Delli, 1972.

de Jong, J. W. *A Brief History of Buddhist Studies in Europe and America*. Tokyo: Kōsei Publishing, 1987.

Deluz, Christiane. *Le livre des merveilles du monde—Jean de Mandeville*. Paris: CNRS, 2000.

DeMartino, Richard. "On Zen Communication." *Communication* 8/1 (1983):13–28.

Deshauterayes, Michel-Ange-André le Roux. "Histoire de Fo ou Boudha." In *Mélanges sur l'Histoire d'Afrique, d'Asie et d'Amérique*, 156–80. Paris: Bibliothèque nationale NAF 22335.

——. *Doutes sur la dissertation de M. de Guignes qui a pour titre: Memoire, dans lequel on prouve que les Chinois sont une colonie egyptienne*. Paris: Laurent Prault, 1759.

——. "Recherches sur la religion de Fo, professée par les bonzes Ho-chang de la Chine." *Journal Asiatique* 8 (1826): 40–49, 74–88, 179–88, 219–23.

Dharampal-Frick, Gita. *Indien im Spiegel deutscher Quellen der Frühen Neuzeit (1500–1750): Studien zu einer interkulturellen Konstellation*. Tübingen: Niemeyer, 1994.

——. "Malabarisches Heidenthum: Bartholomäus Ziegenbalg über Religion und Gesellschaft der Tamilen " In *Missionsberichte aus Indien im 18. Jahrhundert*, edited by Michael Bergunder, 126–52. Halle: Verlag der Franckeschen Stiftungen, 2004.

Diderot, Denis. *Encyclopédie I (Lettre A)*. Edited by John Lough and Jacques Proust. Paris: Hermann, 1976.

Diderot, Denis, and Jean le Rond d'Alembert. *Encyclopédie ou dictionnaire raisonné des sciences, des arts et des métiers*. Vol. 1, 1751; vol. 2, 1752.

Diodorus, Siculus (Diodore de Sicile). *Histoire universelle de Diodore de Sicile*. Translated by Abbé Terrasson. Vol. 1. Paris: De Bure, 1737.

Doi, Tadao. *Nihon daibunten*. Tokyo: Sanshodo, 1955.

Doi [Tadao] sensei shōju kinen runbunshū kankōkai. *Kokugoshi e no michi*. 2 vols. Vol. 2. Tokyo: Sanshodo, 1981.

Dow, Alexander. *The history of Hindostan*. London: T. Becket and P.A. De Hondt, 1768.

Droit, Roger-Pol. *Le culte du néant: Les philosophes et le Bouddha*. Paris: Seuil, 1997.

——. *The Cult of Nothingness: The Philosophers and the Buddha*. Translated by David Streight and Pamela Vohnson. Chapel Hill: University of North Carolina Press, 2003.

Dubois, Jean-Antoine. *Description of the Character, Manners, and Customs of the People of India*. London: Longman, Hurst, Rees, Orme, and Brown, 1817.

——. *Mœurs, institutions et cérémonies des peuples de l'Inde*. Paris: Imprimerie Royale, 1825.

Duchesne-Guillemin, Jacques. "Anquetil-Duperron." In *Encyclopaedia Iranica*, edited by Ehsan Yarshater, 2: 100–101. London: Routledge & Kegan Paul, 1987.

Dupuis, Charles-François. *Mémoire sur l'origine des Constellations et sur l'explication de la fable par l'astronomie*. Paris: Desaint, 1781.

——. *Origine de tous les cultes, ou religion universelle*. Paris: H. Agasse, 1795.

Duteil, Jean-Pierre. *Le mandat du ciel: le rôle des Jésuites en Chine, de la mort de François-Xavier à la dissolution de la Compagnie de Jésus (1552–1774)*. Paris: Éditions Arguments, 1994.

Ebeling, Florian. *Das Geheimnis des Hermes Trismegistos: Geschichte des Hermetismus*. München: C.H. Beck, 2005.

Ebisawa, Arimichi. *Ebora byōbu bunsho no kenkyū*. Tokyo: Natsume, 1963.

Elisseeff, Danielle. *Nicolas Fréret (1688–1749): réflexions d'un humaniste du XVIIIe siècle sur la Chine*. Paris: Presses Universitaires de France, 1974.

——. *Moi, Arcade, interprète chinois du Roi-Soleil*. Paris: Arthaud, 1985.

Ellis, Francis. "Account of a Discovery of a modern imitation of the Védas, with Remarks on the Genuine Works." *Asiatic Researches* 14 (1822): 1–59.

Ernst, Carl W., "Sufism and Yoga according to Muhammad Ghawth." *Sufi* 29, (1996): 9–13.

——. "The Islamization of Yoga in the Amrtakunda Translations." *Journal of the Royal Asiatic Society* 3, no. 13:2 (2003): 199–226.

——. "Situating Sufism and Yoga." *Journal of the Royal Asiatic Society* 3, no. 15:1 (2005): 15–43.

Erskine, William. "On the Authority of the *Desatir*, with Remarks on the Account of the Mahabadi Religion Contained in the Dabistan." *Transactions of the Literary Society of Bombay* 2 (1818): 395–98.

Étiemble, René. *Les Jésuites en Chine: la querelle des rites (1552–1773)*. Paris: Julliard, 1966.

Evans, R. H., ed. *Catalogue of the Library of the Late Sir William Jones*. London: W. Nichol, 1831.

Fabricius, Johann Albert. "Dissertatio de controversiis cum atheis et gentilibus." In *Consideratio variarum controversiarum cum Atheis, Gentilibus, Iudaeis, Mahumedanis, Socinianis, Anabaptistis, Pontificiis et Reformatis*. Helmstedt, 1704.

——. *Codex apocryphus Novi Testamenti*. Hamburg, 1703.

Faure, Bernard. *Bouddhismes, philosophies et religions*. Paris: Flammarion, 1998.

Faust, Jürgen. *Mythologien und Religionen des Ostens bei Johann Gottfried von Herder*. Münster: Aschendorff, 1977.

Fauvel, John, Raymond Flood, Michael Shortland, and Robin Wilson, eds. *Let Newton Be!* Oxford: Oxford University Press, 1988.

Fenicio, Giacomo. *The Livro da Seita dos Indios Orientais (Brit. Mus. Ms. Sloane 1820).* Edited by Jarl Charpentier. Uppsala: Almqvist & Wiksells, 1933.

Firuz bin Kaus, Mulla. *The Desatir; or, Sacred Writings of the Ancient Persian Prophets, in the Original Tongue.* 2 vols. Bombay: Courier Press, 1818.

Fitzgerald, Timothy. *The Ideology of Religious Studies.* New York: Oxford University Press, 2000.

Force, James E., and Richard H. Popkin. *Essays on the Context, Nature, and Influence of Isaac Newton's Theology.* Dordrecht: Kluwer Academic, 1990.

———. *Newton and Religion: Context, Nature, and Influence.* Dordrecht: Kluwer Academic, 1999.

Fortia d'Urban, Agricole Joseph de. *Considérations sur l'origine et l'histoire ancienne du globe.* Paris: Veuve Séguin, 1807.

Foucher, d'Obsonville, and Pillai Maridas. *Bagavadam, ou, Doctrine divine: ouvrage indien, canonique; sur l'Être Suprême, les dieux, les géans, les hommes, les diverses parties de l'univers, &c.* Paris: Veuve Tilliard & Fils, 1788.

Fourmont, Étienne. *Réflexions critiques sur l'origine, l'histoire et la succession des anciens peuples, Chaldéens, Hébreux, Phéniciens, Égyptiens, Grecs, etc., jusqu'au temps de Cyrus.* Paris: de Bure, 1735.

———. *Meditationes sinicae.* Paris: Musier, 1737.

———. "Dissertation sur les annales chinoises, où l'on examine leur époque, & la croyance qu'elles méritent." *Mémoires de Littérature tirés des Registres des l'Académie Royale des Inscriptions & Belles Lettres* 13 (1740): 507–19.

———. *Réflexions critiques sur l'origine, l'histoire et la succession des anciens peuples, Chaldéens, Hébreux, Phéniciens, Égyptiens, Grecs, etc., jusqu'au temps de Cyrus.* Paris: de Bure, 1747.

Francke, August Hermann. *Hallesche Berichte: Der Königl. Missionarien aus Ost-Indien eingesandter Ausführlichen Berichten Erster Theil.* Halle: Waysen-Haus, 1728.

Fréret, Nicolas. "Recherches sur les traditions religieuses des Indiens pour servir de préliminaires à l'examen de leur chronologie." *Histoire de l'Académie Royale des Inscriptions et Belles-Lettres* 18 (1753): 34–48.

Frois, Luis. *Die Geschichte Japans (1549–1578). Nach der Handschrift der Ajudabibliothek in Lissabon übersetzt und kommentiert von G. Schurhammer und E. A. Voretzsch.* Leipzig: Asia Major, 1926.

Gallagher, Louis. *China in the 16th Century: The Journals of Matthew Ricci, 1583–1610.* New York: Random House, 1953.

Gascoigne, John. "'The Wisdom of the Egyptians' and the Secularisation of History in the Age of Newton." In *The Uses of Antiquity: The Scientific Revolution and the Classical Tradition,* edited by Stephen Gaukroger, 171–212. Dordrecht: Kluwer Academic, 1991.

Gaulmier, Jean. *L'idéologue Volney 1757–1820: Contribution à l'histoire de l'Orientalisme en France.* Beyrouth: Imprimerie Catholique, 1951.

———. *Un grand témoin de la révolution et de l'empire Volney.* Paris: Hachette, 1959.

Germann, Wilhelm. *Ziegenbalg und Plütschau: Die Gründungsjahre der Trankebarschen Mission, Zweite Abtheilung: Urkunden.* Erlangen: Deichert, 1868.

Gessner, Salomon. *The Death of Abel.* Translated by M. Collyer. London, 1761.

Giorgi, Antonio Agostino. *Alphabetum Tibetanum Apostolicarum Commodo Editum.* Rome: Sacra Congregatio de Propaganda Fide, 1762.

———. *Alphabetum Tibetanum* (German). Translated by Lindegger Peter. 2 vols. Rikon/Zürich: Tibet-Institut, 1999–2001.

Gladwin, Francis. *The Asiatick Miscellany: consisting of original productions, translations, fugitive pieces, imitations, and extracts from curious publications.* 2 vols. Calcutta: Daniel Stuart, 1785–86.

———. *The Asiatic miscellany.* Edited by Michael J. Franklin. London: Ganesha, 2001.

———. *New Asiatick Miscellany. Consisting of original Essays, translations, and Fugitive Pieces. Volume the First.* Calcutta: Joseph Cooper, 1789.M

Göbel-Gross, E. *Die persische Upaniṣaden-Übersetzung des Moġulprinzen Dārā Šukoh.* Marburg: Erich Mauersberger, 1962.

Goguet, Antoine-Yves. *De l'origine des loix, des arts, et des sciences; et de leurs progrès chez les anciens peuples.* Paris: Desaint & Saillant, 1758.

Golinski, Jan. "The Secret Life of an Alchemist." In *Let Newton Be!*, edited by John Fauvel, Raymond Flood, Michael Shortland, and Robin Wilson, 147–67. Oxford: Oxford University Press, 1988.

Gonzalez de Mendoza, Juan. *Historia de las cosas más notables, ritos y costumbres del gran reyno de la China.* Rome/Madrid, 1585.

Goody, Jack. *The Theft of History.* Cambridge: Cambridge University Press, 2009.

Gorp, Jan van. *Origines Antwerpianae, sive Cimmeriorum Becceselana novem libros complexa.* Antwerp: Christoph Plantin, 1569.

Görres, Joseph. *Mythengeschichte der asiatischen Welt.* 2 vols. Heidelberg: Mohr und Zimmermann, 1810.

Gouk, Penelope. "The Harmonic Roots of Newtonian Science." In *Let Newton Be!*, edited by John Fauvel, Raymond Flood, Michael Shortland, and Robin Wilson, 101–25. Oxford: Oxford University Press, 1988.

Grafe, Hugald. "Hindu Apologetics at the Beginning of the Protestant Mission Era in India." In *Missionsberichte aus Indien im 18. Jahrhundert*, edited by Michael Bergunder, 69–93. Halle: Verlag der Franckeschen Stiftungen, 2004.

Griffiths, Ralph. "Review of Holwell's Interesting Historical Events, Part II." *The Monthly Review; or, Literary Journal* 36, (1767): 7–17

Grimm, Reinhold. *Paradisus coelestis, paradisus terrestris. Zur Auslegungsgeschichte des Paradieses im Abendland bis um 1200.* München: Wilhelm Fink, 1977.

Grose, John Henry. *A Voyage to the East-Indies, with Observations on Various Parts.* London: S. Hooper and A. Morley, 1757.

Gründler, Johann Ernst, and Bartholomaeus Ziegenbalg. *Die Malabarische Korrespondenz. Tamilische Briefe an deutsche Missionare. Eine Auswahl.* Edited by Kurt Liebau. Sigmaringen: Jan Thorbecke, 1998.

Grundmann, Johannes. *Die geographischen und völkerkundlichen Quellen und Anschauungen in Herders "Ideen zur Geschichte der Menschheit".* Berlin: Weidmann, 1900.

Guignes, C. L. J. de. *Mémoire historique sur l'origine des Huns et des Turks, adressé à M. Tavenot.* Paris: Debure l'aîné, 1751.

———. *Histoire générale des Huns, des Turcs, des Mogols, et des autres tartares occidentaux, & c. avant Jésus-Christ jusqu'à présent.* Paris: Desaint & Saillant, 1756–58.

———. *Recherches sur les philosophes appelés Samanéens. Mémoires de Littérature tirés des Registres des l'Académie Royale des Inscriptions & Belles Lettres* 26 (1759): 770–804.

———. *Mémoire dans lequel on prouve, que les Chinois sont une colonie égyptienne.* Paris: Desaint & Saillant, 1760.

———. "Recherches sur les navigations des Chinois du côté de l'Amérique, & sur quelques Peuples situés à l'extrémité orientale de l'Asie." *Mémoires de Littérature tirés des Registres des l'Académie Royale des Inscriptions & Belles Lettres* 28 (1761): 503–25.

———. "Recherches sur les Chrétiens établis à la Chine dans le VIIe siècle." *Mémoires de Littérature tirés des Registres des l'Académie Royale des Inscriptions & Belles Lettres* 30 (1764): 802–19.

———. "Essai sur le moyen de parvenir à la lecture & à l'intelligence des hiéroglyphes Egyptiens." *Mémoires de Littérature tirés des Registres des l'Académie Royale des Inscriptions & Belles Lettres* 34 (1770): 1–55.

———. "Réflexions sur un Livre Indien, intitulé Bagavadam, un des dix-huit Pouranam ou Livres Sacrés des Indiens, dont la traduction a été envoyé en 1769 à M. Bertin, Ministre et Secretaire d'Etat." In *Histoire de l'Académie Royale des Inscriptions & Belles Lettres* (1772): 312–36.

———. "Reflexions sur un Livre Indien, intitulé Bagavadam, un des dix-huit Pouranam ou Livres sacrés des Indiens, dont la traduction a été envoyé en 1769 à M. Bertin, Ministre & Secrétaire d'Etat." *Mémoires de Littérature tirés des Registres des l'Académie Royale des Inscriptions & Belles-Lettres* 38, (1777): 312–36.

———. "Untersuchungen über die Samanäischen Philosophen." *Magazin für die Philosophie und ihre Geschichte* 3 (1780): 53–110.

———. "Recherches historiques sur la Religion Indienne, & sur les Livres fondamentaux de cette Religion, qui ont été traduits de l'Indien en Chinois. Premier Mémoire. Etablissement de la Religion Indienne dans l'Inde, la Tartarie, le Thibet & les Isles." *Mémoires de Littérature tirés des Registres des l'Académie Royale des Inscriptions & Belles Lettres* 77 (1781a): 346–458.

———. "Recherches historiques sur la Religion Indienne. Second Mémoire. Etablissement de la Religion Indienne dans la Chine, & son Histoire jusqu'en 531 de J.C." *Mémoires de Littérature tirés des Registres des l'Académie Royale des Inscriptions et Belles Lettres* 78 (1781b): 1–111.

———. "Recherches historiques sur la Religion Indienne. Troisième Mémoire. Histoire de la Religion Indienne à la Chine, depuis l'an 544 jusqu'en 698." *Mémoires de Littérature tirés des Registres des l'Académie Royale des Inscriptions et Belles Lettres* 78 (1781c): 112–200.

———. "Observations sur quelques points concernant la Religion et la Philosophie des Egyptiens & des Chinois." *Mémoires de Littérature tirés des Registres des l'Académie Royale des Inscriptions & Belles Lettres* 77 (1781d): 302–45.

Halbfass, Wilhelm. *India and Europe: An Essay in Philosophical Understanding.* New Delhi: Motilal Banarsidass, 1990.

Halde, Jean-Baptiste du, S.J. *Description géographique, historique, chronologique, politique et physique de l'Empire de la Chine et de la Tartarie chinoise.* La Haye: Henri Scheurleer, 1736.

Halhed, Nathaniel. *A Code of Gentoo Laws.* London, 1776. Reprint, London: Routledge, 2000.

———. *Code des Loix des Gentoux, ou Réglemens des Brames. Traduit de l'Anglois, d'après les Versions faites de l'original écrit en Langue Samskrete.* Paris: Stoupe, 1778.

Hamilton, Bernard. "Prester John and the Three Kinds of Cologne." In *Prester John, the Mongols and the Ten Lost Tribes,* edited by Charles F. Beckingham and Bernard Hamilton, 171–85. Aldershot: Variorum, 1996.

Hartmann, George W. "A Case Study of the Perpetuation of Error." In *Twentieth Century Psychology: Recent Developments in Psychology,* edited by Philip Lawrence Harriman, 192–99. New York: Ayer, 1946.

Hasrat, Bikrama Jit. *Dārā Shikūh: Life and Works.* 2nd ed. Calcutta: Munshiram Manoharlal, 1982.

Hawley, Daniel S. "L'Inde de Voltaire." In *Studies on Voltaire and the Eighteenth Century,* edited by Theodore Besterman, 139–78. Banbury: Voltaire Foundation, 1974.

Hay, Denys. *Europe. The Emergence of an Idea.* New York: Harper & Row, 1966.

Haycock, David Boyd. *William Stukeley: Science, Religion and Archaeology in Eighteenth-Century England.* Woodbridge: Boydell, 2002.

Hazard, Paul. *La crise de la conscience européenne, 1680–1715.* Paris: Fayard, 1961.

Henderson, G. D. *Chevalier Ramsay.* London: T. Nelson, 1952.

Herbelot de Molainville, Barthélemy d'. *Bibliothèque orientale, ou Dictionnaire universel, contenant généralement tout ce qui regarde la connoissance des peuples de l'Orient.* Paris: Compagnie des libraires, 1697.

Herbelot de Molainville, Barthélemy d', Claude de Visdelou, and A. Galand. *Bibliothèque orientale, ou Dictionnaire universel contenant généralement tout ce qui fait connoître les peuples de l'Orient.* La Haye: J. Neaulme & N. Van Daalen, 1779.

Herbert of Cherbury, Edward. *De religione gentilium, errorumque apud eos causis.* Amsterdam: Blaeu, 1663.

———. *Pagan Religion: A Translation of De religione gentilium.* Translated by John Anthony Butler. Ottawa: Dovehouse, 1996.

Herder, Johann Gottfried von. *Älteste Urkunde des Menschengeschlechts.* Riga: Johann Friedrich Hartknoch, 1774.

———. *Werke. Band III: Ideen zur Philosophie der Geschichte der Menschheit.* Edited by Wolfgang Pross. München/Wien: Carl Hanser, 2002.

Heylyn, Peter. *Cosmographie in Four Books.* London: Henry Seile, 1652.

Holbach, Paul Henri. *Eléments de la morale universelle, ou Catéchisme de la nature.* Paris: de Bure, 1790.

Holbach, Paul Henri (pseud. M. Mirabaud). *Système de la nature, ou des loix du monde physique & du monde moral.* 2 vols. Vol. 2. London, 1770.

———. *Système de la nature, ou des loix du monde physique & du monde moral.* 2 vols. Vol. 1. London, 1770.

Holwell, John Zephaniah. *A Genuine Narrative of the Deplorable Deaths of the English Gentlemen and Others, Who were Suffocated in the Black-Hole in Fort-William at Calcutta in the Kingdom of Bengal; in the Night Succeeding the Twentieth Day of June, 1756.* London: A. Millar, 1758.

———. *Interesting historical events, relative to the provinces of Bengal, and the empire of Indostan.* 3 vols. London: Becket & De Hondt, 1765–71. Reprint (parts 1 and 2 only), with introduction by M. J. Franklin. London: Routledge, 2000.

———. *Événemens historiques intéressans, relatifs Aux Provinces de Bengale, et à l'Empire de l'Indostan.* 2 vols. Amsterdam: Arkstee & Merkus, 1768.

———. *Holwells merkwürdige und historische Nachrichten von Hindostan und Bengalen, nebst einer Beschreibung der Religionslehren, der Mythologie, etc.* Leipzig: Weygandsche Buchhandlung, 1778.

———. *A Review of the Original Principles, religious and moral, of the ancient Brahmins.* London: D. Steel, 1779.

———. *Dissertations on the Origin, Nature, and Pursuits, of Intelligent Beings, and on Divine Providence, Religion, and Religious Worship.* Bath: R. Crutwell, 1786.

Holwell, John Zephaniah (Pseud. A Divine of No Church). *Primitive religion elucidated, and restored.* N.p., 1776.

Hosten, Henry. "Le Bhâgawata—D'après un texte en Tamoul. Nouvelle Traduction de Maridas Poullé de Pondichéry (1793–1795)." *Revue Historique de l'Inde Française* 4, no. 1 (1920): 1–235.

———. "The Ezour Vedam and Father A. Mosac, S.J." *Catholic Herald of India,* June 29, 1921, 499–500.

———. "Report of the Rev. H. Hosten, S.J., of St. Joseph's College, Darjeeling, on his visit to Mylapore, Pondicherry, etc., in connection with the preparation of a history of Jesuit Missions in Bengal." In *Indian Historical Records Commission: Proceedings of Meetings (Fourth Meeting held at Delhi. January 1922),* 57–102. Calcutta: Government Printing, 1922.

Howell, James. *Epistolae Ho-Elianae.* 7th ed. London: Thomas Guy, 1705.

Huart, C., and L. Massignon. "Les Entretiens de Lahore [entre le prince impérial Dârâ Shikûh et l'ascète hindou Baba La'l Das]." *Journal Asiatique* 209 (1926): 285–334.

Hubert, René. *Les sciences sociales dans l'encyclopédie: la philosophie de l'histoire et le problème des origines sociales.* Paris: F. Alcan, 1923.

Huët, Pierre-Daniel. *Demonstratio evangelica.* Paris, 1678.

———. *Traité de la situation du paradis terrestre.* Paris: Jean Anisson, 1691.

———. *Tractatus de situ Paradisi terrestris.* Amsterdam: Boom, 1698.

———. *Alnetanae quaestiones de concordia rationis et fidei.* Frankfurt/Leipzig, 1709.

Hume, David. *The Natural History of Religion by David Hume.* Edited by A. Wayne Colver. Oxford: Clarendon Press, 1976.

Hutter, Peter. *Germanische Stammväter und römisch-deutsches Kaisertum, Historische Texte und Studien, Band 21.* Hildesheim/Zürich: Olms, 2000.

Hyde, Thomas. *Historia religionis veterum persarum, eorumque magorum . . . Zoroastris vita.* Oxford: Theatrum Sheldonianum, 1700.

Ides, Evert Ysbrants. *Three years travels from Moscow over-land to China.* London: Freeman, 1706.

Ilive, Jacob. *The Oration spoke at Joyners-hall in Thamesstreet.* London: T. Cooper, 1733.

Imai, Tadashi. "Engelbert Kaempfer und seine Quellen. Literatur und sonstige Informationen, die Kaempfer für sein Japan-Buch zur Ergänzung seiner Beobachtungen benutzte." In *Engelbert Kaempfer zum 330. Geburtstag: Gesammelte Beiträge zur Engelbert-Kaempfer-Forschung und zur Frühzeit der Asienforschung in Europa*, edited by Hans Hüls and Hans Hoppe, 63–81. Lemgo: F.L. Wagener, 1982.

Irwin, Robert. *For Lust of Knowing: The Orientalists and Their Enemies.* London: Allen Lane/Penguin, 2006.

———. *Dangerous Knowledge: Orientalism and Its Discontents.* New York: Overlook Press, 2006.

Ith, Johann. *Ezour-vedam oder der alte Commentar über den Vedam.* Bern: Typographische Gesellschaft, 1779.

Jenyns, Soame. *A Free Inquiry into the Nature and Origin of Evil.* 4th ed. London: R. and J. Dosdsley, 1761.

Jeyaraj, Daniel. *Bartholomäus Ziegenbalgs "Genealogie der malabarischen Götter".* Halle: Francke, 2003.

Jones, Inigo, and John Webb. *The Most Notable Antiquity of Great Britain Vulgarly called Stone-Heng on Salisbury Plain, Restored by Inigo Jones.* London: D. Pakeman, 1655. Reprint, Menston: Scolar Press, 1972.

Jones, William. *Lettre à Monsieur A*** du P*** [Anquetil du Perron], dans laquelle est compris l'examen de sa traduction des livres attribueés à Zoroastre.* London: Elmisly, 1771.

———. *The Letters of Sir William Jones.* Edited by Garland Hampton Cannon. 2 vols. Oxford: Clarendon Press, 1970.

———. *The Collected Works of William Jones.* Edited by Garland Cannon. Richmond: Curzon Press, 1993.

Jones, William, John Carnac, Warren Hastings, Archibald Keir, Thomas D. Pearse, Antoine Louis Henri de Polier, John Shore, Sir Charles Wilkins, and John Williams. *Dissertations and miscellaneous pieces relating to the History and Antiquities . . . of Asia.* 3 vols. London: G. Nicol/Dublin: P. Byrne & W. Jones, 1792–96.

Jones, William et al. *Recherches Asiatiques, ou Mémoires de la société établie au Bengale pour faire des recherches sur l'histoire et les antiquités, les arts, les sciences et la littérature de l'Asie.* Translated by A. LaBaume; edited by Louis Mathieu Langlès. 2 vols. Paris: Imprimerie Nationale, 1805.

Kaegi, Werner. "Voltaire und der Zerfall des christlichen Geschichtsbildes." *Corona* 8, no. 1 (1938): 76–101.

Kaempfer, Engelbert. *Histoire naturelle, civile et ecclésiastique de l'Empire du Japon*. Translated by François Naude. The Hague: P. Gosse & J. Neaulme, 1729.

———. *Ausführliche Beschreibung des Chinesischen Reichs und der grossen Tartarey, Band 4: Beschreibung des Japonischen Reichs*. Translated by Johann Christian Koppe; edited by Jean-Baptiste du Halde, 1749.

———. *Engelbert Kämpfers Geschichte und Beschreibung von Japan*. Edited by Christian Wilhelm Dohm. Lemgo: Meyersche Buchhandlung, 1777–78.

———. *The History of Japan together with a Description of the Kingdom of Siam, 1690–1692*. Glasgow: James MacLehose & Sons, 1906.

———. *Heutiges Japan*. Edited by Wolfgang Michel and Barend J. Terwiel. München: Iudicium, 2001.

Kailasapathy, K. "The Writings of Tamil Siddhas." In *The Sants: Studies in a Devotional Tradition of India*, edited by Karine Schomer and W. H. McLeod, 385–414. Berkeley, Calif.: Berkeley Religious Studies Series; Delhi: Motilal Banarsidass, 1987.

Kanne, Johann Arnold. *Erste Urkunden der Geschichte oder allgemeine Mythologie*. Bayreuth, 1808.

Kao, Dionysius. "A Short Description of the Vast Empire of China." In *Three Years Land Travels of His Excellency E. Ysbrant Ides from Mosco to China To which is added a New Description of that vast Empire written by a Native*, edited by Evert Ysbrands Ides, 114–73. London: Freeman, 1705.

Katagiri, Kazuo. *Oranda tsūji Imamura Gen'emon Eisei*. Maruzen Library 145. Tokyo: Maruzen, 1995.

Kieffer, Jean-Luc. *Anquetil-Duperron: L'Inde en France au XVIIIe siècle*. Paris: Belles-Lettres, 1983.

King, Richard. *Orientalism and Religion: Postcolonial Theory, India and "The Mystic East"*. London: Routledge, 1999.

Kircher, Athanasius. *Obeliscus Pamphilius*. 1650.

———. *Oedipus Aegyptiacus, hoc est universalis hieroglyphicae veterum doctrinae temporum iniuria abolitae instauratio*. Roma: Vitalis Mascardi, 1652–54.

———. *China monumentis, qua sacris qua profanis, nec non variis naturae et artis spectaculis, aliarumque rerum memorabilium argumentis illustrata*. Amsterdam: Jacob Meurs, 1667.

———. *China Illustrata with Sacred and Secular Monuments, Various Spectacles of Nature and Art and Other Memorabilia*. Translated by Charles van Tuyl. Bloomington: Indiana University Research Institute for Inner Asian Studies, 1987.

Klaproth, Julius Heinrich. "Sur les Clefs chinoises." *Nouveau Journal Asiatique* 1 (1828): 233–37.

Kleuker, Johann Friedrich. *Holwell's merkwürdige historische Nachrichten von Hindostan und Bengalen*. Leipzig: Weygand, 1778.

———. *Das brahmanische Religionssystem im Zusammenhange dargestellt und aus seinen Grundbegriffen erklärt*. Riga, 1797.

Knefelkamp, Ulrich. *Die Suche nach dem Reich des Priesterkönigs Johannes*. Gelsenkirchen: Müller, 1986.

Kopf, David. *British Orientalism and the Bengal Renaissance: The Dynamics of Indian Modernization 1773–1835*. Calcutta: Mukhopadhyay, 1969.

Körner, Josef. *Die Brüder Schlegel: Briefe von und an Friedrich und Dorothea Schlegel*. Berlin: Askanischer Verlag Carl Albert Kindle, 1926.

La Peyrère, Isaac. *Prae-Adamitae. Sive exercitatio super versibus duodecimo, decimotertio, & decimoquarto, capitis quinti epistolae D. Pauli ad Romanos. Quibus inducuntur primi homines ante Adamum conditi*. Amsterdam: Janssonius, 1655.

——. *Men Before Adam*. London: n.p., 1656.

——. *I Preadamiti. Praeadamitae (1655)*. Macerata: Quodlibet, 2004.

Lach, Donald F., and Edwin J. Van Kley. *Asia in the Making of Europe*. Vol. 3: *A Century of Advance*. Book 2: *South Asia*. Chicago: University of Chicago Press, 1998

Lafitau, Joseph François. *Moeurs des sauvages Ameriquains comparées aux moeurs des premiers temps*. Paris: Saugrain, 1724.

Lamennais, Félicité. *Oeuvres complètes de F. de la Mennais*. Vol. 3: *Essai sur l'indifférence en matière de religion*. Paris: Paul Daubrée et Cailleux, 1836.

Lane, Père de la. "Lettre du Père de la Lane, Missionnaire de la Compagnie de Jésus, au Père Mourgues, de la même Compagnie (dated Pondichery, January 30, 1709)." In *Lettres édifiantes et curieuses, écrites des missions étrangères*, edited by Charles Le Gobien, vol. 11: 210–39. Paris: G. Merigot, 1781.

Lange, Joachim. *Merckwürdige Nachricht aus Ost-Indien*. Leipzig & Frankfurt am Main: Johann Christoph Papen, 1708.

Langlès, Louis Mathieu. *Fables et contes indiens: Nouvellement traduits, avec un discours préliminaire et des notes sur la religion, la littérature, les moeurs, &c. des Hindoux*. Paris: Royes, 1790a.

——. *De l'importance des langues orientales pour l'extension du Commerce, les progrès des Lettres & des Sciences. Adresse à l'Assemblée Nationale*. Paris: Champigny; Strasbourg: Koenig, 1790b.

Lardinois, Roland. *L'invention de l'Inde: Entre ésotérisme et science*. Paris: CNRS, 2007.

Launay, Adrien. *Histoire des Missions de l'Inde: Pondichery, Maissour, Coimbatour*. Vol. 1. Paris: Ancienne Maison Charles Douniol, 1898.

Le Clerc, Jean. Review of "Confucius Sinarum Philosophus." *Bibliothèque Universelle et Historique* (December 1688): 332–90.

Le Comte, Louis Daniel. *Nouveaux mémoires sur l'état présent de la Chine*. Paris: Jean Anisson, 1696.

Le Gobien, Charles. *Histoire de l'Edit de l'Empereur de la Chine en faveur de la religion chrétienne; avec un éclaircissement sur les honneurs que les chinois rendent à Confucius et aux morts*. Paris: Anisson, 1698.

——(ed). *Lettres édifiantes et curieuses, écrites des missions étrangères*. 26 vols. Paris: G. Merigot, 1781–83.

Lehmann, Arno. *Es begann in Tranquebar*. 2nd ed. Berlin: Evangelische Verlagsanstalt, 1956.

Leibniz, G. W. *Das Neueste von China (1697). Novissima Sinica.* Edited by by H. G. Nesselrath. Köln: Deutsche China-Gesellschaft, 1979.

———. *Discours sur la théologie naturelle des Chinois.* Edited by Wenchao Li and Hans Poser. Frankfurt am Main: Vittorio Klostermann, 2002.

Lenoir, Frédéric. *La rencontre du Bouddhisme et de l'occident.* Paris: Fayard, 1999.

Leopold, Joan, and Jean Leclant. *The Prix Volney: Its History and Significance for the Development of Linguistic Research.* Dordrecht: Kluwer Academic, 1999.

Letts, Malcolm. *Mandeville's Travels: Texts and Translations.* 2 vols. London: Hakluyt Society, 1953.

Leung, Cécile. *Étienne Fourmont (1683–1745): Oriental and Chinese Languages in Eighteenth-Century France.* Leuven: Leuven University Press, 2002.

Lincoln, Bruce. *Theorizing Myth: Narrative, Ideology, and Scholarship.* Chicago: University of Chicago Press, 1999.

Little, J. H. "The Black Hole—The Question of Holwell's Veracity." *Bengal: Past and Present* 11, no. 21 (1915): 75–104.

———. "The Black Hole Debate." *Bengal: Past and Present* 12 (1916): 136–49.

Lockman, John. *Travels of the Jesuits, into Various Parts of the World.* 2 vols. London: John Noon, 1743.

Longobardi, Niccolò. *Traité sur quelques points de la religion des Chinois.* Paris: Louis Guerin, 1701.

Lopez, Donald S. "Pandit's Revenge." *Journal of the American Academy of Religion* 2000 (2000): 831–35.

Lord, Henry. *A display of two forraigne sects in the East Indies vizt: the sect of the Banians the ancient natiues of India and the sect of the Persees the ancient inhabitants of Persia together with the religion and maners of each sect.* London: Constable, 1630. Critical edition edited by Will Sweetman. Lampeter: Edwin Mellen, 1999.

Lorenzen, David N. *Who Invented Hinduism? Essays on Religion and History.* New Delhi: Yoda Press, 2006.

Loubère, Simon de la. *Du Royaume de Siam.* 2 vols. Amsterdam: Abraham Wolfgang, 1691.

Lubac, Henri de. *La rencontre du bouddhisme et de l'Occident.* Paris: Cerf, 2000.

———. *La postérité spirituelle de Joachim de Flore.* Paris: Lethellieux, 1979.

Lucena, Johannes. *Historia da Vida do Padre Francisco de Xavier.* Lisboa, 1600.

Lundbæk, Knud. *T. S. Bayer (1794–1738). Pioneer Sinologist.* London and Malmö: Curzon Press, 1986.

———. *Joseph de Prémare, 1666–1736, S.J.: Chinese Philology and Figurism.* Aarhus: Aarhus University Press, 1991.

Lütkehaus, Ludger. *Nirwana in Deutschland: Von Leibniz bis Schopenhauer.* München: Deutscher Taschenbuch Verlag, 2004.

Ma Duanlin 馬端臨. *Wenxian tongkao* 文獻通考. 2 vols. Kyoto: Chūbun shuppansha, 1978.

Macpherson, James. *Fragments of Ancient Poetry: Collected in the highlands of Scotland and translated from the Galic or Erse language.* Edinburgh: G. Hamilton and J. Balfour, 1760.

———. *An Introduction to the History of Great Britain and Ireland.* 3rd ed. London: Becket & De Hondt, 1773.

Magaillans [Magalhães], Gabriel de. *Nouvelle relation de la Chine, contenant la description des particularitez les plus considerables de ce grand Empire.* Paris: Claude Barbin, 1688.

———. *A New History of China Containing a Description of the Most Considerable Particulars of that Vast Empire.* London: Thomas Newborough, 1688.

Maigrot, Charles. *Acta causae rituum seu ceremoniarum Sinensium.* Cologne 1715.

Mailla, Joseph Anne Marie de Moyriac de. *Histoire générale de la Chine ou Annales de cet empire; Traduites du Tong-Kien-Kang-Mou.* Vol. 5. Paris: Ph.-D. Pierres/Clousier, 1778.

Maillard, Christine. *L'Inde vue d'Europe. Histoire d'une rencontre (1750–1950).* Paris: Albin Michel, 2008.

Malek, Roman, and Arnold Zingerle, eds. *Martino Martini S.J. (1614–1661) und die China-mission im 17. Jahrhundert.* Sankt Augustin: Institut Monumenta Serica, 2000.

Mallet, Paul Henri. *Introduction à l'histoire du Danemarc.* Copenhagen, 1755.

Mangold, Sabine. *Eine "weltbürgerliche Wissenschaft"—Die deutsche Orientalistik im 19. Jahrhundert.* Stuttgart: Franz Steiner Verlag, 2004.

Manji zokuzōkyō 卍續藏經. Taipei: Xinwenfeng chubanshe, 1976.

Manuel, Frank Edward. *The Eighteenth Century Confronts the Gods.* Cambridge, Mass.: Harvard University Press, 1959.

———. *Isaac Newton Historian.* Cambridge: Cambridge University Press, 1963.

———. *The Religion of Isaac Newton: Fremantle Lectures 1973.* Oxford: Clarendon Press, 1974.

———. *The Changing of the Gods.* Hanover, N.H.: University Press of New England, 1983.

Marana, Giovanni Paolo, Robert Midgley, and William Bradshaw. *Letters writ by a Turk-ish spy.* 8 vols. London: J. Rhodes, 1723.

Marée, Valentin. *Traité des conformités du disciple avec son maître.* 3 vols. Liège, 1658–60.

Maria, Vincenzo. *Il viaggio all'Indie orientali.* Venice: Giacomo Zattoni, 1678.

Marini, Giovanni Filippo de. *Delle missioni de padri della Compagnia di Giesu, nella pro-vincia del Giappone, e particolarmente di quella di Tumkino. Libri cinque.* Rome: Nicolo Angelo Tinassi, 1663.

Marshall, Peter J. *The British Discovery of Hinduism in the Eighteenth Century.* Cambridge: Cambridge University Press, 1970.

Martini, Martino. *Novus Atlas Sinensis.* Amsterdam: Joh. Blaeu, 1655. Reprint, edited by Giuliano Bertuccioli. Trento: Università degli studi di Trento, 2002.

———. *Sinicae historiae decas prima.* München: Lucas Straub, 1658.

Maspéro, Henri. "Le songe et l'ambassade de l'empereur Ming. Étude critique des sources." *Bulletin de l'École Française d'Extrême-Orient* 10 (1910): 5–130.

Masuzawa, Tomoko. *The Invention of World Religions.* Chicago: University of Chicago Press, 2005.

Maurice, Thomas. *Indian Antiquities*. London: Author, 1794–96.

——. *The History of Hindostan: Its Arts Its and Sciences, as connected with The History of the Other Great Empires of Asia, During the Most Ancient Periods of the World*. 2 vols. Vol. 1. London: W. Bulmer, 1795.

——. *Sanscreet Fragments, Or Interesting Extracts from the Sacred Books of the Brahmins, on Subjects important to the British Isles*. London: Galabin, 1797.

——. *A Dissertation on the Oriental Trinities, extracted from the fourth and fifth volume of "Indian Antiquities"* London: Galabin, 1800.

——. *The Indian sceptic confuted, and Brahmin frauds exposed*. London: Bulmer, 1812.

——. *Memoirs of the Author of Indian Antiquities comprehending the history of the progress of Indian literature in Britain during a period of thirty years*. London: The author, 1819.

McGuire, J. E., and P. M. Rattansi. "Newton and the 'Pipes of Pan'." *Notes and Records of the Royal Society London* 21–22 (1966–67): 108–43.

Meinert, J. G. *Johannes von Marignola, minderen Bruders und Päbstlichen Legaten Reise in das Morgenland v. J. 1339–1353*. Prag: Gottlieb Haase, 1820.

Menot, Michel. *Sermons*. Paris, 1506.

Michaud, Joseph François. *Biographie universelle (Michaud), ancienne et moderne*. Paris: C. Desplaces, 1857.

Mickle, William Julius. "Enquiry into the Religious Tenets and Philosophy of the Brahmins." In *The Lusiad: or, the Discovery of India*, 178–251. London: T. Cadell & W. Davies, 1798.

Mignot, Vincent. "Mémoires sur les anciens philosophes de l'Inde." *Mémoires de l'Académie des Inscriptions et Belles-Lettres* 31 (1768): 81–338.

——. "Unité de Dieu reconnue par les anciens philosophes de l'Inde et par les modernes." In *Bibliothèque Académique*, edited by A. Sérieys, 163–65. Paris: Delacour, 1810.

Mignot, Vincent, and Claude de Visdelou. "Authenticité du monument chinois concernant la Religion chrétienne." *Journal des Sçavans* (1760a): 397–410.

——. "Examen de la question: s'il y a eu des Chrétiens à la Chine avant le septième si'ècle?" *Journal des Sçavans* (1760b): 509–26.

Milton, John. *Paradise Lost, Paradise Regained*. New York: Penguin, 2001.

Mohl, Jules. *Vingt-sept ans d'histoire des études orientales: rapports faits à la Société asiatique de Paris de 1840 à 1867*. 2 vols. Paris: Reinwald, 1879–80. Reprint, London: Ganesha; Tokyo: Synapse, 2003.

Monier-Williams, Monier. *A Sanskrit-English Dictionary: etymologically and philologically arranged with special reference to Greek, Latin, Gothic, German, Anglo-Saxon, and other cognate Indo-European languages*. Oxford: Clarendon Press, 1872.

More, Henry. *The Immortality of the Soul, So farre forth as it is demonstrable from the Knowledge of Nature and the Light of Reason*. London: James Flesher, 1662.

Mosheim, Johann Lorenz. *Dissertationes ad historiam ecclesiasticam pertinentes*. 2nd ed. Altona & Flensburg: Korte, 1743.

——. *Institutionum historiae ecclesiasticae libri IV*. 4 vols. Helmstadt: Weygand, 1755.

Moseley, C. W. R. D. *The Travels of Sir John Mandeville*. London: Penguin, 1983.

Mühlberger, Josef B. *Glaube in Japan. Alexandro Valignanos Katechismus, seine moraltheologischen Aussagen im japanischen Kontext*. St. Ottilien: EOS, 2001.

Müller, D. H. "Die Rezensionen und Versionen des Eldad had-Dani." *Denkschriften der Wiener Akademie der Wissenschaften, Philosophisch-historische Classe* 41 (1892): 1–80.

Müller, Friedrich Max. "On False Analogies in Comparative Theology." In *Chips from a German Workshop*, vol. 4, *Essays Chiefly on the Science of Language*, 203–38. London: Longmans, Green, 1895.

——. *The Upanishads*. New York: Dover, 1962.

Müller, Johann Joachim. "De tribus impostoribus (Autographus Mülleri 1688)." In *Österreichische Nationalbibliothek, Handschrift No. 10450*. Vienna, 1688.

——. *De imposturis religionum (de tribus impostoribus)* = *Von den Betrügereyen der Religionen: Dokumente*. Edited by Winfried Schröder. Stuttgart: Frommann-Holzboog, 1999.

Mulsow, Martin. *Moderne aus dem Untergrund: Radikale Frühaufklärung in Deutschland 1680–1720*. Hamburg: Meiner, 2002.

Mungello, David. *Curious Land: Jesuit Accommodation and the Origins of Sinology*. Honolulu: University of Hawai'i Press, 1989.

Murr, Sylvia. *L'Inde philosophique entre Bossuet et Voltaire*. 2 vols. Paris: École française d'Extrême-Orient, 1987.

Navarrete, Domingo Fernandez. *Tratados historicos, politicos, ethicos, y religiosos de la Monarchia de China*. Madrid, 1676.

Newton, Isaac. *The Chronology of the Ancient Kingdoms Amended*. London, 1728.

——. *Opticks: or, a Treatise of the Reflections, Refractions, Inflections and Colours of Light*. 4th corrected ed. London: William Innys, 1730.

——. *Opera quae exstant omnia*. Edited by Samuel Horsley. Vol. 5. London: John Nichols, 1785. Reprint, Stuttgart-Bad Cannstatt: Frommann-Holzboog, 1964.

Niecamp [Niekamp], Johann Lucas [Lukas]. *Kurtzgefasste Missions-Geschichte, oder historischer Auszug der evangelischen Missions-Berichte aus Ost-Indien von dem Jahr 1705 bis zu Ende des Jahres 1736*. Halle: Waysen-Haus, 1740.

——. *Histoire de la mission danoise dans les Indes Orientale*. Translated from German by Benjamin Gaudard. 3 vols. Genève: Henri-Albert Gosse, 1745.

Nock, Arthur Darby, and André-Jean. J. Festugière. *Corpus Hermeticum*. 2 vols. Paris: Les Belles Lettres, 1960.

Okabe, Kazuo. "'Shijūnishōkyō' no seiritsu to tenkai. Kenkyūshiteki oboegaki." *Komazawa daigaku bukkyōgakubu kenkyū kiyō* 25 (1967): 103–18.

Olender, Maurice. *The Languages of Paradise*. New York: Other Press, 2002.

Orme, Robert. *Historical fragments of the Mogul Empire of the Morattoes, and of the English concerns in Indostan from the year MDCLIX*. 2nd ed. London: F. Wingrave, 1805.

Osterhammel, Jürgen. *Die Entzauberung Asiens:. Europa und die asiatischen Reiche im 18. Jahrhundert*. München: C.H. Beck, 1998.

Pailin, David A. *Attitudes to Other Religions: Comparative Religion in Seventeenth- and Eighteenth-Century Britain*. Manchester: Manchester University Press, 1984.

Paine, Thomas. *The age of reason, part the second, being an investigation of true and fabulous theology*. London: H.D. Symonds, 1795.

Palladius, Helenopolitanus et al. *Palladius de gentibus Indiae et Bragmanibus. S. Ambrosius de moribus Brachmanorum. Anonymus de Bragmanibus*. Edited by Edward Bysshe. London: T. Roycroft, 1668.

Palumbo, Antonello. "Dharmarakṣa and Kaṇṭhaka: White Horse Monasteries in Early Medieval China." In *Buddhist Asia 1. Papers from the First Conference of Buddhist Studies Held in Naples in May 2001*, edited by Silvio Vita and Giovanni Gerardi, 167–216. Kyoto: Italian School of East Asian Studies, 2003.

Parfitt, Tudor. *The Lost Tribes of Israel: The History of a Myth*. London: Phoenix, 2003.

Pastine, Dino. "Le origini del poligenismo e Isaac Lapeyrère." In *Miscellanea Seicento*, vol. 1, 7–234. Firenze: Felice le Monnier, 1971.

———. *La nascita dell'Idolatria: L'oriente religioso di Athanasius Kircher*. Firenze: La Nuova Italia, 1978.

Paulinus a Sancto Bartholomaeo: see under Sancto Bartholomaeo

Pauw, Cornelius de. *Recherches sur les Égyptiens et les Chinois*. Vol. 2. Berlin, 1773.

Pennington, Brian K. *Was Hinduism Invented? Britons, Indians and the Colonial Construction of Religion*. Oxford: Oxford University Press, 2005.

Phan, Peter C. *Mission and Catechesis: Alexandre de Rhodes and Inculturation in Seventeenth-Century Vietnam*. Maryknoll: Orbis Books, 1998.

Philipps, Jenkin Thomas. *An account of the religion, manners and learning of the people of Malabar in the East Indies*. London: W. Mears, 1717.

Pilhofer, Peter. *Presbyteron kreitton: Der Altersbeweis der jüdischen und christlichen Apologeten und seine Vorgeschichte*. Tübingen: J.C.B. Mohr, 1990.

Pinkerton, John. *A General Collection of the Best and Most Interesting Voyages and Travels in all Parts of the World*. Vol. 9. London: Longman, Hurst, Rees, Orme, and Brown, 1811.

Pinot, Virgile. *La Chine et la formation de l'esprit philosophique en France (1640–1740)*. Genève: Slatkine, 1971.

Pirenne, Jean. *La Légende du Prêtre Jean*. Strasbourg: Presses de l'Université de Strasbourg, 1992.

Pluquet, Adrien-François. *Examen du fatalisme*. 2 vols. Paris: Didot & Barrois, 1757.

Pocock, J. G. A. *Barbarism and Religion*. Vol. 4, *Barbarians, Savages, and Empires*. Cambridge: Cambridge University Press, 2005.

Polaschegg, Andrea. *Der andere Orientalismus: Regeln deutsch-morgenländischer Imagination im 19. Jahrhundert*. Berlin: de Gruyter, 2005.

Polier, Antoine Louis Henri de. *Mythologie des Indous*. Vols. 1, 2. Rudolstadt & Paris, 1809.

———. *Le Mahabarat et le Bhagavat*. Edited by Georges Dumézil. Paris: Gallimard, 1986.

Pomeau, René. *Essai sur les mœurs et l'esprit des nations et sur les principaux faits de l'histoire depuis Charlemagne jusqu'à Louis XIII*. Paris: Garnier, 1963.

———. *La religion de Voltaire*. Paris: Nizet, 1995.

Pons, Jean François. "Lettre du Père Pons, Missionnaire de la Compagnie de Jésus, au Père Du Halde, de la même Compagnie." In *Lettres édifiantes et curieuses, écrites des missions étrangères*, edited by Charles Le Gobien, 65–90. Paris: G. Merigot, 1781.

Popkin, Richard H. *Isaac La Peyrère (1596–1676): His Life, Work, and Influence*. Leiden: Brill, 1987.

———. *The History of Scepticism*. Oxford: Oxford University Press, 2003.

Postel, Guillaume. *Des merveilles du monde*. Paris, 1553a.

———. *De Originibus, sev, de varia et potissimum orbi Latino*. Basel: J. Oporin, 1553b.

Possevino, Antonio. *Bibliotheca Selecta Qua Agitur De Ratione Studiorum in Historia, in Disciplinis, in Salutem Omnium Procuranda*. Roma: Typographia Apostolica Vaticana, 1593.

Poullé, Maridas, J. B. P. More, and Pierre-Sylvain Filliozat. *Bagavadam ou Bhāgavata purāna: ouvrage religieux et philosophique indien*. Tellicherry: Institute for Research in Social Sciences and Humanities, 2004.

Prasad, Mahesh. "The Unpublished Translation of the Upanishads by Prince Dara Shikoh." In *Dr. Modi Memorial Volume*, edited by Dr. Modi Memorial Volume Editorial Board, 622–38. Bombay: Fort Printing Press, 1930.

Prémare, Joseph-Henri. *Notitia Linguae Sinicae*. Malacca, 1831. Reprint, Hong Kong, 1893.

———. *Vestiges des principaux dogmes chrétiens tirés des anciens livres chinois*. Edited by A. Bonnetty and Paul Hubert Perny. Paris: Bureau des annales de philosophie chrétienne, 1878.

Priestley, Joseph. *A Comparison of the Institutions of Moses with those of the Hindoos and other Ancient Nations*. Northumberland: A. Kennedy, 1799.

Prinz, Otto. *Die Kosmographie des Aethicus*. München: Monumenta Germaniae Historica, 1993.

Purchas, Samuel. *Purchas, his Pilgrimage, or Relations of the World and the Religions Observed in All Ages and Places Discovered, from the Creation unto the Present*. London: W. Stansby, 1613.

Qanungo, K. R. *Dara Shukoh*. 2nd ed. Calcuttta: S.C. Sarkar & Sons, 1952.

Queyroz, Fernão de. *The Temporal and Spiritual Conquest of Ceylon*. Translated by Simon Perera. Colombo: A.C. Richards, 1930.

Rabault-Feuerhahn, Pascale. *L'archive des origines. Sanskrit, philologie, anthropologie dans l'Allemagne du XIXe siècle*. Paris: Cerf, 2008.

Rachewiltz, Igor de. *Prester John and Europe's Discovery of East Asia*. Canberra: Australian National University Press, 1972.

Raleigh, Walter. *The History of the World*. 1st ed. 2 vols. London: Walter Burre, 1614.

Raleigh, Walter, William Oldys, and Thomas Birch. *The Works of Sir Walter Ralegh*. 8 vols. Oxford: Oxford University Press, 1829.

Ramsay, Andrew Michael. *Les voyages de Cyrus, avec un discours sur la mythologie*. Amsterdam: Covens & Mortier, 1728.

———. *The Philosophical Principles of Natural and Revealed Religion Unfolded in a Geometrical Order*. 2 vols. Glasgow: Robert Foulis, 1748, 1749.

———. *The Travels of Cyrus: to which is annexed, A Discourse upon the Theology and Mythology of the Pagans.* Albany, N.Y.: Pratt & Doubleday, 1814.

———. *Les voyages de Cyrus, avec un Discours sur la Mythologie.* Edited by Georges Lamoine. Paris: Honoré Champion, 2002.

Ramsey, Rachel. "China and the Ideal of Order in John Webb's An Historical Essay." *Journal of the History of Ideas* 62, no. 3 (2001): 483–503.

Raspe, Rudolph Erich. *Gesetzbuch der Gentoos, oder Sammlung der Gesetze der Pundits.* Hamburg: C. E. Bohn, 1778.

Rattansi, Piyo. "Newton and the Wisdom of the Ancients." In *Let Newton Be!*, edited by John Fauvel, Raymond Flood, Michael Shortland, and Robin Wilson, 185–201. Oxford: Oxford University Press, 1988.

Raynal, Guillaume-Thomas. *Histoire philosophique et politique des établissements & du commerce des européens dans les deux Indes.* 2nd ed. Vol. 1. Amsterdam, 1773.

Régis, Pierre-Sylvain. "Confucius sinarum philosophus." *Journal des Sçavans* (January 1688): 99–107.

Rhodes, Alexander de, S.J. *Histoire du royaume de Tunquin.* Lyon, 1651.

———. *Cathechismus.* Roma: Congregatio de Propaganda Fide, 1651.

Ribeyro, João. *Histoire de l'Isle de Ceylan.* Paris: Guimard, 1701.

Ricci, Matteo. *De Christiana expeditione apud Sinas suscepta ab societate Jesu ex P. Matthaei Ricci eiusdem societatis commentariis.* Edited by Nicholas Trigault. Agustae Vindecorum (Augsburg): C. Mangium, 1615.

———. *Storia dell'introduzione del Cristianesimo in Cina.* Edited by Pasquale M. d'Elia. Vol. 1, *Fonti Ricciane.* Roma: Libreria dello Stato, 1942.

———. *The True Meaning of the Lord of Heaven.* Edited by Edward J. Malatesta. St. Louis: Institute of Jesuit Sources, 1985.

Ricci, Matthieu, and Nicolas Trigault. *Histoire de l'expedition chrétienne au royaume de la Chine 1582–1610.* Paris: Desclée de Brouwer, 1978.

Ritter, Carl. *Die Vorhalle europäischer Völkergeschichten vor Herodotus, um den Kaukasus und an den Gestaden des Pontus.* Berlin: G. Reimer, 1820.

Rixner, Thaddäus Anselm. *Versuch einer neuen Darstellung der uralten indischen All-Eins-Lehre oder der berühmten Sammlung tôn Oupnek'hatôn: Erstes Stück Oupnek'hat Tschehandouk.* Nürnberg, 1808.

Robertson, William. *A Historical Disquisition concerning the Knowledge which the Ancients had of India.* London: Strahan & Cadell, 1791.

Rocher, Ludo. *Ezourvedam: A French Veda of the Eighteenth Century.* University of Pennsylvania Studies on South Asia 1. Amsterdam/Philadelphia: J. Benjamins, 1984.

Rocher, Rosane. *Alexander Hamilton (1762–1824): A Chapter in the Early History of Sanskrit Philology.* New Haven, Conn.: American Oriental Society, 1968.

———. "Nathaniel Brassey Halhed on the Upaniṣads (1787)." In *Annals of the Bhandarkar Oriental Research Institute, Diamond Jubilee Volume (1977–78)*, 279–89. Poona: Bhandarkar Oriental Research Institute, 1978.

———. *Orientalism, Poetry, and the Millennium: The Checkered Life of Nathaniel Brassey Halhed, 1751–1830.* Delhi: Motilal Banarsidass, 1983.

———. "Sanskrit for Civil Servants 1806–1818." *Journal of the American Oriental Society* 122, no. 2 (2002): 381–90.

Rodrigues, João. *Arte da Lingoa de Iapam.* Nagasaki: Collegio de Iapão, 1604.

———. *História da igreja do Japão.* Macao: Notícias de Macau, 1954.

———. *João Rodrigues's Account of Sixteenth-Century Japan.* Edited by Michael Cooper. London: Hakluyt Society, 2001.

Roger, Abraham. *De Open-Deure tot het Verborgen Heydendom.* Leyden, 1651.

———. *Abraham Rogers Offne Thür zu dem verborgenen Heydenthum.* Nürnberg: Johann Andreas Endrers, 1663.

———. *Le Théatre de l'Idolatrie, ou la Porte Ouverte pour parvenir à la connaissance du paganisme caché.* Translated by Thomas La Grue. Amsterdam: Jean Schipper, 1670.

———. *De Open-Deure tot het Verborgen Heydendom.* 'S-Gravenhage: Martinus Nijhoff, 1915.

Ross, Alexander. *Pansebeia: Or, A View of All Religions in the World.* London: James Young, 1653.

———. *Alexander Rossen unterschiedliche Gottesdienste in der gantzen Welt.* Heidelberg: Wolfgang Moritz Endters & Johann Andreas seel. Erben, 1674.

Ross, Alexander, and David Nerreter. *Der wunderwürdige Juden- und Heidentempel.* Nürnberg: Wolfgang Moritz Endter, 1701.

Rossi, Paolo. *The Dark Abyss of Time. The History of the Earth and the History of Nations from Hooke to Vico.* Chicago: University of Chicago Press, 1987.

Rubiés, Joan-Pau. *Travel and Ethnology in the Renaissance: South India Through European Eyes, 1250–1625.* Cambridge: Cambridge University Press, 2000.

Rudbeck, Olof. *Atlantica sive Manheim.* Uppsala, 1675–98.

Ruiz-de-Medina, Juan. *Documentos del Japon.* Rome: Instituto Histórico de la Compañía de Jesús, 1990.

Rule, Paul A. *K'ung-tzu or Confucius? The Jesuit Interpretation of Confucianism.* Sydney / London / Boston: Allen & Unwin, 1986.

Sabbathier. "Inde." In *Dictionnaire pour l'intelligence des auteurs classiques, grecs et latins, tant sacrés que profanes,* vol. 22, 215–52. Paris: Delalain, 1777.

Said, Edward. *Orientalism.* 1978. 25th anniversary ed. with a new preface by the author. New York: Vintage Books, 1994.

Sainte-Croix, Guillaume Emmanuel. *L'Ezour-Vedam ou Ancien Commentaire du Vedam, contenant l'exposition des opinions religieuses & philosophiques des Indiens.* Yverdon: De Felice, 1778.

———. *Recherches historiques et critiques sur les mystères du paganisme.* Edited by Sylvestre de Sacy. Paris: de Bure Frères, 1817.

Sale, George, George Psalmanazar, Archibald Bower, George Shelvocke, John Campbell, and John Swinton. *An Universal History, from the Earliest Accounts to the Present Time.* 65 vols. London: T. Osborne, 1730–65.

———. *The Modern Part of an Universal History, from the Earliest Accounts to the Present Time.* Vol. 6. London: S. Richardson, 1759.

Sammlung asiatischer Original-Schriften. Indische Schriften. Zürich: Ziegler und Söhne, 1791.

Sancto Bartholomaeo, Paulinus a. *Systema Brahmanicum Liturgicum mythologicum civile Ex monumentis indicis Musei Borgiani Velitris Dissertationibus Historico-criticis.* Roma: Antonius Fulgonius, 1791.

———. *Viaggio alle Indie Orientali.* Roma: Antonio Fulgoni, 1796.

———. *Darstellung der brahmanisch-indischen Götterlehre, Religionsgebräuche und bürgerlichen Verfassung: nach dem lateinischen Werke des Pater Paulinus a St. Bartholomaeo bearbeitet.* Translated by Johann Friedrich Kleuker. Gotha: Ettinger, 1797.

Sancto Bartholomaeo, Paulinus a, Johann Reinhold Forster, Abraham Hyacinthe Anquetil-Duperron, and A. I. Silvestre de Sacy. *Voyage aux Indes Orientales.* Translated by José Marchéna. 3 vols. Paris: Tourneisen fils, 1808.

Santarem, Vicomte de. *Atlas composé de mappemondes, de portulans et de cartes hydrographiques et historiques depuis le VIe jusqu'au XVIIe siècle.* Paris: E. Thunot, 1849.

Scafi, Alessandro. *Mapping Paradise: A History of Heaven on Earth.* Chicago: University of Chicago Press, 2006.

Schlegel, Friedrich. *Über die Sprache und Weisheit der Indier.* Heidelberg: Mohr und Zimmer, 1808.

———. *Briefe an Ludwig Tieck.* Edited by Karl von Holtei. Vol. 3. Breslau: Trewendt, 1864.

Schmidt, Nathaniel. "Traces of Early Acquaintance in Europe with the Book of Enoch." *Journal of the American Oriental Society* 42 (1922): 44–52.

Schmidt-Biggemann, Wilhelm. *Philosophia perennis: Historische Umrisse abendländischer Spiritualität in Antike, Mittelalter und Früher Neuzeit.* Frankfurt: Suhrkamp, 1998.

———. "Heilsgeschichtliche Inventionen. Annius Von Viterbos 'Berosus' und die Geschichte der Sintflut." In *Sintflut und Gedächtnis,* edited by Martin Mulsow and Jan Assmann, 85–111. München: Wilhelm Fink, 2006.

Schurhammer, Georg. *Das kirchliche Sprachproblem in der japanischen Jesuitenmission des 16. und 17. Jahrhunderts.* Tokyo: Deutsche Gesellschaft für Natur- und Völkerkunde Ostasiens, 1928.

———. *Die Disputationen des P. Cosme de Torres S.J. mit den Buddhisten in Yamaguchi im Jahre 1551.* Vol. 24a. Tokyo: Mitteilungen der Deutschen Gesellschaft für Natur- und Völkerkunde Ostasiens, 1929.

———. *Francis Xavier: His Life, His Times (vol. 2: India, 1541–1545).* Translated by Joseph Costelloe. Rome: Jesuit Historical Institute, 1977.

Schütte, Josef Franz. *Valignanos Missionsgrundsätze für Japan.* 2 vols. Vol. 1. Roma: Edizioni di storia e letteratura, 1951.

———. *Valignanos Missionsgrundsätze für Japan.* 2 vols. Vol. 1, part 2. Roma: Edizioni di storia e letteratura, 1958.

Schwab, Raymond. *Vie d'Anquetil Duperron.* Paris: Ernest Leroux, 1934.

———. *La renaissance orientale.* Paris: Payot, 1950.

Scrafton, Luke. *Reflections on the government, &c. of Indostan, with a short sketch of the history of Bengal, from 1739 to 1756, and an account of the English affairs to 1758.* London: G. Kearsley, 1763. Reprint, London: G. Kearsley, 1770.

Secret, François. "Postel et l'origine des Turcs." In *Guillaume Postel, 1581–1981*, 301–6. Paris: Guy Trédaniel, 1985.

Semedo, Alvarez de. *Imperio de la China*. Madrid: Juan Sanchez, 1642.

Sérieys, A. *Bibliothèque Académique*. Vol. 3. Paris: Delacour, 1810.

Sharf, Robert H. "The Scripture in Forty-Two Sections." In *Religions of Asia in Practice: An Anthology*, edited by Donald S. Lopez, Jr., 418–29. Princeton, N.J.: Princeton University Press, 2002.

Sharpe, Eric J. *Comparative Religion: A History*. Chicago: Open Court, 1986.

Shea, David, and Anthony Troyer. *The Dabistán, or, School of Manners*. 3 vols. Paris & London: B. Duprat/Allen and Co., 1843.

Shuckford, Samuel. *The sacred and prophane history of the world connected*. 4 vols. London: J. and R. Tonson, 1740.

Silverberg, Robert. *The Realm of Prester John*. Athens: Ohio University Press, 1972.

Sinner, Jean-Rodolphe. *Essai sur les dogmes de la métempsychose et du purgatoire*. Berne: Société typographique, 1771.

Sirinelli, Jean. *Les vues historiques d'Eusèbe de Césarée durant la période prénicéenne*. Paris: Université de Paris, 1961.

Smith, Wilfred Cantwell. *The Meaning and End of Religion*. Minneapolis: Fortress Press, 1991.

Société de gens de lettres. *Tableau raisonné de l'histoire littéraire du dix-huitième siècle*. Edited by Fortuné-Barthélemy de Félice. Mensuel. Yverdon: de Félice, 1779, 1782–1783.

Sonnerat, Pierre. *Voyage aux Indes orientales et à la Chine*. Paris: Chez l'auteur, 1782.

Soyen, Shaku. "The Sutra of Forty-Two Chapters." In *Sermons of a Buddhist Abbot*, 1–21. New York: Samuel Weiser, 1906.

Spencer, John. *De legibus Hebraeorum ritualibus et earum rationibus libri tres*. Cambridge: John Hayes, 1685.

Spinoza, Benedictus de. *Tractatus theologico-politicus*. Hamburg: Apud Henricum Künraht [sic.], 1670.

Stackelberg, Jürgen von. *Voltaire*. München: C.H. Beck, 2006.

Stausberg, Michael. *Die Religion Zarathustras: Geschichte—Gegenwart—Rituale*. 3 vols. Vol. 2. Stuttgart: Kohlhammer, 2002.

Steuco, Agostino. *De perenni philosophia*. Edited by Charles B. Schmitt. New York: Johnson reprint, 1972.

Stillingfleet, Edward. *Origines Sacrae*. 2 vols. Vol. 1. Oxford: Clarendon Press, 1817.

Stolzenberg, Daniel. "Egyptian Oedipus. Antiquarianism, Oriental Studies and Occult Philosophy in the Work of Athanasius Kircher." Ph.D. dissertation, Stanford University, 2004.

Stroppetti, Romain. *Anquetil-Duperron, sa place et son rôle dans la Renaissance orientale*. Lille: Doctoral thesis, Université de Lille, 1986.

Suzuki, Daisetz Teitaro. *Sermons of a Buddhist Abbot: Including The Sutra of Forty-Two Chapters*. Chicago: Open Court, 1906.

Sweetman, Will. *Mapping Hinduism: "Hinduism" and the study of Indian religions, 1600–1776*. Halle: Verlag Franckesche Stiftungen, 2003.

———. "The Prehistory of Orientalism: Colonialism and the Textual Basis for Bartholomäus Ziegenbalg's Account of Hinduism." *New Zealand Journal of Asian Studies* 6, no. 2 (2004): 12–38.

Tachard, Guy. *Voyage de Siam des pères jesuites, envoyés par le Roy aux Indes & à la Chine*. Amsterdam: Pierre Mortier, 1687.

———. *A relation of the voyage to Siam*. London: J. Robinson & A. Churchil, 1688.

Tavernier, Jean Baptiste (Baron d'Aubonne). *Les six Voyages de Jean Baptiste Tavernier, Ecuyer Baron d'Aubonne, qu'il a fait en Turquie, en Perse et aux Indes*. Paris: G. Glouzier & C. Barbin, 1676.

Temple, William. *The Works of Sir William Temple*. 4 vols. Vol. 3. London: F.C. and J. Rivington et al., 1814.

Thévenot, Jean de. *Voyages de Mr Thévenot*. Paris: Ch. Angot, 1689.

Timmermans, Claire. *Entre Chine et Europe: taoïsme et bouddhisme chinois dans les publications jésuites de l'époque moderne (XVIe–XVIIIe siècles)*. Lille: Atelier national de reproduction des thèses, 2002.

Tindal, Matthew. *Christianity as Old as the Creation; or, the Gospel, a Republication of the Religion of Nature*. London: n.p., 1730. Reprint, London: Routledge/Thoemmes Press, 1995.

Toland, John. *Letters to Serena*. London, 1704.

Torrey, Norman L. *Voltaire and the English Deists*. Hamden, Conn.: Archon, 1967.

Tournemine, René Joseph de. "Projet d'un ouvrage sur l'origine des fables." *Mémoires pour l'histoire des sciences & des beaux Arts (Mémoires de Trévoux)* (November–December 1702): 84–111.

———. "Seconde partie du projet d'un ouvrage sur l'origine des fables." *Mémoires pour l'histoire des sciences & des beaux Arts (Mémoires de Trévoux)* (November–December 1703): 189–212.

Trautmann, Thomas. *Aryans and British India*. Berkeley: University of California Press, 1997.

Trigault, Nicholas. *De christiana expeditione apud Sinas suscepta ab Societate Iesu*. Cologne: Bernard Walter, 1617.

Trousson, Raymond, Jeroom Vercruysse, and Jacques Lemaire. *Dictionnaire Voltaire*. Paris: Hachette, 1994.

Ullendorf, Edward, and C. F. Beckingham, trans. and eds. *The Hebrew Letters of Prester John*. Oxford: Oxford University Press, 1982. {chap 5, 6,}

Ulrich, Jörg. *Euseb von Caesarea und die Juden*. Berlin: Walter de Gruyter, 1999.

Vaissière, Étienne de la. "The Rise of Sogdian Merchants and the Role of the Huns: The Historical Importance of the Sogdian Ancient Letters." In *The Silk Road: Trade, Travel, War and Faith*, edited by Susan Whtifield, 19–23. Chicago: Serindia Publications, 2004.

Valignano, Alessandro. *Catechismus christianae fidei*. Lisbon: Antonius Riberius, 1586.

———. *Monumenta Xaveriana*. Vol. 1. Madrid: Augustino Avrial, 1900.

———. *Historia del Principio y Progresso de la Compañía de Jesús en las Indias Orientales, 1542–1564*. Edited by Josef Wicki. Rome, 1944.

Van der Velde, Paul. "The Interpreter Interpreted: Kaempfer's Japanese Collaborator Imamura Genemon Eisei." In *The Furthest Goal: Engelbert Kaempfer's Encounter with Tokugawa Japan*, edited by Beatrice Bodart-Bailey and Derek Massarella, 44–58. Folkstone: Japan Library, 1995.

Varenius, Bernhardus. *Descriptio Regni Japoniae*. Amsterdam: Ludwig Elzevir, 1649.

———. *Tractatus in quo agitur: De Iaponiorum religione. De Christianae religionis introductione in ea loca. De ejusdem exstirpatione. Adjuncta est de diversa diversarum gentium totius telluris religione brevis informatio*. Amsterdam: Elzevir, 1649.

———. "Bernhardi Varenii Kurtzer Bericht von mancherley Religionen der Völcker." In *Alexander Rossen unterschiedliche Gottesdienste in der gantzen Welt, 941–1040*. Heidelberg: Wolffgang Moritz Endters & Johann Andreas Seel. Erben, 1674.

Vinson, Julien. "Les anciens missionnaires jésuites qui se sont occupés de la langue tamoule." *Revue de linguistique et de philologie comparée* 35 (1902): 263–96.

———. "Notes sur l'Ezour vedam." *Journal Asiatique* 203 (1923): 169–72.

Visdelou, Claude de. "Traduction du monument chinois, concernant la Religion Chrétienne." *Journal des Sçavans* (1760): 340–52.

———. "Notice du livre chinois nommé Y-King." In *Le Chou-king, un des livres sacrés des Chinois*, edited by Joseph de Guignes, 404–36. Paris, 1770.

Visdelou, Claude de, and A. Galand. *Bibliothèque Orientale*. Vol. 4. La Haye: J. Neaulme & N. van Daalen, 1779.

Visdelou, Claude de, and Abbé Mignot. "Traduction du monument chinois, concernant la Religion Chrétienne." *Journal des Sçavans* (1760): 340–52.

Volney, Constantin-François. *Voyage en Syrie et en Égypte, pendant les années 1783, 1784, et 1785*. 2nd ed. 2 vols. Paris: Desenne, 1787.

———. *Les Ruines, ou méditation sur les révolutions des empires*. Paris: Desenne, 1791.

———. *La Loi naturelle, ou, Catéchisme du citoyen français*. Paris: Sallior, 1793.

———. *The Ruins: or a Survey of the Revolutions of Empires*. Translated by Anon. 3rd ed. London: J. Johnson, 1796.

———. *Travels through Egypt and Syria, in the years 1783, 1784, and 1785*. Translated by John Scoles. 2 vols. New York: John Tiebout, 1798.

———. *Leçons d'histoire. Oeuvres de C. F. Volney*, vol. 7. Paris: Parmantier, 1825.

———. *Les Ruines, ou méditation sur les révolutions des empires. Oeuvres de C. F. Volney*, vol. 1. Paris: Parmantier, 1826.

———. *Voyage en Syrie et en Égypte (3 éd., 1799): Considérations sur la guerre des Turcs. Oeuvres*, vol. 3. Edited by Anne Deneys-Tunney and Henry Deneys. Paris: Fayard, 1998.

Voltaire. "Nouveau Plan d'une Histoire de l'esprit humain." *Mercure de France* (April 1745): 3–37.

———. *Sermon des cinquante*, 1749.

——. *Essay sur l'histoire générale et sur les moeurs et l'esprit des nations, depuis Charlemagne jusqu'à nous jours.* Genève: Cramer, 1756.

——. *Essay sur l'histoire générale, et sur les moeurs et l'esprit des nations, depuis Charlemagne jusquà nos jours.* Vol. 1. N.p., 1761.

——. *La philosophie de l'histoire.* Amsterdam: Changuion, 1765.

——. *Les questions d'un homme qui ne sait rien.* Vol. 4, *Nouveaux mélanges philosophiques, historiques, critiques, etc.* N.p., 1767.

——. "Homélies prononcées à Londres en 1765, dans une assemblée particulière." In *Nouveaux mélanges philosophiques, historiques, critiques &c. &c. (Sixième partie)*, 293–358. N.p., 1768.

——. *Siècle de Louis XV. Seconde partie.* Lausanne, 1769.

——. *Fragmens sur l'Inde, sur le Général Lalli, sur le progrès du Comte de Morangiés, et sur plusieurs autres sujets.* London, 1774.

——. *Questions sur l'encyclopédie.* Vol. 4. Geneva, 1775.

——. *Correspondance générale. Oeuvres de Voltaire*, vol. 6. Paris: Baudouin Frères, 1828.

——. *Dictionnaire philosophique. Oeuvres de Voltaire*, vol. 32. Paris: Lefèvre, 1829.

——. *La défense de mon oncle. Oeuvres complètes de Voltaire*, vol. 27. Paris: Hachette, 1894.

——. *Il faut prendre un parti. Oeuvres complètes de Voltaire*, vol. 29. Paris: Hachette, 1894.

——. *Lettres chinoises, indiennes et tartares. Oeuvres complètes de Voltaire*, vol. 30. Paris: Hachette, 1895.

——. *La philosophie de l'histoire.* Edited by J. H. Brumfitt. 2nd ed. *The Complete Works of Voltaire*, vol. 59. Geneva: Institut et Musée Voltaire, 1969.

——. *Voltaire's Correspondence.* Edited by Theodore Besterman. Geneva: Institut et Musée Voltaire, 1953–65.

——. *Correspondance vol. 6 (Octobre 1760–Décembre 1762).* Edited by Theodore Besterman. Paris: Gallimard, 1980.

——. *Dictionnaire philosophique.* Paris: Gallimard, 1994.

——. *Lettres philosophiques; Derniers écrits sur Dieu.* Edited by Gerhardt Stenger. Paris: Flammarion, 2006.

Vossius, Gerardus. *De theologia gentili et physiologia Christiana sive de origine ac progressu idololatriae.* Amsterdam: I & C. Blaeu, 1641. Reprint, New York: Garland, 1976.

Wagner, Bettina. *Die "Epistola presbiteri Johannis" lateinisch und deutsch.* Tübingen: Max Niemeyer, 2000.

Walbridge, John. *The Leaven of the Ancients: Suhrawardi and the Heritage of the Greeks.* SUNY Series in Islam. Albany: State University of New York Press, 2000.

——. *The Wisdom of the Mystic East: Suhrawardi and Platonic Orientalism.* SUNY Series in Islam. Albany: State University of New York Press, 2001.

Walker, D. P. *The Ancient Theology: Studies in Christian Platonism from the Fifteenth to the Eighteenth Century.* London: Duckworth, 1972.

Walter, Xavier. *Avant les grandes découvertes. Une image de la Terre au XVIe siècle: Le voyage de Mandeville.* Roissy: Alban, 1997.

Wasserstein, David J. "Eldad ha-Dani and Prester John." In *Prester John, the Mongols and the Ten Lost Tribes*, edited by Charles F. Beckingham and Bernard Hamilton, 213–36. Aldershot: Variorum, 1996.

Webb, John. *A Vindication of Stone-Heng Restored*. London: J. Bassett, 1665.

——. *The Antiquity of China or an historical Essay endeavoring a probability that the Language of the Empire is the primitive Language spoken through the whole world before the Confusion of Babel*. London: Nath. Brook, 1669.

——. *The Antiquity of China or an Historical Essay Endeavoring a probability that the Language of the Empire of China is the Primitive Language spoken through the whole World before the Confusion of Babel*. London: Obadiah Blagrave, 1678.

Weir, David. *Brahma in the West: William Blake and the Oriental Renaissance*. Albany: State University of New York Press, 2003.

Welbon, Guy R. *The Buddhist Nirvāṇa and Its Western Interpreters*. Chicago: University of Chicago Press, 1968.

Westfall, Richard S. "Isaac Newton's *Theologiae Gentilis Origines Philosophicae*." In *The Secular Mind: Transformations of Faith in Modern Europe*, edited by W. Warren Wagar, 15–34. New York: Holmes & Meier, 1982.

Whiston, William. *A New Theory of the Earth from its Original to the Consummation of All Things*. London: Tooke, 1696.

——. *The Works of Flavius Josephus*. Edited by D. S. Margoliouth. London: Routledge & Sons, 1906.

Wilford, Francis. "On Egypt and other countries adjacent to the Cálí River, or Nile of Ethiopia, from the ancient books of the Hindus." *Asiatick Researches* 3 (1792): 295–367.

——. "On the Sacred Isles of the West." *Asiatick Researches* 8 (1805): 245–367.

Wilkins, Charles. *The Bhagvat-Geeta, or Dialogues of Kreeshna and Arjoon*. London: C. Nourse, 1785. Reprint, London: Ganesha, 2001.

Willson, A. Leslie. *A Mythical Image: The Ideal of India in German Romanticism*. Durham, N.C.: Duke University Press, 1964.

Wilson, Walter. *The History and Antiquities of Dissenting Churches and Meeting Houses, in London, Westminster, and Southwark*. 4 vols. Vol. 2. London: W. Button & Son, 1808.

Windisch, Ernst. *Geschichte der Sanskrit-Philologie und Indischen Altertumskunde*. 4th ed. Berlin: Walter de Gruyter, 1992.

Windischmann, Carl Josef Hieronymus. *Die Philosophie im Fortgang der Weltgeschichte*. Bonn: Adolph Marcus, 1832.

Windschuttle, Keith. "Edward Said's 'Orientalism revisited'." *New Criterion* 17, no. 5 (January 1999).

Winkelmann, F. *Euseb von Kaisareia: Der Vater der Kirchengeschichte*. Berlin: Verlags-Anstalt Union, 1991.

Witek, John W. *Controversial Ideas in China and in Europe: A Biography of Jean-François Foucquet, S.J. (1665–1741)*. Roma: Institutum Historicum S.I., 1982.

Yampolsky, Philip B. *The Platform Sutra of the Sixth Patriarch*. New York: Columbia University Press, 1967.

Yanagida, Seizan (Yokoi Seizan). "Hōrinden-bon Shijūnishōkyō no kadai (About the Bao-linzhuan Version of the Forty-Two Section Sutra)." *Indogaku bukkyōgaku kenkyū 6*, no. 3/2 (1955): 627–30.

Yule, Henry. *Hobson-Jobson: A Glossary of Colloquial Anglo-Indian Words and Phrases, and of Kindred Terms, Etymological, Historical, Geographical and Discursive.* Edited by William Crooke. London: J. Murray, 1903.

Zachariae, Theodor. "The Discovery of the Veda." Translated by Henry Hosten. *Journal of Indian History* 2 (1922–23): 127–57.

Zarncke, Friedrich. "Prester John's Letter to the Byzantine Emperor Emanuel." In *Prester John, the Mongols and the Ten Lost Tribes*, edited by Charles F. Beckingham and Bernard Hamilton, 40–112. Aldershot: Variorum, 1996.

Ziegenbalg, Bartholomäus. *Beschreibung der Religion und heiligen Gebräuche der malabari-schen Hindous, nach Bemerkungen in Hindostan gesammelt.* 2 vols. Berlin: Königlich Preussische akademische Kunst- und Buchhandlung, 1791.

———. *Genealogie der malabarischen Götter: aus eigenen Schriften und Briefen der Heiden.* Edited by Wilhelm Germann. Madras: Selbstverlag Germann, 1867.

———. *Ziegenbalgs Malabarisches Heidenthum.* Edited by Willem Caland, *Verhandlungen der Königlichen Akademie der Wissenschaften Amsterdam, No. 25/3.* Amsterdam: Koninklijke Akademie van Wetenschappen, 1926.

———. *Bartholomäus Ziegenbalgs kleinere Schriften.* Edited by Willem Caland, *Verhandlungen der Königlichen Akademie der Wissenschaften Amsterdam, No. 29/2.* Amsterdam: Koninklijke Akademie van Wetenschappen, 1930.

———. *Bartholomäus Ziegenbalgs "Genealogie der malabarischen Götter".* Edited by Daniel Jeyaraj. Halle: Francke, 2003.

Ziegenbalg, Bartholomäus, Anton Wilhelm Boehme, and Heinrich Pluetscho. *Propagation of the Gospel in the East (Parts 1 & 2).* 3rd ed. London: J. Downing, 1710.

———. *Propagation of the Gospel in the East (Part 3).* London: J. Downing, 1718.

Ziegenbalg, Bartholomäus, and Wilhelm Germann. "Bibliotheca Malabarica." *Missions-nachrichten der ostindischen Missionsanstalt zu Halle* 32, no. 1, 2 (1880): 1–20, 62–94.

Ziegenbalg, Bartholomäus, and Johann Ernst Gründler. *Thirty Four Conferences Between the Danish Missionaries and the Malabarian Bramans (or Heathen Priests) in the East Indies, Concerning the Truth of the Christian Religion: Together with Some Letters Written by the Heathens to the Said Missionaries.* Translated by Jenkin Thomas Phillips. London: H. Clemens, 1719.

Ziegenbalg, Bartholomäus, and Heinrich Pluetscho. *Several Letters relating to the Protestant Danish Mission at Tranquebar in the East Indies.* London: J. Downing, 1720.

Županov, Ines G. *Disputed Mission: Jesuit Experiments and Brahmanical Knowledge in Seventeenth-Century India.* Oxford: Oxford University Press, 1999.

Zürcher, Erik. *The Buddhist Conquest of China.* Leiden: Brill, 1959.

Zvelebil, Kamil Veith. *The Poets of the Powers.* London: Rider, 1973.

———. *Tamil Literature.* History of Indian Literature 10.1. Wiesbaden: Otto Harrassowitz, 1995.

Index

Voyages de Cyrus (Ramsay), 266
Vyāsa, xiv, 50, 243–44, 384, 390

Wagner, Richard, 1
Walker, Daniel Pickering, 8, 31, 254, 260, 267
Walter, Xavier, 496
Wang, Pan, 484
Warburton, William (1698–1779), 170, 344
Wasserstein, David J., 304, 496
Webb, John (1611–1672), 273–79
Welbon, Guy R., 77
Wenxian tongkao (Ma Duanlin), 218, 223–24, 235, 244, 246
Westfall, Richard S., 262–64, 494
Whiston, William (1667–1752), 307, 444
Wicky, André, xviii
Wilford, Francis (c. 1761–1822), 335–36
Wilkins, Charles (1749–1836), 13, 253, 348, 356, 428, 438–39, 460–61, 469
Willson, Leslie, 53, 298–99
Wilson, Walter, 314
Windischmann, Carl Josef Hieronymus, 497
Windschuttle, Keith, 500
Winkelmann, F., 386
Witek, John, 286, 495

Xavier, Francis (1506–1552), 16–18, 90, 127
Xuanzang (c. 602–664), 237

Yama, King of Hell (Jap. Emma ō), 184
Yampolsky, Philip, 227
Yanagida, Seizan (1922–2005), xvii, 225, 251, 435
Yang, Guangxian (1597–1669), 280
Yijing (Book of Changes), xv, 7–9, 12, 29, 62, 76, 202–3, 213, 277–78, 280, 282–84, 287, 290, 367, 484
Yōhō, Paulo, 18
Yule, Henry, 498

Zarncke, Friedrich, 305, 496
Zend Avesta, 76, 78–79, 223, 253, 405, 407, 419, 421, 439, 461, 469, 500
Zhixu (1599–1655), 493
Zhu, Shixing (3rd century), 245
Ziegenbalg, Bartholomaeus (1683–1719), 12, 14, 44–45, 49, 77, 79–80, 85–91, 94–112, 115–16, 118–21, 129, 131, 165, 173, 185, 215–16, 221–22, 240, 398, 415, 432, 434–35, 485–86, 488–89
Zingerle, Arnold, 495
Zoroaster, 1, 6–7, 26, 31, 141, 144, 218, 267, 278, 343, 365, 404–5, 407, 414, 454, 464, 466, 468
Županov, Ines, 371, 485
Zvelebil, Kamil Veith, 85, 97–98